State and
Local Politics

State and Local Politics

The Individual and the Governments

W. B. Stouffer

Cynthia Opheim

Susan Bland Day
Southwest Texas State University

HarperCollins*Publishers*

Sponsoring Editor: Lauren Silverman
Project Editor: Melonie Parnes
Design and Cover Coordinator: Heather A. Ziegler
Cover Design/Cover Illustration: Edward Butler
Photo Research: Mira Schachne
Production: Willie Lane/Sunaina Sehwani
Compositor: Digitype, Inc.
Printer and Binder: R. R. Donnelley & Sons, Co.
Cover Printer: New England Book Company

State and Local Politics: The Individual and the Governments
Copyright © 1991 by HarperCollins Publishers Inc.

Library of Congress Cataloging-in-Publication Data

Stouffer, Willard B.
    State and local politics : the individual and the governments /
W. B. Stouffer, Susan Bland Day, Cynthia Opheim.
        p.   cm.
    Includes index.
    ISBN 0-06-046455-0
    1. State governments—United States.   2. Local government—United States.   3.
Federal government—United States.   4. Pressure groups—United States.   5. Polit-
ical participation—United States.
    I. Day, Susan Bland.   II. Opheim, Cynthia.   III. Title.
JK2408.S857   1991
353.9—dc20   90-5014
                                                                                   CIP

90 91 92 93   9 8 7 6 5 4 3 2 1

Dedicated with love and respect to our strongest supporters:
Sandy, Cinnamon, and Brewer Stouffer
Jeff Opheim
Jo and Wallie Bland

Contents

Features   *xviii*
Preface   *xxii*

CHAPTER 1 **Why?**   1

Why Study State and Local Politics?   1
   It Was Good Enough for Plato and Aristotle   2
   These Governments Are Major Actors in the National
     Political Economy   2
   State and Local Governments Are Major Customers   3
   State and Local Governments Are Major Employers   4
   The Federal Government Depends on State and
     Local Governments   5
   Some State and Local Governments Try Harder   5
   State and Local Governments Are Launching Pads for Careers   6
   State and Local Governments Are Launching Pads for Innovations   6
Why the Individual?   9
   Individual Action Matters   9
   Individuals Matter   13
   Collective Bias of Social Sciences   14
   Humanizing Promotes Understanding   15
   The Obligation to Contribute Our Talents to the Community   15
Why the Governments?   16
Why Yet Another Book on State and Local Government?   18
   How to Pass Tests on This Book   19
   Stretching Minds   20
Conclusion   *21*

Study Objectives   21
Glossary   22

CHAPTER 2   **The State and Local Environment**   24

The Conceptual Environment   24
    Politics   25
    Government and the State   25
    The Nation-State   26
Political Systems: Two Sets of Similarities   28
    Similarities Shared Because They Are Systems   28
    Similarities Shared by Political Systems   29
The Changing Technological Environment   34
    Rapid Technological Change   34
    The Metropolitan Paradox   37
The Environment of Belief: Political Culture   39
    Political Socialization   39
    Three Regional Subcultures   40
    National Identity   46
Conclusion   49
Study Objectives   50
Glossary   51

CHAPTER 3   **Federalism and Intergovernmental Relations**   54

Federalism: A Novel American Compromise   55
    Three Things That Federalism Is   55
    Three Things Federalism Is Not   58
American Federalism: A Four-Dimensional Definition   60
    A Union of Governments   61
    A Union of People   61
    The Government of the Union Exercises Sovereignty   63
    The Union Is Made of Indestructible Parts: Six Guarantees 66
    American Federalism: The Litmus Test   69
Federalism: A Working Vocabulary   70
    Expressed Powers   70
    Implied Powers   71
    Concurrent Powers   72
    Powers Denied the National Government   72
    Obligations of the States to One Another   73
    Powers Prohibited to the States   74
Modern American Federalism: Intergovernmental Relations (IGR)   75
Some of the Solutions in Operation   78
    The ACIR: Advice and Attention   78
    Councils of Government   78

The Council of State Governments   80
Fiscal Federalism   80
Ten Federal Administrative Regions   86
The Essentials: Characteristics That Remain the Same   87
A Union of Sovereign People   88
A Union of Governments   88
Constitutional Guarantees That Still Work   89
A Government of the Union That Still Exercises Sovereignty   89

Conclusion   89
Study Objectives   90
Glossary   90

CHAPTER 4   Foundations of the Governments: State
            Constitutions   95

State and Local Sources of Authority   95
Constitutional Government: Two Ideas in Conflict   98
Four Principles of Limited Government   100
Liberalism   100
Republicanism   102
Separation of Powers   103
Democracy   104
Four Principles: Summary   110
Conditions Promoting Constitutional Government   112
Preparing for the Twenty-first Century: Constitutional Revision   113
State Constitutional Flaws   113
Guidelines for Constitutional Design   114
Constitutional Adaptation   115
Formal Changes in State Constitutions   116
Amendment   117
Revision   119
Revision by Convention   119
Revision by Commission   120
Constitutional Revisions and You   121
Conclusion   122
Study Objectives   122
Glossary   123

CHAPTER 5   Foundations of the Local Governments   126

Are Local Governments Really Necessary?   128
Sources of Local Government Authority   130
State Constitutions   130
State Laws   130

Local Charters   130
Local Acts or Ordinances   131
Structure (and Politics)   131
Executive-Legislative Relations   131
Chief Executive-Executive Branch Relations   132
Five Types of Local Governments   133
The County   134
Towns and Townships   135
Municipalities   137
Independent School Districts   142
Special Districts   143
Reasons for Creating Additional Local Governments   144
Constitutional and Statutory Restrictions   144
Interest Group Power   146
Private Profit   147
Intergovernmental Convenience   149
Defensive Incorporation   149
Alternatives to the Creation of New Intergovernments   151
Are There Too Many Local Governments?   153
Yes, There Are Too Many   153
Kellogg and Battle Creek   155
No, There Aren't Too Many Governments   157
Conclusion   159
Study Objectives   160
Glossary   160

CHAPTER 6   Political Participation—Making the System Work:
             The Options   164

Participation: Conventional and Unconventional   165
The Fox   166
An Individual Can Act Alone   166
Political Participation Involves a Wide Range of Activities   167
You Can Lose Your Battles and Win the War   167
Political Participation Can Be an Enjoyable Experience   171
Participation Can Change the Political System for Better or for
    Worse   171
Who Participates?   172
Opportunity Cost   173
A Hierarchy of Activities   174
Accumulating Activities   175
The Verba-Nie Typology of Participant Types   175
The Birmingham Study   178
Public Opinion   179
Participation Strategies   182

Lobbying 183
Grass-Roots Lobbying 185
Demonstrating 186
Appointmenteering 189
Electioneering 190
Litigation 192
Conditions That Influence Participation 192
Six Conditions You Can Influence That Increase Participation 193
Institutional Factors: Powell's Paradox 197
Conclusion 199
Study Objectives 199
Glossary 200

CHAPTER 7 **Participation Through Institutions: The Interest Group Option** 203
Three Institutions for Political Participation 203
Interest Groups 204
Political Action Committees 204
Political Parties 209
Interest Groups as Institutions 211
The Variety of Interest Groups 211
Business 212
Labor Unions 213
Professional or Occupational Associations 213
Intergovernmental Organizations 215
Public-Interest Groups 216
Organizations of Religious and Moral Concerns 217
Ethnic Organizations 217
Local and Neighborhood Organizations 218
Agricultural Organizations 218
Functions Performed by Interest Groups 219
Informing 219
Representing 222
Balancing 222
Symbolizing 223
Mobilizing 223
Problems Associated with Interest Groups 223
Irresponsibility 223
Government by the Few 224
Undemocratic Decision Making 225
Misrepresentation: The Selective Benefits Problem 226
Diversity 227
Elitism 228
Paralysis of Government: Hyperpluralism 229

The Business Bias   *230*

Controlling the Mischiefs of Faction   231
    Disclosure   *231*
    Regulation   *232*
    Public Financing   *233*
    Strengthening Other Institutions   *233*

Conclusion   **254**

Study Objectives   **234**

Glossary   **235**

CHAPTER 8   **Institutions for Participation: Political Parties and**
Elections   **238**

Political Party: A Definition   239
    Control of Government   *240*
    Two Parties   *240*
    One-Party Regions and No-Party Elections   *240*
The Formal Structure of Political Parties   241
    The Party in Office   *242*
    The Electoral Party Organization   *244*
    The Party in the Electorate   *248*
The Responsible Party Model   253
    Six Assumptions About Politics in Complex Societies *254*
    Two Components of Responsible Party Theory   *258*
The American Party System: Why the Same Two Parties?   260
    Historical Factors   *260*
    Electoral Rules   *261*
    Constitutional Arrangements   *261*
    Career Strategies   *263*
    Socioeconomic Factors   *263*
Why Are Party Labels Excluded from Most City Elections?   265
    Patronage   *265*
    Machine Politics   *267*
    The Structure of Political Machines   *269*
    Politics as a Business   *270*
    Functions of the Machines   *271*
    The Decline of Political Machines   *272*
    The Reform Movement   *275*
Bringing Back the Balance   278
    Partisan Municipal Elections   *279*
    Including Party Identity at Registration   *279*
    Closed Primaries   *279*
    The Straight Ticket Option   *280*
    Endorsing Conventions   *280*
    Allocating Surplus Campaign Funds to State or Local Parties *281*

   Providing Parties with Free Television and Radio Time   281
   Giving Parties the Authority to Organize State Legislatures   282
 Conclusion: Can Parties Adjust?   282
 Study Objectives   283
 Glossary   284

CHAPTER 9 **Legislatures**   289

 The Functions of Legislatures   290
  Lawmaking   290
  Budget Making   291
  Oversight   291
  Judicial   292
  Representation   294
  Amending   296
 State Legislatures   296
  Historical Changes in the Role of State Legislatures   297
  The Modern State Legislature   298
  The Structure and Organization of State Legislatures   306
  How a Bill Becomes Law   311
 Local Legislatures   316
  County Boards   316
  City Councils   318
 Obtaining Access   325
  Strategies of Influence   325
 Conclusion   328
 Study Objectives   329
 Glossary   330

CHAPTER 10 **Chief Executives**   333

 The Functions of Chief Executives   334
  Symbolic   334
  Administrative   334
  Legislative   335
  Fiscal   336
 Governors   337
  Historical Development of the Role of Governor   337
  The Modern Governor   339
  Recruitment, Tenure, and Compensation   342
  The Governor as Manager   343
  The Governor as Chief Legislator   348
  The Governor as Party Leader   352
 Local Chief Executives   353
  Counties: Headless Horsemen   353

Mayors   *354*
City Managers   *360*
School Superintendents   *363*
Conclusion   **365**
Study Objectives   **366**
Glossary   **366**

CHAPTER 11   **The Many Limbs of the Executive Branch**   **370**

Functions of Bureaucracy   373
   Administration   *374*
   Rule Making   *374*
   Revising Rules: Adjudication   *375*
The Nature of Bureaucratic Organization   375
Organization of State Executive Branches   376
   The Lieutenant Governor   *378*
   Department Heads and Top Administrators   *379*
   The Civil Service   *381*
   Reorganization of State Executive Branches *384*
   An Example of State Bureaucratic Organization: The Texas
     Public Education System   *385*
Bureaucrats in the Intergovernmental System   387
   Effects of Federal Dollars   *387*
   Relations of State and Local Administrators *388*
Reforming the Bureaucracy: Current Issues   389
   Budgeting and Budget Reform   *389*
   State and Local Employee Unions   *391*
   Contracting out Public Services: Privatization *394*
   Openness in Government   *396*
   Legislative Control of the Bureaucracy   *400*
Conclusion   **401**
Study Objectives   **403**
Glossary   **404**

CHAPTER 12   **The Search for Justice: Law and the Judiciary** **407**

The Nature of Law   408
   Law and Justice   *409*
   Law in a Federal System   *409*
The Forms of Law   410
   Common Law   *410*
   Equity Law   *411*
   Statute Law or Civil Law   *412*
   Administrative Law   *412*
   Civil Law and Criminal Law   *413*

The Law and the Search for Justice	*414*
The Judiciary: Courts and Cases	414
Civil Cases	*414*
Criminal Cases	*415*
The Judiciary: Courts and Jurisdictions	417
Courts of Last Appeal	*418*
Intermediate Courts of Appeal	*421*
State Trial Courts	*421*
Local Trial Courts	*421*
Justice of the Peace Courts	*423*
Cost of State and Local Court Systems	*423*
The Judiciary: Lawyers and Judges	424
Lawyers: Gatekeepers of the Legal System	*424*
Judges: The Individuals in Charge	*428*
The Judiciary: Court Reform	434
Conclusion	*436*
Study Objectives	*436*
Glossary	*436*

CHAPTER 13 **The Search for Justice: Crime, Police, and Corrections** **441**

Criminal Justice	441
Crime, Victimization, and Imprisonment	442
What Is Crime?	*443*
How Are Crimes Counted?	*443*
How Much Crime Occurs in the United States?	*445*
Who Are the Victims?	*448*
Drugs and Crime	*449*
Who Goes to Prison?	*449*
State and Local Programs for Crime Reduction	*451*
Law Enforcement: The Challenge of Policing a Free Society	453
The Number of Law Enforcement Personnel	*454*
Kinds of Law Enforcement Personnel	*454*
Who Becomes a Police Officer?	*455*
What Do Police Officers Do?	*456*
Why Do Police Officers Do What They Do?	*457*
Civil Liberties and Police Work	*462*
Future of Law Enforcement in the United States	*462*
What Can the Individual Do?	*464*
Corrections: The Challenge of Humane and Effective Punishment	465
The Types of Correctional Facilities	*466*
Imprisonment in the United States	*467*
Incarceration in the United States Today	*468*
How Many People Are in Prison?	*468*

The Corrections Officer	*469*
Probation	*470*
Proposals	*471*
The Debate Revisited: Deterrence, Rehabilitation, or Retribution?	*472*
The Costs of Justice: Pay Now or Later?	*473*
What We Can Do as Citizens in the Community	475
Conclusion	*475*
Study Objectives	*476*
Glossary	*477*

CHAPTER 14 **The Search for Justice: Poverty and Welfare**	**483**
Poverty	483
What Is Poverty?	*485*
How Many Are Poor?	*487*
The Causes of Poverty Among the Deserving Poor:	
Unemployment, Family Disorganization, Low Wages, and the	
Culture of Poverty	*488*
Failure to Work: The Undeserving Poor?	*491*
Consequences of Poverty	*492*
Poverty and the Fifty States	*496*
The System of Welfare	496
Should We Have a Welfare System?	*496*
What Is Welfare?	*498*
Federal, State, and Local Governments: Partnership or Rivalry?	*498*
Federal, State, and Local Welfare Programs for the Poor	*500*
How Much Does the Welfare System Cost?	*501*
Who Receives Welfare?	*504*
Does Welfare Make Any Difference?	*505*
A New Proposal: Workfare	*508*
Conclusion: What We Can Do in Our Communities	*508*
Study Objectives	*510*
Glossary	*510*

CHAPTER 15 **Paying for It: The Revenue-Expenditure System**	**515**
The Budget: A Plan for Paying for It	516
Nine Influences on Governmental Budgets	*516*
Redistribution: What Gets Paid for and Who Pays	*521*
Budget Choices: The Art of the Possible	*522*
The Fiscal Year	*524*
Agency Budget Requests	*524*
The Budget and You	*525*
Expenditures: Where Does the Money Go?	526
Government Contributions to the GNP	*526*

The Growth of Government Spending — 526
Major State and Local Functions: What We Pay For — 527

The Revenue System — 532
No New Taxes: The Promise of Free Lunches — 533
Types of State and Local Taxes — 536
Determining the Mix — 538
Ten Characteristics of a Good State-Local Revenue System — 538
Tax Capacity and Tax Effort: Comparing the Fifty States — 550

Conclusion: Regressivity and Redistribution — 553
Study Objectives — 553
Glossary — 554

Index — 559

Features

CHAPTER 1

Box 1-1 Some of the State and Local Zoos Preserving Endangered Species Through Captive Breeding Programs 4

Box 1-2 Selected Ford Foundation Innovation Winners: 1986–1987 8

Box 1-3 An Incident in a Small Texas Town 12

Box 1-4 The Giraffe Project 16

Box 1-5 Layers of Government in Fridley, Minnesota 17

CHAPTER 2

Box 2-1 Political Resources the Power of Persuasion 30

Box 2-2 The Stoplight and the Long Island Schoolchildren 33

Box 2-3 Year of the Human Race 35

Box 2-4 From the Declaration of Independence 41

Box 2-5 The Anglo Core Culture in *The Federalist* 47

CHAPTER 3

Box 3-1 Unitary, Federal, and Confederal Structure 56

Box 3-2 Federalism and Three Compromises 57

Box 3-3 Countries with a Federal Form of Government 59

Box 3-4 To the Members of the American Nation: Come into the Union and Bring Your State Governments with You 62

Box 3-5 Guarantees of State Viability in the Constitution 67

Box 3-6 The Proliferation of Grant Programs in San Jose 76

Box 3-7 As a Federal Agent, a City Can Take State Property 77

Box 3-8 Publications of the Council of State Governments 81

Box 3-9 Organizations Affiliated with the Council of State Governments 82

Box 3-10   Cooperating Organizations: Nonmembers   83
Box 3-11   A Brief Grants-in-Aid Vocabulary   85

CHAPTER 4
Box 4-1   How to Keep Government on the Sidelines   99
Box 4-2   The "L" Word   101
Box 4-3   Selected Safeguards for Plebiscitary Democracy   111

CHAPTER 5
Box 5-1   Diversity from State to State: Local Governments   127
Box 5-2   The Northwest Ordinance of 1787   137
Box 5-3   Creating Profitable Governments   148
Box 5-4   Recommendations of the Committee for Economic Development   154
Box 5-5   Examples of Functional Cooperation in the St. Louis City—County Area   158

CHAPTER 6
Box 6-1   Greenpeace and Environmental Politics   167
Box 6-2   A Few Individuals Who've Stuck Their Necks Out   168
Box 6-3   Individuals Who Take Action May Start Out Alone, but They Seldom End Up that Way   169
Box 6-4   A Plethora of Participation Options   170
Box 6-5   Myths with Special Meaning: The Consequences of Believing that You Can't Fight City Hall   171
Box 6-6   The Many Meanings of "Lobby"   184
Box 6-7   Boards and Commissions in a Medium-Size City   191
Box 6-8   The Volunteer and Money in the Bank   193
Box 6-9   An Individual is More Likely to Participate if He or She   194

CHAPTER 7
Box 7-1   A Mix of Opinions on PACs   207
Box 7-2   Union Shops for Lawyers in Right-to-Work States   214
Box 7-3   Interest Group Democracy: Common Cause   217
Box 7-4   Better Farming Through Chemistry: A Case Study of Interest Group Conflict   220
Box 7-5   Six Major Sources of Interest Group Funds   225
Box 7-6   Gentle Persuasion   226

CHAPTER 8
Box 8-1   Types of State and Local Elections   255
Box 8-2   Cues Used by Voters in Elections Without Party Labels, Including Primary Elections   256

Box 8-3   The Logic of Patronage   267
Box 8-4   Ambassadorships: Modern Examples of Patronage at the Edge of the Benefit of the Doubt   268
Box 8-5   Boss Tweed: An Odious Individual   269

CHAPTER 9
Box 9-1   Sunset in the States: Mixed Reviews   293
Box 9-2   Partisan Gerrymandering in California   301
Box 9-3   The Saga of Willie Brown   309
Box 9-4   Tips on Writing or Visiting Your Elected Representative   326

CHAPTER 10
Box 10-1   Selling a Vision: Governor Bill Clinton and Education Reform in Arkansas   340
Box 10-2   Different Views of the Governor as Manager   344
Box 10-3   Personality and Mayoral Success: Biracial Politics in Mississippi   357
Box 10-4   Need Neighborhood Services? Try Hiring the Neighbors   361

CHAPTER 11
Box 11-1   The Problems of the Texas State Board of Insurance   372
Box 11-2   Awards for Creative Nonresponsiveness   373
Box 11-3   Public Unions Push for Comparable Worth   394
Box 11-4   A Whistle-Blower Speaks Up   399

CHAPTER 12
Box 12-1   Common Law in Action   411
Box 12-2   The Small Claims Court   422
Box 12-3   So You Want to Be a Lawyer?   425
Box 12-4   The Paralegal: Another Career in the Judiciary   427
Box 12-5   The Election of Judges and Campaign Contributions   431

CHAPTER 13
Box 13-1   *Uniform Crime Report* Definitions   444
Box 13-2   The Calculation of Crime and Victimization Rates   447
Box 13-3   Who Are the Offenders?   450
Box 13-4   AIDS in Prison   470
Box 13-5   The Probation Officer: Social Worker with the Power to Imprison   471

CHAPTER 14
Box 14-1   Who Are the Poor?   489

Box 14-2   Homeless, with Children, in America   494
Box 14-3   A Day in the Life of a Welfare Worker   506

CHAPTER 15
Box 15-1   Budgets Involve Life-and-Death Decisions   517
Box 15-2   Reinforcing Inequality: Selected Examples   523
Box 15-3   Fiscal Year Frustrations   525
Box 15-4   Revenue Sources for State and Local Governments   533
Box 15-5   Collecting the Property Tax   546

Preface

Our point of view is that the individual matters, that individual action makes a difference in what government does. From this premise comes our concern with reform, with providing a lucid book that will encourage individuals to study the institutions and processes on which they are most likely to have an impact — state and local governments. From our concern with the individual also comes our emphasis on the intergovernmental context. To be effective, individuals have to become informed about the interacting, overlapping, and sometimes competing units of government of which they are citizens, voters, and taxpayers.

As teachers, we are concerned about the fact that students come to our text with different skills and levels of preparation. That is why Chapter 1 spends some time addressing this issue and why every chapter ends with a glossary and study objectives on which both learning and testing can be based.

As teachers, we are also aware that some colleagues with whom we hope to be sharing students may find our organization of material a little different. In developing our intergovernmental theme we have tried to avoid causing difficulties for colleagues who may wish to treat local government separately from state government. We have placed the local government portions at the end of chapters that include material on local institutions. We hope that reading assignments can be more easily organized simply by referring to the table of contents instead of skipping all over a chapter to mold our work to your needs.

As idealists, we believe that politically skilled and motivated individuals can increase the rationality and effectiveness of our intergovernmental system. Thus, our book has an unabashed reformist and participatory outlook. We believe that virtually anything humans make can be improved; more important, we believe that it is essential to improve our state and local systems of governing so that we can better deal with the myriad problems that confront us. As we point out more than once, our students — the future leaders of our states and communities — will be asked to make decisions about changing their state and local political systems. Exploring some of these proposals in the classroom as early as possible makes a lot of sense to us.

We are serious about teaching. We feel that we are coteachers with the instructors who adopt this book for their courses. Producing a textbook that challenges students and encourages them to read beyond the assigned text was one of our motivations for taking on this project. We have tried very hard to make this book readable, and we would like to think that at times it's even interesting. Our major intent is to be as lucid and straightforward as possible without sacrificing substance. We've seen too many cute, shallow texts that grab your attention and then don't do much with it. However, we also know how difficult it is to get students to stay with encyclopedia-like texts. We've tried to walk a fine line between being merely interesting and being merely informative. We hope you approve of the result.

We would like to thank all the people who have assisted us during the lengthy course of this project. In particular we'd like to thank Chuck Hickman, our HarperCollins representative, who helped us get rolling many drafts ago and kept after us to finish. Lauren Silverman, the Political Science Editor, is owed our gratitude for her advice and encouragement. We'd also like to thank Melonie Parnes, our project editor, and our colleagues on other campuses who made many helpful suggestions.

J. Edwin Benton
University of South Florida

James Button
University of Florida

Paige Cubbison
Miami Dade Community College

Michael R. Fitzgerald
University of Tennessee

James M. Graham
Carl Sandburg College

James Hanley
Mott Community College

James A. Jarvis
Wayne State University

Eleanor C. Main
Emory University

Ken Mladenka
Texas A & M University

James Morse
Temple University

Albert J. Nelson
University of Wisconsin

David C. Nice
University of Georgia

Lois M. Pelekoudas
Central State University

Richard C. Rich
Virginia Polytechnic Institute and State University

Ronald J. Schmidt
California State University/Long Beach

John R. Todd
North Texas State University

Richard D. Willis
University of Iowa

William Winter
University of Colorado/Boulder

Many of our colleagues at Southwest Texas State have been most helpful. In particular, we appreciate the efforts of Dan Farlow, Patricia Shields, and Landon Curry, who read parts of the manuscript and provided insightful criticisms. The staff members of the Southwest Texas State University library, especially Robert Harris, Ann Blakely, Al Quinn and Magaret Vaverek, were extremely patient in helping us locate necessary documents and useful data. Last but not least, we could not have finished—probably ever but certainly not when we did—had it not been for Lisa Whiteside, Ann Birdsong, and Marie Gutierrez, who contributed countless hours of typing, editing, and duplicating. They made our task infinitely less difficult.

W. B. Stouffer
Cynthia Opheim
Susan Day

Chapter 1

Why?

We begin with an attempt to answer four questions that any reasonable person might ask about this state and local government textbook.

1. Why study state and local politics?
2. Why use the word "individual" in the subtitle?
3. Why use the plural of the word "government" in the subtitle?
4. Why yet another book on state and local government?

WHY STUDY STATE AND LOCAL POLITICS?

There are several answers to this question. In the interest of brevity, we will deal with only eight of them.

It Was Good Enough for Plato and Aristotle

State and local politics is a legitimate and traditional subject of study. The origins of this study can be traced to the founding of the discipline of political science. The founders of political science lived in and studied a type of community called the *polis*, the city-state of ancient Greece. In attempting to develop a science of the well-ordered, harmonious community, Plato and Aristotle dealt with the units of government closest to the individual. Although these communities were often independent of a larger central government, early political scientists were concerned with issues that are still relevant at local and state as well as national levels of governance.

These issues include corruption (why it occurs and how to avoid it), justice (what it is and how to obtain it), the appropriate role of money in politics (should those who have the gold make the rules?), who really governs (the one, the few, or the many?), who ought to govern, and in whose interests they should govern. Is politics the process of getting one's own or using political resources to serve the community?

These Governments are Major Actors in the National Political Economy

The **political economy** is the collection of reward systems that affect the choices available in a given society.[1] The political economy is the part of **society** where **politics** and **economics** overlap. The study of political economy focuses on the variety of taxes, permits, licenses, rules, and regulations (such as those on minimum wages, working conditions, or on the maximum axle weight of trucks) that affect economic decision making by individuals and by organizations. Each social science studies political economy from a slightly different perspective. This book was written by two political scientists and a sociologist. Thus, we may not see things in exactly the same way as your economics or history instructors and textbook authors. This diversity of viewpoints is a healthy thing. It leaves the final decisions on what to believe and what to do about what you believe up to you.

What won't be up to you is making decisions with political and economic consequences. Like it or not, you will face numerous decisions from the obvious — pay your taxes or take your chances on getting caught when you don't — to the subtle — should you work on Saturday morning or sleep in if the next dollar you earn will be taxed at a higher rate? Thus, whatever your choice, you will play a role in the political economy.

However, unless you choose an active role in the political system, you simply leave to others decisions about changing or maintaining the economic regulations, taxes, **tax expenditures**, and legal rights that exist in your state and community. Whether you act politically or not, the political economy will be there to influence you by means of rewards, penalties, choices, and opportunities.

Some dimensions of our state and local political economies are products of foreign competition and decisions by the federal government. For example, a low rate of inflation is maintained in exchange for a nationwide unemployment rate of nearly 10 percent. However, state and local governments make numerous decisions that produce economic rewards and penalties, including decisions about borrowing (selling bonds) instead of taxing to raise revenue and decisions to spend or not to spend money on the maintenance of equipment, buildings, bridges, highways, and sewer lines. These decisions and others like them may offer opportunities for state and local residents to avoid paying higher taxes now, but they ultimately affect the choices that future leaders as well as you and your children will face in the years and decades to come.

The idea that state and local governments are major actors in the political economy is supported by the fact that they spend over $775 billion a year.[2] They are major customers, employers, and providers of services such as police protection, garbage disposal, water, sewage disposal, electricity, emergency medical care, day care, parks, and recreational facilities from gold courses to zoos (Box 1-1).

State and local governments are also major economic regulators in areas such as food inspection, health inspection, building safety, and the licensing of occupations from barbering to neurosurgery. Each of these roles in the political economy is by itself a valid reason for studying state and local politics.

State and Local Governments are Major Customers

Each year state governments alone spend more than $4 billion on equipment; they also spend over $19 billion on construction. In addition to these sums, a goodly portion of the $176 billion spent on current operations goes for purchases of supplies, sometimes from local businesses and sometimes directly from the manufacturer.[3]

Sometimes state and local governments make decisions about their purchases that have effects beyond their borders. The state of California purchases thousands of automobiles and trucks each year. The specifications for pollution control and safety that it requires for fleet purchases have a great influence on auto manufacturers. Some manufacturers find it makes economic sense to use these specifications for all their models; others may decide to modify standard vehicles for the California market.

Each year the textbook committee of the state of Texas Board of Education makes decisions which have a profound effect on the textbook publishing industry because it is making decisions for the one thousand school districts in Texas which purchase about 20 percent of all the schoolbooks bought nationwide in any given year. The decisions of the textbook committee have a profound effect on the decisions made by various publishers about whether to continue publishing editions of certain books. Obviously, this economic decision has other important repercussions for the content of textbooks throughout the United States.

Individuals who anticipate playing a role in the free enterprise system

Box 1-1   # Some of the State and Local Zoos Preserving Endangered Species Through Captive Breeding Programs

State	Zoo	Animal
Alabama	Birmingham Zoo	Red wolf, white rhino
Colorado	Denver Zoological Gardens	Red panda
Connecticut	Beardsley Zoological Gardens	Red wolf
Florida	Discovery Island Zoological Park	Golden lion tamarin
Hawaii	Honolulu Zoo	Black lemur, golden lion tamarin, red crown crane
Kansas	Lee Richardson Zoo	Black rhinoceros
Maryland	Baltimore Zoo	White-naped crane
New York	New York Zoological Park	Chinese alligator
North Carolina	North Carolina Zoological Park	Grevy's zebra
Ohio	Columbus Zoological Park	Puerto Rican crested toad
Oklahoma	Oklahoma City Zoological Park	Arabian oryx, Aruba Island rattlesnake
Oregon	Washington Park Zoo	Asian elephant, Humboldt penguin
Pennsylvania	Philadelphia	Andean condor
South Carolina	Riverbanks Zoological Park	Black palm cockatoo
Utah	Hogle Zoological Garden	Red-ruffed lemur
Washington	Point Defiance Zoo	Golden lion tamarin
Wisconsin	Milwaukee County Zoological Gardens	Snow leopard

Source: Carol Memmott, "Modern-Day Noahs Work to Save Animals," *USA Today*, October 10, 1989.

may consider it useful to know something about one of the biggest markets —or sets of customers—in our economy. State and local governments also affect the economy in terms of licensing requirements and charges, taxing and borrowing activities, and decisions about whether to own and operate economic enterprises such as railroads, liquor stores, and utility companies.[4] Even business majors can learn something useful from a course in state and local government.

State and Local Governments Are Major Employers

There are over 13 million jobs in state and local governments, and approximately 11 million of them are full-time jobs. Naturally, not all these jobs are available at once. In times of economic distress governments may attempt to save money by leaving some important jobs vacant. However, it is unlikely that the state and local government payroll will ever again be less than $18 billion a year. That payroll includes five times as many civilians as the national government employs.[5]

The variety of jobs in state and local governments is about the same as that in the private sector. Therefore, it makes sense for those considering employment after college to take a look at some of the major employers in our economic system.

The Federal Government Depends on State and Local Governments

John Naisbitt, the author of *Megatrends*, has asserted that "in politics, it does not really matter any more who is president, and Congress has become obsolete. . . . State and local governments are the most important political entities in America."[6]

While our belief in the importance of the individual causes us to protest that it *does* matter who is President of the United States, of a university, or of any other organization, we share Naisbitt's optimism about the subject matter of this book — the 50 states and 80,000 local governments. The study of state and local governments as they currently exist is an excellent way to develop the background necessary to make informed choices about whether to change them at all and, if necessary, what to change in the years to come.

Furthermore, while we are inclined to feel that Naisbitt understates the importance of the national government, we agree that state and local governments are a very important part of the American political system. Most national policies, such as care for the aged, assistance for the unemployed, and education for all those able to benefit from it, are carried out by state and local employees. The federal government seldom sets up its own service delivery system. Instead, it usually creates a **grant** program to encourage state and local governments to perform certain important services. In 1987 the federal government channeled $153 billion into the economy via grants.[7]

Most grant money does not arrive automatically but must be applied for by state or local officials. Unless these officials, whom you elect, decide to apply for and accept the terms of a federal grant, your state or community will not receive federal funds for various projects and services. Thus state and local decision makers are key actors in our national political system. They influence how much state, local, and federal money is spent in your state and community. The fact that some leaders are willing to meet the conditions attached to federal grant opportunities and some are not is part of the reason why Arkansas, Louisiana, Oklahoma, New Mexico, and Texas received federal funds amounting to $344 per capita in 1987 while Colorado, Montana, North Dakota, South Dakota, Utah, and Wyoming received $588 per capita, nearly twice as much.[8] Thus, it may be worth taking a little time and trouble to learn how to get state and local decision makers to take a closer look at grant programs.

Some State and Local Governments Try Harder

Some governments offer a wide range of services and programs paid for from their own resources; others do not. As a citizen with many years of paying taxes ahead of you, you may find that it is a good investment of time to learn something about the services your governments provide as well as the costs involved. For example, the tuition fees at state schools, colleges, and universities result from political decisions made by state governments. The average rates for tuition and room and board at state colleges and universities within each of the 50 states range from $5324 in Vermont to $2286 in Nebraska.[9]

State and local governments vary widely in their ability to pay for services and benefits such as low tuition fees and financial assistance for college students. Equally important, if not more so, is the fact that these governments also vary widely in the efforts they make to use their ability of pay for services. We will explore this concept more thoroughly in Chapter 15. For the present, we'll simply note that a state or local government's wealth is not the only factor in determining whether it makes an effort to solve problems involving human needs and human suffering.

Learning more about whether the governments that serve you can "afford" to offer the services you think they should is an important reason for studying state and local government. In the course of this endeavor you may also gain some insight into how to go about influencing the decisions that state and local governments make.

State and Local Governments Are Launching Pads for Careers

If you are considering a political career, state and local governments are good places to get experience. The opportunities are there. More than 500,000 state and local officials are elected in each 4-year election cycle.

If you are thinking in terms of the "number one office" in the land, there are precedents for obtaining state and local experience first. George Washington, for example, served from 1759 to 1774 as a delegate to the Virginia House of Burgesses before taking on the job of commander in chief of the Revolutionary Army.

Among the Presidents in this century who have held state and/or local office one finds

Ronald Reagan—Governor of California

Jimmy Carter—Governor of Georgia

Harry S. Truman—Judge and county executive in Missouri

Franklin Delano Roosevelt—State senator and governor of New York

Calvin Coolidge—City Councilmember, mayor, state senator, and governor of Massachusetts

State and Local Governments Are Launching Pads for Innovations

Franklin Delano Roosevelt referred to the states as laboratories for experimentation. Many of the major problems facing this country today will be ameliorated and even solved by the nationwide application of experiments being planned or taking place as you read this paragraph.

The Ford Foundation's program of annual awards for innovation to state and local governments has brought to light many examples of how this can be done. Some of these examples are replacing the older, "how it should not be done" case studies that abound in graduate schools of public administration. Furthermore, this foundation grant program (as well as some of the examples themselves) provides ample evidence that government, business, and labor are not locked in a permanent adversarial relationship. They can and do work together to promote the ability of individuals and communities to solve difficult problems and occasionally come close to reaching their highest potential.[10]

The STEP (Strive Toward Excellence in Performance) program in Minnesota received an award for promoting innovation and efficiency in several ways. First, executives lent by businesses to state government studied the operations of the agencies to which they were assigned and made recommendations for improvements. For example, a utility company executive's suggestions led to a drastic reduction in the time it took to get a driver's license into the hands of individuals. Second, government workers were encouraged to experiment and make suggestions. Not only were rewards and recognition made available, but marketplace dynamics were introduced into the operation of many state agencies to encourage officials at all levels to view the public as customers to be pleased rather than as merely a herd of complaints and demands to be managed.

When the Minnesota Department of Natural Resources discovered that the use of state parks was declining because credit cards could not be used to pay entrance fees or buy things at camp stores, STEP officials went to bat for the people in the parks department and helped them overcome the resistance of the finance department. Officials in this agency at first didn't want their employees to have to deal with anything but cash and checks. Once plastic was accepted, park usage and revenue increased. The department of natural resources has more money in its budget, the finance department has been able to apply to other departments the changes necessary to accommodate credit cards (thus countering the stereotype of obstructionist bean counters), and the people of Minnesota are happier with their parks.[11] As John Hebers observes,

> Marketplace dynamics is one aspect of an innovative managerial culture that is spreading out of Minnesota to other states and jurisdictions as far away as Hawaii. It is sometimes called a bottoms up strategy because it encourages change and creativity to bubble up from the ranks. It spurs officials to put their own ideas to work, take risks and, in turn, give their subordinates more freedom to be innovative.

Thus, as this example and Box 1-2 indicate, there is a lot more to state and local governments than most people are aware. Whether you help these governments as an active citizen promoting the spread of helpful innovations or as a public servant making them work, state and local governments can put your time and talent to good use.

Box 1-2 # Selected Ford Foundation Innovation Winners:
1986–1987

Program	Purpose	Inquiries	Known replications
Family Learning Center Leslie Public Schools Ingham County, Michigan	Provides child care, transportation to high school, and social services to teenage parents from rural areas	56+ 10 international	None known
Video Disc Catalog Department of Finance Rochester, New York	Uses laser videodisc technology to compile a pictorial record of all local properties in order to enhance the consistency of property valuations	60+ 10 international	25 cities have adopted some portion of the program
Alternative to Incarceration Department of Corrections State of Georgia	Reduces overcrowding in prisons by assigning nonviolent offenders to varying degrees of probationary supervision	Numerous inquiries, including 38 foreign governments	22 states have replicated at least one of the programs
Parents Too Soon Department of Public Health State of Illinois	Reduces teenage pregnancy by educating teens about the realities of child care; also deals with health risks to mothers and infants, high rates of infant mortality, and interrupted education	1 per month	14 states are using the campaign (videos, posters and public service announcements), in which teen parents talk about their experiences
Homeless Services Network Department of Human Services St. Louis, Missouri	Addresses the crisis needs of people living, or at risk of living, on the streets (especially homeless women with children) through city-	73	Fort Worth has a similar system to transport people to shelters, clinics, and job interviews

continued

Box 1-2 *(continued)*

	funded services provided by private agencies		
Open Public Events Network Agency for Public Telecommuni- cations State of North Carolina	Enhances public access and understanding of state government through television coverage, followed by viewer call-ins	100+	Minnesota and Washington have modified versions of the program
Parents as Teachers Program Department of Elementary and Secondary Education State of Missouri	Guides parents through their children's first 3 years of development through home visits by educators and group meetings with other parents and children	4 per day	46 programs in 25 states

Source: John Hebers, "Other Winners Still Solve Problems from Child Care to Water Cleanup," *Governing*, Vol 3.1, October 1989, pp. 33–45.

WHY THE INDIVIDUAL?

There are essentially five reasons why we used the word "individual" in the subtitle of this book: (1) the importance of individual action, (2) the value of each individual, (3) the collective bias of the social sciences, (4) the validity of humanizing the world to increase our ability to cope with it, and (5) the Aristotelian proposition about participation.

Individual Action Matters

A few months after graduation from Vanderbilt University, Marie Ragghianti was hired to work for the Tennessee state board of pardons and paroles. She was a single mother with two children who had spent many years in the threadbare existence of part-time jobs at starvation wages to feed her kids and get herself through school. At long last she achieved a fairly comfortable life-style.

After several months of hard work she was promoted to the position of chairperson of the board. Now she had an office and a secretary in addition to decent pay, reasonable hours, and meaningful work. Once she became chairperson of the board of pardons and paroles of the state of Tennessee, it looked as if Ragghianti could breathe easily for a while. For her, the middle-class dream had arrived: no more tight-pants cocktail waitressing, no more typing dull theses for graduate students who couldn't spell. She could save some money, contribute to her church, buy new clothes for her kids, and take them out to eat in a decent restaurant occasionally.

It soon became clear, however, that her superiors expected Ragghianti to cooperate in a bribery scheme to sell pardons and paroles. All she had to do was sign off on recommendations to Governor Ray Blanton to free or reduce the sentences of undeserving but well-connected criminals. Money, not **rehabilitation**, became the criterion for releasing rapists, drug dealers, and murderers from state prison.

To her superiors, Ragghianti must have seemed perfect for the job. She was a devout Catholic — "Hey, they're used to accepting authority, aren't they?" She had an Italian name — "Those people 'understand' about bending rules, don't they?" She had three kids to support, having left a wife-beating husband to work her way through college — "She needs her paycheck, doesn't she? Besides, she knows the way things are." She had worked in the Tennessee Young Democrats while in college — "Marie? She'll cooperate." Unfortunately for them, her superiors forgot that **stereotypes**, though sometimes useful, are *always* imperfect pictures of reality.

When Ragghianti heard about the payoffs, she thought at first that Governor Blanton was being used. She soon learned better — either he knew what was going on or he didn't want to know. After some fairly explicit warnings from the governor's office to keep quiet about what she had learned, Ragghianti felt certain that if she spoke out she would soon lose her job, maybe more. Friends told her to keep quiet and to cooperate. "'The system' is too big," they said.

To Ragghianti, it just didn't seem right, no matter how big the system, to let the corruption she could see every day continue. As the pressure mounted, she wrote the following entry in her diary:

> I thought back to all the hard times that the kids & I had known, & all the meals of macaroni & cheese, & the cups of milk I'd borrowed, & the post-dated checks that we lived on, & the juggling of bills & the tears, & the marriage proposals, & the other proposals, & how *easy* it would have been, at any time, how *easy* it would have been to 'sell out.'[12]

And so she resolved not to sell out. Against the advice of others, including her priest, Ragghianti told the FBI about the governor, his legal counselor, and the rest of the crew. Pretty soon her diary contained the entry, "I am afraid now, really afraid. In fact, I am terrified."[13] In the course of the next 3 years Ragghianti was fired, a smear campaign was initiated in an attempt to discredit her, and she received death threats. Four people were murdered.

Ultimately the FBI investigation resulted in arrests and convictions of Governor Blanton's legal counsel and other conspirators as well as the termination of Blanton's governorship and the end of his political career. This all took place in the 1970s. Now Marie Ragghianti and her grown children are safe. She was reinstated in her job but left it shortly afterward to seek a law degree. A best-selling book and the sale of film rights have brought her some income and removed any doubts generated by the smear campaign. The governor and his coconspirators have served or are serving time in prison.

The business of pardon and parole selling in Tennessee is bankrupt, as is the liquor license business, for which Blanton ultimately was convicted. It's safe to assume that officials in other states will now think twice about pardons and paroles as sources of income. They will do so not because of recent constitutional amendments, new laws, or new anticorruption strike forces but rather because an individual stood up to say, "No, this is wrong!"

Individual actions, individual choices, individual talents, and individual tenacity matter even in a society of over 240 million people. That is why political scientists and other social scientists tend to employ words such as "frequently," "often," "most," "many," "seldom," and "infrequently" instead of "always," "invariably," "everyone," "all," and "never." Although there are patterns, the patterns do not apply to each individual in a given objective category. Individuals overcome gender, class, ethnic, and religious prejudice to do noble things for their fellow sufferers and sometimes for their ignorant tormentors. Individuals overcome poverty, racism, and physical handicaps to do great things for themselves and for the society of which they are members. Thus, we generalize about human beings very carefully.

While some individuals are clearly superstars or have faced unusual sets of circumstances, most of us are not superstars and never get the opportunity to put a governor in jail. Thus the study of the institutions, processes, and patterns by which our society offers rewards and makes progress possible is important. Whether you are a potential superstar or one of the rest of us, you need to learn about these things in order to discover how an individual can contribute to progress and help prevent the continuation of bad practices or the initiation of new ones that move us backward. The study of both our political system and the individuals who have helped it improve is an obligation to ourselves and to the generations which will follow. We can improve and preserve our state and local communities and our nation by identifying that which is worth saving as well as that which needs changing. If we don't, there are individuals who will make the changes for us in ways we may not appreciate.

To a very great extent the survival of our system depends on individuals standing up for what is right. Without hundreds of individual statements affirming that racial prejudice is wrong, the damage it does today would be far greater. Racial and ethnic prejudice is still here. Unlike the bad old days, there are more individuals around who no longer accept the evils of prejudice as something they can't do anything about. Box 1-3 is not the only

Box 1-3 An Incident in a Small Texas Town

In Texas law, a rear-end collision at a stop sign automatically makes the driver of the second car the guilty party. Thus, in late January 1983 a fender bender just off the square in Chaw, Texas, appeared to be a simple matter of discovering whether there were any injuries, getting the cars moved, and writing a ticket.

As Officer Jones, a former sergeant on the Houston police force and a decorated Vietnam veteran, approached the two vehicles, he had no idea that he was going to provide a lesson in human relations which would be the talk of the town for days and perhaps years to come. He had taken over as police chief in this small town to earn enough money to finish college in a nearby city and put away some money for law school. Teaching human relations was nowhere on his agenda.*****

"Anyone hurt?" he asked. The driver of the first vehicle, an elderly Mexican-American, just shook his head sadly. "Naw, I'm okay," said the driver of the second vehicle, also a senior citizen but an **Anglo** like the police officer. "Guess I was going a little too fast and hit this greaser here."

Officer Jones raised an eyebrow at the "greaser" and then said, "I'm afraid I'll have to issue you a ticket, sir."

"Me, a ticket?" said the driver, somewhat astonished. "But son, he's a Mesakin. They alluz git the tickets, else at leas' a stern talkin' to." Then he smiled knowingly. "Yer new in town, ain't you, son?"

Officer Jones placed his hand on man's shoulder and leaned toward him slightly.

"Could you just step over here a moment, sir?" He motioned to a spot a little farther away, out of the hearing of the other driver and the driver's wife, who was fighting back tears."

"Sure, son, anythin' you say."

When they reached the spot, Officer Jones took a deep breath before he said, "I sure wish you were thirty years younger, sir."

The man smiled. "So do I, son, but why?"

"Because then I could pound some manners into your ignorant, bigoted skull, sir. Now, pay very close attention," he said, carefully articulating every syllable. "When we go back to the vehicles, your language will have improved some. If I hear you utter one more racial slur in the hearing of that couple, you will be amazed at the things I can find to ticket you for. Besides following too closely, there are literally dozens of things wrong with your driving as well as with your vehicle. Furthermore, I had better not hear about any problems with your insurance company paying for the damage to their vehicle." He paused and smiled. "Now, go sit down and behave yourself while I do some paperwork here."

The bug-eyed Anglo swallowed and nodded. Truly white-faced now, he turned and walked slowly back to await his ticket.

The next day the mayor of the small town happened by the police chief's office.

"Understand you gave one of our senior citizens a little talking to."

"Yes, sir, I did."

"You know it's the main topic of conversation in the coffee shop, the post office, and the general store, don't you?"

continued

Box 1-3 *(continued)*

"Yes, sir."

"Keep up the good work, son. But lighten up just a little, okay?"

"I'll try, sir. I truly will, sir."†

---

*The names of town and officer have been changed. The officer is a former student whose language has been tidied up a bit but who affirms that this version of the incident is essentially accurate.

†Food for thought. When you stand up for your beliefs, there are other people involved. You not only affect the situation at hand, you help others, who share your beliefs, realize that they are not alone.

---

example of individuals standing up for what is right on this and many other issues.

Individuals Matter

We used the word "individual" in our subtitle simply as a statement of value. Each individual human being is important. We make no claim to being unique in recognizing this fact. The inherent worth of each individual is a theme that runs through the art, music, and literature of the Western world.

An individual is more than the sum of his or her physical parts and mental urges, trained to speak, dress, and pray in a certain manner or manipulated by the mass media to buy a product or vote for a product-candidate. Not only does it matter who leads, it also matters whether particular individuals choose to follow.

Perhaps no current conflict illustrates this more dramatically than the debate over whether a woman has the right to terminate a pregnancy. Both sides consistently affirm the value of individual human life. The central question is, When does human life begin? This critical question is so well recognized that comedy routines—"Four weeks, four months, foreplay?" —have been built around it. The issue itself is far from comic, and unfortunately, the debate is often far from genteel. Whichever side one takes, however, it is a side that firmly believes in the value of individual human life.

To point out that other human beings merit courtesy and respect even when we don't agree with them is to risk dwelling on the obvious. Civilized behavior toward individuals with whom we intensely disagree has practical consequences, not the least of which is a reduction in the amount of bloodshed and violence. The survival of our political system depends to a very great extent on a nonviolent approach to disagreements on some very big issues. Without this consensus, scarce resources would have to be allocated to keep the peace—resources that could instead be used for hospitals, food, shelter, and protection from activities that everyone agrees are criminal.

A bombed abortion clinic. Our intergovernmental system cannot exist in an open democratic society if violence becomes part of the tool kit for political expression. (Courtesy of Bettmann.)

Collective Bias of Social Sciences

The third reason for using the word "individual" in our subtitle has to do with the social science perspective, the way we must view human behavior. All the social sciences, including political science, emphasize the **collective** rather than the individual. We use collective terms such as "the people," "the electorate," "the public," "social class," and "ethnic group." It is useful to remind ourselves every now and then that a central goal of our scholarly effort is to help individual human beings understand and thus better operate in the social part of their world. We will occasionally provide examples of individuals such as Marie Ragghianti and Officer Jones in an attempt to counter the collective bias built into the subject matter of this book.

Humanizing Promotes Understanding

A fourth reason for including "individual" in the subtitle is to help make the world we are trying to explain not only more understandable but also worth understanding. In a large, complex society such as ours it is often tempting to believe that large, complex entities — the media, big business, government, special interests — rule our lives. If, occasionally, we realize that these entities are made up of individual human beings, we may find the world a friendlier place in which to live and work.

Not only is a such a world a less threatening place, it is also one we may be able to deal with more rationally and effectively. If we deal with other individuals as fellow humans instead of "things" that play roles, such as "bureaucrat" or "clerk," we may find these individuals responding to us as human beings. This may lead to cooperation in getting things done. Marie Ragghianti, you may recall, was a bureaucrat, that is, an employee of the state of Tennessee. Officer Jones is a police officer, also a member of a bureaucracy.

In discussing the future of our federal system, David Beam has observed:

> Although policy analysts have traditionally devoted most of their attention to the investigation of large impersonal forces in determining governmental events, the record shows that a decisive role is also played by personality, interests, values, and commitments of the decision makers themselves. Moreover, it is not just these very few "great" men and women of history, but a great many lesser individuals too, who sometimes have their stamp on governmental trends. Individuals tucked away at strategic locations in the legislature, the bureaucracy, interest groups, in the media, or elsewhere can influence outcomes by pointing out problems or proposing solutions.[14]

The Obligation to Contribute Our Talents to the Community

Our fifth and final reason for focusing on the individual has to do with the obligation to participate. Aristotle put it something like this: If good people don't participate in the affairs of the community, then others will. Because we believe that participating in our political system is worth the time and trouble it takes, we will point out from time to time the ways in which individuals have made a difference. More often than not these individuals have made ours a better system by participating in it.

Because individual actions are so important in maintaining what is good about our political system, an organization called the Giraffe Project (Box 1-4) was created a few years ago to give recognition to the actions of ordinary individuals across the country who've stuck their necks out to help others and reaffirm the values that too many of us take for granted.

Although this is not a how-to-do-it book, one of its major purposes is to equip the individual with a better understanding of how our political system works so that he or she can be more effective in dealing with it. Our basic assumptions about the American political system are that for all its faults, it is a system worth attempting to understand, and that informed participation

---

Box 1-4   **The Giraffe Project**

In 1983 John Graham, a retired foreign service officer, and Ann Medlock, a journalist, founded an organization to recognize people who "stick their necks out for the common good." Sticking one's neck out may involve discomfort, danger, or ostracism or cause one to lose one's job; sometimes it involves devoting time and energy to a long-term project for the good of others when the time could have been spent on more profitable activities. It usually involves some kind of risk.

Almost daily more than 500 radio stations report short accounts of people who are given a Giraffe award. Four times a year *The Giraffe Gazette* reports on the deeds of individuals who have been commended for their actions by a screening committee consisting of Graham, Medlock, and 10 to 15 friends and neighbors. "Each of these individual acts," says Medlock, "teaches the rest of us about learning to cope in an unsafe world."

Through the courtesy of the Giraffe Project, we will report in these pages on a few of the more than 300 Giraffes who have helped keep alive the notion that individuals matter. If you want to nominate someone for a Giraffe award or help the organization in other ways, here is the address:

The Giraffe Project, Box 759, Langely, WA 98260

Sources: *Time*, (August 8, 1988), 8, and *The Giraffe Gazette*.

---

is one of the best ways of understanding it. The more we know about the world of politics, the more comfortable we will be in acting constructively within it.

In sum, we believe that the individual matters because it is important who leads and the direction in which we are led. It also makes a difference when individuals speak up for what is right. Individual actions often have a ripple effect on the way other individuals see the world and thus on the way the world works.

WHY THE GOVERNMENTS?

In the subtitle of this book and from time to time in the pages which follow, we use "governments" in the plural because this word provides an occasional reminder that you, as a citizen, are responsible for electing and keeping track of the leaders in charge of several interacting units of government. Our use of the plural term "governments" also represents an attempt to emphasize the dynamics of the political system in which individuals and governments interact. Quite often, textbook authors use the term in the

Box 1-5 **Layers of Government in Fridley, Minnesota**

11. United States of America
10. State of Minnesota
 9. Metropolitan Mosquito Control District
 8. Minneapolis-St. Paul Metropolitan Airports Commission
 7. Anoka County
 6. Soil Conservation District
 5. North Suburban Hospital District
 4. Minneapolist-St. Paul Sanitary District
 3. North Suburban Sanitary Sewer District
 2. Independent School District
 1. City of Fridley

The individual citizen of: 1, 2, 3, 4, 5 . . .

Believe it or not: A citizen of Fridley, Minnesota, is expected to exercise informed control through the electoral franchise of over 11 superimposed governments and is taxed for their support.

Source: Committee for Economic Development, *Modernizing Local Government*, (New York: Committee for Economic Development, 1966), 12. Reprinted by permission.

singular to refer to any one of or all of the governments with which an individual must deal. When "government" is used in that way, it tends to give the impression of a well-integrated system that the individual must confront in order to get anything done. This, of course, is not the case. The individual confronts, one at a time, a number of units of government which do not necessarily work well together.

State and local governments interact in a number of ways: They make contracts with one another, perform services for one another, sue one another, give money to one another, and compete with one another for new industries and tourist dollars. Not only do many of these governments deal directly with one another, they may also deal with the same citizens. Many governments have authority over and responsibilities to the same land and people.

From our perspective, the fact that the individual may have more than one government to keep track of is an important feature of the political system. For an example of the number of governments with which an individual may interact in a not atypical urban area, see the case of Fridley, Minnesota, in Box 1-5. Each government's tax rate, service offerings, or both will have an effect on other governments and on the individual. Many city residents finance two separate road or street departments (city and county) without ever inquiring whether combined operations or cooperative arrangements might save money. A local newspaper which fails to assign a reporter to look into the intergovernmental dimension of local politics is clearly shortchanging its subscribers. This is something you might think about if you are looking for part-time journalistic employment.

In the years to come it will be up to you to determine how well organized, well integrated, and efficient the system of governments is in your state and community. One of the purposes of this book is to give you a few tools for making informed judgments about your governments.

In recent years a new term, intergovernmental relations (IGR), has entered the vocabulary of political science. This term is another way of suggesting that state and local governments, as well as the national government, are part of a dynamic system of interaction. Whether we call it the study of state and local government, the study of state and local governments, the study of the interaction between the individual and the governments, or the study of intergovernmental relations, the study of this system is both important and quite compatible with our concern for the individual. According to Deil S. Wright, an authority on intergovernmental relations,

> Strictly speaking, then, there are no intergovernmental relations; there are only relations among officials who govern different units. The individual actions and attitudes of public officials are at the core of IGR.[15]

Thinking of governments in terms of the people who run them helps us remember that mistakes are human and sometimes can be corrected. Furthermore, decisions by human beings can be overruled. After all, when the state of Vermont, the city of Los Angeles, or Anoka County "speaks," it is actually a *person* who is saying something, and persons can be fired, voted out of office, or persuaded to change their minds. Thus the individual does not usually confront governments as such. Instead, the individual deals with other human beings who are government officials or employees.

WHY YET ANOTHER BOOK ON STATE AND LOCAL GOVERNMENT?

The authors of this book have been teaching long enough to know that at least two things that ought to be in textbooks cannot be found in many of them.

The first thing is a straightforward admission that textbooks form the basis for test questions. We have taught from textbooks which were well organized but boring and from books which were interesting but didn't seem to have much "meat." The problem with the first kind of book is that students don't want to read it. The problem with the second kind is that instructors find it rather difficult to determine whether their students have actually learned anything. While holding your interest is important to us, providing you with information useful for participating in your governments has a much higher priority. Thus, we tend to favor "meat," or content, over style, or "cute."

How to Pass Tests on This Book

We will try to compensate for our lack of pizzazz by attempting to make it as painless as possible for you to meet one of your highest priorities: getting a decent grade on tests based on this book. To this end we offer four pieces of advice: break your reading into digestible bits, outline, identify and learn study objectives, and use flash cards.

Break Your Reading into Digestible Bits Don't attempt to read any chapter of this book all at once. Since this is a textbook, it lacks a sustained plot and character development. To attempt to read it all at once is to invite sleep. For your convenience, this book has already been broken into digestible bits through the use of chapters, headings within chapters, and subheadings between headings. Therefore, skim each chapter to identify the main courses and major dishes before you start your intellectual meal.

Outline First find the outline we provide by marking our headings with appropriate outline identifiers (I, A, 1, a, and so on), and then write the outline of the chapter in your notebook before attempting to read the chapter. This will provide a road map of where you are going. It will also provide an opportunity to identify many if not most of the study objectives.

Identify and Learn the Study Objectives By study objectives we mean any idea or set of ideas that can be the subject of a test question. You might also call them study questions, learning goals, or behavioral objectives. What you call them matters less than that you identify the meat of a chapter (or a lecture).

While it is possible for an instructor to test you on tiny details, it is more likely that he or she will focus on ideas associated with reasons why, characteristics of, differences between, or definitions of new terms and concepts. In this book we attempt to lead you to most of the study objectives with headings and subheadings. Not all authors do this, however, and sometimes study objectives are buried in the text of a chapter. We've probably done this ourselves a few times in this textbook.

A study objective can be the subject of a vast array of exam questions. Once you have learned the study objective, you are ready regardless of the type of question about it. In most chapters there are usually from 5 to 15 study objectives, sometimes more if the chapter is particularly long. After checking your outline for study objectives, survey the chapter again to find objectives that are hidden in "headless" paragraphs or buried in strings of "reasons why" that haven't been introduced with a topic sentence.

As you will soon observe, if you haven't already, we provide about ten study objectives at the end of each chapter. We hope that this will help. We cannot guarantee, however, that your instructor won't find objectives to add to his or her test question pool that we overlooked. Therefore, don't depend entirely on our list. Make a few more of your own. Remember, we are feeding you a few study objectives in order to teach you how to fish for them by yourself — in this and other texts.

Use Flash Cards   Once you have a list of study objectives, read the chapter, or at least the parts of the chapter in which you've identified study objectives, to see if you understand them. Then isolate each one on an index card.

On one side put the study objective (for example, to identify four steps in studying for a test based on this book). If one or more of the items briefly listed on the flip side of your card requires some elaboration, make a separate card for that idea, concept, or point. For example, after you list our four pieces of advice, you may wish to make a card that defines a study objective or a card that lists three advantages of using flash cards. Thus some study objectives will generate more than one index card.

Flash cards have at least three advantages. The first is to reinforce learning by writing the information out on the card in the first place. Second, making an individual copy of each study objective and its response forces you to concentrate on one item at a time, biting off the information in digestible bits. Ever notice how you lose track of ideas when you "review" a whole page of notes? A third advantage of making flash cards is that it becomes easier to quiz yourself before your instructor tests you. Either you know what is on the flip side of that card or you don't.

If you can pass your own tests, you will probably pass the instructor's. Making cards from lecture notes isn't a bad idea either. It helps separate main points from examples and helps identify places in your notes that need cleaning up or need that fourth "reason why," for which you ought to check someone else's notes or ask the instructor.

Stretching Minds

The second thing we've yet to find in many textbooks is a willingness to confront the fact that there are many bright people who are poorly prepared for college. This lack of preparation may be a product of the wide differences in the resources available to local school districts, or it may have something to do with upbringing or with a late blooming of an individual's motivation to do something with his or her intellectual equipment. Regardless of the cause, the fact remains that the individual applied to and is enrolled in an institution of higher education. Almost by definition this education should challenge and stretch minds. Colleges and universities are about what *can be* as well as what is. If some students have to work a little harder to realize their considerable potential, so be it.

It seems to us that too many texts are dummied down when they ought to challenge, push, and stretch. Some, for example, use a ninth-grade vocabulary to explain college-level material. To avoid this inconsistency we've used our own vocabularies. We identify in boldface type some of the terms we think will be new to you. Whether or not we define them in the text, we have placed a glossary of the terms in boldface at the end of each chapter. Naturally, glossary entries are fair game for test questions. Thus, we recommend that you make flash cards on the glossary terms that are new to you as well as the study objectives at the end of each chapter.

If we miss a term or two in the glossary, we assume that you have a good dictionary and, if not, that you will buy one. There are also several good political science dictionaries available, so we won't recommend one by name. We used our own vocabularies because we assume that no matter how poorly prepared for college an individual may be, he or she has the potential to rise to the occasion and look up a few words in a dictionary or even ask questions in class based on the reading.

Whether or not we really stretch you, make you mad enough to read further in other sources, or simply teach you some facts, we'll never know unless you tell us. Please do. Just write us care of the publishers. They'll forward our mail.

Conclusion

In the course of answering four questions, this chapter has attempted to explain a little bit about this book, its goals, and its approach to the subject matter. The major goal of this book is to encourage you to help make the more than 80,000 governments in this country more effective and more responsive to the public interest. We hope to show that you can do so through informed participation in state and local politics.

Study Objectives

1. Identify seven reasons why studying state and local governments may be important.
2. Identify five reasons why attention to the individual is important in studying state and local governments.
3. Identify Marie Ragghianti and her relationship to the study of state and local governments.
4. Identify the Giraffe Project.
5. Why is the plural word "governments" rather than the singular word "government" used in the subtitle of the book?
6. Identify four steps in effectively preparing for tests based on the material in this book.
7. Identify three advantages of flash cards.

Glossary

Anglo Among the many peculiarities of the political culture of Texas and most of the Southwestern states is the fact that all people of predominantly European heritage are called Anglos (short for Anglo-Saxon) to differentiate them from Mexican-Americans and African-Americans. This term is somewhat disconcerting to newcomers from other states, particularly those who are proud of their non-Anglo-Saxon heritage. Officer Jones, for example, is an Irish-American from Chicago.

collective Collective nouns are used in the singular to describe or refer to a collection of many individuals. Collective nouns take singular pronouns and use the singular form of verbs, e.g., the army . . . it.

economics The study of the relationships in society involving the use, management, or exchange of limited resources.

grant A sum of money given, not lent, from one to another is called a grant or a grant-in-aid. Private foundations, wealthy individuals, and units of government are the sources of most grants.

political economy Relationships in society involving politics and economics. These relationships usually involve regulations which affect economic choices.

politics Any human relationship that involves—to a significant degree—influence or power.

rehabilitation Repairing damage to the mind or body. To rehabilitate a criminal is to convert that person into a productive citizen. Rehabilitation usually involves training.

society Any collection of individuals among whom there exist regular patterns of behavior.

stereotypes Mental constructs used to simplify part of reality in order to cope with it. The more we go beyond merely coping and attempt to understand reality, the less likely we are to operate in terms of stereotypical thought. The problem with stereotypes is not only that they are partially true but that they provide no guidance as to how often they are not true.

tax expenditures Exceptions to tax laws that result in reductions in the amount of tax revenue collected. Tax expenditures result when legislatures give a tax break, or exception, to one category of individual, business, or type of income or property.

Endnotes

1. Edmund S. Phelps, *Political Economy*, (New York: Norton, 1985), 5.
2. Advisory Commission on Intergovernmental Relations, *Significant Features of Fiscal Federalism 1989 Edition*, vol. 1 (Washington, DC: Advisory Commission, 1989), 12.
3. Council of State Governments, *The Book of the States: 1988–89* (Lexington, KY: Council of State Governments, 1988), 273.
4. Ibid., 271.
5. Ibid., 273–274.
6. John Naisbitt, *Megatrends* (New York: Warner, 1982), 97.

7. Ibid., 426.
8. Ibid., 426–427.
9. Ibid., 345.
10. John Hebers, "The Innovators: Where Are They Now?" *Governing* (October 1989), 33–42. See also the October 1988 issue, pp. 30–40.
11. Ibid., 42–43.
12. Peter Maas, "A Woman of Valor," *Parade* (May 29, 1983); see also Peter Maas, *Marie: A True Story*, (New York: Random House, 1983).
13. Peter Maas, "A Woman of Valor," *Parade* (May 29, 1983).
14. David R. Beam, "Forecasting the Future of Federalism," *Intergovernmental Perspective*, (Summer 1980), 7.
15. Deil S. Wright, *Understanding Intergovernmental Relations*, (North Scituate, MA: Duxbury, 1978), 9.

Chapter 2

The State and Local Environment

In this chapter we explore a portion of the environment in which the individual interacts with one or more state and local governments. First, we will indicate the definitions we have in mind when we use terms such as "politics," "political system," "political socialization," "Metropolitan Statistical Area," "nation," and "ethnic group." Second, we will identify three features of individual and governmental interaction which seem important to us: technological change, the metropolitan paradox, and political culture.

THE CONCEPTUAL ENVIRONMENT

The vocabulary of political science owes much to the philosophers of the Golden Age of Greece. Socrates, Plato, and Aristotle were all concerned with the proper way to order the Greek city-state, or *polis*. From this word come the words "politics" and "political system" as well as "policy" and "polite."

Politics

Politics is an awkward word. As any dictionary will tell you, it does not mean more than one politic. Like economics and physics, politics appears to be a plural word without actually being one ("construed as singular" says our dictionary).

We borrow our definition of politics from Robert Dahl. His definition of "political system" contains a definition of politics: any human relationship involving, to a significant extent, influence.[1] Influence is the ability to get someone to do something he or she might not otherwise do. It may involve physical force or various other methods, such as persuasion and the manipulation of rewards and punishments. When the federal government informed the states that they would have to raise the drinking age to 21 in order to receive money from the Highway Trust Fund, it was very persuasive.

Sooner or later nearly all relationships, including the most personal, involve politics. Individuals attempt to influence others and must respond to the attempts of others to influence them. Although political scientists study individual relationships, they usually direct their attention to patterns of influence or systems of political relationships. They also tend to concentrate on those political systems large and complex enough to include a government.

Government and the State

Politics can occur without government. Friends, families, and even small communities use influence to make decisions and resolve conflicts without bothering to organize a government. Governments appear in a society when a set of specialized roles or offices emerge which give those who occupy them more than ordinary influence in making decisions. Political systems such as bowling leagues have governments, as do fraternities, sororities, churches, and business corporations.

A **government** is a set of offices which make and enforce decisions that affect the members of a political system. Governments are usually limited in regard to the subject matter on which they make decisions. We sometimes use the term **jurisdiction** to refer to the subject matter or the territory over which a government (or a government official) can make decisions. The government of the Walla Walla Scuba Diving Club, for example, has rather limited jurisdiction both in terms of territory and in terms of the subject matter about which it makes decisions. Although political scientists are interested in many kinds of governments, they tend to focus on those associated with the state.

The **state** is that political system whose government is able to enforce its claim to unique authority to regulate the use of force among the people living in a defined territory. This does not mean that the government of a state is the only organization that uses force or that it is always able to control the use of force. It means that the *claim* to regulate the use of force is seldom disputed. A state whose government cannot enforce this claim is in big trouble or on the verge of revolution or both.

The word "state" can be used to identify two different types of political units. The first type of state is a member of the international state system. Among the 140 or so other members of this system are Canada, Mexico, and the Union of Soviet Socialist Republics. In this context, the United States of America is the state in which we all live, regardless of which portion of it we call home. To avoid confusion, we will use other terms to refer to this type of state. "Country" is a handy alternative, as in "My Country 'Tis of Thee."

The second type of state is the one to which we will give a lot of attention in this book. In some countries the political unit analogous to one of our 50 states is called a province or a territory. Canada, for example, has ten provinces and two territories. Mexico has 31 states (*estados*). Japan has 47 prefectures.

The 50 states are not the only large subunits of our federal system. The United States of America also includes the District of Columbia (Washington, DC); the Commonwealth of Puerto Rico; the Virgin Islands of St. John, St. Croix, and St. Thomas; the Pacific Territories of Guam and Samoa; Wake and Midway Islands; and the islands in the U.S. Trust Territory of the Pacific, including the Northern Marianas, the Carolinas, and the Marshalls, along with several other small islands. Citizens of virtually all these political units are also citizens of the United States. Unlike citizens of the 50 states, however, not all of them vote in presidential elections, and none of them send voting representatives to Congress. That is about all the attention these areas of the United States will receive, not because they aren't important but because one has to draw the line somewhere. We've taken on enough in attempting to deal with the 80,000 American governments, among which the 50 states and the national government play a dominant role. For your convenience we have listed all 50 states, their capitals, and their population size and rank according to the latest population estimates inside the front cover of this book.

The Nation-State

Although the **nation-state** is the predominant political unit in the international community today, this was not always the case. Not only is it possible for there to be states which aren't nation-states, it is possible for there to be nations whose people do not live together in one state. Italians were once divided into a collection of small separate states including Naples, the Kingdom of Two Sicilies, and Padua. The Vatican in Rome is still an independent Italian state. The two Germanies which are merging into one in this decade were once a single state which was created in the nineteenth century by uniting (through persuasion, force, and guile) a half dozen smaller independent German states, including Prussia, Schleswig-Holstein, Bavaria, and Hanover.[2]

Nation   A **nation** is a collection of people with a common sense of identity who seek to establish or maintain a state of their own.[3] Once created, national identities are difficult to destroy. States, by contrast, can be destroyed by the actions of larger, more powerful states. After World War I, the major powers in Europe agreed to do away with Serbia, which became part of Yugoslavia. Whether a Yugoslavian identity has been developed to replace or at least compete with the Serbian identity in the current generation remains to be seen.

Ethnic Group   We define an **ethnic group** as a collection of people with a common sense of identity who seek to obtain the rights and benefits of citizenship in a larger society or state. Although they do not seek a state of their own, ethnic groups — particularly in new nation-states — make national leaders very nervous. Because ethnic groups and nations are so similar, there is tension between ethnic groups and the larger society in many countries.[4]

This tension is based on at least three similarities between ethnic groups and nations: sources of identity, dependence on elites, and failure to understand operating models. First, the sources of identity for both nations and ethnic groups are very similar. Either type of identity can be based on one or combination of the following: shared historical experiences, myths, political institutions, religion, and language. In short, both ethnic groups and nations are cultural as well as political entities.

Second, the existence of both ethnic groups and nations depends on dynamic leaders who interpret history, communicate myths, and make an ethnic or national identity appealing to a large number of people. Leaders who successfully recruit followers can lead in many directions — toward loyalty to the existing state or toward an independent state. The early history of at least two ethnic groups in the American political system includes leaders who advocate a separate nationalism as well as those who followed the ethnic group path.[5]

Third, ethnic groups and nations tend to use different models of the nation. Since they view the nation differently, they also view ethnic groups differently. For leaders of nations attempting to promote national unity, the idea of an additional political identity is hard to appreciate. "What's wrong with just being one of us?" they ask.

To ethnic leaders (who are by definition loyal members of the nation) this question seems unfair. "We are loyal Americans (or Yugoslavians or whatever), but we are being mistreated, so we've united on the basis of our ethnic identity to get our rights as members of the nation. Can't you understand that?"

It's hard to "understand that" without exploring the differing models or perceptions of the American nation under which both ethnic leaders and national leaders operate. We will do that later in this chapter. At present we turn to another important feature of the conceptual environment in which governments, individuals, and groups of individuals interact: the political system.

POLITICAL SYSTEMS: TWO SETS OF SIMILARITIES

In Chapter 1 we mentioned that Marie Ragghianti's friends told her that "the system" was too big for her to fight. Since she did fight the system and won the battle, we won't worry too much about their definition of system. Instead, we will use a definition by a well-known political scientist, Robert Dahl, who defines a **political system** as "any persistent pattern of human behavior involving to a significant extent control, influence, power, or authority."[6] If this definition looks familiar, it should. On page 25 we defined politics by using a portion of Dahl's definition of a political system. The discussion which follows borrows shamelessly from the vocabulary and concepts developed by Professor Dahl.

Political systems that are complex enough to contain governments have certain important similarities.

Similarities Shared Because They Are Systems

A **system** is a collection of parts that interact in some way. All political systems are similar in that they contain parts that interact. However, we are unlikely to refer to a stamp collection as a system, because stamps do not interact very much.

Systems Are Abstractions   Like all systems, the political system is an abstraction. An **abstraction** is a mental construction, a set of ideas that we use to simplify reality and organize our thinking about it. Since systems are abstractions, they exist independently of physical objects.

For example, without the concept "ignition system" in your head, your adventure under the hood of a car is simply one of looking at, and maybe touching, "things" that have no meaning to you. Putting your finger on why the car doesn't start is as much a mental as a physical act.

Systems Can Be Parts of Other Systems   Our solar system is a subsystem of our galaxy, which is a subsystem of the universe. The political system of Chicago is a subsystem of Cook County's political system, which is a subsystem of the Illinois political system, which is a subsystem of the American political system.

When we discuss the political economy, we are identifying yet another subsystem. Parts of it are generally thought of as being economic (money, land, labor, control of factories), and parts are considered to be political (taxes, government regulations, government purchases).

An Element Can Be Part of More Than One System Just as an individual can have more than one set of friends or be part of more than one social system (family, school, workplace), something that is part of the political system can also be part of the economic system.

This simple idea is useful because sometimes — for example, when election campaigns get rough — attempts are made to imply that one cannot be two things at once. However, the fact remains that an individual can be both a loyal American and a member of an ethnic group, a mother and a county judge, or a civil servant and a member of a labor union. As we will see later on, one can even be a Republican nationally and a Democrat locally or vice versa.

It is worth noting that to be active in a political system does not mean that one gives up all other pursuits. When one enters the political system, one does not have to *leave* some other system.

Similarities Shared by Political Systems

Among the characteristics shared by virtually all political systems, we have identified nine which seem most useful in understanding the relationship between the individual and the governments.[7]

Uneven Distribution of Political Resources A political resource is anything that can be used to obtain power or influence. Political resources come in many forms. The more politically sophisticated you become, the better able you will be to recognize and make use of your own political resources.

Among the most obvious political resources are money, intelligence (Box 2-1), charm, the ability to communicate, information, physical stamina, weaponry, and access to people who have political power. Other resources, depending on the particular political system, might be membership in an ethnic group, a labor union, or a service organization. With such a variety of political resources and contexts in which they may be either advantages or disadvantages, it is no surprise that these resources are not distributed equally in any political system.

Just as political resources are distributed unequally among individuals so are they distributed unequally among the governments. Some governments have wealthier tax bases than others, some have more authority then others, and some benefit from advantages ranging from climate to political institutions.

Uneven Distribution of Political Power In addition to the fact that political resources are distributed unequally, there are other reasons why political power or influence is distributed unequally in virtually all political systems. Among them are occupational specialization, inheritance, and personality.

Box 2-1   # Political Resources: The Power of Persuasion

In the Brer Rabbit stories of Uncle Remus we find an example of political power based on mental resources. When Brer Rabbit pleads, *"Please* don't throw me in the brier patch," and gets what he *really* wants from Brer Bear — to be thrown in the brier patch — we can observe physical power being influenced by the power to persuade (through reverse suggestion).

The Brer Rabbit stories that Joel Chandler Harris told through Uncle Remus provide some heavy political lessons. These stories, like Aesop's fables, can be traced to African folktales in which the poor and weak frequently use unlikely resources to outdo the rich and powerful, teach them moral lessons, or both.

The strategic lesson taught by Brer Rabbit did not got unlearned by African-Americans. A hundred years after the Civil War ended, most blacks were still not free to act as full citizens because of segregation laws and restrictive customs, which in most Southern states were enforced subtly as well as violently and sometimes at night.

During the 1960s, in front of television cameras in broad daylight, civil rights demonstrators seemed to say as they defied segregation laws, "Please don't hit us with that ax handle, please don't squirt us with that fire hose, please don't show the world how nastily you've been treating us for generations."

When the demonstrators were beaten and blasted on the evening news for all America and the world to see, American public opinion changed, and the injustice of legally enforced segregation finally began to come to an end.

Conflicting Aims   In all political systems there are disagreements over conflicting aims. The more complex the society is, the more likely it is that individuals will fail to agree on important matters. The sources of conflict are limitless. Families with children want the neighborhood quiet by nine o'clock while singles may want to play their stereos full blast until 2 A.M.; chemical industries want to save money by dumping wastes directly into the river while environmentalists want the river to be clear.

While other political systems, such as the neighborhood, the workplace, the church, and social organizations, may find ways to resolve some conflicts, state and local governments are frequently involved in conflict resolution. Many observers consider this to be one of the main functions of government.

The more complex our society becomes, the more likely it is that both sides in a dispute will try to use government to resolve the dispute in their favor. Thus, knowledge about government becomes an ever more important tool for maintaining and improving the quality of life as well as influencing the activities in which governments become involved.

Competition for Political Power   Competition occurs for different reasons: Some people compete for the fun of it, some to keep a job they enjoy, some to accomplish a single goal, and some simply to be in a position to protect advantages that already have been won. Few individuals compete for political power for only one reason.

There is competition in nearly all political systems. To attempt to reform competition out of politics is to embrace frustration. When there does not appear to be competition, look for arrangements which transfer it behind the scenes, where it can be managed by those who stand to lose from it.

Cooperation in the Use of Power   Just as there is competition in all political systems, so there are various patterns of cooperation. People cooperate in different ways and for different reasons. Some do it selflessly, for **altruistic** reasons. Some cooperate because they feel a sense of obligation, others do so because they enjoy the social interaction of group activity, and some do so only when they know that benefits will result. Cooperation in most political systems involves mutual accommodation, favor trading, assistance, or exchange of information both in and outside government. It takes cooperation to get power, and it takes cooperation to keep it.

A Leadership That Seeks Legitimacy   In every political system those in charge of the government seek to base their claim on something other than brute force. **Legitimacy** is the quality of being accepted as right, fair, proper, or in accordance with agreed upon standards. Political power which is legitimate is called **authority**. Political power based on blackmail or threats is not usually regarded as legitimate.

Legitimacy enables governments and individuals to get things done without using other political resources such as money, troops, weaponry, and a lot of time and effort shouting, pleading, and cajoling. Thus, legitimacy is itself a political resource.

Max Weber identified three sources of legitimacy: tradition (this is the way our ancestors did it), rational-legal norms (we are doing it according to practical rules that we all agreed to), and **charisma** (this individual is a very special person). Of the three, charisma is regarded as the least stable, lasting a lifetime at best; thus it is the most difficult form of legitimacy to transfer from one generation to the next.

In rapidly changing societies such as ours it is important to remember that the terms "legitimate" and "legal" are not synonymous. We hope that our laws are legitimate, but sometimes a law regarded as appropriate by one group or generation is not regarded as legitimate by another. In a political system with a legitimate government, the population is more likely to work within the established procedures to change laws. When it becomes clear that legitimacy and legality are seriously out of step, many political leaders tend to get nervous. This is why political leaders watch public opinion very closely.

The Development of a Belief System   In almost every political system one finds a body of beliefs and attitudes about how the political system works and ought to work. Political leaders understand and attempt to conform their behavior to this belief system, which is the source of their legitimacy, their claim to rule.

Some authors discuss belief systems in terms of ideology, and some in terms of political culture. At the risk of some oversimplification, let's assume that while there may be an area where ideology and political culture overlap or mix, the two can be differentiated.[8]

Scholars, political leaders, and others with a fair amount of education can state a goodly portion of their political beliefs with clarity and can apply these beliefs with some consistency to the real world. This version of a belief system, one which is manifest and mentally available, we'll call an **ideology**.

In most political systems, very few people operate at the level of ideology. The vast majority of citizens in major political systems around the world can explain very little of what they believe. Their version of the ideas that make up the political culture or belief system of a country is latent. The latent version of a belief system is characterized by words and phrases such as "ah," "um," "er," "uh," and "ya know."

Thus, very few people operate at the level of ideology. Despite vast efforts to promote the Marxist-Leninist ideology in the Soviet Union, the average Russian has just as much trouble explaining his or her belief system as does the average American.[9] The relatively few members of the population who operate ideologically in any political system are those who are active participants, leaders, and would-be leaders.

Even though they share the same basic beliefs, or political culture, members of this political elite find many things about which to disagree. Furthermore, there is often more disagreement among the leaders than there is among the members of the general population. The leaders see clear distinctions between various courses of action, and because they want their interpretations of how to apply the belief system everyone shares to be the ones that get enacted into law, they may find themselves manipulating not only ideas but other people.

Assuming that it is better to have a population that is able to choose wisely among those making proposals about how to apply what we all believe, most governments spend a fair amount of money on education. Further assuming that it is better to be a manipulator than a manipulatee, we encourage you to learn more about your belief system and, of course, how to apply it to the politics of state and local governments.

Permeable Boundaries   All systems have boundaries, and it isn't always easy to determine exactly where they are. We assume, however, that somewhere out there in space is a boundary between the earth's atmosphere and the rest of our solar system or between our solar system and the rest of the galaxy.

The fact that units of government have identifiable territorial boundaries is sometimes a deceptive oversimplification of our political system. People, ideas, commerce,and pollution pass over these boundaries with ease. State and local governments can neither keep people out nor keep them in. When businesses decide to take jobs and investments out of a unit of state or local government, there is little that the government can do.

Box 2-2 **The Stoplight and the Long Island Schoolchildren**

When more than one local government has jurisdiction over different matters in the same geographic area, it can be very confusing for ordinary citizens. It raises questions such as, How many political systems does one have to contact to get something done? Who's in charge? and Is *anyone* in charge?

In an article titled "The Balkanization of Suburbia," written more than ten years ago, Samuel Kaplan told of the troubles he and his neighbors encountered attempting to sort through the various local governments which shared jurisdiction over all or part of an area containing some 35,000 people located in the Port Washington peninsula of Long Island, New York.

Their objective was to get a traffic light installed on Main Street to make it safer for children to go from the elementary school on one side of the street to the library on the other side. Briefly, this is what they learned in 1971 about the boundaries of their various political systems:

The school on the south side of the street was located in an unincorporated area of Port Washington and therefore was controlled by the township. The library on the north side was located in the village of Baxter Estates. The street itself was a county road but was located in and patrolled by the Port Washington Police District, which is independent of the village, town, and county. Traffic lights on county roads are the responsibility of the county. However, parking on a street that is also a county road falls under the jurisdiction of the town.

Although Mr. Kaplan wrote as much in sorrow as in anger (and with enviable style and charm), his cause was not lost. While it did take time ("A lot of time," Mr. Kaplan might say), the governments did respond.

First, the township of North Hempstead passed a parking ordinance. This at least gave the children and motorists a better view of one another. Second, the Nassau County Board of Supervisors ordered a traffic study.

Whether the traffic flow was great enough, according to existing standards, for it to order its public works department to install a traffic light or whether the Nassau County board simply caved in to public pressure, we don't know. We do know that an official of the Nassau County board told us on the phone that there is now a traffic light on Main Street between the school and public library. We didn't ask when it was installed.

Source: Samuel Kaplan,"The Balkanization of Suburbia," *Harper's* (October 1971), 72–74.

For the individual, one of the most vexing boundary problems occurs when one unit of government decides that it doesn't have the authority to deal with a problem. "That's beyond our jurisdiction" is the official response. Sometimes the jurisdictional boundary is territorial, and sometimes it is a question of subject matter. Too often the problem is not jurisdiction but the willingness of public officials to respond to important problems, as the case study in Box 2-2 suggests.

The Possibility of Change   The good news is that political systems can change for the better. The bad news is that they can change for the worse. Each new generation of citizens and leaders concerns itself with new issues and brings new insights and new interpretations to political roles and institutions.

In considering change in the American political system — whether the good old days were really all that good — it is worth noting that when our nation was founded, slavery was tolerated and women couldn't vote. During the industrial revolution leaders who proposed laws prohibiting child labor were regarded as enemies of the free enterprise system. In short, our system has changed, and for the better in many ways.

Where it goes from here depends on you. Whether you become a leader willing to make tough decisions or an individual willing to do your homework and let your leaders know you are watching, you will affect some part of the political system. In doing so, you will affect the whole because political systems neither exist in isolation nor remain forever the same.

THE CHANGING TECHNOLOGICAL ENVIRONMENT

The individual and the governments interact in a rapidly changing world. A critical feature of the rapid changes to which they must continue to adjust is the fact that human beings create technology faster than they create methods for dealing with it constructively. In this section we will attempt to put rapid technological change in a meaningful context by discussing its pace and some of its consequences.

To help you appreciate the speed with which change occurs, we have provided in Box 2-3 a brief version of human history collapsed into one calendar year. As you will observe, most of the technological advances we have come to take for granted occurred rather late in that year.

Rapid Technological Change

The American system of government was born in an agricultural era. It is still adapting to the consequences of industrialization and metropolitan living even as it enters the era of computers, robots, and the twenty-first century.

Box 2-3   **Year of the Human Race**

Homo sapiens appears at the last stroke of midnight as the new year begins. Fire is domesticated in early February. The agricultural revolution occurs in March, but most of the earth is still sparsely populated by hunters and gatherers clear through the summer. Recorded history begins about November. By this time the agricultural revolution has spread more widely. People begin a long adjustment to urban living which was not possible before the discovery of the science of seed collection.

Sometime after Thanksgiving, the pyramids are built. The navigational equipment to carry Columbus and later the Pilgrims across the Atlantic becomes available about the second week in December. On December 29 James Watt gets his steam engine to run in the morning. In the afternoon America wins its independence. The industrial revolution gets rolling just before dawn the next day.

It's a pretty full day. By the time it is over, the slaves will be free and telephone lines will connect Europe and America. Ships made of steel (which actually float!) — each carrying a hundred times as many people from Europe to America as the *Mayflower* did — will cross the Atlantic in one-third the time it took the *Mayflower* to make the same trip.

Mass production of the automobile starts about noon on December 31. By dinner-time, electricity is beginning to reach rural America through the cooperatives financed by Roosevelt's New Deal. Television (black and white) becomes available only to the affluent about the time the New Year's Eve parties are under way.

The countdown is well along when the first commercial nuclear reactor begins to generate electricity and two Americans land on the moon and return safely. The first stroke of midnight has already sounded as Apple builds its first computer. The echoes of the last stroke are dying out as most of you graduate from high school.

It isn't even two o'clock in the morning, dawn is a long way off, and you are now enrolled in state and local government as another 60,000 years of human history begin.

Technology can be defined as the knowledge available to make, store, use, or transmit energy, matter, or information. The root word of technology is *techne*, meaning "skill." The discovery that people could make and use fire resulted in technology for dealing with the materials for producing and using it — spits for cooking over it, pots for cooking on it, hearths and chimneys to manage and disperse heat and smoke, and developments in metallurgy, fuel discovery, and the preparation and refinement of fuels.

The social and political consequences of the next major technological discovery — agriculture — were enormous. The agricultural revolution made it possible for many people to live in one place all year. It no longer mattered whether game and wild plants were available. Because one farm family could feed many other families, not everybody had to be a farmer.

Thus, while it involved the development of techniques for planting, harvesting, and storing crops, the agricultural revolution also made economic and other social specializations possible. The agricultural revolution also created a type of city to which the human race has had over 10,000 years to adapt. Plato, Christ, Charlemagne, Shakespeare, and Thomas Jefferson all lived in essentially the same type of urban place. It was a walking city; that is, one could walk completely around it in less than a day. Its area was about 2 square miles. The metropolitan areas of the automotive revolution, by contrast, have been here for only about 50 years. Thus, in the context of human history, it will take some time to adapt to them.

Technological change may once have permitted a long, leisurely process of getting used to new ways of doing things, but it no longer does. Because new problems and new opportunities arise long before we've fully solved the problems or explored the possibilities of the previous ones, rapid technological change is an important part of the environment in which individuals and their governments find themselves.

The industrial revolution, which really got rolling in the United States after the Civil War (about 1865), changed cities all over the world as well as the world itself. Manufacturing activities required unskilled labor, thus increasing the size of the city's population. Technology made it possible for cities to grow both up (steel frameworks to build skyscrapers and elevators so that people could use them) and out (steel made light-rail streetcar systems possible, first horse-drawn and then electric). The city of the industrial revolution was bigger and more complex, with more opportunities and more problems than the human race had been adapting to for over 10,000 years.

Reprinted with special permission of North American Syndicate.

The opportunity to adjust to this type of city did not last very long, because in the second decade of the twentieth century the mass production of the automobile began. We are still adjusting to the automotive revolution. Three of the many adjustments we have made are as follows:

First, for certain activities there is no difference between an automobile, a hotel room, a movie theater, and a restaurant. The implications in terms of morals and manners are considerable.

Second, our perception of time has changed dramatically from the days when journeys were calendar events, not stopwatch events. People who walk or use horses and buggies (or even mass transit) are accustomed to waiting a few minutes here and there. People in cars become very quick tempered if the car ahead of them doesn't move within ten seconds after the light changes. Sitting through an entire 90-second light cycle without moving causes some people to come unhinged.

Third, our relationship to the land has changed in at least two major ways as a result of the automobile. First, more people view land as an economic quantity to be divided and sold for a profit. Fewer people view it as a sacred trust from generations of the past and to generations of the future. Second, urban land is put to more different uses than ever before. The walking city and the city of the streetcar devoted a relatively small amount of space to transportation. Today, our tendency toward two- and three-car families requires vast amounts of land for parking and for service locations as well as for roads, bridges, and interchanges.

When a unit of government considers requiring developers to set aside land for parks, in many communities this is viewed as confiscation of private wealth rather than enforcement of a responsible use of the land.

Given the short time we have had to adjust to rapid change, it is no wonder that new metropolitan areas containing hundreds of homes, businesses, malls, and shopping centers sprawling for miles in every direction under the jurisdictions of dozens of different units of government present us with organizational challenges we have yet to meet adequately.[10]

The Metropolitan Paradox

Metropolitan Statistical Areas (MSAs) contain over 30 percent of the governments in this country, yet most metropolitan areas have no government. This is the metropolitan **paradox**. To appreciate the importance of this paradox, we must examine a definition and a process.

Metropolitan Statistical Area An MSA is an area consisting of a county in which there is a city (or twin cities) with a total population of 50,000 people and any contiguous counties which are socioeconomically integrated with the core county.[11] Socioeconomically integrated means that unless a contiguous county meets certain standards regarding population density, urban population, and close economic and social ties with the core county, it is not included in the MSA.

Not only do MSAs include numerous communities and governments, many of them also form larger **agglomerations** called Consolidated Metropolitan Areas (CMAs). There are now nearly 20 CMAs. Some observers refer to this phenomenon as a **megalopolis.** Whether we call it a megalopolis, a CMA, or an MSA, it is a large complex of people and governmental units struggling to cope with traffic jams; air pollution; stray animals; water shortage in the summer and floods in the spring; fire, sewage, and solid waste management; juvenile delinquency; and a host of other problems that ignore the boundaries between one government and the next.

County boundaries are used to define MSA and CMA boundaries in all but six states (Connecticut, Rhode Island, Massachusetts, Vermont, New Hampshire, and Maine). In those states, statistical data are collected by towns and cities. Most states designate their county governments to be the agency for collecting birth, death, land ownership, and other statistics.

While the more than 300 MSAs in the United States account for only 16 percent of the land area, they contain about 75 percent of the population and most of the wealth, jobs, cultural centers, and problems in our political economy.

Because county boundaries are used to define MSA boundaries in most states, many parts of metropolitan America are not completely urbanized. Thus, while it is probably useful to know that not every square foot of metropolitan America is densely populated, paved, and polluted, it is probably more important to remember that metropolitan areas are gobbling up some of the best farmland on the continent.[12] Furthermore, although metropolitan areas occupy a relatively small land area, what happens on that land area affects the rest of the country in terms of air pollution, acid rain, and finding places to dump household, industrial, hazardous, and nuclear waste.

The Process of Metropolitan Sprawl   **Metropolitan sprawl** is the uncoordinated spread of economic, recreational, residential, and governmental development beyond the legal limits of the core cities of the metropolitan areas of America. Metropolitan sprawl is also known as suburban sprawl or urban sprawl. It means traffic jams, water shortages, pollution, vast shopping centers with asphalt parking lots smothering good farmland, downstream flooding because the land upstream can't absorb as much water, and large populations crowding inadequate parks and recreational facilities.

According to urban historian Lewis Mumford, "The city has burst open and scattered its complex organs and organizations over the entire landscape."[13] Not only have affluent urban workers migrated to live outside the central city, but many jobs have left as well. Furthermore, new units of government have been created outside the central city. These new units add to another problem found in the intergovernmental environment: the fragmentation of authority.

The Fragmentation of Authority   Authority, as noted earlier, is legitimate power. When power is divided into many small parts, at least two things can happen, one good and one bad. If individuals or units of government which have a small part of power have a common vision of what they want to do with it, they can cooperate in accomplishing great achievements. It is of course a major premise of democracy that the bits of power we each possess will be used for a common good. If power is used in such a way that each power holder is in a position to cancel out the effort of others, like a collection of clowns all fighting to get through a narrow doorway, the fragmentation of authority can be very wasteful. Not only are resources lost, but so ultimately is legitimacy.

One source of fragmentation of authority in metropolitan America is the creation of approximately 500 new special districts a year for the past 20 years. Between the 1962 and 1982 Censuses of Governments 10,000 new special districts and 1,077 new municipalities were created. That is a great many new offices, new officials, and new jurisdictions.

Examples of both governmental cooperation and wasteful competition in metropolitan areas are available. To the frustrated citizen who doesn't want to take a short course in local jurisdictions and responsibilities, the frequent examples of inaction and irresponsibility seem to outweigh any advantages of numerous local governments. A question that needs asking in many of the more than 300 MSAs is whether we can produce good results through a democracy of governments in metropolitan America or whether we need to create a single metropolitan government and hold it responsible by holding the individuals in charge of it responsible.

Different solutions will be appropriate to different conditions. For the present, it is sufficient to note that the metropolitan paradox, together with metropolitan sprawl and the fragmentation of authority, has yet to be eliminated in any MSA to the point where a model solution has emerged. Thus individuals and their governments will be experimenting with potential solutions for a long time to come.

THE ENVIRONMENT OF BELIEF: POLITICAL CULTURE

Political culture consists of attitudes, beliefs, values, and patterns of behavior which influence the way we see the world and the way we deal with it. In this section we will examine political culture in terms of three concepts: political socialization, regional subcultures, and three models of our national identity. The notion of political culture is important not only because it helps us understand ourselves but because it helps us understand the people we may wish to influence. If you understand the models and values that other individuals use to operate within the real world and you attempt to communicate in their terms instead of your own, not only will those individuals seem less irrational, so will you.[14]

Political Socialization

Political socialization is a process through which we learn our political culture—the beliefs, ideas, and attitudes about politics that are accepted as appropriate for our society. We are taught our political culture throughout our lives, but for many Americans the early years are most important because the

> political orientations of most individuals are simply not challenged very frequently. It is well known that politics in the conventional sense is not salient for most people on a day-to-day basis. . . . Therefore, since politics is most often a peripheral concern, change typically comes about rather slowly; because the questions raised are seldom about the foundation of the political system, basic political beliefs are most likely not to shift.[15]

Thus, change can occur, and when it does, it may affect the entire adult population of a society, not only the 18-year-olds or the gray panthers.

We have observed that the fact of change in all political systems is both good news and bad news. The notion that the individual members of a society are much more open to change in their basic political beliefs and values than earlier research indicated is also good and bad. The patterns laid down over a generation can be changed for the better or for the worse.

This potential malleability of individual beliefs increases the importance of the individual both in terms of affecting change in others and in terms of being more aware of one's own vulnerability. Openness to change also increases the importance of leadership. As Jennings and Niemi have noted,

> Perhaps the most important implication of all this is the emphasis it places on political leadership. Citizens are willing to change with the times, and occasionally demand change. But the possible directions of change are many. The task of political leadership is to channel development in a way that proves to be satisfactory.[16]

This makes it even more important for us to attempt to understand these patterns laid down over time. First, we need to know what is worth saving if others attempt to change the patterns. Second, confident in the knowledge that change for the better is possible, we need to know what it is that needs improving.

Three Regional Subcultures

The beliefs and values which most Americans share as the central part of their political culture are based largely on the writing of John Locke, a seventeenth-century English philosopher. Locke's ideas were adapted by the political leaders who led the revolution which created the American political system. This ideology has become the core of American political culture. Perhaps the most concise statement of this cultural core is found in the Declaration of Independence (Box 2-4). Political leaders in the government may argue over the application of these principles in the real world, but they base their arguments on the same system of ideas and beliefs. Thus, even liberals and conservatives have more in common than would appear to be the case, especially in the heat of debate.[17]

Although the terms "liberal" and "conservative" are frequently used in the American political context, another set of differences may be equally if

Box 2-4   **From the Declaration of Independence**

We hold these truths to be self-evident, that all men are created equal, that they are endowed by their Creator with certain unalienable rights, that among these are life, liberty, and the pursuit of happiness. That to secure these rights, governments are instituted among men, deriving their just powers from the consent of the governed, — That whenever any form of government becomes destructive of these ends, it is the right of the people to alter or to abolish it, and to institute new government, laying its foundation on such principles and organizing its power in such form, as to them shall seem most likely to effect their safety and happiness.

not more important in understanding the environment of the governments. Daniel Elazar has identified three American subcultures which he and his students have demonstrated to be important in shaping the way we think about politics. These subcultures are three versions of the same overarching American political culture. Elazar identifies them as traditionalistic, individualistic, and moralistic.[18]

These three cultures (or subcultures) are found in various combinations in each of the 50 states. As Figure 2.1 indicates, few states have only one of these cultures and the pattern of distribution reflects migration out of the states in which the cultures originated. Each culture embraces values which are part of the Lockean-American political culture, but some emphasize some aspects more than others. In light of our concern about change for the better, Elazar's caveat is worth noting: "Each of the three political subcultures contributes something important to the configuration of the American political system and each contains certain characteristics that are inherently dangerous to the survival of that system."[19]

Each of these three political cultures emerged in a particular area of pre-Revolutionary America. Although they are all preindustrial (in fact, pre-Civil war), they continue to be important elements in the environment of the individual and the governments.

The Traditional Culture   The traditional political culture is associated with the southern tier of the original 13 states. It emerged in a plantation society where a landed gentry with large holdings dominated. Political institutions in this society were closely linked to the family system.

In the traditional political culture, elite members use their power to provide jobs and other kinds of help to distant cousins who may have fallen on hard times. Political parties and elections are considered unwelcome intrusions. Political competition is thought of as occurring between extended families. As a "family affair," political competition is viewed as an

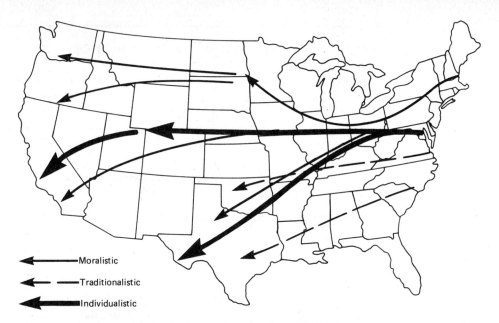

Figure 2.1 Distribution of three American political cultures. Emerging in preindustrial colonial America, these cultures have been modified by time and transportation to new places. However, they still influence our views about politics. (*Source:* Daniel Elazar, *Federalism: A View From the States,* 2nd ed. (New York: Harper & Row, 1972), 110–111.)

almost private rather than public concern. Open discussion of issues, names in the paper, and ordinary people deciding which faction or family is going to win are somewhat foreign to the traditionalist culture.

The traditionalist elite bases its legitimacy on tradition (their families arrived first) and on superior education and experience in governance. It mistrusts the marketplace and the "pushiness" of commercial competition or of individuals (nobodies) attempting to better themselves. It also mistrusts the efforts of moralists to help the disadvantaged "rise above their station." The traditionalist values a quiet, rural society in which everyone knows his or her place and those at the top of the social hierarchy control things.

The traditional values include the notion that along with certain benefits there are obligations associated with elite status: charity, civic involvement, and the recruitment and training of new leaders. Accomplishment is valued, though little of it is expected to occur in the lower orders. Thus, equal opportunity and equality before the law are valued, as is the notion of inalienable rights. The elite members of this society, however, also assume that some are better able to exercise their rights than others are.

The positions of most, if not all, traditionalists are fairly predictable on issues such as civil rights, women's liberation, gay rights, bilingual education, and labor unions. Traditionalists value education, however, and many of the sons and daughters of the traditional elite have provided enlightened leadership at the community, state, and national levels.

The Moralistic Culture   The moralistic political culture is associated with the small farming communities of New England, in which almost everyone attended one of a handful of Protestant churches in the community. In these homogeneous societies, everyone was supposed to participate in community decision making. Political participation in this type of culture is regarded as a noble calling. One participates because of an obligation to do so, just as one is obligated to do what is right. Through broadly based participation in community affairs, the common good can be better perceived and more effectively brought about.

Certain American political institutions are not welcome in moralistic communities. For example, moralists tend to see parties as alien to the notion of men and women of goodwill sitting down to reason together in search of the common good. Votes cast because of party loyalty are thought of as uninformed votes. Thus, the moralist and the traditionalist share a common suspicion of political parties, but for entirely different reasons.

The moralist is particularly outraged by corruption. One's participation in the affairs of the community arises from one's obligation and concern for the community (the public interest). Thus, anyone who attempts to reap personal benefit is betraying the whole community.

"To the victors belong the spoils" and the notion that people support issues out of self-interest are alien concepts in a moralistic political culture. Thus, the moralist who supports an issue believes that he or she supports it out of concern for what is right, not just because the moralist or his or her friends, family, or life-style peers will benefit.

The Individualistic Culture   The individualistic political culture is associated with the problems of survival in the new cities of eighteenth-century America and with the code of "every man for himself" that emerged in the struggle to push the frontier westward into new lands, breaking treaties with the Native Americans along the way.

The individualistic political culture views the political system as a marketplace. Government is a source of opportunities for bettering one's condition economically as well as politically. Those who gain control of government obtain benefits for their efforts. They are also obligated to distribute rewards to those who help them get this control. Thus, while the moralist sees obligation in terms of the community, the individualist is likely to see it in terms of the party, the faction, the family, or whatever group he or she regards as politically helpful.

Although the individualistic political culture is based to some extent on participation for individual gain, it recognizes that individuals banded together often have a better chance of winning prizes than do individuals competing alone. The individuals one is most able to trust are members of one's own family or tribe. Thus, as in the traditional political culture, to individualists, politics and family feuds have much in common.

In the individualistic political culture, politics may be seen as essentially a dirty business practiced by professionals who have to grease a few palms to get things done. The individualist who could be making money in the marketplace sees time spent on community affairs as wasted unless material benefits are involved. The individualistic political culture is as appropriate for the contemporary individual who is interested in getting his or hers as it was for the supporters of the nineteenth-century urban political machines that we shall examine in Chapter 8.

The individualistic political culture is more tolerant of corruption than is the moralistic culture. It simply considers corruption an unfortunate part of political life. Similarly, many of us tolerate bent garbage cans and parking lot dings on our cars.

Because they are more inclined to view politics as a game, individualistic participants have trouble understanding why moralists get so hot under the collar and behave in such an uncompromising fashion when a little trade-off here and a little payoff there would send everybody home with something. Politics, of course, is not the only American game in which people may get a bit dirty or at least sweaty.

Political Culture and Political Action   For many participants in the political system, regardless of their political culture, politics is a lot of fun. Even if it gets messy on occasion, it has its exhilarating moments. Sometimes one feels pretty good about accomplishing something in politics whether it's for the ordinary working stiff or for posterity.

The three political cultures we have summarized are combined in several ways in different states and communities. The resulting combinations help shape what people expect of their governments and what they will tolerate from them.

A growing body of research testifies to the importance of political culture as an influence on the actions of state governments and individuals. Ira Sharkansky, for example, using data on the contiguous 48 states, indicates that high levels of traditionalism were associated with low voter turnout, lower government expenditures on social programs, a low tax effort, and lower levels of expenditure on education.[20] Others have shown relationships of political culture to party competition and innovation government policies. Even the way candidates campaign in elections appears to be influenced by the political culture in which the campaign takes place.[21]

The equal rights amendment for women has been adopted by some state legislatures in each type of culture. However, states with a predominantly traditionalistic political culture have lagged behind other states in terms of the percentage of states ratifying. As Table 2.1 indicates, only 25 percent of traditionalistic states have ratified the amendment, while 88 percent of moralistic and 76 percent of individualistic states have done so.

In concluding our discussion of the three subcultures, it is useful to note that Elazar cautions us against "hasty judgments" of any or all of the political cultures. Each has contributed something worthwhile to the American political system:

Table 2.1 POLITICAL CULTURE AND THE EQUAL RIGHTS AMENDMENT

	Predominant state political culture*							
	M	MI	IM	I	IT	TI	T	TM
Not Ratified	Utah		Illinois	Nevada	Missouri	Alabama Arkansas Florida Georgia Louisiana Oklahoma	Mississippi South Carolina Virginia	Arizona North Carolina
Ratified and Rescinded		Idaho	Nebraska				Tennessee	
Ratified	Colorado Maine Michigan Minnesota North Dakota Oregon Vermont Wisconsin	California Iowa Kansas Montana New Hampshire South Dakota Washington	Connecticut Massachusetts New York Ohio Rhode Island Wyoming	Alaska Indiana New Jersey Pennsylvania	Delaware Hawaii Maryland	Kentucky New Mexico Texas West Virginia		

*Predominant culture is listed first.

M = Moralistic

I = Individualistic

Source: John Kincaid, ed. Political Culture, Public Policy and the American States (Philadelphia, PA: Institute for the Study of Human Issues, 1982), 21. Reprinted with permission.

The moralistic political culture, for example, is the primary source of the continuing American quest for the good society. At the same time, there is a tendency toward fanaticism and narrow-mindedness noticeable among some of its representatives. The individualistic political culture is the most tolerant of out-and-out political corruption, yet it has also provided the framework for the integration of diverse groups into the mainstream of American life. The traditionalistic political culture contributes to the search for continuity in a society whose major characteristic is change, yet in the name of continuity, its representatives try to deny blacks (or Indians, or Hispanic-Americans) their civil rights.[22]

Elazar also notes that sometimes one political culture serves to limit the excesses of another, as in the individualistic culture's protection, "though not for any noble reasons," of personal freedom in the face of moralistic efforts to use the power of government to produce a better social order. Adherents of the moralistic and traditionalistic cultures have also been known to limit the individualistic tendency to stretch liberty into license.

National Identity

All three subcultures identified by Elazar were created during the early years of American history, before the industrial revolution and before massive immigration changed the nature of American society. Thus, they do not address the problem of defining the American nation. The three subcultures do not attempt to answer the question of who we are because they all were created when the only view of the American nation was that of a society most of whose members shared a common British heritage.[23]

The question of who we, the American people, are is an important one for the study of state and local government. Our common bond of membership in a nation is an essential link in holding together a political system in which there is a great deal of real and potential divisiveness. The potential breakup of the Soviet Union is only one example in modern times of the difficulty of keeping large political units from falling apart.

Today there are three competing myths or models of who we are: the Anglo core culture, the melting pot, and cultural pluralism. Like all attempts to simplify reality in order to deal with it or understand it better, each myth or model leaves out part of the picture. Each is partially true and partially false. The trick is in determining which part is which. A discussion of different models of who we are would not be very important if not for the fact that these models serve both as explanations for how things *are* and as patterns for how things *ought to be.*

It is the "ought to be" dimension of each model that has important political consequences. To jump ahead a bit, people who operate in terms of the melting pot see bilingual education as a useful tool to promote assimilation. They are uncomfortable when it is used as part of a state-financed program to preserve and promote ethnic heritage. Those who think in terms

---

Box 2-5   **The Anglo Core Culture in** *The Federalist*

Providence has been pleased to give this one connected country to one united people; a people descended from the same ancestors, speaking the same language, professing the same religion, attached to the same principles of government, very similar in their manners and customs.

The Federalist Papers, which we will learn more about in Chapter 3, were written by three of the founding fathers—John Jay, Alexander Hamilton, and James Madison—all writing under the pseudonym Publius. *The Federalist Papers* first appeared as a series of newspaper articles written to convince the people of New York that they ought to elect Federalists to the constitutional ratifying convention in New York. They are generally regarded not only as one of the finest statements of American constitutional principles but also as a classic in the field of political theory.

Source: "Paper Number Two" in Roy P. Fairfield, ed., *The Federalist Papers* (Baltimore: Johns Hopkins Press, 1981), 6.

---

of cultural pluralism are more likely to see this as a perfectly legitimate way to use state and local funds because America is a collection of ethnic groups.

The Anglo Core Model The Anglo core cultural model is based on the fact that our language is a dialect of English and our basic political institutions and basic political values can be traced to the English philosopher John Locke. Thus, certain core symbols, institutions, and practices are so central to our self-concept that to alter them would be to risk severe damage to our national identity.

Although the Anglo core culture model was based on fact, it ignored other facts. Even as John Jay wrote Paper Number Two of *The Federalist* (Box 2-5), Americans of non-British or non-Anglo-Saxon European cultural heritage were making contributions to the American nation. African-Americans were also adding to the national wealth through their labor, their music, and their contributions to our language.

Recognition of the importance of the Anglo core does not mean, however, that these values cannot be taught to people who weren't born here or whose heritage is not Anglo-Saxon. Unfortunately, for many years this point was not understood. The Anglo core culture became identified with the emergence of political movements such as the Know-Nothings and the Klu Klux Klan.[24]

Thus, the main reason for the limited appeal of the Anglo core culture as the operating model for the American nation today is the fact that this model does not adequately recognize the contributions made by people of other cultural heritages.

The Melting Pot Model The melting pot is the model which we celebrate most often in a culinary way. The selection of ethnic foods available and the entry of ethnic words into the language testify to the ability of the American society to accept new ways of doing things. The concept of assimilation—adopting a new culture and contributing to it—is central to the melting pot model. In this model, the American national identity is the result of contributions by individuals as well as other cultures.

This interpretation also has some problems. The major one is that it is does not contain a place for ethnic groups. In fact, it is rather impatient with them. Ethnic identity is viewed as something that should disappear a generation or so after immigration to this country. The so-called English–only movement is as much a melting pot as an Anglo core culture phenomenon. Many of its adherents are first- and second-generation Americans who believe that the melting pot model is not only an explanation of how things are but a prescription for how things ought to be.

Although many American families and individuals have shed their ethnic identity and thus provide ample evidence that the model is partly true, others have not. Many Americans are proud of their ethnic identity. They do not wish to give it up and resent the notion that being ethnic somehow means not being ready for prime-time Americanness.

The Cultural Pluralism Model Cultural pluralism is perhaps the most popular image of America today. Because it is the most recent, there is a tendency to think of this model as being better than the others instead of simply being the newest imperfect explanation of who we are.

Cultural pluralism gives respectability to ethnic identity. It accurately reflects the notion that many Americans wish to keep and sometimes rediscover their pre-American ethnic heritage. According to this model, everyone is a part of an ethnic salad in which every ingredient maintains its identity. In *Megatrends*, John Naisbitt asserts, "We have moved from the myth of the melting pot to a celebration of cultural diversity."[25]

The pluralist model, for all its many advantages, has some disadvantages as well. The most important one for the purposes of this discussion is that the model has no place for the fact that many Americans do not have and do not want an ethnic identity. To the cultural pluralist this is not the way things ought to be. In the following passage Ricardo Garcia, a cultural pluralist, indicates the difficulty that this model of America has in dealing with a freestanding American national identity:

> The dominant ethnic group in American society is made up of much-maligned white, Anglo-Saxon Protestants (WASPs). The power of our WASP heritage is still potent, manifested in major institutions, in people's attitudes and behaviors. The WASP group is so deeply embedded in American society that its attitudes and values are perceived by some to be the American core ethos.[26]

The implications of this quote are both interesting and potentially troublesome. First, it forces on a **category** of persons a group identity they may not want. Many people classified as WASPs are neither of British heritage nor of particularly devout Protestant faith. WASP is a sort of catchall category for nonethnic whites. If everyone must have an ethnic identity, what do we do with people who say they don't have one? Do we honor that claim or not? Many Americans identify with the American nation and have no additional ethnic identity, though they may have other identities based on their schools, professions, sports, hobbies, astrological signs, food preferences, and so on ("I'm a lactovegetarian." "You are? Well, that's interesting. I'm a Sagittarius").

For many Americans, ethnic identity is rather incomplete. After the 1970 Census, the U.S. Bureau of the Census found in a series of reinterviews conducted in 1973 that only 64.7 percent of the surveyed individuals reported the same ethnic responses that they had less than five years earlier.[27]

A second problem with cultural pluralism is the difficulty of dealing with the notion of a national identity. If everyone is ethnic, what do we do with George Washington and Abraham Lincoln? Are they merely WASP heroes? Clearly they are more than that, just as Martin Luther King is both an ethnic and a national hero.

The tendency of cultural pluralism to force an ethnic identity on everyone brings us to the issue raised much earlier in this chapter: the tension between nationalists who use the melting pot (or something very much like it involving assimilation into the whole) as their model of the nation and ethnic leaders who use cultural pluralism (or something involving an ethnic identity for each individual) as their model.

Each of these models is flawed. Each is useful for many individuals but not for others. Each deserves respect, and in some societies, such as ours, each receives respect. One of the tragedies of other societies is that they lack political institutions that make it possible for people with different views on important matters to work out solutions peacefully.

As future leaders at the state, local, and national levels, you will have to deal with people who have models different from one another's and from yours. Our major reason for bringing this to your attention is to prepare you to respect those models and to communicate in terms of shared goals and beliefs rather than to insist on ideological uniformity.

Conclusion

In this chapter we have introduced some terms and concepts we think are useful in the study of the individual and the governments. We have attempted to avoid jargon as much as possible. However, we find it extremely difficult to have readers "know what we mean" if they do not share a working vocabulary and a common frame of reference.

It is important to emphasize that the frame of reference in this book is simply one of many. We do not claim that our definitions or sets of concepts are the best for everyone. We offer them because you need to know that they exist and need to come to terms with them if you want to operate effectively in your state and community. Later in this book we will explain some institutions — such as political parties — and some policies — such as welfare and taxation — from a particular point of view. We do this to encourage you to think, to challenge yourself, and to prepare yourself for dealing with the decisions you will be asked to make in the political system of your state and community. We do not do it to persuade you that a particular point of view is the right one.

A few paragraphs ago we asked somewhat rhetorically whether George Washington and Abraham Lincoln were American heroes or merely WASP heroes. Equally significant is the question of whether Harriet Tubman, Sojourner Truth, Cesar Chavez, and Martin Luther King can be American as well as ethnic heroes. The answer, we hope, is that they not only can be but *already are* American heroes.

Respecting the right of other individuals to differ from us ideologically and then working with them through our state and local political institutions to peacefully resolve the consequences of our differences have been necessary for the survival of our political system and our nation for over two centuries. Understanding how they work and endeavoring to make them work better will improve the chances that they'll be around for another 200 years.

Study Objectives

1. Compare and contrast ethnic group and nation. Identify three similarities and one essential difference.
2. Identify three sources of tension between leaders of new nation-states and leaders of the ethnic groups within them.
3. Define "political system" and identify some major similarities shared by all or most political systems.
4. Identify ways in which all systems are similar whether or not they are political.
5. Identify nine similarities shared by all political systems.
6. Identify three dimensions of the human environment of the governments.
7. Define "technology" and identify three technological changes that have profoundly affected the social environment of the human race.
8. Explain what the metropolitan paradox is.
9. Explain the relationship between metropolitan sprawl and the fragmentation of authority.
10. Define "political culture." How does it affect politics?
11. Identify the three American political cultures or subcultures.
12. Describe the three models that are used to describe American society (or define who "we the people" are).

Glossary

abstraction A mental construction, a set of ideas that we use to simplify reality and organize our thinking about it.

agglomeration A collection of mixed items. In the metropolitan context it refers to areas of hundreds of square miles that include a hodgepodge of cities, towns, villages, trailer parks, slums, industrialized areas, and commercial areas.

altruistic The quality of being unselfish and concerned with the well-being of others.

authority Political power which is legitimate.

category A part of a classification scheme. Although "category" and "group" are used interchangeably by many people, we use this term to refer to items or individuals included in a classification scheme because they share a characteristic. A group is a collection of individuals who share an identity or have some connection to one another other than simply sharing a characteristic. "Category" is objective; "group" is subjective.

charisma The gift of grace; a quality of having special personality characteristics that enable one to lead other people. Charismatic individuals are usually believed to have superior moral qualities.

ethnic group A collection of people with a common sense of identity who seek to obtain the rights and benefits of citizenship in a larger society or state. Members of ethnic groups can also be members of nations.

government A set of offices which make and enforce decisions which affect the membership of a political system.

ideology A set of beliefs about politics. It comes in two forms: manifest and latent.

jurisdiction The subject matter or territory over which an individual or government has authority.

legitimacy The quality of being accepted as right, fair, proper, or in accordance with agreed upon standards.

megalopolis A large complex of people and governmental units struggling to cope with traffic jams; air pollution; stray animals; water shortages in the summer and floods in the spring; fire, sewage, and solid waste management; juvenile delinquency; and a host of other problems that ignore the boundaries between one government and the next.

Metropolitan Statistical Area (MSA) An area consisting of a county in which there is a city (or twin cities) with a total population of 50,000 people and any contiguous counties which are socioeconomically integrated with the core county.

metropolitan sprawl The uncoordinated spread of economic, recreational, residential, and governmental development beyond the legal limit of the core cities of the metropolitan areas of America.

nation A collection of people with a common sense of identity who seek to establish or maintain a state of their own. Members of nations may also be members of ethnic groups.

nation-state The predominant political unit in the international community today. It consists of a self-governing political unit—a state—in which a nation constitutes the majority of the politically relevant population.

paradox Something that appears to be false or absurd but is true once one understands it.

political resource Anything that can be used to obtain power or influence.

political system Any persistent pattern of human behavior involving to a significant extent control, influence, power, or authority.

politics Any human relationship involving to a significant extent influence or power.

state A political system whose government is able to enforce its claim to unique authority to regulate the use of force among the people living in a defined territory.

system A collection of parts that interact in some way.

technology The knowledge and skill available to make, store, use, or transmit energy, matter, or information.

Endnotes

1. Robert A. Dahl, *Modern Political Analysis*, 3rd ed., (Englewood Cliffs, NJ: Prentice-Hall, 1976), 3. The most lucid portions of our section on politics and political systems are based on this excellent book.

2. For a discussion of the arbitrary and artificial nature of nation-states, see Mostafa Rejai and Cynthia H. Enloe, "Nation-States and State-Nations," *International Studies Quarterly* 13–2 (June 1969), 140–158, and the introductory chapter of Cynthia Enloe, *Ethnic Conflict and Political Development*, (Boston: Little, Brown, 1973).

3. Karl Deutsch, *Nationalism and Social Communication*, (Boston: MIT Press, 1966). On p. 105, Deutsch observes that "nationalities turn into nations when they acquire the power to back up their aspirations."

4. For a discussion of ethnic-nationalist tensions, see Cynthia H. Enloe, 35–84.

5. See, for example, Edmund David Cronon, *Black Moses: The Story of Marcus Garvey and the Universal Negro Improvement Association* (Madison: University of Wisconsin Press, 1955), and James A. Gregor, "Black Nationalism: A Preliminary Analysis of Negro Radicalism," *Science and Society*, 27 (Fall 1963), 415–432. For a discussion of nationalism in the Mexican-American community, see Joseph L. Love, "La Raza: Mexican-Americans in Rebellion," in Edward Simmen, ed., *Pain and Promise: The Chicano Today* (New York: New American Library, 1972), 271–286.

6. Dahl, 3.

7. For eight of these nine we express our gratitude once again to Professor Dahl. "Cooperation" is our contribution.

8. Lorand B. Szalay and Rita Mae Kelly, "Political Ideology and Subjective Culture: Conceptualization and Empirical Assessment," *American Political Science Review*, 76:3 (September 1982), 585–602. As the authors observe on p. 585, "The study of ideology and the study of culture have too often been separated."

9. The Russian or East European students you may meet in your travels or as exchange students are an entirely different matter. Their survival in the elite world of state-supported education depends on ideological correctness.

10. For an excellent overview of the history of the city and the emergence of the metropolis, see Mark Schneider, *Suburban Growth: Policy and Process*, (Brunswick, OH: King's Court, 1980). The American classic is, of course, Louis Mumford, *The City in History* (New York: Harcourt Brace and World, 1961).

11. U.S. Bureau of the Census, *County and City Data Book, 1988*. (Washington, DC: U.S. Government Printing Office, 1988).

12. Edward H. Glade, Jr., and Keith Collens, "State Agriculture," in *The Book of the*

States: 1982–83, (Lexington, KY: Council of State Governments, 1982), 620–631.

13. Mumford, 34.

14. The two essential sources on political culture are Daniel J. Elazar, *American Federalism: A View from the States*, 2nd ed., (New York: Harper & Row, 1972), 86–126, and Gabriel A. Almond and Sidney Verba, *The Civic Culture: Political Attitudes and Democracy in Five Nations*, (Boston: Little, Brown, 1965).

15. M. Kent Jennings and Richard Niemi, *Generations and Politics* (Princeton, NJ: Princeton University Press, 1981), 390.

16. Ibid., 391.

17. Donald J. Devine, *The Political Culture of the United States: The Influence of Member Values on Regime Maintenance*, (Boston: Little, Brown, 1972), 46–65.

18. Elazar, 93.

19. Elazar, 125.

20. Ira Sharkansky, "The Utility of Elazar's Political Culture: A Research Note," *Polity* 5 (Fall 1972), 139–141.

21. An excellent collection of essays and research reports on political culture can be found in John Kincaid, ed., *Political Culture, Public Policy and the American States* (Philadelphia: Institute for the Study of Human Issues, 1982).

22. Elazar, 125.

23. Edgar Litt, *Ethnic Politics in America: Beyond Pluralism*, (Glenview, IL: Scott, Foresman, 1970), 8–13. See also Milton M. Gordon, "Assimilation in America: Theory and Reality," *Daedalus*, XC (Spring 1961), 263–283. This article also appears as a chapter in a useful volume edited by Brett W. Hawkins and Robert A. Lorinskas, *The Ethnic Factor in Amrican Politics*, (Columbus, OH: Merrill, 1970). Additional sources on this topic include Stanley Feldstein and Lawrence Costello, eds., *The Ordeal of Assimilation: A Documentary History of the White Working Class*, (Garden City, NY: Anchor/Doubleday, 1974), Joseph Rothschild, *Ethonopolitics* (New York: Columbia University Press, 1981), Stephen Steinberg, *The Ethnic Myth: Race, Ethnicity, and Class in America*, (New York: Antheneum, 1981), and Anthony D. Smith, *The Ethnic Revival*, (Cambridge and New York: Cambridge University Press, 1981).

24. For an example of the literature which probes the wrongs caused by Anglo-Saxons in particular and whites in general, see Lewis H. Carlson and George A. Colburn, *In Their Place: White America Defines Her Minorities, 1850–1950*, (New York: Wiley, 1972).

25. John Naisbitt, *Megatrends*, (New York: Warner, 1982), 244.

26. Ricarado L. Garcia, *Fostering a Pluralistic Society Through Multi-Ethnic Education*, (Bloomington, IN: Phi Delta Kappa Educational Foundation, 1978), 12.

27. Stanley Lieberson, "Unhyphenated Whites in the United States," *Ethnic and Social Studies* 8 (January 1985), 174.

Chapter 3

Federalism and Intergovernmental Relations

The theme of this chapter is the development of federalism as an American contribution to the science of politics. *E Pluribus Unum*, it says on the Great Seal of the United States, which appears in many places, including the back side of the dollar bill. That Latin phrase means "from many, one." Creating an *unum* out of a plurality of peoples and governments was no small accomplishment; the process still continues.[1]

Suggestions for reforming, restructuring, and altering the unity which is our federal system have included abolishing the states, granting statehood to major metropolitan areas, and proposing a constitutional amendment favoring a states' rights doctrine.[2] To make wise decisions about altering the American federal system, it makes sense to start with a fairly clear picture of the essential nature of that system. This chapter will sketch some of its most salient features and some of the major changes which have occurred since it began in 1787.[3]

FEDERALISM: A NOVEL AMERICAN COMPROMISE

Definitions can be short or long, simple or detailed. Our short definition of federalism is as follows: a system of government in which power is divided between a central government and regional or subdivisional governments.[4] Before we inflict on you a longer definition, we will examine three things that it is and three things that it is not.

Three Things That Federalism Is

A Relatively New Concept The language of political science can be traced at least as far back as the ancient Greeks; thus any concept invented in the past 200 years is relatively new. While discussions of federalism can be found in medieval European as well as classical Greek political theory, the term "federalism" was traditionally used interchangeably with the term "confederation" to refer to any association of independent political units.[5] Until the system of government established by the American Constitution had been in operation for several decades, this practice continued. For that reason, the debate over the ratification of the U.S. Constitution took place not between federalists and confederalists but between federalists and antifederalists.

Alexis de Tocqueville, writing in the 1830s, attempted to explain the American system to Europeans. He observed that "a form of government has been found out which is neither exactly national or federal . . . the new word which will one day designate this novel invention does not yet exist."[6]

Tocqueville was unaware that he had employed the word which was eventually to identify "this novel invention." The word "federalism" already existed, but its new meaning had been invented only recently. Tocqueville was one of the first to point out the existence of this contribution to the science of politics. It soon became clear that the American Constitution really had created something more than a league of independent governments. Because of this we now have two distinguishable concepts — **federal** and **confederal** — which are discussed briefly in Box 3-1.

An American Contribution to the Science of Politics Other countries which have created their own versions of federalism have used the American model. Not only was it the oldest one available in written form, but a series of essays setting forth the philosophical underpinnings of the federal system was available.

The Federalist Papers is one of the most widely read books on politics worldwide. It consists of 85 newspaper articles written between 1787 and 1789 to persuade the people of the state of New York to elect delegates to

---

Box 3-1 # Unitary, Federal, and Confederal Structures

Representative Political Units

Unitary	France, Japan
Federal	United States, Canada
Confederal	The United Nations, the European Economic Community

The Sovereign

Unitary	The people
Federal	The people
Confederal	The states that created the union

Autonomy of Governments in the Union

Unitary	All subunits are local governments which can be overruled and abolished by the central government
Federal	Subunits and the central government are partners in the union, sharing power
Confederal	States can abolish or restructure the union and/or the central government

Relationship of the Central Government, to the Individual

Unitary	Direct: Individuals are citizens of the central government
Federal	Direct: Each individual is a citizen of both the central government and a member government
Confederal	Indirect: Individuals are citizens of member governments only; the confederal government deals with individuals with the permission of the member governments

---

the state ratifying convention who would approve the proposed constitution. This classic was written by three delegates to the Constitutional Convention in Philadelphia—James Madison, John Jay, and Alexander Hamilton—writing under a single pen name, Publius. Their work is as well known among college students in Canada, Germany, India, and Australia as it is in the United States, perhaps even more so.[7]

A System of Government Based on Compromise Federalism itself is a compromise. The government of the United States of America exists because advocates of a strong central government and advocates of state sovereignty were able to compromise. As we noted earlier, the federal system as we know it did not exist as an option among many from which the authors of the Constitution could choose. They created it. American federalism was the only way to get the states to enter a union with a real central government.[8]

Most students of American government are aware of at least one or two of the three great compromises briefly sketched in Box 3-2; the Connecticut, three-fifths, and slave trade compromises. What is sometimes understated is

Box 3-2 ## Federalism and Three Compromises

THE CONNECTICUT COMPROMISE

Also known as the Great Compromise, this involved the distribution of seats in the national legislature. There would be a two-house legislature. Representation in the upper house was to be based on equal representation for every state; in the lower house, it was to be based on population. Each state was given two seats in the Senate and was guaranteed, regardless of population, at least one seat in the House of Representatives.

This compromise between large and small states made it possible for the Constitutional Convention to break out of an almost hopeless deadlock. Without some protection, the guarantee of representation in both houses, and significant representation in the Senate, small states would not have entered the union. Representatives from large states, on the other hand, felt that they were being underrepresented in the national legislature.

THE THREE-FIFTHS COMPROMISE

This was also about representation. It was decided that the formula for distributing seats in the House of Representatives among the states would use the census figures for three-fifths of the slave population of each state. The Northern representatives did not want to reward slaveholding states by giving them representation based on the slave population. The Southern representatives at the convention naturally wanted the entire slave population counted for the purposes of allocating seats.

Thus, slaveowners, who could vote while their slaves could not, were overrepresented in the national legislature while working people in nonslave states were underrepresented. Without this compromise the Southern states would not have entered the union.

THE SLAVE TRADE COMPROMISE

This allowed the slave trade to go untaxed and unregulated until 1808. After that it could be regulated and taxed and probably abolished. Representatives of slaveholding interests believed that by that time the imported population of slaves would be large enough to maintain itself by natural increase.

This compromise involved several principles: abolishing the slave trade altogether; taxing the importation of slaves; taxing the export of slave-grown products such as sugar, cotton, and tobacco; and using the word "slave" in the Constitution.

Source: Catherine Drinker Bowen, *Miracle at Philadelphia*, (Boston: Little, Brown, 1966; reprint, Atlantic Monthly Press, Little, Brown, 1986).

the fact that these compromises involved real issues to which strong emotions were tied. Take the three-fifths compromise. Delegates from Northern states weren't sure that it was right to let slaveholders in South Carolina and Virginia have a stronger voice in Congress than the numbers of free men in those states warranted. Since slaves, even though they were property, were also to be counted for purposes of representation, Elbridge Gerry of Massachusetts asked, "Why then should not horses and cattle have the right of representation in the North?"[9] As Box 3-2 indicates, the three-fifths compromise meant that the votes of free men in states such as Pennsylvania and New York were diluted. Southern slave owners ended up with a proportionately larger influence in Congress than citizens in the Northern states had.

For American federalism to come into existence, people of strong convictions had to suspend judgment and consider the possibility that they might not know everything. In the closing hours of the convention, when a complete document had been prepared for signing, Benjamin Franklin advised reluctant delegates to set aside their reservations and sign. He said:

> I confess that there are several parts of this constitution that I do not at present approve, but I am not sure I shall never approve of them. . . . The older I grow, the more apt I am to doubt my own judgment, and to pay more respect to the judgment of others. . . . On the whole, I cannot help expressing a wish that every member of the Convention who may still have objections to it would with me on this occasion doubt a little of his own infallibility and to make manifest our unanimity, put his name to this instrument.[10]

Compromise is essential for the American federal system to work. The possibility of doubting the **infallibility** of our political wisdom is an important thing to remember in an age of nonnegotiable demands and political principles that seem carved in stone. We do not suggest that one's personal moral and ethical principles bend with every passing breeze. We simply emphasize the fact that if the founding fathers had not agreed to leave some issues that were very important to them for future generations to resolve, there probably would be no United States of America.[11]

Having examined federalism as an American political invention based on compromise, we now consider three things with which federalism is often confused.

Three Things Federalism Is Not

After a decade or so of discussing federalism with students, it seems apparent to us that there are at least three concepts with which federalism is frequently confused.[12] Most of the confusion comes from the temptation to define federalism in terms of qualities with which it is often but not always associated: democracy, separation of powers, and decentralization.

Democracy Many a blue book over the years has testified to the confusion that exists in many undergraduate (and graduate) minds about the

---

Box 3-3 ## Countries with a Federal Form of Government

State	Number and Name of Divisions
Argentina	22 provinces
Australia	6 states
Austria	9 provinces
Brazil	27 federated states
Canada	10 provinces
Federal Republic of Germany	10 Lander
India	22 states and 9 territories
Malaysia	13 states
Mexico	31 states
Federal Republic of Nigeria	19 states
Switzerland	22 cantons (19 full, 6 half)
United States	50 states
Union of Soviet Socialist Republics	15 union republics containing 20 autonomous republics, 6 territories, 120 regions, and 8 autonomous regions
Venezuela	20 states
Yugoslavia	6 republics

Source: Mark S. Hoffman, *The World Almanac and Book of Facts 1990* (New York: Pharos Books, 1989).

---

relationship between federalism and democracy. Although most apples are red when ripe, it does not follow that *all* ripe apples are red. Thus, while it can be argued that federalism works best when combined with democracy, it does not follow that federalism and democracy are the same thing.[13]

Not all the federal systems listed in Box 3-3, for example, are democracies. Federal systems may become dictatorships temporarily or permanently. The Weimar Republic of Germany, for example, was a federation and a democracy until Hitler took power in 1932 and dispensed with both principles. Given its formal structure, the Union of Soviet Socialist Republics is a federation. One could argue that it is also a democracy, but even after peristroika and glasnost, one would do so with limited success.

The Principle of Separation of Powers This principle divides power *within* a government, whereas federalism divides power *between* governments. In the U.S. Constitution, **separation of powers** means that the power of the national, or federal, government is divided into three branches: executive, legislative, and judicial.

At the state and local levels, governments may or may not employ this principle. Virtually all state constitutions separate the powers of state government. The laws and charters that establish local government may or may not employ this principle. In most counties, for example, the officials who approve the budget (a legislative function) are the same officials who are in charge of spending money (an executive function).[14]

The confusion between federalism and separation of powers seems to arise from a failure to appreciate the fact that power can be divided or shared in a number of dimensions. Federalism looks at power sharing in terms of the whole and its parts. Separation of powers is concerned with power within a single government, whether the government of the whole or the government of a part.

Decentralization   Federalism is not the only system of government in which there is a national government as well as regional and local governments. The first part of our brief definition of federalism—a system of government in which power is divided between a central government and regional or subdivisional governments—certainly allows one to **infer** that in other types of systems such lesser or more local governments do not exist. However, this inference is wrong. In all large political systems there are local as well as central governments. Not only do local governments exist in unitary systems of government, they also exercise power and spend a fair amount of money.

An essential difference between federal and unitary systems of government lies in the way in which power is formally distributed. In a unitary system the central government has the right to claim all power but delegates some of it to the subordinate units of government in the interests of efficiency. This is called **decentralization**. Decentralization can be reversed unilaterally by the central government.

In contrast, in many federal systems of government the formal distribution of powers cannot be changed by the central government acting alone.[15] To do this, the constitution must be amended. This requires action at the state (or provincial) level. It may not be necessary for all the states to approve, but it usually requires a majority, sometimes a special majority. In the United States, for example, three-fourths of the states must ratify a proposed constitutional amendment before it can go into effect.

We now turn to our four-part definition of federalism. We will not back into very many definitions in this book, but federalism is a rather special term and deserves special treatment. Our discussion of three things it is and three things it is not has provided a context which is intended to make our definition a little more understandable.

AMERICAN FEDERALISM: A FOUR-DIMENSIONAL DEFINITION

We define American federalism as a dynamic political system in which a union of governments and a union of people establish a constitution that guarantees the continued existence of the member governments and creates a central government that exercises sovereignty for the union.

This is not the only and certainly not the best definition of federalism available, but it serves our needs because it enables us to point out four features of the American political system. Some but not all of these characteristics are shared by other federal systems.[16]

A Union of Governments

An important feature of the American federal system is the fact that each of the 50 states could exist as an independent country. Looking at the bigger states, we see that California's gross domestic product in 1987 ranked fifth in the world after that of the United States, Japan, West Germany, and France. Twenty-three states have economies ranked in the top 50 worldwide.[17]

Rhode Island, the smallest state in area, is larger in square miles and in population than are 16 independent countries, including Liechtenstein, Luxembourg, Malta, and Monaco. The least populous state, Alaska, with a population of about 400,000, still ranks ahead of more than a dozen countries.[18]

Some federations include parts which were once independent, such as the princely states of Germany.[19] Before becoming a part of the United States, Texas was an independent republic for nearly a decade. Vermont, which declared itself a republic independent from England and from New York in 1777, was the first new state created after the federal constitution was ratified by the original 13 states.[20]

The concept of a union of separate polities is an essential aspect of federalism. If the unique identity of each part is not recognized, then the parts are in danger of becoming mere administrative subunits of the central government.[21] Daniel J. Elazar expresses the notion of a union of governments very nicely in his definition of federalism:

> The mode of political organization that unites separate policies within an overarching political system by distributing power among general and constituent governments in a manner designed to protect the existence and authority of both.[22]

A Union of People

Implicit in the meaning of American federalism is the notion of a single nation. Its citizens may have additional ethnic, class, religious, or geographic identities, but they share or are encouraged to share a single national identity. Thus, American federalism is nationalistic, as John Jay, the author of Paper Number Two of *The Federalist*, candidly admits in Box 3-4. The **nationalism** built into American federalism is one reason for the tension, discussed in Chapter 2, between the notion of America as a union of people —one people—and America as a union of peoples—ethnic groups. This tension is neither unique to America nor necessarily unhealthy.

An essential difference between a union of governments that is a federation and a union of governments that is a confederation is the citizenship of

---

Box 3-4   **To the Members of the American Nation: Come into the Union and Bring Your State Governments with You**

I have often taken notice that Providence has been pleased to give this one connected country to one united people . . . who, by their joint counsels, arms, and efforts, fighting side by side throughout a long and bloody war, have nobly established their general liberty and independence.

    This country and this people seem to have been made for each other, and it appears as if it was the design of Providence that an inheritance so proper and convenient for a band of brethren, united to each other by the strongest ties, should never be split into a number of unsocial, jealous, and alien sovereignties.

Source: John Jay, "Federalist Number Two," in James Madison, Alexander Hamilton, and John Jay, *The Federalist Papers,* (New Rochelle, NY: Arlington House, circa 1975), 38.

---

the people, as Box 3-1 indicated. In a federation there may be state, provincial, or territorial citizenship, but the people are also citizens of the national (federal) government. In the American federation and most others, the central government has a claim to the loyalty of its inhabitants and a claim to the right to regulate or tax them because they are its citizens.

The notion that the citizens of a federation have rights as well as responsibilities was the basis for the civil rights movement in America. Some American citizens demanded that the federal government meet its obligations to its citizens by enforcing the requirement that those citizens be treated equally in every state regardless of state law and custom. Thus, in the 1960s the federal government became deeply involved in traditionally state and local matters such as education and voting registration. The idea of a united people sharing a single national identity helps us appreciate the practical value of federalism. It is as if the authors of the Constitution had declared, "If the only way to bring the people of a single nation together under one government is to bring their separate governments into a union of governments, then that's the way we'll have to do it." Hamilton observed in *The Federalist* that "a nation without a national government is, in my view, an awful spectacle."[23]

In some federations, the customs, language, religion, geography, and other sources of identity may interfere with the recognition of a common identity. When these separate sources of identity reinforce one another, as in Yugoslavia and the Soviet Union today or in the slaveholding states in the American South over 100 years ago, the federation may confront problems severe enough to threaten its continued existence.[24]

National identity can be created in at least two ways. First, individuals are taught to think of themselves as members of the nation by education (and, if you will, propaganda). They are taught stories about national heroes and heroines, myths, symbols, a common language, and a common set of laws and customs.

The second way in which a national government can bring new people into the nation is by expanding the idea of what the nation—or union of people—really is. This expansion of the definition of the American nation occurred during the 1960s and 1970s and to some extent is still going on. It involved educating both those who were included in the old definition of nation and those who had accepted their exclusion as being part of the nature of things.

The union of people—the American nation—was redefined during the civil rights era by the blood, sweat, and tears of many individuals and the martyrdom of a few. The new union included, as full citizens, millions of people (African-American, Hispanic-American, Native American, and Asian) who previously were treated as second-class citizens in terms of the ability to buy property, ride where they chose in public vehicles, attend the public schools and colleges of their choice, and participate in electoral politics.

This process of **national integration**, bringing all Americans into the same society, continues. Ultimately it does not matter whether they come into the nation singly or in groups. Thus, the idea that America is a union of peoples may help make our political system work better for them. The ultimate objective, whatever our model of it, is a union of individuals who each possess a national identity that links all of us to individuals in the 80,000 units of state and local government within our federal system.

The Government of the Union Exercises Sovereignty

Sovereignty is a concept which includes two notions: supremacy in one's own sphere of influence and independence from the rule of others. In democratic political theory, sovereignty resides with "the people."[25] The people delegate power to one or more governments to exercise on its behalf. In practice, when one wishes to define an entity in the larger political system which can act *as if it were* sovereign, one usually refers to government. However, it is worth the effort to remember that in federal systems which are democratic, the people, not the government, is sovereign. This is why we used the phrase "exercise sovereignty" in our definition.

One Sovereign, One Government In a unitary system only one government—the national government—exercises sovereignty. It makes rules which affect the other governments in the political system as well as the people.

In confederal systems, the central government does not exercise sovereignty: it cannot act independently of the member governments. Under our first constitution, the Articles of Confederation, for example, there was no executive branch at the national level. The U.S. Congress could pass laws but had no means to enforce them.

A modern confederacy, the United Nations, has an executive branch, but it has no power to carry out resolutions passed in the General Assembly unless the member governments give it permission and money. When the executive branch of the UN acts, it offers services in accordance with the laws of the state in which it happens to be acting, whether it is distributing food in Ethiopia or distributing birth control information in India.

Three Dimensions of Sovereignty   In the American federal system the national government exercises sovereignty in three ways. First, it is independent of the control of the governments within its boundaries. When an agency of the U.S. government carries out the functions assigned to it by the Constitution or by law, it does not need the permission of a state government to act. The FBI, for example, does not have to get the permission of the government of Michigan to arrest someone in that state who is suspected of breaking a federal law. Usually courtesy and custom result in cooperative action, but it is not legally necessary.

A second way in which the national government exercises sovereignty is as an actor in the international state system, independent of the rule of any foreign government. In the American federal system, the national government is the only government empowered to deal with foreign states. Article I, Section 10, of the Constitution says, "No State shall, without the consent of Congress . . . enter into any agreement . . . with a foreign power." State and local governments deal with foreign governments in terms of ceremonial matters, exchanging representatives with sister cities, attending international conferences of legislators, and promoting economic links including giving aid or receiving it. However, binding agreements with the force of law between cities or states and foreign governments must have the approval of Congress.

It is worth noting that while the national government officially represents the people of the United States in the international community of nations, it has no control over the behavior of mayors or governors in social settings. Although these officials cannot make binding agreements, they can be as pleasant or unpleasant as they wish with foreign dignitaries. From time to time the national government, and presumably the American people, has been alternately embarrassed and filled with pride by the independent actions of maverick state and local officials.

Third, in conflicts between the national government and member governments of the union, one way or another the federal government exercises sovereignty. When the U.S. Supreme Court tells Congress or the executive branch that it has lost in a court case with a state, it is still a branch of the national government which has decided the issue, not the states.

The Constitution and Supremacy   The supremacy of the national government is stated in Article VI:

This Constitution, and the laws of the United States which shall be made in pursuance thereof; and all treaties made, or which shall be made, under the authority of the United States, shall be the supreme law of the land; and the judges in every State shall be bound thereby, any thing in the constitution or laws of any State to the contrary notwithstanding.

The intent here is both clear and impressive. The fact that the representatives of 13 sovereign states agreed to this clause reminds us that some heavy compromising went into the construction of the constitution.

Closer examination of this clause indicates that the laws of the United States which are capable of becoming the "supreme law of the land" must be in accord with the Constitution. Since the Constitution can be amended and the Supreme Court can change its interpretation of the Constitution, it is clear that the process of exercising sovereignty is a dynamic, ongoing process.

If a federal law is enacted to which enough people (state officials included) are strongly opposed, the constitutionality of the law may be tested (it remains supreme until it fails the test of constitutionality) or the law can be repealed or modified by a responsive Congress. Furthermore, the President can modify the executive branch's interpretation of the law by executive order.

Once the objections to a law have been clarified, it is not unusual for Congress to pass new laws refining the old, particularly in cases where unforeseen hardship may be placed on state or local governments. The "final say" of the supreme law of the land can take generations to determine. For example, the final say on whether small children could be employed in factories and mines was not determined until 1941, when the Supreme Court upheld the Fair Labor Standards Act of 1938. Decades earlier the Court had found similar laws, both state and federal, unconstitutional. Attempts to abolish child labor in factories and mines by means of a constitutional amendment also failed. By 1937 only 28 states had ratified the child labor amendment that had been proposed in 1924.[26]

Forbidding the employment of children to pick crops such as onions and apples has yet to be settled by our political system. Whether or not this practice is eventually abolished, it seems clear that the sovereign people of the United States are not interested in reversing the process and making it legal once more to employ children in steel mills and coal mines or in requiring state and local employees to work overtime with no compensation.

Throughout the history of the development of the federal system there has been an effort to determine the boundary between the exercise of sovereignty by the national government and the powers of the states. The most recent opinion of the Court on this matter is that no subject matter is reserved to the states and denied to the national government. According to the Court, the states are protected by the dynamics of the federal system, not by drawing a line which the national government cannot cross. In *Garcia* v. *San Antonio Metropolitan Transit Authority*,[27] Justice Blackmun speaking for the majority, stated that the founders of the Constitution chose to rely on a federal system in which special restraints on federal power over the States inhered principally in the workings of the National Government itself, rather than in discrete limitations on the objects of federal authority. State sovereign interests, then, are more properly protected by procedural safeguards inherent in the structure of the federal system than by judicially created limitations in federal power.[28]

The receptiveness of Congress to demands by state and local officials for legislative relief after the *Garcia* case was decided provides a good example of the safeguards to which Justice Blackmun alluded. The Supreme Court decided in 1985 that the overtime provisions of the Fair Labor Standards Act apply to virtually all state and local government employees, including those working for mass transit systems. State and local officials protested that paying cash bonuses for overtime required of public employees would create an undue financial hardship. They were, however, willing to reward employees who worked overtime with compensatory paid time off. In response to this cry for help, Congress came to the aid of the governments. It enacted the Fair Labor Standards Amendments of 1985 to buffer the effect of the Court's ruling, setting forth conditions under which compensatory time could be used in lieu of a cash payment by a state or local government.[29]

Several other safeguards provide us with a clearer understanding of American federalism. Nothing more clearly indicates the political skill of the framers of the Constitution than the guarantees they built into the union to ensure that its parts would be indestructible.

The Union is Made of Indestructible Parts: Six Guarantees

The fourth feature of our definition of American federalism is that the viability of the parts must be maintained. The U.S. Supreme Court observed in 1869:

> The preservation of the states, and the maintenance of their governments are as much within the design and care of the Constitution as the preservation of the Union and the maintenance of the National government. The Constitution in all of its provisions, looks to an indestructible Union, composed of indestructible States.[30]

As Box 3-5 indicates, there are numerous guarantees in the Constitution which promote the continued existence and vitality of the states. The six safeguards we discuss by no means constitute the complete list. They provide enough evidence, however, to demonstrate that even though the central government possesses powers that sometimes appear awesome, there is some basis for the belief that states are unlikely to become mere administrative subdivisions in a unitary system.

Territorial Integrity   The territorial boundaries of a state cannot be altered without the consent of that state's legislature. Minor boundary dis-

Box 3-5 Guarantees of State Viability in the Constitution

Article I

Section 2 No person shall be a Representative. . . . who shall not, when elected, *be an inhabitant of that State in which he shall be chosen.**

Section 2 *[E]ach State shall have at least one Representative.**

Section 3 The Senate of the United States shall be composed of *two Senators from each State. . . .*

Section 3 No person shall be a *Senator* . . . who shall not, when elected, *be an inhabitant of that State for which he shall be chosen.*

Section 5 *Each House shall be the judge of* the elections, returns and qualifications of *its own members. . . .*

Section 7 *Every bill* which shall have passed the House of Representatives *and the Senate*, shall, before it becomes a law, be presented to the President of the United States. . . .

Article II

Section 1 *Each state, shall appoint*, in such manner as the legislature thereof may direct, a number of electors, equal to the whole number of Senators and Representatives to which the State may be entitled in the Congress. . . .

Section 1 The electors shall meet *in their respective States*. . . . The person having the greatest number of votes shall be the President, if such number be a majority of the whole number of electors appointed; and if there be more than one who have such majority, and have an equal number of votes, then *the House of Representatives shall immediately choose by ballot* one of them for President; and if no person have a majority, then from the five highest on the list the said House shall in like manner choose the President. *But in choosing the President, the votes shall be taken by States, the representation from each State having one vote. . . .*

Article IV

Section 1 Full faith and credit shall be given in each State to the public acts, records, and judicial proceedings of every other State.

Section 2 The citizens of each State shall be entitled to all privileges and immunities of citizens in the several States.

Section 3 [N]o new State shall be formed or erected within the jurisdiction of any other State; nor any State be formed by the Junction of two or more States, or parts of States, *without the consent of the legislatures of the States concerned* as well as of the Congress.

continued

Box 3-5 *(continued)*

> *Section 4   The United States shall . . . protect each* of them [the states] against invasion; *and on application of the legislature*, or of the Executive (when the legislature cannot be convened) *against domestic violence*.

Article V

> The Congress, whenever *two thirds of both Houses* shall deem it necessary, *shall propose amendments to this Constitution*, or on the application of the legislatures of two thirds of the several States, shall call a convention for proposing Amendments which . . . shall be valid . . . *when ratified by the legislatures of three fourths of the several States, or by conventions in three fourths thereof. . . .*

*Emphasis added throughout.

putes between states — and such disputes have been numerous — are decided by the U.S. Supreme Court acting as umpire of the federal system. Although the creation of the state of West Virginia during the Civil War may appear to be an exception to the notion of territorial integrity guaranteed to the state of Virginia, it is worth recalling that at that time the Commonwealth of Virginia was in a state of rebellion against the United States of America. Upon the conclusion of hostilities, in the course of officially recognizing that it had never left the Union, the Virginia House of Burgesses formally approved of the creation of West Virginia.[31]

Representation in Congress   Every state is guaranteed three seats in Congress — two in the Senate and one in the House of Representatives — regardless of its population. Thus, it is difficult for any legislative action to occur in the absence of participation by the representatives elected in each of the states. In other words, the states and portions of the states are the electoral units for the national legislature.

While the actual number of seats in the House of Representatives allocated to a state may change as national population patterns change or as the Constitution is amended, representation in the Senate can be changed only with the consent of the state involved. Article V not only says that "no State, without its consent, shall be deprived of its equal suffrage in the Senate," it also exempts that clause from constitutional amendment.

Members of Congress Must Be State Residents   The likelihood that Congress will pay at least some attention to the problems of the states is increased by the fact that the Constitution requires that members of Congress be inhabitants of the states they represent.

In some political systems the residence of members of the national legislature is irrelevant. The national party finds safe constituencies for party leaders somewhere regardless of their places of residence. Imagine, for example, the kinds of decisions the national government might make if the legislature were elected not from state-based constituencies but on a party ticket that could obtain a majority of the popular vote nationwide.

The National Legislature is Truly Bicameral The requirement that all laws and proposals to amend the Constitution must pass both houses means that the House cannot overrule the Senate and vice versa. In the U.S. Congress each house must approve of a bill or proposed constitutional amendment in exactly the same language or the bill fails. Thus, all the built-in protections for the states must be dealt with in the creation of the supreme laws of the land.

The relationship between the Senate and the House of Representatives stands in contrast to that found in many other national legislatures, including the British Parliament, where the upper house can only delay legislation. The House of Commons can in effect pass a law whether the House of Lords likes it or not.

The Electoral College Chooses the President Each state is guaranteed three Electoral College votes regardless of its population. To be elected President or vice president, a candidate must win a majority of the votes cast in the Electoral College, not just more votes than anyone else receives. This forces some attention to be paid to the wishes of a fairly large number of states in constructing a majority coalition. If there is no majority in the Electoral College, the decision goes to the House of Representatives, with each state having equal voting weight. Each state delegation, regardless of its size, gets one vote for President.

The Constitution Cannot Be Amended Without State Participation To say that the U.S. Constitution cannot be amended unless the states are consulted is to understate the point. The Constitution requires that any proposed amendment be ratified by a special majority of the states. Three-fourths of the state legislatures (or, if special ratifying conventions are used in each state, three-fourths of them) must ratify the amendment before it takes effect (Figure 3.1). Moreover, the source of all proposed amendments since the Constitution went into effect has been Congress, a body in which the states have some influence, as we have suggested.

American Federalism: The Litmus Test

We summarize our four-part definition of American federalism with a test which can be used to determine whether another federal system approximates American federalism. Although all six guarantees we have identified would have to be in place to protect the member governments, the simple

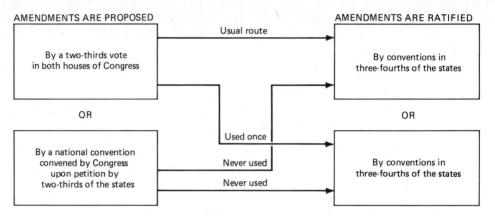

Figure 3.1 The steps in amending the U.S. Constitution. Not only is this a two step-process, two levels of government are always involved. Even when state conventions are used, as they were on one occasion, the state legislature is still involved in financing them and deciding how their delegates will be chosen.

litmus test would be whether the member governments have to approve formal amendments to the constitution. If at least a majority must approve, then the system in question may resemble American federalism: a union of governments and a union of people under a central government exercising sovereignty, all three of which are established in a constitution that guarantees the continued existence of the member governments.

FEDERALISM: A WORKING VOCABULARY

Thus far we have introduced several terms which are necessary for a better understanding of American federalism in particular and American politics in general. We add to that list six concepts which are found in the Constitution or which emerged very early in the development of our federal system and continue to be relevant today.

Expressed Powers

Expressed powers are also called enumerated or delegated powers. They are expressed, or enumerated, in Article I, Section 8, of the Constitution as subjects on which Congress has the power to make laws. Elsewhere in the Constitution, Congress is given the power to approve or reject certain actions that state governments may wish to take, such as entering into compacts or agreements with one another or with foreign nations. Congress is also given the power to admit new states to the Union under conditions which protect the territorial integrity of the states.

A point worth emphasizing about powers given to the national government, whether expressed or otherwise, is that they come from a constitution created by a sovereign people, not from the states. The Constitution is very clear on this point. "We the People of the United States," it says, "in order to form a more perfect Union . . . do ordain and establish this Constitution for the United States of America."

The delegated powers of the national government can be altered or taken away by constitutional amendment but not by the states. What the states did not give, they cannot take away. A leading states' rights advocate, James Kilpatrick, has observed, somewhat wistfully, "The States have very few rights; as the Ninth and Tenth Amendments make clear in their perfect choice of nouns, people have rights; States have powers."[32]

Implied Powers

This concept is such an important aspect of the history of intergovernmental relations in the United States that it merits a chapter by itself. In the interest of brevity, this discussion is limited to a few paragraphs here. The "foregoing powers" mentioned below are the enumerated powers we have already discussed. The constitutional source of implied power is Article I, Section 8, which contains the statement that Congress shall have the power

> to make all laws which shall be necessary and proper for carrying into execution the foregoing powers, and all other powers vested by this Constitution in the Government of the United States, or in any department or officer thereof.

The phrase "to make all laws which shall be necessary and proper" is also known as the elastic clause because it allows the expressed (enumerated) powers of the national government to apply to new topics and situations unforeseen by the authors of the Constitution.

The implied powers doctrine was set forth in the landmark case *McCulloch* v. *Maryland* (1819), in which Chief Justice John Marshall observed that the authors of the Constitution did not limit the power of Congress to enumerated subjects. He wrote:

> Let the end be legitimate, let it be within the scope of the Constitution, and all means which are appropriate, which are plainly adapted to the end, which are not prohibited, but consistent with the letter and spirit of the Constitution, are constitutional.[33]

The doctrine of implied powers makes it possible for federal power to stretch to subjects unforeseen by the founding fathers. More than that, however, it provides a basis for arguing that almost anything is traceable to an enumerated power.

Imagine, for example, that Congress only had the power to regulate interstate commerce, that it had no other enumerated or specific power. With the doctrine of implied powers, the regulation of interstate commerce can be stretched to cover almost anything on which Congress now legislates.

The regulation of interstate commerce is meaningless, it can be argued, if foreign countries an invade our shores and disrupt this commerce. Thus, Congress must regulate immigration and create a defense force to protect interstate commerce. Congress cannot do this without the power to tax and spend. Furthermore, healthy commerce requires a transportation network to carry goods and information. It also requires educated employees and informed consumers. Healthy commerce also requires protection from foreign competition and/or the opportunity to compete in foreign markets. Thus, as long as one interprets the phrase "necessary and proper" in a flexible manner, the elasticity of the implied powers of the national government seems almost limitless.

This scenario is only partially imaginary. The regulation of interstate commerce has been the basis for extending federal involvement into many areas, from labor relations and industrial safety to inspections of food-processing plants and the nondiscriminatory provision of motel accommodations and transportation.

Although it appears that Chief Justice John Marshall issued a book of blank checks in 1819, each of these checks still has to be cashed in a political system in which Congress is not the only check writer. Thus, what Congress does with implied powers depends to a great extent on what the public and the President think it ought to do, what the courts decide is a "legitimate" end and a legitimate means to that end, and the willingness of state and local officials to (enthusiastically or reluctantly) enforce a law that Congress claims is "necessary and proper."[34]

Concurrent Powers

Concurrent powers are powers that both the states and the federal government may exercise. For example, the Constitution gives to the federal government the power to tax and to regulate commerce. Since it does not deny that the states also have taxing authority and the power to regulate commerce, the two levels of government may both engage in these activities. If the concurrent exercise of power in a certain area becomes unworkable, the regulations of the federal government are supreme. Without a specific statement by Congress that it intends to pre-empt a field of law, it is up to the Supreme Court to decide whether federal laws overrule state laws.[35]

Powers Denied the National Government

Both Article I, Section 9, and the Bill of Rights specifically list certain things that the national government cannot do. Furthermore, Article IV, Section 3, prohibits the creation of new states from the territory of existing states without the permission of the state legislatures. The prohibitions found in Article I, Section 9, such as to suspend the writ of habeas corpus, pass ex post facto laws, and give preference to the ports of one state over those of another, seem to be fairly straightforward. However, the limitations on the national government in the Bill of Rights are the source of a vast body of constitutional law dealing with the interpretation of the meaning of terms such as "unreasonable searches" and "cruel and unusual punishments" and stating whether there really are limits to what one may call a religion, how freely one may exercise it, and at what point state and federal governments may or may not assist religious institutions in promoting education or care for the elderly.[36]

Obligations of the States to One Another

In discussing the relationships among the 50 states, the term "horizontal federalism" sometimes is used to differentiate this dimension of our Constitution from the state-national dimension ("vertical federalism"). The Constitution places three major interstate obligations on the states. The first is that each state must give full faith and credit to the public acts, records, and judicial proceedings of every other state. The importance of this is apparent if one imagines taking an automobile trip from Bangor, Maine, to San Diego, California, without interstate obligations of full faith and credit. In each state one must stop at the border to take a test for a driver's license and have one's vehicle inspected to make sure that one and one's vehicle pose no threat to the safety and health of the residents of that state. Naturally, one would do a fair amount of hanging around service stations and government offices, filling out forms and paying fees.

For the most part, states recognize one another's public acts, records, and judicial proceedings. The exceptions are what help keep lawyers employed and occasionally make the newspapers. Technical matters, such as whether a resident of State A has lived long enough in State B to establish residency there so that a divorce, recognized in the courts of State A, can be obtained in State B are the reason why this part of the Constitution is sometimes referred to as "the lawyer's clause."

The second interstate obligation is for each state to grant to the citizens of other states the same privileges and immunities enjoyed by its own citizens. The Supreme Court has recognized some exceptions. For example, states are allowed to charge out-of-state students a higher tuition for attending state colleges and universities than students who are residents of the state. The same exception is applied to hunting or fishing license fees, which can be higher for those from out of state. The justification for this is that state taxpayers subsidize higher education and game management activities and thus have earned the right to lower costs.

The third interstate obligation is to release to officials of another state any person accused of a crime who has fled from that state. This action is sometimes referred to as rendition. More commonly, the complete process of rendering up, or handing over, a person to be taken from one state to another is also called extradition. It also happens between countries.

Extradition, a process which is usually routine, sometimes involves headline-making exceptions. Those exceptions give the impression that extradition is a rare and delicate matter. From time to time governors have refused to "render up" persons who have fled from another state because over a period of several years those persons have become model citizens, because it appears that they have more than paid for their crimes through the time already served in the other state's prison system, or because there is strong evidence that the individual was not dealt with fairly in the first place.

When asked to umpire these situations, the Supreme Court has found no machinery to force a state to render a person to another state. It is a moral duty, the Court has declared, not a legal one. Thus, it seems that the federal government has no power to require state officials to behave morally.[37]

The federal government wisely stayed out of the case of Mr. Moke, who was taken from his cage at the St. Louis Zoo by a person who fled to Florida with him. The state of Missouri asked the governor of Florida to return Mr. Moke, a chimpanzee, and the person who had kidnapped him. The governor of Florida learned the chimpnapper was Mr. Moke's former owner. After selling Mr. Moke to the St. Louis Zoo, the former owner had tried unsuccessfully to buy him back once he realized how much he missed his hairy little friend. Furthermore, the former owner had left $1000 in the cage as partial payment.

If you were the governor, what would you do? The enthusiasm of the governor of Florida for meeting his "moral" obligation to render up Mr. Moke and his owner was well under control: Florida did not extradite.[38] Most extradition cases are not this exceptional. Usually, officials are happy to see the last of the persons sought in another state and cheerfully turn them over; sometimes they even deliver.

Powers Prohibited to the States

Article I, Section 10, lists several things states cannot do, such as coin money, and a few things they can do only if permitted by Congress, such as enter into agreements or compacts with other states. One of the most important sources of constitutionally imposed limitations on state government is the clause in the Fourteenth Amendment which says: "nor shall any State deprive any person of life, liberty, or property, without due process of law; nor deny to any persons within its jurisdiction the equal protection of the laws."

The "due process" and "equal protection of the laws" provisions have been interpreted in the last third of this century to mean that almost the whole of the Bill of Rights applies not only to the national government but also to state and local governments. *Brown* v. *The Board of Education* is perhaps the best known example of the application of the Fourteenth Amendment's "equal protection of the laws" clause. In 1954, the Supreme Court declared that state laws enforcing segregated education were unconstitutional. This case marked the end of legally enforced segregation in public schools and the beginning of the end of segregation, period.[39]

MODERN AMERICAN FEDERALISM: INTERGOVERNMENTAL RELATIONS (IGR)

Intergovernmental relations (IGR) is a term which focuses our attention on the dynamic nature of our federal system. It embraces the notion of change and the idea that more than two levels of government interact. American federalism began in preindustrial America as a compromise between those who wanted to create a national government and those in each of 13 independent states who feared the loss of state sovereignty. Today, American federalism had been so altered by national and international events that it would be almost unrecognizable to those who designed it. The accomplishment of the framers can be appreciated if we note that the foundation they laid was for a 13-state federation that now includes 50 states. Not only do the 13 original states cover less than 10 percent of the area of United States, the state of Alaska would include them all with room to spare.

Our intergovernmental system is a system of relations between more than 80,000 interdependent units of government of which only a small fraction existed in 1789.[40] Boxes 3-6 and 3-7 provide brief snapshots of examples of developments which have altered our federal system. Each one indicates that our system is no longer simply a matter of one-dimensional national-state relationships. It now involves cooperation and conflict among more than 80,000 governments, the numerous agencies and offices in each one, the interest groups which represent them, and additional coordinating bodies.

The proliferation of grants within the city of San Jose (Box 3-6) suggests that not only is this interaction sometimes confusing, but complexity is often a product of local action. After all, it was the San Jose city officials who applied to state and federal agencies for these grants. Furthermore, as often as not, grant programs are created in response to demands by local officials from communities in the individual states.

The relationship between grants and the federal system indicates that this system has become extremely complicated, first because of the proliferation of governments and second as a result of the proliferation of interest groups representing various types of governments as well as interest groups representing types of specialists within those governments. There are now hundreds of organizations of public officials (elected and appointed) which lobby state and national legislatures for laws and for grant programs to advance the goals of those governments and agencies, whether they are township supervisors, waste management technicians, fire marshals, or nursing home supervisors. Few state or local chief executives are aware of what all these intergovernmental spokespersons are asking of Congress. Keeping track of the consequences of these requests is a challenging and more or less permanent feature of intergovernmental relations.[41]

The Tacoma Dam case (Box 3-7) suggests another dimension of the intergovernmental system. Not only does the federal government now inter-

Box 3-6 **The Proliferation of Grant Programs in San Jose**

In 1970, to find out where he stood in terms of matching requirements that committed local funds, office space, and employee time, Mayor Norman Mineta of San Jose, California (population in 1970, 450,000), got a $200,000 grant to discover the number of grants in which his city was involved.

From this study came two revelations which were unsettling, to put it mildly. First, it was virtually impossible to see the total picture in detail. No local, state, or federal agency had the data on how many federal grants entered the city of San Jose. Not only were school districts, the county, and other special districts involved, there was no way to find out the total dollar amount even for city government agencies. It took every penny of that grant to put together a booklet summarizing the known commitments involving the city of San Jose.

Second, to Mayor Mineta's surprise, it was learned that San Jose was committed to come up with matching money of about $20 million in order to get $56.4 million from various federal agencies for a range of services and programs which the mayor and the city council had never sat down to review and approve.

Source: Deil S. Wright, *Understanding Intergovernmental Relations*, (North Scituate, MA: Duxbury, 1978), 57–58.

act directly with cities, counties, and townships, but in some circumstances the local-national alliance can lead to conflict with the state. In Washington, the city of Tacoma acquired the authority to seize state property for the purposes of building a dam. Although the dam was never built, the principle that a city operating under a federal license can act independently of its state was established.

The way in which the state of Washington finally won its battle further indicates the complexity of the intergovernmental system. The state of Washington enlisted the aid of the U.S. Environmental Protection Agency, which is part of the Department of the Interior. The secretary of the interior, Morris Udall, took the Federal Power Commission to court to require it to rescind the license it had issued to the city of Tacoma. The Supreme Court upheld the Interior Department in *Udall* v. *Federal Power Commission* on the grounds that the Federal Power Commission had not prepared or required the city of Tacoma to prepare an environmental impact statement before issuing the license.

The intergovernmental principle established in the Tacoma case still stands. Thus a federal agency can still issue a license granting certain kinds of authority to a city whether or not the state in which the city is located approves. Acting within the authority granted by the license, a city can use

---

Box 3-7　**As a Federal Agent, a City Can Take State Property**

City of Tacoma v. *Taxpayers:* Supreme Court of the United States, 1958

MR. JUSTICE WHITTAKER delivered the opinion of the Court.

This is the latest episode in litigation beginning in 1948 which has been waged in five tribunals and has produced more than 125 printed pages of administrative and judicial opinions. It concerns the plan of the City of Tacoma, a municipal corporation in the State of Washington, to construct a power project on the Cowlitz River, a navigable water of the United States, in accordance with a license issued by the Federal Power Commission under the Federal Power Act. The question presented for decision here is whether under the facts of this case the City of Tacoma has acquired federal eminent domain power and capacity to take, upon the payment of just compensation, a fish hatchery owned and operated by the State of Washington, by virtue of the license issued to the City under the Federal Power Act. . . . The project cannot be built without taking the hatchery because it necessarily must be inundated by a reservoir that will be created by one of the project's dams.

The Court found in favor of the city of Tacoma's authority under a license issued by the Federal Power Commission to build the dam and take the state fish hatchery in the process.

Source: 3576 U.S. 320, 78 S. Ct. 1209, 2 L.Ed. 2d 1345. Cited in William D. Valente, *Local Government Law: Cases and Materials*, 3rd ed. (St. Paul, MN: West, 1987), 310–313.

---

the power of eminent domain to take state property — with just compensation — whether or not the state approves, as long as it makes sure it has filed the proper environmental impact statements and held public hearings.[42]

Although the Tacoma case indicates something about the complexity of IGR, the civility of IGR is equally important. As far as we are aware, no one was kneecapped or had his or her car bombed in this controversy. In some parts of the world, wars are fought over disputes of this magnitude.

As we noted in Chapter 1, the pace and volume of technological and demographic change have become so great that we tend to lose sight not only of what we have accomplished but also of the fact that we *can* accomplish constructive change. A brief overview of some of the solutions which have been introduced to reduce confusion and render the intergovernmental system more manageable will help indicate what has been accomplished. Thus, with some knowledge of what seems to be working, we will be in a better position to evaluate future suggestions for making the federal system more accountable to the needs of individuals and more effective in attempting to meet them.

SOME OF THE SOLUTIONS IN OPERATION

Among the many significant features of modern federalism, we have identified five which seem most appropriate for our discussion of efforts to make this system more understandable by the average citizen, a bit more efficient, and a little more sensitive to the needs of individuals.

The ACIR: Advice and Attention

The Advisory Commission on Intergovernmental Relations (ACIR) was created in 1959. It is composed of 25 members. Nine of them represent the federal government: three from the Senate, three from the House, and three from the executive branch. Fourteen represent state and local governments: four mayors, three governors, three state legislators, and three county officials. Three are private citizens.

Most of the members are chosen by the President with the advice of appropriate organizations: the National Governor's Association, the National Conference of State Legislatures, the National League of Cities, and the National Association of Counties. The Senate and House members are chosen by the presiding officers of those bodies.

The commission members who serve part time are assisted by a full-time staff of approximately 20 persons headed by a full-time executive director. The director is usually someone with excellent academic credentials who has studied or served in government (or both) for a long time.

The purpose of the ACIR is to study the workings of the federal system and make recommendations for improving it. The considerable body of research which the commission has published is available, at least in part, in most university libraries and upon request by writing to the ACIR, Washington, DC, 20575. Although the ACIR is a relatively small federal agency, it is a very influential one whose studies and recommendations are taken seriously at all levels. Many of these recommendations have been enacted into law at the national and state levels.

The success of the national ACIR in identifying and suggesting solutions to problems has led to the creation of state-level ACIRs in 25 states.[43]

Councils of Government

Councils of government (COGs) are an excellent example of encouragement of local innovations by the national government. A **council of government** is a voluntary association of local governments. The first council of government began in 1954 in the multicounty metropolitan area of Detroit, Michigan. It was called the Supervisor's Inter-County Committee. By 1968 it evolved into the Southeast Michigan Council of Governments, including cities and townships as well as the original three county governments.[44] Today there are nearly 600 COGs nationwide, serving their regions and regional governments in a variety of ways, from managing a zoo in the

Portland, Oregon, area to developing programs for at-risk children in a 12-county area of San Antonio, Texas.[45]

The basic idea of COGs is coordination. The proliferation of governments, particularly in metropolitan areas, has made it difficult for decision makers in each government to keep track in the normal course of a nine-hour day of how their actions may affect or be affected by the actions of neighboring governments. The council of government idea formalizes interaction between these decision makers.

Representatives of each government meet once or twice a month with one another to discuss mutual problems and review reports and proposals from a staff devoted to helping them plan and coordinate everything from highway and drainage construction to human service activities.

The national government helped promote the spread of the COG idea by building rewards and requirements for planning and metropolitan area coordination into various grant programs, beginning with Section 701 of the Housing Act of 1954. The ACIR studied COG activities and accomplishments and recommended in 1962 that state and local governments use COGs to reduce confusion and fragmentation of resources in metropolitan areas.[46]

In 1963 the Office of Management and Budget (OMB) moved the COG concept forward. The OMB is located in the Executive Office of the President and is responsible for coordinating the activities of the various federal departments and agencies. Its ability to get their attention is enhanced by the fact that it is also the agency that prepares the budget that the President submits to Congress. In 1965 the OMB issued circulars A-85 and A-95 to promote coordination both within states and within the national government.

Circular A-85 attempted to help elected chief executives from governors to mayors regain control over the coordination of grant programs, which, as we observed in the San Jose case, was sorely lacking. Circular A-85 established the chief executive review and comment procedure. In essence this meant that most federal agencies could not even begin to deal with a grant application unless the chief executive of the state or local government from which the grant application came had approved it. Naturally, A-85 did not eliminate confusion altogether, but it has reduced it, particularly because of the link between it and A-95.

OMB circular A-95 attempted to promote coordination within each state by requiring that the states create or designate existing agencies as clearinghouses for reviewing grant applications. These agencies could prevent the advancement of applications that interfere with long-range planning.

A-95 attempted to deal with the fact that in each MSA as well as each state hundreds of overlapping governments might be pursuing conflicting goals or duplicating programs without consulting one another or working toward general goals for the whole MSA. It was rather like asking the sewer and street departments to coordinate their work so that one didn't pave a street the day before it was scheduled to be torn up for sewer repair.

The mechanism which states almost universally adopted to act as clearinghouses for federal grant applications was the council of governments. Busy chief executives serving on these councils found them to be a useful source of information in conducting their own oversight functions. Many states have now designated state planning regions, using county lines as boundaries, and have assigned major coordinating functions to the COG for that region.[47]

Federal funding for COGs was virtually eliminated by the Reagan administration, and in 1983 the A-95 requirements were replaced by Executive Order 12372, which reduced federal pressure to use COGs as designated coordinating bodies while still requiring federal agencies to use whatever clearinghouse the state designated. In 37 states COGs have proved to be so useful that the A-95 procedures are still used by the statewide clearing agencies.[48] The member governments in many states have found COGs to be valuable not only for coordinating grant applications but for actually performing services on an areawide basis. A few COGs have been given authority usually assigned to local governments, such as taxing (16 COGs), zoning (15 COGs), and the power of eminent domain. More often, however, the activities of COGs consist of planning (highways, mass transit, water and solid waste management), disseminating information, and coordinating services.[49]

Naturally, some COGs are more successful at coordination than others, just as some local governments are more successful at service delivery than others and some local government officials are more likely than others to cooperate with one another. Furthermore, a badly run COG will probably do more harm than good. The point remains, however, that it is a technique for promoting coordination that can work.

The Council of State Governments

For more than 50 years the Council of State Governments (CSG), a voluntary organization, has operated as an information broker for the states. From its national headquarters in Lexington, Kentucky, and from regional offices in Atlanta, Chicago, New York City, and San Francisco, the CSG has attempted to "synthesize the complex political, cultural, geographical, and philosophical differences inherent in our federal system into cohesive and constructive regional and national approaches."[50]

The scope of interaction and the variety of tasks performed by state governments are indicated in Boxes 3-8 through 3-10.[51] Box 3-8 lists publications by the National CSG which are available to public officials and interested citizens. Box 3-9 indicates the variety of other organizations which are affiliated with the CSG. Box 3-10 reinforces the notion of variety by indicating the kinds of functions that public officials perform.

Fiscal Federalism

A thorough study of fiscal federalism is far beyond the scope of this book and certainly the scope of this chapter. Every year the ACIR publishes a

---

Box 3-8   **Publications of the Council of State Governments***

The Book of the States: a biennial reference book

State Elective Officials and the Legislatures: a directory of names, addresses, and telephone numbers

State Administrative Officials Classified by Function: a directory of names, addresses, and telephone numbers

State Government News: a monthly magazine about state innovations and issues

Suggested State Legislation: an annual volume of draft legislation selected by a committee of state officials

The Journal of State Government: a quarterly publication that provides a forum for discussing state issues from the viewpoints of academics, political leaders, and practitioners

Conference Calendar: a monthly listing of conferences held by the various affiliated and cooperating organizations of state officials

*Selected list, available in most university libraries.

---

two-volume work titled *Significant Features of Fiscal Federalism* which consists almost entirely of tables and charts measuring, in billions of dollars, the flow of funds via several hundred grant-in-aid programs between the federal, state, and local levels of government.

At the beginning of this century the national government had five grant programs which distributed $3 million. Today the national government sends many times that amount of money to state and local governments — over $100 billion in 1987. This increased role of the national government is sometimes called **fiscal federalism.** Currently the national government provides 17 percent of the funds that finance the activities of state and local governments.[53] These funds are a major reason why there are so many intergovernmental relationships.

Superior Federal Resources   Fiscal federalism represents an attempt to take advantage of the superior financial resources of the national government to deal with the tremendous diversity of the American intergovernmental system.

Among the national government's superior resources are its powers to (1) tax individuals and business firms, (2) borrow, (3) print money to pay off what it has borrowed, and (4) regulate interest rates. State and local governments can tax and borrow, but they have no control over the money supply and very little control over interest rates.

An important point to remember about the national government's power to tax the incomes of corporations and individuals is the fact that the national government is more or less immune to intergovernmental conse-

Box 3-9   **Organizations Affiliated with the Council of State Governments**

Representatives of these organizations serve on the 175-member CSG governing board, which includes two legislators from each state and all 50 governors. Many of these organizations also publish their own newsletters and journals.[52]

Conference of Chief Justices

Conference of State Court Administrators

National Association of Attorneys General

National Association of Secretaries of State

National Association of State Auditors, Comptrollers, and Treasurers

National Association of State Purchasing Officials

National Conference of Lieutenant Governors

National Conference of State Services Officers

National Conference of State Legislatures

quences of levying taxes. Whether or not it works out this way in practice, many state legislatures and governors believe that if they were to raise taxes to provide services, businesses and/or wealthy individuals would leave their states for a state that levies a lighter load. When the national government levies a tax, there is no other government within the American political system to which an individual or business can go to escape it. For this reason, the national government is in a better position to tax at a higher rate than are state and local governments. This gives the national government the potential to have a great deal of influence in the intergovernmental system.

Fiscal Disparity and Social Diversity   These two important features of our complex socioeconomic system have made it almost imperative that the national government use its superior fiscal resources on behalf of our 80,000 units of government and the individuals within them. Social diversity means that the distribution of economic and social problems in our country is uneven. Not all units of government have to deal with droughts or hurricanes, teenage drug gangs, or nuclear or hazardous waste. Fiscal disparity means that the resources to solve problems are not equally distributed among these governments.

Many states and communities are not equipped to deal with the incredible array of problems arising from technological advances, social change, and

Box 3-10 Cooperating Organizations: Nonmembers

Selected items from the list of the 32 organizations which work with but are not on the governing board of the Council of State Governments.

Adjutants General Association of the United States

Association of Juvenile Compact Administrators

Association of State and Interstate Water Pollution Control Administrators

Conference of State Sanitary Engineers

National Association of Extradition Officials

National Association of State Departments of Agriculture

National Association of State Foresters

National Association of State Personnel Executives

National Association of State Units on Aging

National Conference of States on Building Codes and Standards

National Criminal Justice Association

National Reciprocal and Family Support Association

environmental diversity. This fact might remain just a fact, like the lack of air on the moon, if it weren't for another fact we've already discussed: The 50 states and the communities within them are inhabited by a single people, a nation. The government of that nation has pledged itself to promote opportunities for each American to realize his or her highest potential— "We the People of the United States, in order to form a more perfect Union. . . ."[54]

Not only do Americans live in rich states as well as poor states, but within each state there are also tremendous differences in the resources available for problem solving. In many states the richest school districts spend ten times as much money per pupil as do the poorest districts. Rich school districts aren't necessarily inhabited by rich families. Big houses aren't the only source of a tax bases; the source can be oil reserves, industrial plants, shopping centers, or simply the business district of a large city.

It is generally agreed that the national government has an obligation within the intergovernmental system to promote equal opportunities for Americans regardless of the state in which they are born. A consensus is emerging that states also have obligations to provide equal opportunities to each state resident regardless of the county, city, or school district in which that individual lives. In 1989, the state of Massachusetts took over the Chelsey, Massachusetts, school system and assigned its management to Boston University. New Jersey's board of education took over the 28,000-school system of Jersey City, the state's second largest school system, and California took over the 53,000-student Oakland school system, that state's fifth largest school system. Some of these takeovers are applauded by local residents; for example, over 50,000 Oakland residents signed petitions urging passage of the takeover bill in the California legislature. The reasons for these takeovers vary from a declining tax base to corruption and mismanagement, but in every case the objective is the same: to provide equal educational opportunity to all the state's citizens.

Grants-in-Aid Grants-in-aid are one of the two essential features of fiscal federalism (Box 3-11). As you may recall, a grant-in-aid is a transfer of funds from one unit of government to another. It is not a loan. There are a variety of ways in which governments distribute money. The type of grant used has consequences that may have an impact that goes beyond the grantor and grantee. For example, from 1972 to 1986 the national government's General Revenue Sharing Program distributed over $60 billion to states and certain kinds of local governments, including municipalities.

The fact that virtually no conditions were attached to this money encouraged many unorganized communities to create their own municipal governments instead of continuing to depend on country and township governments for services. In 1985 there were 1098 more municipal governments than there had been in 1972, an increase of about 6 percent. It is probably not a coincidence that the rate of municipality creation has declined since the General Revenue Sharing Program was canceled.[55]

Mandates The conditions or requirements that grant recipients must meet are called **mandates**. By using mandates, the national government has altered the way state and local governments do business. It has introduced requirements intended to increase accountability and efficiency. For example, many grants now require that public hearings be held before decisions are made about spending federal grant money. This has increased participation in government by local citizens. Affirmation action efforts must be made by state and local officials who spend grant money to hire new employees. In some cases state and local budgeting has been improved by the installation of effective accounting methods to keep track of federal funds.

In recent years, however, it has been observed that the pendulum may have swung too far. There is real concern that mandates may interfere with the realization of the goals they are intended to achieve.[56] The ACIR has reported that the total number of federal mandates imposed as conditions for receiving federal aid grew from 4 in 1960 to 1034 in 1978. These conditions include detailed record keeping to demonstrate that age, gender, and race discrimination has not occurred in hiring decisions and the require-

Box 3-11 A Brief Grants-in-Aid Vocabulary

Category	Scope of Activity
Project	Specific activity such as a sewage treatment plant or a summer program for children
Categorical	Narrow range of activities within a functional area
Block	Broad range of activities within a functional area
General revenue sharing	Virtually anything except to match funds for other federal grants

Category	Federal Commitment
Fixed-amount	Limited to a specific amount of money
Open-ended	Unlimited as long as the recipient meets criteria such as matching money for unemployment compensation or aid to dependent children

Category	Method of Allocation
Formula	Units of government are allocated funds according to formulas that take into account factors such as unemployment or the school-age population
Competitive	Usually applies to project grants for which a limited amount of money is available and only a few applicants receive grants

Category	Recipient Participation
Matching	Recipient government supplies some funds or the equivalent of funds in the form of hours of work by personnel or supplies or the use of facilities such as buildings or equipment
Nonmatching	Recipient government simply meets guidelines for spending money

Source: George F. Break, "The Economics of Intergovernmental Grants," in *American Intergovernmental Relations*, ed. Laurence J. O'Toole, Jr. (Washington, DC: Congressional Quarterly Press, 1985), 144–145.

ments that archaeological and historic preservation studies and environmental impact studies be conducted before construction can take place. Recent examples include the conditions attached to grants from the Highway Trust Fund which forced several states to enact seat belt and drinking age laws in order to avoid reductions in their formula share of the money.

During the eight-year Reagan administration, although much was said about reducing red tape, the number of mandates did not decrease significantly while the amount of money given to state and local governments did. As Robert B. Hawkins, Jr., observed, "Federal regulation of state and local governments is outpacing federal financial support."[57]

Not only does the federal government make requirements of the state and local governments, state legislatures do the same thing to local governments. A partial solution to the resulting multiplication of mandates would be to require that the price tag be attached.

Fiscal Notes   A statement attached to any proposed piece of legislation, whether a grant program or not, that includes an estimate of the dollar cost of carrying out that legislation is called a **fiscal note**. A no-cost provision is a commitment by the mandating government to pay for the costs of carrying out the new regulation. While the first requirement is nice, the second is even nicer from the point of view of officials who are required to meet mandates. Thus far, only California, Massachusetts, New Hampshire, and New Mexico have both provisions. A few other state legislatures require fiscal notes but provide no funds to reimburse local governments for the cost of carrying out state mandates.[58] It will be interesting to see if the national government ever requires states to enact these provisions before receiving federal money.

Whether the federal government itself will reimburse the states for the cost of meeting this and other federal requirements remains to be seen. In 1984 the ACIR recommended "full federal reimbursement to state and local governments for all additional direct expenses legitimately incurred in implementing new federal statutory mandates."[59] This recommendation has not yet been acted upon.

In sum, at least four dimensions of fiscal federalism are important in the study of the individual and the governments. First, the amount of money involved is very large and constitutes a considerable portion of the revenues of some units of government. Second, federal government grant money has promoted national unity by making it possible to offer programs to all Americans which raise the standards of services and social justice regardless of the local or state jurisdiction in which an individual lives. Third, legitimate efforts by the federal government to make sure this money is spent properly have expanded to a wide range of mandates, some of which involve serious interference in state and local decision making. Fourth, some state and local governments have successfully influenced Congress to create new programs or change formulas for allocating grants. This success has encouraged other governments to do the same. As a consequence, fiscal federalism has become an integral part of the dynamics of intergovernmental contact and communication.

Ten Federal Administrative Regions

For the purposes of administering federal programs, including grants-in-aid, each of the 50 states has been placed in one of ten Standard Federal Regions. Most major federal agencies which deal with the state and local governments have been required to adopt the same regional map and put their own regional headquarters in the cities which have been designated for the ten regions.[60]

The top executives of these agencies constituted the membership of each of the ten Federal Regional Councils. Until 1983, when the Reagan administration abolished them, their mission was to improve the coordination of federal activities, including grant programs, in each region. Whether the regional councils are ever reconstituted, the continued existence of the standard regional headquarters has greatly reduced travel and confusion for state and local officials. Prior to the establishment of the regions in 1972, each

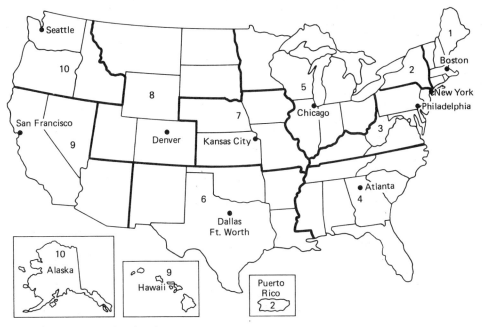

Figure 3.2 Ten Federal Administrative Regions. Not all federal Agencies use them, but enough do so that life has been made less complicated for state and local officials. (*Source:* Study Committee on Policy Management Assistance, *Strengthening Public Management in the Intergovernmental System*, [Washington, DC: Executive Office of the President, 1975], 15.)

different federal agency divided the country into its own regions without consulting the others.[61]

For example, Idaho, as Figure 3.2 indicates, was located in a region for one agency whose regional headquarters was in San Francisco, another agency located Idaho in a region whose headquarters was in Denver, and yet another agency required Idaho officials to look to Kansas City for advice and guidance on the programs it administered.

Individuals who had to travel to regional headquarters to put together a grant package for their state, city, or county greatly appreciated the stream-lining of regional arrangements (Figure 3.3 on p. 88). Thus, while state officials might have had mixed emotions about abolishing another coordinating agency — the federal councils — they are likely to let the White House know their feelings pretty quickly if the Standard Federal Regions are abandoned by the agencies they deal with most often.[62]

THE ESSENTIALS: CHARACTERISTICS THAT REMAIN THE SAME

Although our nation-state has become an intergovernmental system, it is still a federal system as well. Among the many indicators of consistency, one finds at least four essential characteristics which have remained the same.

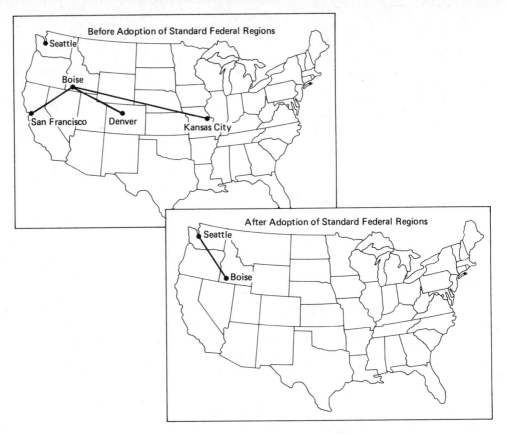

Figure 3.3 An example of the impact of Federal Administrative Regions. Imagine how many mayoral, gubernatorial, and staff miles and hours have been saved by simplifying travel, especially for projects involving more than one agency. These savings include dollars, fuel, and hotel bills. (*Source:* Study Committee on Policy Management Assistance, *Strengthening Public Management in the Intergovernmental System*, [Washington, DC: Executive Office of the President, 1975], 15.)

A Union of Sovereign People

The American nation is still a union of people. It is a union of people among whom there are occasional disagreements, some of which are based on the fact that we do not all define ourselves using the same model. However, more people and more kinds of people are members of our nation, enjoying full citizenship rights than our founding fathers ever imagined.

A Union of Governments

Originally a union of 13 states and a new national government, today the federal system includes 50 states. When some people use the term "federal," they refer only to the state-national relationship outlined in the Constitution, while others include all the governmental entities involved in the intergovernmental system. Whichever governments one includes, one is talking about a system that is still a union of governments after 200 years.

Constitutional Guarantees that Still Work

The parts of the Union remain indestructible. The states are still the key units within the federal system. The states have so many internal and inter-governmental responsibilities that the overload created by multiplying mandates has resulted in part from asking states to administer national responsibilities as well. Veteran journalist Neal R. Pierce puts it this way:

> Virtually all 50 states today are strong enough entities to take on almost any program the national government might hand over to them. Twenty or 30 years ago this wasn't the case. [However,] a quiet revolution of state-level reform, centered on new constitutions, broad-scaled executive branch reorganizations, "one-man, one vote" reapportionment, and professionally staffed legislatures has changed all that.[63]

Today the states are better equipped then ever before, and as observed earlier, all of them could stand alone in the world community of nations. Thus, our system is still a union of state and national governments.

A Government of the Union that Still Exercises Sovereignty

The government of the Union exercises sovereignty. The notion that the government of the Union may or may not exercise too much sovereignty will continue to be debated as long as the system exists. The task that we, the sovereign people, face today is to make sure that the reforms we support are dedicated to strengthening the whole system, not simply weakening a particular part of it.

Conclusion

The American federal system involves not only tension between the center and its parts but also competition and conflict among the parts themselves. The governor of California and the agriculture commissioner of Texas once got into a name-calling contest over Mediterranean fruit fly control. (Many observers agreed that they were both right.) The frost belt and sun belt disagree over the location of federal military installations, and communities within states as well as states themselves compete with one another and with foreign countries to attract new industries. We argue among ourselves over federal purchasing contracts which benefit local industries, the formulas of major grant programs, and the ability of states to tax the exploitation of natural resources such as oil, gas, and coal. These are all serious matters with interstate as well as intergovernmental consequences. Conflict in various forms is a continuing feature of a large, complex society. Fortunately, in our federal system compromise and negotiation are built in. The federal system itself is part of the conflict-resolving equipment.

Study Objectives

1. Identify three things which federalism is and three which it is not.
2. Identify the three compromises that were necessary for the creation of the U.S. Constitution.
3. Identify the four parts of our definition of federalism.
4. Identify three dimensions of sovereignty.
5. Identify the significance of *Garcia* v. *San Antonio Metropolitan Transit Authority*.
6. Identify the six protections guaranteed to the states.
7. Identify the litmus test of federalism.
8. Identify and define the terms in a working vocabulary of federalism.
9. Identify five changes in the American federal system which have helped it deal with the fact that it has become a system of intergovernmental relations.
10. Identify the major features of fiscal federalism.

Glossary

confederal A system of government in which the central government is subordinate to the parts that make up the whole.

council of government A voluntary association of local governments.

decentralization The process of delegating functions (education, fire protection) to a local unit of government in the interests of efficiency.

federal Describes a system of government in which power is divided between a central government and specific subunits of government.

fiscal federalism The dimension of our federal system which involves the use of superior financial resources at the national level to assist units of government with fewer financial resources.

fiscal note A statement attached to a proposed law which indicates what it would cost to carry out that law.

infallibility The characteristic of not being subject to error.

infer To deduce or reason from. We point this out because many people use "imply" and "infer" interchangeably. What you infer from someone's words is not necessarily what that person meant to imply.

mandates The conditions or requirements that grant recipients must meet to receive funds. A mandate is a command; thus mandates are not always grant-related.

Laws that assign new responsibilities or limitations on other governments are also called mandates.

national integration The process of bringing all Americans into the same society.

nationalism A belief system whose central value is the nation-state.

salient The quality of being noticeable. A salient issue is one of which many people have become aware.

separation of powers A principle of government that divides power within a single level of government. The usual division is three branches: executive, legislative, and judicial.

sovereignty A concept which includes two notions: supremacy in one's own sphere of influence and independence from the rule of others. In democratic political theory, sovereignty resides with "the people."

Endnotes

1. While all 11 volumes of the comprehensive overview of the federal system, *The Federal Role in the Federal System: The Dynamics of Growth*, would be heavy going, the serious student is encouraged to examine the summary volume, *An Agenda for American Federalism: Restoring Confidence and Competence*, vol. 10 (Washington, DC: U.S. Government Printing Office, 1981), A-86, and Richard Leach, *American Federalism*, (New York: Norton, 1970).

2. "Amendments Are the Talk of the Season," *Governing* (October, 1988), 13. See also Robert T. Golembiewski and Aaron Wildavsky, *The Costs of Federalism*, (New Brunswick, NJ: Transaction, 1984), Roy V. Peel, *State Government Today*, (Albuquerque: University of New Mexico Press, 1948), Stanley D. Brunn, "Geography and Politics of the United States in the Year 2000," *Journal of Geography*, (April 1973), 42–49, and G. Etzel Pearcy, *A 38 State U.S.A.*, (Fullerton, CA: Plycon, 1973).

3. Students interested in keeping abreast of significant changes in the federal-intergovernmental system are advised to monitor the following two quarterly publications: *Intergovernmental Perspective*, published by the Advisory Commission on Intergovernmental Relations, and *Publius*, published by the Center for the Study of Federalism.

4. K. C. Wheare, *Federal Government* (Westport, CT: Greenwood Press, 1980).

5. Martin Diamond, "What the Framers Meant by Federalism," in Robert A. Goldwin *A Nation of States* 2nd ed, (Chicago: Rand McNally, 1974), 26–27. See also David F. Epstein, *Political Theory of the Federalist*, (Chicago: University of Chicago Press, 1984).

6. Alexis de Tocqueville, *Democracy in America*, vol.1, trans. Henry Reeve (New Rochelle, NY: Arlington House), 144.

7. Ivo D. Duchacek, *Comparative Federalism*, (New York: Harper & Row, 1970). See also David F. Epstein, *Political Theory of the Federalist*.

8. For a very readable account of the negotiations and compromises in Philadelphia in 1776, see Catherine Drinker Bowen, *Miracle at Philadelphia*, (Boston: Little, Brown, 1986).

9. Ibid., 92.

10. Ibid., 255–256.

11. Bowen, quoting Hamilton on the three-fifths compromise, without which "no union could possibly have been formed." Ibid., 200.

12. For a more elegant example of ex adverso definition, see "What Democracy is Not," in Giovanni Sartori, *Democratic Theory*, (Detroit: Wayne State University Press, 1962), 135–157.

13. Franz Neumann, "Federalism and Freedom: A Critique," in Arthur W. MacMahon, ed., *Federalism: Mature and Emergent*, (Garden City, NY: Doubleday, 1955), 44–57. See also William H. Riker, *Federalism, Origin, Operation, Significance*, (Boston: Little, Brown, 1964).

14. Herbert S. Duncombe, *Modern County Government*, (Washington, DC: National Association of Counties, 1977), 51

15. See Murray Greensmith Forsyth, *Unions and States: The Theory and Practice of Confederation*, (New York: Leicester University Press, 1981).

16. For additional definitions of federalism, see K. C. Wheare, *Federal Government*, and Arthur Maas, ed., *Area and Power*, (Glencoe, IL: Free Press, 1959).

17. Daniel J. Elazar, "A View from the Commission," *Intergovernmental Perspective*, (Fall 1988), 2.

18. John W. Wright (ed.) *The Universal Almanac, 1990*, (Kansas City: Andrews and McMeel, 1989), 161, 448–456. With an area of 1049 square miles, Rhode Island is more than twice the size of all but 4 of those 16 countries.

19. Ivo D. Duchacek, *Comparative Federalism*, (New York: Harper & Row, 1970).

20. Ralph Nading Hill, *Yankee Kingdom: Vermont and New Hampshire*, (New York: Harper and Brothers, 1960), 170, and Clifton McCleskey, Allan K. Butcher, Daniel E. Farlow, and J. Pat Stephens, *The Government and Politics of Texas*, 7th ed. (Boston: Little, Brown, 1982), 3. See also T. R. Fehrenbach, *Lone Star: A History of Texas and Texans* (New York: Macmillan, 1968).

21. For a discussion of attempts to create and maintain federalism in new nations, see Thomas Franck, ed., *Why Federations Fail* (New York: New York University Press, 1968).

22. Daniel J. Elazar, *American Federalism: A View from the States*, (New York: Harper & Row, 1972), 2.

23. Alexander Hamilton, "Federalist Number 85" in James Madison, Alexander Hamilton, and John Jay, *The Federalist Papers*, (New Rochelle, NY: Arlington House, circa 1975), 527.

24. Karl Deutsch, *Nationalism and Social Communication: An Inquiry Into the Foundations of Nationality*, (Boston: MIT Press, 1966), 162–166, 181–186.

25. James Bryce, *Modern Democracies* (New York: Macmillan, 1924), 20.

26. John A. Garraty, *The American Nation*, vol. 2 (New York: Harper & Row, 1983), 573. See also Walter I. Trattner, *Crusade for the Children*, (Chicago: Quadrangle, 1970), Viviana A. Rotman Selizer, *Pricing the Priceless Child*, (New York: Basic Books, 1985), and Ronald B. Taylor, *Sweatshops in the Sun*, (Boston: Beacon, 1973).

27. *Garcia* v. *San Antonio Metropolitan Transit Authority*. Supreme Court of the United States, 1985. 469 U.S. 528 S.Ct. 1005, 83 L. Ed. 2nd 1016.

28. William D. Valente, *Local Government Law: Cases and Materials*, 3rd ed. (St. Paul, MN: West, 1987), 325.

29. Ibid., 330–331.

30. *Texas* v. *White*, (1869). Quoted in C. Herman Pritchett, *The American Constitutional System* (New York: McGraw Hill, 1981), 21.

31. Oscar D. Lambert, *West Virginia and Its Government*, (Boston: Heath, 1951).

32. James Jackson Kilpatrick, "The Case for States' Rights," in Robert A. Goldwin,

ed., *A Nation of States: Essays on the American Federal System*, (Chicago: Rand McNally, 1974), 24.

33. Quoted in Joseph T. Keenan, *The Constitution of the United States: An Unfolding Story*, (Homewood: Dorsey, 1988), 98.

34. In *South Carolina* v. *Baker*, 1988 48 CCH S. Ct Bull. Justice Brennan's majority opinion included the following: "States must find their protection from congressional regulation through the national political process, not through judicially defined spheres of unregulable state activity," 1646–7.

35. Pritchett, 18.

36. Ibid., 91–101.

37. Ibid., 23.

38. Thomas H. Eliot, *Governing America*, 2nd ed. (New York: Dodd, Mead, 1964), 759.

39. The Court, as is its practice, combined similar cases from several states in deciding this one. The school district of Topeka, Kansas, was not the only intergovernmental litigant.

40. Among the excellent overviews of the shift from federalism to intergovernmental relations on which this chapter has relied are David B. Walker, *Toward a Functioning Federalism* (Cambridge: Winthrop, 1981), Daniel J. Elazar, *American Federalism: A View from the States* (New York: Harper & Row, 1972), David C. Nice, *Federalism: The Politics of Intergovernmental Relations*, (New York: St. Martin's, 1987), and Deil S. Wright, *Understanding Intergovernmental Relations*, (North Scituate, MA: Duxbury, 1978).

41. For a similar example in Muncie, Indiana, see David B. Walker, *Toward a Functioning Federalism* (Cambridge, MA: Winthrop, 1981), 3.

42. Valente, 314.

43. Michael Tetelman, "State-Local Panels: An Overview," *Intergovernmental Perspective* (Summer–Fall 1987), 26–29. Recent issues of *Intergovernmental Perspective* have each featured an article on one of the 25 state ACIRs.

44. Tetelman, 25.

45. National Association of Regional Councils, *News and Notes* (November 18, 1988), 2, and telephone interviews with Al Notzen, executive director of the Alamo Area Council of Governments, San Antonio, Texas, and Carole Anne Boileau, communications associate, National Asociation of Regional Councils, Washington, DC, November 18, 1988.

46. National Association of Regional Councils, *News and Notes*, 39.

47. *Intergovernmental Perspective*, (Fall 1984), 5.

48. Office of Management and Budget, *Implementation of Executive Order 12372: The First Year: Background Document for the Report to the President*, (Washington, DC: Executive Office of the President, March 1985), Appendix 4.

49. National Association of Regional Councils, *Regional Council Programs and Activities: 1988 Survey*, (Washington, DC: National Association of Regional Councils, 1988), 4.

50. "The Council of State Governments," *The Book of the States: 1986–87*, (Lexington, KY: Council of State Governments, 1987), 455.

51. Ibid., 456–457.

52. See Jack Sulzer and Roberta Palen, *Guide to the Publications of Interstate Agencies and Authorities*, (Chicago: American Library Association, 1986).

53. Advisory Commission on Intergovernmental Relations, *Significant Features of Fiscal Federalism, 1989* ed., vol. 1 (Washington, DC: ACIR 1989), 26.

54. David C. Nice identifies 11 reasons for grants, of which "service assurance" and

"equalization of needs and resources" are the first two. *Federalism*, 51–54.

55. Joel C. Miller, "Muncipal Annexation and Boundary Change," in *The Municipal Year Book 1988* (Washington, DC: International City Management Association, 1988), 62.

56. Walker, 193.

57. Robert B. Hawkins, Jr., "Rebalancing the Federal Budget and the Federal System," *Intergovernmental Perspective* (Fall 1988), 13.

58. Joseph F. Zimmerman, "Developments in State-Local Relations: 1984–85," *The Book of the States: 1986–87*, 433.

59. Advisory Commission on Intergovernmental Relations, *Regulatory Federalism: Policy, Process, Impact and Reform*, (Washington, DC: ACIR, 1984), quoted in Hawkins, 14.

60. *U.S. Government Organization Manual, 1988–89* (Washington, DC: Office of the Federal Register, National Archives and Records Administration revised June 1, 1988), 784. See also Office of Management and Budget circular A-105 for restrictions on agencies seeking to use other regional arrangements.

61. For a brief history of Federal Regional Councils, see "Federal Regional Councils," in Martha Derthick, *Between State and Nation: Regional Organizations of the United States*, (Washington, DC: Brookings Institute, 1974), 157–181.

62. Among them are the Environmental Protection Agency, Housing and Urban Development, Department of Transporation, Health and Human Services, Department of Labor, and the General Services Adminisration; see individual agency listings in the *U.S. Government Organization Manual: 1988–89*, (Washington, DC: Office of the Federal Register, National Archives and Records Administration, revised June 1, 1988). See also Office of Management and Budget, "Circular A-105, Standard Federal Regions."

63. Neal R. Pierce, *Public Administration Times*, (December 1, 1981), 2.

Foundations of the Governments: State Constitutions

STATE AND LOCAL SOURCES OF AUTHORITY

The 50 state constitutions are the source of authority on which each of the 50 state governments bases its claim to exercise the sovereignty of the people of that state. Like the U.S. Constitution, the state constitutions establish the structure of government by identifying the major offices, the qualifications of those eligible to hold them, the method of selecting public officials, and the procedures for amendment. For these reasons alone, an examination of state constitutions is worthwhile. However, there are at least five additional reasons for studying the constitution of your state in particular and state constitutions in general.

1. *There are significant differences between state constitutions and the U.S. Constitution which are useful in understanding both.* According to Janice C. May, these differences are so numerous that "we may be justified in speaking of 'two constitutional traditions.'"[1] May pays particular attention to three differences between state constitutions and the U.S. Constitution. The first is that only governments or conventions selected by governments are involved in amending the U.S. Constitution. However, the people are involved in amending the state constitution in all but a few states. The second difference is the frequency of amendment. Most state constitutions have more than three times as many amendments as the 26 additions to the U.S. Constitution. The third is that the U.S. Constitution tends to serve as a set of guidelines for conducting politics; many state constitutions are part of the prize for political victory.

2. *Since the 1970s, legal scholars have "rediscovered" state constitutional law.* In large part this has occurred because state judges have used the state constitution to extend the individual rights of state citizens.[2] For example, in *Robinson* v. *Cahill* (1973), the New Jersey Supreme Court found that since the New Jersey constitution guarantees equal educational opportunity to every New Jersey schoolchild, the state's method of financing education was unconstitutional. It then ordered all the state's schools systems shut down until the legislature found a way to finance them equitably.[3] Not only do judges influence state constitutional interpretation, so do state attorneys general. Thomas R. Morris reports that although opinions about the legality or constitutionality of a proposed action are not binding, "they are regularly sought and almost always followed by state officials."[4]

3. *Not all state constitutions are the same.* There are significant differences among state constitutions, and these differences are worth noting. Daniel Elazar, for example, has identified six constitutional patterns "rooted in the original constitutional conceptions of the founding era plus differences among types and goals of pioneers who first settled the [13 colonies] of the New World."[5] Numerous other differences resulting from the impact of both groups and individuals are based on these six patterns.

4. *State constitutions are critical to the study of the intergovernmental system.* In addition to setting forth the structure of state government, they also are the ultimate source of authority for local government. Perhaps nothing symbolizes the linkage between state constitutions and the fate of local government better than the fact that since 1921, when it published its first model state constitution, the National Municipal League has sponsored research on state constitutional issues.[6]

Some state constitutions devote a few pages to local government but give the authority to create local governments to the legislature. Other state constitutions describe some dimensions of the local government system in copious detail. Usually county government is described in some detail, including the officers who must be elected. For the citizens of a given county to restructure their county government, in many states they must push a constitutional amendment through the legislature and get it approved by all the voters in their state.

5. *In your lifetime, we are confident that you will be asked to change your state's constitution.* Listing "frequent amendment" as one of the major differences between the U.S. and state constitutional traditions, Janice C. May reports that the 50 state constitutions had 5198 amendments as of 1985.[7] In the period 1986–1987 alone, an additional 275 amendments were proposed, of which 204 were adopted (Table 4.1).[8]

Table 4.1   STATE CONSTITUTIONS

State	Date ratified	Number of words	Number of amendments
Alabama	1901	174,000	452
Alaska	1956	13,000	20
Arizona	1911	28,876	104
Arkansas	1874	40,720	71
California	1879	33,350	449
Colorado	1876	45,679	108
Connecticut	1965	9,564	23
Delaware	1897	19,000	115
Florida	1969	25,100	41
Georgia	1983	25,000	10
Hawaii	1959	17,543	77
Idaho	1890	21,500	103
Illinois	1971	13,200	3
Indiana	1851	9,377	36
Iowa	1857	12,500	45
Kansas	1861	11,865	80
Kentucky	1891	23,500	26
Louisiana	1975	36,146	15
Maine	1820	13,500	153
Maryland	1867	41,134	195
Massachusetts	1780	36,690	116
Michigan	1964	20,000	15
Minnesota	1858	9,500	109
Mississippi	1890	23,500	54
Missouri	1945	42,000	62
Montana	1973	11,866	10
Nebraska	1875	20,048	183
Nevada	1864	20,770	100
New Hampshire	1784	9,200	141
New Jersey	1948	17,086	36
New Mexico	1912	27,200	104
New York	1895	80,000	203
North Carolina	1971	11,000	24

continued

Table 4.1   STATE CONSTITUTIONS *Continued*

State	Date ratified	Number of words	Number of amendments
North Dakota	1889	31,000	119
Ohio	1851	36,900	142
Oklahoma	1907	68,800	114
Oregon	1859	25,965	174
Pennsylvania	1968	21,675	19
Rhode Island	1843	19,026	44
South Carolina	1896	22,500	454
South Dakota	1889	23,300	92
Tennessee	1870	15,300	32
Texas	1876	62,000	283
Utah	1896	17,500	73
Vermont	1793	6,600	49
Virginia	1971	18,650	16
Washington	1889	29,400	76
West Virginia	1872	25,600	59
Wisconsin	1848	13,500	118
Wyoming	1890	31,800	51
United States	1787	10,000	26

Source: The Book of the States 1988–89, (Lexington, KY: Council of State Governments, 1988), 14.

Thus, a little knowledge about your state's constitution as it is now, how it compares with models such as the U.S. Constitution, and how it compares with other state constitutions is in order. With this information you will be better equipped to make informed decisions and perhaps influence the decisions made by others. In the pages which follow we will compare and contrast major features of state constitutions, leaving a closer examination of your state constitution to you and your instructor.

CONSTITUTIONAL GOVERNMENT: TWO IDEAS IN CONFLICT

The idea of government implies that there is a need for something to be done. This usually results in the selection of a set of officials to exercise power in the name of the community. The idea of constitutional government implies limits on the use of that power so that individuals or the community as a whole will be protected from arbitrary behavior on the part of those who govern.

The conflict between the idea of government (using power to do something) and the idea of limits (preventing the abuse of power) cannot be resolved easily. Anything that weakens the ability of government to do mischief also weakens its ability to act in the public interest. The status quo

---

Box 4-1　# How to Keep Government on the Sidelines

1. Fragment power within the executive branch of government. Distribute it among numerous officials; it becomes so difficult for any of them to get much done that they either stop trying or conserve their energy for a very few projects (Chapter 10).*

2. Create numerous veto points. Before any significant action takes place, require formal approval from numerous actors in the political system: the legislature, the governor, the courts, and/or the public via a referendum (Chapters 4 and 5).

3. Make it easy to remove officials by providing a recall system that is easy for a small number of people to put into motion (Chapter 4).

4. Keep officials busy doing nonproductive activities by giving them short terms of office, thus requiring them to spend a lot of time and energy running for reelection (Chapters 4, 9, and 10).

5. Provide no resources for taking action (money, personnel, equipment). Keep the budget low (Chapter 15).

6. Limit the grant of power in the constitution to a short list of enumerated powers. Without a "necessary and proper" clause, public officials must get the constitution amended to do anything new (Chapter 5).

*Indicates the chapter or chapters in which this item is discussed.

---

is seldom preserved, because change always takes place. Thus weak government does nothing, and other parts of the political system (major polluters, organized crime, strip miners, and a host of businesses that do not want the public inquiring too closely into how they prepare food, make chemicals, dispose of waste products, build buildings, or treat their employees) may be allowed to change it to suit themselves.

John P. Wheeler, Jr., believes that a weak government does not provide protection from arbitrary rule but rather is more likely to encourage irresponsible government.

> This approach has consistently proved self-defeating for it has prevented states from meeting the needs of a dynamic society. It is better to give power to the organs of government and then seek means to keep public officials honest and responsible than seek to deny them power. The constitution is a poor place to seek complete insurance against irresponsible government.[9]

Weak government does little to assure that change occurs in the public interest. In the game of politics, weak government simply stays on the bench and keeps its uniform clean (Box 4-1).

If one is concerned about protecting the environment or promoting social justice, it really doesn't matter whether one has a government too weak to provide these things or a government strong enough to provide them but controlled by the "wrong" people. Confronting either of these conditions is bad news, but the latter may be preferable because once there is control of government, individuals can bring about their goals by using the power that is available without first having to revise the constitution to grant government the power to act and *then* putting that power to use.

The authors of the 145 or more constitutions which have been in force in the 50 states since 1776 have used a variety of methods to reduce the risks of excessive strength and excessive weakness. Throughout this book we will compare the results of these experiments. However, all 50 state constitutions currently employ four basic principles to resolve the too weak/too strong dilemma of constitutional government.

FOUR PRINCIPLES OF LIMITED GOVERNMENT

State constitutions all embrace, with some variation, four principles which serve to limit government: liberalism, republicanism, separation of powers, and democracy.

Liberalism

Liberalism (Box 4-2) is a term used to identify both an ideology whose central value is the freedom of the individual and a basic principle of constitution making that is consistent with that ideology: the protection of individuals from the abuse of power. The notion that governments are created to protect individual freedom is firmly established in all state constitutions by a bill of rights.

For many years state constitutional bills of rights were regarded as virtually useless because the national government seemed to be more able and more willing to protect individual freedom than were many state governments. During the 1970s, however, the U.S. Supreme Court began to identify limits to the rights the U.S. Constitution guarantees under the equal protection clause of the Fourteenth Amendment. Thus, in *San Antonio Independent School District* v. *Rodriguez* (1973), the Supreme Court ruled that education is *not* a fundamental right guaranteed by the national constitution and that it therefore could not find the method of financing schools in Texas to be in violation of the U.S. Constitution.

The possibility remained, however, that state constitutions might guarantee equal educational opportunity. During the past two decades the state supreme courts of California, Connecticut, New Jersey, and Texas have declared that the methods for financing public schools conflicted with the constitutions of those states. According to their state constitutions, not the U.S. Constitution, individuals are guaranteed the right to equal educational opportunity.

It may be too early to tell, but it appears that in the years to come state constitutions are more likely to be looked to for individual protection than in times past and a whole new field of scholarship and law will be explored.[10]

Box 4-2   # The "L" Word

Given the controversy over the "L" word in the 1988 presidential election, it seems appropriate to define one's use of it carefully. We have attempted to do that in the text: Liberalism is an ideology or a principle of government. However, it may be useful to elaborate slightly on the additional assumptions that govern our use of the term.

1. It is important to remember that conservatives and liberals are members of the same ideological family. The process of getting liberal proposals enacted into law is sometimes a family feud in which the rhetoric of each side may be emotional and uncomplimentary. This is unfortunate, but given the different views of each side about government and capital and given the fact that not all liberal proposals are worthy of enactment, it is understandable.

2. Liberalism originated in the era of John Locke and Adam Smith, when government was viewed as the personal property of kings, dukes, earls, and czars, many of whom used it to take property, and sometimes life, away from individuals without due process of law.

3. Conservativism is a first cousin to, not the opposite of, liberalism. After the French Revolution (1789), when the Parisian mobs began to use the guillotine with reckless abandon, Edmund Burke wrote a critique of liberalism, which he believed the French philosopher Jean-Jacques Rousseau had carried to extremes, thus leading to the carnage of the French Revolution. On the whole, Burke agreed with Locke more than he disagreed with him. Burke rejected French, not English, liberalism.

4. After the industrial revolution, a new social institution emerged upon which liberals and conservatives disagreed. That social institution was capital, defined as the ownership of large-scale economic enterprises. To conservatives, the factory was simply another form of private property, to be afforded all the protections Adam Smith had intended for a small family business. To liberals (and a lot of others: progressives, utopian socialists, Marxists, nihilists, and Luddites), the factory was a new kind of power that could be used to dominate and destroy workers and whole communities.

5. Since conservatives and liberals disagreed about what capital is, they disagreed about what to do about it. Conservatives wanted it left alone. Liberals wanted it regulated in the interests of free enterprise (the Sherman Antitrust Act), employees (child labor acts, collective bargaining agreements, minimum wage laws), and the next generation (environmental protection laws).

6. Their disagreement about how to respond to the industrial revolution has affected the responses of liberals and conservatives to government. Liberals see government as the only available tool to control the damage that can be done by capital. Conservatives, by contrast, continue to mistrust government and are more inclined to trust capital than to trust government to deal with major social problems. Thus, conservatives are prepared to give large tax breaks to corporations and wealthy individuals in the hopes that this will promote economic development, which in turn will provide jobs, which in turn will enable everyone to rise from poverty. Liberals, by contrast, are more prepared to tax the wealth of corporations and wealthy individuals in order to provide services directly to individuals for whom the economy does not seem to be working.

continued

Box 4-2 *(continued)*

> **7.** Over time, many conservatives have come to accept liberal proposals once they are convinced that these proposals will not destroy society, the free enterprise system, or individual freedom. Although liberals value individual freedom and society far more than they value the free enterprise system, they are prepared to go along with conservative proposals to preserve the free enterprise system as long as the other two values are not endangered.

Republicanism

The term **republicanism** is associated with two related but separable concepts: representative government and community.

Representative Government   Representative government limits the abuse of power by making power harder to get. It limits the abuse of the power by reducing the likelihood that government will be overly responsive to short-run enthusiasms or to the whims of temporary majorities. The republican principle requires that government decisions be made by representatives of the people, not by the people themselves. This slows the decision-making process and allows representatives to deliberate about government action toward making the current demands of the general public the law of the land. The republican principle builds in delay. It prevents a majority — whether moral, amoral or immoral — from having all its goals instantly become law.

Of course, if a majority stays around long enough to elect representatives to control the government, it may enact policies for which there seems to be public enthusiasm. In short, the first meaning of republicanism attempts to limit the abuse of power by removing control of government at least one step from the hands of a temporarily aroused public.

A Community of Enlightened Citizens   The second meaning of republicanism involves the notion of a community of enlightened citizens who share many of the same values. This form of republicanism views participation in the affairs of the community as an obligation, not merely a right. Government is not the enemy or something to be taken "off our backs" but a tool for accomplishing agreed upon goals.

The republican idea of a community in which politics consists in the search for the common good is found most frequently in states with a moralistic political culture. Daniel Elazar notes that the constitutions of the New England states "are basically philosophic documents designed first and foremost to set a direction for civil society and express and institutionalize a theory of republican government."[11] According to this theory, the abuse of power can best be checked by an active and informed citizenry deciding who governs and advising the representatives how to govern. The phrase "the price of liberty is eternal vigilance" is consistent with the notion of republicanism. People stay free by carefully watching those who govern them.

Stripped to its essentials, this definition may sound somewhat idealistic. However, it is no more so than the idea of politics as dirty and the idea that only the worst people participate and win. Republicanism simply views the glass of water as being half full instead of half empty. Ideals by their nature are difficult to attain; that we do not always attain them does not mean we should not try. Ideals provide goals to achieve and a yardstick by which to measure our behavior. Without some idea of what the community *should* be, we leave government unchecked, because then whatever is, is right.

This little essay on ideals is not limited to republicanism alone. Democracy (trust the people) and liberalism (free the individual) both imply that "the people" and "the individual" can be trusted to use power or freedom wisely. We know, of course, that freedom and power have been used unwisely from time to time. That is probably why state constitution makers often build more than one principle into their documents. The possession of ideals does not prevent realistic behavior. Trust your fellow citizens, but count your change.

Separation of Powers

Separation of powers, as noted in Chapter 3, is a principle that divides power at a single level of government. At the state level, separate branches of government are created, and each branch is assigned certain specific functions. All 50 states have three branches: legislative, executive, and judicial. By dividing control over the different functions — rule making, rule administration, and adjudication — and by assigning them to the different branches of a government, we can check the abuse of power by those who hold it because these people don't have all of it. The division of power makes it difficult for a majority to gain complete control of a government. In addition to the division of power and responsibilities, the length of terms of office, the qualifications, and the method of selecting officials in each branch may differ.

The principle of separation of powers is usually coupled with the principle of checks and balances; that is, each branch is supposed to serve as a check on the abuse of power by the others. At the state level, for example, the governor, who is chief of the executive branch, is given the power to veto laws passed by the legislature. The legislature is given the power to make or approve the budget and can deny operating funds to executive agencies and to the judicial branch. The judicial branch can be appealed to by citizens or public officials who believe that laws are not being enforced in accordance with the state's laws or that a particular law is not consistent with the state constitution.

Democracy

All state constitutions embrace this principle, some more thoroughly than others. **Democracy** is a term which we shall use first to indicate the source of authority on which both state and local governments base their claim to rule and second to describe the method by which decisions are made.

A Source of Authority   Many ancient and medieval governments were theocracies. In a **theocracy** those in power base their claim to rule on the will of God. They assert, as did the Ayatollah Khomeini in Iran, that God put them in power and that only God can hold them responsible for their actions. Although in the very long run this may work out, as the Ayatollah doubtless discovered, the very long run may take decades. In the meantime a lot of human potential and even lives may be wasted.

Most modern governments base their claim to rule on the permission of those whom they govern—the people. Although we invoke divine blessings on our currency and in the Pledge of Allegiance—"one nation, under God, with liberty and justice for all"—state governments in America depend on a source of authority that is quite limited and imperfect. The source of authority for state constitutions is "we the people." The entire system of governments based on national and state constitutions has the power to make laws and collect taxes because it has received our permission to do so.

Democracy as a Method of Governing   As a principle of government, democracy is essentially the principle of majority rule. When combined with republicanism and liberalism, democratic systems of government are those in which the members of a community attempt to make decisions by means of a majority vote after a free and open discussion of the issues.[12] Without the concern of liberalism for the rights of individuals who may or may not be in the minority and without the concern of republicanism for the long-run survival of the community, democracy can be reduced to mob rule. Indeed, the Greek word *demos*, which is the source of the word "democracy," is also the source of the word **demagogue**. Untutored by liberal and republican guidance, democracy can result in whatever a majority of ill-informed, self-centered nitwits want at any particular point in time.

Nevertheless, considerable social science research has confirmed that the vast majority of the American public supports in the abstract the general principles we have identified.[13] About 20 years ago, before the civil rights revolution, Prothero and Grigg surveyed a sample of adult voters in Ann Arbor, Michigan, and Tallahassee, Florida, in an attempt to measure their commitment to liberal democratic values. They found that there was a consensus in support of the principles of democratic government, majority rule, and minority rights. However, only the more educated citizens indicated significant agreement on certain items which applied these principles to hypothetical situations, such as "Would you allow a Communist (or an atheist or a socialist) to give a speech in your community?"[14]

Although we have no data on whether Americans faced with the same questions might change their answers if the linkage between the principles involved and the issues were explained on the spot, the behavior of the residents of the Southern community studied suggests that the linkage between our responses to (1) questions on abstract principles, (2) hypothetical applications of these principles, and (3) real behavior is worthy of a great deal of study. Prothero and Grigg reported that 42 percent of their Southern respondents said that "a Negro should not be allowed to run for mayor of this city," but they also reported that no negative action was taken by "white people" when an African-American actually did run for mayor just a few months before the survey was taken.[15]

Since 1970, when given the opportunity to change state constitutions in the direction of individual freedom and tolerance, more often than not the voters have made such a change. In examining the impact of state constitutional amendments on civil rights, Janice C. May has observed that

> In a democracy, support for civil rights must ultimately find an anchor in public opinion. For better or worse, the state constitutional tradition tips the scales toward voter participation in preserving or reducing civil rights. The record of civil rights protection during the past 15 years, while mixed, holds out hope for the state amendment process.[16]

Two attempts to apply the principle of democracy to the practical world of politics continue to influence state constitutions and thus the way in which individuals and the governments deal with one another. They are called Jacksonian democracy and plebiscitary democracy. Since they will affect the way constitutions change in the future, it is worth spending some time examining them.

Jacksonian Democracy   Early state constitutions embraced the republican idea of government in the name of, but not by, the people. They limited the ability of all adult citizens to participate in decision making. Age, property ownership, gender, and race were criteria which kept many adults from voting or governing. During the early nineteenth century several states introduced changes in their constitutions and laws which are traditionally characterized by the term **Jacksonian democracy**. Recent scholarship suggests, however, that Andrew Jackson and his supporters were beneficiaries of democratic changes rather than initiators of them.[17] We will use this term to describe a cluster of changes that made state constitutions written during the last three-quarters of the nineteenth century more democratic.

Jacksonian democracy uses two criteria or standards for evaluating political systems. These criteria involved two basic questions: Can the adult population vote to choose public officials? and Can everyone in the adult population actually compete to be a public official?

The opportunity to choose public officials was greatly expanded in the nineteenth century. The property qualification was not used in the constitutions of the new states in the West, and the Eastern states soon revised their constitutions to eliminate it also. Jacksonian democracy embraced this practice and went beyond it in two ways: by encouraging the average citizen to actually govern and by increasing the opportunities to do so.

Andrew Jackson, elected in 1828 and again in 1832, was the first President born west of the Appalachian Mountains. More important, although he became a wealthy man, he wasn't born that way. Associated with neither the Virginia planter aristocracy nor the New England merchant-banker elite, Old Hickory had little patience with the idea that leaders should be chosen from families that could provide formal education for their sons and subsidize them while they served an apprenticeship in governance. "No man has any more intrinsic right to official station than another," said Jackson. "The duties of all public officers are so plain and simple that men of intelligence may readily qualify themselves for their performance."[18]

However, the legacy of Jacksonian democracy went beyond providing an opportunity to serve in the jobs that existed. It also changed the structure of government to provide more elective offices. This change had several consequences. First, it provided more opportunities to obtain a government job through the ballot box. Second, and perhaps more important, it placed upon each individual more responsibility for keeping track of those in government. Instead of electing one chief executive official at the county or state level who hired and fired the rest, the public was expected to be responsible for the hiring and firing of a multitude of public officials through the ballot box.

Jacksonian democracy lives on in the constitutions of the many states which were influenced by it. Eighteen states still place supreme court judges on the ballot, and even more elect lower court judges. A majority of states elect more than six executive officials, including the governor and lieutenant governor. In California, for example, voters choose the governor, secretary of state, attorney general, treasurer, and the comptroller as well as the four members of the board of property tax equalization. In Colorado, voters who want to be responsible must become informed about the qualifications of the three elected members of the University of Colorado Board of Regents. The clerk of the supreme court is elected in Montana, and in Oklahoma and seven other states the voters elect a commissioner of insurance.[19]

The Jacksonian belief is still expressed by many opponents of constitutional reform who believe that the best way to keep a public official honest is to make his or her job elective rather than appointive. This aspect of Jacksonian democracy can be summarized in the dubious proposition "More is better."

Sometimes the public responds to all these elective offices and all this responsibility by making a joke of it. From 1940 until his death in 1977, a man named Jesse James was regularly reelected to the office of state treasurer in Texas. While this Jesse James was not guilty of robbing the banks of cash, he did cost the taxpayers money by leaving large amounts of state funds in non-interest-bearing checking accounts in various banks around the state. This practice continued under his successor, Warren G. Harding, but was halted by the first female elected on her own to statewide office in Texas, Ann Richards.[20]

Plebiscitary Democracy   Plebiscitary democracy (PD) is an attempt to provide the general public with an opportunity to make decisions directly by voting yes or no in elections. Plebiscitary democracy attempts to approximate the direct democracy associated with rural communities in which the adult population is small enough that its members can meet to talk things over and make collective decisions. The New England town meeting, in which the whole community makes major budgetary and personnel decisions once a year, is reminiscent of PD.[21]

There is a limit, however, on how effective direct democracy can be when large numbers of people are involved, even in New England.[22] A large football stadium packed with citizens aroused and divided over an issue does not leap immediately to mind as the best way to make decisions on important public matters.

In many large communities and at the state level there are institutions which attempt to provide an element of direct democracy. Public hearings and open meetings at which the public is invited to bring information and testimony to help public officials make decisions are ways to provide elements of direct involvement in decision making by the public. However, those who attend public hearings and open meetings don't make legally binding decisions on the issues they have discussed. Their elected representatives make these decisions after talking over the issues with their legislative colleagues and following established legislative procedures.

Plebiscitary democracy differs in many ways from representative government, but perhaps the most significant difference is that PD has no built-in process of deliberation such as that found in the legislative process of representative government. Plebiscitary democracy is a method of making decisions in which there is no provision for exploring alternatives, talking things over, or seeking compromises. Plebiscitary democracy involves direct elections on yes or no questions.

Deliberation on and discussion of the propositions to be voted on may take place during the period between the announcement that a referendum will take place and the time of the vote. Sometimes, on particularly important issues, in communities where there is a civic organization such as the League of Women Voters, a public meeting may be held at which advocates for each side debate the issues, but PD itself does not include a formal deliberative process. As David B. Magleby observed, "One of the most persuasive criticisms of direct legislation is that it allows us to vote our passions and our prejudices."[23]

Before discussing PD further, it is important to emphasize two reasons why we are devoting this much space to it. First, for all its apparent shortcomings, PD is here to stay (Figure 4.1). Forty-nine states use at least one dimension of PD in the constitutional amendment process — referendum — when they refer proposed amendments to the voters. Only Delaware uses

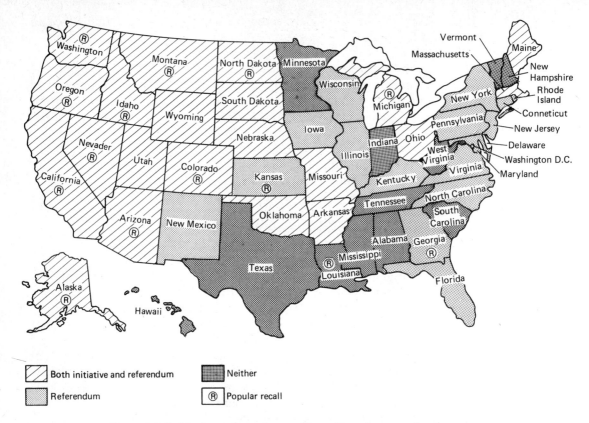

Figure 4.1 Initiative referendum and recall at the state level.

the legislature alone to propose and ratify amendments to its constitution.[24] Twenty-one state constitutions contain a provision for PD to be used to propose legislation, and 37 provide for the referral of state law to the voters before it goes into effect.[25]

Second, PD is widely used at the local government level, particularly in municipalities. Local PD is found in many states which do not use PD at the state level. Thus, it is likely that there will be constitutional amendments proposing the adoption of various PD procedures for decision making at the state level as well. Hence, we invoke the familiar refrain "This subject is important for you to know something about because you will be tested on it, in life if not in the classroom." To this observation we can confidently add, "In the 1990s you will be asked to make a decision using PD."

The three terms most commonly associated with plebiscitary democracy are **initiative, referendum,** and **recall.**

An *initiative* is the process of getting propositions on the ballot. These proposals or propositions are initiated by individuals and groups using petitions signed by an appropriate number of citizens. The propositions may involve constitutional amendments, laws, or proposals to remove (recall) public officials.

An initiative involves at least three steps: (1) writing a petition for government action, (2) circulating copies of the petition for registered voters to sign, and (3) making sure all the legal formalities have been followed before submitting the petitions to the appropriate government official.

The initiative process usually requires a certain percentage of the electorate to sign the petition; the signatures are then verified by a designated public official such as the secretary of state or the county clerk. When enough people sign the initiative petition and the number of valid signatures is declared sufficient, the proposal or proposition is put on the ballot and referred to the voters.

Referendums are sometimes referred to as elections because the public uses balloting to make a decision. The distinction between a referendum and an election is further blurred because they often occur on the same day. A referendum is the process of referring decisions to the public. In a referendum the public votes yes or no on propositions which can be placed on the ballot by at least three different procedures. The one traditionally associated with referendum is the initiative process. A second procedure exists because some state or local constitutions require that certain measures automatically be referred to the people. In addition to the ratification of proposed constitutional amendments and laws, referendums may be required for the approval of bond issues (the pledging of public credit for a loan to government). A third procedure occurs when a legislative body wants a formal but nonbinding statement by the public to guide it. Instead of taking public opinion polls, the legislators hold a nonbinding referendum. Thus, referendums come in two styles: binding and nonbinding. When the government must abide by the results of the vote in a referendum such as the ratification of a constitutional amendment, the referendum is binding.

In some states and many local governments, legislative bodies can put a proposal before the public in the form of a nonbinding referendum. In this case the legislature is seeking guidance, asking for the advice of the general public. Nonbinding referendums in which the vote is overwhelmingly for or against a course of action provide the clearest kind of guidance. However, a 50-50 split is almost worse than no guidance at all. It implies that no matter how legislators vote, they will offend half the public (or half of that portion of the public that cares about the issue).

A *recall* is a process that involves both an initiative and a referendum. A petition is circulated (initiative) proposing to remove an elected public official in a specially called referendum. Usually recall referendums occur in local governments, particularly municipalities. However, in 1984 for the first time in 30 years in the United States, a recall election at the state level resulted in the removal of a public official. Two state legislators who had voted to raise the income tax to help pay for increased educational spending and welfare payments were recalled in Michigan. In 1988 the governor of Arizona, Evan Mecham, was hit with a double whammy. A recall petition drive obtained more than enough signatures to force a referendum, but before it took place he was impeached.

Mixed Reviews   Proponents of PD argue that it provides an opporuntity to force legislatures dominated by powerful interest groups to pay attention to the public interest.[26] Opponents argue that PD simply gives wealthy interest groups even more influence because voters already overwhelmed by other electoral decisions respond to referendums by voting for the side with the biggest advertising budget and the cleverest slogans.

Betty Zisk reports that in 78 percent of the campaigns she studied in four states between 1976 and 1982, the biggest spenders won. In 20 of 32 cases on which polling data were available before the campaign began, an "initial majority approval of voters was changed in the direction of the high-spending side to create electoral victory for the spenders."[27]

Magleby summarizes his effort to empirically test some of the assertions in favor of PD with the following observation:

> The practice of direct legislation has by and large fallen short of the reformer's expectations and is prone to abuse. The people who rule in direct legislation are those who have mastered the process at the petition-qualification and voting stages. Large numbers of citizens are effectively excluded from participation, and what issue concerns they might have do not reach the direct legislative agenda. Because of the participation biases fostered by the direct legislation process and the inability of many voters to translate their opinions in to policy, the process has fallen short of the mark in the areas of participation and representation as well.[28]

In short, PD is not universally admired. As Thomas Cronin, the author of the most recent study of PD, suggests, there are many points worth considering before deciding whether PD is appropriate for a given state or community. Box 4-3 lists a few of his suggestions for improving the way PD works. If you live in a state that already has it, Cronin has some excellent suggestions for improving the way PD operates.

Cronin concluded his analysis of PD by observing that while he favors it for some state and local governments, he does not recommend it at the national level:

> Not until these processes can be proved to work with greater integrity at the subnational level should anyone seriously consider amending the [U.S.] Constitution to permit them for the national government.[29]

One might conclude from this that a process that has not yet proved to have sufficient integrity at the national level needs to be looked at very carefully before being adopted at any level.

Four Principles: Summary

The four principles found in all 50 state constitutions are combined in different ways to limit the abuse of power. Each state bill of rights limits the

Box 4-3   **Selected Safeguards for Plebiscitary Democracy**

1. *Sponsorship.* A petition for an initiative should have a number of sponsors before it is registered to begin the signature collection process. Requiring a significant number of sponsors discourages frivolous use of the process. This requirement ultimately saves taxpayers a good deal of money and helps preserve the integrity of the process.

2. *Filing fee.* A fee between $200 and $1000 to file the petition before initiating the process further discourages frivolous and publicity-seeking efforts.

3. *Official statements.* Too many initiatives use inflammatory and emotional language to get public attention. To prevent this from interfering with an objective view of the issue, a public agency should be charged with the task of preparing the language of the petition before it is circulated.

4. *Geographic distribution.* Some states limit the percentage of signatures that come from one area to make sure that the petition reflects the wishes of the general public. In Massachusetts no more than 25 percent of the signatures can come from one county. At the local level this can apply to voting precincts.

5. *Hearings.* One of the most serious shortcomings of PD is that no required deliberative process is involved. Screening out frivolous petitions prepares the way for requiring appropriate governing bodies (state legislative committees, county commissioners courts, city councils) to hold public hearings on petitions which have completed the initiative stage. These hearings should take place early in the referendum campaign. Thus the media have an opportunity to report the facts and issues raised by the hearings.

6. *Voter information pamphlets.* These are officially prepared digests of the issues, the pros and cons. Some newspapers take a position on an issue, and local residents only hear one side. Thus, although this costs money in the short run, it may save money in the long run by promoting a fully informed vote.

7. *Financial disclosure.* The source and amount of funds that organizations spend in initiative and referendum campaigns should be reported. Any contribution or expenditure over a minimum amount, say, $200, should be reported.

8. *Fairness in the media.* Disclosure is of little use if the information is not made readily available to the public in an easily understood format. Thus, it may be necessary to require the press to publish this information in accordance with a prescribed format. In addition to reporting expenditures, the mass media should be required to make an effort to give both sides a fair hearing.

Source: Thomas E. Cronin, *Direct Democracy: Initiative Referendum, and Recall*, (Cambridge: Harvard University Press, 1989), 234–238.

use of the power by the governments in their dealings with the individual, thus tempering the impact of majority rule. Separation of powers limits the ability of any individual or group to control all three branches of government at the same time. It also makes it difficult for any branch to dominate a state government.

Representative government requires deliberation and discussion before action. By removing the levers of power from temporary majorities and requiring that the people act indirectly through representatives, it reduces the abuse of power through miscalculation or appeals to emotion.

Democracy requires the popular election of those who do the deliberating. Thus, those in power are limited by the possibility that they will be held to account by the public at the next election. In many states not only the chief executive but many other officials who carry out the laws are elected. Furthermore, the people are consulted in amending the constitution in every state but Delaware. In 23 states, if elected representatives fail to enact laws supported by the public, the public can enact laws and amend the constitution without involving the legislature.

None of these limitations alone or in combination make it impossible for abuse of power to occur or for circumstances to arise in which a majority or a large determined minority can impose its will on the rest of a state's inhabitants. Indeed, it can be argued that it is impossible to design such a constitution unless human nature is redesigned.

CONDITIONS PROMOTING CONSTITUTIONAL GOVERNMENT

Constitutions are mere pieces of paper unless certain conditions are met. Three practical limits on power which help make constitutions meaningful are as follows:

1. Public officials themselves accept the rules of the game as set forth in the constitution as legitimate. They accept the ideals which the constitution attempts to promote because they believe in them.

2. Public officials know that other political actors both in and out of government have political resources which can be used to punish them for breaking the rules. A few people may get away with breaking the rules because no system is perfect. However, if the abuse of power frequently results in punishment, those who want to behave themselves will feel better about doing so and those who are tempted to abuse their power will be more circumspect. This principle also holds true, of course, in the political economy. Businesspeople who want to pay fair wages are more likely to do so if everyone is required to do so. Chemical firms which want to install expensive refining equipment to prevent the escape of toxic gases or chemicals are more likely to do so if all chemical firms are required to do so.[30]

3. Public officials know that both the rules of the game and their own

activities are a matter of record. If the rules of the game are secret, who's to know if they are being followed? Even when the rules are available, if the actions of public officials are not a matter of public record, who's to know whether these actions were done according to the rules? Thus, in a society with open meetings, open records, a free press, and an informed and active public, government officials are more easily held accountable when they attempt to misuse their power.

4. The public—"we the people"—learns the rules and insists that they be followed, pays attention to and remembers the promises of candidates and reminds them occasionally what they promised to do or not do, votes the rascals out when it seems appropriate, attends and participates in public hearings, and occasionally runs for public office. In short, if people do not attend the open meetings, read the open records, consult the free press, or make themselves heard, government officials and, for that matter, people with a lot of power in the political economy can operate pretty much as they please.

These four conditions do not guarantee a liberal democracy. They simply increase the likelihood that one will survive and adapt successfully to changes in its environment.

PREPARING FOR THE TWENTY-FIRST CENTURY: CONSTITUTIONAL REVISION

There seems to be a consensus among most students of state government that many state constitutions are badly in need of revision. Terry Sanford, a former governor of North Carolina and later president of Duke University, has referred to state constitutions as "drag anchors of state progress, and permanent cloaks for the protections of special interests."[31]

State Constitutional Flaws

The major problem with state constitutions is that they are too restrictive, keeping state and local government from dealing with the problems that confront them. Numerous scholars have added to the list of shortcomings, building on this main problem. On most lists one finds the following observations about state constitutions.

1. *They are too long because they are too detailed.* The average state constitution is 26,150 words long, three times as long as the U.S. Constitution. As Table 4.1 (see pp. 47 to 98) indicates, there is a considerable range in the length of state constitutions. Note that while the Alabama constitution is approximately 174,000 words long, that of Alaska contains only 13,000 words.

2. *They are too detailed and therefore too long.* The details come from restrictions on the state legislature, on the executive agencies, and on local

government and from topics best left to laws (or even interoffice memos within agencies). The Oklahoma constitution, for example, requires that "stock feeding" be taught in public schools.

Excessive detail can make a constitution more of a legal code than a concise statement of principles. The excessive detail involved is one reason why state constitutions have to be amended so frequently. It isn't age that makes a constitution obsolete or difficult to adapt to modern conditions, it is detail. The oldest state constitution, Vermont's, has been amended "only" 49 times since its adoption in 1793. As you will note from examining Table 4.1, the Vermont constitution is also the shortest of the state constitutions.

3. *They contain numerous obsolete references.* Once state constitutions have become too long and detailed *and* too frequently amended, it becomes expensive and time-consuming to identify parts that everyone agrees are outmoded and therefore removable.

4. *They contain numerous empty phrases such as the following from Pennsylvania's constitution*: "the sessions of each House and of committees of the whole shall be open, unless when the business is such as ought to be kept secret."[32]

5. *They are often repetitive, poorly written, and poorly organized.* This, of course, adds to their length.

The notion that the "average" state constitution needs improvement tends to imply that all states have seriously flawed foundations, but this just isn't so. Some state constitutions are models of brevity and have needed relatively little change since their adoption. Among them one finds constitutions from three different centuries: Connecticut (1965), Indiana (1851), and Vermont (1793). All these documents contain less than 10,000 words. The Vermont constitution is shorter by about 1000 words than the U.S. Constitution, which itself is a model of brevity.

Guidelines for Constitutional Design

In *McCulloch* v. *Maryland*, Justice John Marshall provided us with good reasons why a constitution should not be as detailed as a legal code: "It would probably never be understood by the public." He also suggested that in writing a constitution, "only its great outlines should be marked, its important objects designated."

Thus, the generation which writes a constitution should create a document which describes in general terms (1) its goals, (2) the most important offices and institutions of government, (3) their selection, and (4) the method of adopting and amending the constitution itself. Then it should allow each succeeding generation to interpret the meaning of the constitution and make its own mistakes.

Constitutional Adaptation

Constitutions which follow Justice Marshall's advice are flexible. They can be adapted to changing conditions without being revised or added to. Such constitutional change usually occurs in one of three ways.

Legislative Elaboration Flexible constitutions allow state governments to deal with nuclear power, toxic waste, theft by computer, and other problems which the constitution framers never dreamed of simply by passing laws or statutes. Each new law is based on a legitimate grant of general authority in the constitution (to promote the general welfare, to regulate commerce, and so on). In turn, the new law grants authority and/or resources to a new or existing state or local agency. No constitutional amendment is required.

Judicial Interpretation As conditions change and as new judges are chosen, the interpretation of the constitution and the laws which elaborate on it also change. State bills of rights which didn't mean much in the 1950s have been interpreted by state courts in the 1980s to guarantee equal educational opportunity. By interpreting the constitution or laws in a new way, the courts help adapt the constitution to changes in the environment of the governments.

Executive Action Governors and other executive officials use the powers of their offices in new ways to change the meaning of those offices as well as the constitution which created them. Naturally, some of the laws passed by the legislature and some actions by executive officials will be challenged by individuals and groups opposed to them. These individuals and groups can attempt to remove the offending officials by recall (if that is available) or challenge the constitutionality of the law in the courts.

The more general and brief is the constitution on which a government is founded, the easier it is for the system of government to adapt to change.

Rigid restrictions on government can be responded to in several ways. If the constitution puts government in a straightjacket, three unpleasant things can happen. Each type of response can have unfortunate consequences.

First, public officials can solve problems by bending or ignoring the rules. As the rules are bent, the four conditions we have mentioned may gradually disappear. This can result in a loss of respect for the rules of the game among officeholders and eventually the general public. Breaking the rules in a situation where it is necessary can lead to breaking the rules because it is merely convenient, then breaking them because one can get away with it, and finally breaking them because everyone else is doing it.

A second reason why an overrestrictive constitution is not healthy for a political system is that crucial problems may not get solved. Public officials may justify their inability to solve problems by blaming the constitution for things such as polluted aquifers, crime in the streets, and child abuse. Under these conditions respect for the rules of the game declines, and the foundation on which government bases its claim to rule begins to crumble.

A third and far more likely situation is that an inflexible constitution will be amended frequently to help adjust it to changing conditions. Although this sounds like a good idea, it has one disadvantage. The difference between the fundamental rules of the game — the constitution — and the rules and regulations made in the course of governing can easily become confused. Some state constitutions have been amended more than 250 times. Not all these amendments were intended to streamline or modernize the document. Some were done to protect special interests which used their political resources to build advantages into the basic foundation of state government.

In contrast to the numerous state constitutional amendments, the U.S. Constitution, written in 1786, has been amended only 26 times. Of those 26 amendments, the first 10 constitute the Bill of Rights.

In a state where the public is frequently asked to amend the constitution, the constitution itself is in danger of becoming merely one of the tools of government instead of a check on the misuse of those tools.

Under these conditions it becomes easier for those with wealth and power to promote their own interests. Those with less wealth and power — consumers, debtors, the working and middle classes, the poor, minority groups, and women — are not likely to benefit from this sort of situation.

Building special advantages into the constitution for the haves creates a double hurdle to the solutions of problems suffered by the have-nots, who must organize their political resources to do two things, not just one. First, they must get the right people elected to office. Second, they must get the constitution changed so that their elected officials can keep the promises they made about solving problems such as poverty; housing; health care; limited environmental protection; regressive taxes; discrimination in the workplace, in schools, and in the courts; and limited protection for workers injured on the job or unemployed through technological change or bad corporate decision making.

It is hard to get people elected to the legislature who will pass progressive legislation and to get a governor elected who will help move it along or at least won't veto it. However, when one also has to change the constitution, the difficulties double. After they have come close once or twice, it becomes increasingly harder to convince the powerless that they can make the system work.

FORMAL CHANGES IN STATE CONSTITUTIONS

Formal changes involves altering the written constitution. This can be done by means of amendment or revision. There is no strict boundary differentiating one from the other; it is rather like the difference between a little and a lot. When the voters of Louisiana were asked to pass judgment on 53 constitutional amendments at the same election in 1970, it was not clear whether they were involved in amendment or revision. They might have felt that 53 decisions amounted to a lot of amendments in print too small to read, because a majority of them voted no on all 53 proposals.

Constitutions are divided into articles just as books are divided into chapters. When proposals dealing with more than one or two articles are offered, revision rather than amendment is probably occurring. As a rule of thumb, amendment usually involves adding to the constitution; revision usually involves rewriting all or a significant number of articles.

AMENDMENT

The amending process involves two steps: proposal and ratification. All state constitutions provide for the legislature to propose constitutional amendments. Each house must approve of the amendment by a **special majority**. A special majority is larger than a simple majority, which is one-half plus one. Special majorities are usually two-thirds or three-fourths of each house. The larger the majority required, the more difficult it is to approve amendments (Table 4.2). Some states require that two successive legislatures approve a proposed amendment before it goes to the people.

Table 4.2 STATE AMENDMENT PROCEDURE: LEGISLATIVE ROLES

State	Vote required to propose	Number of legislative sessions
Alabama	3/5	1
Alaska	2/3	1
Arizona	Majority	1
Arkansas	Majority	1
California	2/3	1
Colorado	2/3	1
Connecticut	[a]	[a]
Delaware	2/3	2
Florida	3/5	1
Georgia	2/3	1
Hawaii	[b]	[b]
Idaho	2/3	1
Illinois	3/5	1
Indiana	Majority	2
Iowa	Majority	2
Kansas	2/3	1
Kentucky	3/5	1
Louisiana	2/3	1
Maine	2/3	1
Maryland	3/5	1

continued

Table 4.2 STATE AMENDMENT PROCEDURE: LEGISLATIVE ROLES *Continued*

State	Vote required to propose	Number of legislative sessions
Massachusetts	Majority	2
Michigan	2/3	1
Minnesota	Majority	1
Mississippi	2/3	1
Missouri	Majority	1
Montana	2/3	1
Nebraska	3/5	1
Nevada	Majority	1
New Hampshire	Majority	2
New Jersey	c	c
New Mexico	Majority	1
New York	Majority	2
North Carolina	3/5	1
North Dakota	Majority	1
Ohio	3/5	1
Oklahoma	Majority	1
Oregon	Majority	1
Pennsylvania	Majority	2
Rhode Island	Majority	1
South Carolina	d	2
South Dakota	Majority	1
Tennessee	e	e
Texas	2/3	1
Utah	2/3	1
Vermont	f	f
Virginia	Majority	1
Washington	2/3	1
West Virginia	2/3	1
Wisconsin	Majority	2
Wyoming	2/3	1

[a]Connecticut: 3/4 vote in each house at one session or a majority vote in each house in two sessions between which an election has intervened.

[b]Hawaii: 2/3 in each house in one session or a majority vote in two.

[c]New Jersey: 3/5 in one session or a majority vote in two.

[d]South Carolina: 2/3 in each house for first passage and a majority after approval in a referendum.

[e]Tennessee: Majority at the first passage and 2/3 in the second.

[f]Vermont: 2/3 in the senate for the first passage plus a majority in the house; a majority in both houses on the second passage.

Source: The Book of the States: 1988–89, (Lexington, KY: Council of State Governments, 1988), 16–17.

It would seem that the rules for amending may affect the amendment process in ways that have not been fully explored. Data for this research are available since 8200 amendments have been proposed to state constitutions, 62 percent of which have been adopted.[33]

In 17 states amendments also can be proposed by initiative. An initiative involves obtaining a required number of eligible voters to sign a copy of a petition. The number of signatures varies from state to state, but commonly it is some percentage of the vote for governor in the previous election. Usually there are several hundred copies in circulation and several thousand signatures. Once the petition has been certified, in most states by the secretary of state, the proposal is placed on the ballot for consideration by the public.

The second step in the amendment process is ratification. This is done by referendum. (The term "election" is commonly used for both a referendum and candidate selection, though technically it should only be used for the latter.)

REVISION

Constitutional revision involves even more variety than does amendment. Essentially it involves writing a new constitution. Sometimes, however, large-scale amendment of an existing constitution is also called a revision.

Revision by Convention

Fourteen state constitutions require that the electorate be asked periodically to vote on whether it wants a constitutional convention to meet for the purpose of revising the constitution or proposing a new one. The periods vary from 20 years in eight states to 9 years in Hawaii.

In the other states, constitutional conventions are called as the occasion arises. There have been at least 230 state constitutional conventions in our history, 60 of them in this century. They come in two forms: limited and unlimited.

A limited constitutional convention differs from an unlimited one in that it cannot touch certain portions of the constitution, such as the bill of rights, or it may be limited to a single subject, such as the apportionment of the state legislature or education. According to Albert Sturm about half the 40 state constitutional conventions since 1938 have been limited and about half have been unlimited.[34]

As in everything with a beginning, a middle, and an end, important decisions are made at each stage of the convention process. We use the term "process" to suggest that the actual convention is the middle stage, even though it too has a beginning, middle, and end.

Chief among the decisions to be made before calling a convention is determining the scope of the mandate. Is it to be an unlimited or a limited convention? If it is to be a limited convention, will it have a broad or a narrow focus?

Other important preconvention decisions involve methods for selecting delegates to the convention and for compensating them. Will delegates be elected from small single-member districts which give minorities and the poor a better chance at serving as delegates or from large districts, or will they be appointed? If they are appointed, by whom?

Constitutional conventions are highly political activities. Not only do advocates of various causes clash, but realists who see politics as the "art of the possible" but support the same causes as "true believers" may disagree on tactics and on what can realistically be accomplished.

During the convention technical decisions are made which influence the final outcome on controversial matters. Should the voters be presented with an all-or-nothing package or a series of choices? Although in recent years all-or-nothing choices on a wholly new constitution have done less well than have series of choices on separate resolutions, the 53-item package that faced Louisiana voters in 1970 was voted down.[35]

The third stage in the process is the ratification campaign. Whether one is revising a city charter, restructuring a county government, or promoting state constitutional reform, there is an important lesson to be learned from the experiences of several efforts at state constitutional reform: An all-out campaign effort involving as many people as possible will significantly improve the chances of adoption.

Revision by Commission

Commissions are created in various ways: by executive order, by law, by legislative resolution, and (in Florida) by constitutional provision. Members of constitutional commissions are usually appointed, but convention delegates are usually elected. Commissions often include ex officio members, that is, members such as the speaker of the house of representatives, the chief justice of the supreme court, the governor, and other occupants of important statewide offices.

There are two major types of commissions associated with constitutional revision: study commissions and preparatory commissions.

Study commissions hold public hearings around the state, commission research suggestions from the public, and prepare a report which usually includes a list of recommendations and/or a draft of suggested revisions. The report is then submitted to the state government, usually the legislature and/or the governor. Such reports are usually published and made available to the general public. Then the work of the commission is usually finished. It is up to the legislature to make formal revision proposals.

The fact that study commissions usually report to the legislature, which can then decide whether to act on their recommendations, makes this approach much more attractive to most legislators than a state convention in which the proposals usually go directly to the public and are beyond the

Table 4.3   SELECTED INDICATORS OF CONSTITUTIONAL CHANGE: 1960–1980

Feature	Number of state constitutions	
	1960	1980
Two-year terms for governors	15	4
Governors prevented from running for successive terms	16	5
Short executive ballot (four offices or less)	3	9
Legislature meets every other year (biennial sessions)	31	14

Source: David B. Walker, "The States and the System: Changes and Choices," *Intergovernmental Perspective*, 6:4 (Fall 1980), 7.

reach of the state legislature or other state officials. Burying a recommendation in committee, for example, is a lot easier than confronting it as a proposal in a ratification campaign.

Preparatory commissions are usually created to make arrangements for constitutional conventions. They take care of a number of necessary details, such as arranging for printing, acquiring space for the convention and its several committees to meet, arranging for press credentials and media participation, scheduling, staffing, and perhaps even establishing the interim rules and regulations for conducting the first day or so of the convention.

As Table 4.3 indicates, there has been some progress in recent years toward the reduction of the Jacksonian ballot and the removal of various restrictions on the ability of governors and legislatures to deal with modern problems.

In the 40-year period prior to 1960 only five new constitutions were created, two of which were those of Hawaii and Alaska. In the 20-year period since 1960 there have been 11 new state constitutions and no new states.

CONSTITUTIONAL REVISIONS AND YOU

The opportunity to participate in revising a state constitution does not come along every year or even every decade. However, when it does arrive, it is worth considering some of the ways in which you can participate. In addition to the role of voter, there are other possibilities. We suggest only three.

First, the early stages of most attempts at constitutional revision involve a series of public hearings held at various locations around the state. They may be conducted by a legislative committee or a revision commission. This is an excellent opportunity for the average citizen (you) to see how political leaders in the state operate and to influence the course of events.

In most states, elaborate efforts are made to promote attendance. Participation in commission hearings provides a real opportunity to influence events. It is for this reason that organized interest groups make sure they have a local representative at each public hearing in each city.

Hearings are sometimes carefully organized to make the optimum use of time. A common arrangement is for staff members to circulate a sign-up sheet or distribute forms on which individuals who want to addresses the commission identify themselves and the topics they wish to address. Staff members then use this information to make a schedule for calling on people.

Second, all conventions require a staff. Once it is announced that a commission will be formed, the creation of the staff begins. Although many staff members are borrowed from existing agencies and legislative staffs, it is possible to serve on the commission staff or work on a more temporary basis helping make arrangements for the hearings which will take place in one's home community.

Third, today's volunteer is tomorrow's indispensable employee. Volunteering to work in the ratification campaign or in another phase of the constitutional revision process is not the worst way to spend some time. The pay isn't great, but the opportunity to meet interesting people and learn about the political process from the inside not only looks good on job application forms later in life but also provides some interesting stories to tell one's grandchildren. A volunteer effort may lead to useful contacts; you might simply obtain material for a term paper or two or even meet Mr. or Ms. Right.

Conclusion

In concluding our introduction to state constitutions, it is worth noting that while our discussion has been biased in the direction of change, we are aware that change can be for the worse as well as for the better. In fact, the 50 states have operated under 145 different constitutions, not all of which were improvements over the previous ones.

Nevertheless, knowing something about constitutional revision is important since you may want to help the revision process have a happy ending in your state.

Study Objectives

1. Identify five reasons for studying state constitutions.
2. Identify the ratification dates, the number of words, and the number of amendments added to your state constitution.
3. Identify the two ideas in conflict in most state constitutions.
4. Identify six ways to keep government on the sidelines.
5. Identify four principles of limited government.

6. Identify the similarities and differences between conservatives and liberals in America.
7. Identify republicanism and the two terms associated with it.
8. Identify the major features of Jacksonian democracy.
9. Identify the consequences of making more offices elective rather than appointive.
10. Identify plebiscitary democracy and the three procedures that go along with it.
11. Identify the advantages and disadvantages of plebiscitary democracy.
12. Identify six ways to promote the integrity of plebiscitary democracy.
13. Identify the conditions that promote constitutional government.
14. Identify the major shortcomings of most state constitutions.
15. Identify the guidelines for writing a constitution which are found in *McCulloch* v. *Maryland.*
16. Identify the three ways in which constitutional change usually occurs.
17. Identify the formal methods for changing a state constitution.
18. Identify three ways in which you might participate in amending a state constitution.

Glossary

demagogue One who appeals to the emotions and lesser instincts (selfishness, greed, fear of strangers) of others.

democracy A system of government in which the majority rules. In America we usually think of liberal democracy (majority rule and minority rights) when we use the term. To the ancient Greeks and to some of the authors of the U.S. Constitution, however, democracy meant little more than mob rule (rule by the *demos*).

initiative The process of getting propositions on the ballot.

Jacksonian democracy A term used to describe a number of changes in our political system which took place during the early nineteenth century. Among them are the long ballot, universal suffrage, and short terms of office, all of which were intended to make government more democratic.

liberalism A term which is used to identify both an ideology whose central value is freedom of the individual and a basic principle of constitution making consistent with that ideology.

plebiscitary democracy (PD) An attempt to approximate the direct democracy associated with rural communities in which the adult population is small enough that its members can meet to talk things over and make collective decisions.

recall A process that involves both an initiative and a referendum. A petition is circulated (initiative) proposing a referendum to remove an elected public official in a specially called referendum.

referendum The process of referring policy decisions to the public. It is sometimes referred to as an election because the public uses balloting to make a decision.

republicanism A principle which is most often associated with representative government. It also implies a community of enlightened citizens who share many of the same values.

special majority Larger than a simple majority, which is one-half plus one. Special majorities are usually two-thirds or three-fourths of the relevant body (house, senate, or electorate). They are required for procedures that do more than routine business: propose a constitutional amendment, suspend the rules, impeach a governor, and so forth.

theocracy A system of government in which those in office claim that their authority is based on the will of God, not on election or heredity.

Endnotes

1. Janice C. May "Constitutional Amendment and Revision Revisited," *Publius*, (Winter 1987), 153.
2. Thomas C. Marks, Jr., and John F. Cooper, *State Constitutional Law*, (St. Paul, MN: West, 1988), 48–49.
3. *Robinson v. Cahill*, cited in John J. Harrigan, *Politics and Policy in States and Communities*, (Glenview, IL: Scott, Foresman, 1987), 300–301.
4. Thomas R. Morris, "State Attorneys General as Interpreters of State Constitutions," *Publius* (Winter 1987), 133–152.
5. Daniel Elazar, "Principles and Traditions," *Publius* (Winter 1982). 18. The six patterns are commonwealth, commercial republic, southern contractual, civil code, frame of government, and managerial. See pp. 18–22.
6. National Municipal League, *Model State Constitution*, 6th ed (revised) (New York: NML, 1968). Since 1921 the NML model has been significantly revised six times. The sixth edition was published in 1963 and then further revised for a 1968 publication. The Alaska constitution is cited by the NML as being the state constitution that comes closest to its model, and Elazar identifies Alaska as an example of a managerial pattern constitution.
7. May, 162.
8. Albert L. Sturm and Janice C. May, "State Constitutions and Constitutional Revision: 1986–1987," in *The Book of the States 1988–89*, (Lexington, KY: Council of State Governments, 1988), 7.
9. John P. Wheeler, Jr., ed., *Salient Issues of Constitutional Revision*, (New York: National Municipal League, 1961), xiii.
10. See, for example, Bradley D. McGraw, ed., *Developments in State Constitutional Law* (St. Paul, MN: West, 1985).
11. Daniel J. Elazar, *American Federalism: A View From the States*, 2nd ed. (New York: Harper & Row, 1972), 96.
12. For more sophisticated attempts to define democracy and liberal democracy, see Robert A. Dahl, *A Preface to Democratic Theory*, (Englewood Cliffs, NJ: Prentice-Hall, 1956) See especially p. 84 for a concise presentation of the definitional characteristics of what Dahl calls "polyarchy, an inadequate, incomplete, primitive ordering of the common store of knowledge about democracy."

13. Donald J. Devine, *The Political Culture of the United States*, (Boston: Little, Brown, 1972), 286. For an opposing view, see James A. Stever, *Diversity and Order in State and Local Politics*, (Columbia, SC 1980), 24–26.

14. James W. Prothero and Charles M. Grigg, "Fundamental Principles of Democracy: Bases of Agreement and Disagreement," *Journal of Politics*, 22 (1960), 278–294. This is one of the classic studies on elite-mass support of democratic values. See also Herbert McCloskey, "Consensus and Ideology in American Politics," *American Political Science Review*, (Winter 1964), 361–382.

15. Prothero and Grigg, 240.

16. May, 178. A 1970 study conducted for CBS News found that things had not changed very much; see Robert Chandler, *Public Opinion: Changing Attitudes on Contemporary Political and Social Issues*, (New York: Bowker, 1972), 6–13.

17. Edward Pessen, *Jacksonian America*, rev. ed. (Champagne-Urbana: University of Illinois Press, 1985), 150. For a capsule account of the impact of Jacksonian democracy on state constitutions, see Albert L. Sturm, "The Development of American State Constitutions," *Publius* (Winter 1982), 63–65.

18. John A. Garraty, *The American Nation*, 5th ed., vol. 1 (New York: Harper & Row, 1983), 238–239.

19. *The Book of the States 1986–87*, 51–52.

20. Ronnie Dugger, *Texas Observer*, (October 1983).

21. Joseph F. Zimmerman, *The Massachusetts Town Meeting: A Tenacious Institution*, (Albany, NY: Graduate School of Public Affairs, 1967), 15–24.

22. Ibid., 57.

23. David B. Magleby, *Direct Legislation: Voting on Ballot Propositions in the United States* (Baltimore: John Hopkins University Press, 1984), 191. See also Thomas E. Cronin, *Direct Democracy* (Cambridge, MA: Harvard University Press, 1989).

24. *The Book of the States 1987–88*, 16. As do ten other states, Delaware requires approval of a proposed amendment in two different legislative sessions.

25. *The Book of the States 1988–89*, 217–219.

26. For a summary and discussion of reform assertions in favor of PD, see Magleby, 27–28; for the opposing assertions, see Magleby, 29–30.

27. Betty Zisk, *Money, Media, and the Grassroots: State Ballot Issues and the Electoral Process*, (Newbury Park, CA: Sage, 1987), 245.

28. Magleby, 199.

29. Cronin, 251.

30. See Edmund S, Phelps, *Political Economy*, (New York: Norton, 1985), 183, for a discussion of the logic of collective action and problems of public choice.

31. Terry Sanford, *Storm over the States*, (New York: McGraw-Hill, 1967), 189.

32. Advisory Commission on Intergovernmental Relations, *The Question of State Government Capability*, (Washington, DC: Advisory Commission on Intergovernmental Relations, 1985), 39.

33. May, 158.

34. Sturm, 81–82.

35. Ibid., 80.

Chapter
5

Foundations of the Local Governments

Nothing testifies to the diversity of the American intergovernmental system more than the variety of local governments found within it. As Box 5-1 indicates, not only are there different forms from state to state, but different functions are assigned to them.

The purpose of this chapter is to examine a few questions about local governments: Are local governments necessary? Where do local governments get their authority? Who creates local governments and why? Do we need 83,000 of them? In seeking answers to these questions we will attempt to identify some regularities among the local governments that exist in the American intergovernmental system.

Box 5-1   Diversity from State to State: Local Governments

The following quotations from the U.S. Census of Governments provide examples not only of the variety of types of local government in any one state but also the many ways in which different states define and limit local government.

Although town governments exist in each county in New Hampshire, they do not cover the entire area of each county. Cities, gores, grants, purchases, unorganized locations, and unorganized townships exist outside the town.[a]

Iowa townships may provide fire protection, cemeteries, community centers, and township halls. Township trustees also serve as fence viewers and resolve animal trespass problems upon request. Although Iowa township trustees may levy taxes, and may issue anticipatory bonds, the compensation of township trustees is paid by the county government. For this reason, townships in Iowa are classified as administrative subdivisions of the counties and are not counted as separate governments in census statistics on governments.[b]

The entire state of Indiana is encompassed by 91 county governments except for the former county of Marion. Effective January 1, 1970, Marion County and the City of Indianapolis were consolidated to operate as one government, designated the city of Indianapolis.[c]

California law provides for the following types of school districts: elementary, high school, unified, and community college. Among the types of elementary districts are city districts, regular districts, union districts, joint districts, and joint union districts.[d]

In Louisiana, county governments are legally designated "parish" governments. The entire state is accounted for by parish governments, except for the parishes of East Baton Rouge, Orleans, and Terrebonne. These three parishes are substantially consolidated for government purposes with the cities of Baton Rouge, New Orleans, and Houma, respectively. The governing body of a parish is called the police jury, except in Jefferson Parish, which has a parish council, and Plaquemines Parish, which has a commission council.[e]

The entire state of Virginia is accounted for by county government, except for areas located within the boundaries of the 41 cities. Cities in Virginia exist outside the area of any county, and are counted as municipal rather than county governments, . . . [although] cities perform county-type as well as municipal functions. . . . In localities where a city and a county share the same clerk of circuit court, commissioner of revenue, commonwealth's attorney, sheriff, or treasurer, the officials involved are classified for census purposes as county officials. . . .[f]

[a]U.S. Bureau of the Census, *1987 Census of Governments, Government Organization* (Washington, DC: U.S. Government Printing Office, 1988), 141.
[b]Ibid, 76.
[c]Ibid, 72.
[d]Ibid, 20.
[e]Ibid, 89.
[f]Ibid, 215.

Source: U.S. Bureau of the Census, *1987 Census of Governments, vol. 1: Government Organization* (Washington, DC: U.S. Government Printing Office, 1988), A-1–A-235.

ARE LOCAL GOVERNMENTS REALLY NECESSARY?

If you stop and think about it a moment, we could get along without local governments. The 50 state governments could offer all the essential services through state agencies. With more personnel the state police, highway department, health department, and education department could provide local services.

This is not to say that we would be happier or better served without 80,000 units of local government. It simply suggests that what we take for granted as being what is does not exhaust the possibilities of what could be. There are at least six reasons why local government is preferred over the delivery of services at the local level by an agency headquartered elsewhere.

1. *Delegation.* From the point of view of national leaders, local government (and state government) is a necessary part of any large system for making decisions. Some responsibility for decision making must be delegated to local decision makers whether the system governs, makes cars, or sells hamburgers.

2. *Personnel management.* When the local community takes responsibility for choosing or removing local decision makers, it takes pressure off the leaders of the wider political system, who have enough hiring and firing problems of their own.

3. *Maintaining system legitimacy.* Local government places some of the responsibility for making tough decisions about services and taxes in the hands of locally elected officials. These decisions are more likely to be accepted if they are made locally. Furthermore, these decisions can be overruled by local political action without disrupting the wider system.

4. *Resource management.* Taxes raised locally may be managed a little more carefully than are funds raised and redistributed by the state or by the national government.

Tax dollars go further when labor, supplies, and even cash are donated voluntarily to make local projects work. Most people are more likely to volunteer for local projects than for national or state projects. It is easier to donate a few hours on something near one's home than to work on a project involving a long commute or an overnight stay. Instances of statewide and nationwide responses to a tragedy or a dramatic case of need are newsworthy because they are unusual. Less often reported are the millions of dollars worth of labor and resources donated by members of local churches, synagogues, temples, Lions, Elks, the League of Women Voters, B'nai Brith, Shriners, and other organizations that plug away all year long. Every service or project they offer is one that a public official does not have to raise taxes to pay for.

5. *Access.* Local government provides individuals with convenient access to decision makers to express needs and seek explanations. Although a relatively small percentage of the population takes advantage of these opportunities, it is

important that the opportunity is there. It is easier to get to city hall or the county courthouse than to the state capital or Washington, DC.

6. *Local autonomy.* In many communities a desire arises to be independent of other communities. Before the rapid urbanization of America, this desire was expressed in terms of the creation of new county governments. Now it is usually expressed in terms of municipal authority.

If you look at a map of county lines in states settled during the eighteenth and early nineteenth centuries, when population growth was fairly rapid in rural areas, you will find many counties with boundaries that were designed to fit local geographic and settlement patterns. In contrast to this, observe the straight lines of surveyors that define the much larger counties farther west (Figure 5.1).

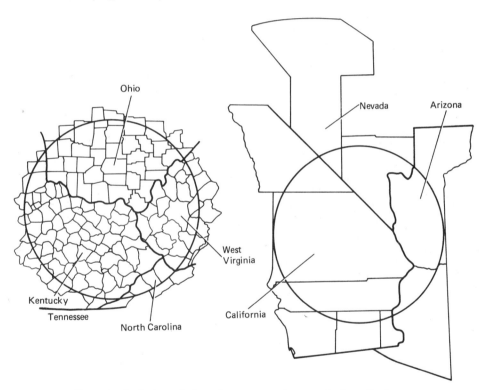

Figure 5.1 Counties before and after the automotive revolution. Each area represents the same number of square miles — about 20,000. In the horse and buggy days, every good-sized community wanted its own county, with a centrally located county seat where most legal, financial, and political business would be conducted. After the automobile made travel to the county seat much easier, it seemed more practical for a community to have its own municipal government empowered to offer urban services. The county became at least temporarily less relevant. Thus, new small counties were no longer created as communities grew in the postautomotive area. (*Source:* Rand McNalley, County Map of the United States.)

Many of the eastern counties were created for local autonomy and convenience—usually the convenience of two locales. When an existing county found itself with two population concentrations—an older settlement the population of which had run things for years and a new settlement which threatened to take over the politics of the county through sheer force of numbers—the sporting thing seemed to be to divide the county: "Let the newcomers have their own county. Besides, if we don't, they'll take over ours." (When an old country boy offers a deal, he seldom loses on it.)

The machinery for creating new counties still exists in most states. However, few of the states which were settled after the industrial revolution, and especially after the automobile went into mass production, have very many counties that are small in area, defining a community. The creation of a new county in the United States is an unusual event; only five were created in the 1980s. During the same period 249 municipalities were incorporated.[1]

SOURCES OF LOCAL GOVERNMENT AUTHORITY

Among the sources of authority for local governments in various states one finds state constitutions, state laws, local charters, and local ordinances.

State Constitutions

Specific Governments   Articles in or amendments to many state constitutions create specific governments by name. For the first century of our existence this was the usual method for creating cities. In some states special districts have been created by constitutional amendment. This, of course, contributes to the length and clutter of state constitutions.

Required Procedures   Most state constitutions today contain procedures for creating various types of local government. Some states set up a classification system according to population size. In most of these systems, the larger the government, the more authority it can be given. Usually these governments are cities. However, in some states counties are also classified. The state of Washington, for example, has a scheme that places counties in 11 categories from ninth (fewer than 3300 inhabitants) to AA (500,000 inhabitants or more).[2]

State Laws

As with constitutions, state laws also create specific local governments and procedures to be followed for creating types of local government.

Local Charters

Charters are local constitutions and are usually given to cities. Although some states give this opportunity to counties or to city-county consolidations, the more common reference is to cities. These charters are granted in accordance with any of the procedures we have mentioned. Charters create two basic types of governments: general law and home rule.

General law governments follow a pattern set forth in state law or the state constitution. Thus, to change anything in a general-law city's charter requires at a minimum an act of the legislature, if not a constitutional amendment.

A *home-rule* charter enables the community to revise its local government constitution without returning to the legislature for a law or constitutional amendment.

Thus, if a city ordinance is declared null and void by a court because it is not consistent with the city's charter, the remedy is local instead of at the state level. The city charter can be amended, and then the ordinance can be passed again if that is what the community wants. No state law or constitutional amendment has to be guided through the state legislature.

Local Acts or Ordinances

In many states, county governments are empowered to create authorities and special districts. New Jersey empowers its counties to create beach erosion control districts, county bridge commissions, county improvement authorities, county industrial pollution control financing authorities, and county recreation authorities.[3] Thus, the source of authority for these governments is an act or ordinance passed by another local government.

In each of the 50 states it is ultimately the state constitution on which these various laws, enabling acts, and procedures for creating local governments are based. Thus, each state constitution provides a context for the study of local government — a study, we hasten to add, that is of more than passing importance.

STRUCTURE (AND POLITICS)

At the risk of some oversimplification of their almost infinite variety, local government structures can be classified in two basic dimensions: the relationship of the executive branch to the administrative branch and the relationship of the executive departments to the chief executive.

1. In the legislative-executive dimension there are three basic types: commission, council-manager, and an independent executive and council.
2. In the executive branch-chief executive dimension there are two basic types: fragmented and unified.

Executive-Legislative Relations

In most of the governments we have discussed the government is empowered, and sometimes required, to offer services which it finances in part by taxing and borrowing.

The legislative branch sets the tax rate and approves the budget. The executive is responsible for carrying out the services.

The Commission Form   In the commission form the two functions are wholly or partially combined in one body. The commissioners may each take charge of all the departments within the government or may be assigned a few. In many county governments the commissioners collectively are the legislature and individually are in charge of a portion of the county road system. In some cities that use the commission form, each commissioner takes charge of one or more departments.

The Council-Manager Form   In this form the legislature retains indirect control over the executive branch through an administrator whom it appoints and can remove. Some examples of this form include the elected school board and the appointed school superintendent, the elected city council and the manager it appoints, and an elected county commission and appointed county executive.

For a city government to have a council-manager form of government, according to the International City Management Association, its charter or constitution must allow the manager "to serve as chief administrative officer, to oversee personnel, development of the budget, proposing policy alternatives, and general implementation of policies and programs adopted by the council."[4]

County governments rarely give this much authority to the manager, although many special districts do. School district superintendents also have much the same authority over principals, teachers, and other district employees as city managers have over department heads and the rest of the city government.

Elected Chief Executive   This form of government follows most closely the principle of separation of powers (Chapter 4). In theory, it places control of the executive branch in the hands of one elected official who is responsible to the voters rather than to the legislature. In cities this form is referred to as the strong mayor form. In counties it is usually referred to as the elected executive form.

Whether the mayor of a city is elected by the electorate or by the city council is less important than the control that mayor has over the heads of the major departments in the executive branch. Many cities with elected mayors are really commission or council-manager cities. Some council-manager cities also have an elected mayor who presides over council meetings. That official, however, is not an elected *chief* executive, because he or she has no control over the executive branch.

Chief Executive-Executive Branch Relations

The amount of influence the chief executive has over the executive branch may be limited by the source of authority, by law, or by politics. The most common distinction involves the relationship of the chief executive to the rest of the executive branch.

Fragmented and Unified Executive Branch   In a unified executive branch the chief executive can hire, fire, and give direction to the heads of the various departments. In a fragmented executive branch the chief executive may not have much formal influence because another person or authority chooses the heads of the major departments.

Political Limits and Opportunities   Politics may modify the ability of a chief executive to get things done. Although they can hire, fire, and direct department heads, many city managers must deal with powerful city councilpersons who attempt to meddle in administrative matters instead of sticking to their legislative role. School superintendents may find it politically necessary to remove a coach who is an excellent teacher but can't win football games or to keep a poor teacher in the classroom because of his or her connection to a school board member. Furthermore, executives at all levels must make personnel decisions in the context of affirmative action, civil service regulations, state and federal grant mandates, and the realities of the political situation.

Political skill can also make it possible for an official without much formal authority to persuade, motivate, and lead a government and community to accomplish important goals.

CAOs and Political Leaders   The job of chief executive requires both technical and political skills. Some executive branches separate the political and the administrative roles. Many strong mayor cities have a chief administrative officer (CAO) who operates almost like a city manager in the council-manager system, except that he or she is hired and fired by the mayor, not by the council. The mayor in a strong mayor system takes charge of the coalition building, the negotiation, and the promotion of projects and plans as well as the ceremonial functions associated with serving as the head of a unit of government.

The need to devote time and talent to both the technical-administrative and political roles is one reason why Charles R. Adrian, an authority on city government, has observed that the council-manager system and the mayor-council system are becoming more alike.[5] Now that we have examined sources of authority and some of the possible relationships between the executive and legislative branches, let us examine the types of local governments.

FIVE TYPES OF LOCAL GOVERNMENTS

Although all people may be created equal, all local governments are not. The U.S. Bureau of the Census identifies five types of local governments: counties, townships, municipalities, school districts, and special districts. Counties and municipalities (or cities) are usually considered **general-purpose**

governments. They offer a wide range of services and contain all three branches of government: legislative, executive, and judicial.

Townships, which exist in 21 states, lie somewhere between general-purpose and special-purpose governments, depending on the way in which they are structured in each state. In Iowa, for example, townships are sub-units of county government and are not considered to be separate governmental units (Box 5-1). In other states, townships offer a wide range of services.

Special-purpose governments include independent school districts and special districts such as municipal utility districts (MUDs), soil conservation districts, rural fire control districts, and mosquito abatement districts as well as metropolitan transit authorities and port authorities. Most of these governments specialize in a limited number of services and lack a judicial branch. However, some, such as the New York Port Authority, which was created by an interstate compact between New York and New Jersey, have become incredibly complex.[6] As Table 5.1 indicates, special-purpose governments outnumber general-purpose governments. Furthermore, they are increasing at a much faster rate. In the past 25 years 10,000 special districts have been created. In this chapter we hope to shed some light on why so many of these governments have been created.

The County

County governments are found in all but two states: Connecticut and Rhode Island. In two other states they exist under different names: boroughs in Alaska and parishes in Louisiana. Because they are the largest unit of government in terms of land area, there are fewer counties than any other form of local government. Of the 83,000 local governments, there are only 3042 of the county type in the United States. After the state and the national govern-

Table 5.1 GENERAL-PURPOSE AND SPECIAL-PURPOSE GOVERNMENTS: 1987

Type	Number
General purpose	38,984
National	1
State	50
County	3,042
Municipal	19,200
Township	16,691
Special purpose	44,253
School district	14,721
Special district	29,532
Total	83,237

Source: U.S. Bureau of the Census, *1987 Census of Governments, vol. 1: Government Organization* (Washington, DC: U.S. Government Printing Office, 1988), vi.

ments, county governments include more people than any other type of government, yet for many Americans county government remains a "Dark Continent of American Government."[7]

Dual Identity   The county serves two basic purposes: an agency of state government and a unit of local government. Most counties were created in the eighteenth and nineteenth centuries as arms of state government to provide limited services to an essentially rural population. As an agent of the state, a county government provides courts, jails, roads, bridges, schools, welfare services, and record keeping (land sales and vital statistics) and conducts the general election every other year in November. County government enables the state to provide a more or less uniform system of law and order and a basic minimum standard of some services throughout the state.

County as Local Government   Counties are units of local government for three reasons. First, the officials who run them are locally elected. An alternative to local election is selection by a state agency, such as the state highway engineer or the state police personnel assigned to your area. Those officials are state employees who are selected and assigned by the state.

Second, each county determines its own budget and has the power to tax and spend. These powers, of course, may be limited by the state constitution or state laws.

Third, many if not most counties were created as a result of local efforts. In an existing county the citizens of one or more population concentrations combined to ask the state to establish a separate county government. In unorganized geographic counties, the process was essentially the same.

An important role of county government is to determine the range of services that county residents receive. Besides the services that counties are required to perform for the state, a county may choose to offer a wide range of additional services. As Table 5.2 indicates, some services are offered as a result of counties contracting with other units of government or private enterprise to offer them. While counties in metropolitan areas are likely to offer more services, some rural or nonmetropolitan counties go considerably beyond the traditional functions of law and order and roads.

Whether a county offers a service depends on political action by the citizens within it, even those who live in cities. As county citizens, they can demand services paid for by the county government rather than by the city government alone. If the county is prohibited from performing a service by state law or the state constitution, the citizens of the county can, as we observed in Chapter 4, get those changed. County citizens, after all, are also state citizens.

Towns and Townships

In some states the town is part of a classification scheme for urban locations. In those states, towns are cities; some of these towns are of considerable size, but they have fewer powers and responsibilities than do large cities. In 21

Table 5.2 A FEW SERVICES OFFERED BY AMERICAN COUNTIES

Service	County-operated	Contracted out
Airports	585	264
Electric power	18	50
Fire protection	607	191
Gas supply	14	49
Hospitals	476	259
Landfills	1261	359
Libraries	1128	202
Nursing homes	489	167
Public transit	148	98
Sewerage system	310	75
Stadiums and convention centers	140	40
Water supply	312	86

Source: U.S. Bureau of the Census, *1987 Census of Governments, vol. 1: Government Organization* (Washington, DC: U.S. Government Printing Office, 1988), 11.

states and for over 52 million people the terms "town" and "township" refer to a unit of local government that is not simply a small city. Two terms are used in discussing towns and townships: the New England town and the congressional township. The latter was created with the former as a model.

The New England Town   The New England town (or sometimes township) is from 20 to 40 square miles in area, about half the size of the average county in New England. These towns include both rural and urban populations. New England town government existed even before the American Revolution.[8] It was designed for the technologically simple needs of a fairly homogeneous rural population most of which lived on small farms.

Today in many parts of New England, annual town meetings still set the tax rate and the budget and make major decisions that affect the community, including the election of officials such as the town clerk, the treasurer, selectpersons, auditors, a road commissioner, a sewer commissioner, a tree warden, constables, members of the board of health, and a school committee. The major town official who is the moderator of the meeting may be elected for a term of as many as three years or on a meeting-by-meeting basis.[9]

The Congressional Township   In 1787, when the Continental Congress set up procedures for surveying and selling public lands in the Northwest Territory, which ultimately became the states of Michigan, Ohio, Indiana, and Wisconsin, it created a geographic unit known as the congressional township (Box 5-2).

In short, the **Northwest Ordinance** attempted to set up New England town-sized blocks of land which might become future units of local govern-

---

Box 5-2   **The Northwest Ordinance of 1787**

The system of measuring land in the Northern states from the Great Lakes to the Pacific was one of the last official acts of the Continental Congress under the old Confederal Constitution. The public lands in the Northwest Territory (Michigan, Ohio, Indiana, and Wisconsin) were to be divided by surveyors into townships of 36 square miles. Each township was then divided into 36 sections of land, each with its own identifying number. These 1-square-mile sections were then divided into quarters of 160 acres each. These in turn were divided into four fields or farms of 40 acres each.

Once established, these procedures were carried westward with the migration of residents of these states.

Source: Ferris E. Lewis, *State and Local Government in Michigan, 8th ed.* (Hillsdale, MI: Hillsdale Educational Publishers, 1979), 127–140.

---

ment. Thus, much of Ohio, Michigan, and Indiana and some of the land farther west which had yet to be purchased from France or taken by force or guile from Native Americans was destined to be divided up into townships, each the same size — 36 square miles.

Since lines on a map often ignore rivers, ridges, hills, valleys, and other geographic features that help shape communities, it is a wonder that any of these uniformly shaped townships actually became units of local government. Many did, however. The process was helped by two political phenomena to which we have already referred: political culture and "the rules of the game." The political culture of New England was carried into the congressional townships in the heads and hearts of the early settlers, many of whom had been born and raised in New England. Along with the moralistic version of American political culture, they brought familiarity with the township as the "natural" form of local government.

The process of making the township part of the state pattern of local government rather than establishing geographically convenient boundaries was helped by the requirement, established quite early in the laws of most states, that when the citizens of an area wished to set up a new county, they had to include whole townships.

Today there are over 16,000 township governments in the 21 states that stretch along the northern third of the United States from Cape Cod in Massachusetts to Puget Sound in Washington.

Municipalities

A **municipality**, or city, is a unit of general-purpose local government created to meet the needs of an urban population. In the era of the walking city, when the urban population was located in a fairly small area, it made sense

Reprinted with permission of James L. Ballard of the National Trust for Historic Preservation.

for urban residents to have their own government, separate from the county or township. Such a government could offer services that the rural population didn't need and deal with problems (for example, fires in tall buildings) that the rural population didn't have.

Until the industrial revolution American cities were few and far between, islands in an agricultural sea. Terms such as "village," "town," and "city" provided a useful way of differentiating urban places in terms of population size, complexity of problems to be dealt with, range of services offered, and appropriate local government structure. The industrial revolution and the automotive revolution promoted the dispersion of urban businesses and the spread of residential concentrations into the countryside.

Today distinctions among local governments which were appropriate for an agricultural America are difficult to apply consistently. There are some very large villages and some very small cities. This confusion is also reflected in the fact that some counties as well as townships offer urban-type services to their "rural" as well as suburban and urban residents.

If this is so, why should we even have separate municipal governments? Why can't county or township government do it all?

There are two answers. First, in some circumstances a county or township government probably can do it all. It depends on the constitution and laws of the state. Second, to understand the special role of the municipality, we have to summarize some intergovernmental history. This summary will involve three terms: "incorporation," "Dillon's rule," and "home rule."

Incorporation of Municipalities   A corporation is an artificial entity created by a group of people. It has legal standing. A corporation can sue and be sued, own property, buy and sell goods and services, and borrow money. It exists independently of the individuals who create it. For people in the business world, incorporation—the act of creating a corporation—puts a buffer between the individual businessperson and liability for anything done in the name of the corporation. Thus, a corporation can go bankrupt, and that's that. The individuals who own the corporation aren't liable for its debts or for other obligations that the corporation cannot meet.

For most of the nineteenth century a distinction existed between municipalities and other local governments that was based on the belief that only municipalities were corporations. For better or worse, the act of municipal incorporation was viewed as a local act, whereas the creation of a county (or township) government was regarded as state act. When counties and townships tried to do the things that cities did—pass local ordinances to deal with health problems, regulate traffic, or offer certain services—they were stopped by many state courts because they were not corporations. The Ohio Supreme Court explained it this way in 1857:

> A municipal corporation proper is created mainly for the interest, advantage, and convenience of the locality and its people; a county organization is created almost exclusively with a view to the policy of the state at large with scarcely an exception, all the powers and functions of the county organization have a direct and exclusive reference to the general administration of that policy.[10]

Similar court decisions during this era existed in many other states. At the national level, Chief Justice Roger B. Taney, whose place in history is linked forever to the Dred Scott decision, declared that "the several counties are nothing more than certain portions of the territory into which the State is divided for the more convenient exercise of the powers of government."[11]

Thus, for individuals to use government to deal with the problems of industrial America at the local level rather than going through the state legislature, it became necessary to create municipal governments. No other form of local government had the authority to offer urban-type services and deal with the problems of densely populated areas.

Lest we give the wrong impression about courts and mislead you about local politics, we hasten to point out that the courts did not decide on their own to interfere with local government. Courts become involved in questions of the ability of governments to do something because individuals sue to prevent the government from acting to regulate or perform some activity. There are, after all, individuals (and businesses) who find it profitable to dump chemicals in lakes and streams or employ children in the fields and factories or who feel that city parking garages, utilities, and day care centers will compete unfairly with theirs. Thus, they go to court to stop a local unit of government from acting.

Today the distinction between locally-created and state-created governments seems somewhat specious. New governments are created at all levels usually because local citizens ask the state to allow them to be created (or to create them). Nevertheless, for a goodly period of our history it appeared that city (municipal) governments could make regulations (also called ordinances or local laws) just because they were a special entity called a corporation.

Dillon's Rule   The authority provided to cities through their corporate status alone was weakened if not destroyed by an Iowa Supreme Court judge named John F. Dillon. His specialty was a relatively new area of public law called municipal law. In the 1880s, when the judge was writing his influential *Commentaries on the Law of Municipal Corporations*, which by 1911 had gone through five editions, America was industrializing rapidly and experimenting with the best way to bring order to its expanding urban areas.

Judge Dillon influenced the use of power by municipal government by interpreting its legal powers in a rather narrow fashion. **Dillon's rule**, as a famous passage from his commentaries is now known, states that

> It is a general and undisputed proposition of law . . . that a municipal corporation possess and can exercise the following powers, and no others: First, those granted in express words; second, those necessarily or fairly implied in or incident to the power expressly granted; third, those essential to the accomplishment of the declared objects and purposes of the corporation — not simply convenient, but indispensable. Any fair, reasonable substantial doubt concerning the existence of power is resolved by the courts against the corporation, and the power is denied.[12]

In short, Judge Dillon interpreted Iowa state law to mean that municipal governments had virtually no implied powers. Any individual or business which sued a city to stop it from doing something and could raise a reasonable suspicion that a city was doing something for convenience rather than necessity would win in court.

To those suspicious of the way some urban politicians were using their power, Judge Dillon's rule was very appealing (no pun intended). Therefore, Dillon's rule was widely accepted as the way things ought to be in most states during the late nineteenth and early twentieth centuries.

Dillon's rule is worth remembering for at least four reasons. First, it provides an excellent example of the fact that expertise is important in the real world. With no legal power beyond the borders of Iowa other than widespread respect for his expertise, Dillon shaped the future of American intergovernmental relations as well as the content of textbooks on the subject. Knowledge can be a political resource. This is a point worth remembering during the sometimes tedious process of acquiring it.

Second, Dillon's rule indicates the importance of the rules of the game. Constitutions, charters, and other basic political documents constitute the rules of the game by which the political process of rule making and enforcement is played. State constitutions and city charters determine whether a city council or county commissioner's court has the authority to regulate a new activity (massage parlors, junkyards, fireworks, video games) or perform a new function (building sports stadiums and parking lots, providing day care facilities). If someone doesn't want to be regulated or thinks tax money shouldn't be spent on activities that offend his or her sensibilities, he or she can take a local government to court. Following Dillon's rule, the courts for many decades ruled against new activities unless the government had express authority from state law or a clause in its charter that expressly granted or "clearly implied" that the local government had the authority to engage in the activity in question.

Third, Dillon's rule made the careful drafting of local government charters very important. If a power wasn't in the original charter, getting it could be a time-consuming process. In most cases it meant that the state legislature had to amend the charter (if it was a charter granted to a specific city by name) or change the laws affecting all general-law municipalities. In some cases the state constitution might have to be amended. All these were potentially expensive and time-consuming procedures.

Fourth, Dillon's rule made the distinction between home-rule government and general-law government an extremely important one. Home rule became virtually essential for growing cities that were likely to have the problems associated with urban development. With home rule, the charters drafted by local charter commissions could be more easily and locally amended or revised. General-law cities might have to wait years to get the authority they needed from either state law or state constitutional amendments.

Home Rule Home rule means that the citizens of a local government choose the charter of that government and can amend or revise it without consulting the state legislature or the statewide electorate. Home rule has two basic dimensions.

First, it allows the local community to determine the structure of the unit of local government. This structure can follow the Jacksonian long ballot model or can use any of the other models which were discussed earlier. Second, the community can decide whether the local government should have the power to pass ordinances, also known as local laws. The community can decide, within the limits of the state laws and constitution, how much authority to give its government and on what subject matters. Home rule invariably means that a local government can make and enforce ordinances. Although there are limits, ordinance authority gives local governments considerable flexibility in dealing with local problems.

Local ordinance-making authority can be granted by the state to units of government which don't have home rule. However, home rule makes ordinance authority a sure thing. In the absence of ordinance-making authority, general-law governments can only enforce the laws passed by the state.

Thus, a local problem such as hazardous waste disposal would require action by the state legislature and the governor.

Home-rule governments can react to new situations quickly by passing and enforcing local laws. If its home-rule government lacks the authority to deal with a specific situation, the local community can still amend its charter to grant that authority a lot more quickly than it can get it from the state.

In many states home rule is available only to cities of a certain size. Although cities with populations of 5000 or more usually have home rule, very few counties and townships have it.[13] Thus, a county with a population of several hundred thousand may be stuck with a structure more suited for an earlier period of American history and may have little power to deal with modern conditions such as the sprawl of populations and problems beyond the boundaries of the home-rule cities within it.

In many states, county and township governments lack the power to deal with modern problems, and so other units of government (cities and special districts) are created to deal with them. Although municipalities with home rule are equipped to deal with modern problems within their borders, they are still vulnerable to problems originating outside those borders. The units of government (county and/or township) within whose boundaries the sources of some of these problems lie unfortunately lack the authority to deal with them. Many city officials would like to see township and/or county governments equipped with the authority to take appropriate action. The vulnerability of cities and the incapacity of some counties constitute one of the major pairs of misfortunes in the intergovernmental scene.

This pair of misfortunes will not go away until the intergovernmental system is modified by means of state and local action. The suggested solutions range from city-county consolidation to simply granting counties home rule.

Independent School Districts

In five states and the District of Columbia, primary and secondary education are provided by general-purpose governments: counties, townships, or municipalities. The school systems run by these governments may have a board and be divided into geographic areas called districts for administrative purposes. These school districts are not considered separate units of government; they are merely agencies of the local government that controls them.

In 30 states elementary and secondary education is given special recognition in the state constitution through the requirement that schools be administered by special units of government which are independent of county, city, or township supervision. Generally referred to as school districts, these units of government are more correctly called independent school districts.

A "mixed" situation exists in 15 states where general-purpose governments provide education in some places and independent school districts provide it in others. Furthermore, in some states the school boards of cities or counties may be elected rather than appointed by the city council or the county board of supervisors.

Special Districts

Sometimes called nonschool special districts, these units of local government perform a range of services which is usually narrower than those performed by cities, counties, and townships. Many special districts perform only one service. As Table 5.3 indicates, special districts are created to perform many different types of functions. Most special districts are located within a single county, and one-fourth of them have the same boundaries as an existing general-purpose government. However, more than 2400 special districts have territory in two or more counties, and some cross state lines. The latter are usually involved in parks, bridges, ports, mass transit, or airports.

The significance of special districts for many observers of the intergovernmental scene is that the public knows so little about them and takes little interest in seeing that they wisely use their considerable powers to tax, spend, borrow, and duplicate efforts. Of the 19,675 special districts on which the U.S. Census Bureau has financial data, nearly 40 percent have

Table 5.3 SPECIAL DISTRICT GOVERNMENTS BY FUNCTION: 1987

Function	Number	Percent
Single-function districts:		
Natural resources*	6,360	21.5
Fire protection	5,070	17.2
Housing and community development	3,464	11.7
Water supply	3,060	10.4
Cemeteries	1,627	5.5
Sewerage	1,607	5.4
Parks and recreation	1,004	3.4
Libraries	830	2.8
Hospitals	783	2.7
Education buildings	713	2.4
Highways	621	2.1
Health	484	1.6
Airports	369	1.3
Other†	1,489	5.0
Multiple-function districts	2,051	7.0
Total	29,532	100

*Includes drainage and flood control, irrigation, and soil and water conservation.
†Includes parking facilities, water transport and terminals, solid waste disposal, utilities, and industrial development.

Source: U.S. Bureau of the Census, *1987 Census of Governments, vol. 1: Government Organization* (Washington, DC: U.S. Government Printing Office, 1988), xi.

outstanding debts of more than $1 million. Over a thousand have debts of $5 million or more.[14]

Although we are inclined to share the view that special districts make the intergovernmental landscape more complex than need be, we think it is important for future leaders of the system to keep in mind the possibility that the proliferation of special districts is a sign that something needs attending to rather than a direct cause of the problem.

Just as there are a variety of causes for a puddle of liquid on the floor during a soap opera—a leaky roof, an untrained puppy, a spilled beverage, an overflowing bathtub, a freshly used umbrella, a defective dishwasher, copious weeping—so there are a variety of causes for the creation of so many units of local government, special districts or otherwise.

REASONS FOR CREATING ADDITIONAL LOCAL GOVERNMENTS

In the past 25 years the population of the United States has grown by 25 percent. The number of municipalities has grown by 5 percent. However, the number of special districts has grown by 60 percent. In other words, special districts have increased at more than twice the rate that the population has.

Early in this chapter we mentioned several reasons for having local government (delegation, local autonomy, access, personnel management, system legitimacy, and resource management). Although an increase in population may require some new units of government, it seems reasonable to look beyond population increase and the general advantages of local government for an explanation of the proliferation of special districts.

There are at least five reasons for creating new local governments: constitutional and statutory restrictions, the power of interest groups, private profit, intergovernmental convenience, and defensive incorporation. In many if not most cases, more than one reason is involved.

Constitutional and Statutory Restrictions

Not all states create governments equal. As Table 5.4 indicates, some states give more authority to local governments than do others. Furthermore, while cities nearly always have more flexibility than counties do, the degree of flexibility varies considerably among the states. At a minimum this means that in some states, communities facing new problems may not be able to use existing governments such as the county or the township to solve their problems. Thus, they may create new units of government such as municipalities and special districts.

In some states it is easier to create a new unit of local government than it is to go through the state political system to change the state law or constitutional provision that restricts one's local government. Table 5.5 shows the

Table 5.4   STATES RANKED BY DEGREE OF AUTHORITY GRANTED TO LOCAL GOVERNMENT

State and composite rank*	State rank by cities	State rank by counties
28. Alabama	23	37
5. Alaska	13	2
25. Arizona	14	38
21. Arkansas	34	6
18. California	17	17
42. Colorado	37	45
4. Connecticut	4	†
9. Delaware	26	5
26. Florida	30	14
30. Georgia	18	32
40. Hawaii	‡	22
50. Idaho	47	44
12. Illinois	10	19
37. Indiana	40	24
44. Iowa	39	30
14. Kansas	15	11
29. Kentucky	36	16
10. Louisiana	16	8
2. Maine	2	20
6. Maryland	7	9
43. Massachusetts	41	48
16. Michigan	3	2
17. Minnesota	19	12
45. Mississippi	31	35
19. Missouri	8	47
31. Montana	38	18
41. Nebraska	24	41
46. Nevada	45	33
22. New Hampshire	27	36
36. New Jersey	35	31
48. New Mexico	49	23
35. New York	44	25
3. North Carolina	5	3
24. North Dakota	25	21
27. Ohio	11	42
13. Oklahoma	12	27
1. Oregon	6	1
7. Pennsylvania	20	4
38. Rhode Island	42	†
15. South Carolina	21	7
47. South Dakota	43	39
34. Tennessee	32	34
11. Texas	1	43

continued

Table 5.4   STATES RANKED BY DEGREE OF AUTHORITY GRANTED TO LOCAL
GOVERNMENT *Continued*

State and composite rank*	State rank by cities	State rank by counties
20. Utah	28	10
39. Vermont	48	46
8. Virginia	9	13
32. Washington	33	29
49. West Virginia	46	40
23. Wisconsin	22	15
33. Wyoming	29	26

*A rank of 1 means that this state gives a particular type of local government a high degree of discretionary authority.
†There are only 48 states ranked in the county column because neither Connecticut nor Rhode Island has organized county governments.
‡There are only 49 states ranked in the city column because in Hawaii all four local governments are either counties or city-county consolidations.

Source: Advisory Commission on Intergovernmental Relations, *Measuring Discretionary Authority*, (Washington, DC: ACIR, 1981), 59.

12 states which lead the country in the number of special districts. Although there are parallels between population rank and interest group rank, it would appear that there are also additional reasons why these states contain 61 percent of the special districts in the intergovernmental system.

Interest Group Power

As Table 5.4 indicates, Texas ranks first among the states in terms of the discretionary authority given to cities. However, it ranks forty-third among the states in terms of the authority given to counties. With the most restricted county governments in the nation, communities in Texas organize other units of government to obtain services and acquire the power to regulate various legal and illegal entrepreneurial activities. Texas led the nation in new municipal incorporations in the 1980s and ranks third in the total number of special districts.

There have been attempts to better equip counties in Texas to deal with urban problems. However, a few powerful interest groups have been able to prevent legislation which would strengthen county government; thus, late in December and around the Fourth of July, roadside stands selling fireworks spring up just outside the boundaries of most Texas cities. These cities can regulate fireworks and usually ban their sale in the interest of health and fire prevention. However, Texas counties do not have that authority, even though they try to get it in almost every session of the legislature. Thus, the power of interest groups not only dooms Texas county governments to budget for and fight grass fires every January and July, it also encourages communities to create additional governments.[15]

Table 5.5   LEADING SPECIAL DISTRICT STATES

State	Rank in population	Rank in special districts	Number of special districts
California	1	2	2734
New York	2	10	978
Texas	3	3	1892
Pennsylvania	4	4	1805
Illinois	5	1	2783
Indiana	12	12	836
Missouri	15	6	1217
Washington	20	7	1177
Colorado	28	9	1085
Oregon	30	11	876
Kansas	32	5	1387
Nebraska	35	8	1119

Source: U.S. Bureau of the Census, *1987 Census of Governments, vol. 1: Government Organization* (Washington, DC: U.S. Government Printing Office, 1988), x.

Private Profit

In some states the creation of a special district is a very profitable activity. It usually involves gaining control over several aces of land within commuting distance of a good-sized city and then developing that land using money borrowed by a government one has created for one's own purposes. As Virginia Marion Perrenod observes in her detailed study of Houston-area developer districts,

> The old axiom of "never use your own money to make money" is certainly true for the developer who has discovered a bonanza for financing his development. Enabling laws that allow districts to be formed either by a percentage of property holders or by a percentage of holders in value are the key to this public development for private purposes.[16]

These governments are special districts and are registered under a variety of titles, such as municipal utility district and water development district. The process usually involves the steps listed in Box 5-3. If all goes well, the developer sells all the improved land at a handsome profit and moves on, leaving behind a unit of government which owes a lot of money and a community of property owners to run that government and tax themselves to pay off the debt. Of course, all may not go well.

First, all the property may not be purchased. Those who did purchase the land, including the developer, may have to shoulder the tax burden to pay off the bonds issued by the special district. Since the district (not the developer) owes the debt, the developer may decide he or she doesn't want to own the

---

Box 5-3 **Creating Profitable Governments**

Major steps followed by developers in creating a special district in unincorporated areas:

1. The developer acquires control over a parcel of several hundred acres, usually by buying a little and purchasing an option to buy the rest.

2. The developer moves employees onto the land and begins the survey and development work. While this is going on, the employees establish residency to be able to vote. As soon as residency has been established, the developer makes sure they register.

3. The developer initiates the legal procedures set forth in state law to create a special district. This usually involves a public hearing that few attend and a referendum to determine whether the residents of the area approve. Since most of the voters are employees of the developer, little money is invested in public opinion polls to predict the outcome.

4. When the special district is finally created, the developer has control of a virtually private government. This government can borrow money by issuing bonds. The bonds are attractive to people in certain income tax brackets because the interest is not subject to income tax.

5. Having obtained the money to pay for engineering work, street construction, water lines, and so forth by borrowing, the special district then hires the developer or someone the developer approves of to put in these improvements.

6. When all or most of the improvements are installed, the developer advertises and sells the land to prospective home builders.

Source: Woodworth G. Thrombley, *Special Districts and Authorities in Texas*, (Austin: Institute of Public Affairs, University of Texas, 1959).

---

land anymore and simply fail to pay off the mortgage owed to the bank. The bank then becomes the owner of the land. Other landowners may not be in so flexible a position. They may have invested their life savings in the land and the new house that is on it.

A second possibility is that the development work in the district may be poorly planned or improperly performed. In unincorporated areas, land is cheaper than it is in cities but there is no city government to make inspections to ensure that utility construction and home building are performed properly. If the "improvements" don't last very long, in addition to paying off the bonds, the taxpayers of the special district may have to pay for expensive repairs and maintenance.

These unhappy scenarios are not the usual case. Nevertheless, many observers of the intergovernmental scene are less than enthusiastic about creating more special districts in the intergovernmental system, especially "developer-owned" districts.

Intergovernmental Convenience

Special districts sometimes are created by other units of government. The two major reasons are to coordinate a large expensive service and to avoid taking responsibility for offering new functions.

Coordinating a Large Expensive Service   A major reason local governments may find it convenient to create a new special district is to offer a service such as mass transit to an area larger than that of any of the local governments involved. Large special districts offer four noteworthy political advantages.

First, a multigovernment special district can move the day-to-day aggravations of offering the service a step farther away from the elected officials.

Second, large special districts have a broader tax base. Furthermore, because they are taxing authorities, the bills they send do not reflect negatively on the "no-new-taxes-read-my lips" promises of the local government officials.

Third, special districts can borrow money to build improvements. Therefore, the debt burden of existing governments won't be increased, and their ability to borrow for their own projects is less likely to be directly affected.

Fourth, in cases where a metropolitan area crosses state lines or when a complex of numerous local governments already exists, a large multigovernment special district may be a valuable coordinating device.[17]

Avoiding Responsibility for New Functions   The traditions, the rules of the game, and the personal preferences of some public officials may encourage them to avoid taking responsibility for offering a new service. Thus, they may promote the creation of a special district to offer the service within their territorial jurisdiction. This is one reason for the proliferation of fire districts and road districts in some counties. The county is empowered to offer the service or improvement, but the county board must raise the tax rate to pay for it. Raising taxes takes more fortitude than many officials appear to possess.

Defensive Incorporation

To incorporate, as we recall from our discussion of Dillon's rule, is to create a new municipality. Defensive incorporation is the process of creating a new municipality to avoid annexation by a nearby larger city.

Annexation is the act of adding land to an existing unit of government. In the American context we usually think in terms of unincorporated areas when we discuss annexation.

An **unincorporated area** is land that lies outside the boundaries of an existing municipality. A municipality, you may recall, comes into being by means of incorporation.

In some states, such as Texas, it is very easy for a city to grow by annexing. The city simply follows a procedure established by the state. Residents and businesses can be annexed whether they like it or not. In other states, such as Michigan, it is very difficult for a city to annex adjacent land because a review board that is generally hostile to annexation must approve. In many states the residents of the unincorporated area must approve of the process, sometimes by a special majority.

Whether annexation is easy or hard, one condition always exists: The land to be annexed must be outside the boundaries of an existing city. Even though it lies within a special district, township, or county, unincorporated land usually can be annexed. For this reason, residents of areas outside the boundaries of large cities may find it useful to protect themselves from annexation by incorporating a city of their own.

From the point of view of those who think that these residents are trying to avoid responsibility for helping the larger city deal with its problems, the act of incorporation is sometimes called **defensive incorporation**.

Defensive incorporation is associated with pejorative terms such as "exclusionary zoning" and "parasitism." **Exclusionary zoning** is the practice of passing land use regulations which make it very difficult to build high-density, low-cost housing of the sort that would enable some of the less affluent population of the central city to move to the suburban city.

Parasitism is sometimes used to describe actions such as defensive incorporation and exclusionary zoning when practiced by people who own businesses in or have high-salaried jobs in the central city of a metropolitan area. The idea is that these individuals are taking profits and salaries out of the city without putting very much back into it.

Since most central cities have many expensive problems to solve, people who locate their homes outside the city and prevent their inclusion in the central city's tax base are not highly regarded by central-city political leaders.

Most of the terms we have just introduced are judgmental in that they attribute selfish motivations to the actions of others. Whether or not these are the true motivations is not for us to decide. We simply introduce these terms because they are part of the intergovernmental scene, especially in metropolitan areas.

A less judgmental view of defensive incorporation involves the consideration of three facts about community decision making. First, not everyone in a community is involved in making every decision. Second, decisions are usually made for more than one reason. Third, wrong decisions are sometimes made for altruistic reasons just as right ones are made for selfish reasons. When a local population decides something, it is neither a unidimensional nor a totally homogeneous act. Defensive incorporation stripped of its emotional weight simply means that a suburban community goes through the procedures required by the state to become a municipality in order to avoid becoming part of a large city.

The central cities of many metropolitan areas today are completely surrounded by small and medium-size cities. Some of the surrounding cities are products of defensive incorporation. Others were there all along; the big city just grew out to meet them.

It is not our purpose here to decide whether suburban residents incorporate out of good motivations such as the desire for community self-government, a government whose headquarters are located within a few miles of one's residence, lower taxes, better services, a better chance to influence decisions that affect the community, and a safer environment in which to raise children or incorporate because of irresponsibility, selfishness, narrow-mindedness, or bigotry.

In sum, it is fair to say that many people believe that defensive incorporation is not a noble act. The fact that they believe this has an impact on the way they deal with the political system, the kinds of policies they promote at the state and national levels which may affect local politics, and the way they view the residents of these newly incorporated areas.

ALTERNATIVES TO THE CREATION OF NEW INTERGOVERNMENTS

For most of this century it has been convenient for urban populations to create new units of local government to obtain one or more urban-type services. The alternatives that follow are usually less convenient but are worth reviewing briefly. Yesterday's inconvenience may be tomorrow's opportunity.

1. Do without the service. For example, instead of twice-weekly trash pickup, one can recycle most of one's own trash, make a compost heap in the backyard and take the rest to the nearest landfill. For apartment dwellers, a compost heap is not usually an option. Other services may be less easy to do without or to improvise on one's own.

2. Through the existing local government, contract with private business for the service. Privatization is a growing trend; in many states local governments are offering some services through private contractors rather than using local government employees. Table 5.2, for example, indicates not only the variety of services offered by counties but also the fact that every one of the 12 services listed is sometimes offered via contracts with private firms.

3. Demand that one of the existing governments use its authority to offer the service even if this means an increase in taxes. Adding a city police department when one already has a sheriff's department costs money. It may be chapter to increase the sheriff's budget so that more deputies can be hired and trained to patrol urban areas.

If the existing county legislative body won't vote more funds or if the existing sheriff won't even ask for them, new county officials can be chosen through the electoral process. This means entering the political arena. There's a first time for everything.

The tremendous potential for the 3000 county governments to serve as areawide units of government and thus reduce the proliferation of special districts is best represented by the Lakewood plan in California. There, Los Angeles County, which first contracted with the city of Lakewood to offer urban-type services, eventually offered services such as trash collection and fire and police protection to many of the small towns and cities within the county.

4. If the existing government doesn't have the authority to do something, it can be helped to get to that authority through the passage of state laws or a constitutional amendment.

This is how the home-rule movement began. Many cities created in the eighteenth century were given restrictive charters by the state legislature or were created by general laws which provided only expressed powers. Dillon's rule didn't help the situation very much. The individuals and groups who organized the movement to get home rule for cities succeeded in getting it for counties in a few states. However, most states have yet to allow county and township governments to obtain home rule.

5. Consider the Virginia system. As some states do, Virginia empowers counties to perform many urban functions, including regulation of land use. However, Virginia also allows cities to become, in effect, counties.[18] This system is not used in any other state. Perhaps that is why Virginia, although it ranks fourteenth in the United States in terms of population, ranks *last* in terms of units of government per county and forty-fourth in terms of total governments.

In Virginia, urban communities above 5000 inhabitants decide whether they wish to be towns or cities. When a town or an unincorporated area with 5000 or more inhabitants decides to become a city, it takes on all the legal powers and responsibilities of a county, including welfare and educational services. Even though it may be surrounded geographically by the county of which it was formerly a part, the city ceases to be part of that county.

Virginia towns, by contrast, remain in the county. The decision whether to become a town or city in Virginia is essentially a decision about taking on more responsibility. In Virginia, counties have the authority to perform many of the functions that cities perform, and thus there is less motivation to incorporate or create special districts. As James Campbell of the Virginia Municipal League has observed, "Our city-county separation is probably the reason why there are fewer taxing authorities in Virginia than any other state."[19] As a result, Virginians appear to have an easier job keeping track of their governments.

ARE THERE TOO MANY LOCAL GOVERNMENTS?

As Table 5.6 indicates, the total number of governments is lower than it has been since the early 1960s. Virtually all this reduction has been the result of a state-by-state consolidation of rural school districts that was completed by the early 1970s. After the process was completed, the number of units of local government began a steady increase. Municipalities and special districts have been the major source of this growth. If this trend continues, it is very likely that we will someday be back up to a total number of units of government that exceeds 90,000. There are several possible answers to this question.

Yes, There Are Too Many

The trend toward more local governments which has become apparent since the 1970s (11,000 more special districts and over 1000 more municipalities) is of concern to business, political, and scholarly observers. These observers believe that the multiplication of local governments can lead to citizen confusion, fragmentation of authority, wasted resources, and ultimately a decline in legitimacy.[20]

Over 20 years ago, the Committee for Economic Development, a prestigious organization consisting of top executives from major corporations and other leading American institutions, issued a two-part report on their analysis of the governmental system. The local government portion included the nine recommendations listed in Box 5-4. Similar recommendations can be found in the literature of the ACIR and the National Municipal League.

We point out the work of the Committee for Economic Development to indicate the concern of the business community with the intergovernments. Naturally, these executives all value economy and efficiency, especially in the governments to which their firms pay taxes. However, the thrust of their

Table 5.6   GOVERNMENT UNITS: 1962–1987

Type	1987	1982	1977	1972	1967	1962
National	1	1	1	1	1	1
State	50	50	50	50	50	50
County	3,042	3,041	3,042	3,044	3,049	3,043
Municipal	19,200	19,076	18,862	18,517	18,048	18,000
Township	16,691	16,734	16,822	16,991	17,105	17,142
School district	14,721	14,851	15,174	15,781	21,782	34,678
Special district	29,523	28,078	25,962	23,885	21,264	18,323
Total	83,237	81,831	79,913	78,269	81,299	91,237

Source: U.S. Bureau of the Census, *1987 Census of Governments, vol. 1: Government Organization* (Washington, DC: U.S. Government Printing Office, 1988), vi.

Box 5-4 **Recommendations of the Committee for Economic Development**

1. The number of local governments in the United States, now about 80,000, should be reduced at least 80 percent.

2. The number of overlapping layers of local government found in most states should be severely curtailed.

3. Popular election should be confined to members of the policy-making body and to the chief executive in governments where the strong mayor form is preferred to the council-manager plan.

4. Each local unit should have a single chief executive, either elected by the people or appointed by the local legislative body, with all administrative agencies and personnel fully responsible to him or her; election of department heads should be halted.

5. Personnel practices based on merit and professional competence should replace the personal or partisan spoils systems found in most counties and many other local units.

6. County modernization should be pressed with special vigor, since counties—everywhere except New England—have a high but undeveloped potential for solving the problems of rural, urban, and most metropolitan communities.

7. Once modernized, local governments should be entrusted with broad legal powers permitting them to plan, finance, and execute programs suited to the special needs, interests, and desires of their citizens.

8. The 50 state constitutions should be revamped either by legislative amendment or through constitutional conventions concentrating on modernization of local government to provide for boundary revision, extension of legal authority, and elimination of unneeded overlapping layers.

9. The terms and conditions of federal and state grants-in-aid should be revised to encourage the changes recommended in this statement.

Source: Committee for Economic Development, *Modernizing Local Government: To Secure a Balanced Federalism*, (New York: Committee for Economic Development, 1966), 17–19.

argument is that American communities need to deal with the problems facing us and that it is the obligation of those who derive advantages from the system to take on this task:

> [T]he need for action is urgent; the responsibility of each citizen to share, to participate, and to exert initiative in constructive endeavors cannot be evaded. And that responsibility bears most heavily upon those favored in education, wealth, and positions of trust. . . . To shirk this challenge is to deny our birthright of freedom and self-government.[21]

As Box 5-4 indicates, the first suggestion the committee made was to reduce the number of local governments by more than 75 percent.[22] This point is worth considering for three reasons.

First, it indicates a fairly distant goal that may take a generation or more of state and local leadership to achieve. These executives are well aware that the dismantling or consolidation of 64,000 units of local government in the near future is highly unlikely.

Second, it may be a realizable goal. From 1962 to 1987, the number of school districts did decrease by more than 50 percent. Furthermore, between 1980 and 1986, 62 places surrendered their separate municipal identity, 42 by dissolution and 20 by consolidation. Although these 62 dissolutions ran counter to the trend of 249 new cities, it is worth noting that the creation of a city is not an irreversible act.[23]

Third, it is important to consider the suggestions of the committee not only on their merits but because they indicate that local government reform is not merely a parochial concern or one limited to starry-eyed idealists. Hardheaded businesspeople who lead national corporations are concerned with the shape of the intergovernmental system, just as we are.[24]

Kellogg and Battle Creek

Since actions sometimes speak louder than lists of recommendations, the Kellogg Company's use of its political resources in Battle Creek, Michigan, is worth some attention. In 1978, Kellogg decided that it needed to expand its corporate headquarters. It had been in Battle Creek for over 70 years and wanted to stay. However, its executives were discouraged by the urban-sub-urban bickering which took place between the city of Battle Creek and Battle Creek Township. Furthermore, Kellogg was having trouble recruiting executive talent because of a reluctance to bring families into a no-growth economically depressed area.

The company lacked the political resources to get the state to change the restrictive annexation laws which made it virtually impossible for a city in Michigan to extend its boundaries and thus acquire the tax base to finance needed service improvements. However, the company did have influence in Battle Creek (city and township) and decided to use it.

First, it looked around at other areas with bickering urban and suburban governments where consolidations had led to **economies of scale** and economic growth. The mergers of Toronto, Nashville, Minneapolis, Indianapolis, and a few others all indicated that mergers were difficult but not impossible. If political resources (including carrots, sticks, leadership skills, and lots of time and energy selling the idea to the public) were carefully invested, consolidations could and did occur. Second, Kellogg commissioned a Michigan law firm in another city to study the procedures for merging the city (population 35,700) and the township (20,600) and to prepare a precise timetable for announcement and publicity prior to the referendum which would have to take place before the merger.

Third, it prepared a plan for merger which would bring maximum benefits to as many political actors as possible. The plan included the creation of a fund to provide seed money for the creation of small businesses and equal city and township representation on an expanded city council which would include all incumbent councilpersons. No one's seat would be at risk until the 1984–1985 elections. The showpiece of the plan was that Kellogg and its more than 700 headquarters staff members would not leave Battle Creek for a better offer elsewhere. Not only would Kellogg stay, it would build a new $20 million to $30 million worldwide headquarters and put the tax savings resulting from the merger into the seed money fund. The tax savings and thus the seed money fund would amount to more than $1.6 million over a five-year period.[25]

In May 1982, with no advance notice, Kellogg revealed its plan. The message was simple. In effect, Kellogg told the citizens of Battle Creek Township and the City of Battle Creek:

> Allow your governments to keep on bickering over who gets new economic development opportunities, or merge them and start thinking about the whole area of Battle Creek as one interconnected community. We have been, and we will be a responsible citizen of this community; that is why we are going to all this trouble.[26]

On November 2, 1982, the citizens of Battle Creek voted yes to the merger of city and township and to economic development. Since that referendum, the area has attracted new jobs and domestic and foreign plants, has become a regional retailing center, and is now another success story of corporate-government partnership.[27]

Shortly after the election, noted intergovernmental reporter Neal R. Pierce, observed that

> For years, good government groups, lacking clout, have fought a lonely battle for metropolitan consolidations — rarely succeeding. But if forward looking corporations enter the ring, the odds could start to change dramatically.[28]

Since 1982, few corporations have entered the intergovernmental arena to promote rationalization. Too many have used the competition for new jobs and industry to play off one community against another. As a responsible corporate citizen, Kellogg went to a lot of trouble to give Battle Creek a chance to keep a major resource in its political economy. It is worth noting that Tony the Tiger acted a little differently from the tiger Exxon is trying to put in your tank. Exxon quietly left New York for Dallas in 1989, apparently having made no effort to use its resources to promote reforms in exchange for staying. That Battle Creek is much smaller than New York and that Exxon's influence might thus be proportionately smaller are noteworthy factors in the corporate-government relationship.

Nevertheless, the Kellogg example is worth some attention in that it indicates that corporate America is not united in either altruism or greed. It depends in part on the individual in charge of the corporation. Gary Costley, the vice president of Kellogg in charge of the merger project, asked a question worth asking in many corporate boardrooms:

> We said to ourselves, we've been here 70 years. It is fair just to pull up stakes and leave without giving the citizens of this community a chance to do something about what we regard as a fixable problem?[29]

The response, of course, depends on who is answering the question.

No, There Aren't Too Many Governments

It is important to note that not all students of the intergovernmental system are equally committed to reforming local government by means of consolidation or dissolution. Some take the position that the proliferation of overlapping units of local government represents a rational response of local communities to their problems. If government is a tool for solving a community's problems, their argument goes, why shouldn't some communities choose a variety of tools instead of just one?

In 1988, two studies of the St. Louis, Missouri, metropolitan area, were released. Numerous governments compete for economic resources and development in this metropolitan area. The two studies came to radically different conclusions. One was sponsored by the ACIR. Its principal investigators were Ronald J. Oakerson and Roger B. Parks. The title of their study is *Metropolitan Organization: The St. Louis Case*. Its purpose was to learn how a system with extensive jurisdictional fragmentation actually worked. After a careful examination of the 91 cities and many special districts in the St. Louis County area, the authors found a great deal of cooperation through formal and informal agreements among political leaders and public officials in the St. Louis area. Box 5-5 provides some examples of these cooperative arrangements.

What did they not find, however, was a system in place to deal adequately with distressed communities. As the authors expressed it,

> A complex metropolitan area that has performed well in terms of service responsiveness and in finding efficient ways to deliver services may not perform equally well in assisting distressed communities.[30]

The residents of most distressed communities tend to be racial minorities who are taxing themselves at relatively high rates but are unable to raise revenues to deliver the kinds of services enjoyed by their more advantaged neighbors. This disparity in fiscal resources is not specific to St. Louis or to Missouri. It is one of the major problems confronting state and local government today.

In contrast to the ACIR study was one submitted by a group of local citizens who were appointed to make reform recommendations. The Board of Freeholders consisted of 19 members: 9 appointed by the mayor of St. Louis, 9 appointed by the St. Louis County executive, and 1 appointed by the governor of Missouri. Their plan suggested a radical reorganization of the St.

Box 5-5   **Examples of Functional Cooperation in the St. Louis City–County Area**

POLICE AND FIRE SERVICES

1. An areawide major case squad pools investigative resources from a large number of separate police departments to respond to serious crimes.

2. The St. Louis County Police and Fire Training Academy supplies recruit training for all police and fire departments in the county.

3. Mutual aid agreements link all fire departments in the county and St. Louis City.

4. Joint dispatching arrangements are common among both police and fire departments.

5. The Regional Justice Information System (REJIS) links all police dispatchers in the city and county to a common data base for information related to crime and criminals. An areawide 911 system operates throughout the county.

6. The Greater St. Louis Fire Chiefs' Association facilitates the sharing of specialized equipment among fire departments.

PUBLIC EDUCATION

1. The Cooperating School Districts of the St. Louis Suburban Areas supplies members with a large audiovisual collection and provides for joint purchasing of supplies and equipment.

2. The Regional Consortium for Education and Technology supplies members with computer technology, software, training, and maintenance.

Source: Roger B. Parks and Ronald J. Oakerson, "St. Louis: The ACIR Study," *Intergovernmental Perspective.* (Winter 1989), 9–10.

Louis County area. It pointed out that approximately 400,000 residents in unincorporated St. Louis County were not being well served largely because the county did not have an adequate tax base to provide municipal-type services at anywhere near the quality offered in many of the municipalities.[31]

In his comparison of the freeholders' plan and the ACIR study, Donald Phares noted that the resource disparity between rich and poor municipalities and between municipalities as a whole and the county has been worsened by "land grab annexation" and incorporation activity. "The most fiscally productive areas in unincorporated St. Louis County are literally being grabbed up," he observed, "while the less resource rich areas remained for the county to take care of as its diminishing resources allow."[32]

The freeholders recommended the creation of 37 new municipalities to cover the entire county. Some of these municipalities would consist of both a formerly unincorporated area and one or more existing cities that would be consolidated into a larger new city. Although the freeholders' plan was supposed to be voted on by all the residents of St. Louis County in spring 1989, legal action by individuals and organizations threatened by the plan successfully prevented the vote.

There is no reason to believe, however, that if the vote had taken place, it would have led to an overwhelming victory for the reorganization advocates. In 1926 a proposal to merge the city and county under a city government failed, and since that time efforts to deal with the limited resources of the county have been defeated at the polls.[33]

The scholarly debate over consolidation versus proliferation will not be decided in the near future in St. Louis or in very many other metropolitan areas of the United States. Unless political actors with considerable power can be persuaded to act, as Kellog did in Battle Creek, the real-world debate will continue to be resolved in favor of proliferation.

We leave it up to you to decide whether the saturation point has been reached in your state and community and where to take it from there. We recommend that you take a close look at both studies of St. Louis County as you prepare to make a positive contribution to the debate in your community. Whether you come down on the side of proliferation, on that of consolidation, or somewhere in between, it will be useful for you to know something about the dynamics that lead to the creation of additional units of government because those dynamics will continue to operate for a long time.

Conclusion

In addition to the seven reasons for the study of local government listed in Chapter 1, it is worth noting that some top executives of corporate America have long expressed a concern with the effectiveness and efficiency of local government. This concern goes beyond decisions about where to locate new facilities. It involves an interest in the shape of the national pattern of local governance.

Restructuring efforts are under way in several states. As a result, it is very likely that sooner or later you will be asked to vote on or perhaps help promote state and local reforms which affect the number, structure, and powers of local governments. Therefore, it makes sense to prepare for informed discussion on remodeling, dismantling, or leaving as is.

We began this chapter by observing that 83,000 governments may be more than we need. Although social, economic, and even political changes beyond the boundaries of any state or community have created pressures for the establishment of more and more governments, we have attempted to indicate that there are ways of slowing the growth and even reducing the number of units of local government.

The thrust of our argument has been that the foundation of a unit of government and its source of authority set limits on what that government can and cannot do. In some states, general-purpose governments such as the county are not allowed to deal with certain types of problems. If the problems are to be dealt with, either these existing units will have to be given the authority or new ones will have to be created. We are suggesting that giving adequate power to existing units may be a way to slow the growth in the number of units of government. A logical way to begin the process of intergovernmental reduction is to examine the foundations of local governments, the power available to them, and the methods or procedures for altering, consolidating, or abolishing them.

In sum, it matters who runs our local governments. These governments have great potential for problem solving. The question is whether our needs for local governance require 80,000 units of government smaller in area than a county.

Study Objectives

1. Identify the major types of local government. Have they all increased in numbers in the past 25 years? If so, have they all increased at the same rate?
2. Identify the reasons why we have local government.
3. Identify the sources of authority for local governments.
4. Identify the basic types of local government structure in terms of the legislative-executive dimension and the chief executive-executive branch dimension.
5. Identify reasons for creating new local governments.
6. Identify the steps in creating a special district.
7. Identify Dillon's rule and its relationship to home rule.
8. Identify the Virginia system of towns and cities.
9. Identify alternatives to the creation of new local governments.
10. Identify some of the reasons for merging existing governments or slowing the rate of creation of new ones.
11. What did the Kellogg Company do to promote intergovernmental progress?
12. Identify the two different views of fragmentation in the St. Louis area.

Glossary

annexation The act of adding land to an existing unit of government, usually a municipality (city). Since cities cannot take land from one another, only unincorporated land can be annexed. In some states it is very easy for cities to annex land; in others it is almost impossible.

charters Local constitutions that are usually given to municipalities (cities).

defensive incorporation The act of creating a new municipality in order to avoid annexation by a large one nearby.

Dillon's rule A principle of law that states that cities do not have implied powers; they can do only that which is specifically granted by their charters.

economies of scale Savings from consolidation and reduction in duplication that arise in any large enterprise whether it is a government or a business. At a minimum, these savings occur first from buying at wholesale rather than retail prices and second because one set of decision makers and procedures rather than several is involved in doing the buying or offering the service. Economies of scale have limits. They decline after a certain size is reached. The size varies from one type of service or function to another.

exclusionary zoning The practice of passing land use regulations which make it very difficult to build high-density, low-cost housing of the sort that would enable people of modest means to live in an area.

general-purpose government A unit of government that offers a wide range of services and contains all three branches of government: legislative, executive, and judicial.

general-law cities Municipalities which do not have home rule. A contemporary term might be "generic cities." These are cities whose charters or constitutions all follow a pattern established by the state law or constitution.

home rule The citizens of a local government choose the charter of that government and can amend or revise it without consulting the state legislature or the statewide electorate.

municipality A unit of general-purpose local government created to meet the needs of an urban population—a city.

Northwest Ordinance One of the last official acts of the Continental Congress. Passed in 1787, this law organized the lands ceded by several of the states to the confederation. These lands included the Northwest Territory, which now includes Ohio, Indiana, Illinois, Michigan, Wisconsin, and Minnesota.

parasitism A pejorative term sometimes used to describe the suburbs of large cities. It asserts that individuals who work or own businesses in the city and live in the suburbs are taking profits and salaries out of the city without putting very much back into it.

special-purpose governments Governments that specialize in a limited number of services.

unincorporated area Land outside the boundaries of a municipality. In virtuality all states the general-purpose government responsible for unincorporated areas is the county; in some states it is the township or the township and county.

Endnotes

1. Joel C. Miller, "Municipal Annexation and Boundary Change," in *The Municipal Yearbook 1988* (Washington, DC: International City Management Association, 1988), 60–61.
2. U.S. Bureau of the Census, *1987 Census of Governments*, vol. 1: *Government Organization* (Washington, DC: U.S. Government Printing Office, 1988), 221.

3. Ibid., 145–146.
4. *The Municipal Yearbook 1988* (Washington, DC: International City Management Assoociation, 1988), xvi.
5. Charles R. Adrian, "Forms of City Government in American History," in *The Municipal Year Book 1988*, 9–10. This is an excellent essay. In addition to the five trends toward convergence, one finds a thorough up-to-date overview of city governance in the 1980s.
6. John C. Bollens, *Special District Governments in the United States* (Berkeley: University of California Press, 1957), 71.
7. For an exploration of this theme see, Henry S. Gilbertson, *The County, the 'Dark Continent' of American Politics* (New York: The National Short Ballot Association, 1917).
8. David Thomas Konig, "English Legal Change and the Origins of Local Government in Northern Massachusetts," and Bruce C. Daniels, "The Political Structure of Local Government in Colonial Connecticut," in Bruce C. Daniels, ed., *Town and County* (Middletown, CT: Wesleyan University Press, 1978), 12–43, 44–71; Edward Cooke, Jr., "Local Leadership and the Typology of New England Towns, 1700–1785," *Political Science Quarterly* (December 1971), 586–608.
9. Joseph F. Zimmerman, *The Massachusetts Town Meeting: A Tenacious Institution*, (Albany, NY: Graduate School of Public Affairs, 1967), 20, 30–35.
10. Cited in Robert Norwood, *Texas County Government: Let the People Choose*, (Austin: Texas Research League, 1984), 46–47.
11. Ibid., 46.
12. John F. Dillon, *Commentaries on the Law of Municipal Corporations*, 5th ed. (Boston: Little, Brown & (O., 1911).
13. Vincent L. Marando and Robert D. Thomas, *The Forgotten Governments* (Gainesville: University Presses of Florida, 1977), 134–135.
14. *1987 Census of Governments*, vol. 1, 22.
15. David McNeely, "Bills Bottled Up on Construction Rules in Unincorporated Areas," *Austin American-Statesman*, May 5, 1985.
16. Virginia Marion Perrenod, *Special Districts, Special Purposes: Fringe Governments and Urban Problems in the Houston Area* (College Station: Texas A&M University Press, 1984), 44.
17. Bollens, 66–70.
18. Chester W. Bain, *A Body Incorporate: The Evolution of City-County Separation in Virginia*, (Charlottesville: University Press of Virginia, 1967), 37. Bain differentiates cities in terms of first class and second class, according to size. However, the *Municipal Yearbook* and common practice use the town-city distinction adopted in our brief overview. See the *Municipal Yearbook 1988*, 211. James Campbell, Director of Intergovernmental Affairs, Virginia Municipal League, personal communication, December 1988.
19. Campbell, Personal Communication, December 1988.
20. See, for example, Nicholas Henry, *Governing at the Grass Roots: State and Local Politics*, 2nd ed., (Englewood Cliffs, N.J.: Prentice-Hall, 1984) 22–23.
21. Committee for Economic Development, *Modernizing Local Government: To Secure a Balanced Federalism*, (New York: Committee for Economic Development, 1966), 19.
22. Ibid., 67.
23. Miller, 61–62.
24. *1987 Census of Governments*, vol. 1, vi.

25. Neal R. Pierce, "Kellogg to Battle Creek: Merge Governments or We Leave Town," *Today*, (November 26, 1982), 5.

26. "Innovative Options in Local Governance: Annexation in Battle Creek," and "Merger of the City of Battle Creek and Battle Creek Township," unpublished documents provided to the authors by Gordon Yager of the Cereal City Development Corporation, November, 1989.

27. Interviews with the current Battle Creek city manager, Rance L. Leader, and the city manager at the time of the merger, Gordon Yager, November 10, 1989.

28. Pierce, 5.

29. Ibid.

30. Roger B. Parks and Ronald J. Oakerson, "St. Louis: The ACIR Study," *Intergovernmental Perspective.* (Winter 1989), 11.

31. Donald Phares, "Reorganizing the St. Louis Area: The Freeholders Plan," *Intergovernmental Perspective.* (Winter 1989), 12–15.

32. Ibid., 14. See also Donald Elliott, "Reconciling Perspectives on the St. Louis Metropolitan Area," *Intergovernmental Perspective.* (Winter 1989), 17–19.

33. Phares, 13.

Chapter
6

Political Participation—Making the System Work: The Options

Political participation can be defined as any activity which attempts to influence decisions about public issues. Each chain of political activities is linked eventually to government officials. Implicit in most definitions of political participation is the notion that attempting to influence the government does not necessarily involve direct contact with it.[1]

Thus, attempting to influence public opinion on a political issue and recruiting individuals to work in campaigns are political activities even though no public officials are involved. Even volunteers who empty wastebaskets to make campaign headquarters presentable to the public or who baby-sit a fellow campaign worker's kids are engaged in a political activity. Influencing one or more of the governments may be the ultimate objective of political activity, but political participation occurs whether government is directly involved or not.

PARTICIPATION: CONVENTIONAL AND UNCONVENTIONAL

Many observers divide participation activities into two types: conventional and unconventional. Margaret Conway, for example, defines conventional participation as "those activities that are accepted as appropriate by the dominant political culture." The activities she identifies as appropriate include voting, running for office, working in a campaign, and corresponding with a public official. Unconventional activities, she points out, are those which are not regarded as appropriate even though they may be perfectly legal.[2]

The problem with this distinction is that marches and demonstrations may be examples of inappropriate behavior in one community while being almost passé in another. This is one of the major themes in Golembiewski, Moore, and Rabin's *Dilemmas of Political Participation*. Not only is there growing disagreement about what constitutes appropriate behavior, it is also true that "these new demands for what people want often strain available resources."[3] In this chapter we will focus on participation rather than on "available resources." The latter is an important concern, and we will take it up in Chapter 15 when we discuss whether we can afford to do better at providing social justice, protection of the environment, and some of the government services that individuals and organizations are demanding.

Although there may be disagreement about appropriate and inappropriate types of participation, it makes sense to identify some patterns of activity as being more central than others. Whether we call them traditional, conventional, or essential, there are certain activities with which we must become familiar in order to begin to understand how the political system works. Although our list of conventional activities includes demonstrations while Conway's does not, there is considerable agreement among political scientists on most of the conventional strategies for political participation. Besides being a subject on which political scientists have produced a great deal of literature, conventional participation has an additional practical virtue: without it, unconventional participation seldom works very well.

Saul Alinsky, author of *Rules for Radicals* and *Reveille for Radicals*, is both an inventor of unconventional ways to influence decision makers and a great respecter of the need to organize, do one's homework, and understand the rules of the game. He regards these activities as necessary so that one can gain ground through conventional participation after the explosions of unconventional participation have cratered the mental landscape of the establishment. During the violence outside the 1968 Democratic convention in Chicago, where police and National Guard personnel bashed demonstrators, his response to students who asked him if he still believed in working within the system was classic Alinsky:

> Do one of three things. One, go find a wailing wall and feel sorry for yourselves. Two, go psycho and start bombing — but this will only swing people to the right. Three, learn a lesson. Go home, organize, build power and at the next convention, *you be the delegates.*[4] (Italics in original.)

Having put forward the notion that informed conventional participation is a good place to start acquiring practical knowledge about how the system works, we now introduce you to a participant who is far from conventional. He will help us explore five facts about political participation on which this chapter, and indeed this book, are based.

THE FOX

On a cool autumn morning in September 1970, a stocky middle-aged man filled a 50-pound milk can with sewage that had floated downstream. He got it from the Fox River, near the outfall pipes of the U.S. Reduction Company's aluminum-recycling plant in Aurora, Illinois.[5]

That afternoon in East Chicago, Indiana, the man with the milk can entered the headquarters of the U.S. Reduction Company. After crossing the clean, tiled floor, he tipped the milk can and slowly emptied it near the reception desk. The contents, which had warmed and ripened somewhat since being collected that morning, oozed across the floor in an ever-spreading surface of stinking slime.

The man handed a note to the receptionist, one of the few who had yet to flee choking and gagging from the nauseating smell. Then the man with the milk can exited. The note he left demanded that the pollution of the river cease immediately.

The note was signed "The Fox."

The Fox is an appropriate character for our chapter on political participation because he illustrates five facts about political participation which, though often overlooked, are worth serious consideration as you decide whether to participate and, if so, how.

An Individual Can Act Alone

Politics by definition involves more than one individual. Nevertheless, an ordinary individual acting alone can influence decision making in and outside the government.

The Fox did not bring about an immediate change in water quality in the Fox River. However, he gained national publicity for the environmental movement and was featured in *Newsweek* for this and other acts, such as climbing smokestacks which annually dump tons of particles into the sky and then sealing them with homemade metal lids. Although no direct connection has been made, many of the guerrilla tactics of an international organization called Greenpeace (Box 6-1) are reminiscent of the guerilla tactics the Fox used on behalf of the environment.

Individuals are the essential political actors. Each decision to participate or not is made by an individual. As you may recall from Chapter 1, the purpose of the Giraffe Project, which provided the examples in Box 6-2, is to give recognition and publicity to individual acts of courage and integrity on

---

Box 6-1 **Greenpeace and Environmental Politics**

On September 7, 1988, Greenpeace demonstrators placed a dead seal on the doorstep of the prime minister's residence in Great Britain (10 Downing Street) to protest Britain's pollution of the North Sea. Britain is the only nation to dump partially treated sewage sludge, roughly 5 million tons a year, directly into rivers flowing into the North Sea.

Source: Andre Carothers, "The Seal Plague: Pollution and the Collapse of the North Sea," in *Greenpeace* magazine, (November-December 1988), 7.

---

behalf of others.[6] The motto of the organization is "Nobis est," which means "It's up to us." The interesting thing about individual acts of participation is that they often lead to the mobilization of many other individuals who were there waiting for an individual spark to ignite them, as Candy Lightner's experience indicates (Box 6-3).

Political Participation Involves a Wide Range of Activities

Pouring raw sewage on a corporate headquarters floor is not what most people have in mind when they think about political participation. We mention it not to register approval but to indicate that imagination is about the only limit on the methods used to participate in politics — imagination *and* one's sense of fair play. After all, the top-level decision makers at the U.S. Reduction didn't mop up the mess in the reception room (and perhaps in the rest rooms nearby). Although it would have been more appropriate if the Fox had picked on a major polluter, the facts about whether or not U.S. Reduction was guilty was not the major feature of the *Newsweek* story; the activities of the Fox were.

Box 6-4, on p. 170, touched on only a few of the possibilities, including some we've already mentioned. As noted in Chapter 2, almost anything can be a political resource. It logically follows that almost any activity can be a form of political participation.

You Can Lose Your Battles and Win the War

The Fox was unsuccessful in putting an immediate end to the pollution of the Fox River and had little impact on the U.S. Reduction Company. Thus, he lost his battle. However, he probably advanced the winning of a larger war by helping to draw state and national attention to the Fox River and to environmental problems elsewhere. Eventually state and federal officials took notice of the problem, and efforts were made to clean up the river.

Box 6-2 A Few Individuals Who've Stuck Their Necks Out

Vicki Ceja, a mother of four, got tired of living on a muddy street, so she organized her community and got the city to pave it. Getting results felt pretty good, so she kept going. Now, as president of Metropolitan Organizations for People, she's leading the fight against polluted water and hazardous wastes, a serious problem in Denver.

If you got mugged by a bunch of street kids, would you go to bat for them? Steve Mariotti did. He figured they were street-smart, tough, and independent—maybe they would do well in the business world, as he was. Eventually, after working part time with the young entrepreneurs and then going to work full time, Mariotti quit his business altogether and now teaches teens in New York City public schools to be entrepreneurs. His students have started 45 legitimate profit-making companies.

Ray Profitt patrolling the Delaware River for polluters. (Reprinted with permission of Neal Menschel, staff photographer, *The Christian Science Monitor*, Boston, MA.)

Ray Profitt of Delaware is known as "the river vigilante." A former test pilot and stockbroker, he has appointed himself protector of the Delaware River and its tributaries. Originally he cruised along the waterways in a small plane or amphibious vehicle to spot violations of state and local ordinances such as untreated sewage outfall, a new unregistered drainpipe pouring out industrial waste, and dumping in the marshlands. Now that he has a hovercraft, he traces the pollution to its source and lets the offender know that he has photographed and documented the violation and is prepared to take the violator to court if the mess isn't cleaned up. His success in court has led to lots of scrambling into compliance with the laws. So far he has a perfect record.

Source: Giraffe Broadcasting Services, Giraffe Spot 128, Giraffe Spot 145, and *The Giraffe Gazette*, (Spring 1988), 1–3. Reprinted by permission.

Box 6-3 **Individuals Who Take Action May Start Out Alone, but They Seldom End Up That Way**

Candy Lightner mobilized thousands of parents, many of whom had lost loved ones in accidents involving drunk drivers. Ms. Lightner's 13-year-old daughter, Cari, was killed in an accident caused by a frequently arrested but seldom punished drunk driver. Ms. Lightner dealt with her grief in part by creating Mothers Against Drunk Drivers and soon heard from hundreds of parents who had had a child killed or permanently handicapped by a drunk driver.

There are now over 300 chapters in over 40 states. Recent victories have included laws in several states against open alcoholic beverage containers in vehicles and mandatory jail time for drunk drivers and the federal law that requires states to raise the drinking age to 21 to receive money from the Federal Highway Fund. Just as important as laws and law enforcement is the change in attitude. "We're seeing Fortune 500 companies providing taxi service for employees who had too much to drink at office parties," Ms. Lightner reports.

Source: *Time* (January 7, 1985), 41, and *People* (July 9, 1989), 102.

Today, there are water skiing contests as well as an annual canoe race on the Fox River.[7]

Although we can grant the Fox a long-run victory, a more important thing to keep in mind about losing in the short run is that each political battle is often part of a larger war. Even when your side loses a battle, you have influenced the opposition in at least three important ways that will help win the war.

First, you have forced the opposition to use political resources. They have had to make promises, expend funds, and use time and energy dealing with you that might have been invested elsewhere. Second, by fighting and losing you've also made the opposition think about the price of making you unhappy next time. Next time they may negotiate. Third, you have required the opposition to go on record for or against something. Because of this, the opposition's behavior may come to the attention of others who agree with you, perhaps even a group of individuals who are already organized. Those individuals and that group may be allies in the next battle.

If you had not participated, few people would know that the opposition turned down a worthy proposal. Unless you bring up a matter, place it on the public agenda, power holders don't have to establish a public record on an issue (Box 6-5). They can quietly do it their way. Simply by making your opponents take a position you have acquired valuable information about what they really want.[8]

Box 6-4 A Plethora of Participation Options

Write a letter, send a telegram, make a phone call

Organize the production of dozens, hundreds, or thousands of the above

Hand out literature, type envelopes, stuff envelopes

Join a political party or interest group, found a party or interest group, or attend a meeting of a party, interest group, or candidate selection committee

Walk a neighborhood door to door to hand out literature, register voters, or get signatures on a petition

Tend a card table or booth in a public place where literature is distributed, contributions are collected, or petitions are signed

Baby-sit for someone so the parent can participate

Organize a group of baby-sitters for one or more fellow workers

Provide transportation for voters, people walking neighborhoods door to door, or fellow workers

Put up yard signs or assemble yard signs for someone else to put up

Deliver speeches, write speeches, photocopy and mail speeches

Run for office

Recruit people to run for office

Organize meetings

Report violations of rules to police officers, pollution control agencies, better business bureaus, election commissions, or newspapers

Give a party to let a candidate meet potential campaign workers or contributors

Negotiate a compromise between two individuals or groups

Organize contributions to pay for a newspaper ad, radio spot, or television spot

Write a newspaper ad, radio spot, or television spot

Write articles about or take pictures of tragedies, victories, violations, community problems, things to be rewarded, or things to be stopped

Testify before a committee, commission, or council

Attend a council meeting

Do library research on a public issue

Express an opinion or provide information to a decision maker who is a government official, a voter, a friend, a staff member for a governmental decision maker, a decision maker outside government (such as a party leader), a newspaper editor, a reporter, an interest group leader, or an interest group member

> ## Box 6-5 Myths with Special Meaning: The Consequences of Believing That You Can't Fight City Hall
>
> If power holders can convince you that participation is hopeless because you cannot win, then they are winning three battles, not just one.
>
> 1. They get their way.
>
> 2. They get to economize on the use of their political resources.
>
> 3. They don't have to take public action against a reasonable request.
>
> In short, they win cheaply, and quietly.
> Remember: You can fight city hall, but you have to know where it is first.

Political Participation Can Be an Enjoyable Experience

It may sound silly to say something like "Dumping raw sewage can be a lot of fun," but for the Fox it must have been so. The adrenaline flow of adventure, the glee of sticking it to the smug, and the satisfaction of doing something about an important problem are rich sources of enjoyment.

We hasten to point that sewage distribution is not high on our personal list of political activities. It is mentioned as evidence that some pretty far-out activities can be considered political participation. Thus, there are many possibilities for finding enjoyment in politics.

Participation Can Change the Political System for Better or for Worse

Because your battles are part of a larger war and because all political contests take place within a framework of rules and customs, it is a good idea to keep in mind that what you do in your current battles can affect not only your credibility and chances of making alliances and achieving success in battles to come but also the political system itself.

We point this out at the risk of some redundancy because we've seen leaders who failed to impress their own values of fair play and common sense on less informed followers. (Our premise, you may recall, is that you are a future leader; thus we assume you will have this opportunity.)

In you keep in mind the notion that the less people know about politics, the less respect they have for it, you will appreciate the fact that beginners break the rules more often than experienced, politically active people do. Naturally, when leaders break the rules, they get lots of unwelcome publicity. However, local political arenas are littered with the mistakes of amateur zealots who believed political activity is something dirty and behaved that way.

The Fox, depending on your point of view, may be a zealot or a folk hero.

The point here is not to judge him but to point out that political systems can be seen as fragile environments which can be poisoned for a long time by what we do now.

The Fox broke some rules and made life unpleasant for the innocent as well as the guilty. On the state and national scene, the Fox may be remembered as a hero among environmentalists for bringing discomfort to the polluters and publicity to the environmentalist cause.

On the local scene, however, he may have done as much harm as good to the prospects for communication, compromise, and constructive action. As an outdoorsperson and nature lover, the Fox doubtless understands the importance of preserving fragile systems and would not approve of fishing with dynamite sticks.

As an environmental activist, he would be chagrined to learn, if he did not know already, that the U.S. Reduction Company was involved in an environmentally constructive business, the recycling of aluminum scrap.[9] The company claims that the only thing the outfall pipe dumped into the Fox River was warm water from the noncontact pipes of the cooling system. Thus, the pollution the Fox collected was floating to, not coming from, the outfall pipes. Whether the pipes carried pollution or not, the fact remains that the Fox's mess on the reception room floor was cleaned up by custodians who had nothing to do with corporate decision making.

The political system probably needs a few Foxes every now and then.[10] However, many more people must do their homework to make the system responsive and responsible. After a dramatic event has focused attention on an issue, somebody has to draft a bill and get a legislator to introduce it, guide it through the legislative committees and through both houses, and then get it enforced. Before all that can happen, it may even be necessary to nominate and elect some somebodies to do it.

To briefly summarize the connection of the Fox to our five facts about participation, the Fox

1. Acted alone
2. Acted innovatively
3. Contributed to the winning of a larger war
4. Probably got some enjoyment out of participating in politics
5. Will have a long-term effect on the political systems in which he acted

WHO PARTICIPATES?

Nearly every conceivable type of person can and does participate in politics. However, some categories of people participate more than others do. To put it another way, there seems to be a considerable amount of unmobilized resources in the American political system. For example, Table 6.1 indicates a difference of over 30 percent in voting rates between those with a college education and those with less than a junior high school education.

Table 6.1   RATE OF VOTING PARTICIPATION AMONG SELECTED CATEGORIES OF AMERICANS IN PRESIDENTIAL ELECTIONS

Category	Percentage of group voting	
	1976	1988
Male	59.6	56.4
Female	58.8	58.3
White	60.9	59.3
Black	48.7	51.5
Hispanic surname		28.8
Age 18–24	42.2	36.2
Age 45–64	68.7	67.9
Education		
8 years or less	44	36.7
9–11 years	47	41.3
12 years	59	54.7
More than 12 years	74	70.7

Sources: U.S. Bureau of the Census, *Statistical Abstract of the United States, 1977* (Washington, DC: U.S. Government Printing Office), 508, and U.S. Bureau of the Census, *Current Population Reports: Voting and Registration in The Election of November 1988*, (Washington, DC: U.S. Government Printing Office, 1989), 1–2.

Although many types of people vote, not nearly as many people get more involved than that. The proportion of the general public considered politically active is rather small. In fact, according to Lester Milbraith,

> About one-third of the American adult population can be characterized as politically apathetic or passive; in most cases they are unaware, literally, of the political part of the world around them. Another 60% play largely spectator roles; they watch, they cheer, they vote, but they do not do battle. The percentage of gladiators does not exceed 5 to 7 percent.[11]

In order to better understand why some individuals participate more than others do, it is necessary to deal with three related concepts: opportunity cost, the notion that political participation is hierarchical, and the notion that it is cumulative.

Opportunity Cost

The **opportunity cost** of political participation can be looked at in two ways. First, it can be seen as the political resources one invests in a political activity; second, it can be seen as the political resources one uses or gives up to engage in political activity. From the first perspective, time spent on a political activity is time invested in good government, goals one hopes to achieve through electoral victory, or self-satisfaction because one has done one's duty as a citizen. From the second perspective, time spent voting or engaging in any political activity is time given up that might have been used to do other things. An important point to understand about political participation is that it has a great deal to do with the way people think about it. Furthermore, just as political resources are unequally distributed in every society, so are opportunity costs, Thus, for a worker on the night shift attending an evening city council meeting means wages lost, while for a daytime worker it simply means recreational opportunities forgone.

Although the cost of participating in the same activities may have different meanings to different people in terms of how it affects their lives, most activities can be measured in terms of the amount of time involved, the amount of money involved, or the degree of effort.

A Hierarchy of Activities

It levies no great tax on one's mental equipment to figure out that some of the activities presented in Figure 6.1 require a greater investment of political resources than do others.

Activities at the top of the list require a larger investment of political resources such as time and energy than do those at the bottom. For this reason, we can state that political participation is hierarchical: Political activities can be arranged in a hierarchy according to increasing opportunity costs.

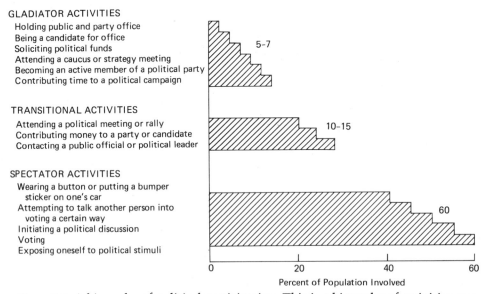

Figure 6.1 A hierarchy of political participation. This is a hierarchy of activities, not of people. More political resources must be invested in activities near the top of the hierarchy. Thus the percentage of the population willing to make that investment declines as the opportunity cost of activities increases. (*Source:* Lester Milbraith, *Political Participation*, [Chicago: Rand McNally, 1965], 18–19.)

This hierarchy also indicates that decreasing percentages of the population engage in high-cost activities. It is important to note the difference between a hierarchy of activities in which people from all walks of life participate and a hierarchy of people according to **socioeconomic status** (SES). The first is a ranking of activities in terms of opportunity costs; the second is a ranking of individuals in terms of their wealth, the status of their occupations, and the amount of formal education they have.

Accumulating Activities

Political participation is also **cumulative** in that people who participate in activities involving high opportunity costs usually participate in lower-cost activities as well. Political participation is cumulative, or additive. The opposite principle would be that of exchange or substitution: As people move from low-cost to high-cost activities, they will stop doing the former. In politics, however, people add activities instead of replacing one type with another. Candidates for governor still remember to vote and have been known to express an opinion about politics now and then.

In short, when we say that political participation is hierarchical and cumulative, we mean that

1. We are ranking *activities*, not people.
2. Activities can be arranged in a hierarchy of increasing opportunity costs or declining number of participants.
3. People participating in high-opportunity-cost activities such as running for office are also likely to participate in lower-cost activities such as voting in presidential elections.

The notion that participation is hierarchical and cumulative is a useful generalization that is accurate most of the time. However, recent studies have indicated that it is not accurate all the time. One of the most important of these studies is that of Sydney Verba and Norman H. Nie (Table 6.2).

The Verba-Nie Typology of Participant Types

Verba and Nie analyzed data gathered from interviews with a sample of over 3000 adult Americans concerning their involvement in four basic modes of political activity: voting, campaigning, communal participation, and personal contacting of public officials. Using statistical techniques, the authors looked for patterns of individual participation and identified six basic types of political participants.

1. *Inactives* (22 percent). This group corresponds to Milbraith's apathetics. Members of this category seldom vote and rarely engage in any other political activities.

2. *Voting specialists* (21 percent). This term does not mean that mem-

Table 6.2   INVOLVEMENT IN POLITICAL PARTICIPATION

Activity	Percentage
1. Regularly vote in presidential elections	72
2. Always vote in local elections	47
3. Active in at least one organization involved in community problems	32
4. Have worked with others in trying to solve some community problems	30
5. Have attempted to persuade others to vote their way	28
6. Have ever actively worked for a party or candidates during an election	26
7. Have ever contacted a local government official about an issue or problem	20
8. Have attended at least one political meeting or rally in the last three years	19
9. Have ever contacted a state or national government official about an issue or problem	18
10. Have ever formed a group or organization to attempt to solve a local community problem	14
11. Have contributed money to a party or candidate	13
12. Presently a member of a political club or organization	8

Source: Sidney Verba and Norman H. Nie, *Participation in America: Social Democracy and Social Equality*, (New York: Harper & Row, 1972), 31. Reprinted by permission.

bers of this category are somehow expert at voting. Rather, it means that voting is about the only activity in which these people participate.

3. *Parochial participants* (4 percent). This group contains such a small percentage of the population that it hardly seems worth bothering with. However, Verba and Nie regard this category as the most interesting.[12] Parochials engage in few activities other than contacting public officials to solve specific problems that affect them personally.

Since it requires a certain amount of initiative and self-confidence to contact a public official, members of this category seem well equipped to participate in the political sytem in other ways. They seldom do, however. Very few parochials belong to service clubs or community organizations, and other than voting, they rarely participate in political activities which appear to have low opportunity costs, such as wearing a campaign button, displaying a bumper sticker on one's car, and contributing to political campaigns. In short, parochials appear to be a category of persons who are well equipped to contribute to the political system on which they are willing to make demands.

The discovery of the parochial category suggests that political participation is neither cumulative nor hierarchical for everyone. It also encourages one to be a little optimistic. Parochials, after all, constitute only 4 percent of the sample. This approach seems to be consistent with the somewhat cynical "What's in it for me? . . . want mine now . . . Me first . . . Don't volunteer, just take" philosophy that the popular media have attributed to a mythical category of Americans called yuppies.[13] Thus it is refreshing to find that behavior consistent with this philosophy is not widespread among those who participate in the political system. If subsequent research finds that parochials are growing in numbers, we may have cause for some concern.

4. *Communalists* (20 percent). Communalists provide further evidence of the need to qualify the notion that political participation activities are cumulative. Communalists participate in many activities involving attempts to deal with community problems. They belong to and are active in various community services and charitable organizations.

As Table 6.3 indicates, Americans report membership in a wide range of organizations. Organizations involved in campaigning or electoral competition are those to which communalists are least likely to belong; they are much more likely to belong to charitable organizations or those involving the volunteering of services in response to community problems.

Communalists vote, but that is about the extent of their role in electoral politics. A communalist may invest political resources such as time, energy, and money in the affairs of his or her community but seldom participates in even those campaign activities which are regarded as having low opportunity costs.

Table 6.3 PERCENTAGES OF THE ADULT POPULATION REPORTING MEMBERSHIP IN 16 TYPES OF ORGANIZATIONS

Type of organization	Percentage reporting membership
Labor unions	17
School service groups such as the PTA and alumni groups	17
Fraternal groups such as Elks, Eagles, and Masons and their women's auxiliaries	15
Sports clubs	12
Political groups such as Democratic or Republican clubs and the League of Women Voters	8
Veterans' groups such as the American Legion	7
Youth groups such as Boy Scouts and Girl Scouts	7
Miscellaneous groups not fitting the categories in this list	7
Professional or academic societies such as the American Dental Association and Phi Beta Kappa	7
Church-related groups*	6
Service clubs such as Lions, Rotary, Chamber of Commerce, Zenta, and Optimists	6
Hobby or garden clubs	5
Farm organizations such as the Farmer's Union, Grange, and Farm Bureau	4
Literary, art, discussion, or study clubs	4
School fraternities and sororities	3
Nationality groups such as the Sons of Herman, League of Latin American Citizens, and Hibernian Society	2

*Does not include church membership but rather associations emerging around the church or religion.

Source: Sidney Verba and Norman H. Nie, *Participation in America: Social Democracy and Social Equality*, (New York: Harper & Row, 1972), 42. Reprinted by permission.

The discovery that there appear to be about five times as many cooperation-oriented communalists as there are parochials reinforces our optimism. We'd rather live in a community where communalists outnumber parochials than one in which it's the other way around.

5. *Campaigners* (15 percent). This group is the mirror image of communalists. Activities that are without competition do not seem to interest them. Verba and Nie suggest that the conflict dimension differentiates communalists from campaigners. Both are active in the affairs of the community, but they tend to deal with different dimensions. Campaigners are more likely to

Try to persuade others how to vote

Work actively for a party or candidate

Attend a political meeting or rally

Contribute money to a party or candidate

Belong to a political club

Communalists are more likely than any of the previously mentioned groups to

Work with others on a local problem

Form a group to work on local problems

Be an active member of a community problem-solving organization

6. *Complete activists* (11 percent). Individuals in this category engage in all the dimensions of activity we have studied. In terms of campaign and community activities, they perform at a higher rate than do the other groups in almost every dimension.

Among the various dimensions of political orientation that Verba and Nie analyze in relation to their typology is civic-mindedness, or willingness to give time and effort to the needs and problems of the community.[14] Only two types of participants score high in terms of this orientation: communalists and complete activists.

Thus the complete activist can be thought of as being both a civic-minded campaigner and a communalist, willing to enter the world of politics to promote the common good. If the complete activist seems somehow familiar, it may have something to do with the fact that this whole book is oriented toward encouraging you to become one.

The Birmingham Study

Philip B. Coulter's study of citizens' contacts with the government of Birmingham, Alabama, was conducted about eight years after the Verba-Nie study. It closely analyzed one activity: contacting public officials. Coulter's study is instructive to students of political participation for at least three reasons. First, it supports the view that contacting is somehow different from other political activities. Second, it indicates that contacting has more than one dimension. Third, it provides ample evidence that only a few of those who make personalized contact with public officials are parochials.

Contacting Is Different   In reinforcing the findings of Verba and Nie that citizen-initiated contacting is different from other participation activities, Coulter explains that

> Through contacting, a citizen takes the initiative, in other words, chooses the nature, content, referent, target, level of government, and timing of the contact. Contacting is harder than most participatory acts, because the citizen must set the policy agenda of a contact, the subject matter is automatically important and salient to him/her.[15]

Contacting Has More Than One Dimension   Coulter identifies two different types of contact with public officials: expressing an opinion on a public issue (we will discuss this later as part of the larger strategy of lobbying) and **particularized contacting**.

Particularized contacting involves three types of interaction with an official: (1) complaining about a specific problem that directly affects the individual, (2) requesting help, and (3) demanding that "something be done" about a more general problem that affects directly the individual.[16]

Particularized Contacters Are Not All Parochials   Coulter's findings suggest at least one important modification of the findings of Verba and Nie about participation.

One modification is that particularized contacting, and therefore contacting in general, is a more common occurrence than Verba and Nie found it to be. Coulter observes that individuals may do much more particularized contacting than Verba and Nie reported in their study. After reviewing more than a dozen studies of cities across the country, Coulter found that the average rate of contacting reported was 33 percent, which is noticeably higher than the 20 percent reported by Verba and Nie.[17] However, Coulter confirms their view that most contacters are not parochials. Among those who contact are a large percentage of individuals who participate in many other political activities.

Coulter's data are consistent with the Verba-Nie finding that political activists do even more contacting than parochials do. In fact, Table 6.4, on p. 180, indicates that many of the Birmingham contacters fit the political activist model rather than the parochial model. Though contacting may be somehow different and may not fit the cumulative model that applies to most other political activities, contacting (both particularistic and general) is still engaged in by the most active political participants.

PUBLIC OPINION

Sooner or later most strategies of political participation involve attempts to influence public attitudes on an issue or toward a candidate and to promote the expression of those attitudes as opinions. **Public opinion** can be defined

Table 6.4   BIRMINGHAM CONTACTERS COMPARED WITH A NATIONAL SAMPLE REPORTING PARTICIPATION IN POLITICAL ACTS

Activity	National	Birmingham
1. Regularly vote in presidential elections	72	88
2. Always vote in local elections	47	58
3. Active in at least one organization involved in community problems	32	31*
4. Have worked with others in trying to solve some community problems	30	68
5. Have attempted to persuade others to vote as they do	28	58
6. Have ever actively worked for a party or candidate during an election	26	49
7. Have ever contacted a local government official about an issue or problem	20	100
8. Have attended at least one political meeting or rally in the last three years	19	46
9. Have ever contacted a state or national official about an issue or problem	18	31
10. Have ever formed a group or organization to solve a local community problem	14	31
11. Have ever given money to a party or candidate during an election campaign	13	51
12. Presently a member of a political club or organization	8	18

*The response for item 10, a higher-opportunity-cost activity, is used here.

Sources: Sidney Verba and Norman H. Nie, *Participation in America: Social Democracy and Social Equality*, (New York: Harper & Row, 1972), 31, and Philip B. Coulter, *Political Voice: Citizen Demand for Urban Public Services* (Tuscaloosa: University of Alabama Press, 1988), 67–70.

as the expression of an attitude on an issue or matter of public concern.[18] As Bernard Hennessy observes,

> Words, spoken or printed, are the most common form of expression of opinion, but at times, gestures—the clenched fist, a stiff-arm salute, even the gasp of the crowd—will suffice to express opinion. . . . For public opinion at any given moment of measurement, expression is necessary.[19]

This approach assumes that if attitudes or feelings aren't expressed, they aren't opinions yet. Others make no distinction between attitudes and opinions.[20] This does not mean that they are unaware of the difference between volunteering an opinion to a friend or coworker and giving an opinion in response to a public opinion poll. In explaining "what every citizen should know" about public opinion polling, Herbert Asher (who uses "attitude" and "opinion" interchangeably) pays considerable attention to "nonattitudes," which are held by people with limited information about or commitment to an issue.[21]

However one defines public opinion, the move from having an attitude and/or opinion to actually expressing it clarifies one's orientation toward an issue or individual. This is why some people have been known to observe, "I really don't know what I think about that until I hear what I have to say on it."

Four dimensions of public opinion are of particular concern to those who wish to get things done in the intergovernmental system: public awareness, distribution (or direction) of opinions, intensity of opinions, and stability of opinions.

Public Awareness Awareness can be measured in terms of the percentage of the public aware of an issue or individual. Not everyone has an opinion on every issue. The portion of the general public which is aware enough of an issue to have an opinion on it can be identified as the **issue public**. The size of the issue public can be changed by making more people aware of the issue. One way to do this is to make the issue more **salient**, or noticeable to the general public, in the hope that some members of that public will become concerned enough to express an opinion on it.

For individuals who are thinking about running for office, public opinion analysts use the term **name recognition** to identify public awareness. Potential candidates often have polls taken to discover the percentage of the public aware of their names. Potential candidates with high name recognition (a large issue public) are more likely to decide to run.

Distribution of Opinion Distribution can be measured in terms of percentages of the public who have a particular position on an issue or candidate.

When public opinion polls are presented in the media, the "don't knows" and "have no opinions" are sometimes left out. This tends to "harden the data," disguise the size of the issue public, and make the distribution of opinion appear more dramatic than it really is. To overstate things a bit, if 20 percent are for a course of action, 10 percent are against it, and 70 percent don't care, it is somewhat less than totally honest to report only that the proportion of those favoring an issue is twice that of those against it.

In discussions of opinion distribution, the term "direction" is sometimes used to indicate the guidance given to policymakers. On an issue that is divided 50-50 no guidance is given. What matters is how many people are actually aware of the issue. A small issue public split evenly can be more safely disregarded than can a large issue public split evenly.

Intensity Intensity of opinion on an issue can be measured in terms of percentages of the public who feel strongly about their position on an issue.

Individuals whose opinions are strongly felt are most likely to express them by taking action to support them. The fact that some people are willing to act implies that others may be almost ready to. Thus, when you participate as an individual, you force decision makers to at least consider the possibility that you are the tip of an iceberg. This is because intensity can also be measured in terms of the number who are willing to do more than merely express an opinion.

Stability   Stability is the degree to which the other three dimensions of public opinion remain unchanged. Decision makers who ignore changes in public opinion are in danger of not being reelected. Thus, they are sensitive to changes in the size of an issue public, the distribution of opinion, and the intensity of opinions.

The polling firm of Yankelovich, Skelly, and White has developed a **mushiness index** to estimate the stability of public opinion measured in a survey. The index is based on four facts about the relationship of each respondent to the issue:

1. How much the issue affects the respondent personally
2. How well informed the respondent feels on the issue
3. How much the respondent discusses the issue with family and friends
4. The respondent's own assessment of how likely it is that his or her views will change[22]

In a 1981 survey on attitudes about restricting imports, the responses were 54 percent in favor, 41 opposed, and 5 percent unsure. However, after an examination of all the opinions in terms of the mushiness index, it was found that among the mushiest group, only 39 percent were in favor of restrictions. Thus, few of those who didn't know much and didn't care were in favor of import restrictions. Among the firmest group, by contrast, 62 percent were in favor of them.[23]

This sort of information is useful to policymakers who are attempting to do what the public wants, avoid making the public dissatisfied with them, or both. It is also of interest to those concerned with changing public attitudes and opinions. Thus, it is useful to know that many individuals have little information or are unaware of how an issue affects them, especially if you have the facts and a lucid explanation ready.

Building the mushiness index into every poll is time-consuming and expensive. Thus, political leaders are more likely to augment polling results with information about the willingness of members of the public to act on their opinions by participating in the political system.

PARTICIPATION STRATEGIES

Political strategies combine and direct an almost infinite number of political activities toward a political goal. The strategy an individual or an organization chooses depends on the type of decision to be influenced. For example, influencing an appointment to the state supreme court involves tactics and techniques different from those involved in getting a bill passed in or a candidate elected to the state legislature.

Six of the most well known strategies are **lobbying, grass-roots lobbying,** attendance at **public hearings, demonstrating, appointmenteering, litigation,** and **electioneering.** Organizations such as political parties and interest groups use these strategies; individuals acting independently can use them as well. Even when organizations act, they do so through individuals—their leaders, spokespersons, chairpersons, lobbyists, and sometimes ordinary members.

Lobbying

"Lobbying" is a term which can be defined to embrace a number of activities. As Box 6-6 suggests, it is a much misunderstood and misused term. We define it as any activity which involves personal communication with a decision maker which is intended to influence a decision on a public issue.

Thus, writing a letter, sending a telegram, making a personal visit to the office of a decision maker, and talking to a decision maker about an issue at a social gathering are all lobbying activities. Although it is analytically possible to differentiate particularized contacting—"Fix the pothole in front of my house"—from lobbying—"Fix the potholes in our neighborhood"—the distinction becomes less important in the practical world of getting things done. A leader cares more about the fact that you are willing to act than about why you are acting.

If you want the potholes in your neighborhood fixed, make sure to get all kinds of people to contact the decision makers regardless of their motives or private agendas.

Rationale   Since lobbying involves a higher investment of political resources than does responding to a public opinion poll or voting, decision makers pay more attention to it. Those willing to lobby are likely to be willing to work for another candidate if lobbying doesn't pay off. Thus, the number and types of individuals involved in lobbying are sometimes used as a measure of the intensity as well as direction of public opinion. Lobbying serves decision makers as a source of information about the political environment. It also conveys other kinds of information—technical, legal, economic, and even ethical—that may not otherwise be readily available to decision makers.

The importance of information is so great that many decision makers not only employ a staff to gather it, but also hold hearings to provide additional opportunities for information to be presented. Granted, some decision makers don't really care what the public thinks. However, since they are required to listen anyway by laws which require public hearings, by their colleagues who do care, or both, they sometimes learn something useful.

Box 6-6 **The Many Meanings of "Lobby"**

1. *Verb.* To attempt to influence a decision on a public issue by personally contacting a decision maker.

"Mr. Councilperson, don't vote for the ordinance on leashing dogs," barked A. Jones over the phone.

"I won't fence with you, Mr Jones," replied the councilperson bitingly. "I'm tired of stepping into things without any warning. I'll make my decision after I read the staff report."

2. *Verb.* Any method of attempting to influence a decision of government.

"Now rub this magic lantern," said the elf, "and the city council will grant your wish."

"Are you sure this is lobbying?" asked Charles Credulously.

"Would a person with ears like mine lie to you?" the Elf asked pointedly.

3. *Verb.* To attempt to influence any decision.

Item: Fenwick lobbied his father for a new sports car.

"Please, Daddy, all my friends have one."

"Not until you floss more regularly," said his father.

"Aw, gee, Dad," said Fenwick, "you are really mean."

"That's tough love, son," said his father indulgently.

4. *Noun.* A collection of well-financed organizations or well-dressed individuals representing them.

News item: The lobby won a major victory today when the legislature voted not to tighten restrictions on the amount of effluents that can be discharged into rivers and streams. The Sierra Club, an organization which supported the limitations, got no support from any legislator up for reelection.

"Golly, the legislature sure is mean," said Fred Frosted, a spokesperson for the Sierra Club.

"That's tough," said Bubba Stud, a lobbyist for the Nasty Chemical Corporation.

5. *Noun.* All organizations that try to influence decisions by government.

"The lobby sure is confusing," said Melvin Generalization sweepingly. "I can never tell what it wants government to do."

6. *Noun* (archaic). A waiting area, antechamber, or passageway leading from a meeting room to the rest of a building.

"You get the tickets, Sue, while I park the car. No sense in this precipitation moisturizing both our apparel," said Maxwell Savecoin dryly. "I'll meet you in the lobby."

"Golly, Max," said Sue Knot brightly, "you sure know a lot of big words."

7. *Noun* (fictional). A part of the abdomen between the foyer and the vestibule.

News item: The popcorn thief surrendered after a quick-witted usher hit him in the lobby.

"I figured I might hurt my hand if I hit him in the teeth," explained the usher.

Attendance at Public Hearings Public hearings are essential and often overlooked opportunities for participation. A public hearing is an official meeting held by a decision-making body to gather information about a problem or a proposed course of action.

Legislatures at all levels (county, city, school district, and state) hold public hearings, as do many state and local administrative agencies. Decision makers may not do exactly what the participants in hearings want them to, but the decision-making process is usually influenced by the testimony presented. Each source — professional lobbyists, experts, and ordinary citizens — is important in its own way.

Part of the skill of lobbying is being able to find out when and where public hearings on one's topic of interest will take place. While notices of public hearings are often published in the newspaper, people active in politics often contact public officials to find out if any hearings are planned on matters of interest to them and to get on the mailing list of those who provide advance notice.

Rational Attending a public hearing not only gives one the opportunity to express opinions and influence public officials, it also gives one the opportunity to see what the opposition is up to and get informal feedback about the reactions of public officials to you and to your opposition. At the local level many decisions can be influenced by what goes on at public hearings before the school board, city council, or county commissioners court.

Grass-Roots Lobbying

Grass-roots lobbying involves attempting to get others to act, to lobby. It is sometimes called public relations work. Grass-roots lobbying is a strategy directed toward directing opinions, increasing the size of an issue public, and increasing the intensity of opinion among those who agree with the position for which one is lobbying. It has two dimensions: long term and short term.

Two Time Frames Short-term grass-roots lobbying is action-oriented. It attempts to get other people to act very soon, if not immediately: "Mail your message *today!*"

The long-term dimension seldom involves calls for action. It is basically a public relations exercise. Long-term grass-roots lobbying often uses advertisements in the mass media to promote the notion that an individual or group is trustworthy and legitimate. Long-term grass-roots lobbying is sometimes referred to as the bank account approach.

By investing in a bank account of goodwill among the general public, an individual or group may be able to make withdrawals later on. A good reputation (credibility, public image) is a political resource for an individual or a group. Organizations can enhance their public image by using meaningless "feel good" slogans or by actually doing something altruistic. Individuals can enhance their reputations though volunteer and charity work. Candidates for public office are often individuals with established reputations.

It goes without saying that community public service is a good thing in and of itself. However, the practical benefits may not be so obvious. When individuals with a bank account of goodwill eventually become involved in a public issue, they start out with a little more credibility than do those who were too busy to do public service work; furthermore, those who volunteer have a lot more personal contact with the people who make decisions in that community because the decision makers are probably also volunteers.

Rationale   Grass-roots lobbying is important because decision makers are accustomed to being contacted by professional lobbyists and are often impressed when an ordinary individual takes the time and trouble to contact them about an issue. Because contacts from ordinary individuals are not as common as contacts from professional lobbyists, decision makers often give these contacts from people "at the grass roots" a little extra weight.

Well-financed interest groups and their professional lobbyists use direct mail and mass media campaigns to encourage ordinary people to contact public officials. Not all decision makers have become so sophisticated that they disregard hundreds or thousands of letters or cards that say exactly the same thing. Even if these items are were mailed from different addresses by different individuals as part of a computerized direct-mail campaign, the fact that these individuals took the time to put those items in the mail says something about the intensity of their opinion on the issue.

Two Messages   Grass-roots lobbying usually sends two messages to decision makers. The first message is the content, the overtly expressed message. The second message is indirect. It says, "Hey, look at all the people we can get to contact you and maybe even vote for or against you in the next election."

Regardless of the level at which you operate, you can multiply the weight of your political opinions by bringing along a few friends to a hearing or encouraging them to contact public officials themselves. When you do this, you are doing grass-roots lobbying, and it often works. When local legislative bodies, for examples, find their usually empty chambers filled with people concerned about an issue, they are likely to pay extra attention. Some members may even change position on an issue in the presence of a significant number of citizens who cared intensely enough or were organized skillfully enough to show up.

Demonstrating

A demonstration is an activity designed to get attention for a cause. It is a symbolic act. Marches, picket lines, sit-ins, or building a shanty on campus, are all demonstrations. A picket line may act as a fence to keep customers, workers, or supplies out, but it is a symbolic fence. A shanty built to demonstrate against apartheid may actually keep someone dry, but it is not intended to be a domicile.

Since the Boston Tea Party, demonstrations have been part of the American political scene. Attempting to influence decisions by means of attention-getting behavior has become such a frequently used technique that it can probably be considered a conventional form of participation.

Rationale   A demonstration is a tactic with one or both of the following goals: to increase the number of people aware of an issue or to provide decision makers with evidence of the intensity of opinion on an issue.

The Fox's demonstration helped bring attention to the environmental issue and thus increased the size of the issue public. A march or sit-in helps indicate the size of the issue public and the intensity of feeling on an issue.

Individuals or groups which demonstrate are usually short on political resources such as money and prestige. If they had more money, they could buy media time. If they had more prestige, they could spend an extended period of time with a decision maker. Sometimes, however, even prestigious figures use a demonstration as a tactic to bring attention to an issue. Thus, when John Thompson, the coach of the Georgetown University basketball team, walked off the court before a game, he brought national media attention to the National Collegiate Athletic Association's Rule 42 which denies athletic scholarships to freshmen who fail to meet minimum academic requirements.

Risk   Demonstrations can be illegal or legal. Either way, the individual or organization which chooses this strategy takes a risk. If things get out of hand, it can make the demonstrators and the cause look dumb, selfish, or even nasty. A recent demonstration by teachers in Austin, Texas, involved great risk and careful organization. Several thousand teachers came to that city to march on the state capitol to petition the legislature for higher wages and educational reforms. Great care was taken to make sure that no teacher carried a sign with misspelled words on it.

Greater risks are taken when a group decides to engage in illegal demonstrations. It works sometimes, but only if conditions are right.

Civil Disobedience or Illegal Demonstration   Most states and communities have laws which in the interests of public safety require that a parade permit be applied for before marches, parades, or mass demonstrations take place. They also have laws dealing with trespass and damage to private property. They may also have other laws which you regard as wrong.

To demonstrate against laws one regards as wrong, one must usually get permission from the appropriate authorities. Sometimes the authorities do not cooperate. Organizers of demonstrations thus face the choice between not demonstrating at all and demonstrating illegally. The decision to disobey the rules in order to bring attention to one's cause is not an easy one to make.

Civil Disobedience: Conditions for Success   Civil disobedience in particular and any demonstration in general are most likely to be successful in bringing public attention and sympathy to one's cause if all the following conditions are met:

1. The cause is perceived by the general public as just. If the law one is breaking or the situation one is disturbing the peace to dramatize conflicts with the basic principles of the larger society, it makes sense to create a large issue public. Civil rights demonstrators who sat in at segregated lunch counters in North Carolina during the 1960s were breaking laws that conflicted with the principle of equality, a value supported by the larger society.

2. The public can be made aware of one's actions. If the media are not present, the message is unlikely to get to many people. The media may be somewhere else, reporting other events. This is why one takes a chance with demonstrations, legal or illegal. In short, demonstrations work best on a slow news day when plenty of reporters and camera crews are available.

3. There is a simple, acceptable remedy. Passing laws prohibiting discrimination is an action that decision makers can take. However, a demonstration against sickness or poverty is much less likely to be successful than one in favor of a particular antipoverty program or a specific bill to fund medical research.

4. The demonstrators must be willing to accept the consequences of their actions. Individual members who hit back, resist arrest, or violently refuse to be carried away in a police van are very likely to damage rather than help their

Demonstrating is a tactic that works best when the purpose is clear and there is a realizable remedy, a positive course of action that a government can take. (Reprinted with permission of Kim Bradley, staff photographer, *San Marcos Daily Record*, San Marcos, TX.)

cause. The key to successful demonstration is passive resistance whether the demonstration is legal or illegal.

Demonstrators who refuse to take their lumps either don't understand why demonstration was chosen as a tactic or are really attempting to use a different tactic. Demonstration is not the same thing as rioting, hand-to-hand combat, or revolution. Thus, an organization which builds a shanty on campus without first getting permission and then defends that shanty with baseball bats is likely to do its cause more harm than good.

The individuals who participated in civil disobedience during the civil rights era of the 1960s took their lumps and went to jail. In doing so, they demonstrated their faith in the American system of justice and their commitment to moving America in the direction of becoming a more just society.

Appointmenteering

Appointmenteering is any activity intended to influence political appointments. Many nonelective positions in government are filled by following civil service regulations and procedures. Many, however, are filled by a process of recruitment and selection that is neither systematic nor well publicized.

The term "appointmenteering" is used here to emphasize the fact that there are many appointed positions in state and local government that have a great deal of influence in the political economy and the wider society. Thus, it matters who gets appointed to the civil service commission.

Many appointed positions in state and local government involve making decisions that affect other people's income. Local planning and zoning commissioners sometimes make decisions that affect the opportunities for developers to get very rich or just moderately rich and may even encourage them to look elsewhere for land to develop. Textbook selection committee members on state or local school boards make decisions which affect the income not only of local publishers' representatives but of whole publishing companies.

Appointmenteering involves most of the same elements that lobbying does — bringing facts and opinions to the attention of decision makers. In this context facts about the record and qualifications of people you support or oppose are most relevant. Another way to influence appointments is to volunteer to be appointed. Box 6-7 lists a few options on p. 190.

Local governments use lots of volunteer time and talent on various boards and commissions. In many communities the pool of volunteers is small. To make yourself available, all you need to do is contact a unit of local government to find out which boards and commissions are of interest to you and then submit your name to the county clerk, the city secretary, or the secretary to the superintendent of the schools. In most communities you will find boards or commissions that deal with the library (an important board to

Box 6-7 **Boards and Commissions in a Medium-Size City**

Airport Commission

Parks and Recreation Board

Fair Housing Commission

Senior Citizens' Advisory Board

Historic Preservation Commission

Human Services Agency Board

Citizen's Storm Drainage Advisory Board

Personnel Appeals Board

Plumbing Board of Adjustments and Appeals

Municipal Electrical Utility Board

Main Street Advisory Board

Mayor's Conservation Committee

Cemetery Commission

Commission for Minorities

Sunset Advisory Commission

Commission for Women

Emergency Medical Service Committee

Ethics Review Commission

Building Code Board of Adjustments and Appeals

Zoning Board of Adjustments and Appeals

Charter Review Commission

Industrial Development Board

Minority Business Enterprise Committee

City-County Joint Airport Zoning Board

Housing Authority Board

Electric Utility Board

Civil Service Commission

Library Board

continued

Box 6-7 *(continued)*

> Tourist Development Council
>
> Planning Commission
>
> Zoning Commission
>
> Public Transportation Committee
>
> Convention Center City-County Task Force
>
> Examining Board of Heating and Air-Conditioning Contractors
>
> **Source:** City secretary, San Marcos, Texas (November 1989).

be on if you wish to help prevent censorship or book burning), planning (land use, transportation, and social services are a few of the things for which there may be specialized planning commissions), and zoning (an important board which attempts to separate family-style residences from a wide range of other kinds of land use, including industrial and commercial use, while promoting the most efficient use of land) as well as a civil service commission, a commission on human rights, a charter review commission, an airport commission, and a variety of commissions created to meet local needs.

Electioneering

Electioneering is any activity directed toward influencing electoral decisions by individuals eligible to vote. At least three different decisions are subject to influence: (1) whether to register, (2) whether to vote, and (3) how to vote on each item on the ballot. In addition to influencing the voting decision, many electioneering activities also attempt to persuade people to help in the election campaign by contributing money, time, or other resources.

Registration   To prevent voting fraud, most democracies require some form of registration. In this country, states make and enforce registration laws usually, but not always, through county government. States vary greatly in their registration hours and places and in the degree to which their laws and procedures make registration easy.

In 21 states citizens can register to vote by mail. In a few more states one must have a good reason (absent on business, disabled, absent for religious reasons, and so on) to register in absentia. Otherwise, one must appear before an election official to register. Regardless of the ease of registration, in nearly every state one must reregister to vote if one's residence has changed since the last election.

Since in any five-year period almost 50 percent of the American popula-

Box 6-8   ## The Volunteer and Money in the Bank

While lots of money is spent in elections, some of that money is spent on buying personal services. When the services are volunteered, money is saved. The volunteer who works unpaid for an hour is contributing many times the hourly wage he or she might be paid. This is because no one else had to spend time raising the money to buy those services and no one else had to keep books on how that money was spent.

tion has changed residence, this means that in every election year several million Americans who have failed to reregister become ineligible to vote.[24] Therefore, one way to promote voting is to promote registering. Registration drives are thus an important part of any election campaign.

Voting   Campaigning is critical to voter turnout. The major task in a campaign is to bring the election or referendum to the attention of the eligible voters, to convince them that they ought to act. Most campaigns spend a fair amount of money in the weeks before the election finding out where the supporters are and then concentrating on getting them to vote (Box 6-8). If all the votes in a geographic area are for the other candidate, not much campaigning will be done there. Contrary to popular opinion, much more effort is directed toward finding and motivating one's supporters than toward attempting to convert the followers of the opposition.

Litigation

Litigation is the act of using the court system to influence decisions. In Chapter 12 we will discuss state and local court systems, but for now we will simply suggest that sometimes ordinary people can use the legal system at relatively low cost.

In most cities there are law firms which take on a few cases involving the public interest at low fees or for free. They get good publicity if they win. In most states there is also an organization which specializes in giving legal aid to those who cannot afford regular attorney's fees. "Cannot afford" is a flexible term which can be better defined by contacting your state or local legal aid society.

Using the courts does not mean that you need to accuse someone of a crime or sue that person for damages. You may simply ask the judge to issue an order (a writ) that tells someone to stop doing something (writ of injunction) or tells a public official to do something he or she should do anyway (writ of mandamus). If the court issues a writ, a person who refuses to comply with it is in contempt of court. At that point, the behavior of this individual becomes a government matter and you have acquired an important ally. In most states there are also small claims courts and justice of the peace courts which operate without attorneys. Thus, if you have a problem that is not likely to be solved by contacting the legislative or executive branches of government, keep in mind the fact that the legal system is there for people who can't afford $150-an-hour attorney fees as well as for people who can.

CONDITIONS THAT INFLUENCE PARTICIPATION

In addition to political culture, at least two sets of conditions influence participation. The first involves socioeconomic status (SES), which places individuals in categories according to the prestige of their occupations, the amount of formal education they have completed, and the size of their incomes. The second set involves the social and political institutions available to promote participation and the rules and regulations for participating.

Even though individuals in each socioeconomic category participate, it is a well-documented fact that people with higher SES characteristics are more likely to participate than are those with low SES characteristics. As an individual, you cannot do very much about increasing the participation of others by improving their SES. Therefore, we turn our attention to six conditions that you may be able to influence to increase the participation of others.

Six Conditions You Can Influence That Increase Participation

When socioeconomic characteristics are held constant, that is, when we compare poor whites and poor African-Americans or middle-class whites and middle-class African-Americans (instead of all African-Americans and all whites), an interesting fact emerges. African-Americans participate at a higher rate than does the rest of the American population. A major causal factor for this difference is the existence of African-American organizations and leaders who attempt to influence the six conditions we are about to discuss.[25] These conditions are summarized in Box 6-9, on p. 194.

Value Rewards of Participation   Individuals are more likely to participate when they believe that the rewards of participation are valuable. Political scientists identify three basic types of rewards associated with political participation: **material benefits, purposive benefits,** and **solidary benefits.**[26] Though many activities may involve more than one type of reward, it is useful to identify the types separately.

Material rewards come in a variety of forms with different meanings for different people. Owners of businesses may participate in politics by making campaign contributions or supporting candidates in other ways in order to receive government contracts or freedom from regulations which may ultimately cost them money. Other individuals may participate by attending a rally because free food or door prizes are available there. People may volun-

Box 6-9   **An Individual Is More Likely to Participate If He or She**

1. Values the rewards to be gained

2. Thinks the alternatives are important

3. Is confident that he or she can help change the outcome

4. Believes the outcome will be unsatisfactory without his or her action

5. Believes that he or she possesses knowledge or skill that bears on the question at hand

6. Thinks the barriers (opportunity costs) are not too high

Source: Robert A. Dahl, *Modern Political Analysis* (Englewood Cliffs, NJ: Prentice-Hall, 1970), 85.

teer to work in a campaign in part because today's indispensable volunteer is tomorrow's employee. People are encouraged to join organizations because of discounts on insurance or equipment, or the availability of a professional journal that provides useful information. Though you may not have material rewards to offer, you may be able to encourage others to participate because of material rewards you know about. Information, as we observed earlier, is a political resource.

Purposive rewards are those which come to individuals who have worked for a particular goal and achieved it. The goal might have been the election of a candidate, the passage of a state law that requires people to take a course in gun safety before buying a firearm, or an item in the city budget that will pay for paving a street.

Purposive rewards operate at two levels: the immediate psychological lift from having accomplished something one worked hard for and the long-term benefits that come from better government, smooth streets, or a safer society.

Solidary benefits are those which come from being part of a group of people one enjoys being with. Simply belonging is a psychological benefit that means a great deal to many people. Solidary benefits may also include the fellowship or camaraderie of people engaged in a meaningful activity.

One of the functions of a political leader is to shorten the time it takes for others to make the connection between rewards and participation. You can increase the participation of others if you can help them see the rewards of politics. In some situations people with little or no formal education or political experience can benefit from the education and experience of others.

These others are identified in various ways. They have been called activists, subleaders, leaders, radicals, gadflies, busybodies, party hacks, and many other colorful but uncomplimentary things which we leave for you to learn as you become more politically experienced.

Perception of Significant Differences   Individuals are more likely to participate in politics when they believe that there are significant differences among political alternatives. The less informed one is about a subject, the fewer distinctions one will be able to make when confronting it.

People who don't know much about the votes of various city council members on specific issues such as expenditures for street repairs in poor districts tend to see city council members as being pretty much the same.

An individual who explains to several dozen citizens in a poor neighborhood the differences in the voting records of the candidates is likely to improve not only the ability of those citizens to see the differences among council members but also the likelihood that those citizens will participate in the next city council election.

Efficacy or Confidence   The characteristic of believing that one can affect one's surroundings, that one can change things, is called a sense of efficacy. When it involves politics, we call it **political efficacy**. Individuals with a high sense of political efficacy are ones who believe that they can influence the political environment. People with a high sense of political efficacy are more likely to participate in a wide range of political activities.

Efficacy can often be transferred from one area of subject matter to another. When people feel good about themselves, they are more likely to venture into new areas, such as politics. During the civil rights era, African-American leaders indicated their awareness of this fact by promoting the phrase "Black is beautiful." The reasoning was that if you are "beautiful", you'll be more likely to register to vote, sit in at the lunch counter, ride in the front of the bus, or even run for sheriff.

Outcome Uncertainty   Some individuals who are confident that the outcome of an event will be satisfactory without their participation may find other things to do with their time. The more uncertain the outcome appears, the more likely people are to participate.

This is particularly important in the late stages of a campaign, whether it is an election or a referendum. If potential voters are convinced that their side will win without their votes or if potential participants are convinced that their side will win without their participation in various volunteer activities, it is very likely that significant numbers of them will not participate, and the contest may be lost. Thus, it is important for leaders to make followers aware that the race is still close, that every vote counts, and that every hour of volunteer activity is needed.

Relevant Knowledge or Skill   Individuals who believe they have something to contribute to a discussion are likely to partake in it. The hard part is convincing people who have something to contribute in the political arena but don't believe they do.

One way to deal with this situation is to take away excuses by pointing out that no special skills are needed for the activity involved: "You don't have to do anything for our candidate, just be there. That way the media won't take pictures of empty seats in the auditorium." Occupying a chair is a skill that most people possess. In short, the fact that those with relevant knowledge or skill are more likely to participate tends to provide an excuse for nonparticipation. Therefore, you must take away that excuse by explaining that skill or knowledge is not important. The irony is, it takes skill and knowledge to do that.

Reasonable Opportunity Costs   Individuals are more likely to participate in politics when they believe the opportunity costs are relatively low.

Opportunity costs are to a considerable extent a product of the institutional context in which the individual operates. Thus, in some communities one must stand in long lines to vote because those in charge of the election didn't hire enough people to run it or just didn't plan very well. The opportunity cost of a 5- or 25-minute wait is subjectively measured by one individual as being unreasonable and by another as being perfectly acceptable.

Thus, one of the jobs of a political leader is both to work to lower opportunity costs and to persuade those whom one wishes to participate to perceive that the existing opportunity costs are reasonable.

Much has been written about alienation and apathy as sources of nonvoting in American elections.[27] However, since a large number of Americans are proud of their system and believe it works pretty well, some observers are inclined to interpret their nonparticipation as a sign of satisfaction.[28] The only European democracy in which the voting turnout is lower than that of the United States is Switzerland, a nation whose citizens are noted for their support of their system.[29] Thus, a certain amount of nonparticipation can be seen as a vote of confidence in the status quo.

It is reasonable to assume, however, that individuals who attempt to motivate the less fortunate are not going to operate on the assumption that nonparticipation is a sign of contentment. Political activists who confront satisfaction or complacency have a delicate job to perform. To overcome the inertia created by the belief that everything is going just fine, someone must create dissatisfaction by pointing out things that are wrong with the way things are now so that we will act to fix them. In so doing, that person must avoid appearing to criticize very much beyond the things for which immediate action is required.

This is not an easy task. People who point out too many things that need correcting are easily written off as chronic complainers and sometimes are accused of being disloyal to the "American way." More often the response is, "If you don't like it here, why don'cha go someplace else?"

Each of the six conditions we have discussed can be influenced by an individual working to change the beliefs, feelings, and perceptions of others.

In a sense, these conditions can be seen as levers to pry people out of apathy or handles that one can grasp to move people into the political arena.

Institutional Factors: Powell's Paradox

The second set of conditions that influence individual participation consists of the political institutions with which and through which most individuals participate. In discussing voting turnout in America, G. Bingham Powell has observed that

> Seen in comparative perspective, American voter turnout presents an interesting paradox. Americans seem to be more politically aware and involved than citizens in any other democracy, yet the levels of voter turnout in the United States are consistently far below the democratic average.[30]

After seeking answers to this paradox, Powell found a major part of the explanation in the nature of our state registration laws. As Table 6.5, on p. 198, indicates the United States and France are the only two democracies which have neither required nor automatic registration. France requires registration for the equivalent of an identity card, and this facilitates voting registration.

In the United States, the registration laws of the 50 states determine whether it is easy or difficult to register. According to Powell, if the states were to employ some form of automatic registration, the turnout in national elections would increase by about 14 percent.[31]

Same-day registration in the United States is not the same thing as automatic registration. Furthermore, it hasn't been in place very long in the few states which have it. Nevertheless, some indication of the potential for increased turnout which may occur as states simplify registration procedures is found in Table 6.6, which compares turnout in the four states with same-day registration with the national average of turnout for the 1984 presidential election. A difference of 11.6 percent is somewhat less than the 14 percent that Powell predicted but close enough to suggest that reforms in voter registration laws in the United States might have some effect in terms of increasing turnout.

Another important institutional factor that influences voting turnout is the party system. According to Powell, a more competitive and dynamic party system would increase voter turnout in national elections by 13 percent. State regulation, as we shall note in Chapter 8, has a considerable influence both on the nature of the party system and on the ability of political parties to operate independently of the interest group system.

Thus, Powell's paradox is resolved somewhat by understanding that although we have a political culture and an ideology that promote participation, some of our rules and political institutions do not promote voting. Voting is only one of many political activities. It is the one, however, that enables many people to pool their limited resources in order to have more influence on their governments.

Table 6.5   TURNOUT AND REGISTRATION REQUIREMENTS IN 20 DEMOCRACIES IN THE 1970s

	Registration method*	Percent eligible registered	Percent eligible voting
Australia	Required	86	91
Austria	Automatic	88	96
Belgium	Automatic	88	95
Canada	Automatic	68	93
Denmark	Automatic	85	98
Finland	Automatic	82	100
France	Optional†	78	91
West Germany	Automatic	85	94
Ireland	Automatic	77	100
Israel	Automatic	80	100
Italy	Automatic	94	100
Japan	Automatic	72	100
Netherlands	Automatic	82	98
New Zealand	Required	83	95
Norway	Automatic	82	100
Spain	Automatic	78	100
Sweden	Automatic	88	97
Switzerland	Automatic	44	85
United Kingdom	Automatic	75	100
United States	Optional	54	61
Average		78.45	94.7

*In order to prevent vote fraud, all 20 democracies use some kind of registration system. The following three types are found among them: Required registration means that eligible voters are subject to fines or penalties if they do not register. Automatic registration means that governments attempt to register all eligible voters who come into contact with government agencies; for example, when one applies for a driver's license or a hunting license, one is automatically registered to vote. Optional means that eligible voters can choose not to register and therefore not to vote.

†French law requires citizens to apply for identification cards; this process facilitates voter registration.

Source: G. Bingham Powell, "American Voter Turnout in Comparative Perspective," *American Political Science Review* (March 1986), 38. Reprinted by permission.

Table 6.6   VOTING TURNOUT IN STATES WITH SAME-DAY REGISTRATION: 1984 PRESIDENTIAL ELECTION

State	Percent of registered voting	Percent of voting age voting
Maine	68.2	65.0
Minnesota	72.1	68.5
Oregon	76.2	62.6
Wisconsin	Not available	63.4
Four-state average		64.9
National average		53.3
Difference		11.6

Sources: Voting statistics, *The World Almanac 1987*, (New York: Scripps Howard, 1986), 307, and "Registration Laws," in *The Book of the States, 1986–87*, (Lexington, KY: Council of State Governments, 1986), 208.

Conclusion

In this chapter we have dealt with individual participation and with ways in which politically active individuals can affect the participation of others primarily by dealing with the way they think about themselves and about their relationship to the political system.

In previous chapters we touched on some of the objective conditions which reduce participation. Two of the most salient are the long ballot of Jacksonian democracy, which presents so many choices that nonparticipation becomes a logical way to reduce confusion and frustration, and the numerous levels of government which confront the individual with a host of officials to elect and a variety of different elections in which to choose them (state, county, city, school board, water district, flood control district, park district, soil conservation district, and so on). For some observers, the number of choices represents a real barrier to participation.

The fact remains, however, that until informed individuals participate in the system, reform is not likely to occur. This presents us with an interesting situation: One cannot make the system easier to participate in until one participates in it.

We encourage you to take part in politics if only to find out for yourself whether we have overstated the need for reform. However, you may find that the agenda for reform is so long that in your lifetime only one or two items can be dealt with successfully. Either way, the fact that you have become an informed participant is a step in the right direction. The more you play the game of politics, the better you will understand the way it works, and the better equipped you will be to explain, defend, or correct it.

Study Objectives

1. Define political participation.
2. Identify the advantages of conventional participation.
3. Identify the five facts about political participation the Fox illustrates.
4. Explain why political participation can be described as hierarchical and cumulative.
5. Identify the six categories of participants in the Verba-Nie typology.
6. Identify the six types of participation strategies.
7. Identify the two time dimensions of grass-roots lobbying.
8. Identify the conditions associated with success in the use of a demonstration as a political strategy.
9. Identify the six conditions you can influence to increase the likelihood that an individual will participate.
10. Give two reasons why Americans vote at a lower rate than do citizens of most other democracies.

Glossary

appointmenteering Any activity intended to influence political appointments.

cumulative Increasing by successive additions. In the case of political participation, this means adding rather than substituting activities.

demonstrating Any activity in which individuals by their presence or action attempt to gain public attention and support for a cause or issue.

electioneering Any activity directed toward influencing electoral decisions by individuals eligible to vote. It is sometimes called campaigning. However, since recruitment of candidates is not always included in the definition of "campaigning," electioneering has a separate meaning for some political scientists.

grass-roots lobbying A strategy which involves attempting to get other people to contact public officials on behalf of one's issue or cause.

issue public The portion of the general public which is aware enough of an issue to have an opinion on it.

litigation The act of using the court system to influence decisions.

lobbying Any activity which involves personal communication with a decision maker which is intended to influence a decision about a public issue.

material benefits Rewards such as income, goods, or services which one receives for participating in an activity.

mushiness index An attempt to estimate the stability of opinion expressed by the respondents to a survey or an issue. The index is based on four facts about the relationship of each respondent to the issue.

name recognition The characteristic of having many people aware of one's name. It is related to the notion of the issue public. One increases the salience of an issue or an individual's name by demonstrating or using the mass media. Potential candidates often have polls taken to discover the percentage of the public aware of their names.

opportunity cost The political resource or resources one invests in a political activity; political resources used or given up to engage in a political activity.

particularized contacting This involves three types of interaction with an official: (1) complaining about a specific problem affecting the individual directly, (2) requesting help, or (3) demanding that something be done about a more general problem affecting the individual directly.

political efficacy The belief that one can influence one's political environment. It is a characteristic found in varying degrees; those with a high sense of political efficacy are the most willing to participate.

public hearings Official meetings held by a decision-making body to gather information about a problem or proposed course of action.

public opinion The expression of an attitude on an issue or matter of public concern.

purposive benefits Benefits that come to individuals who have worked for a particular goal and achieved it.

salient Noticeable. A salient issue is one about which many people are aware.

socioeconomic status The placement of individuals in categories according to the prestige of their occupations, their incomes, and their levels of education. Social scientists prefer this term when talking about rich and poor people. Since social scientists are usually middle class, it reduces ambiguity and the pressure to choose sides.

solidary benefits Benefits which come from being part of a group of people one enjoys being with. Simply belonging is a psychological benefit that means a great deal to many people. Solidary benefits may also include the fellowship or camaraderie of people engaged in a meaningful activity.

Endnotes

1. See, for example, the definitions of Sidney Verba and Norman H. Nie, *Participation in America: Social Democracy and Social Equality*, (New York: Harper & Row, 1972), 2, and M. Margaret Conway, *Political Participation In The United States*, (Washington, DC: Congressional Quarterly Press, 1986), 2.
2. Conway, 3.
3. Robert Golombiewski, J. Malcom Moore, and Jack Rabin, *Dilemmas of Political Participation*, (New York: Prentice-Hall, 1973), 8.
4. Saul Alinski, *Rules for Radicals*, (New York: Random House, Vintage Books edition, 1972), xxii. See also *Reveille For Radicals* (New York: Random House, Vintage Books edition, 1969), 54.
5. *Newsweek*, (1970), reprinted in Golombiewski et al., 76–78.
6. *Time*, (August 8, 1988), 8.
7. Sponsored by the Aurora, Illinois, Chamber of Commerce each June.
8. Robert A. Dahl, *Modern Political Analysis*, 2nd ed. (Englewood Cliffs, NJ: Prentice-Hall, 1970), 21.
9. Telephone interview with Tom Hendon, Director of Environmental and Engineering Services, U.S. Reduction Company, January 30, 1989.
10. The notion that radical individuals and organizations are helpful in paving the way for the success of moderates is well developed in Herbert H. Hines, *Black Radicals and the Civil Rights Mainstream, 1954–1970*, Knoxville: The University of Tennessee Press, 1988. See especially pp. 3–5.
11. Lester Milbrath, *Political Participation*, (Chicago: Rand McNally, 1965), 16.
12. Verba and Nie, 11.
13. Douglas Foster, "Post-Yuppie America," *Mother Jones* (February-March 1989), 16–18.
14. Verba and Nie, 85.
15. Philip B. Coulter, *Political Voice: Citizen Demand for Urban Public Services*. (Tuscaloosa: University of Alabama Press, 1988), 6.
16. Ibid., 4.
17. Ibid., 14.
18. For a similar definition, see Bernard Hennessy, *Public Opinion*, 4th ed. (Monterey, CA: Brooks/Cole, 1981), 4.
19. Ibid., 6–7.
20. Herbert Asher, *Polling and the Public: What Every Citizen Should Know*, (Washington, DC: Congressional Quarterly Press, 1988), 37.
21. Ibid., 21–36.
22. Ibid., 34.
23. Karyln Keene and Victoria A. Sackett, "An Editor's Report on the Yankelovich, Skelly and White 'Mushiness Index,'" *Public Opinion* (April-May 1981), 50–51.
24. Council of State Governments, *Book of the States, 1986–87* (Lexington, KY: CSG, 1986), 208.

25. Verba and Nie, 171.
26. Peter Clark and James Q. Wilson, "Incentive Systems: A Theory of Organizations," *Administrative Science Quarterly*, 6:3 (September 1961), 126–166. See also Robert Salisbury, "An Exchange Theory of Interest Groups," *Midwest Journal of Political Science* 13:1 (February 1969), 1–32.
27. See, for example, William Crotty, *American Parties in Decline*, 2nd ed. (Boston: Little Brown, 1984), 276.
28. Furthermore, some regard a high rate of participation as a sign of dissatisfaction and a threat to the stability of the system. See, for example, Seymour Martin Lipset, *Political Man: The Social Bases of Politics*, (Garden City, NY: Doubleday, 1960), 185.
29. G. Bingham Powell, "American Voter Turnout in Comparative Perspective," *American Political Science Review* (March 1986), 23.
30. Ibid., 17.
31. Ibid., 36.

Chapter 7

Participation Through Institutions: The Interest Group Option

If you became an active participant in the political system, sooner or later you will join, ally yourself with, or oppose (on some issue or other) a political party, interest group, or political action committee—probably all three. Dealing with these institutions is not an option. Choosing to join or create one is. To deal skillfully and choose wisely, one must have some background information about these three types at organizations.

THREE INSTITUTIONS FOR POLITICAL PARTICIPATION

Political parties, interest groups, and political action committees are not the only institutions for political participation. One can also participate in the three branches of government which will be discussed in Chapters 9 through

13. In this chapter and Chapter 8 we focus on parties, interest groups, and political action committees — their similarities, differences, and roles in the political system.

Interest Groups

An **interest group** is an organization which seeks to influence government decisions without taking responsibility for running the government. This definition has three dimensions: organizing, seeking to influence government decisions, and not taking responsibility.

The first dimension sets interest groups apart from interests. Not all interests (the unemployed, victims of child abuse, college students, residents of a particular neighborhood) are organized to influence government; interest groups are. Interest groups have a structure, leaders, names, addresses, and usually phone numbers. You can mail a letter to an interest group. Interests are harder to correspond with.

The second dimension brings under this definition many types of organizations that did not start out to influence government. Many religious, charitable, and ethnic organizations as well as corporations, labor unions, and professional associations were not created to influence government. However, once they attempt to do so, they are treated analytically as interest groups.

Thus, when a corporate chief executive appears before a congressional committee to ask for a loan guarantee for his or her firm or before a state legislature to testify against new regulations, that executive is not likely to be acting as a private citizen. He or she is there to represent an interest group which also happens to be a corporation.

The third dimension differentiates interest groups from parties. Parties seek to control government by getting their candidates elected. Interest groups seek to influence the decisions made by public officials, elected and appointed. Political action committees (PACs) tend to specialize in raising funds to contribute to candidates; they focus on political campaigns. As we shall observe presently, interest groups and PACs have much in common.

Political Action Committees

A **political action committee** is an organization created to collect money in order to influence elections through campaign contributions. Although PACs have been around since the 1940s, their numbers expanded radically between 1974 and 1984. At the national level they grew from 608 to more than 3000 in that ten-year span.[1]

Proliferation of PACs in Your Lifetime   State-level PACs have been growing rapidly in numbers and in the amounts of money they contribute to campaigns. In Oregon, for example, only 36 PACs existed in the early 1970s; they contributed a total of $200,000 to candidates. In 1980, 151 such committees in Oregon contributed close to $1 million. In North Carolina, the number of PACs grew from 29 in 1974 to 259 in 1984.[2]

Reasons for PAC Proliferation   There are at least three reasons for the proliferation of PACs at the state and local levels. The first has to do with the increasing importance of the role of government in dealing with many of the complex problems that confront our society and an increasing awareness in the business community of the relationship between profit margins and regulation by state and local governments.

At the local level, a change in the inches of asphalt or base required for roads in a new subdivision can cost a developer thousands of dollars. In Agoura Hills, a growing suburb 40 miles outside Los Angeles with a population in 1986 of about 20,000, contributions by developers seeking to elect a friendly council led to expenditures by some candidates of over $20,000.[3]

On the state level, races in which at least one candidate for governor spends over $3 million are no longer limited to the three biggest states.[4] Noted authority on campaign finance Herbert Alexander reports that expenditures on statewide and legislative races (excluding congressional races) were $228.9 million in 1984 and had risen to $312.9 million two years later.[5]

At both levels the principle of borrowing from the rich instead of taxing them is worth a lot of money to investment law firms and banking firms. These firms help state and local governments through the complicated process of selling bonds to investors who usually buy them in denominations of $5000 or more. For example, in 1985, five investment banking concerns which had collected fees of $4.8 million on bond issues in the state of New Jersey since 1982 contributed $257,250 to assist in the reelection of the governor.[6] As of 1987, state and local governments owed $265.7 billion to investors.[7] Virtually all that debt was incurred through the sale of bonds in large denominations, and a percentage of it went to banking and law firms.

A second reason for the growth of PACs has to do with the growth of the political consultancy profession. Political consultants are individuals or firms which manage political campaigns, not only election campaigns but grass-roots lobbying campaigns and fund-raising campaigns. Money, large amounts of it, is necessary to pay political consultants and buy television time, and PACs are the vehicles for raising and handling this money. The California Commission on Campaign Financing reported that in 1986 over $57 million was spent on 100 California races. Twelve of those races cost more than $1 million each. Ninety-two percent of the money received by legislative candidates came from outside their districts, largely from wealthy individuals and PACs.[8] Thus, many individuals are concerned about the role of money in our democratic system.

An aide to former Florida governor Ruben Askew tells the story of an old-style rally in a rural north Florida town where the governor, who relished these rare occasions away from the big-money people — time he could spend with the ordinary voter — was approached by a withered dirt farmer with a

$100 check in his hand. "I want you to have this," said the farmer, his voice trembling with awe and respect. "I have supported you for years, and I'm behind you now." That farmer's $100 check paid for about half a second of television in the Tampa market, where a 30-second television spot costs around $6000.[9]

Not all PACs have the same amount of money to contribute. The competition is not among equals. In the 1984 legislative elections in North Carolina, for example, ten PACs made over half the contributions received from all PACs. The North Carolina Medical Society PAC contributed $36,300. The tenth-ranking PAC, representing the Virginia Electric and Power Company, contributed $16,450.[10] During the 1988 election cycle alone, 81 PACs in the state of Texas each contributed $20,000 or more to legislative and local races, for a combined total of $8,930,000.[11] The number of PACs has increased radically at the local level as well.

The third reason for the increase of PACs has to do with changes in election laws at the state and local levels. In 1974, Congress passed the Federal Election Campaign Act, which attempted to regulate the use of money in elections. In that law, the federal government continued its ban on direct contributions from corporate and labor union treasuries. Many states also apply this ban to state and local elections. In the course of clarifying the relationship between corporate treasuries and political activities, the Federal Election Campaign Act allowed for the creation of PACs by corporations and other interest groups. PACs had to maintain separate funding, but they could be assisted by an existing corporation without breaking the law or by an existing interest group without that group sacrificing its tax-free status. Thus, nonprofit educational interest groups which seek to inform the public about important issues can continue to receive contributions which are tax-deductible for the contributors. If the contributors choose to contribute to the PACs of that interest group, their contributions are not tax-deductible.

Thus, two separate treasuries have to be maintained. The organizations which choose to create PACs can assist those PACs in a number of ways. They can provide them with office space, personnel, and funds for expenses such as phones; they can also give them very valuable resources, such as a list of corporate executives and members of the board and a list of all the members of the interest group. These lists are very important to any political organization seeking to raise funds by direct mail. Sometimes they are provided in a way that makes it very easy to prepare direct mail-outs. For example, a corporation or interest group would probably give its PAC the names and addresses of members or stockholders on a computer tape or disk.

As Box 7-1 indicates, the recent growth of PACs has led to the expression of opinions about PACs and their influence that are not only mixed but rather strong. Although PACS can be distinguished from interest groups because PACS all have separate budgets and tend to specialize in electioneering, there are many similarities between PACs and interest groups (or labor unions and corporations acting as interest groups).

Box 7-1   # A Mix of Opinions on PACs

Walter Mondale: "I think it is time to declare that the government of the United States is not up for sale. . . . Let's plan controls on these PACs."

Fred Wertheimer, Common Cause: "Alarming. Outrageous. Downright dangerous. That's the only way to begin to describe the threat posed by the torrents of special interest campaign cash being offered up to our representatives and senators by the special interest political action committees. This democracy threatening trend must be stopped."

Patrick Buchanan, columnist: "Destroy the PACs and you constrict the voice of small business, and restrict the political access of the millions who support them —enhancing the clout of Big Media, Big Business, Big Labor and their ilk who can afford to maintain permanent lobbying representation in [Washington]."

John Glenn, US senator, R–Ohio: "The PACs and the people's support of them is a vital part of our political process."

Ann Lewis, political director of the Democratic National Committee: "When you look at in on paper, it would seem that PACs and the parties should be rivals. But in practice, we've come to very important accommodations. . . . Our party has become a broker, a facilitator, and a sometime matchmaker for the PACs."

Joe Gaylord, executive director of the National Republican Congressional Committee: "If we ever were rivals, we're not anymore. . . . We see ourselves as the people in the middle. To PACs we try to offer ourselves as a service organization to provide information about Republicans who are running for Congress. For our candidates we try to help match them to PACs."

Former U.S. representative William Brodhead, D-Michigan: "They're trying to buy votes. There's no other purpose to it. Labor unions, trade associations are all doing the same thing."

Lee Ann Elliott, Federal Elections Commission: "Saying 'PAC money buys votes' is the equivalent of looking at the obituary page and concluding that people die in alphabetical order. There is not a quid pro quo. . . . The presumption is that congressmen are dishonest and on the take, that PAC givers are sleazeballs, in the business of bribery—and neither is the case."

Justin Dart, Dart industries, confidant of President Reagan: Talking to politicians "is a fine thing but with a little money they hear you better."

continued

Box 7-1   *(continued)*

Representative Barney Frank, D-Massachusetts: "We are the only human beings in the world who are expected to take thousands of dollars from perfect strangers on important matters and not be affected by it."

Representative Andrew Jacobs, Indiana: "The only reason it isn't considered bribery is that Congress gets to define bribery."

Source: Larry J. Sabato, *PAC Power: Inside the World of Political Action Committees*, (New York: Norton, 1984), 122–124, 141.

PACs and Interest Groups: Similarities   Four similarities between PACs and interest groups explain why we occasionally refer to both types of organizations as interest groups.

1. Both share the political goal of influencing government decisions without taking responsibility for the consequences of those decisions. Thus, when the National Rifle Association (NRA) successfully lobbies against the banning of AK-47s or Teflon bullets, there is no way the American government or American voters can hold either the NRA or its PAC responsible for any murders committed by people wielding "legally" acquired automatic weapons; nor can police officers whose bulletproof vests are pierced by Teflon bullets do anything about the NRA's success at lobbying or its PAC's success at electioneering. In the 1981–1982 campaign cycle the NRA Political Victory Fund raised $2 million.

To attempt to do anything to the NRA or its PAC through government action would be to deny the NRA and any other organization which seeks to operate in the political system freedom of speech, freedom of assembly, and the right to petition the government for the redress of grievances. All three of these rights are guaranteed by the U.S. Constitution and by state constitutions.

Furthermore, in several states the NRA has been able to have the state constitution amended to include a much less restrictive claim to the right to bear arms than is guaranteed in the U.S. Constitution. The Second Amendment, you may recall, includes the phrase "a well regulated militia, being necessary to the defense of a free-state."

2. PACs and interest groups often share the same roof. With a few exceptions, most PACs are departments of an interest group. The federal election campaign laws of the 1970s established fairly detailed rules for reporting campaign contributions, and many interest groups, including corporations and labor unions, established PACs to facilitate the preparation of these reports. For practical purposes, a corporate PAC is as much a part of the corporation as is the corporation's public relations department.

3. Some PACs behave like interest groups. According to Larry Sabato, "The most important single trend in PAC development is not the swelling of the committees' treasuries but their increased emphasis on political education and grassroots activism."[12] In short, PACs perform many activities traditionally associated with interest groups. Thus, if it walks like a duck, quacks like a duck, and swims like a duck, let's call it a duck.

4. Interest groups and PACs both help create and extend services to PACs. According to a leading scholar on PACs, the U.S. Chamber of Commerce has a PAC called the National Chamber Alliance for Politics (NCAP) which does not make campaign contributions at all. Instead of engaging in the one activity with which PACs are commonly identified, the NCAP devotes its considerable resources to providing a variety of services to other business-oriented PACs. For example, staff research and analysis of the several thousand candidates competing in primary and general elections for the 435 House seats and the 33 or more Senate seats up for election every two years results in the preparation of a list of opportunity races in which business-oriented candidates have a good chance of winning. It has been estimated that getting on the NCAP's opportunity list is worth about $100,000 in contributions from other PACs which follow the Chamber PAC's advice.[13]

The Federal Elections Commission (FEC), to which all PACs making contributions to candidates in federal elections must report, is the best source of data on PACs. Since most PACs operating at the state level make contributions to federal as well as state candidates, FEC data provide us with a fairly accurate overview of the PAC picture. A few states require financial reports similar to those required by the FEC and make them available to the general public at the county seat or state capital.[14] One of the problems with these financial reports is that government funds are not spent on preparing summaries that enable voters to make comparisons. Thus, in the absence of summary reports, voters must go through the campaign reports of all the candidates running for a particular office in order to develop a clear view of who's getting big contributions from whom.

Political Parties

A **political party** is an organization that seeks to control the government. In democracies, a political party does this by winning elections rather than through coups and terrorism. When the candidate of a party wins an election, then in a sense the party "controls" that office. Naturally, the successful candidate has something to say about how he or she is going to operate in that office. However, on issues of importance to the party, members of the party vote together more often than not in most legislatures. Political parties are different from interest groups in four important respects.

1. Parties attempt to control the whole government; interest groups merely attempt to influence a few particular decisions. If the party in control of

the government doesn't do a good job, then in theory we can hold it responsible by electing candidates from the other party in the next election. There is no similar mechanism even in theory for holding an interest group responsible. Interest groups which obtain decisions which benefit them at the expense of the public interest are not elected by the general public.

2. Parties offer slates of candidates at the county, state, and national levels; interest groups do not. Interest groups may attempt to influence particular elections and may even influence the process by which individuals seek party nomination. However, an interest group does not nominate a slate of candidates to appear on the ballot under its label.

3. Parties are heavily regulated by state governments; interest groups are not. The election codes of most states describe in some detail how parties are supposed to operate, nominate candidates, and choose their officers. Except for requiring PACs to report how much money they receive and then contribute to candidates and requiring lobbyists to register and report expenditures, few states regulate the internal operation of interest groups in a significant way. Unlike party leaders, interest group leaders may make decisions on the use of group resources without consulting their members, and leadership selection is not regulated at all.

4. Parties are organized geographically from the precinct level to the national level. Although interest groups such as state medical associations may be organized on the county level, very few interest groups are organized at all major geographic levels in the electoral system (precinct, ward, county, state, national) as parties are.

Although political parties are significantly different from interest groups, they do share at least three features. First, they are organizations. True, some parties appear to be more organized then others. Will Rogers once observed, "I belong to no organized political party. I am Democrat." Nevertheless, both major parties have some kind of structure, officers, formal rules for conducting business, and state and local party headquarters that are open during election years if not permanently.

A second similarity is that both parties and interest groups create PACs. In each house of Congress and in several state legislatures, the members of both parties have organized PACs which raise funds intended to help the party keep the seats it has and gain more.

A third similarity was noted at the beginning of this chapter: They are both institutions which promote political participation. In this similarity, however, there is a major difference. Political action committees attempt to promote participation only among their members and thus are somewhat selective in their efforts. Political parties, by contrast, are virtually the only institutions in the political system which attempt to mobilize the general public to participate in the electoral process. The relationship between a viable political party system and popular participations in elections was discussed in Chapter 6. According to G. Bingham Powell, participation in general elections would increase by more than 10 percent if we had a stronger political party system in the United States at the state and local levels. We will touch on this issue in Chapter 8 when we deal with the responsible party model.

INTEREST GROUPS AS INSTITUTIONS

The major difference between an organization and an institution is longevity. Institutions are organizations which have lasted a long time. In the American political system, parties and interest groups are institutions which are almost as old as government. Particular interest groups and parties may come and go, but the general practice of creating such organizations is well established at the national, state, and local levels. Both James Madison and Alexis de Tocqueville regarded them as necessary parts of our political system.

Madison referred to interest groups as factions and regarded them as "sown in the nature of man." Because factions "are united . . . by some common impulse of passion, or of interest, adverse to the rights of other citizens, or to the permanent and aggregate interests of the community," there needs to be a method for "curing the mischiefs of faction." In Paper Number Ten of *The Federalist* he observed that "the regulation of these various and interfering interests forms the principal task of modern legislation and involves the spirit of party and faction in the necessary and ordinary operations of government."[15]

De Tocqueville referred to interest groups as associations. He was impressed by the way Americans made use of them, although he made it clear that our rudimentary parties and interest groups could be threats to, as well as promoters of, the general good. Even for an enlightened nineteenth-century aristocrat like de Tocqueville, the grant of permission to form political associations to the common people was seen not as a right but as a privilege, to be taken away or modified when abused. "The unrestrained liberty of association for political purposes is the privilege which a people is longest in learning how to exercise," he noted.[16] But once learned it becomes a vital check against tyranny. Thus for two of the major contributors to modern American political theory, the notion of regulating both parties and interest groups seemed quite acceptable. An interesting term paper topic might be a comparison of the regulation of parties and that of interest groups in your state.

THE VARIETY OF INTEREST GROUPS

There are many types of interest groups. No single classification scheme can capture them all, and many groups belong in more than one category. The categories and case studies which follow merely represent an attempt to promote an exploration of the variety of interest groups and gain some understanding of their role in the political system.

Business

Although businesses compete with one another in the free enterprise system, they have many interests in common. Most are employers. Nearly all have to spend time and money dealing with various government regulations. All are subject to various kinds of local, state, and national taxes. Many seek government assistance in a variety of ways and at all levels, from getting permission to block city streets so that trucks can unload equipment conveniently to government loans and tax breaks.

There are three basic types of business interest groups: (1) individual firms, (2) trade associations, and (3) peak associations.

Individual Firms This category includes large enterprises which may operate at local, state, and national levels, such as General Motors, Exxon, and Boeing Aircraft, as well as smaller businesses of various sizes, many of which operate only at the local level.

Trade Associations In every town there are a variety of businesses (automobile dealerships, flower shops, and grocery stores) each of which can be linked to others like it across the state or at the national level through a trade association. In recent years trade associations have developed to link similar firms in large cities and metropolitan areas. Check the Yellow Pages sometime; there are a lot of businesses of the same type in a big city. Each type may have particular set of issues on which it seeks state or local government help or freedom from regulation.

Peak Associations These organizations include businesses in different fields which still have many shared interests. The U.S. Chamber of Commerce, which is organized at the state and local levels, is perhaps the best known, representing a wide range of firms. Others include the National Association of Manufacturers, which is also organized in many states, and the Business Roundtable, which tends to represent very large corporations.

Local chapters of many business organizations are as much social organizations as they are economic or political ones. Here local businesspeople gather to share experiences as employers, as taxpayers, and as people competing with big out-of-town enterprises.

In towns with populations of around 10,000 or less this function is often served by an almost ritual gathering for midmorning coffee at chosen restaurant, drugstore, or café. Sooner or later talk turns to the latest gossip about city hall, the courthouse, and the wider world of politics. Without taking a vote or running an opinion poll, leaders of the business community sometimes develop a consensus on many matters which will be discussed later in other forums.

One of the first things that happens when small towns begin to grow is that the business community becomes too large and diverse to meet in a coffee shop. More formal arrangements have to be made. Among them is the creation of one or more business organizations linked to state and national groups.

Labor Unions

Labor unions tend to be found in large economic enterprises where personal friendships and family-style relationships between employers and employees are hard to maintain. Among the central concerns of labor unions in the political arena is the issue of the legal right to create or maintain a union shop. A union shop is a factory or business establishment in which the employees, by majority vote, have created an organization to represent them in negotiating with the employer.

An essential feature of unions is that they can claim to represent employees only when a majority of the employees have voted to organize. A majority vote can end the organization as well. In a union shop one must join the union and pay dues shortly after becoming employed.

The purpose of a union shop is to avoid situations where an employee can get benefits without paying dues. Organizations require resources to do their job. Free riders ultimately weaken the ability of an organization to get the resources necessary to pursue its goals.

Right-to-work laws make union shops illegal. In other words, these laws encourage free riders. If only some of the workers pay dues to a collective-bargaining organization, the employers will still grant benefits won by the union to all employees whether they are union members or not. That way, the unity of the employees is weakened and so is their organization. Free riders are the key to breaking up labor unions: "Hey, why pay dues when I can get all these benefits for nothing?"

In addition to representing employees in particular shops, mines, and factories, many local unions combine to form statewide and nationwide organizations. These organizations promote legislation designed to help both union members and have-nots. Thus, many labor unions lobby for legislation to provide public housing, mass transit, minimum wages, strict regulation of child labor, education assistance, Social Security, and medical assistance for the disadvantaged.

Whereas business organizations tend to see government as a source of regulations and interference with the free enterprise system, labor unions tend to see government as an ally or weapon in the fight against the misuse of economic power by employers. Both unions and businesses support the free enterprise system. They simply see the role of government in that system a little differently.

Professional or Occupational Associations

This category contains numerous groups. Some of them, like the American Medical Association and the American Bar Association, are very influential

Box 7-2 **Union Shops for Lawyers in Right-to-Work States**

In many states the professional association for lawyers (the state bar association) is actually in charge of determining who gets to practice law and who doesn't. This is sometimes called an integrated bar. In this context, the term "integrated" has no relationship whatsoever to how many female, African-American, or Hispanic lawyers practice law in that state. It means that the professional association for lawyers is integrated with the government. In integrated bar states, obtaining a law degree and passing the exam designed and administered by the bar association aren't enough. One must also be admitted to the bar, and one must pay dues to the bar association.

This union shop for lawyers is often found in right-to-work states. It is one of the interesting features of state politics that many states which give this kind of control to the state bar association do not give it to organizations of blue-collar workers.

at the local, state, and national levels. It also contains organizations of more modest influence, such as the American Political Science Association.

The term "profession" can be defined as "a calling requiring specialized knowledge and often long and intensive academic preparation." It is on the basis of "intensive academic preparation" that physicians, lawyers (Box 7-2), and college professors claim to have a profession rather than an occupation. Nevertheless, in practical terms most professional and occupational associations have essentially the same political goals: control over entry to the profession or occupation, control over standards in the profession or occupation, and the development of mechanisms through law or custom which provide economic benefits for those already in the profession or occupation.

A major goal of many professional or occupational interest groups is to get the state legislature to create a board or commission to "regulate" them. The members of the board are usually practitioners of the occupation or profession and have close ties to the interest group to which most of the other practitioners belong.

While it is true that some professional or occupational interest groups represent people who are nearly always employees—teachers, nurses, and college professors, for example—many of the more affluent and powerful professional organizations represent people who are both professionals *and* business owners.

Some lawyers, physicians, and accountants are full-time employees of governments, corporations, and hospitals. Most, however, have a private practice which is essentially a business. In addition to owning or leasing an office, furniture, sophisticated phone systems, and office equipment, this business also has employees. As business owners, these lawyers, accountants, and physicians have an interest in profit, labor-management relations, tax policies, and government regulation which aligns them with the business community.

Intergovernmental Organizations

Many organizations represent either units of government or public officials. In Chapter 3 we presented a list of a dozen or more which are affiliated with the Council of State Governments. They include the National Association of Counties, the U.S. Conference of Mayors, the National League of Cities, the International City Managers Association, the National Governors' Association, and the National Conference of State Legislatures.

Two of the several intergovernmental interest groups which publish reference works that are of use to professionals, scholars, and private citizens are the Council of State Governments (CSG) and the International City Management Association (ICMA). The CSG publishes *The Book of the States*, which contains many tables comparing the governments and policies of several states. It is revised every other year and can be found in the reference section of most libraries. Also found there is *The Municipal Yearbook*, published by the ICMA, which contains articles on topics of current interest to city officials as well as tables and charts reporting surveys of city government structure, policies, and expenditures.

In addition to publications, intergovernmental interest groups promote the sharing of ideas and information through workshops, conferences, and annual conventions. They also coordinate efforts to influence other levels of government. A state association of mayors, for example, keeps its members informed about bills before the legislature which may affect cities.

As elsewhere in the interest group system, some organizations have more influence than others, especially when they form coalitions. The National Association of Towns and Townships (NAT&T) and the National Education Association (NEA) have lost several battles with interest groups representing the larger general-purpose governments. These two associations have attempted several times to get Congress to pass legislation to expand the membership of the Advisory Commission on Intergovernmental Relations (ACIR) to include seats for a township official and a school board member. Since this prestigious federal agency's recommendations on public policies are carefully considered by decision makers in all branches of government, it would be helpful for school districts, towns, and townships to be represented on it.

The commission has consistently recommended that Congress not increase its membership and Congress has followed this advice. Thus, just as all business organizations are not united on every issue, so it is with members of the intergovernmental family. Not only are there differences based on government type — city, townships, county, special district, state, and so on — there are also possibilities for alliances and disagreements based on size, wealth, diversity, and social problems. This makes it very difficult for intergovernmental organizations to always present a united front on issues.

Public-Interest Groups

Jeffrey M. Berry defines a public-interest group as "one that seeks a collective good, the achievement of which will not selectively and materially benefit the membership or activists of the organization."[17]

This definition does not mean that all other groups are against the public interest; it simply suggests that the public interest is not the primary focus of most organizations.[18] One of the functions of public-interest groups is to create coalitions of individuals and interest groups which can agree on "the public's" side of a specific issue.

Included in the broad category of public-interest groups are consumer, social-justice (civil rights and poverty), and environmental organizations. Women's organizations of general membership, including the League of Women Voters and the National Organization for Women, are also included in this category.

Two of the best known public interest organizations are Common Cause and the Public Interest Research Group. Common Cause (Box 7-3) was created in the 1970s by John Gardner, a former member of President Johnson's cabinet. The Public Interest Research Group was created by Ralph Nader, a lawyer whose book *Unsafe at Any Speed*, revealed dangerous design and production flaws in the Chevrolet Corvair.

The Public Interest Research Group is a staff-run organization which seek contributions from foundations and the general public. Common Cause is a membership organization, with over 200,000 members across the nation. This distinction is worth pointing out, since many organizations among the various types we are examining are run by their staff and make decisions with little or no consultation with their members. Some of these organizations are referred to as checkbook organizations. They have no participatory membership base but simply appeal to the public for donations. Some members of the public donate more often than do others.

Public-interest groups such as Common Cause, the Public Interest Research Group, the Sierra Club, and the Environmental Defense Fund do not claim to be infallible judges of the public interest. What they do claim is that on various issues, such as air pollution, water contamination, unsafe drugs, and unsafe cars, the public has not had an opportunity to consider *all* the facts.

Thus, public-interest groups are as interested in getting members of the general public to take the time to learn about these issues and make up their own minds about them as they are in attempting to tell people what is good for them.

In short, public-interest groups are concerned with getting certain issues on the public agenda. If, after careful consideration, the general public decides to tolerate air pollution and unsafe cars as trade-offs for economic growth and cheap transportation, it is possible that public-interest groups will have done their job on those issues and turn to others. There are plenty of important issues on which the public appears to need more information.

Box 7-3 **Interest Group Democracy: Common Cause**

Common Cause is not the only democratically run interest group; it does, however, offer a basis for asking questions about other interest groups which claim to be so.[19] Each year Common Cause does two things that few other interest groups do.

First, it distributes a mailed questionnaire to its members, giving them the opportunity to identify issues which concern them. The questions are worded to seek information, not to exert influence. No inflammatory rhetoric is used, as in some interest group polls. The results of this poll are reported in *Common Cause* magazine and are a major source of guidance for the board of directors and the executive director in terms of allocating resources in the coming year.

This contrasts significantly with the usual method by which interest groups communicate with their members. In many if not most interest groups the leadership chooses the issues and then presents one side to the membership through literature designed to motivate both contributions and letters to government officials.

A second way in which Common Cause differs from most interest groups is that its members nominate and elect the 60-member board of directors by mail. The terms are staggered so that no one has to make decisions about 60 offices all at once. Months before elections are scheduled, the Washington office sends out requests for nominations and then prepares and distributes brief biographical sketches of each candidate for the board of directors and ballots for voting.

Democracy through the mails is not the only or necessarily the best method of choosing leaders. Some interest groups choose their leaders through a system of state, regional, and national conventions. Both methods indicate that interest groups can be operated democratically.

Organizations of Religious and Moral Concerns

Included in this category are local churches, synagogues, and temples of various denominations; the organizations which link them at district, regional, state, and national levels; and various associations to which several denominations may belong, such as the National Council of Churches. Religious organizations attempt to influence government at all levels on many issues, such as social justice, hunger, racism, poverty, human rights, and the separation of church and state. In addition to traditional church-based organizations, a number of groups link television evangelists and secular conservative organizations.

Ethnic Organizations

Ethnic organizations are interest groups which help keep ethnic groups and ethnic identity alive. As we noted in Chapter 2, an ethnic group is a collection of people with a shared sense of identity which may be based on common language, religion, historical experiences, historical figures, and myths about ancestry.

The difference between an ethnic group and an ethnic organization or ethnic interest group is essentially the same as the difference between an interest and an interest group. The difference is organization. Ethnic groups are not organizations; ethnic interest groups are organizations. Identifying with an ethnic group involves an emotional commitment. Joining an ethnic interest group involves additional political resources such as time and even money.

Among the better known ethnic interest groups are the National Association for the Advancement of Colored People, the League of Latin American Citizens, B'nai B'rith, and the American Indian Movement. In addition to ethnic interest groups which are overtly political, many churches provide an organizational base for ethnic political activity.[20] Thus, some organizations can be classified as both religious and ethnic interest groups.

Local and Neighborhood Organizations

There are thousands of neighborhood interest groups at the state and local levels. Some represent the disadvantaged, some represent middle-class homeowners, and some represent exclusive neighborhoods. Some deal only with city or county government; others operate from the neighborhood to the state level.

In New York, the Queens Citizens Committee Organization (QCCO), an independent local neighborhood organization, has influenced decisions by the Port of New York Authority as well as the city council.[21] Neighborhood organizations have a stake in state and national policies in fields such as housing, historic preservation, urban redevelopment, economic development, and social justice. Thus, far from being small-time or parochial, many are true grass-roots organizations.

Agricultural Organizations

This category includes organizations which represent individuals and enterprises associated with farms, dairies, orchards, ranches, and food-processing plants. Among the variety of agricultural groups, there are two more or less clear types: general and commodity.

The three largest general organizations are the American Farm Bureau Federation, the National Grange, and the National Farmers Union. Each of these organizations is stronger in some regions than in others and has closer ties to some crops than to others.

Among the commodity organizations are the big three marketing cooperatives which link dairy farming: the Associated Milk Producers Incorporated, Mid-American Dairies, and Dairymen Inc. Each is organized at the state level and is stronger in some regions than it is in others.

Federal farm programs are of great interest to these organizations, but there are many things that state and county government do which affect them as well. At the county level, government may or may not provide adequate office space for the county extension agent or vote funds for acquiring or maintaining a fairgrounds and show barns to assist in the marketing of the county's agricultural produce.

At the state level, the opportunities for involvement are virtually endless, including promoting major state agricultural products abroad, controlling pests and diseases, and dealing with the physical and financial consequences of droughts and freezes. In the summer of 1985, for example, watermelon growers in California suffered a setback because of the improper application of pesticides which contaminated their crops. Fixing the blame, apportioning the costs, and avoiding future occurrences will take a decade to sort out in the state courts and legislature.

In 1985 a series of events involving agricultural, industrial, and ethnic interest groups in Texas, the state department of agriculture, and the state legislature provide us with a case study that illustrates at least five noteworthy dimensions of interest group activity in the political system (Box 7-4).

FUNCTIONS PERFORMED BY INTEREST GROUPS

A function can be defined as a contribution to the maintenance of a system. Thus we use the word "function" to differentiate strategies such as lobbying, electioneering, and appointmenteering from the effect they have on the political system. Among the functions performed by interest groups which help our political system operate the way it does are five which are particularly important: informing, representing, balancing, symbolizing, and mobilizing.

Informing

Interest groups bring information to decision makers who lack the staff resources to get it for them. Giving testimony at public hearings is an important part a lobbyist's job. Some of this testimony involves raw data, and some involves interpretations of what the data mean.

Some interest groups have resources for public relations and lobbying activities which are greater than the entire city hall payroll of the average city. In most state legislatures, staff resources are not available to research all issues. There are barely enough staff members to handle the flow of paperwork involved in drafting bills, reporting on hearings, and coordinating amendments and revisions. Thus, technical information on complex tax issues or the economic consequences of environmental regulation are valuable to decision makers. It doesn't matter whether it comes from an ordinary citizen, a group representing have-nots, or a group representing haves. Technical information is a valuable resource.

Box 7-4   # Better Farming Through Chemistry: A Case Study of Interest Group Conflict

In 1985, Jim Hightower, the commissioner of agriculture for the state of Texas, approved new regulations on aerial spraying of pesticides. This action was preceded by lengthy hearings at which various interest groups representing farmers, farm workers, chemical companies, aerial spraying firms, and environmentalists testified.

The chemical industry, the aerial spraying firms, and the leaders of the Farm Bureau Federation were particularly offended by two features of the new regulations. First, appropriate notice of intent to spray was required: Signs were to be posted in fields 48 hours in advance. Thus, neighbors could plan accordingly by bringing the washing in, keeping their kids indoors, and not working in nearby fields that day. The second offensive feature was that farm laborers were not to be sent out to work in chemically "hot" fields. A waiting period was required after aerial spraying.

Aerial spraying involves tons and gallons of toxic chemicals, in contrast to spraying from backpacks, which involves pounds and quarts. On family farms where there is enough money to afford aerial spraying, no farmer sends his or her family to work in hot fields. However, a large agribusiness farm owner or manager may not be reluctant to send members of someone else's family into hot fields.

Shortly after Hightower's pesticide regulations were announced, the battle lines were drawn. On one side was the Farm Bureau Federation, the Texas Chemical Council, and the aerial spraying firms. On the other was a loose coalition of environmentalists, farm worker organizations, and the Texas Farmers' Union, which represents small family farms.

After each biennial session of the state legislature, the influential *Texas Monthly* publishes an analysis of the session which features nominations for the ten best and ten worst legislators. Among the ten worst was the chairman of the House Agriculture and Livestock Committee, a leading ally of the Chemical Council and the Farm Bureau. One reason for including him among the ten worst (from among 150 representatives and 31 state senators) was "his zeal to serve their power struggle with Hightower the way a tractor serves its driver: unquestioning, unrelenting, its only duty to go where it is pointed."

The *Texas Monthly* summarized the 1985 legislative struggle as follows:

But the battle with Hightower was not over personalities or budgets or pesticides but over power: whether the "good-ol-boy" network and the agricultural lobbies could mortally wound the first agriculture commissioner who was not beholden to them.[22]

This struggle over pesticide regulation indicates five facts worth considering about interest group politics not only in Texas but elsewhere:

1. Labor-management conflicts occur outside the factory, store, and construction site. Many labor disputes involve working conditions. The working conditions in rural America for many farm laborers involve exposure to toxic chemicals.

continued

Box 7-4 *(continued)*

2. Significant disagreements are found within a single interest. Small farmers and large agribusiness firms do not agree on what government should and should not do. The Farm Bureau Federation represented large agribusiness firms in Texas; the Texas Farmers' Union represented small family farms.

3. Interest group spokespersons don't always represent their membership accurately. In the middle of the legislative session the *Texas Observer* published the findings of an investigation of the Texas Farm Bureau's claim that it represented the typical family farmer. The reporter found that the Farm Bureau was more of an insurance conglomerate than a representative of the family farm. The Farm Bureau was supposed to sell insurance only to its members, but many customers had their membership fees rebated to encourage them to buy insurance. Nevertheless, the Farm Bureau tended to report all its insurance customers as members. So carelessly did the Farm Bureau interpret its membership figures that it claimed to represent more Texas farm families than there are farms in the whole state. Furthermore, the Farm Bureau owned stock in several chemical companies which produced pesticides.

4. Economic firepower does not always win. The Texas Farm Bureau and the Texas Chemical Council had far more money to spend in lobbying the legislature and at the grass roots than did the coalition that supported Hightower. Nevertheless, at the end of the 1985 legislative session, Hightower's budget remained intact and the agricultural department remained in charge of pesticide regulation.

5. Conflicts over regulations that affect profits tend to become long-term wars. Thus, the Farm Bureau and the chemical industry will be after Hightower in many future battles. In 1989 they did manage to trim his budget slightly and modify his control of pesticide regulation. Nevertheless, they failed in their main goals of removing Hightower from office and denying him any influence in pesticide regulation.

   As we go to press Hightower is still in charge, an individual making a difference. He even survived a 1990 effort by the Farm Bureau-chemical alliance to defeat him in the Democratic party primary. This relentless partnership ran six candidates in order to confuse the voters. It didn't work. The Farm Bureau "six-pack" became a joke, and in the March election voters gave Hightower the nomination with approximately a 60 percent majority.

Sources: Mikkel Jordahl, "The Texas Farm Bureau," *Texas Observer*, (April 19, 1985), 10, and *Texas Monthly*, (July 1985), 126.

Obviously, technical information is not the only thing that influences decisions. Information about the political consequences of certain decisions is also important, and interest groups can supply this as well. That is one reason why the political consulting business has grown so much in recent years. Public opinion polling conducted by consultants paid by interest groups provides data about what the public wants, what it will tolerate, and how much discretion is available to decision makers on certain issues.

Representing

A system of representation based on geographic districts is likely to overlook interests which do not form a majority in any particular electoral district. Interest groups provide a means for those who constitute a numerical minority to obtain representation in the decision-making process.

If 10 percent of a state's population feels strongly about something, unless that 10 percent forms a majority in a particular constituency, it cannot elect even one representative in most state and local election systems. Although in a close election race 10 percent of the vote represents a significant number, many elections are not all that close. Furthermore, unless that interest organizes to try to prove that its 10 percent made the difference between winning and losing, the significance of its vote will be lost. Winning candidates like to think that "all the people" have spoken, not 41 percent plus some interest's 10 percent.

An interest group which combines (aggregates) the resources of 10 percent of the population in terms of campaign contributions and volunteer activity is much more likely to get the attention of candidates. Candidates may even compete for the endorsement (formal expression of support) of an interest group.

Interest groups which have the attention of a candidate during the campaign usually have access to that candidate when he or she becomes an officeholder. In this way interest groups can represent numerical minorities.

Balancing

Interest groups inclined toward the "mischiefs of faction" are counterbalanced by two other kinds of interest groups: real and potential.

Real interest groups promote the public interest out of their own self-interest. They may inform the public or appropriate officeholders about what the other side is attempting. Organized labor thus counterbalances various business groups, environmentalists act as a check on industries which pollute, consumer groups act as a check on producers, and so on.

Potential interest groups, according to David Truman, also keep interest groups from throwing the political system out of balance. Truman maintains that interest groups are aware that if they go too far in the pursuit of their goals, members of the general public will organize in protest and may successfully compete with them for influence over government decisions. These nonexistent potential groups, says Truman, thus act as a check on the abuse of power by the interest groups which do exist.[23] Available evidence suggests that potential interest groups do not materialize automatically and are often not there when needed most.

Symbolizing

Symbols can promote self-respect, encouraging individuals to believe in themselves and in a system which really doesn't seem to be working for them. Interest groups serve as symbols for individuals that they are somebody, that their values and identity are shared by others.

Ethnic, cultural, religious, and other organizations increase the likelihood that their members will participate in the political system in a positive way. They achieve this by providing these individuals with a positive identity and the knowledge that they are not alone, that there is an organization to channel their talents and resources as well as their grievances into the political system.

The symbolizing function is performed in many ways: by pooling resources to build, buy, or rent a meeting place; publishing newspapers or newsletters informing members of events, individual achievements, and group victories; and organizing events such as meetings and social or ritual occasions which increase group solidarity and commitment.

Mobilizing

Mobilization is the process of getting people to act, to move from passive watching to active participation. In one sense this is simply another way of looking at grass-roots lobbying. Interest groups influence decisions about matters important to them by getting their members and supporters to act, write letters, attend rallies, contact decision makers, and vote.

In another sense, mobilization is an important function which keeps a political system dynamic, alive, and open. Some interest groups perform an important function for the system as a whole. By mobilizing the passive, recruiting and training new leaders, and bringing new people into the political system, these organizations provide new energy, new ideas, and fresh insights that make state and local governments more responsive and thus more effective.

PROBLEMS ASSOCIATED WITH INTEREST GROUPS

Although interest groups are both unavoidable and advantageous for our political system, they present problems about which informed observers of the political system ought to be aware.

Irresponsibility

Interest groups almost by definition are not responsible, not accountable to the general public for the results of the government decisions they influence. When lobbyists for an interest group get a wrinkle written into a tax law that makes it more profitable for tax purposes to close a mine or a factory than to keep the enterprise going, we cannot hold that interest group responsible for the lost jobs and human suffering produced. Elected officials who approved the law may be held responsible, but not the lobbyists who promoted it.

Many interest groups are not even responsible to their members. As Box 7-5 indicates, dues-paying members and voluntary contributors are only one source of funding for interest groups. Thus, when members who are unhappy with the actions of group leaders leave an interest group, substitutes for lost dues can be found from other sources. Many interest groups depend heavily on dues, but many do not.

The realities of mass-mailed solicitations are such that many organizations can survive on less than a 10 percent response to a 200,000-item mailing. Thus, rejection by 90 percent of those solicited still allows interest group leaders to claim that they have received several thousand contributions and letters supporting their position.

Government by the Few

Robert Michels observed the tendency for small numbers of people within organizations to run them. He called it the **iron law of oligarchy**.[24]

Michels was saying much more than the fact that large numbers of people have to choose representatives to handle the details of day-to-day organization. He was concerned with the fact that in many cases small numbers of individuals take over organizations and abolish the linkages which hold them accountable to their members. Elections are held at inconvenient times, nomination becomes a complex or secret process, and election procedures such as proxy voting, which allows one person to cast votes for other people, are introduced.

On the face of it there is nothing wrong with the fact that once they are in office, many interest group leaders tend to stay there for an entire career. One way to recruit talented people and get them to make a commitment to the organization is to offer job security. However, when the procedures for making sure that the leaders are doing what the members want them to do begin to erode, the iron law of oligarchy takes on ominous features.

If many organizations run by small elites which are not responsible to their members exist in a society, they may present no great problem. However, when those organizations marshal considerable political resources to influence the selection of government officials and the decisions those officials make, they may become a problem. Government unduly influenced by irresponsible organizations can become irresponsible government.

Box 7-5 **Six Major Sources of Interest Group Funds**

1. Members' dues and contributions

2. Selective benefits*

3. Television and direct-mail solicitations

4. Publications and fees

5. Foundations and wealthy contributors

6. Government grants

*Selective benefits are those provided only to members, such as an organization's magazine or identity card. As a source of income, some selective benefits of considerable value, such as car insurance and airplane tickets, are sold at a discount to members.

Source: Jeffrey M. Berry, *The Interest Group Society*, (Boston: Little, Brown, 1984), 88–90.

Undemocratic Decision Making

No one expects corporations and financial institutions to be run democratically. Many act as interest groups and organize PACs to raise political campaign funds "voluntarily" (Box 7-6 represents an exception, not the rule) from executives and stockholders. Thus, it is no surprise that undemocratic institutions operate in our political system.

However, we might have some expectations about interest groups that are voluntary membership organizations. Common Cause provides an example of how an organization can give its members the opportunity to influence the selection of issues and strategies on which group resources will be expended. Every year a detailed survey of membership positions on issues is taken. The questions are neutrally worded, and members can indicate the direction and intensity of their opinions on these issues.

The results of the poll are printed in an issue of *Common Cause*. Furthermore, many issues of the magazine contain pro and con debates on an important public question that is likely to be of concern to the membership. Thus, the leadership of Common Cause is as concerned with accurately reflecting the opinions of its members as it is with mobilizing the members to influence government decision makers.

Common Cause is, however, as much a departure from norm as is the behavior of the bank official in Box 7-6. The much more common practice of leaders in voluntary association interest groups is to use the journal of an interest group to promote a hard-line, uncompromising position on issues and to send out mailings that are disguised as surveys but are not really legitimate efforts to survey opinion. Many "surveys" mailed out by interest

Box 7-6   **Gentle Persuasion**

When the president of Mutual Bank in Boston found out that some of the bank's 64 officers had failed to contribute to the banking industry's state and federal political action committees, he fired off a memo to all of them, saying in no uncertain terms why they should ante up:

> This is unacceptable. . . . All of you are fully aware of the importance to this bank of the issues being voted on this year. I hope none of you is so naive as to think that political contributions—even those from PACs, despite all the pious rhetoric—do not play a vital part in the progress of such matters. . . . Every single officer of this institution should—must—consider it a part of his or her position to contribute. . . . Even if you give substantially to individual candidates, you should, as officers of this bank, all support the PACs.

Before the memo, only 19 of 64 officers had been persuaded to contribute to banking industry PACs; afterward, the number jumped to 48.

Source: *Common Cause* (January-February 1985), 8.

groups are actually attempts to mobilize members to take action and at the same time to raise funds.

Misrepresentation: The Selective Benefits Problem

In some interest groups the members are more like customers than supporters of interest group causes. The reason for this is that selective benefits attract both members and customers.

Selective benefits, you may recall from Chapter 6, are rewards provided to individuals for belonging to an organization. Selective benefits for interest group members can be distinguished from the collective benefits that a large category of individuals or perhaps everyone in society is able to enjoy. Some people are more likely to pay dues to join an interest group if they get something in return. These selective benefits may include journals (professional and recreational) and discounts on various purchases (insurance, travel, medicine, and items used in one's business whether one is farmer or a physician).

The point here is that many interest group members belong primarily because they have purchased a package of selective benefits, not because they want to promote a cause or enjoy the company of other group members. Table 7-1 provides a basis for making these observations. The Farmers Union is an organization that represents farmers whose land holdings are relatively small (in effect, the traditional family farm). As the table indicates, the Farmers Union would lose about half its membership if it stopped

Table 7.1 MEMBERS OR CUSTOMERS? DIMENSIONS OF MEMBER MOTIVATION IN TWO MINNESOTA FARM ORGANIZATIONS

Item	Farm Bureau members (%)	Farmers Union members (%)
1. Importance of feelings of responsibility	35	50
2. Main reason for joining was services	54	34
3. Forced to choose between service and lobbying; chose service	66	44
4. Would drop out if organization provided lobbying but no services	56	45
5. Would drop out if organization provided services but no lobbying	23	46

Source: Terry M. Moe, *The Organization of Interests*, (Chicago: University of Chicago Press, 1980), 205–217. Reprinted by permission.

lobbying (item 5). The members apparently are aware of what the organization stands for, and that is a major reason why they belong to it. In addition, more Farmers Union members join out of a sense of responsibility to help the organization that helps them (item 1).

The Farm Bureau Federation is both a major insurance company and a group which looks after the interests of large corporate farms, collectively referred to as agribusiness. The federation would keep over 75 percent of its membership if it stopped lobbying. Clearly, many Farm Bureau members are not concerned and perhaps not even in agreement with the policy stands taken by the leadership. This may be because many Farm Bureau members joined to get their cars insured.[25] Items 2 and 3 support the notion that Farm Bureau members are customers as much as or more than they are members of an organization that attempts to influence government decisions on matters that concern them.

The implications of this for you as a future decision maker are important. When spokespersons for groups financed largely by the sale of selective benefits tell you that their membership wants something done or not done, a good question to ask is, "How do you know what your members want?"

Diversity

Given the consensus reaching back to Madison and de Tocqueville that regulation of interest groups is a valid and necessary activity, the sheer numbers and variety of types of interest groups make it extremely difficult to design a method of regulation which is rational, effective, and fair.

All states regulate political parties. This is easier because there aren't very many parties. However, the task of regulating the "mischiefs of faction" is more complex in the case of interest groups. For example, the

Southern Baptist Convention, with some 14 million members, is a potent organization. It takes positions on issues which involve decisions by the government. The fact that it is primarily a religious organization raises some difficult questions. How much government involvement should there be in making sure that the Southern Baptist Convention is run democratically and that members get a chance to hear both sides of issues on which the power and influence of the organization are brought to bear? If we are to design laws for interest groups that govern their leadership selection and decision-making processes, how should churches and religious organizations be treated?

One way might be to exempt religious organizations and use some kind of threshold in terms of economic resources. Thus, a neighborhood organization or public-interest group might not have to spend scarce resources on member surveys, as Common Cause does. However, an organization with a budget of over $60 million such as the National Rifle Association might be required to spend some of its resources on unbiased member surveys and on increasing the level of information about both sides of issues of concern to NRA members as well as NRA leaders.[26]

Elitism

For democracies to work, not all institutions within them have to be operated democratically, nor do they have to promote democratic attitudes. However, for those who must make decisions about keeping state and local governments democratic and making them more so, it is wise to know a little bit about the mixture of institutions at work in the political system. Interest groups are a case in point.

Although they operate in a democracy, many interest groups by accident or design promote an attitude that can be summarized as elitist. It is a view that is somewhat the opposite of the "trust the people" doctrine of liberal democracies. Some elitist attitudes border on contempt for the ability of the average person to make a wise and unselfish decision once the issues have been explained. They promote the view that a small group of leaders ought to decide what is best for its followers and the general public.

The late Terry Dolan, who once exercised virtual one-man control of the National Conservative Political Action Committee (NCPAC), bragged about the power of his PAC to a televised audience: "We could elect Mickey Mouse to the House or Senate."[27] This attitude toward democracy is not unique among interest group leaders. As Robert Billings, formerly of the Moral Majority, observed, "People want leadership, they don't want to think for themselves."[28]

The elitist practices of a few organizations and a few antidemocratic sentiments among some interest group leaders do not present a "clear and present danger" to our system. They are, however, patterns about which we ought to be aware as we confront choices about reforming the political system to increase or decrease the comparative influence of one or another set of institutions. Whether state government should exercise the same degree of control over interest groups with large amounts of political resources and influence that it exercises over political parties is a question that may confront you in the years to come. It bears far more discussion than we have presented here. However, one has to start somewhere.

Furthermore, as we shall observe in the chapters to come, an alternative to interest group domination is strong parties and viable institutions of government that act as alternatives to actually regulating the activities of large interest groups and the way they use their resources.

Paralysis of Government: Hyperpluralism

The process by which well-financed interest groups operate as a loose network of mutually supporting seekers of self-interest can ultimately lead to a situation in which particular groups gain control of the portion of the government that affects them most closely. The officials in charge, whether appointed or elected, both owe their positions to and agree with the interest group which got them there and helps keep them there.

This can, as Theodore Lowi suggests, result in the paralysis of government. No action is taken in the public interest because it might interfere with a particular group's private interest.[29] Interest groups can thus be issued licenses to pollute streams, underground water supplies, and the air and produce unsafe products, maintain unsafe working conditions, and engage in competitive practices which destroy small businesses or institutions which benefit the general public, such as mass transit systems and parks, beaches, and other recreational areas.

Two ways in which interest groups have helped close doors on policies and programs at the state and local levels which might have been in the public interest involve mass transit and public housing.

Early in this century, at a critical stage in the development of urban transportation, when a variety of policy choices were available, a consortium of corporations strongly influenced the decision-making process by buying up and then destroying electric trolley systems in about 50 large American cities. When they did this, there weren't all that many large American cities. Thus they set a pattern for how things would be done in growing cities. In 1949, in a Chicago courtroom in a federal court, a jury found General Motors guilty of conspiracy in restraint of trade. General Motors was fined $5000, and its treasurer was fined $1.[30] The 50 mass transit systems were never rebuilt.

The current condition of mass transit in American cities is not wholly due to the effect of this conspiracy. However, by destroying electric trolley systems and channeling talent and energy into other methods of moving people and goods, the conspiracy doubtless shaped the options considered and the decisions made. At that time in our history, the governments of the states and cities affected were unable to deal with this interest group assault on the public interest.

In the area of public housing, real estate and building industry lobbyists have been able to keep public housing projects relatively small and stigmatized as welfare-type services. In other countries public housing is rented by members of the middle and upper classes as well as by people on welfare. It is located in coordination with mass transit and serves as an alternative to private housing. Thus, public housing serves as a check on high prices and excessive profiteering in the housing market.[31]

The implications of a strong public housing system and mass transit systems for reducing urban sprawl and the inefficient use of time and fuel are too many to develop here. However, it seems fairly obvious that urban sprawl has been rather expensive for the state and local taxpayers who foot the bill for education, police, fire, sewer, and water services as populations spread haphazardly across the landscape.

The Business Bias

One of the most important features of the interest group system is that it is not balanced. There are more business interest groups than any other kind. Furthermore, as we have indicated, many people in high-prestige professions are in effect operators of businesses enterprises such as law firms and medical practices. On the whole, in struggles between business and nonbusiness interest groups, business interest groups are better equipped. They have more money, more prestige, and more resources to offer elected and appointed government officials. Business interests can employ experienced, skilled full-time professionals to communicate their positions on various issues and write their salaries and expense accounts off as part of the cost of doing business.

This imbalance should come as no surprise, but one needs to confront it early on and take it as a feature of the interest group system rather than the result of an evil plot. In a landmark survey of state political systems, Sarah McCally Morehouse examined the dominant types of interest groups in each of the 50 states and the degree to which interest groups as a whole influenced the state political system.[32]

Although other institutions in the 50 states, such as local governments, political parties, the legislature, and the governor, all influence the decision-making process, it is possible to identify states in which interest groups are more influential than they are in others (Table 7.2).

The table indicates two characteristics of the relationship between business interest groups and the system of interest groups found in every state. First, regardless of the comparative strength of the interest groups in each state political system, business groups predominate. They are regarded by legislators, journalists, executive officials, and other informed sources as having more influence on the political system than do other types of interest groups. Second, in states where interest groups are strongest, business inter-

Table 7.2   APPARENT BIAS IN STATE INTEREST GROUP SYSTEMS

Type of group	Percent of interest group type in states where interest group systems are		
	Strong*	Moderate	Weak
Business	75	71	58
Labor	5	7	15
Farm	7	13	14
Education	7	7	13
Government	5	2	

*Columns may not add up to 100 percent because of rounding.

Source: L. Harmon Zeigler, ''Interest Groups in the States,'' in Virginia Gray, Herbert Jacob, and Kenneth N. Vines, eds., *Politics in the American States*, 4th ed. (Boston: Little, Brown, 1984), 103.

ests are even more predominant. The stronger the interest group system, the stronger the business interest groups within it.

The fact that the interest group system is biased in favor of business would not be very important if most Americans were owners of or executives in businesses. However, most Americans are employees and/or consumers. Thus, there are times when the interests of the business community and the interests of the general public do not coincide. If the strongest institutions in the political system are biased in favor of business, it is not likely that the general public interest will be looked after adequately.

CONTROLLING THE MISCHIEFS OF FACTION

There are four basic methods of limiting the damage interest groups can do to the political system while allowing these groups to continue making positive contributions to the political system: disclosure, regulation, public financing, and strengthening other institutions.

Disclosure

Disclosure involves letting the public know about sources of money and uses of money in attempts to influence public decisions. Disclosure requires interest groups as well as parties and candidates to make clear where they get their financial resources and what they do with them. By requiring that the use of money in politics take place in the public eye instead of behind the scenes, disclosure requirements may help voters and public officials decide whether they want to support a given candidate or course of action.

At the very least, disclosure may suggest to some people that a careful look be taken at a proposal or candidate receiving heavy financial support from a particular interest group. The two activities interest groups engage in which are most subject to disclosure requirements are electioneering and lobbying.

Disclosure may be more effective when there is an adequately financed independent agency which both enforces the reporting requirements and makes information about contributions easily available to the public before an election. Twenty-two states have such agencies.[33]

Disclosure can occur, of course, without doing much good. Collecting file cabinets full of reports which enterprising citizens, journalists, and scholars can read only if they come to the office of the secretary of state in the state capital and request them is better than no disclosure at all. This arrangement works much better in a small state than in a large one.

Disclosure can be even more effective, however, if periodic reports are published which can be more easily digested and transformed into newspaper stories or questions to ask at candidate forums.

Regulation

This approach involves requiring an interest group to do something or forbidding it to do something. Usually regulation involves the amount of money an interest group or PAC can contribute to a candidate or party.

In addition, federal regulations and some state regulations make it illegal for corporations and labor unions to contribute directly to a candidate from company funds or union dues. This is one reason why PACs are created: to provide a fund-raising organization separate from the corporation, union, or interest group.

Other limitations may involve the internal operation of the interest group itself. The Landrum-Griffin Act is a federal law that requires labor unions to make detailed reports of union constitutions and rules. Furthermore, certain types of persons are forbidden to hold union office: ex-convicts, Communists, and people with conflicting business interests (a union member who owned a printing company might be tempted to benefit his or her business through control of union funds). One of the intentions of the Landrum-Griffin Act was to make union leaders accountable to union members.[34]

The same kinds of controls over the internal affairs of various wealthy PACs and large interest groups might further accountability in those organizations as well. Thus far, however, little effort has been made to require by law that elections in organizations other than unions and political parties be held democratically, that members who disagree with interest group leaders get an opportunity to be heard by the rest of the membership, or that both sides of important issues be represented in interest group journals and other mailings.

Public Financing

The federal government, 17 states, and a few cities provide resources for the election campaigns of certain candidates or their parties. Presidential candidates who meet qualifications indicating that they have a significant amount of public support can receive federal funds if they promise to adhere to limitations on their campaign expenditures.

In 13 states taxpayers indicate whether they want a portion of their state income taxes to be placed in a fund for public funding of election campaigns. In seven states taxpayers can add a contribution called a surcharge to the state campaign financing fund. In California the surcharge is matched by the state.

In some states these funds are turned over to political parties; in others they are given directly to candidates for various offices, usually statewide rather than legislative. In Utah the county central committee of the party designated by a voter gets 50 percent of that voter's checkoff funds. Hawaii appropriates funds for all nonfederal elective offices. New Jersey provides funds only for gubernatorial elections, while three other states make funds available to campaigns for more than one state office.[35]

In Seattle, Washington, and Tucson, Arizona, candidates for city council and mayor receive public funds if they agree to limit the total amount of money they spend in their campaigns.[36] As we have observed, money is not the only political resource. Instead of providing funds in exchange for limits on candidates' expenditures, at least one city is considering the provision of free time on cable TV, office space, and polling, printing, and secretarial services.[37]

Strengthening Other Institutions

Although it is not a perfect relationship because many factors are involved, the stronger the interest groups in a state are, the more likely it is that institutions such as political parties, the legislature, and the executive branch of government will be less able to govern, deliver on campaign promises, and promote policies for the have-nots.

Thus, if you wanted to limit the imbalance in a state political system between interest groups and other institutions, you would probably not want to introduce reforms that weaken other institutions. On the contrary, you would be advised to attempt to (1) dilute the relative influence of interest groups by raising the level of education and awareness of the general public, (2) strengthen other institutions such as political parties, (3) increase the resources available to state and local legislatures, and (4) make it easier to hold the heads of executive agencies accountable to the chief executive rather than to the interest groups with which they deal most closely.

In the chapters that follow, we will discuss these institutions and ways to strengthen them. The purpose of strengthening other institutions is not to obliterate interest groups or even render them powerless but simply to let them continue doing the good things they do well while preventing them from advancing the mischiefs of faction.

Conclusion

In this chapter we have identified one type of institution through which you can influence government: interest groups. We have attempted to demystify PACs, treating them essentially as interest groups. We have broadly sketched the wide variety of interest groups and used several case studies to identify important lessons about interest groups and their role in state and local politics.

Our discussion of the advantages and disadvantages of interest groups doubtless gives the impression that we believe the latter often outweigh the former. This was not an accident. However, it was not intended to suggest that interest groups and PACS are illegitimate institutions or that they should be removed from the political system.

The possibility that the disadvantages of interest groups outweigh their advantages is partly a product of the fact that the political system is out of balance. When interest groups are too strong, other institutions, including government, are likely to be weak, unable to promote the public interest. Furthermore, these other institutions are unable to help interest groups correct their own problems. Take, for example, the problem of misrepresentation. Many businesspeople would be appalled by the extreme positions taken by interest group leaders in the name of the business community, just as many responsible gun owners would be embarrassed by, or at least unsympathetic to, some of the positions taken by the National Rifle Association. When interest groups predominate, parties and government have little opportunity to require interest group leaders to act more responsibly toward their followers.

These observations will be tested in the pages to come. Naturally, since we chose the evidence, it won't be an unbiased test. Therefore, we urge you to conduct your own tests in the course of deciding how to participate in politics.

Study Objectives

1. Identify the three dimensions of our definition of "interest group."
2. Compare and contrast interest groups and parties.
3. Identify four similarities between PACs and interest groups.
4. Identify the difference between an interest and an interest group.

5. Identify the three major types of business interest groups.
6. Identify the major issue which concerns labor unions.
7. Identify two examples in which the language of politics helps shape our views on issues.
8. Identify two publications associated with intergovernmental interest groups.
9. Identify "public-interest group" and differentiate it from one or more of the other types of interest groups.
10. Differentiate "ethnic group" and "ethnic interest groups."
11. Identify "the mischiefs of faction."
12. Identify the functions performed by interest groups.
13. Identify four ways to reduce the effect of problems associated with interest groups (control the mischiefs of faction).

Glossary

disclosure This involves letting the public know about sources and uses of money in attempts to influence public decisions. Disclosure requires interest groups as well as parties and candidates to make clear where they get their financial resources and what they do with them.

ethnic organizations Interest groups which help keep ethnic groups and ethnic identity alive.

interest group An organization which seeks to influence government decisions without taking responsibility for running the government.

iron law of oligarchy The tendency for small numbers of people within organizations to run them.

political action committee An organization created to collect money in order to influence elections, largely through campaign contributions.

political party An organization that seeks to control government. In democracies a political party is an organization that seeks to control government through winning elections rather than through coups and terrorism.

potential interest groups Groups which, according to some theorists, will emerge from the general public if existing interest groups misbehave excessively. The effectiveness of this threat is demonstrated in part by the level of air pollution, homelessness, and the fairness of state and local taxes. In other words, your assessment of the condition of society is a measure of your assessment of the effectiveness of potential interest groups.

real interest groups This is another term for "interest groups." It is used in the discussion of potential interest groups to differentiate that which could be from that which is.

Endnotes

1. Larry J. Sabato, *PAC Power: Inside the World of Political Action Committees*, (New York: Norton, 1984), 12.

2. Malcom E. Jewell and David M. Olson, *Political Parties and Elections in American States*, 3rd ed. (Chicago: Dorsey, 1988), 163–164.
3. California Commission on Campaign Financing, "Money and Politics in the Golden State: Financing California's Local Elections," cited in Joel L. Swerdlow, ed., *Media Technology and the Vote: A Source Book*, (Washington, DC: Annenberg Washington Program in Communications Policy Studies of Northwestern University, 1988), 86–87.
4. Carl E. Van Horn, ed., *The State of the States*, (Washington, DC: Congressional Quarterly Press, 1989), 186.
5. Herbert Alexander and Brian A. Haggerty, "Campaign Spending is Going Up, but Who's Keeping Score?" *Governing*, (November 1987), 74.
6. W. John Moore, "Buying State Access," *National Journal* (April 30, 1988), 1116–1121, cited in Bruce Stinebrickner, *State and Local Government*, 4th ed. (Guilford, CT: Dushkin, 1989), 56.
7. Advisory Commission on Intergovernmental Relations, *Significant Features of Fiscal Federalism*, 1989 ed. (Washington, DC: ACIR, 1989), 14.
8. Swerdlow, 82.
9. Dexter Filkins, "For Senate Candidates, the Only Issue Is Money," *Washington Post* (May 25, 1988), A19, cited in Swerdlow, 82.
10. Jewell and Olson, 165.
11. Kevin Williams, "Introduction," in *Political Action Committee Contributions in Texas: 1988*, (Austin, TX: Kevin Williams, 1989).
12. Sabato, 165.
13. Ibid., 47.
14. Ibid., 164.
15. James Madison, Federalist 10 in Roy P. Fairfield, ed. *The Federalist Papers* 2nd ed., (Baltimore: Johns Hopkins University Press, 1981), 17.
16. Alexis de Tocqueville, *Democracy in America*, Vol. I translated by Henry Reeve, (New Rochelle, NY: Arlington House, 1971), 182.
17. Jeffrey M. Berry, *Lobbying For The People: The Political Behavior of Public Interest Groups*, (Princeton, NJ: Princeton University Press, 1977), 7.
18. Some authors use the term "public-interest group" to refer to organizations which represent units of government or government officials. See, for example, Deil S. Wright, *Understanding Intergovernmental Relations*, (North Scituate, MA: Duxbury, 1978), 61. While it is true that we are all in big trouble if these organizations do not keep the public interest in mind, we have chosen to use Berry's definition.
19. For an excellent theoretical treatment of Common Cause in the larger interest group context, see Andrew S. McFarland, *Common Cause: Lobbying in the Public Interest*, (Chatham, NJ: Chatham House, 1984).
20. Edgar Litt, *Ethnic Politics in America*, (Glenview, IL: Scott, Foresman, 1970), 49–59.
21. For a discussion of QCCO and its successful confrontation with the powerful Port Authority of New York and New Jersey, see Michael Dorman, "The Bigger They Are," *Empire State Magazine*, (1983) collected in, Bruce Stinebrickner, ed., *State and Local Government 84/85*, (Guilford, CT: Dushkin Publishing Group, Inc., 1984), 68–71.
22. *Texas Monthly*, (July 1985), 126.
23. David Truman, *The Governmental Process*, (New York: Knopf, 1951), 33.

24. Robert Michels, *Political Parties* (New York: Dover, 1959); see especially "Democracy and the Iron Law of Oligarchy," pp. 377–393.
25. Mikkel Jordahl, "The Texas Farm Bureau," *Texas Observer*, (April 19, 1985), 9–12.
26. National Rifle Association, annual financial report for 1987 to the New York Department of State. The NRA's largest opponent is Handgun Control. In contrast to the $69 million in revenue of the NRA, Handgun Control's report to the New York Department of State indicates $3 million in revenues.
27. Sabato, 96.
28. James L. Guth, "The Politics of the Christian Right," in Allan J. Cigler and Burdett A. Loomis, eds., *Interest Group Politics*, (Washington, DC: CQ Press, 1983), 73.
29. Theodore J. Lowi, *The End of Liberalism*, 2nd ed. (New York: Norton, 1979), 60.
30. Testimony of Tom Bradley, mayor of Los Angeles, before the U.S. Senate Subcommittee on Antitrust and Monopoly, Judiciary Committee, U.S. Senate, 93rd Congress, February 26–March 1, 1974. Quoted in Mark Schneider, *Suburban Growth: Policy and Process*, (Brunswick, OH: King's Court Communications, 1980), 32–33.
31. Arnold J. Heidenheimer, Hugh Heclo, and Carolyn Teich Adams, *Comparative Public Policy: The Politics of Social Choice in Europe and America*, (New York: St. Martin's, 1983), 93–94. See also Barry Checkoway, "Large Builders, Federal Housing Programmes, and Postwar Suburbanization," *International Journal of Urban and Rural Research*, (March 1980), 21–45.
32. Sarah McCally Moorehouse, *State Politics, Parties and Policy*, (New York: CBS College Publishing, 1981).
33. Council of State Governments, *The Book of the States, 1986–87*, (Lexington, KY: Council of State Governments), 185–189.
34. Richard B. Morris, ed., *The Encyclopedia of American History*, 6th ed. (New York: Harper & Row, 1982), 526.
35. *The Book of the States, 1986–87*, 206–207.
36. *Austin American-Statesman*, July 23, 1985.
37. Ibid., A-10.

Chapter 8

Institutions for Participation: Political Parties and Elections

Political parties are organizations for political participation. They are defined in terms of, and are almost impossible to analyze apart from, elections. Parties, interest groups, and PACs have names, addresses, and members. These institutions for political participation constitute a system for influencing government decisions. A body of literature emerged during the 1980s suggesting that this system is out of balance. Titles such as *The Party's Over*, *American Parties in Decline*, and *Where Have All the Voters Gone: The Fracturing of America's Political Parties* imply that parties are not doing very well.[1] There is a fair amount of evidence that states with strong interest groups are far more numerous than are states with strong two-party systems.[2] Furthermore, parties play little or no role, and party labels do not even appear on the ballot, in most city and virtually all school board elections.

Table 8.1 ATTITUDES TOWARD INSTITUTIONS FOR PARTICIPATION

In general, which one of the kinds of organizations listed below do you feel best represents the political interests of people like you?

1. Organized groups concerned with specific issues, such as business, labor, environmental, and civil rights groups
2. The two major political parties: the Democrats and the Republicans
3. Other political parties
4. Don't know

	Percentages			
	1	2	3	4
Total public	45	34	3	17
Male	45	38	3	14
Female	45	32	3	20
Birth year*				
1959–1965	56	21	5	17
1949–1958	56	27	4	13
1939–1948	44	41	3	12
1919–1938	41	40	2	17
1918 or earlier	27	42	2	29

*Survey was taken in 1983, using age groups. Conversion to birthdates done by authors.

Source: Advisory Commission on Intergovernmental Relations, *Changing Attitudes on Government and Taxes*: (Washington, DC ACIR, 1988), 71.

In the pages which follow we will attempt to explain why the system seems to be out of balance and what can be done about it. As elsewhere in this book, our discussion is from a particular point of view. It is clearly pro-party. However, if you have serious reservations about political parties, two things are clear. First, you are not alone, as Table 8.1 indicates. The generations born before 1939 have a much more positive attitude toward political parties. Your generation and those born since the end of the Great Depression tend to see interest groups as the institutions most likely to be representative of your concerns. If you share your generation's doubts, a second clear response to the bias in this chapter is that you may want to consider working against any suggestions we make for changing the status quo.

POLITICAL PARTY: A DEFINITION

A **political party** in the American intergovernmental system is an organization which attempts to take control of government by means of winning elections. This definition has three implications.

Control of Government

When we say "attempts to take control," we do not mean to suggest that a party in charge of a unit of government ever becomes fully responsible for everything that goes on in that government. If we were to do so, we would be denying the basic argument of this book: that individuals as well as institutions matter. However, when a party criticizes incumbent officeholders during electoral campaigns and promises to do better, that party and its candidates give the impression that once in office they will take responsibility for making government work in the interests of the larger society.

Two Parties

Our definition applies to the major parties in the American two-party dominant system: Republicans and Democrats. We do, however, recognize the existence of minor, or "third," parties in the American political system, many of which contest elections in order to promote various causes or protest the failures of the two major parties. Some minor parties are successful in getting candidates elected locally and even at the state level. Many do not last more than one or two election cycles before one of the major parties adopts their issues and even recruits their candidates. A few minor parties —sometimes referred to as ideological parties—continue to exist for decades with no electoral victories.

One-Party Regions and No-Party Elections

An organization does not have to win elections frequently or even occasionally in every constituency to be considered a political party. This notion is based on two facts about the American political system. First, a party may habitually lose elections in one county or portion of a state but frequently win in other counties or portions of the state. For the first half of this century the states of the former Southern Confederacy were referred to as the Solid South because elections there were consistently won by the Democratic party. That long string of victories, however, did not remove the Republican party from the American or even the Southern political system. When the Solid South was a feature of the American political system, the farm belt states were predominantly Republican. Thus, the Republican party had a base in the Midwest from which to help Republicans in the South, and the Democrats had a base in the South from which to help Democrats in the Midwest.

It used to be said in Iowa that "Iowa will go Democratic when hell goes Methodist."[3] As Figure 8.1 indicates, at least in terms of elections for governor, the South is no longer solid. Furthermore, in Iowa, despite Republican control of the governorship and the office of state auditor, Democrats control both houses of the state legislature and the five statewide elective offices, including lieutenant governor.[4]

A second fact about the American political system that makes parties uncompetitive in many constituencies is that parties are formally excluded from the ballot in about half the elections held in this country. These **nonpartisan elections** do not use party labels on the ballot as a guide to voters. In a nonpartisan election parties may offer candidates and try to inform the public about which ones are Democrats and which are Republicans, but when the voter walks into the voting booth in a nonpartisan election, there are no party labels on the ballot.

The general election in November is the one election in which party labels are included in most states. An exception is Nebraska, where the legislature is elected without party labels. As we shall observe later, party primaries are also nonpartisan elections; there are no party labels to guide voters in making electoral decisions.

THE FORMAL STRUCTURE OF POLITICAL PARTIES

According to Frank J. Sorauf, each of the two major American parties contains three major components: the party in office, the electoral party organization, and the party in the electorate.[5]

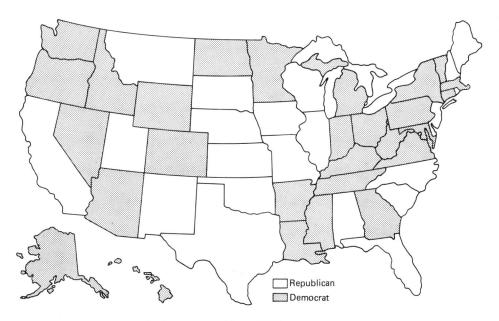

Figure 8.1 Party control of governorships: 1989.

The Party in Office

The **party in office** consists of officials in government who were elected under the party label or appointed because of party affiliation. These are the individuals who attempt to organize the government and take responsibility for running it. In the best of circumstances it is difficult for the party in office to become unified enough to carry out the comprehensive programs that were promised in party platforms and campaign literature. In addition to the fact that each party is made up of individuals with their own personalities, career objectives, and values, six major sources of difficulty face party leaders in promoting unity in the party in office: (1) federalism, (2) separation of powers, (3) institutional loyalty, (4) PACs and interest groups, (5) political consultants, and (6) the rules of the game.

The Federal System   When one party controls the national government, states governed by the other party can expect that in close-call decisions involving grants, appointments, and the location of economic benefits such as new federal facilities, the benefit of the doubt probably will not go their way. Even when the parties are the same at the national and state levels, the national government may promote policies and programs that are not consistent with state and local goals and objectives. For example, Alaska and California are attempting to protect their coastal environments while the federal government allows unsupervised oil shipments and offshore oil drilling. One governor is a Republican, the other a Democrat.

The Principle of Separation of Powers   One party may control the governorship but not both houses of the state legislature. From 1965 to 1986 this occurred at least once in virtually every state.[6] As we pointed out in the case of Iowa, not only is it common for one party to have the governorship while the other controls at least one house of the legislature, but the executive branch itself may be divided between the two parties, if executive offices other than the governorship are elective.

Institutional Loyalty   Even when one party controls the governorship and both houses, difficulties arise from the fact that party members in each branch develop a loyalty to their own agency, house, or branch of government. They tend to perceive things differently than do fellow party members from elsewhere in the government.

PACs and Interest Groups   In many states the interest group system is so strong and the party system so weak that each officeholder is obligated to PACs for finances to get the party nomination. Many candidates have won a general election without much help from their party. Thus these members of the party in office may owe as much or more loyalty to the coalition of interests and individuals that constituted their campaign organizations as they do to the party under whose label they won office.

Political Consultants   Originally **political consultants** were individuals or firms that offered professional expertise in the new technology of political campaigning: computer-assisted mass mailings to target particular literature or issues to particular demographic areas within a city, county, or state for campaigning, fundraising, or both; public opinion polling; television and radio advertising; and press relations. The increased dependence of candidates at all levels on consultants to raise money and help spend it has also increased the cost of campaigns. From 1984 to 1988 about $6 billion was spent on campaigns.[7]

In recent years these consulting firms have begun to lobby the public officials they helped to elect, which raises some interesting ethical questions. Also worth our attention is the fact that some consultants are now engaged in candidate recruitment. According to Larry Sabato, two political consultants were primarily responsible for getting Dan Quayle chosen as George Bush's running mate: "Bob Teeter, Bush's pollster, and Roger Ailes, his media consultant, had both handled Dan Quayle's previous congressional campaigns in Indiana. And they both knew just how attractive and malleable Dan Quayle was." They advocated his selection, says Sabato, because "Dan Quayle is a consultant's kind of candidate."[8]

The influence of the more than 12,000 people in America who earn part or most of their living by political campaign consulting bears careful scrutiny by individuals concerned with responsive and responsible government. It is one of the factors which may increase the independence of incumbents from the influence of party and from the discipline of the electorate.[9]

However, if the parties hire consultants, this may tend to work the other way. According to political consultant Celinda Lake, "We are likely to see many more consultants in permanent relationships with state party organizations. . . . Frankly the consultants desire these relationships because parties . . . are there forever."[10]

Under these conditions, promoting agreement among the diverse elements in each party in government is a challenging and ongoing part of the political process. The ability of a party to promote unity in government and thus deliver on the party's campaign promises is enhanced by a state's political culture, traditions, constitution, election laws, and rules for organizing government as well as the skills of party leaders in taking advantage of new technologies and resources such as those offered by political consultants.

The Rules of the Game   An example of the importance of the rules for organizing a legislature is found in the U.S. Congress. There the parties are important to each member because assignments to the 20 or more standing committees in each house are made by party committees. In each house the seats are assigned to each party in proportion to its membership in the whole body. Then the Republicans assign the Republican seats and the Democrats assign the Democratic seats through a party committee. Since choice committee assignments are important to the careers of individual legislators, the party becomes more important to members of the House and Senate.

By contrast, the role of the party in making committee assignments is not as great in most state legislatures. This power usually resides in the hands of the speaker of the house and the president of the senate.[11] In the absence of a strong party organization, there is likely to be a tendency toward making one powerful person and the interest groups which helped that person along the way more important to members of the legislature than are party goals or programs.

In spite of the limited role assigned to parties, many state legislatures have at least a rudimentary party organizational structure. The basic elements are the positions of the majority and minority leaders elected by party caucuses. A **party caucus** is a meeting of all the members of a party in a legislative body. Thus, there could be a house party caucus of Democrats, a house party caucus of Republicans, and two senate party caucuses. Jewell and Olson found that in 43 states party caucuses play a role in the legislative process. They identify six types of party caucuses:[12]

Caucuses with votes binding on members

Caucuses used by strong leaders to affect policy

Caucuses that contribute significantly to party cohesion

Caucuses that contribute significantly to policy-making

Caucuses that serve primarily to keep the membership informed

Caucuses designed to give members control over leaders

Although state legislatures often contain four different party organizations, two in each house, there is usually at least one significant party in the executive branch: the governor's party. This is the coalition of local and state party leaders, interest groups, and individuals that helped the governor get elected. The ability of a governor to deliver on promises and get reelected depends to a great extent on the governor's ability to promote harmony and cooperation not only between his or her party and fellow party members in the house and senate, but also between the entire party in office and the electoral party organization.

The Electoral Party Organization

The **electoral party** consists of (1) individuals who campaign, attend party meetings and social functions, and contribute to the party, (2) officials of the party at the state and local levels, and (3) staff members. The vast majority of the individuals in an electoral party are volunteers. Very few staff members or officials are on the payroll. The electoral party can be viewed as a set of permanent organs which keep the party going year-round and organize the temporary organs — the primaries and conventions at which party members interact and make decisions.

The Permanent Organs   These organs consist of the chairs and the executive committees at the national, state, county, and precinct levels. The organizational structure of a party is determined largely by state law. The **state election code** (the collection of laws dealing with elections) usually requires that certain officials be designated and often requires the party to choose them in a certain way. Unlike interest groups, parties are highly regulated by state government.[13]

The electoral party in many states is not organized at the grass roots in every geographic area. Figure 8.2 indicates the way state chairs would like it to be. In a state with 200 counties, there may be dozens of precinct chairs and one or two county chairs open at any given time. Although this is bad news for a state chair and for candidates who would like party help, the good news is that individuals eager to learn the political process can become party officials fairly easily in some places.

The basic pattern of organization is for the chair of the executive committee at one level to serve as a member of the executive committee at the next highest level. Thus, a county executive committee would consist of precinct chairs and the county chair. In states with townships and states where counties include cities large enough in population to have more than one state senate or congressional district, the pattern would be a little different.

Just as there is variation and incomplete development of the party structure in some states, there is also considerable variation in the formality of organization at party headquarters. Although most state party headquarters

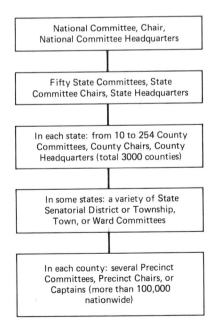

Figure 8.2 Party organization. Not every office is filled in every precinct and county, but few state offices are vacant for long in either party.

have two or three full-time staff members and an office in the state capital, many county and precinct organizations operate out of someone's business office or home. Meetings of the county executive committee at a kitchen table are not unheard of in suburban and rural areas.

Organizational charts imply hierarchy. In political parties, however, there is as much bottom-to-top influence as there is top-down influence. County chairs are not hired and fired by state chairs. If the state chair is involved at all, it is likely to be as one of the people who cajole and persuade a reluctant individual to take the job of county chair. Usually, the selection of a county chair occurs at the local level. Chairs are usually individuals who have been active in the party for a considerable period of time, know the personalities and history of the party at the level at which they operate, and are respected for "paying their dues" because they work hard within the organization.

Periodic Organs: Primaries and Conventions   In most states parties are required by state law to nominate candidates for most public offices by means of primary elections rather than at party conventions.[14] In a **primary election** voters who may or may not be active in the party can help determine whom the party will nominate. In many states even party officials such as precinct and county chairs are chosen in a primary.

The laws for getting on the ballot in primaries are so open in some states that the party's most precious resource — the nomination — is placed at the disposal of the general public and thus of any interest groups eager to influence the selection process. Because of this required openness to non-members, a tragicomedy of major proportions occurred in 1986 in the state of Illinois.

Two candidates from a far-right-wing organization led by Lyndon Larouche ran in the Democratic primary and received enough votes to win nomination to statewide offices. Party leaders could do nothing about it because they had no control over the nominations. So distasteful was the prospect of running on the same ticket with these candidates and being associated with the policies they supported that the Democratic party's candidate for governor — former U.S. Senator Adlai Stevenson III — withdrew from the Democratic ticket and attempted to organize an independent slate. To no one's surprise, Republicans won in the general election.

The requirement of nomination by primary election is a major difference between parties and interest groups. The general public has virtually no role in telling interest groups whom to choose as leaders or how to use their major resources.

Political party conventions are held at the precinct, county, state, and national levels. Even when state conventions do not nominate candidates, they are regarded as important institutions because they

Obtain publicity for the party and its candidates

Afford prestige to local party leaders who attend them as delegates

Provide opportunities (not always realized) for building party unity for the forthcoming campaign

Select delegates to the national conventions and the national committee

Select or certify the selection of the party members who will serve as presidential electors if the party's candidate wins in that state

Select the state chair (usually by ratifying the choice of the party's candidate for governor)

May also pass rules affecting party operations and organization

Make policy decisions including the state party platform

In addition to the factors listed above, in some states there is an additional reason: These states hold endorsing conventions, which have the effect of promoting party unity and party strength.

Endorsing Conventions   In nine states the electoral party still has a major role in influencing the nominating process for governor and other major offices. The mechanism for this is the preprimary convention. In these conventions members of the electoral party decide which candidates to endorse for the primary election. In Connecticut a clear winner at the convention becomes the party's nominee and does not need to run in a primary unless a rival who received at least 20 percent of the convention vote challenges him or her. In Colorado the candidate endorsed by the convention is listed first on the primary election ballot. Thus primary voters in that state can safely assume that ballot position means something in the governor's race — the preference of those active in the party.[15]

Although not all candidates endorsed by a party convention win the nomination in the primary, most do. As a result, candidates endorsed by the convention are much more likely to pay attention to the party after they are elected. Further differences are noticeable between states which have endorsing conventions and those which do not. States with endorsing conventions are about twice as likely to have uncontested primaries because unsuccessful candidates frequently withdraw from the primary. Uncontested primaries promote party unity. According to Jewell and Olson, in states with conventions for endorsing party candidates for governor, primary contests occurred 49.3 percent of the time in the period 1960–1986. However, in the rest of the states nearly 80 percent of the primary races for governor were contested.[16]

According to Morehouse, the ability of the electoral party to have such a strong influence on the nomination for a state's highest elective office helps strengthen the party and increase the likelihood of cooperation between the party in office and the electoral party.[17]

The Party in the Electorate

At least one of the following three categories of people are included in most definitions of the **party in the electorate**: (1) those who say they identify with the party and in some states those who stated their party allegiance when they registered to vote, (2) those who vote in the primary election of a party, and (3) those who usually vote for a party's candidates in general elections.

Since there are no lists of dues-paying members or formal procedures for joining and since many states do not require voters to indicate party preference when they register to vote, any attempt to measure the size of the party in the electorate is usually indirect. It depends on which of the foregoing dimensions one wishes to stress. We now examine each dimension of the party in the electorate to gain a better understanding of the nature of parties and their role in the political system.

Party Identifiers   **Party identification** is the willingness to express a feeling of support for and identity with a political party. Party identity performs two important functions in promoting a stable, coherent political system. One function is performed for the individual, and one for the electoral process.

In terms of the electoral process, the fact that 60 percent of the population has a party identity and usually acts on it means that each party starts every election with a fairly predictable share of the vote on which to build. From its portion of the electorate, each party can recruit candidates and volunteer workers and appeal for campaign contributions. If each party started each election cycle from zero with no foundation on which to build, the electoral process would probably involve even more blatant appeals to emotion and greater use of attention-getting activities than it already does.

The recent concern about landslide elections at the presidential level as an indicator of party decline can also be interpreted as an indicator of the tenacity of party identity. In 1984 one of the most popular Presidents in our history won nearly every state in an election that was referred to frequently in the media as a landslide. However, this most recent landslide was only the fifth highest in our history. Four other Presidents (two Republicans and two Democrats) received larger margins. The first landslide occurred in 1920, when Warren G. Harding won with 60.3 percent of the popular vote. The biggest was that of Franklin Delano Roosevelt, who in 1936 won 60.8 percent of the popular vote. During the era in which those elections took place, the party system was considered to be alive and well.

In the language of the scholars at the Survey Research Center at the University of Michigan, the 1984 presidential election was a "deviating election," one in which a significant portion of the largest party in the electorate (the Democratic party) deviated from its normal vote. In the context of party loyalty it is important to remember that in 1984 over half the voters stayed loyal to their parties. Eighty-nine percent of the strong Democrats stayed with the Democratic party, and 91 percent of the strong

Republicans stayed with the Republican party. The importance of party identity to participation is further demonstrated by the fact that a much smaller percentage of the independents actually voted.

In terms of the individual, party identity provides a set of cues for use in making decisions, particularly when no other information is available. Although the number of voting-age Americans who identify with parties is smaller than it was 30 years ago, when the following words were written, they still ring true:

> In view of the fact that very few Americans have any deep interest in politics, it is a mild paradox that party loyalties should be so widespread. A partial key to this puzzle is that these identifications perform for the citizen an exceedingly useful evaluative function. To the average person the affairs of government are remote and complex, and yet the average citizen is asked periodically to formulate opinions about those affairs. . . . Having the party symbol stamped on certain candidates, certain issue positions, certain interpretation of political reality is of great psychological convenience.[18]

Every two years since 1952 the Survey Research Center at the University of Michigan has asked a nationwide sample of voters the same question: "Generally speaking, do you think of yourself as a Republican, a Democrat, an independent, or what?" For party identifiers this question is followed up by one which probes for the strength of party identity.[19] In the late 1980s well over half of the voting population still identified with one of the major parties. As Table 8.2 indicates, two trends support the notion of party decline. First, an increasing portion of the electorate is choosing an independent identity. Second, fewer party identifiers are indicating a strong attachment to their parties. Neither trend, however, supports the idea that parties are dying political institutions.[20]

A trend that is not apparent in the table is somewhat ambiguous for the future of the parties. It seems that some individuals identify with one party at the national level and the other party at the state and local level. Recent

Table 8.2   PARTY IDENTIFICATION

	1956 (%)	1966 (%)	1976 (%)	1986 (%)
A. Democrat	50	55	52	50
B. Republican	37	32	33	36
C. Independent*	9	12	15	12
D. Partisan total†	87	87	85	86
E. Strong Democrats	21	18	15	18
F. Strong Republicans	14	15	14	10
G. Strong Party Identifiers	35	33	29	28

*Excluding Democratic and Republican leaners, i.e., pure independents.

†Including Democratic and Republican leaners, i.e., all party preferences of any strength.

Source: Larry Sabato, *The Party's Just Begun*, (Glenview, IL: Scott, Foresman, 1988), 114–115.

research has indicated the existence of fairly stable dual party identities for about 20 percent of the electorate.[21] In the South, for example, some conservative Democrats continue to vote in "their" party's primary to nominate candidates for state and local office while consistently voting for Republican presidential candidates and sometimes Republican gubernatorial and U.S. senatorial candidates. While the significance of this pattern in terms of reported party identity (or independence) has yet to be established, Jewell and Olson suggest that many persons probably call themselves independents because they register with one party (and vote in its primary) while voting more often in the [general election for] the other party."[22] Thus, there may be fewer independents than meets the eye. As Wolfinger and Arseneau observe, many independents are "really closet Democrats and Republicans, not people without attachments to a party."[23]

Voters in Party Primaries   Both parties shrink considerably in size if one measures the party in the electorate in terms of voters in primary elections. Although 65 percent of the voting-age population identifies with a party, only 30 percent of the electorate votes regularly in a party primary. This smaller category of individuals is a focal point for political consultants and party leaders. The rolls of primary voters are very useful sources of information about those most likely to vote at all as well as those most likely to work for a party's candidate. Thus, the basic data used for preelection polling and "get-out-the vote" activities in general elections are the lists of primary voters. These lists are usually available for individual voting precincts in each county. They can be purchased in most states at the county clerk's office or the office of the county election administrator.

State law governing the conduct of primary elections affects the way one interprets the primary vote totals for a party in a given state. In 11 **open primary** states one can vote in either party's primary regardless of whether one identifies with the party.[24] Thus, figures from these primaries may include, along with dual identifiers, independents who cared enough to vote in a party primary for a single candidate they liked without having any allegiance to the rest of the slate that the party (through the primary process) nominated.

This type of primary is sometimes called an open primary because it is open to all eligible voters, including those who do not publicly identify themselves with a party. In 9 of these 11 states one obtains all party ballots at the same voting place and then makes one's choices for one party's candidates in the privacy of the voting booth. In the other two—Washington and Alaska—one can vote in more than one primary, though one can choose only one candidate per office.

In more than 20 states, however, one must declare party affiliation from 15 days to a year before voting in a party's primary. In 14 other states one can declare one's party identity on the day of the primary by voting in that party's primary.[25] In these states the polling places for the parties are usually in different locations. Needless to say, the rules for the conduct of primary elections affect not only the usefulness of the voting rolls but also the coherence and viability of political parties within a given state.

Party Identity and General Elections   If we measure the party in the electorate in each state by the number who support its candidates for statewide offices or elect its candidates to the state legislature, we obtain a picture of the party system that indicates far greater stability and increasing opportunities for the parties to promote responsible government. Since 1976 political scientists have been using a scheme of analysis developed by Austin Ranney to measure interparty competition within the states.[26] This measure, or **index of competition**, involves three dimensions: (1) proportion of success, (2) duration of success, and (3) frequency of divided control.

Proportion of success is the average of the combined percentage of the total gubernatorial vote and the percentage of seats in the state legislature won by a party in a given time period. The more competitive the state is, the closer each party is to 50 percent. *Duration of success* is the percentage of a given time period during which each party controls the governorship and/or the legislature. *Frequency of divided control* is the percentage of a given time period in which control of the governorship and legislature has been divided between the parties. The numbers generated by these dimensions are than adjusted to develop an index with a range of zero (consistent Republican success) to 1 (consistent Democratic success). Between these two extremes one finds the index scores for all 50 states.

Another way of viewing this index is to think of it in terms of an overall percentage Democratic victory index. In other words, a score of 0.8500 means that the Democrats win 85 percent of the time and the state is viewed as a one-party Democratic state. If a Republican had invented the index, the orientation might have been reversed, with 1 representing Republican success. Ranney has suggested the following categories and cutoff scores for classifying state party systems:[27]

One-party Democratic	0.8500 or higher
Modified one-party Democratic	0.6500 to 0.8499
Two-party	0.3500 to 0.6499
Modified one-party Republican	0.1500 to 0.3499
One-party Republican	0.0000 to 0.1499

One indication that the parties now battle more evenly than they did in the days of the Solid South is the fact that by 1980, as Figure 8.3 indicates, two-party states far outnumbered one-party states and that in some Southern states the parties had become competitive.

Table 8.3 provides the index scores for 1980. All the states from the original Confederacy had lower one-party Democratic scores than ever before, and only five were one-party-dominant. Now that you know the method, you may wish to update this table for all the states or at least for your own state.[28]

Figure 8.3 State-level party competition: 1980. (*Source:* John F. Bibby, Cornelius P. Cotter, James L. Gibson, and Robert J. Huckshorn, "Parties in State Politics," in Virginia Gray, Herbert Jacob, and Kenneth N. Vines, eds., *Politics in the American States*, [Boston: Little, Brown, 1983], 66.)

Whichever of its many dimensions we focus on, the party in the electorate consists of the people to whom the party in government and the electoral party have meaning. Whether it offers candidates to the party in the electorate who appear to be capable of governing better or offers better programs or positions on important issues of the day, each party promises something. The ability of the people in a state to make sure that the parties keep those promises depends to a great extent on the degree to which the rules for conducting elections and organizing government conform to a model of political behavior known as the responsible party model.[29]

Before we examine that model, a disclaimer is necessary. Like all models, it is an abstraction that exists in perfect form nowhere on earth. Furthermore, it is virtually impossible to realize in the American political system because of the constitutional principle of separation of powers, a point we'll develop later. Nevertheless, the responsible party model provides a goal — government accountable to the electorate — and a means of measuring progress toward it. Some states are much closer to it than are others. Since the model promotes a worthwhile goal, it is worth learning about so that you can better evaluate proposals you may someday be asked to vote on which may strengthen parties or weaken them and thus lead to further imbalance in the relationship between parties and interest groups.

Table 8.3 COMPETITION SCORES OF THE STATES: 1980

State	Index score*	State	Index score*
Alabama	0.9438	Montana	0.6259
Alaska	0.5771	Nebraska	0.5166
Arizona	0.4482	Nevada	0.7593
Arkansas	0.8630	New Hampshire	0.3916
California	0.7081	New Jersey	0.7330
Colorado	0.4429	New Mexico	0.7113
Connecticut	0.7336	New York	0.5390
Delaware	0.5490	North Carolina	0.8555
Florida	0.7524	North Dakota	0.3374
Georgia	0.8849	Ohio	0.5916
Hawaii	0.7547	Oklahoma	0.7841
Idaho	0.3898	Oregon	0.6954
Illinois	0.5384	Pennsylvania	0.5574
Indiana	0.4145	Rhode Island	0.8506
Iowa	0.4539	South Carolina	0.8304
Kansas	0.4671	South Dakota	0.3512
Kentucky	0.7907	Tennessee	0.6648
Louisiana	0.8762	Texas	0.7993
Maine	0.5164	Utah	0.4653
Maryland	0.8509	Vermont	0.3612
Massachusetts	0.7916	Virginia	0.7162
Michigan	0.6125	Washington	0.5806
Minnesota	0.6680	West Virginia	0.8032
Mississippi	0.8673	Wisconsin	0.6634
Missouri	0.6932	Wyoming	0.3879

*0.0000 = One-party Republican state; 0.5000 = a competitive two-party state; 1.0000 = a one-party Democratic state.

Source: John F. Bibby, Cornelius P. Cotter, James L. Gibson, and Robert J. Huckshorn, "Parties in State Politics," in Virginia Gray, Herbert Jacob, and Kenneth N. Vines, eds., *Politics in the American States*, 4th ed. (Boston: Little, Brown, 1983), 66.

THE RESPONSIBLE PARTY MODEL

The central goal of the **responsible party model** is government held accountable to the public through meaningful elections. Parties make elections meaningful by performing at least five functions: (1) identifying and explaining issues to the electorate, (2) developing a program on which to campaign for election, (3) recruiting and nominating candidates, (4) organizing election campaigns, and (5) organizing government to carry out the program on which they campaigned.[30]

The responsible party model is based on the notion of two competing parties, each with a program and a slate of candidates to carry it out. Voters can hold the governing party responsible for its behavior by electing the opposition party in the next election. Although it sounds reasonable if not simplistic, responsible party theory is based on sophisticated notions about government in complex societies such as ours.

Six Assumptions About Politics in Complex Societies

The Public Interest Exists   Large complex societies consist of a variety of people and organizations, each with different needs and wants and different views on what government should do. Nevertheless, some goals are in everyone's interest. The struggle to identify the public interest and obtain agreement on how to achieve it is a major feature of the political process.

Direct Democracy Is Inappropriate for Large Complex Societies   Inappropriate in this case is another way of saying virtually impossible to achieve. Most individuals within a society do not have the time or opportunity to get to know one another in order to establish the rapport and trust necessary for a community to exercise direct democracy. The town meeting setting is not possible with large numbers of people. Few individuals have the opportunity to discuss at length with anyone, much less all their neighbors, many important public issues. Thus, representative government is appropriate if not essential for government to make decisions that identify and promote the common interest in complex societies.

Mediating Institutions Are Necessary   Even though representative government reduces the burden of decision making for the individual, it is still a heavy burden. As noted in Chapter 3, each individual has three or more units of government to keep track of and, in some units, a dozen public officials or more. If initiative, referendum, and recall are available, the voter has numerous proposals to decide on. In addition, the electoral process itself adds to the variety of decisions facing the individual because there are several types of elections, as Box 8-1, on p. 255, indicates. Thus, there is a need for organizations which specialize in making elections a manageable, meaningful activity.

Voters Use Cues in Making Decisions   A cue is a guide or even a shortcut to decision making. We don't know anything about each restaurant we encounter on our travels, but if it is part of a national or regional chain, we can make reasonable assumptions about its menu and prices and the quality of its food. The name of a restaurant in a particular town thus provides a cue, as do brand names in stores. Party labels are similar cues.

Critics of the use of the party as a cue for decision making often make the unwarranted assumption that if party labels are removed from the ballot, voters can make more informed decisions. Responsible party theory asserts that it is unrealistic to assume that in the absence of party labels most voters will enter the polling place with complete information about every candidate and thus have only to register their well-thought-out choices by voting.

The assumption that voters are always informed and rational is more elegantly stated as the **rational-comprehensive model** of decision making. This is the unexpressed alternative to the responsible party model; we en-

Box 8-1   **Types of State and Local Elections**[a]

Jurisdiction or type	Representative offices or subject matter	Time of year
Partisan (party labels serve as decision cues)		
General	President, Congress, state, county, and township legislatures and executives	November
Municipal	Mayor and council in a few large cities	Spring
Nonpartisan (no party labels as decision cues)		
Municipal	Mayor and city council in most cities	Spring
School district	Board members in most school districts	Spring
Special	Called to replace officials who have resigned, died, or been impeached or recalled	Varies
Referendum	Bond issues, amendments to city charters and state constitutions, proposed laws	Varies
Recall	Public votes to remove officials	Varies
Primary[b]	The general public (open) or party members (closed) vote to choose the candidates who will get the party's nomination for the general election in November	Spring-summer
Runoff	A special election held in jurisdictions where a majority rather than a plurality is required to win the nomination in a primary or an election to office; the top two candidates run to determine which one can get a majority	

[a]Some elections combine partisan and nonpartisan elements. In the general election, a few judicial offices may be nonpartisan and referendums may also appear on the ballot with no party labels to guide voting decisions. Some special elections use party labels.

[b]Except for the office of President, the Louisiana primary is essentially the general election for national, state, and local offices. All candidates appear on a nonpartisan ballot in a September election. Candidates with a majority win election to office. For offices which did not produce a majority, the top two candidates compete in a November runoff, which in presidential years is held the same day as the presidential election.

Sources: Jack C. Plano and Milton Greenberg, *The American Political Dictionary*, 8th ed. (New York: Holt, Rinehart & Winston, 1989), and *The Book of the States, 1986–87* (Lexington, KY: Council of State Governments, 1986), 212.

counter it in observations such as "I don't support a political party. I support an individual."

The belief that a voter should make an independent judgment about every candidate for every office is both noble and widespread. Unfortunately, in the real world of supermarket aisles and the voting booth, this does not always happen, as Box 8-2 indicates. Thus, as many voters read down the ballot, past the candidates about whom they have fairly complete information, they find the exercise of informed judgment becoming more and more difficult with each unfamiliar name and office.

In the absence of party labels, other cues are used as substitutes for complete information. For all its shortcomings, the responsible party model is based on the assumption that party labels serve as valid cues for voters. They are guides to a reference group which has attempted to apply the rational-comprehensive model in nominating a candidate for office in the first place. If you agree with the values of the reference group, you vote according to this reference group's (or party's) label.

In elections without party labels it is not unusual for intelligent and reasonably well-informed people to use cues such as those found in Box 8-2 in making voting decisions when they lack relevant information.[31] In elec-

---

Box 8-2   # Cues Used by Voters in Elections Without Party Labels, Including Primary Elections

After voters have made their decisions about the offices at the top of the ballot, the following cues are often used in the absence of other information, such as the name of the candidate's party:

1. Position on the ballot. Being listed first can be worth about 5 percent of the vote to a candidate, all other things being equal.

2. Recognition of the names of candidates whom the voter knows in the community.

3. Recognition of the names of candidates because of radio or TV spots, newspaper ads, billboards, or campaign literature.

4. Recognition of the name of a person who isn't the candidate. Some voters know that they aren't voting for that historical person, and some aren't sure.

5. Name characteristics such as the name of a person, place, or thing which seems appropriate or even humorous.

6. Name characteristics associated with ethnicity or gender.

7. Nicknames or name characteristics associated with images of folksiness, power, or competence.

tions to some offices, these cues become critical factors in determining winners and losers, particularly in elections which present numerous choices to make.

Given the difficulty of applying the rational-comprehensive decision-making model to every candidate for every office, the use of party labels may make sense. Knee-jerk party voting seems just as rational and informed as knee-jerk voting for whoever is listed first on the ballot or voting for people because they have the same names as bank robbers or are called Bubba or Doc. At least when one votes for a party, one is voting for a person with whom one is likely to share a general set of principles. That is the way it is supposed to be—*in theory.*[32]

Preelection Coalitions Are Superior to Postelection Coalitions   In order to win elections, it is necessary to build coalitions consisting of individuals and organizations with differing agendas but some agreement on basic principles. Within each major coalition, negotiations and compromises may take place. In a sense, the two national parties are coalitions of 50 state parties, and these state parties are coalitions of local parties (county, township, and city). The public is best served when coalitions are created before rather than after elections. In this way voters can identify the party whose candidates and issues they want to support.

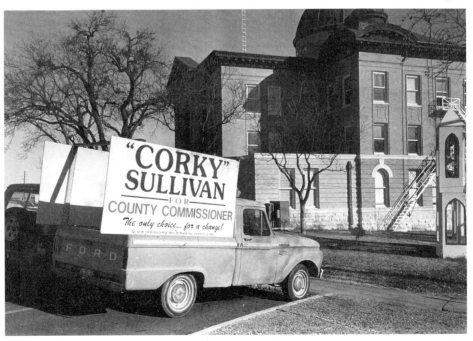

In nonpartisan elections, name characteristics are important cues used by some voters. (Reprinted with permission of Kim Bradley, staff photographer, *San Marcos Daily Record*, San Marcos, TX.)

Parties Are Necessary to Mobilize Voters   In states where parties are weak and in elections where party labels are missing altogether, voters are more likely to use cues such as those in Box 8-2. More important, fewer voters turn out.

One of the major functions of strong political parties is to **mobilize** the have-nots to use their votes to influence the political system. Thus responsible party theory assumes that the interest group system is biased in favor of the haves and that the party system is biased in favor of the have-nots. However, it can be biased in favor of the have-nots only when both parties are strong and the conditions of responsible party theory are met to a significant extent.

Two Components of Responsible Party Theory

The responsible party theory might be called the responsible government theory. Certainly responsible government is its central value. Responsible party theory describes a method for making government accountable to the public through the electoral process. Two or more parties offer candidates who promise to carry out programs. If, once elected, these officials don't keep their promises or if what they promised to do doesn't work, the voters can remove them in the next election and put another party in office.

Responsible party theory involves two essential conditions: competition and cohesion.

Competition   Competition between two or more parties is essential for two reasons. First, it offers a realistic possibility of "throwing the rascals out" at election time. Party competition exists when there are at least two parties with a realistic chance of winning control of major government offices in an election. Although many states are competitive, in terms of Ranney's index of party competition, there are counties and even whole regions within many states which do not have realistic party competition for local and state legislative elections. Thus, a state may consist of one or more one-party systems.

One-party systems are virtually the same as no-party systems. In one-party governments there is no mechanism for voters to replace one set of officeholders with another. Instead, each voter at each election must make a long series of separate decisions on all the candidates for office. In such circumstances it is very difficult for voters to hold officeholders and therefore government accountable.

Second, an organized **loyal opposition**, informed about the mistakes of the governing party and aware of the governing process, must be available to offer the voters an alternative. One cannot throw the rascals out unless there is something to replace them with.

Thus, the loyal opposition performs at least two functions which increase the accountability of government to the governed. First, it provides an ongoing source of information about the way the governing party is doing its job. A free press and various interest groups may help in the investigation and publication of government misdeeds and mistakes. However, they are outsiders. In a competitive party system at least some members of the loyal opposition get elected to the legislature, if not to other offices. Thus, they are in a position to provide an additional degree of insight into the performance of the governing party.

A second function performed by the loyal opposition is to serve as a viable alternative to the party in power. Neither the press nor interest groups offer voters an alternative governing party at election time. A loyal opposition not only offers alternative policies, it also provides a set of candidates to carry them out.

In one-party systems politics and parties operate differently than they do in competitive party states. When only one party's nomination is really valuable, that party is not likely to be a coalition of individuals and interest groups sharing common principles; it is more likely to be a battleground in which all individuals and interests compete for office and influence.

The governing party in a one-party system ends up being the arena instead of a contestant. Victory is a matter of winning the party nomination, because the general election is automatic. Thus, interest groups, factions of the party, and individuals compete within the party for the nomination. Once the nomination is won, party leaders can do little to encourage loyalty to party programs. For the voter, democracy becomes a heavy chore of monitoring all the elected officials and then deciding whether to support them in the next primary. There is no mechanism for throwing out all the rascals.

Cohesion   **Party cohesion** means that within each of the three components of the party there is considerable unity, and that each of the three components supports the goals of the party. For a party to be collectively responsible to the electorate, the parts must be responsible to one another. In order to achieve cohesion:

1. Members of the party in office should support the party program despite attempts to influence them by appealing to other loyalties (institution or constituency), values (ideology, religion, friendship), and interests (personal advancement, campaign resources, the career goals of close associates). The party was put in office to deliver. Members of the party in office who do not support the party should be held responsible to the party in terms of the distribution of benefits (committee assignments, promotions, legislative support). Furthermore, the electoral party should be in a position to deny endorsement.

2. The electoral party should use resources effectively to advance the interests of the party. In performing its traditional functions of managing election campaigns and mobilizing voters, the electoral party must support those who support the party. Although it may choose to be charitable about withholding endorsement from a few elected officials who do not support it, the electoral party must recruit candidates who will support it.

3. The party in the electorate should support all or at least most of the party's candidates in the interests of party unity despite appeals from the other party based on gender, ethnicity, personality, regionalism, friendship, shared values, ideology, issue preferences, and the attractiveness of particular candidates.

Party cohesion may mean that the party has to support an occasional unappealing candidate in order to accomplish greater goals. As one party loyalist put it, "He's an SOB but he's *our* SOB." However, party cohesion also means that there are goals and objectives on which party supporters agree and which they attempt to make apparent to the voters. The responsible party model does not ask the voters for a blank check to be filled in later.

THE AMERICAN PARTY SYSTEM: WHY THE SAME TWO PARTIES?

A remarkable feature of the American political system is that although there are 50 states and 3000 counties in which parties contest elections, there are only two major parties. Furthermore, it hasn't always been the same two. We started out with the Federalists and the Anti-Federalists, then came the Democrats and the Whigs, and finally, after 1860, the same two parties that we have today emerged. More importantly for our purposes, they are the same two parties in nearly every state and county. The question "Why the same two parties?" is really two questions: (1) Why the same two parties in election after election at the national level? and (2) Why the same two parties in every state?

These are questions to which anyone serious about understanding our political system ought to have some answers, if only to show appreciation of the fact that in the social sciences complete and final answers are hard to find. There are basically five reasons why we have a state and national two-party system with the same two national parties operating in nearly every state: (1) historical factors, (2) electoral rules, (3) constitutional arrangements, (4) career strategies, and (5) socioeconomic factors.

Historical Factors

Two historical factors which have shaped our party system are the inheritance of British political institutions and the existence of several major two-sided issues in our history that attracted large nationwide coalitions. At the time of this nation's founding many leaders accepted the legitimacy of a two-party system consisting of the government and the loyal opposition regardless of the actual names of the parties. Among the major issues around which two opposing coalitions could rally were the ratification of the Constitution (Federalist and Anti-Federalist), slavery (Republican and Democratic parties), and the use of big government as a check on the abuse of power by big business (Republican and Democratic parties).

Electoral Rules

Established patterns can be changed. However, when a pattern is reinforced by the actions of those who value it and when these actions involve making the pattern part of the rules of the game, that pattern is more likely to survive. For example, most states require that candidates who seek a place on the ballot have petitions signed by a significant number of voters, sometimes as much as 10 percent of those who voted in the last gubernatorial election. The refinements of this general rule include a deadline for submission long before the election, and some states disallow signatures on the petitions of third-party candidates by people who are registered as members of or who recently voted in a major party's primary.

Many of these rules are reasonable. After all, it takes time and costs money to print ballots, and one doesn't print names on them for frivolous reasons — "Hey, Fenwick, let's all go down to the courthouse and file for sheriff. Buffie and Angela will just *die* when they see our names on the ballot!"

However, even reasonable rules have effects. Whether the primary intention of these regulations was to inhibit third parties or prevent frivolous use of the electoral process or whether it was intended to require candidates and parties to demonstrate that they really have some popular support, it is more than likely that few legislators were aware that the rules would have the effect of reinforcing the existing two-party system.

Constitutional Arrangements

Other arrangements affecting elections were built into the U.S. Constitution or into the political systems of the 13 original states before an American two-party system emerged. The single-member district system, plurality election of legislators, the separate election of the chief executive, and the requirement for an absolute majority in the Electoral College have all increased the likelihood of a two-party system.

Single-Member Districts The fact that we elect our legislators at the state and national levels from single-member districts tends to make it difficult for parties which come in third or fourth to gather much support for contesting elections. A party which comes up empty too often will lose most of its followers to a more successful party, one that has a realistic chance of at least some first-place finishes.

Plurality Election   Electing by plurality rather than by majority eliminates the need for a runoff election. Runoff elections are often necessary if a clear majority is required to win. When minor parties can deny victory to other parties, they are in a position to negotiate between the first election and the runoff. With plurality election there is only one general election that counts. The coalition must be created before, not after, the election. There is no point holding on to the loyalties of a small portion of the electorate for later negotiations. The coalitions created before the election are our two major parties. Once they were able to win some offices, their appeal to members of other smaller organizations to stay in the coalition or join it became difficult to resist.

Separate Election of the Chief Executive   At the state and national levels we vote for the chief executive and the legislature on the same day and the same ballot. However, these votes are separate decisions. We can split our tickets.

In contrast, voters in the parliamentary form of government choose the legislature, and then the legislature chooses the chief executive and the cabinet. Minor parties with only 10 percent of the seats in the parliament may be major players in negotiating at least one cabinet post in exchange for their support of a larger party's candidate for prime minister.

Another contrast between the method of electing state and national representatives in the United States and that in some other democracies is the fact that we do not use proportional representation. This system is almost always associated with parliamentary government.

Proportional representation uses large multimember districts from which numerous legislators are elected according to the percentage of the total vote they receive. Followers of small parties are encouraged to stick with their parties in this system. As long as the small party can get at least a minimum percentage of the vote (usually about 10 percent), it will have at least one seat in parliament, and thus voters for that party will see their party win something. In the discussions to create a governing coalition, a small party's small percentage of seats can be a potent negotiating resource.

A consequence of proportional representation is that in a few countries which use it, there is seldom a government run by a majority party. Instead, the government consists of a coalition of parties which have traded votes in the parliament for a cabinet position or for specific legislation. In our system, although each party may not be as unified as some would prefer, it represents a governing coalition created before rather than after the election.

The Electoral College and Majority Election   To win the presidency, an individual must put together a national coalition consisting of enough people elected from the several states to produce a majority in the electoral college. Otherwise, the election goes to the House of Representatives. Many individuals are quite willing to work very hard to keep the decision out of the hands of the U.S. House of Representatives.

The effort to build a national coalition to win in the electoral college is enormous and is well beyond the resources of a single individual. Thus, an organization must be constructed to contact individuals state by state and make sure they are willing to vote for the candidate, make sure they filed as electors, and so on. The easiest way to operate is to appeal to existing state parties and build a coalition around them. If there is no state party in a particular state, national coalition builders must find people willing to start one that is linked to the national party.

The dynamic of the electoral college combined with some basic features of human nature has at least two consequences: a relatively small number of national coalitions and the same national coalitions for several consecutive elections. First, the desire to be part of a large winning coalition tends to reduce the number of organizations competing at the national level. Few individuals want to invest a great deal of time and energy in coming in second, much less third. People tend to avoid investing political resources in long shots. Thus, while this does not guarantee the creation state by state of two and only two national coalitions, it does keep the number of coalitions rather small.

Second, once a national coalition or party has been created, the individuals from the several states who have participated in it are naturally reluctant to start over from scratch for the next election. Thus, human contacts once made tend to persist over time, and a natural tendency to conserve energy results in the maintenance of an existing, though imperfect, coalition. Furthermore, there are political careers at stake.

Career Strategies

Morehouse suggests that career strategies encourage state political leaders to maintain their links to a national political coalition. Many governors run for the U.S. Senate as well as the presidency, and many state legislators run for statewide office. Even if they do not choose to run at a particular time, they may wish to keep their options open and have access to those who do achieve higher office. Thus, statewide electoral coalitions tend to be linked to national political parties.

Socioeconomic Factors

Although it has been fashionable from time to time to observe that there is not a dime's worth of difference between the two major parties in the United States, there is ample evidence that each party has recognizable base of categories and groups of people within the larger society.

Not every blue-collar worker, African-American, Jewish-American, Mexican-American, Irish-Catholic, rural Southerner, or liberal professional supports the Democratic party all the time. But more often than not a large majority of individuals with these characteristics and their associated goals and needs votes for Democratic candidates.

Likewise, the Republican party does not claim every vote from white-collar workers, suburban dwellers, Protestants from small towns outside the South, accountants, physicians, lawyers, bankers, corporate executives, and small businesspeople. However, the Grand Old Party can count on the support of most of these people most of the time.

Thus each party has an identifiable socioeconomic and regional base in the general population. The fact that many categories and groups identify with one of the two major parties is significant when one recalls that among the most important agents of political socialization are families, friends, coworkers (or fellow professionals), churches, and schools. Thus, individuals grow up with a party identity associated with being a Baptist, a Mexican-American, a doctor's daughter, a banker's son, or a member of a union family. At the dinner table we may hear things like "Republicans are good for business" and "The Democrats are for the little guy."

The Dynamics of Change: Dealignment   According to dealignment theory, the political socialization process tends to weaken party ties during periods when things don't seem to be going right in the American political system — Watergate, the Vietnam war, and Irangate, for example. The likelihood increases that dinner table conversation may involve unpleasant things about politics in general and parties in particular, thus promoting a nonpolitical or "independent" political identity.[33] Individuals who leave their families and set up housekeeping on their own with no partisan identity are very likely to identify with the party which seems to be the most attractive or have the most attractive candidates at the time of their first voting experience.

Once an individual links up, however tenuously, to a party, he or she tends to stay there. Thus when several hundred thousand new voters cast their first vote, realignments of the distribution of party identity may occur. Thus, the Democratic party, the majority party from the Great Depression to the 1960s, could be in the process of losing a portion of its base. If Watergate and Irangate had been Democratic instead of Republican fiascoes, the process might have been accelerated.

The relationship between socioeconomic bases, political socialization, and the party system in America has an added dimension that is worth noting. Since each American party must appeal not only to the individuals within its base but also to independents and people weakly associated with the other party, political campaigns often appear to pay too little attention to issues and put too much stress on superficialities. Although this feature finds few defenders, the disadvantages of the other extreme make it even less attractive. Highly ideological campaigns involving more and smaller parties consisting of intensely devoted and more homogeneous followers who agree on everything in a diverse society like ours could tear it apart.

After an election in such a system, no single party wins and a coalition must be created. Getting the monarchists, the Serbian nationalists, the socialists, and the Goat Worship party to compromise and cooperate in governing is difficult and sometimes impossible. Thus, more elections are held, more time is spent creating fragile coalition governments, and less time is spent using government to accomplish something. In these systems compromise is built out; in the more loosely structured American system compromise is built in.

An Incomplete Explanation   In sum, no single factor or combination of factors guarantees that we will have a two-party system. Historical experience further indicates that the two parties may not always be the same. Nevertheless, our electoral arrangements promote a pattern of a relatively small number of broadly based parties. No one of these features guarantees a national two-party system, with each party based on 50 state parties sharing the same name. No single feature fully explains why we have such a system. However, in combination, these features provide a pretty good start for understanding why our system works as it does.

Two implications of this incomplete explanation are worth noting. First, rules which are made can be changed; second, to affect an outcome is not the same as to determine it. Too often the media give the impression of inevitability. Words like "affect" and "influence" are abandoned in favor of words like "dictate," "determine," and "control." As a result, we are often discouraged from challenging the "forces of history." If you want to start a third party or help one out, you are not facing an impossible task, just a difficult one. After all, some third parties have replaced one of the major ones in our national two-party system. Furthermore, a three-party system is not unthinkable. Britain, a source of our two-party system, has had one from time to time.

WHY ARE PARTY LABELS EXCLUDED FROM MOST CITY ELECTIONS?

Although we have a two-party system at the state and national levels, in most municipal government elections, political parties do not appear on the ballot. To understand why these differences exist we must review the place of political machines and the reform movement in American political history. We begin with a "dirty" word—patronage.

Patronage

Patronage, to put it mildly, is a much abused word. It is so heavily laden with negative connotations that a paragraph or two is necessary in order to gain some perspective. We begin by pointing out that patronage is a rather ancient practice. The Latin root for "patronage" is *patronus*, meaning, "protector." That word in turn comes from the Latin word for "father," *pater*.

A patron is someone who protects, supports, or advances the cause of someone else. The nature of a patronage relationship varies with the context in which it is found. Patrons are customers in stores and restaurants; they are the financial supporters of art museums and charitable enterprises. Sometimes specialized words are used to describe patrons. Backers of Broadway shows are called angels. In some police departments a person who looks after the career of a subordinate is called a rabbi. "Rabbi" means "teacher," and teachers or patrons provide guidance, insight, and information about other people, about how to get things done, and about where the opportunities lie.

Patronage can involve a virtually inexhaustible array of benefits or political resources, and those benefits vary according to the context. Information about where a bridge will be built is useless to an unemployed laborer but very valuable to a real estate speculator. In the context of political parties, jobs, contracts, and opportunities are sometimes provided to individuals and firms which support the party in office. This is not always unethical or illegal and certainly is not always a simple barter relationship.

Although fathers care for their children and may in their old age be cared for by them, no one seriously advances the father-child relationship as merely involving the exchange of child rearing for old-age benefits. However, it is easy to be cynical about patron-client relationships. Thus patrons of art museums can be dismissed as rich people trading money for social status. It is as unhealthy to reduce complex human relationships to self-interested barters, exchanges, or purchases as it is naive to deny that a variety of dimensions are involved in many honorable human relationships.

Although we extend the benefit of the doubt to patron-client relationships in the realm of charitable, educational, and religious institutions, political relationships are particularly vulnerable to oversimplification and cynical assessment. Thus, people with little familiarity with the human relationships involved in politics, are very likely to see patronage as illegitimate or corrupt rather than as a way of promoting a number of legitimate goals. As Box 8-3 suggests, given the choice between two equally qualified candidates for a job, it seems rational for a person with a job to fill to choose the candidate whose political loyalty and enthusiasm have been demonstrated.

Patronage not only involves making decisions in favor of one's supporters, it also may include encouraging or inducing people to become supporters. All things being equal and without evidence of party activity in the case we have just mentioned, one might choose a candidate who comes from a politically active family or is recommended by a political supporter. Political patronage can thus be one of several criteria used in making a decision, all other things being equal.

In an abstract world where all other things are equal, it is possible to practice patronage in a very moral way. In the real world, particularly the world of politics, all other things are seldom equal. Thus, the practice of

---

Box 8-3   **The Logic of Patronage**

You are a busy elected official. Among the decisions you have to make this morning is which of two equally qualified people to hire as one of your administrative assistants. Both applicants are of the same sex and ethnic identity, and both have attached letters of recommendation and impressive résumés indicating that they worked hard to put themselves through school. Both make the same positive impression. However, applicant A has the following in his or her application file, and applicant B does not:

1. A letter from a county judge in your party testifying that applicant A worked hard for the party during the recent election campaign

2. A letter from one of the major contributors to your campaign asking you to give ''every consideration'' to applicant A and indicating that the contributor is an uncle of the applicant

3. A note, included by your secretary, that the governor's office called to put in a good word for applicant A

Which applicant will get the job?

---

patronage requires and is sometimes given the benefit of the doubt. At the national level we have come to expect ambassadorships to go to party supporters (Box 8-4). As *Newsweek*, observed, "The ambassadorship as political pay-off — it's a presidential tradition that goes back to Andrew Jackson."[34]

When the benefit of the doubt is abused; when clearly unqualified individuals are given preference over others for jobs, contracts, or career advancement; or when laws are broken or procedures designed to ensure fair treatment are ignored, such as those designed to promote competitive bidding for government contracts, the practice of patronage and the people engaged in it are corrupted and we move into the realm of machine politics.

Machine Politics

A **political machine** is an organization which practices machine politics, usually after taking control of a state or local political party. According to Raymond Wolfinger, **machine politics** and political machines are "two quite different phenomena."

> Machine politics is the manipulation of certain incentives to partisan political participation: [for example] favoritism based on political criteria in personnel decisions, contracting, and in the administration of the laws. A "political machine" is an organization that practices machine politics, i.e., that attracts and directs its members primarily by means of these incentives.[35]

Box 8-4   **Ambassadorships: Modern Examples of Patronage at the Edge of the Benefit of the Doubt**

''I saw the new Italian Navy. Its boats have glass bottoms so they can see the old Italian Navy.''
—Peter Secchia, nominee for U.S. Ambassador to Italy

Secchia, a multimillionaire lumber tycoon, is a controversial appointment for an ambassadorship. Apparently Bush is grateful to him for a crucial primary victory in Michigan that earned him valuable publicity and delegates to the 1988 Republican presidential nominating convention.

Other Bush ambassadorial nominees include

J. Giffen Weinmann, president of Waverly Oil Corp. A top fund-raiser for Bush, Weinmann has been nominated as ambassador to Finland, a country with few oil reserves.

Melvin Sembler, a Florida shopping center mogul and $100,000 Republican party contributor, has been nominated as ambassador to Australia.

Source: *Newsweek* (June 5, 1989), 25–26.

Wolfinger's distinction between machine politics and political machines contains two important points. First, the term "incentives to partisan participation" clearly implies forms of corrupt patronage. Thus, selective enforcement of the law and hiring practices based *solely* on party (or partisan) loyalty exceed the ethical boundaries of the ancient and honorable practice of patronage. Second, influencing individuals *primarily* by means of these incentives is associated with machine politics and political machines. For Wolfinger and for us, a political machine is a type of party, not a typical party. It is a type of party that operates *primarily* by unethical and sometimes illegal means to get and keep power. Political parties encourage their followers to vote in each election; political machines encourage their followers to vote often in each election.

Although the political machine can be identified as a particular type of political party, a corrupted form so to speak, the average citizen and the media frequently refer to any strong party organization as a political machine. Whether they are engaged in poetic license, simile, metaphor, or simply sloppy thinking, the effect is the same. The impression is perpetuated that a strong political party is the moral equivalent of the notoriously corrupt Tweed Ring that robbed New York City taxpayers of millions of dollars in the nineteenth century (Box 8-5).

Box 8-5   **Boss Tweed: An Odious Individual**

Political machines included honest politicians making the best of a bad thing and charming rascals who enjoyed the game and intended no one any harm. Some, however, were grossly corrupt. One of the most egregious sinners was William Marcy Tweed (1823–1878), a man who gained control of a traditional political machine in New York and used it to become very rich at the expense of the taxpayers.

The amount of money Boss Tweed and his colleagues stole is estimated to have been between $25 million and $200 million. In the 1870s this was enough to operate several state governments for a year. Thus, it was a considerable and shocking sum. The political cartoons of Thomas Nast, the sensational stories reported in *The New York Times*, and an aroused public embarrassed the federal and state governments into action.

Most members of the Tweed Ring were arrested, indicted, found guilty, and imprisoned. The scandal was kept on the front pages when Boss Tweed escaped prison, fled to Spain, was recaptured, and returned to the United States, where he spent the rest of his life behind bars.

Source: Richard B. Morris, ed., *The Encyclopedia of American History*, 6th ed. (New York: Harper & Row, 1982), 298.

The Structure of Political Machines

The "courthouse gang" in rural counties and the classic urban political machine both practiced machine politics and were rural and urban variations of the same phenomenon, a collection of officeholders and hangers-on who practiced machine politics. Nevertheless, the term "political machine" is usually associated with a particular type of organization which existed in a particular period of American history: the late nineteenth and early twentieth centuries.

The structure of the fully formed political machine consisted of a hierarchy in which there was a fair amount of top-down discipline from the boss, through ward leaders, to the hundreds of precinct captains. The boss usually held an official party position, for controlling party nominations was the key to control of the party, just as control of elected office was the key to control of the government. Some but not all bosses held the office of mayor, as did the late Richard M. Daley of Chicago.

Many cities were divided in small single-member districts called wards. These districts elected an alderman to the city council. The ward leaders, who often served as aldermen, were not merely the representatives of a geographic area of the city; they also represented the dominant ethnic groups in those small electoral units. Machine bosses attempted to create a ticket of citywide offices that was balanced ethnically while at the same time running at least one or two "blue-ribbon" middle-class candidates near the top to appeal to the reform elements within the party.

The foundation on which the machine rested was the precinct captain, a party worker who was responsible for getting out the vote in his precinct. Just as important, however, was the precinct captain's service as a link between the people in the neighborhoods and the machine. The precinct captain kept his superiors (ward boss or alderman) advised of opportunities to make public appearances at weddings, funerals, and family celebrations as well as less structured occasions. George Washington Plunkitt, a machine politician, indicated both the importance of precinct captains and the advantages of being able to assist those in need:

> If there's a fire in Ninth, Tenth, or Eleventh Avenue, for example, any hour of the day or night, I'm usually there with some of my election district captains as soon as the fire engines. If a family is burned out, I don't ask whether they are Republicans or Democrats, and I don't refer them to Charity Organization Society, which would investigate their case in a month or two and decide they were worthy of help about the time they are dead from starvation. I just get quarters for them, buy clothes for them if their clothes were burned up, and fix them up til they get things runnin' again. It's philanthropy, but it's politics, too—mighty good politics. Who can tell how many votes one of these fires bring me? The poor are the most grateful people in the world, and let me tell you, they have more friends in their neighborhoods than the rich in theirs.[36]

The relationship between precinct captain and his boss was as personal and nonideological as the relationship between the precinct captain and the people he recruited for the machine. Loyalty to the machine was more personalized than loyalty to the party. The machine was men and friendships; the party (particularly the party of the reformers) was rules and procedures. To some extent machines represented the fatal flaw of depending on a government of men, instead of the rule of law.

Politics as a Business

In a sense, the classic urban political machine was an entrepreneurial device for processing favors, friendship, and patronage (or incentives to participation) into votes, and votes into political power. Many machine politicians referred to it as a business for professionals who understood the "real world."

The political power acquired by the machine was used in part to promote the continued acquisition of incentives, to protect the machine from disruption by electoral challenges and outside interference. If the state attorney general owed his or her job to the machine, the likelihood of an investigation of machine practices was somewhat more remote.

The process was circular. It had no explicit purpose in terms of policies or ideology other than to continue to win control of the government through the electoral process. Just as a business has no explicit purpose other than to make a profit for its owners, thus enabling them to enjoy a comfortable life-style, so machines existed to enable their bosses to enjoy the spoils of office. As George Washington Plunkitt, a successful Tammany Hall politician, observed at the turn of the century, "Politics is as much a regular business as the grocery or dry-goods . . . business."[37] If along the way useful social functions were performed by the machine, so much the better. Most machine politicians believed they were serving the greater good, just as most members of the business community believe they are.

Functions of the Machines

In a classic study of the role political machines played in urban society, Robert K. Merton described several functions they performed which helped bring order and stability to the rapidly growing urban centers of nineteenth and early twentieth-century America.[38]

Perhaps other institutions could have operated in their place, perhaps order would have been possible without them, but most political scientists agree that Merton's observations, to which we have added one or two of our own, are valid. There is some dispute, however, about whether having these functions performed by the machine was worth the cost.

Centralize Decision Making   When numerous decisions had to be made in a hurry, it helped to have someone in charge to make them. Without a mechanism for bringing some sort of discipline to the collection of elected officials created by the Jacksonian long ballot, nineteenth-century urban centers might have become even more disorderly than they were.

Personalize Government   The need still exists for most of us to relate to people as fellow human beings instead of role players. In cities of strangers, those who were not equipped with literacy or a very strong self-image appreciated the fact that the precinct captains and the political machine provided a human source of information and support. If impersonal bureaucrats frighten even you and me, what was it like for a peasant fresh from rural Poland, Italy, Alabama, or West Virginia?

Socialize Newcomers   It can be argued that American cities remained American largely because of the ability of political parties to bring newcomers into the political process and to make that process meaningful. By stimulating participation and arousing interest in the political process, parties helped bring people from very undemocratic societies such as the Hapsburg Empire and czarist Russia gradually into the American political system without doing it too much damage. Political machines were an integral part of the process that gave the melting pot its appeal as an explanation of America and enabled America to adapt to rapid social change.[39]

Provide Welfare   Political machines were not the only source of help for the poor at the time. There were private charities. However, there was virtually no national commitment to social problems until the Great Depression of the 1930s. Until then, welfare assistance was seen as a private and local matter. Thus, with precious little national and state-level effort, the assistance offered by political machines was all the more important, however inefficiently it might have been provided.

Reduce Ethnic Conflict   According to Milton Rakove, a student of the Daley machine in Chicago,

> Every ethnic, racial, religious, and economic group is entitled to have some representation on the ticket. Thus, in Chicago, the mayor's job has been an Irish job since 1933. The city clerk's job belongs to the Poles. The city treasurer can be a Jew, a Bohemian, or a black. A judicial slate is made up of three or four Irishmen, two or three Jews, two or three Poles, several blacks, a Lithuanian, a German, a Scandinavian, several Bohemians, and several Italians.[40]

The Decline of Political Machines

Mayor Richard Daley of Chicago was the last "traditional" urban political machine boss.[41] When he died in 1978, the classic American urban political machine entered history, perhaps never to emerge again. The fact that he was able to keep his machine in operation long after machines had ceased to dominate other major American cities is a tribute to the ability of an individual to affect the political process. The inability of any of his successors to hold the machine together further testifies to the fragility of a system based on a particular individual rather than on laws. In 1989 Daley's son, Richard, was elected to the mayoralty after a period of instability that made many Chicagoans look back on the Daley era with nostalgia.

At least seven factors led to the decline of the political machine: (1) reduction in the salience of politics, (2) assimilation and the decline of white ethnic block voting, (3) decline in the use of unskilled labor, (4) rise of the union movement, (5) federal involvement in the welfare system, (6) corruption, waste, and scandals, and (7) the success of the reform movement.

Reduction in the Salience of Politics   Politics is no longer the only game in town. It interests many of us, but there are other recreational opportunities, other contests, and other teams to root for. Thus, the salience of politics may have experienced the kind of decline one would expect in a society which has grown more complex and affluent.

Assimilation and the Decline of White Ethnic Block Voting   The melting pot image of America discussed in Chapter 2 is based largely on the experience of the European immigrants of the late nineteenth and early twentieth centuries. European ethnic identities still exist and are still important, but the ability of ethnic leaders to deliver large blocks of votes in local elections is a much less common occurrence.

The white ethnics who made up the base of support for urban machines have demonstrated less rather than more solidarity, losing potential leaders to mainstream American political institutions and losing sons and daughters to the suburbs, where their votes don't influence city elections even though ethnic identities persist in some cases.

Decline in the Use of Unskilled Labor   Technological change has led to the mechanization of many construction and maintenance functions performed by city government, reducing the number of jobs available for a patronage machine. Given their limited education and vulnerability to easy replacement, unskilled workers have been the most likely to trade political loyalty for employment.

Rise of the Union Movement   In the building industry and in the public employment sector itself, labor unions have been so successful that union leaders have helped remove the influence of political machines on the job market. The rise of unions to protect workers from employer abuse also protected the hiring and firing process from outside influence, further reducing the patronage that could be distributed by political leaders.

Federal Involvement in the Welfare System   Before 1932 the federal government used few of its considerable resources to provide aid or encourage state governments to provide aid to the needy. After 1932 the federal government, working through state and local governments, encouraged the development of a system of delivering welfare assistance that was impersonal, involving neither loyalty nor gratitude to a local political leader or organization.

Corruption, Waste, and Scandals   The skepticism with which the country bumpkin views the city slicker is an almost universal phenomenon. In America in the nineteenth century, machine leaders who abused their power and authority did more than increase the rural-urban dichotomy; they contributed to the loss of the legitimacy of the machine (and the political party). That is, the corruption, waste, and scandals associated with the machine were a sort of pollution of the political environment that weakened the ability of machine leaders in some cities to claim that the disadvantages of machine rule were outweighed by the advantages.

Political machines did not exist in freestanding isolation. They were part of a system of intergovernments, and they were tolerated if not actively supported by a significant portion of the community for the benefits they offered. When scandals involving machine corruption, waste, and inefficiency became widely known, the machines lost public support and came under careful scrutiny by the other governments in the intergovernmental system.

The Success of the Reform Movement   Antimachine urban reform organizations emerged in the late nineteenth century as part of the larger, more broadly based progressive movement.[42] The progressives protested and attempted to do something about the suffering that occurred as American cities industrialized rapidly and civilized slowly. The broadly based reform movement was concerned with the abuse of the concentration of power in large enterprises. As Richard Hofstadter observed in his Pulitzer Prize-winning work, *The Age of Reform,*

> At bottom, the central fear was fear of power, and the greater the strength of an organized interest, the greater the anxiety it aroused. Hence it was the trusts, the investment banking houses, the interlocking directorates, the swollen private fortunes, that were the most criticized, and after them the well-knit, highly disciplined political machines.[43]

However fascinating the story of the efforts to break up corporate monopolies, regulate railroads, and force social responsibility on slumlords and robber barons, we must focus our attention on that portion of the progressive movement which attacked the political machine for its abuse of concentrated power. It is worth noting that just as there were captains of industry who were not robber barons, there were also party leaders who promoted reform. Hazen Pingree in Michigan, Ed Crump in Tennessee, Samuel "Golden Rule" Jones in Ohio, Hiram Johnson in California, and Robert La Follette in Wisconsin were party leaders who promoted reform by means of their own disciplined party organizations.[44]

Although we have included the reform movement as one factor in the decline of political machines, some scholars discount this movement, asserting that the machine simply became obsolete as society changed. Tari Renner has observed that "there is little systematic, empirical evidence to indicate that they actually caused the decline."[45] Whether its contribution to the decline of urban political machines was great or small, it seems clear that the reform movement contributed to the weakening of political parties by failing to differentiate machines from political parties and by introducing a number of reforms which denied resources to the political parties that might have emerged in new communities. By weakening parties, the reform movement helped shift the balance in the political system in favor of interest groups.

The Reform Movement

The word "reform" means to make better, to remove abuses, to correct wrongs. Thus, any effort to change society or the political system is in the eyes of those who suggest the changes a reform. In the years to come there will be many efforts to improve state and local governments, revise constitutions, change the tax structure, and introduce new ways of financing election campaigns. Many of these efforts will sooner or later be referred to as the reform movement.

In the context of this chapter we use the term the **reform movement** to refer specifically to the collection of individuals and groups concerned with defeating political machines in nineteenth- and twentieth-century urban America. Some of their reforms were applied to other units of government. Today in Nebraska, where the movement was particularly strong, elections to the state legislature are nonpartisan. In virtually all states the direct primary is used for most if not all state and local offices elected on partisan ballots. However, the focus of the reform movement was municipal elections. To wreck the urban political machines, the reform movement concentrated largely on making it difficult for any leader or group of leaders to build or maintain a cohesive, disciplined political party.

The six reform proposals which had greatest effect on political parties were nonpartisan elections, the short ballot, at-large election of city council members, spring elections, merit standards and civil service, and the nomination of party candidates by direct primaries.

Nonpartisan Elections   A nonpartisan election is one in which party labels do not appear on the ballot. In some cities where this reform was introduced, parties still contest the election and work hard to inform voters about which candidates represent the party. Chicago, for example, conducted its elections without party labels on the ballot throughout the mayoralty of Richard Daley.

The motivation for keeping party or group labels off the ballot was to prevent the clients of the machine from using party labels as cues to help them make decisions. In theory this should make it harder for party leaders to manipulate large numbers of uneducated people.

Although nonpartisan elections had mixed results in cities where machines already existed and channels of communication were in place, they had a large impact on the development of new cities in the West, many of which have grown from villages to urban centers in the past 50 years. One indication of success in this area is the fact that over 70 percent of American cities with populations of over 25,000 have nonpartisan elections. Virtually all cities created after 1910 use the nonpartisan ballot.[46]

The differences between partisan and nonpartisan elections provide an opportunity for a quick review of two of the most important functions promoted by political parties: (1) They promote participation through preelection registration and election day get-out-the-vote drives. Partisan elections usually turn out about twice as many voters as do nonpartisan elections. (2) Partisan elections provide voters with meaningful cues. Parties may not be ideologically homogeneous or even united on all issues, but they do stand for something.

By contrast, nonpartisan elections (with no cues on the ballot except names and offices) give the voter less useful guidance: name recognition, name characteristics, position on the ballot, and spurious linkages between the office and a candidate's name, such as Jesse James for state treasurer.

The Short Ballot   There were at least three reasons for the short ballot, a reform which had its own organization, the National Short-Ballot Association. The first reason was to simplify the voting decision. With smaller city councils, and fewer executive officials, voters would be better able to keep track of the performance of a few officials. Not only would the greater good be looked after if the citizens could more easily keep track of the council, but citizens would have less need of a party to recruit and sponsor a slate of candidates. Second, by reducing the number of offices for which nominations had to be made, the machine bosses would no longer play the role of brokers and slate makers. A third reason was to promote accountability by increasing the likelihood that the elected chief executive really would be in charge of the executive branch.

The reduction in the size of legislative bodies at the city level was particularly important to urban reformers. Large councils (sometimes more than 100, seldom less than 25 members) which consisted of collections of representatives of wards (which were usually ethnic neighborhoods) were accused of turning the process of passing the city budget into an expensive process of vote trading. If each representative had to have something for his or her ward, lots of wards meant lots of representatives and lots of somethings.

Reformers felt that creating small councils (seven to nine people) would stimulate more concern for the interests and needs of the city as an entity. In a small council, reformers believed, representatives would have a better chance to get to know one another and would be more likely to work together in the common interest.

At-Large Elections   The use of the **at-large principle** for choosing representatives to legislative bodies such as city councils and school boards was supported in the belief that it would reduce the parochial influence of neighborhood leaders, each taking a narrow view of city governance. Reformers believed that candidates elected at large to a city council would have to build a citywide coalition of support and would be more inclined to look after the interests of the whole city, not just a small part of it.

It is worth nothing that once the city council has been reduced in size by the short ballot, single-member districts are larger and thus the need for at-large elections is reduced significantly.

Spring Elections In addition to removing parties from the ballot in municipal elections, the reformers wanted to separate municipal elections from elections to other levels of government. Thus, whereas in most states the general election takes place in November, city (and often school board) elections take place after the first of the year, usually in the spring. Thus, nonpartisan elections are less likely to be "contaminated" by issues and concerns raised in partisan state and national elections.

Merit Standards and Civil Service The object here was to remove the power of patronage from those in charge of government by means of two requirements. First, officials had to hire public employees on the basis of merit, which often consisted of any or all of the following: passing a test, surviving an interview, and demonstrating that one had at least minimal qualifications related to the job. Second, public employees had to be protected from losing their jobs when a new group of elected officials came into office. Although public employees could be dismissed for cause, they could not be dismissed for belonging to the wrong political party.

Nomination by Direct Primary This reform was intended to reduce the ability of party leaders to influence party nominations. It has played a major role in helping to tip the balance between parties and interest groups in favor of interest groups. By reducing the role of the electoral party in the nominating process, reformers opened the door for money and interest groups to play a larger role. By requiring two campaigns, one for the nomination and one for election, the reformers increased the cost of electoral politics and the influence of those with contributions to make.

The success of reformers in getting their entire program enacted varied from state to state and from region to region. Success depended on many factors — the ability of individual reform leaders to put together an effective coalition, the political culture of the state or region, and the behavior of the local machines, some of which were fairly honest and popular while others were both dishonest and unpopular.

In general, the impact of the reform movement on political parties has been enormous. In terms of political culture, the movement helped establish the notion that it is more respectable not to have a party loyalty than to have one. It encouraged the view that to be an independent is to be a self-directed person, while to be a party loyalist is to be a prisoner of habit or emotion. By aiming at machines and hitting parties, the reformers have established the notion that to strengthen the party is to bring back the worst of the old urban political machines. In introducing the direct primary the reform movement denied the electoral party its most valuable resource for influencing the party in office and rewarding hard work and loyalty. Now potential candidates look to interest groups and to the campaign organizations they create as much as or more than they look to party leaders. Once elected, public officials have absolutely no fear that party leaders will deny them renomination. The party label is won in the primary in part because of name recognition; incumbents are way ahead of challengers on that score, and further-more, they are in a better position to attract campaign contributions from interest groups and corporate PACs.

One of the ironies for those attempting to introduce changes that might correct the imbalance between parties and interest groups is the fact that antimachine reformers and strong party reformers share a common objective: to reduce the role of money in politics and weaken the linkage between business and government decision making. In 1910 William Allen White observed in his influential reformist book *The Old Order Changeth,*

> It is safe to say that the decree of divorce between business and politics will be absolute within a few years. . . . Now the political machine is in a fair way to be reduced to mere political scrap iron by the rise of the people. . . . Under the primary system any clean, quick-witted man in these states can defeat the corporation senatorial candidate at the primary if the people desire to defeat him.[47]

As we have observed more than once, the imbalance between interest groups and parties is an imbalance in favor of a set of organizations in which business groups dominate; the stronger the interest group system, the stronger the business interests within it. By attempting to weaken the link-age between economic power and political power, neither the urban re-formers nor the present-day advocates of strong parties are antibusiness or anti-free enterprise. For example, the leadership of the American Assembly, an educational organization that has advocated strengthening the party sys-tem, includes executives from major corporations and law firms as well as academics and party leaders.[48]

BRINGING BACK THE BALANCE

Many individuals and organizations are concerned about the condition of American political parties. Several have made suggestions for strengthening political parties and thus righting the balance between political parties on the one hand and interest groups, PACs, and political consultancy firms on the other. The objective of this improved balance is government more ac-countable to the electorate and thus more responsive to the individual. As the American Assembly observed in its final report, "Many of us are con-cerned that the balance between parties and interest groups has been upset in recent years . . . and that active steps need to be taken to restore the parties to a more vigorous role in the electoral process.[49]

Although some of the technical points about ballots may be new to you, most of our list of suggestions for strengthening parties is based on material already introduced in this and earlier chapters and thus constitutes a sum-mary of major points raised: (1) partisan municipal elections, (2) including party identity at registration, (3) closed primaries, (4) the straight ticket option, (5) promoting endorsing conventions, (6) requiring that a portion of surplus candidate funds be allocated to state or local parties, (7) during the general election, providing parties with free television and radio time, and (8) giving parties the resources to organize state legislatures. Our eight reforms by no means exhaust the possibilities raised by much longer lists found in the literature, which we urge you to read.[50]

Partisan Municipal Elections

Allowing parties to nominate slates of candidates to appear on the ballot in city elections would enhance both the legitimacy and the active base of parties. It would also improve the linkage between individuals and the governments of which they are supposed to keep track. This reform not only would help the state parties in recruiting and establishing linkages between leaders in county and city political arenas, it also would be good for the community.

David Price has observed that in addition to helping structure electoral decision making and promoting the accountability of local government, "local parties [can] play a broader role as 'mediating institutions,' as focal points of community life, and as links between the community and the larger political world."[51] Although many precinct and county party members already play a role in the politics of their municipal governments, this "reform" would increase the likelihood that they would do so.

There is ample evidence that partisan elections involve higher turnout and would thus promote more participation in municipal elections. In addition, this reform might also promote cooperation between county and municipal officials and place more urban issues on the agendas of state political leaders.

Including Party Identity at Registration

By requiring voters to identify their party, or choose to be independent, at the time of registration, the membership base and the awareness of parties are likely to increase, as would general awareness of the parties among the general public.[52]

More important, this reform would make it easier to administer closed primaries.

Closed Primaries

As a general rule, **closed primaries** limit participation in the nomination process to individuals who have at least chosen to identify with the party.

Twenty-six states already have closed primaries.[53] In these states independents who wish to influence party nominations can do so by joining a party. Otherwise, they can wait until the general election and make their selection from among the slates of candidates nominated by the parties. Nonmembers of interest groups have the same type of choice in influencing the way interest groups operate. They can join, or they can remain outside and deal with the results of interest group actions after the fact.

Closed primaries not only increase party membership and identity, they also are likely to make candidates more aware of the people who make the party work. Consequently, parties are better able to compete with interest groups and PACs for the loyalty and attention of candidates.

The Straight Ticket Option

The straight ticket option makes it easier for a voter to support his or her party. In 20 states the straight ticket option is already available. In 30 states, including those 20, the party column ballot is used. Both options make it easier to use the party as a cue to voting. The most awkward ballot and the one most likely to discourage voters from even voting on offices further down is the office block ballot. This type of ballot increases the likelihood that extraneous cues such as location and name recognition will be used in place of party.[54]

Endorsing Conventions

Endorsing conventions give the electoral party a larger role in the nominating process. This in turn increases the ability of party leaders to compete with interest groups, PACs, and political consultants for the attention of successful candidates. In 38 states party conventions play no role at all in the nominating process. In 12 there is some involvement of party leaders in nominations.[55]

The endorsed candidates are designated on the primary ballot. The importance of the endorsement would be enhanced if the candidates could be listed in order of finish at the convention. This reform will improve the ability of the electoral party to promote party cohesion. Potential candidates who have worked hard for the party in the past or served it well in lesser offices can be rewarded with endorsement for higher office. Given the importance of name recognition and the reality of PAC contributions, public officials elected under a party label who have not helped the party enact its program will probably not be denied reelection every time. However, if endorsements are denied to officeholders, party regulars can encourage them to work a little harder on the party's behalf in the next term of office.

Furthermore, even if a primary contest did occur, the use of endorsing conventions could make ballot location more meaningful by reserving first place for the endorsed candidate.

Allocating Surplus Campaign Funds to State or Local Parties

Party candidates elected to office under the party label should contribute a portion of surplus campaign funds to the state or local party. In this way the parties can be given resources to help candidates who are unable to raise funds via the PAC route or unable to take advantage of incumbency. Furthermore, surplus campaign funds are an open invitation to abuse by officeholders who may use them to increase their personal influence within the party or make it too expensive for anyone else to offer future electoral challenges. In this way officials who are able to build large war chests become isolated not only from the influence of party but also from the discipline of the electorate.

If advancement in the electoral party is based on service and loyalty to the party and if nomination to public office is based in part on a record of party service, the electoral party is strengthened. If, however, advancement in the party or nomination to public office has little or no relationship to party service, the electoral party is weakened.

Political parties need money. A large proportion of the funds contributed by PACs and wealthy individuals goes to candidates who don't need it. These lucky candidates are usually incumbents from safe seats, election districts where their party usually wins by comfortable margins of 10 percent or more. Many of these lucky candidates run unopposed. If funds are made available to the electoral party to use for the recruitment of candidates to run in districts held by the opposition and in support of legislators who *do* need party help for reelection, the party system will become more competitive and the candidates elected will pay at least as much attention to advice and counsel from the party as they do to advice from interest groups, wealthy individuals, and political consultants.

By only requiring that a portion of the *surplus* be given, well-funded incumbents would still be left with a surplus and those with no surplus would not be required to contribute. A fitting irony in this proposal is that the PAC funds which have weakened the party system would be used to strengthen it.

Providing Parties with Free Television and Radio Time

The mass media are an essential part of municipal, county, state, and national elections. Newspapers cannot be required to provide free ads, but radio and television operate as publicly licensed monopolies. The government enforces laws which make it a crime to broadcast on a frequency for which someone has bought a license to use. Thus, as a condition of receiving or keeping a license, the government could require that as a public service each party be given air time during the month or weeks before an election. With free air time to allocate, the parties would increase their ability to promote party unity and then make a more vigorous effort to carry out party platforms after the election. This could further reduce the dependence of candidates on PACs for money to buy the time.

Giving Parties the Authority to Organize State Legislatures

The rules of state legislatures that are not organized along partisan lines could be revised to allow each party caucus to allocate the party's share of committee assignments. Furthermore, the election of leaders by secret ballot instead of roll-call vote might promote the rise to legislative leadership of people whose power base is within the majority party instead of within a small number of powerful interest groups.

In some states, presiding officers with no involvement of a party caucus choose committee members and chairs. In some states, the presiding officers are not chosen by the body in secret ballot. Many lieutenant governors who serve as presidents of state senates are given considerable legal and/or customary power beyond the influence of the majority party members in the state senate.

When the state legislature is organized so that only one person makes committee assignments, only one person decides who will be the committee chairs, and only one person decides who gets staff assistance and who gets choice offices, that person is likely to operate beyond the influence of the party of which he or she is a member. Conversely, if all the members of the party have to approve of major committee assignments and the allocation of other resources and benefits, the party in office is a more meaningful organization. The stronger the party in office is, according to Morehouse, the more likely it is to attempt to deliver the party's platform.

Conclusion: Can Parties Adjust?

Political machines are organizations which gained control of political parties in many American cities during the post-Civil War era and dominated most large cities during the first half of this century. Many of them were so powerful and corrupt that American political culture has reacted (and sometimes overreacted) to them ever since. The failure to differentiate political party from political machine creates an image problem for the political party. More specifically, it creates problems for those who attempt to promote the notion that strong political parties can serve as counterforces to strong interest groups. The mass media exacerbate the situation by indiscriminately using the term "machine" for virtually any local party, campaign organization, or group that seems to have its act together.

As we have already seen, in strong interest group systems one set of interest groups usually predominates. The interests of that set of groups are not always the same as the interests looked after by political parties appealing to the entire electorate for support.

The list of ways to strengthen parties is based largely on features of existing state and local political systems. Thus, in some parts of our federal system parties are being nurtured by the political system, and sometimes, though not always, the public interest is better served.

The future of political parties as promoters of meaningful electoral choices and as counterforces to the influence of interest groups and PACs is not as grim as it appeared a few years ago. There is mounting evidence that while political party identity may have declined, the decline is leveling off. Thus, the party in the electorate may be weaker than it was, but it isn't going to disappear. Furthermore, the electoral parties in many states are stronger than ever. This is one reason for the increase in the proportion of states that have competitive party systems.

It remains to be seen whether state and local political parties will be able to develop their own PACs to raise funds, come to terms with the power of those already established, hire or recruit political consultants willing to promote issues and support candidates of substance instead of candidates who project a photogenic image, and work successfully for reforms that will even the balance between the two major sets of political institutions for political participation.

A great deal will depend on the willingness of individuals to work within the parties and help influence state legislatures. It is in these political institutions that funds are allocated and laws are passed to make government more responsible to the electorate.

Study Objectives

1. Identify the central argument of this chapter.
2. Identify the three components of a political party.
3. Identify the functions of parties.
4. Identify the reasons why we have a two-party system.
5. Identify reasons why patronage is a tradition that won't go away.
6. Differentiate machine politics and the political machine.
7. Differentiate political party from political machine.
8. Identify the reasons political machines came to power.
9. Identify the functions performed by political machines.
10. Identify the reasons why political machines declined.
11. Identify the cues used by voters in place of party labels.
12. Identify the assumptions on which responsible party theory is based.
13. Identify the major components of responsible party theory.
14. Identify the major proposals of the reform movement and their effects on political parties.
15. Identify the ways in which state and local political party systems could be strengthened.

Glossary

at-large principle A principle in which all seats in a legislative body are apportioned to the entire unit of government that the legislature serves. In an at-large city council, all the citizens in the city vote on candidates for each seat. The governor of a state is elected at large; members of the state legislature, by contrast, are elected from single-member districts.

closed primaries Participation in the nomination process is limited to individuals who have chosen to identify with the party.

electoral party Consists of (1) individuals who campaign, attend party meetings and social functions, and contribute to the party, (2) officials of the party at the state and local levels, and (3) staff members.

endorsing convention A convention that takes place before the primary election. It promotes party unity and gives the electoral party a larger role in the nominating process. Delegates to the convention vote to endorse one of the people seeking the nomination for governor or any other office the convention is empowered to endorse. Voters know which candidate in the primary has the approval of the active party members.

index of competition Measures interparty competition within each state. This measure involves three dimensions: proportion of success, duration of success, and frequency of divided control of government.

loyal opposition A party loyal to the political system but opposed to the governing party. As the minority party in the legislature, it is aware of the governing process and is prepared to take over the government if it wins the next election.

machine politics The manipulation of certain incentives to partisan political participation, for example, favoritism based on political criteria in personnel decisions, contracting, and the administration of laws.

mobilize To arouse, to call to action. A major feature of a competitive two-party system is that more voters are mobilized to participate than is the case in a one-party or no-party system.

nonpartisan elections Such elections do not have party labels on the ballot as a guide to voters.

one-party systems There is no mechanism for voters to replace one set of office-holders with another. Instead, each voter at each election must make a series of separate decisions on candidates for each office.

open primary Enables people to vote in either party's primary regardless of whether they identify with that party.

party caucus A meeting of all members of a party in a legislative body.

party cohesion Within each of the three components of the party, there is considerable unity; each component supports the goals of the party.

party identification The sense of identity and willingness to express support for a political party.

party in the electorate Consists of any or all of the following: (1) those who say they identify with the party and, in some states, those who stated their party allegiance when they registered to vote, (2) those who vote in the primary election of a party, (3) those who usually vote for a party's candidates in general elections.

party in office Consists of officials in government who were elected under the party label or appointed because of party affiliation. These are the individuals who attempt to organize the government and take responsibility for running it.

patronage The practice of protecting, supporting, or advancing the cause of someone else. In politics, patronage means that decisions are made in favor of an individual or party's supporters. Few critics of patronage make the distinction between situations in which all other things are equal and situations in which favoritism overrides important factors such as qualifications for the job and the lowest bid to provide a product or service.

political consultants Individuals or firms that offer professional expertise in the new technology of political campaigning.

political machine An organization which practices machine politics and usually has taken over an existing local party.

political party An organization which attempts to take control of government by winning elections.

primary election Enables voters who may or may not be active in the party to help determine whom the party will nominate for the general election.

proportional representation Uses large multimember districts to elect numerous legislators according to the percentage of the total vote the party received.

rational-comprehensive model A model of decision making that assumed that voters are always informed and rational.

reform movement The collection of individuals and groups concerned with defeating political machines in nineteenth- and twentieth-century urban America.

responsible party model A model of party-governmental relationships that allows voters to hold government accountable through meaningful elections.

state election code The collection of laws dealing with elections.

Endnotes

1. David Broder, *The Party's Over: The Failure of Politics in America*, (New York: Harper & Row, 1971), William Crotty, *American Parties in Decline*, 2nd ed. (Boston: Little, Brown, 1984), and Everett Carll Ladd, *Where Have All the Voters Gone: The Fracturing of America's Political Parties*, 2nd ed. (New York: Norton, 1982). Thomas R. Dye begins the chapter on parties in the sixth edition of his widely read textbook *Politics in State and Communities*, with the heading "American Political Parties in Disarray" (Englewood Cliffs, NJ: Prentice-Hall, 1988), 116.

2. Sarah McCally Morehouse, *State Politics, Parties, and Policy*, (New York: CBS College Publishing, 1981), 117.

3. Harlan Hahn, *Urban-Rural Conflict: The Politics of Change*, (Beverly Hills, CA: Sage, 1954), 17. It appears that Hahn was correct in predicting that "political competition in Iowa probably will be influenced most significantly by the growing Democratic vote in urban centers and by the strength of urban party organizations," 213.

4. Council of State Governments, *State Elective Officials and the Legislatures 1989–90*, (Lexington, KY: Council of State Governments, 1989), 38.

5. Frank J. Sorauf, *Party Politics in America*, 2nd ed. (Boston: Little, Brown, 1972), 9–10.

6. Malcom E. Jewell and David M. Olson, *Political Parties and Elections in American States*, (Chicago: Dorsey, 1988), 226–227.

7. Walter Devries, "American Campaign Consulting: Trends and Concerns," *PS: Political Science and Politics*, (March 1989), 21.

8. Larry Sabato, "Political Influence, the News Media and Campaign Consultants," *PS: Political Science and Politics*, (March 1989), 15.

9. Mark Petracca, Larry Sabato, Benjamin Ginsberg, Walter Devries, and Celinda Lake, "Political Consultants and Democratic Governance," *PS: Political Science and Politics*, (March 1989), 11–29.

10. Celinda Lake, "Political Consultants: Opening Up a New System of Political Power," *PS: Political Science and Politics*, (March 1989), 26.

11. Council of State Governments, *The Book of the States, 1988–89*, (Lexington, KY: Council of State Governments, 1988), 123. In only nine states is party leadership or the party caucus assigned a formal role in the committee selection process.

12. Jewell and Olson, 236–237.

13. The election code for most states is several hundred pages long. The 1988 Texas Election Code is over 750 pages long.

14. *The Book of the States 1988–89*, 184–185.

15. Morehouse, 186.

16. Jewell and Olson, 105.

17. Morehouse, 186–187.

18. Donald Stokes, "Party Loyalty and the Likelihood of Deviating Elections," in Angus Campbell, Philip E. Converse, Warren E. Miller, and Donald E. Stokes, *Elections and the Political Order* (New York: Wiley, 1966), 126–127.

19. Angus Campbell, Philip E. Converse, Warren E. Miller, and Donald E. Stokes, *The American Voter* (New York: Wiley, 1960), 122.

20. See, for example, Larry Sabato, *The Party's Just Begun*, (Glenview, IL: Scott, Foresman, 1988).

21. Richard G. Niemi, Stephen Wright, and Lynda W. Powell, "Multiple Party Identifiers and the Measurement of Party Identification," *Journal of Politics*, (November 1987), 1097.

22. Jewell and Olson, 42.

23. Raymond Wolfinger and Robert B. Arseneau, "Partisan Change in the South, 1952–76," in Louis Maisel and Joseph Cooper, eds., *Political Parties: Development and Decay*, (Beverly Hills, CA: Sage, 1978), 197.

24. *The Book of the States, 1988–89*, 186–187.

25. Ibid., 183–184.

26. Austin Ranney, "Parties in State Politics" in Herbert Jacob and Kenneth N. Vines, eds., *Politics in the American States*, 3rd ed. (Boston: Little, Brown, 1976), 51–92.

27. Ibid., 87.

28. John F. Bibby, Cornelius P. Cotter, James L. Gibson, and Robert J. Huckshorn, "Parties in State Politics," in Virginia Gray, Herbert Jacob, and Kenneth N. Vines, eds., *Politics in the American States*, 4th ed. (Boston: Little, Brown, 1983), 66.

29. The classic statement is in American Political Science Association, *Toward a More Responsible Two-Party System* (New York: Rinehart, 1950). For a more recent reformulation, see David Broder, "The Case for Responsible Party Government," in Jeff Fishel, ed., *Parties and Elections in an Anti-Party Age* (Bloomington: Indiana University Press, 1978), 22–33. For a devastating critique of the APSA report, see Evron Kirkpatrick, "Toward a More Responsible Party System: Political Science, Policy Science, or Pseudo-Science?" in Fishel, 33–55.

30. Jack C. Plano and Milton Greenberg, *The American Political Dictionary*, 8th ed. (New York: Holt, Rinehart & Winston, 1989), 85–86.

31. V. O. Key, *Politics, Parties, and Pressure Groups*, 5th ed. (New York: Crowell, 1964), 383, 644.

32. See David E. Price, *Bringing Back The Parties*, (Washington, DC: Congressional Quarterly Press, 1984), 104–107 for an overview of responsible party theory.

33. Paul Allen Beck, "A Socialization Theory of Partisan Realignment," in Richard G. Niemi, ed., *The Politics of Future Citizens: New Dimensions in the Political Socialization of Children*, (San Francisco: Jossey-Bass, 1974), 199–219.

34. *Newsweek*, (June 5, 1989), 25.

35. Raymond E. Wolfinger, "Why Political Machines Have Not Withered Away and Other Revisionist Thoughts," *Journal of Politics*, (May 1972), 365–398.

36. William L. Riordan, *Plunkitt of Tammany Hall*, (New York: E. P. Dutton & Co., 1963), 27–28.

37. Ibid., 19.

38. Robert K. Merton, "The Latent Function of the Machine," in Robert K. Merton, ed., *Social Theory and Social Structure*, (New York: Free Press, 1957), 71–81. See also Theodore J. Lowi, "Machine Politics: Old and New," *Public Interest* (Fall 1967), 83–92.

39. William A. Schultze, *Urban and Community Politics*, (North Scituate, MA: Duxbury, 1974), 176.

40. Richard Rakove, *Don't Make No Waves—Don't Back No Losers: An Insider's Analysis of the Daley Machine*, (Bloomington: Indiana University Press, 1978), 96.

41. Two excellent and very readable studies with differing points of view on Daley and his machine are Rakove, *Don't Make Waves*, and Mike Royko, *Boss: Richard J. Daley of Chicago*, (New York: Dutton, 1971).

42. Richard Hofstadter, *The Age of Reform*, (New York: Vintage, 1955), 5–7.

43. Ibid., 241.

44. Hofstadter uses the term "machine" to describe these organizations. Our definition makes the notion of a reform machine something of an oxymoron, as in "honest crook" or, as Plunkitt might prefer, "honest graft." Among the many excellent biographies of these complex and interesting individuals, of special merit are the following: Melvin C. Holli, *Reform in Detroit: Hazen Pingree and Urban Politics*, (New York: Oxford University Press, 1969), and William D. Miller, *Mr. Crump of Memphis*, (Baton Rouge: Louisiana State University Press, 1964).

45. Tari Renner, "Municipal Election Processes: The Impact on Minority Representation," in International City Management Association, *The Municipal Yearbook 1988*, (Washington, DC: International City Management Association, 1988), 13.

46. Charles R. Adrian, "Forms of City Government in American History," in *The Municipal Yearbook 1988*, 8. See also Eugene C. Lee, "Municipal Elections, A Statistical Profile," in *The Municipal Yearbook 1963*.

47. Quoted in Hofstadter, 258.

48. American Assembly, "Participants in the Sixty-second American Assembly," in *The Future of American Political Parties*, (Harriman, NY: American Assembly, 1982), 13–14.

49. The final report of the sixty-second American Assembly, 11; this report includes 19 suggested reforms.

50. In addition to the American Assembly's final report, many of the papers prepared for it appear in Joel L. Fleishman, ed., *The Future of American Political Parties: The Challenge of Governance*, (Englewood Cliffs, NJ: Prentice-Hall). Two excellent monographs to which this chapter owes a heavy debt are David E. Price, *Bringing Back the Parties*, (Washington, DC: Congressional Quarterly Press, 1984), and Larry Sabato, *The Party's Just Begun*. The credentials of these two authors are particularly noteworthy. Price is a political science professor (Duke University), a U.S. Representative (North Carolina), and a former state party chair. Sabato, also a political science professor (University of Virginia), has written extensively on political action committees and campaign consultants.

51. Price, 110–111.

52. Steven E. Finkel, and Howard A. Scarrow, "Party Identification and Party Enrollment: The Difference and the Consequence," *Journal of Politics*, (1985), 621.

53. *The Book of the States, 1988–89*, 186–187.

54. Sabato, 224.

55. *The Book of the States, 1988–89*, 184–185.

Chapter
9

Legislatures

Legislative power is the cornerstone of American democracy. John Locke described the power of the "legislative" as the most basic and important,[1] and James Madison declared, "In republican government, the legislative authority necessarily predominates."[2] Unlike many democracies, our constitutional system gives the legislature an exalted position through the concept of separation of powers; Congress, state legislatures, and many local legislatures possess power bases separate from and independent of those of executives.

Legislatures play a fundamental role in state and local governments. Despite increasingly powerful executives, state legislatures, city councils, school boards, and other legislative bodies are key policymakers. They are also generally accessible to the individual. Individuals who are familiar with the procedures and organization of legislative bodies have ample opportunities to initiate or block government action. We see examples of this every day. Citizens angry about rising utility rates attend city council meetings to express their displeasure. Students lobby the legislature and testify at public committee hearings to try to prevent tuition increases. A businessperson concerned about the lack of vocational programs in local schools calls a member of the elected school board.

To influence legislative bodies, you must understand the functions they perform, how their members are chosen, and how they are organized. Since local legislative bodies differ in many ways from those at the state level, you should be aware of some of the major differences. This chapter examines the functions of legislative bodies and looks specifically at the characteristics of state and local legislatures. It ends with advice and strategies for gaining access to these legislatures.

THE FUNCTIONS OF LEGISLATURES

Legislatures perform unique functions in the American political system. The following discussion examines some of the most important of these functions.

Lawmaking

If you were to ask legislators what the purpose of a legislature is, you would get a variety of answers: "Our job is to represent our constituents." "We resolve important issues through compromise." "We try to find the best way of providing important services to the citizens of this city (or state)." All these answers would be correct, of course, but the most basic answer is, "We pass laws." Lawmaking, or enacting legislation, is the unique task of the legislature.

Legislators perceive lawmaking to be their primary function. A recent survey asked legislators in Minnesota and Kentucky to rank in importance the functions of lawmaking, oversight, and constituency service. Two-thirds ranked legislating as the most important.[3] Almost all the activities of a legislator revolve around the process of making laws. A legislator introduces bills; deals with bills in committee; listens to public testimony; consults with lobbyists, constituents, and bureaucrats; makes speeches; and even socializes with those interested in a specific law or the lawmaking process.

One should not be misled into believing that legislative bodies do *all* the legislating. Other actors, especially bureaucratic experts, become more involved in the lawmaking process as the size and complexity of the city or state increase. The executive often suggests or initiates laws, and many bills are actually drafted by executive agencies or interest groups. Bureaucrats implement laws, and their decisions are often formalized as orders or rules. The courts interpret statutory and constitutional laws.

Nevertheless, the basic responsibility for resolving conflicts and creating laws lies with the legislature. As one scholar says, "The moment of truth comes when the vote is taken from those people who have been properly elected to the legislature."[4]

Budget Making

Although budget making is a form of lawmaking, it is so important that it deserves to be mentioned separately. When students think about budgeting, they generally think of a dreary bureaucratic process that is complex, hard to understand, and mechanical. Although budgeting is a complex process, it is far from mechanical; it is a highly charged political process. Legislatures deal with important policy questions when they decide how much citizens will be taxed and what programs government will fund. The budget is a government's ultimate statement of its policy choices. When a state legislature decides to raise teachers' salaries, it is making a statement about the high priority of education. A city council that decides to build a municipal convention center rather than a public housing project is making a statement that economic development and tourism are more important than are direct services to the poor.

As with lawmaking in general, developing budgets is not the sole function of legislatures. Often state legislatures rely on the governor's plan for taxing and spending, while local legislature's rely on a city manager, school superintendent, or other administrator. Legislatures do not always follow the executive's plan, but in the absence of any other systematic plan, they find it convenient to use that plan. Executives are assisted in developing the budget by their own staff and by executive agencies that are extremely familiar with the details of budgeting, while legislatures often have less time to deliberate over the budget.

Still, the final decisions about the flow of funds are made by legislatures, and their greatest power is the power of the purse. It is important to remember that only legislatures possess the final authority to tax. This authority, potentially the most abusive held by government, is the key to understanding the dominant role of legislatures in state and local governments.

Oversight

A thoughtful, well-drafted law or budget offers no guarantee that the policy intentions of legislatures will be carried out. To ensure that this happens, legislatures review and evaluate the actions of the executive and oversee the administration of state and local programs. This process of reviewing the implementation of laws and policies is referred to as the **oversight** function.

Until recently oversight was thought of as the neglected stepchild of the policy process. Creating and passing legislation was much more interesting and rewarding than checking to see if that legislation was being implemented properly. In the past few years, however, legislatures have been paying increasing attention to oversight. Both state and local governments are going beyond such traditional measures as budget hearings and audits and are applying oversight to the whole legislative process. They are looking more closely at the efficiency and effectiveness of the programs through performance reviews. Over half the states and many cities have established separate evaluation agencies to conduct oversight of programs and budgets.

Thirty-five states have established some form of **sunset laws**. This typically means that unless the legislature acts to renew an executive agency, that agency will cease to exist after a certain date. In general , sunset laws have not resulted in the termination of many agencies, but they have served as an incentive for agencies to improve their performance.[5] Agencies that know they are going to be reviewed and possibly terminated are moved to improve their performance (Box 9-1).

Although legislatures are becoming more aggressive about oversight, they are still not fully motivated to perform this function. Oversight often becomes a burden which produces no political rewards. One legislator admits that "most of us are elected to be legislators with the thought that we're there to correct the ills of the world, and we usually start by filing bills on every idea we have."[6] Taking action on these bills means creating public policy, engaging in the excitement of combat, and stimulating the attention of the media. In contrast, oversight is a boring or tedious process for legislators, who must attend lengthy hearings, consider the details of complicated programs, and read voluminous reports. Often they face defensive administrators and entrenched interest groups that distrust their motives and consider them incompetent to judge their programs. In an ideal world the oversight process would be a continuous and integral function of the legislature. In the real world it is often the last to receive attention.

Judicial

Legislatures perform judicial functions directly through the impeachment of executive officials and judges and indirectly through the confirmation of judicial appointments. Most state legislatures have the power to remove executive officials and judges through a two-step process. The house of representatives decides whether to **impeach**, that is, bring formal charges against these officials, and the senate tries them to see if they are guilty. Conviction generally requires a two-thirds vote of the senate and results in removal from office.

In many states, legislatures influence the judicial process indirectly through the confirmation of judicial appointments. The state senate confirms gubernatorial appointees to the bench, usually through a two-thirds vote. Even in states where judges are elected, governors frequently appoint judges to fill vacancies on state courts. These appointees must also be approved by the senate.

Thus legislatures exercise checks and balances over the executive and judicial branches. Impeachment is a final weapon against executive unre-

Box 9-1   # Sunset in the States: Mixed Reviews

Sunset legislation had its birth in Colorado in 1976 and quickly caught the imagination of legislatures throughout the country. By 1980 it had spread to more than 30 states and was highly touted as a promising new instrument of legislative oversight.

It sounded so simple. A number of state agencies—around 30—would be scheduled for termination each year. Those agencies would be subjected to a review by the legislature to determine whether they should be continued, modified, or terminated, that is, ''sunsetted.''

The distinguishing feature of sunset and the reason for its catchy name was its automatic termination feature. Agencies not specifically reauthorized by statute before the scheduled sunset deadline would simply cease to exist. For the first time the burden of proof for performance and effectiveness was placed squarely on the agency, and for the first time thorough reviews of the bureaucracy would actually take place. Legislators who were always too busy or too uninterested in oversight would be forced to review agencies and take positive action to see that those agencies continued to operate.

Like most reforms, sunset was oversold. It was supposed to reduce the size of state bureaucracies, but the only agencies terminated were small and insignificant ones. It was supposed to cut down on the increasing costs of state government, but the cost of the sunset review itself was often higher than anticipated. Additional legislative staff had to be hired to conduct the reviews, which required a large amount of time for both the legislature and the agency.

The biggest costs, however, were political. Sunset unleashed a wave of lobbyists who descended on state capitals to protect their favorite agencies and programs. Sunset reviews often opened up enormous controversies. These controversies went beyond questions of how an agency operated; they often revolved around important state policies. Legislators realized the high price of trying to change or eliminate powerful state bureaucracies.

Enthusiasm for sunset waned. By the early 1980s four states had repealed their sunset statutes or let them fall into disuse. All but five states have made changes in their legislation. No states have adopted sunset laws since 1981.

States that have maintained sunset laws have a lowered level of expectations. Many states modified their statutes to limit the scope of sunset reviews. For example, Kansas and Florida review only regulations and programs, not agencies. Some states extended the length of the review cycle in order to lower the costs of the reviews. A longer review cycle also allows more careful scrutiny of agencies.

As sunset moves into its second decade, it has become a reasonably effective tool for legislative oversight. Although it does not often result in the termination of agencies, it does result in their modification. Agencies anticipating sunset reviews usually attempt to get their house in order to minimize the criticism or changes that an unfavorable review might bring. Sunset does seem to encourage more efficient and effective agency operations. More important, the process opens up the possibility of addressing important issues and remedying flagrant bureaucratic abuses. Thus, it seems that in a modified form, sunset may be around for a while.

sponsiveness, although it is cumbersome to employ and is seldom used. Judicial confirmation means that executives must share control over the appointment of judicial personnel.

Representation

Cities and states share with the nation the idea that they should be governed as republics. You'll recall from Chapter 4 that an important aspect of republicanism is the notion of representative government. In Madisonian theory, competent citizens are chosen to represent the community and help it realize its ideals; decision making that is "filtered" through these competent individuals helps preclude tyranny by temporary and irrational majorities. Representatives consider the demands of each issue in light of the whole community. Thus representation is an important function of an elected legislator.

Theories of Representation   Exactly who a legislator represents and how he or she represents them are matters of speculation. Imagine that you have been elected to the state legislature. What would be your philosophy about the way you represent your voters? Would you vote on bills the way you think your constituents want you to vote or the way you think you ought to vote on the basis of your conscience and judgment? The question is not as simple as it sounds.

There are three classic views of the legislator: the **trustee role**, the **delegate role**, and the **politico role**.[7] In making decisions, trustees claims to follow their convictions and principles, doing what they consider right or just even when this means opposing the views of a majority of their constituents. Trustees believe that they are generally in a position to be more knowledgeable about the issues and therefore are elected to use their own judgment. Delegates, by contrast, reflect the views of a majority of their constituents. Their job, as they see it, is to represent the interests of a majority of their voters.

The role of politico combines features of both the trustee and the delegate. Depending on the circumstances, a representative may hold the view of a trustee on one issue and that of a delegate on another. If a representative has aspirations to reelection — and most representatives do — he or she cannot afford to consistently ignore constituency views. However, most voters know very little about most bills. Attempts to mirror the majority view of one's constituents makes no sense if there is no majority view.

Constituents who do have a strong and informed view are likely to be an organized minority, that is, a special-interest group. The demands of special-interest groups may cause conflict in the decisions of a politico. A representative who wants to accommodate the demands of a special-interest group may not believe these demands are in the best interest of the entire community. In this situation, a politico must choose between the role of trustee and that of a delegate.

Certainly the concept of representation is complex. As one state legislator observed, "Each member casts a vote on a bill, resolution, or procedural question based on how he or she reckons that particular problem at that particular moment. Just as the moments change, so do the rationales."[8]

Responding to Constituents   Representation goes beyond promoting the policy views of citizens. Constituents want a legislator who gives them attention and assurances and attends to their individual needs. Most state legislators and all local legislators live and work close to those who elect them. As they go about their business, they are expecte co mix with their constituents at work, parties, the barber shop, or the supermarket. They nurture support by listening and responding to individuals' opinions.

Like their congressional counterparts, state and local legislators spend more and more time helping individual constituents. This individualized assistance is called **casework**. Casework may involve a variety of activities, but a substantial portion of them require that the legislator intervene with a government agency on the constituent's behalf. A single mother may feel she should qualify for food stamps. A college graduate may want a job working for a city or county agency. A parent may feel her son or daughter has been treated badly by a coach or principal. Some legislators enjoy this function of representation not only because it builds electoral support but because they feel they are having a direct impact on people's lives.

How Representative Is the Typical Legislator?   Some people argue that in a democracy such as ours, the representatives we elect to public office should mirror society in general. The idea is that people elected to public office should resemble those who vote for them because this makes them more responsive to the needs of the "common" people. A legislature that reflects the social, economic, and cultural composition of society will be more sensitive to the needs of citizens in that society.

Legislators do tend to possess certain characteristics of a majority of their constituents, such as ethnicity, race, and religion. A legislator representing a district where the majority of voters are Roman Catholic also is likely to be a Catholic. Beyond these basic characteristics, however, legislators are not likely to reflect the general characteristics of their constituencies. Your chances of being elected to a legislature increase substantially if you are white, male, Protestant, upper middle class, and well-educated and work in a business or profession that allows you time for legislative service. However, the portrait of the "average" legislator has been changing slowly over the years. Women and minorities have gained more seats in state and local legislatures, although their numbers are still not overwhelming. Women held about 8 percent of the 7500 state legislative seats in 1975; today they have doubled this to about 16 percent. Minority membership in state legislatures now exceeds 400 seats (5.4 percent).[9]

Table 9.1 shows that lawyers and independent business owners are still the categories most heavily represented in state legislatures, but in recent

Table 9.1 OCCUPATIONAL CATEGORIES OF STATE LEGISLATORS

Occupation	Percent
Attorney	16
Business owner	14
Full-time legislator	11
Agricultural occupation	10
Educator	9

Source: Council of State Governments, *The Book of the States* (Lexington, KY: CSG, 1988), 80.

years their numbers have been decreasing gradually. The number of legislators who define their occupation as legislator is increasing. Indeed, the category of full-time legislator would exceed 20 percent if those who list themselves as retired, homemaker, or student were included. One reason for this increase is the longer session lengths of many state legislatures; being a legislator in many states is now virtually a full-time job.

Amending

One function that all state legislatures and most local legislatures have in common is the ability to change fundamental laws that govern state or local government; these laws are embodied in state constitutions and local charters. States legislatures *propose* amendments to state constitutions that are ultimately approved by the voters. State legislatures also have the authority to approve amendments to the U.S. Constitution.

The fact that legislatures have the potential to alter basic laws embodied in their constitutions demonstrates the importance of legislative bodies in American democracy.

STATE LEGISLATURES

Until recently state legislatures have had a bad reputation. Charges of corruption, malapportionment, and other abuses come frequently from the press and other political observers. Critics also charge that state legislatures are poorly organized and technically ill equipped to do what is expected of them. They are the prime examples of "institutional lag," largely nineteenth-century organizations that must address themselves to twentieth-century problems.[10]

In the past several years, however, state legislatures have instituted wide-ranging changes or reforms. They have reapportioned themselves, increased their capacity to make informed decisions, and passed laws to reduce ethical conflicts. The rapid and dramatic transformation of many state legislatures makes them fascinating targets for study.

Not only are state legislatures more progressive these days, they are also more significant actors in our intergovernmental system. Changes in the federal system since the early 1980s have given the states stronger positions. As states have become more prominent, state legislatures have strengthened their position within the states. These legislatures have assumed more responsibility for state and local matters and are more heavily involved in implementing federal programs.

Historical Changes in the Role of State Legislatures

American state legislatures have been affected by a number of historical changes. Although these changes have been continuous and complex, certain stages in the role of legislatures can be identified.

The Rise and Fall of State Legislatures   Early in American history, legislatures were the symbol of America's democratic struggle against the arbitrary British Crown. For 25 years after the Declaration of Independence, state legislatures dominated. Governors represented political tyranny to American citizens, who viewed the American Revolution as a revolt against executive authority.

For the next 100 years state legislatures suffered a gradual decline that resulted primarily from two factors: the strengthening of executive power and the incompetence and corruption of legislatures. As memories of autocratic royal governors faded, states gradually realized the need for stronger executives. Slowly, hostility toward governors was replaced with a growing trust in executive power. States took steps to strengthen their governors and created a variety of new executive offices that augmented the role of the executive branch in state affairs.

However, the state legislatures brought about their own demise. Over time legislatures fell into disgrace. With the election of Andrew Jackson in 1828, a new breed of legislator appeared on the state political scene. Jackson was elected President because of support from the new masses of propertyless, semiliterate voters. With the rise of Jackson and his breed, the character of people serving in state legislatures changed profoundly. Gradually, as democratization progressed, service in the legislature ceased to be an activity of the wealthy and the able. This trend was heightened by the fact that politics offered little financial reward, except, of course, for bribes. Most competent educated people therefore preferred busines or other professional activities.

The incidence of corruption and bribery in state legislatures seemed to increase toward the end of the nineteenth century. The new industrial giants that emerged in the latter half of that century — manufacturing, oil, mining, and investment, to name a few — were well aware of how greatly they could be hurt or helped by what state legislatures did. Many of these business leaders were as prone to give bribes as state legislators were to accept them.

The Progressive Movement   The most predictable response to abuse of power by governmental bodies is to limit that power. So it was with the reformers who addressed the corruption and incompetence of state legislatures. The progressive movement emerged around the turn of the century, led by William Jennings Bryan, Robert M. La Follette, Theodore Roosevelt, and Woodrow Wilson. These reformers helped institute several measures that limited the power of legislatures and put it into the hands of the people.

The progressives introduced the referendum, the recall, and the initiative. These measures, which were discussed in Chapter 8, gave the people more direct control over elected officials. Many state constitutions were revised. Legislative sessions in many states were limited to one every two years (biennial sessions). Reformers assumed that the less often legislators got together, the less damage they could do. By 1940 only four states had annual legislative sessions.[11] Less frequent legislative sessions provided a reason for lower salaries, and many states restricted legislators' pay. Debt limitations were introduced to control the financial power of legislatures.

The Age of the Executive   Prompted by progressive reform, interest in the period from the mid-1930s to the mid-1960s was focused on state executive organization and administration. During this period new or revised state constitutions enhanced the powers of governors, who were given longer terms, more appointment power, more control over budgets, and greater resources to manage larger bureaucracies. Meeting biennially, state legislatures were dependent on the executive for information, staff support, and direction. Often legislatures voted yes or no to gubernatorial requests, with little revision. They rarely proposed substitute legislation or "marked up," that is, amended legislation in committee.[12]

The Modern State Legislature

Facing stronger executives and possessing fewer resources of their own, state legislatures could be described by the word "amateurish." Throughout the first half of the twentieth century part-time "amateur" legislatures continued to be the standard. Legislators were poorly paid, sessions were short and infrequent, staff support was in short supply, and in many states legislators had no office space. About 20 years ago things began to change.

Reapportionment   Probably the most important reason for criticism of state legislatures was their failure to reapportion. **Apportionment** is the allocation of legislative seats to geographic areas; it means that legislative districts (both state legislative and U.S. congressional districts) are drawn so that they are about equal in population. **Reapportionment** therefore refers to the process of redrawing the boundaries of state and congressional districts to reflect changes or shifts in population. For years states experienced gradual population shifts from rural to urban areas, yet legislatures continued to be dominated by rural legislators who had little interest in addressing the problems and concerns of urban areas. Often rural residents felt that city people were not as virtuous, clean, or God-fearing as those living in rural areas and didn't really deserve state aid.

State legislatures are responsible for redrawing the geographic boundaries for voting districts in the two houses of the state legislature as well as for state seats in the U.S. House of Representatives. Reapportionment is supposed to take place every ten years, after a census is taken. However, as time passed, almost every state failed to perform this function. Reapportionment may sound like a technical process in that entering new census data into the appropriate computer program can easily and quickly yield evenly distributed districts. It is *not* a technical process, however, but a complicated and controversial political process that takes months or even years of planning, bargaining, and scheming to accomplish. It sends waves of anxiety through legislators who almost always have nothing to gain and everything to lose from uncertain results.

Until the 1960s the courts refused to force state legislatures to act, maintaining that reapportionment is a political issue that should be settled by political rather than legal means. Finally in 1962, the Supreme Court heard the landmark case *Baker* v. *Carr* and ruled that malapportionment in the lower house of the state legislature of Tennessee was a violation of the equal protection clause of the Fourteenth Amendment to the U.S. Constitution.[13] Thus challenges to legislative apportionment in Tennessee and other states were issues that should be addressed by federal courts. In 1964, the Court handed down six closely related decisions that ultimately led to the redistricting of nearly every state legislature in the United States.[14] These decisions established the **one person, one vote doctrine**, that is, the idea that state legislative districts must be equal in population according to the most recent census.

Even after the reapportionment requirement, legislative boundaries were often subject to gerrymandering to give unfair advantage to the party in control. **Gerrymandering** is the practice of drawing the lines of the legislative districts to magnify the power of a particular group. It is usually perpetrated by the dominant political party to give electoral advantage to its representatives. Figure 9.1 shows a hypothetical example of gerrymandering. A geographic area might have an equal number of Republicans and Democrats (in our example there are six of each). In the first box, the district lines are drawn so that Republicans form a majority in three of four districts; in the second box, Democrats control three of the four districts. In the third box, the districts are divided so that Republicans and Democrats each control two districts. Contrary to what you might expect, the straightforward solution in the third box is not always easy to achieve.

When gerrymandering occurs, the injured party will generally sue in federal court (Box 9-2). Courts sometimes strike down legislative reappor-

A *Republican*-controlled
gerrymander

A *Democratic*-controlled
gerrymander

A *compromise solution* to the
apportionment districting task

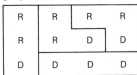

R	R	R	R
R	R	D	D
D	D	D	D

R	R	R	R
R	R	D	D
D	D	D	D

R	R	R	R
R	R	D	D
D	D	D	D

Figure 9.1 Examples of political gerrymandering.

tionment plans if the plaintiffs can prove that gerrymandering was deliberate. The courts are quickest to invalidate racial gerrymandering, or reapportionment plans that obviously discriminate against the election chances of
minorities. Intentional racial gerrymandering is a violation of the fourteenth
amendment's equal protection clause, and is, therefore, unconstitutional.
The courts are not as eager to invalidate political gerrymandering, that is,
reapportionment plans that discriminate against a political party. In fact,
before the early 1980s, federal courts refused to hear cases involving political gerrymandering. Lately the courts have become more receptive to charges
of political gerrymandering, although they have yet to invalidate a redistricting plan on that basis. In 1986, the Supreme Court declared in *Davis* v.
Bandemer that partisan gerrymanders could be unconstitutional. However,
the Court upheld the Indiana redistricting plan that was being challenged
and failed to spell out clear standards that political parties could use to
challenge a plan. In 1989, the Court again failed to invalidate a California
redistricting plan that gave obvious advantages to Democrats running for
the House of Representatives (see Box 9-2).

Reapportionment has made a difference in the way state funds are allocated. The distribution of state aid has shifted to favor urban areas. As urban
constituencies gain representation, there is more emphasis on spending for
the kind of services urban dwellers demand: education, welfare, health, and
hospitals.[15] Democrats have gained some seats mostly in northeastern states,
and a marked increase in the representation of ethnic minorities has accompanied the increase in urban representation.

Despite these changes, the effects of reapportionment have not been as
dramatic as many people expected. Reapportionment was largely a liberal
cause; studies had shown that cities were much more liberal than rural areas.
However, shifts in the population in the last two decades have largely been
from cities to suburbs. Wealthy suburbs tend to elect Republicans who side
with rural representatives against more state involvement in urban
problems.

Legislative Professionalism In 1969–1970 a group known as the
Citizens Conference on State Legislatures conducted a study to determine
the quality of state legislatures. The group evaluated each state legislature

Box 9-2 **Partisan Gerrymandering in California**

After the 1980 Census, California Republicans felt they were the victims of a flagrant case of gerrymandering, and many people agreed. The state's redistricting plan abolished or merged several GOP districts, shored up weak Democratic seats, and created several open seats that provided obvious opportunities for Democrats.

Population growth in California during the 1970s guaranteed two additional seats in the U.S. House of Representatives. Most of this increase occurred in Republican-minded suburban areas. However, after the 1982 elections, the Democrats' 22 to 21 margin in the state's U.S. House delegation jumped to 28 to 17. So effectively were the districts redrawn that in 1984 Republican candidates won a higher share of the aggregate House vote in California but could pick up only one seat.

After numerous challenges, the Republicans filed suit in federal court, but the case, *Badham* v. *Edu*, was dismissed by a federal district court in the spring of 1988. The dismissal was upheld by the Supreme Court in January 1989. The Court's decision was a big disappointment for Republicans, who felt that the California case was about as good an example of partisan gerrymandering as they would get.

The Court's decision made it clear to Republicans in California and across the country that they cannot count on the courts as part of their post-1990 redistricting strategy. If Republicans are to gain seats in the U.S. House and in state legislatures after 1990, they are going to have to rely on political rather than legal strategies.

and made both general and specific recommendations for improvement. In its evaluation, the group determined that legislatures should be functional, accountable, informed, independent, and representative (FAIIR). It suggested structural, procedural, and staffing reforms to improve the performance of state legislatures in these five areas. As part of the study, the Citizens Conference ranked all 50 states according to how they met the five FAIIR criteria. Both the overall ranking and the rankings for each FAIIR criterion are shown in Table 9.2. Although the state rankings, figured about 20 years ago, may no longer be accurate, the criteria for legislative professionalism established in this ground-breaking study are still applicable.

In almost 20 years since the Citizens Conference's study we have seen many states progressively change from a "citizen" legislature to a "professional" legislature. For example, we are witnessing longer and more frequent sessions. Most states have switched to annual sessions; only seven state legislatures meet biennially. Legislators are receiving higher salaries with more substantial benefits. Only nine states still impose constitutional restrictions on legislative salaries. Staff support is increasing in terms of both quantity and quality. There are now more than 16,000 full-time employees, with an additional part-time complement of approximately 9000. Com-

Table 9.2 RANK ORDER OF STATES BY FAIIR CRITERIA

Overall rank	State	Functional	Accountable	Informed	Independent	Representative
1	California	1	3	2	3	2
2	New York	4	13	1	8	1
3	Illinois	17	4	6	2	13
4	Florida	5	8	4	1	30
5	Wisconsin	7	21	3	4	10
6	Iowa	6	6	5	11	25
7	Hawaii	2	11	20	7	16
8	Michigan	15	22	9	12	3
9	Nebraska	35	1	16	30	18
10	Minnesota	27	7	13	23	12
11	New Mexico	3	16	28	39	4
12	Alaska	8	29	12	6	40
13	Nevada	13	10	19	14	32
14	Oklahoma	9	27	24	22	8
15	Utah	38	5	8	29	24
16	Ohio	18	24	7	40	9
17	South Dakota	23	12	15	16	37
18	Idaho	20	9	29	27	21
19	Washington	12	17	25	19	39
20	Maryland	16	31	10	15	45
21	Pennsylvania	37	23	23	5	36
22	North Dakota	22	18	17	37	31
23	Kansas	31	15	14	32	34
24	Connecticut	39	26	26	25	6
25	West Virginia	10	32	37	24	15
26	Tennessee	30	44	11	9	26
27	Oregon	28	14	35	35	19
28	Colorado	21	25	21	28	27
29	Massachusetts	32	25	22	21	23
30	Maine	29	34	32	18	22
31	Kentucky	49	2	48	44	7
32	New Jersey	14	42	18	31	35
33	Louisiana	47	39	33	13	14
34	Virginia	25	19	27	26	48
35	Missouri	36	30	40	49	48
36	Rhode Island	33	46	30	41	11
37	Vermont	19	20	34	42	47
38	Texas	45	36	43	45	17
39	New Hampshire	34	33	42	36	43
40	Indiana	44	38	41	43	20
41	Montana	26	28	31	46	49
42	Mississippi	46	43	45	20	28
43	Arizona	11	47	38	17	50
44	South Carolina	50	45	39	10	46
45	Georgia	40	49	36	33	38

Table 9.2 RANK ORDER OF STATES BY FAIIR CRITERIA (continued)

Overall rank	State	Functional	Accountable	Informed	Independent	Representative
46	Arkansas	41	40	46	34	33
47	North Carolina	24	37	44	47	44
48	Delaware	43	48	47	38	29
49	Wyoming	42	41	50	48	42
50	Alabama	48	50	49	50	41

Source: Citizens Conference on State Legislatures, *State Legislatures: An Evaluation of their Effectiveness* (New York: Praeger, 1971), 40.

puters and modern information systems are now used routinely as part of the state legislative process.[16]

In addition, many more legislators identify themselves as professionals. Until recently state legislative service was purely part time for lawyers, independent businesspeople, farmers, independently wealthy individuals, or anyone who had extra time to devote to public service. As discussed earlier in this chapter (Table 9.1), the number of legislators who define their occupation as legislator is increasing. A recent survey of state legislators conducted by the National Conference of State Legislatures found that more than half the legislators in New York and Pennsylvania defined their occupation as legislator.

The biggest changes tend to occur in the large industrialized states. The legislatures of California, Illinois, Massachusetts, Michigan, New Jersey, New York, Ohio, Pennsylvania, and Wisconsin have lengthy sessions, relatively high legislative salaries, and many members whose primary profession is legislator. However, modernization is occurring in some small states as well. Alabama, Connecticut, Mississippi, and North Carolina have improved or expanded legislative office space and staff. Alabama, Kentucky, and North Carolina recently made major improvements in their legislative computer information systems. In Table 9.3 we identify the most and least professional state legislatures, using much more limited but recent criteria than those used in the Citizens Conference study. The most professional legislatures were those which paid higher salaries and had longer sessions.

Perhaps the most significant development in the modern legislature is the increase in personal staff assistance. Legislative staffing was originally very centralized; it was organized in one or a few central staff agencies which performed all legislative support functions. Often legislative leaders exercised strong control over the staff and used staffing or the lack of it to reward or punish staff members. This is still true in many states, but in recent years staffing has became more decentralized and specialized. About half the states provide professional or support personnel for individual legislators. Separate committee staffs exist to some extent in many legislatures.

Table 9.3 PROFESSIONALISM IN THE STATE LEGISLATURES BASED ON LEGISLATIVE PAY AND SESSION LENGTH

Most professional state legislatures	Least professional state legislatures
California	Alabama
Delaware	Idaho
Illinois	Kentucky
Massachusetts	New Hampshire
Michigan	New Mexico
New Jersey	North Dakota
New York	Rhode Island
Ohio	South Dakota
Pennsylvania	Utah
Wisconsin	Wyoming

Source: Cynthia Opheim, "State Regulation of Lobbies: Professional versus Citizen Legislatures," presented at the annual meeting of the Southwestern Social Science Association, Little Rock, AR, March 29, 1989.

Staffers are also noticeably more partisan. Often staff members are hired on a partisan basis to work for legislative caucuses, leaders, and individual members. Following the pattern of Congress, legislators in some states now have offices and staff in their home districts to help them attend to the needs of their constituents. Although these district offices are not established for blatantly partisan reasons, they certainly contribute to a legislator's re-election.

The goal of these reforms was to work toward the FAIIR criteria, that is, to encourage more informed, deliberative, and independent legislatures. Legislators would have adequate time to consider the measures before them. Salary increases would help retain good people. Specialized and personalized staffers would help legislators handle increasing amounts of legislation more competently and service constituents more conscientiously. Legislators would also become less dependent on special interest groups for information since they themselves would be better informed. With higher salaries, they would be more likely to isolate themselves from the pressure and support of powerful economic interests. Professionalization also meant increased legislative independence from executives.

Despite the optimism of these arguments, there is increasing speculation about the benefits of professionalism. Some people question the efficiency of full-time legislatures, arguing that legislators don't use the extra time to educate themselves and still put off making critical issues until the last minute. Others feel that part-time citizen legislators are more in touch with their constituents. Michigan State Representative Vic Krouse says, "When you spend all your time in Lansing, you're more influenced by the lobbyists than by your constituents."[17] One argument holds that career legislators are more dependent on special-interest groups precisely because serving in the legislature is their job. Legislators with only one means of livelihood place more emphasis on raising money to win reelection.[18]

This debate cannot be resolved by asking if professionalism has any impact on the kinds of policies state governments produce. Research on this question has yielded mixed results. One study showed that professional legislatures tend to produce more liberal redistributive policies.[19] This is not surprising, since the most professional legislatures tend to be in urban industrialized states. However, other scholars found that legislative reforms have little measurable impact on policy.[20]

It seems that as state legislatures handle increasingly complex problems, they will continue to expand their capacity to make decisions. The impact of these reforms on the kinds of decisions they make and the types of influence they consider is still unknown. However, we do know that reforms have helped state legislatures become more dominant players in state government.

Legislatures and Federal Grant Funds   Modern state legislatures are taking a much more active role in overseeing the federal funds given to their states. The growth of federal grants-in-aid to states has been immense, from 160 programs in 1962 to more than 600 in 1981. The cost increased from $24 billion in 1970 to $82.9 billion in 1980. Federal grant monies accounted for almost one of every four dollars in state and local budgets by 1980. After 1981 the Reagan budgets cut funding for many kinds of aid to state and local governments, but in 1986 state and local aid was still $112 billion.

For many years most state legislatures ignored the handling of federal funds in their states. Governors or designated state agencies submitted a "state plan" to federal agencies, outlining how federal money would be spent and identifying the state agencies responsible for spending that money. The legislature, with its constitutional power to appropriate funds, was bypassed completely. Strong links were forged between federal and state bureaucrats, who ignored the traditional authority of the legislature to authorize programs and appropriate money for them.

In the mid-1970s, however, the legislatures began to assert themselves. By 1981, 36 state legislatures actively appropriated federal funds. This means that federal funds are "itemized" in the state budget and are discussed, debated, and prioritized in a normal budget review process. Reduced federal aid has prompted legislatures to consider the impact of federal funds so that they will be less vulnerable to reductions and cutoffs. It is critical to know where federal dollars are going and what might happen if certain programs were cut back or terminated by Washington. States may be left in charge of programs but have empty pockets to fund them.

Legislative appropriation and oversight of federal funds is a major issue of the 1980s and 1990s; it has already caused conflict between state legislative and executive branches. In Pennsylvania the legislature challenged the governor's power to spend funds that had not been officially appropriated by the legislature, and Pennsylvania court upheld the legislature. Consideration of federal funds is also taking more of the legislature's time. More professional state legislatures, however, are better equipped to handle this new function.

The Structure and Organization of State Legislatures

Bicameralism Bicameral, or two-house, legislatures are characteristic of every state but Nebraska. Every state calls the upper house the senate, and most states call the lower house the house of representatives. Several states, including California, New York, Nevada, and Wisconsin, call the lower house the assembly. Ostensibly the rationale behind the two-house legislature is that it is designed to foster a more deliberative process.[21] Since both houses must pass legislation, rash or careless action is less likely. In reality, most state legislatures have a bicameral legislature because Congress set the example. However, one cannot compare the need for bicameralism in Congress with that in state legislatures. The congressional model resulted from the need for a compromise between the big and small states at the Constitutional Convention of 1787 — the Great Compromise. The U.S. Senate was established to satisfy the small states' desire for equality, while the House was established to satisfy the big states' desire for representation based on population. There was no such compelling political circumstances for the states. Indeed, the United States Supreme Court declared that representation in *both* houses in state legislatures has to be based on population.[22]

We generally take for granted the superiority of a two-house legislature, but there are some drawbacks. Although careless or stupid action is less likely, wise or sensible action is more difficult to accomplish. These days the biggest problem in modern legislative bodies is slowness or inability to act. The passage of bills is a slow, often tortuous procedure made even more complex by having two houses. Lest we think that unicameral (one-house) bodies are rare, we should remember that all city councils and other local governing boards are unicameral bodies.[23]

Size The size of the legislature varies a great deal from state to state. The average upper house has about 40 members; the average lower house has about 113. Not surprisingly, the smallest legislature is the unicameral body in Nebraska, where only 49 members serve in the single house. More surprisingly, tiny New Hampshire has the largest legislature, with 400 members. One reason for this may be the tradition in some New England states of giving every town representation.

Large size does not mean that a legislature will be more democratic or representative. Indeed, larger bodies must often become more oligarchic or dictatorial. In a large group it becomes necessary for a few individuals to assume power in order for the group to accomplish anything. Certainly small groups tend to be more personal and informal, and it is easier for individuals to exercise direct influence on decision making. If you doubt this, consider the differences in the two houses of Congress. While the House of Repre-

Nebraska's unicameral legislature in session. (*Source:* Unicameral Information Office.)

sentatives with its 435 members is heavily regulated by procedural rules (there is even a rules committee), the Senate with its 100 members is much more informal.

Larger legislative bodies must organize themselves to get anything done. Size therefore means organizational complexity. A complex organization is less responsive to the public in general and more responsive to special-interest groups. Special-interest groups have the resources, time, and motivation to learn what it takes to operate in a large and complex system. The general public, however, is often too intimidated or unconcerned to make the effort to participate in such a system. Thus bigger does not always mean more democratic or more representative.

Leadership Structure Leadership in a majority of state legislatures, as in Congress, is based primarily on party. The two most important leaders are the speaker of the house and the president or president pro tem of the senate. The major and minor parties in each house select a majority leader and a minority leader. These officers are assisted by majority and minority whips. The leaders and whips sometimes have assistants.

One interesting difference between state and national governments is the role of the lieutenant governor. Although the lieutenant governor is an officer of the executive branch, he or she still presides over the senate in 30 states. Several states recently curtailed the lieutenant governor's power. Eleven states ratified constitutional amendments rescinding the lieutenant governor's authority as presiding officer of the senate.

In most states the lieutenant governor, like the vice president of the United States, presides over the senate, receives assignments from the governor, and waits in the wings for a shot at being governor. However, in some states the lieutenant governor exercises substantial power. In Texas, the lieutenant governor is the major force in the legislature, controlling committee assignments and chairs, assigning bills to committee, and serving as the key figures in budget negotiations. This power is not given to the lieutenant governor by the Texas constitution, but it has evolved because Texas does not have a viable two-party system—there is no competition from minority leaders.

Shyness and modesty are not qualities that propel one to leadership in a state legislature. Members must campaign aggressively to win support from a majority of their party members or chambers. In states with viable parties, leaders are chosen by party caucuses after the general election and before the start of the legislative session. When the legislature meets, the candidate of the majority party is chosen on a straight-line party vote to be speaker of the house or president of the senate. The candidate of the minority party then becomes the minority leader. In states without active parties, the two leaders must win support from majority coalitions.

Leaders' primary responsibility is to move bills through the legislative process. To do this effectively they must manage the committee system by influencing the number and types of committees, determining the number of majority and minority members, and referring bills for deliberation. Most important, leaders control the appointment of the chairs and members of standing committees. Friends and allies are placed on strategic committees, while those who have been less than loyal are banished to less powerful domains (Box 9-3).

It is the responsibility of the leaders of the majority party to move major bills and resolve conflicts that might endanger the passage of key legislation. This is not an easy task. The minority party and its leaders may find it useful to oppose the leaders in the hopes of creating issues that will help the minority party in the next election. Problems with crucial legislation such as the budget and education bills are not easily resolved, especially if funds are short. Effective leaders attempt to resolve conflicts before they arise; often it is necessary for them to meet with opposition leaders and members behind the scenes to work out important stumbling blocks.

Legislative Committees   Imagine that you have been elected to the state legislature. Chances are, you will have knowledge and experience in a few areas. If you are from a rural area, you may be an expert on agricultural policy; if you are a teacher, you are likely to be familiar with educational issues. You will have neither the time nor the knowledge to study in depth the vast array of policy questions that state legislatures consider.

Box 9-3 **The Saga of Willie Brown**

Willie Brown has been speaker of the California Assembly longer than anyone else — almost eight years. Brown, a Democrat and black, was elected speaker by forging a coalition of his supporters and house Republicans. His election came after years of struggle and persistence.

In 1974 Brown, then chairman of the powerful Ways and Means Committee, competed against Leo McCarthy for the leadership position. McCarthy won a majority in the Democratic caucus, and Brown then asked his supporters to back McCarthy in a unanimous vote. Nevertheless, McCarthy stripped Brown of his chairmanship of Ways and Means. After the 1974 elections Brown renewed his challenge. Although the majority of Democrats stood behind McCarthy, Republicans cast a solid vote for Brown. McCarthy, however, won reelection.

Two years later, in 1976, Brown tried once again to unseat McCarthy with Republican support and again failed. McCarthy vented the full power of the speaker on Brown, removing him from all important committee assignments and relegating him to a relatively minor role. But in 1980, by virtue of his political skills and status as a black leader, Brown was again playing a major role in California politics. Shortly thereafter he was elected speaker, and he has held the post ever since.

However, this intriguing story is not over. Although Brown was initially elected speaker with the support of house Republicans, he eventually solidified support within his own caucus. Recent observers say, however, that Brown is once again having problems controlling the various factions of the Democratic party. To maintain his power, it looks as if Brown may once again have to turn to his old allies: the Republicans.

State legislative committees allow specialization, making it possible to give every subject some degree of expert treatment. As our society grows more technological and complex, such specialized treatment becomes more necessary.

Committees are critical to legislative decision making because they provide the mechanism for screening legislation. Legislators review bills assigned to their committees and decide whether those bills should be killed, revised, or voted out with a favorable recommendation. Bills which are never placed on the agenda are simply put aside, or "pigeonholed." In most states, bills that are given a favorable recommendation by the committee are very likely to be passed on the floor.

To help them make decisions, committee members seek and receive information from a variety of sources, including the staff of the committee (if there is one), interest groups, lobbyists, and administrative agencies. If the bill is important enough, the committee will hold public hearings and listen to testimony from interested parties. Although lobbyists and bureaucrats are likely to be the ones who testify, concerned citizens may ask or be asked to give information and opinions. For example, when state legislatures consider increases in tuition fees, college students often testify.

Committee systems vary in power and organization. In some states committees are passive about screening legislation, allowing almost all bills to reach the floor for consideration. In others they are very restrictive. In general, committees are more important in state houses than they are in state senates because the house is larger and more impersonal; representatives are more specialized and have less contact with their colleagues.[24] States vary in the number of committees, but the range for houses and senates is 10 to 20.

Following the suggestion of reformers, the overall number of legislative committees has been reduced in the last few years. Some states formally limit the number of committees to which members can be assigned so that legislators can concentrate on fewer issues and become more specialized. Nevertheless, even a few assignments can sometimes be difficult. Legislators often devote more time to committees they perceive to be more important to their interests.

Multiple committee assignments serve an important function in addition to allowing specialization; they allow the legislative leadership to exercise power. In almost all states, leaders appoint both members and chairs. Though they often try to appoint members to the committees for which they are best qualified, the number one criterion for committee assignments is political support. Leaders occupy positions on the most powerful committees, such as budget and appropriations, and appoint their friends and supporters to these choice assignments as well. The more committees that are available, the more they can be used for reward or punishment.

Although the power that state legislative leaders exercise over members may seem arbitrary and undemocratic, it does help state legislatures to be more efficient. More important, it allows the public to assign responsibility to the legislature. Legislative leaders and the parties or factions they represent are held accountable for the decisions made by the state legislature.

Greater accountability in state legislatures becomes apparent when we compare the committee system in state legislatures with that in Congress. Congressional committee chairs get their jobs by virtue of seniority, not by being in favor with the leadership. Although members are appointed to congressional committees by the leadership, once appointed, they generally continue to serve as long as they wish. The independence of congressional committees from the leadership makes Congress a kind of "headless horse." Although the public may be disillusioned about the performance of Congress in general, it is rarely possible to assign blame to congressional leaders or parties, because they have little control over the actions of committees and subcommittees.

The Role of Parties   Although Chapter 8 provided a thorough description of the role of parties in the states, the specific role of parties in state legislatures deserves attention. We have already seen that most state legislatures are organized and managed along party lines and that most legislative leaders are also party leaders, but the strength of parties and their degree of competitiveness vary from state to state. In a majority of states one party or the other tends to dominate. The most consistent case of one-party dominance has been the Democratic control of Southern legislatures. Republicans have at least 60 percent of the seats in the North Dakota, Utah, and Wyoming legislatures and at least 55 percent in Colorado, Idaho, Indiana, Kansas, New Hampshire, South Dakota, and Vermont.[25] A dominant party often becomes highly factionalized, however, and may split into ideological, regional, or urban-rural wings. Some states, such as California, Pennsylvania, Iowa, and New York, have strong party competition.

In the last few years parties have become more important in the legislative process. Evidence for this is provided by party caucuses for both majority and minority parties that exist in most state legislatures. In addition to selecting leaders, caucuses may perform other functions in varying degrees. One of these functions is *positioning*, or taking official positions on important issues raised before the legislature. Positioning can vary in frequency and in the firmness of the stands taken. For example, in about one-fourth of the states, binding votes may be taken in party caucuses requiring party members to vote as a bloc on the house or senate floor.[26] Attempts to bind occur only in the most partisan states, however, and in most cases members of the party caucus try to build a consensus on an issue. Another function of the party caucus is providing members with information about bills and legislative strategy. Members exchange views with one another, leaders get feedback from the rank and file, and the rank and file get opinions and cues from the leaders. Strategies and tactics for passing or killing legislation are planned so that the caucus's position is advanced.[27]

How a Bill Becomes Law

The lawmaking function in state legislatures is a complicated process governed by a series of complex and detailed rules and procedures. Although some of the details vary from state to state, the lawmaking process can be summarized in general. In many states, the process resembles that of Pennsylvania, as presented in Figure 9.2. One thing becomes clear as we examine the process of passing a bill into law: It is much easier to kill a bill than to get it passed. The legislative process in the states gives an advantage to determined majorities and minorities that feel strongly that a bill should *not* be passed. Numerous obstacles create a hazardous course for the small percentage of bills that are eventually signed into law by the governor.

Introducing Legislation   There are many different sources of influence on legislators: interest groups, executive agencies, the governor, and, as we have pointed out often in this text, the determined individual. Hence, the ideas for initiating legislation as well as the drafting of the bills themselves may come from sources other than a legislator. However, legislators have the sole power to introduce and sponsor legislation.

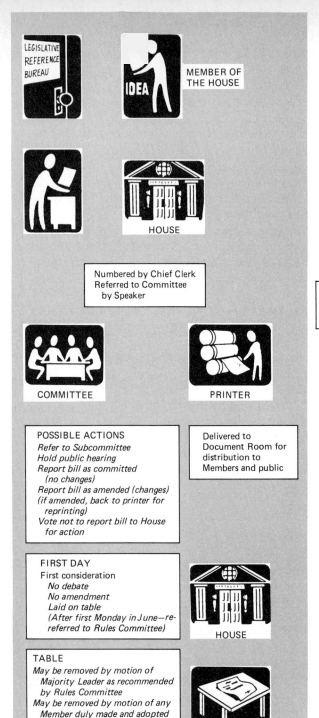

LEGISLATIVE REFERENCE BUREAU

MEMBER OF THE HOUSE

IDEA

HOUSE

Numbered by Chief Clerk
Referred to Committee
by Speaker

COMMITTEE

PRINTER

POSSIBLE ACTIONS
Refer to Subcommittee
Hold public hearing
Report bill as committed
(no changes)
Report bill as amended (changes)
(if amended, back to printer for
reprinting)
Vote not to report bill to House
for action

Delivered to
Document Room for
distribution to
Members and public

FIRST DAY
First consideration
No debate
No amendment
Laid on table
(After first Monday in June—re-
referred to Rules Committee)

HOUSE

TABLE
May be removed by motion of
Majority Leader as recommended
by Rules Committee
May be removed by motion of any
Member duly made and adopted
Automatically removed after 15
Legislative Days

SECOND DAY
Second consideration
Must be called up for
consideration
Debate permitted
Amendment permitted (if
amended, back to printer)
Vote permitted

HOUSE

THIRD DAY
Third consideration and final
passage
Amendment permitted on third
consideration
Debate permitted on final passage
Bill need not be printed with
last amendments for final
passage
102 votes needed for final
passage

HOUSE

Secretary of the Senate
receives bill
Referred to Committee
by President

SENATE

COMMITTEE

Committee action in Senate
is similer to that of
the House

FIRST DAY
First consideration
No debate
No amendment
No vote

SECOND DAY
Second consideration
Debate permitted
Amendment permitted (if
amended, back to printer)
Vote permitted

THIRD DAY
Third consideration and final
passage
No amendment on third
consideration except by
unanimous consent (if
amended, back to printer)
No amendment on final
passage
Debate permitted or final
passage
Bill must be in printed form
and on desks of Senators
26 votes required for final
passage

Figure 9.2 How a bill becomes law. (*Source:* General Assembly of the Commonwealth of Pennsylvania, *The Biography of a Bill* [Harrisburg, PA: Chief Clerk of the House].)

HOUSE

TRANSMITTED BACK TO HOUSE
IF AMENDED—SEE DESCRIPTION OF ACTION ON REVERSE SIDE

IF NOT AMENDED
Signed by Chief Clerk
Signed by Speaker

SENATE

TRANSMITTED BACK TO SENATE

Signed by President

STATE DEPARTMENT

TRANSMITTED TO STATE DEPARTMENT FOR RECORDING

GOVERNOR

TRANSMITTED TO GOVERNOR BY STATE DEPARTMENT

ATTORNEY GENERAL

GOVERNOR REFERS BILL TO ATTORNEY GENERAL FOR OPINION AS TO LEGALITY AND CONSTITUTIONALITY

GOVERNOR

GOVERNOR APPROVES

GOVERNOR PERMITS BILL TO BECOME LAW WITHOUT HIS SIGNATURE
If not signed within ten days when Legislature is in session—bill becomes law
If not signed within 30 days when Legislature has adjourned since die—bill becomes law

GOVERNOR VETOES

TRANSMITTED BY GOVERNOR'S OFFICE TO STATE DEPARTMENT FOR CERTIFICATION, ASSIGNMENT OF ACT NUMBER AND FILING

If vetoed—bill is given a veto number by the State Department and returned to House of origin for possible further action.
If vetoed—bill may be re-passed by a two-thirds vote of the Members elected to both Houses

STATE DEPARTMENT

COPY TRANSMITTED TO LEGISLATIVE REFERENCE BUREAU FOR PREPARATION FOR PRINTING OF LAW

PRINTER

The first step is for the legislator to submit ideas in writing to the bill-drafting agency of the legislature, which drafts and types it in the proper legal form. The legislator files this typed version of the bill with the clerk, who reads aloud the title of the bill in what is called the *first reading*. The bill is then assigned to a standing committee by the presiding officer of the chamber where it has been introduced (bills can be introduced in either the house or the senate in sequence or at the same time). For example, bills relating to law enforcement are referred to the criminal justice committee, while those which deal with taxes are referred to the committee on ways and means. Assigning bills to standing committees is a source of power for the presiding officers, who may assign a bill to a sympathetic or a hostile committee depending on their view of the bill.

Committee Action   To a large extent, the fate of a bill assigned to committee is determined by the chairperson of the committee because the chair decides on the committee's agenda. If the chairperson chooses, he or she may put the bill at the bottom of the committee's agenda; chances are that the committee will never get to the bill, which will die from inaction. Bills that are considered by the committee are usually given public hearings at which lobbyists and other interested individuals may testify. After deliberating, the committee may take one of several possible actions: (1) report the bill favorably in its original form, (2) report the bill favorably with amendments, (3) report favorably a "substitution," or a revised form of the original bill, or (4) report the bill unfavorably. An unfavorable report will in most cases effectively kill the bill. Committees, in the view of most legislators, act as screening mechanisms, and legislators are reluctant to challenge the actions of most committees. Because legislatures are becoming more complex and specialized, committee decisions are often *the* decision in a legislative body. Still, if there is enough sentiment in favor of a bill, an extraordinary majority vote of the members (usually two-thirds) will force the bill out of committee and onto the floor for a vote.

In many cases legislative committees are broken down into subcommittees that represent specific areas within a committee's jurisdiction. Thus bills assigned to a committee are then assigned to a subcommittee; the subcommittee may take any of the actions that we described for committees. At this point, you may have a clearer appreciation of the obstacles faced by a bill on its tortuous journey through the legislative process.

Rules Committee   Most bills reported favorably by a standing committee go to the floor of the legislative house. Bills that involve an expenditure of money, however, may be referred to another committee, such as appropriations, finance, or ways and means, that assesses the cost of the legislation. If the bill is being considered by the house of representatives, it will most likely go to a **rules committee** (or calendars committee as it is referred to in some states), where it is scheduled for house debate. The rules committee has the power to kill a bill by scheduling it so far down the agenda that there is no time for consideration before the end of the session. In some instances, standing committees fearful of the wrath of interest groups report a bill out of committee, knowing full well that the bill will die in the calendars committee.

Consideration on the Floor   Once on the floor, the bill is given a second reading, which in some states signals the beginning of debate on the merits of the bill. After the bill is debated and perhaps amended, a third reading is taken, followed by a final vote. In a bicameral legislature, the bill must go through a similar process in each chamber. If the versions of the bill passed by the two houses are different, one house must concur with the amendments of the other. If this concurrence does not take place, the bill goes to a **conference committee**, where representatives from each house try to iron out the differences. At this point it is still possible for the bill to be killed if the members of the conference committee cannot work out a compromise that ultimately can be approved by both houses.

Action by the Governor   Once both houses approve the bill in the same form, it is ready to go to the governor. If the governor approves, he or she signs the bill and it becomes law. In most states the governor may allow the bill to become law by not signing it within a certain number of days (usually seven to ten). If the governor disapproves, he or she will veto the bill (except in North Carolina, the only state which does not give the governor veto power). This action effectively kills the bill unless two-thirds of the members of each house vote to override the veto. In many states the governor is given special veto power over money bills. This power is called the **line-item veto**; it means that the governor can veto individual items in the appropriations bill rather than rejecting the whole bill.

Passing a Budget Bill   In the state legislative process, the budget is the most important "law" that is passed by the legislature. Many of the details of state budgets are described in Chapter 15; here we will concentrate briefly on a description of budget making in the legislative process. In putting together the budget, legislators consider estimates of available revenue to decide whether they will have to make the most painful of political decisions: raising taxes to meet spending demands. They consider requests from state agencies as well as requests from various sources for funding of new programs.

At a very early stage in the consideration of budget proposals, the revenue and spending portions are separated and sent to entirely different standing committees in each house for careful scrutiny. The spending portion becomes one or more appropriations bills and is sent to the appropriations or budget committee. Some appropriations committees are rather large and include the chairs of all the major subject matter standing committees. This committee and its subcommittees then hold hearings on the proposed appropriations bill or bills. The revenue, or tax, portion is sent to tax committees —usually called ways and means—in each house.

It is not uncommon for individual legislators to submit additional spending bills which also make their way to the appropriations committee. These bills may fulfill campaign promises or may be submitted at the request of individual constituents, campaign contributors, local governments within a legislator's district, or the officials of executive or judicial agencies whose programs were left out of the budget submitted to the legislature.

LOCAL LEGISLATURES

Chances are, an individual's first and most direct political experience in our intergovernmental system is his or her attempt to influence a local governing board. Not only are local legislatures much more accessible than are their state and national counterparts, they make decisions that have a direct and immediate impact on local citizens. County and city board members adopt budgets that specify the services people receive and the amount of taxes they pay. They see or fail to see that streets are maintained, health care is provided, police and fire protection is sufficient, and garbage is collected. They regulate the use of land, the operation of schools, and the disposal of wastes.

There are important differences between state and local legislatures. Local legislatures are usually unicameral rather than bicameral bodies. The concept of separation of power between legislative authority and executive authority is not as distinct in local legislatures. Some local legislatures have executive responsibilities—the extent of those responsibilities varying from one local government to another. In many local legislatures the chief executive presides: The mayor presides over the city council; the county judge presides over the county commission. With the exception of the lieutenant governor, who serves as the presiding officer of some state senates, executive and legislative authority are more well defined at the state level.

As we learned in Chapter 5, the lawmaking authority of local legislatures is limited by state constitutions and state laws. Hence, local governments are entirely creatures of the state. State governments delegate powers to local governments for reasons of convenience and because it is politically popular with the citizens of the state to do so. Local governing boards, unlike state legislatures, act within the authority of state constitutions and state legislatures.

In this chapter we focus largely on the legislatures of the two general-purpose governments: the county and the city. However, since special districts and school districts possess taxing and spending authority, the boards that govern them merit some attention as well.

County Boards

Counties are set up to serve as the state's administrative arm. Until the Depression, counties concerned themselves primarily with carrying out state programs such as tax assessment and collection, law enforcement, judicial administration, road maintenance, administration of state and county elections, and record keeping. For the last decade or more, however, counties have been the fastest-growing general-purpose governments in terms of budgets, employees, and constituents and have expanded their activities to provide more local services. Counties run parks and recreation centers, libraries, airports, utility systems, economic development programs, hospitals, and a host of services that old-time county commissioners would never have imagined. The larger and more densely populated a county is, the more extensive its local services are likely to be. Metropolitan counties in particular are being forced to take the lead in dealing with the problems of rapid growth.

Counties vary not only in size but in how the county government is organized. Although an elected county board or board of supervisors is the official governing body of the county, county board members and commissioners are elected at large by all the voters in the county or by district by voters in different districts within the county. Many large metropolitan counties, such as Palm Beach County, Florida, where the population has tripled since 1960 to 800,000, have gone to electing board members at large, with an appointed county administrator. This system is meant to professionalize the operations of county boards that find themselves tangled in metropolitan growth. Of the nation's 3106 counties, 798 are run by an appointed manager while 391 now have an elected executive.[28]

The variety of size and organization in counties is highlighted by the variety of titles given to county boards and their members. Some county boards are called courts and have names such as court of county commissioners or commissioner's court. In Texas, county boards are called county commissioner's courts and are presided over by the county judge. In California, county boards are referred to as boards of supervisors. County board members are jurors in Louisiana, freeholders in New Jersey, and county legislators in New York. One New York county legislator remarked, "If I tell somebody from New York I'm a commissioner, they think I'm the dog catcher."[29] Although county boards are legislative bodies, their power to legislate is severely restricted by the state. Instead of making new laws or ordinances, they are generally concerned with carrying out state laws and setting the county budget. Indeed, many county boards are given no ordinance-making power by their state governments.

The power of county boards is also limited by the many separately elected officials who run their own departments without supervision from any authority higher than the voting public. These officials, like the board, are local administrators for the state. For example, the sheriff enforces state law and operates a county jail, and the county clerk registers voters, administers state and local elections, and keeps important records such as births, deaths, marriages, and divorces. With popular support and state authority, these officials may feel free to make their own decisions about personnel and procedures. However, the power of county boards over county departments has expanded as counties have come to have more and more local functions. New departments whose functions are primarily local in nature owe their existence to the county, not the state.

County boards also have some power over elected officials through the budget. The board gives these officials their money and may also have the power to revoke, amend, or shift appropriations once they are made. Though they rarely exercise it, most boards have the authority to approve every expenditure made by county officials.[30] However, county boards have to be very careful about punishing officials through the budget since these officials may quickly and convincingly blame the board if services deteriorate. A county sheriff who is denied funds by the board will make sure the voters know who is to blame for an increase in the crime rate.

City Councils

As you learned in Chapter 5, municipal governments are somewhat different from county governments. County governments are created by the state to localize the administration of state policy; municipalities result from actions by local constituents who want to see services provided to the local community. Municipalities come in all sizes in all states. All municipalities are governed by local legislatures called councils or commissions.

A city council in action. (Courtesy of Sidney, Monkmeyer.)

City councils are usually small, with five to nine members. In general, the larger the city, the larger the council, although large cities such as Dallas and Boston have councils with only seven to nine members. Council members usually serve part time, meeting once a week or less. The salaries paid to these local legislators reinforce their amateur status in that most receive either nominal fees or nothing at all. "Professional" city councils exist in some larger cities. Their members meet frequently and are paid enough to make service to the city a job. Council members in Austin, Texas, for example, meet several times a week in televised sessions and receive a salary of $35,000 a year.

Election of City Council Members   City council members are chosen by voters in separate **district elections** or by the voters of the whole city in at-large elections. Each system has advantages and disadvantages. Most studies have concluded that district elections give more representation to ethnic minorities and the poor, who often live in well-defined areas of the city. At-large elections diffuse the strength of those groups and make it harder for them to elect a representative. One study examined several factors that might affect black representation on city councils and found that the switch from an at-large to a district or "ward" election system is the most important factor in increasing black representation.[31] Because of this, federal courts have tended to look unfavorably at recent attempts by cities to switch from district to at-large systems; in some cases the courts have forced cities to modify at-large elections to guarantee minority representation on the council.

District elections allow members of the city council to be in closer contact with constituents and to attend to the specific needs of the district. Supporters of district elections also argue that at-large elections make it easier for wealthy people to dominate city government since the wealthy and well educated have the time to become involved in politics and the money it takes to win a citywide campaign.

Supporters of at-large elections argue that council members in at-large systems are forced to think about the community as a whole, not simply the selfish needs of their own districts. This emphasis on the interests of the whole city has led many reformers to urge the adoption of at-large elections. Just as at-large elections encourage participation by the wealthy and well educated, they also result in better-qualified council members. At-large systems, say their proponents, result in more informed decision makers who evaluate what is best for the entire community.

You'll recall from Chapter 8 that at-large elections resulted from actions by progressive reformers in the early twentieth century who wanted to dilute the power of party bosses over certain districts or wards within the city. Often the voters in these wards were largely poor immigrants who were organized and mobilized by party machines. Thus many historians and political observers point out that at-large election systems were initiated to give the middle and upper-middle classes more power in city politics.

Although council members are elected through the at-large system in approximately 60 percent of municipalities, this pattern is less common as the size of a city increases. Table 9.4 shows the results of a sample of almost 4000 cities. As you can see, the proportion of municipalities using at-large systems declines as the population increases.

In addition to at-large systems, reformers called for nonpartisan elections. Nonpartisan elections — those in which the party affiliation of candidates does not appear on the ballot — grew dramatically during the 1920s and 1930s. Over 70 percent of cities use them, and they are found in every state except Hawaii. As noted in Chapter 8, nonpartisan elections were supposed to be a solution to the corruption of urban party machines. Party bosses who controlled powerful party organizations dominated city government in large cities such as Chicago. More and more middle-class voters developed a distaste for those machines and demanded changes. Reformers argued that nonpartisan elections not only would reduce corruption, they also would focus the voter's attention on issues and candidates rather than party affiliation.

Nonpartisan elections have some effects that the reformers might not have anticipated. Incumbency has become more important. With party eliminated as a cue for how to vote, people rely more on the familiarity of the candidate. This gives an advantage to incumbents, who have greater name recognition. Like at-large elections, nonpartisan elections are also class-biased in favor of the middle and upper classes; this is the case because nonpartisan elections discourage participation by lower-class voters. References to party give poorer, less-educated people more understanding of and interest in elections.

Parties also help support the campaigns of those without money or connections. The Democratic party in particular gives "organizational encouragement" to poor and uneducated voters. It seems clear that nonpartisanship works to the advantage of the Republican party, since Republicans

Table 9.4   METHOD OF ELECTION IN MUNICIPALITIES

Population of city	Election method (%)		
	At large	District	Mixed
500,000 and over	15	23	62
250,000–499,999	35	17	48
100,000–249,999	38	17	45
50,000–99,999	53	11	36
25,000–49,999	56	11	33
10,000–24,999	58	12	30
5,000–9,999	63	12	25
2,500–4,999	67	15	19

Source: International City Management Association, *The Municipal Yearbook*, vol. 55 (Washington, DC: International City Management Association, 1988), 14.

typically have higher voter turnout and rely less on organized efforts to stimulate participation.

Forms of City Government   Legislative bodies in city government are usually found in one of three major forms. The major differences among these forms is the location and responsibility of executive power. Each form places executive power in a different place and gives the legislative body different amounts of executive authority. The three forms are the council-manager, mayor-council, and commission types of government.

The **council-manager** form is the fastest growing type of city government, and like at-large and nonpartisan elections, it was a product of the reform movement that began in the 1920s and 1930s. In theory, the council makes decisions and a city manager is hired to see that those general policies are carried out. The city manager is a professional, that is, someone who has technical expertise about budgets and management and may even have a graduate degree in public administration. The manager is hired and can be fired at any time by the council.

Under this system, mayors are generally weak. They preside over the council but rarely have the power to hire or fire anybody, even the manager. The manager works for the council, not the mayor. To be effective, the manager must be able to detect and serve the council consensus in administering city policies. Thus the council-manager form of government is very vulnerable to conflict. If the council's decision is not clear or changes, the manager may find that he or she has misread the council. This places the manager's job in jeopardy.

The council-manager form is most popular in midsized cities with populations ranging from 25,000 to 250,000. Cities with less than 25,000 people usually find it too expensive to hire a manager. Cities with more than 250,000 people have a number of conflicting interests interested in city administration, making a consensus harder to achieve. City managers work best in cities where there is a broad consensus in the way local government should work. As cities become larger, a broad consensus is harder to achieve because the number of interest groups increases. Larger cities also tend to have more heterogeneous populations which put conflicting demands on the city government and administration, especially if the council is elected from districts rather than at large. By contrast, in midsized cities, especially those where the ethnic and political composition of the population is relatively homogeneous, such as many suburban cities, the city manager form of government is much more popular.[32]

The advantage of the council-manager form of government is that an "expert," the manager, helps the city government run efficiently and professionally. However, there are disadvantages. Although in theory the manager implements council policy, in reality the manager often originates and sets policy behind the scenes. This occurs because council members often do not have the technical expertise of the manager so that the city bureaucrats may feel the need to go along with the manager's recommendations on policy and budget. This is not what proponents of representative democracy have in mind.

The mayor-council system (Figure 9.3) maintains the traditional separation of powers between the legislative and executive branches of government, but these governments differ substantially in the amount of formal power given to the mayor. Therefore, these governments can be classified as strong mayor or weak mayor systems.

A **strong mayor-council** system usually calls for a full-time mayor and a part time council (Figure 9.4). The council may be full time in large cities. The mayor is elected at large and has a very strong executive role. He or she assumes the responsibilities of a manager, appointing department heads, administering city programs, hiring and firing city employees, preparing the budget, and evaluating the performance of city agencies. A strong mayor may also have extraordinary veto power that can be overridden only by a two-thirds or three-fourths majority of the council. The mayor's power and independence from the council are underscored by a large staff of administrative assistants, auditors, legal counsels, city planners, or other professionals. Strong mayors are generally found in large cities. Large cities need a strong mayor who combines administrative and political power to hold a city with many powerful and heterogeneous interests together. A city manager has trouble dealing with powerful interests because he or she is an appointee, not a political figure.

A **weak mayor-council** system places legal restrictions on the mayor (Figure 9.5). Although the mayor may have influence, it is not through his or her formal powers. The council, not the mayor, has control over the budget. The mayor's appointment power is limited; the council appoints key department heads directly. In addition, the mayor may be required to submit all appointments to the council for approval. Weak mayors are usually found in small towns where the business of government is limited. Small towns may have little need for city managers or strong mayors.

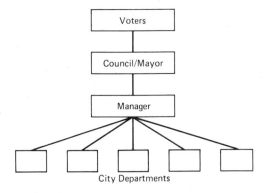

Figure 9.3 The council-manager form of city government. The manager appoints department heads and prepares budgets.

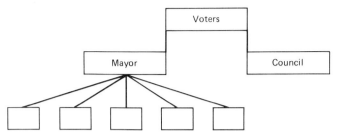

Figure 9.4 The strong-mayor form of city government. City departments are supervised by the mayor.

The **commission form** is the least common major form of city government; it is found in approximately 100 cities around the nation. The distinguishing characteristic of the commission form is its union of executive and legislative powers. It consists of elected council members or commissioners who are also the heads of key executive departments. The typical commission city has five commissioners who head five departments. One commissioner, for example, may head the public safety department — fire and police services. Another may direct parks and recreation. Commission members wear two hats. As members of the legislative body, they set policy for the municipality. At the same time they act as department heads, hiring and firing personnel and preparing budgets.

The advantage of this decentralized system is that the persons in charge of making policy — the commissioners — are also in charge of carrying it out. Commissioners don't have to worry that bureaucrats are violating the intent of the policy or that top-level administrators are getting too much power. However, there are problems. Elected commissioners are full-time politicians and do not always have the competence or expertise to be department heads. Municipal departments handle complex and technical problems and often require administrators with engineering, accounting, planning,

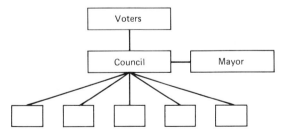

Figure 9.5 The weak-mayor form of city government. The city departments are supervised by council (mayor is a member).

budgeting, and management skills. Since the mayor has no real power, there is no executive to coordinate the various departments. There is also a tendency for commissioners to adopt a live-and-let-live attitude toward the other departments so that there is little accountability and no system of checks and balances.

Another major disadvantage is the difficulty of getting commissioners who also serve as heads of major departments to come up with a city budget. Citywide decisions, especially those which involve the allocation of scarce resources, often require bargaining among outspoken strong supporters of major departments; in some instances, commissions have been unable to develop a budget after weeks of wrangling.

Special District Boards   Although special districts are called by a variety of names — district, authority, corporation — all are governed by boards. With the exception of school districts, most special district boards are appointed by city or county officials. Since special districts usually are established to provide services that require high level of expertise, many feel that "professionals" should be appointed to their governing boards. Once appointed, boards vary in the degree to which they are independent of their parent governments. Some city or county boards, for example, may require special districts to submit their budgets for approval. If a special district board's members are elected, the board is likely to be an autonomous unit of government, raising and spending its own funds without interference from general-purpose governments.

The typical board is made up of three to five members serving three- or four-year terms. Most of the board members serve part time, meeting only once or twice a month. Compensation for service is usually minimal or nonexistent. Board members usually serve more than one term, being reappointed or reelected without opposition. Elected members often step down before the election so that a successor can be appointed to fill the vacancy. The successor then has the advantage of running for election as an incumbent.

Recruitment of board members illustrates the lack of visibility that is characteristic of special districts (Chapter 4). The public is often unaware of these boards and uninformed about their functions even though special district boards possess significant powers, including the most significant of all: taxing authority.

The most numerous of the special district boards are school boards. The vast majority of school districts are "independent," that is, administratively and fiscally independent of any general-purpose government. Independent school districts are organized much as council-manger municipal governments are. Voters elect the members of the board on an at-large basis, and elections are usually nonpartisan. The school superintendent is hired by the school board as a professional administrator of the schools and, like a city manager, can be fired by the board at any time.

Unlike most special district boards, school boards are highly visible.

Some say that "school boards are the essence of grass-roots democracy."[33] They represent the strongly held belief in local control of the schools. Popularly elected boards provide comfort for citizens who fear that "outside experts" — school superintendents and other administrators — may overstep their bounds. Although the at-large system of electing school boards leads to boards dominated by elites or "prominent" citizens, broad support exists for school boards in their present form.

OBTAINING ACCESS

Imagine that you are a student at a state university faced with the possibility of tuition increases that you or your parents cannot afford. The state legislature has not raised tuition fees for some time, and some legislators feel that an increase is due. What are some of the strategies you might use to influence the legislature's decision? How can you get the ear of certain key legislators to let them know the hardships this increase will create for you and thousands of other college students in your state? Remember that even though our example focuses on state legislatures, the strategies described here apply to local legislatures as well.

Strategies of Influence

Letters, Phone Calls, and Personal Visits   The first thing you will probably do is find out the name of your state representative and write him or her a letter. You should try to make the letter appear personal, that is, hand-written or typed on your own typewriter with your signature. Personal letters usually have more of an impact on an elected representative than do impersonal or form letters. You will want to get as many of your friends as possible to write because the larger the number of letters, the more influence they will have. In fact, a letter-writing campaign is what you are really trying to achieve.

If you really hate writing letters or want to do something in addition to writing a letter, you can call your legislator. Chances are, you will not speak to the representative but to a legislative aide who will promise faithfully to relay your feelings to the representative. Again, get as many friends as possible to call. It is also a good idea to call more than once if you have the time and money. If you are persistent, you will probably get to speak directly to the representative (Box 9-4).

The next step is to write and/or call key legislative leaders and committee chairs, such as those who chair the house and senate committees on higher education. These people are probably far more crucial in determining tuition increases than is your own legislator (unless you are lucky and he or she is one of them). You should be aware that these leaders are less likely to be influenced by your calls and letters since you do not determine their electoral fate.

Box 9-4 # Tips on Writing or Visiting Your Elected Representative

If you are considering writing or visiting your state representative, there are important things to remember to make your contact more effective, that is, more persuasive. The most ineffective thing one can do to influence a legislator is to send him or her a random form letter or petition.

Suggestions for an effective personal letter include the following:

- State that you are a constituent, voter, or supporter (if true).
- Cite specific bill numbers so that staff members can find and trace them.
- Give personal examples and creative arguments that may shed new light on an old subject, but keep it short and concise.
- Ask for a response. This ensures that the letter will be read and filed.
- Consider sending a telegram. Carefully timed and targeted telegrams are real attention getters. Few people can help but yield to the pressure of 50 to 75 telegrams from local constituents, especially when they all come the morning of the vote.

A personal visit with your representative is, of course, much better than a letter. It demonstrates dedication and the sort of commitment that is irresistible to most elected officials. If you plan to visit the capitol or city hall, here are some tips to make your visit effective and positive.

- Dress as if you were going to court or a job interview. Your issue is more important to you than your freedom of attire.
- Study the voting record of those you will visit. Be informed.
- Be polite and friendly with administrative aides. They read your letters and are informed on the issues and their employer's position. If they like what you have to say, they can ensure an audience with the elected official.
- Stick to one issue.
- Do not debate, argue, intimidate, or threaten. Do not get offended by ignorance about your issue.
- Beyond a doubt, the most influential way to visit a representative is to be accompanied by a major contributor, known campaign volunteer, or personal friend of the legislator. These people are going to be persuasive because they have already established points of credibility and agreement.

Source: Debra Danburg, "How to Lobby," *Breakthrough*, (June 1979), 19.

If you have the determination, time, and energy, you may want to try to see your representative in person. This may not be that hard to do. In most states, representatives spend a lot of time in their districts and attend all sorts of public events; their presence is usually publicized. Find out where they will be and show up yourself. Since public officials attend these events to get and keep votes, most will not mind giving you a minute or two to express your feelings. It is usually more difficult to see a legislator in his or her office at the capitol (if he or she has one), although it is certainly possible. Be sure the secretary or legislative staffer knows that you are a constituent; this important fact will encourage a legislator to work you into his or her busy schedule.

Campaign Work   If you are really concerned about the possibility of higher tuition fees, you will want to get into the political ball game a little sooner and a little more seriously. Individuals and groups experienced at politics know that the most important influence is established *before* a legislator is elected to office.

There are two ways to gain access to legislators during the election process. The first is through campaign contributions. Legislators, like most of us, are inclined to help the people who help them. With this in mind, you may want to make a contribution to your representative's campaign. To be really effective, however, you will have to organize other students concerned about tuition increases and form a political action committee (PAC). You will give your PAC a catchy name, one that forms a clever acronym, such as STUPAC: Student's Political Action Committee. You and your friends who form this PAC will solicit voluntary contributions from other students. You will have to decide as a committee how the funds you have collected will be spent. A wise way to distribute the funds would be to give a percentage to your representative and then distribute the rest to key legislative figures.

The second way to be effective in the election process is to volunteer to work in a legislative campaign. This may involve stuffing envelopes with campaign literature, making phone calls, registering other students to vote, or just hanging around the campaign headquarters. As you work in the campaign, you will get to know the people who are close to the candidate as well as the candidate. Obviously, this is going to help you gain access to your representative.

Note that campaign work involves an element of risk that your candidate may not get elected and that the opposing candidate will not feel obligated to support your cause. There are ways to minimize this risk. For example, PACs sometimes contribute to *both* candidates. However, it is important to remember that like a lot of other things, the greater the risk, the greater the return. A representative who knows that you helped him or her when help was needed the most is going to be more receptive than is one who first hears from you when he or she is deciding an important issue.

Public Testimony   A crucial time for deciding whether to increase tuition fees comes when the house and senate committees on higher education meet. Because members of these committees specialize in matters of higher education, their colleagues in the legislature are inclined to honor their recommendations. To help gather information and formulate recommendations, committees hold public hearings and invite interested individuals to testify. If you are lucky, the chairperson of the committee is opposed to any tuition increases and places the bill at the bottom of the committee's agenda (a place reserved for unwanted bills that never come up).

When and if the tuition increase bill does come up, you may be asked by the committee to testify. By this time you will have written, called, or talked in person to your legislator. You may have also made a name for yourself by organizing a PAC or working in an election campaign. You are seen by some as a knowledgeable and certainly an interested individual, one whose views deserve formal consideration. But keep in mind that the committee will also be hearing from those who feel a tuition increase is warranted.

Organizing a Group   You can see that individuals who are committed and energetic can gain access to legislative decision making, but it is also apparent that individuals who form an *organization* are more likely to be influential than are those who act alone. Organizations are able to contribute more money and time to a cause. They are usually able to hire professionals, that is, lobbyists, who are experienced at influencing legislators. Individual members of organizations can rely on each other for the motivation it takes to participate in the political process. Even if your involvement in politics is only temporary — to oppose higher tuition fees — you will be more effective if you persuade others to get involved with you.

Conclusion

Legislatures at all levels — federal, state, and local — have common functions. All make laws, approve taxing and spending policies, and oversee the actions of the bureaucracy. All are traditionally the most representative and democratic institutions in government.

Modern state legislatures have done a great deal to overcome their reputations as corrupt and ineffective bodies. Reapportionment means that urban problems are getting more attention, although population growth in conservative white suburbs has reduced the influence of urban interests. The professionalization of state legislatures, particularly those in large urban states, has increased their capacity to make competent decisions. Legislators have higher salaries and more staff members and are staying in session longer; many more are identifying themselves as professionals. Professionalization has also made it possible for legislatures to compete more effectively with executives to control increased federal aid.

There is an ongoing debate, however, over the effectiveness and desirability of legislative professionalism. Some feel that part-time "citizen" legislatures are closer to the people and less susceptible to pressure from organized interest groups. The gradual trend toward professionalization means that this debate may become sharper in the near future.

All state legislatures but one (Nebraska) are bicameral, and their size varies from state to state. Leadership in most state legislatures is based on party, and leaders enjoy a much more powerful role in state legislatures than do their counterparts in Congress. State legislative leaders control the assignment of committee chairs and memberships and often use this power to discipline unsupportive members. Although this power may seem arbitrary, it does give state legislatures more accountability in comparison to Congress.

Unlike state legislative bodies, local governing boards are unicameral and are authorized by a higher authority: the state. County boards exercise some legislative functions but are primarily administrative arms of the state. Most county boards function without centralized executive authority, although recently some large urban counties have appointed or elected county administrators. Variation in municipal boards depends on the extent to which they exercise executive powers. Although the emergence of a professional city manager is apparent in many midsized cities, strong mayors are more likely to govern large cities in which there are many powerful and competing interests.

The system of electing city council members has a dramatic impact on how a city is governed or, more specifically, on who has power in the city government. Reforms in the 1920s and 1930s called for nonpartisan, at-large elections to reduce the influence that powerful party machines had on districts or wards within the city. These reforms give advantages to incumbent politicians and are class-biased in favor of the middle and upper-middle classes. At-large elections diffuse the power of minorities and the poor, who tend to be concentrated in certain areas of the city. Nonpartisan elections eliminate the ability of parties—the Democratic party in particular—to mobilize poor and uneducated voters.

Individuals who are determined to influence the decisions of state and local governments use a variety of participatory strategies to influence the legislative process. These strategies include letters, phone calls, personal visits, campaign work, and testifying before legislative committees or local governing boards. This is fitting in light of the fact that legislatures were originally designed to be the most democratic political institutions in American politics.

Study Objectives

1. Describe functions that are unique to legislatures.
2. Describe the difference in the two classic models of representation and explain why neither is entirely accurate.
3. Identify at least three trends that are making state legislatures more professional.
4. Define "reapportionment." What have been the consequences of reapportionment of state legislatures?
5. Explain why one could argue that the leadership and committee

systems of most state legislatures make them more accountable than is the U.S. Congress.

6. The role of the city council varies according to the structure of city government. Distinguish the similarities and differences in the three major forms of city government.

7. Explain why most school boards resemble the council-manager form of city government.

8. Discuss effective strategies for gaining access to state and local legislatures.

Glossary

apportionment The allocation of legislative seats to geographic areas.

Baker v. *Carr, 1962* The landmark Supreme Court ruling that found that malapportioned districts may violate the equal protection clause of the Fourteenth Amendment. It also established the jurisdiction of federal courts over lawsuits challenging the apportionment of legislative districts.

casework The individual assistance legislators give to their constituents; the most frequent example is intervention with a government agency on the constituent's behalf.

commission form of city government The least common form; consists of elected council members who are also the heads of key executive departments.

conference committee A joint legislative committee where representatives from the house and senate try to iron out the differences in a bill.

council-manager form of city government The fastest growing form of city government. A professional city manager is hired to carry out the decisions of the city council.

Davis v. *Bandemer* A 1986 case in which the Supreme Court declared for the first time that partisan gerrymandering can be unconstitutional. However, the Court has not invalidated a redistricting plan on that basis.

delegate role of representation The model of representation in which elected representatives attempt to mirror the views of a majority of their constituents.

district election The system of electing representatives who represent districts within a city or county to the city council or county board.

gerrymandering The practice of drawing the lines of legislative districts so as to magnify the power of a particular group, usually the dominant political party.

impeach To bring formal charges against executive officials and judges. In state legislatures and Congress, this is done by the house of representatives.

line-item veto The power of a governor to veto individual items in the appropriations bill rather than reject the whole bill.

one person, one vote doctrine The principle established in a series of Supreme Court decisions that state legislative districts must be equal in population according to the most recent census.

oversight The legislature's function of reviewing the way laws and policies are implemented by the bureaucracy.

politico role of representation The model of representation that combines features of the trustee and delegate roles. Representatives attempt to mirror the views of their constituents when those views are strongly and clearly expressed but otherwise use their own best judgment.

reapportionment The boundaries of legislative districts (both state legislative districts and U.S. congressional districts) are drawn so that they are about equal in population.

rules committee The powerful committee, found in most legislative houses of representatives, that schedules bills for debate on the house floor.

strong mayor-council form of city government Found in many large cities; it consists of a strong full-time mayor elected at large and a part-time city council.

sunset laws Unless the legislature acts to renew an executive agency, that agency will cease to exist after a certain date.

trustee role of representation The model of representation in which representatives use their best judgment to make decisions about the issues at hand.

weak mayor-council form of city government Found in most small towns; it consists of a mayor whose formal powers are limited by a strong city council.

Endnotes

1. John Locke, *Second Treatise on Civil Government* (Cambridge: The University Press, 1960), 373.
2. Alexander Hamilton, James Madison, and John Jay, Paper Number Fifty-one, *The Federalist.* (Toronto: Bantam Books, 1982), 263.
3. Richard C. Elling, "The Utility of State Legislative Casework as a Means of Oversight," *Legislative Studies Quarterly* 3 (August 1979), 353–379.
4. Sarah McCally Morehouse, *State Politics, Parties, and Policy* (New York: Holt, Rinehart & Winston, 1981), 260.
5. Advisory Commission on Intergovernmental Relations, *The Question of State Government Capability* (Washington DC: ACIR, 1985), 116. See also Cynthia Slaughter, "Sunset and Occupational Regulation: A Case Study," *Public Administration Review* 46 (May-June 1986), 241–245, for an evaluation of the effectiveness of sunset laws in Texas.
6. Ralph Craft, "Successful Legislative Oversight: Lessons from State Legislatures," *Policy Studies Journal* 10 (Autumn 1981), 161–171.
7. John C. Wahlke, Heinz Eulau, William Buchanan, and Leroy C. Ferguson, *The Legislative System* (New York: Wiley, 1962), chaps. 12 and 13.
8. Chase Untermeyer, "The Lone Star Legislature," in Wendell M. Bedichek and Neal Tannahill, *Public Policy in Texas*, 2nd ed. (Glenview, IL: Scott, Foresman, 1986), 204.
9. William T. Pound, "The State Legislatures," in *The Book of the States*, (Lexington, KY: Council of State Governments, 1988), 78.
10. Alexander Heard, "Introduction—Old Problems, New Context," in American Assembly, *State Legislatures in American Politics*, ed. Alexander Heard (Englewood Cliffs, NJ: Prentice-Hall, 1966), 1–2.
11. Pound, 79–83.
12. John N. Lattimer, "The Changing Role of Legislative Staff in the American State Legislature," *State and Local Government Review* 17 (Fall 1985), 244–250.
13. *Baker v. Carr*, 309 U.S. 186 (1962).

14. *Reynolds* v. *Sims*, 377 U.S. 533 (1964), *WMCA, Inc.* v. *Lomenzo*, 377 U.S. 633 (1964), *Maryland Committee for Fair Representation* v. *Tawes*, 377 U.S. 656 (1964), *Donis* v. *Mann*, 377 U.S. 678 (1964), *Roman* v. *Sincock*, 377 U.S. 695 (1964), *Lucas* v. *Forty-fourth General Assembly of Colorado*, 377 U.S. 713 (1964).

15. H. George Frederickson and Yong Hyo Cho, "Legislative Apportionment and Fiscal Policy in the American States," *Western Political Quarterly* 27 (March 1974), 5–37.

16. Pound, vol. 26, 76–81.

17. Quoted in Andrea Paterson, "Is the Citizen Legislator Becoming Extinct?" in Thad L. Beyle, ed., *State Government: CQ's Guide to Current Issues and Activities, 1987–88* (Washington DC: Congressional Quarterly, 1987), 77.

18. Sherry Bebitch Jeffe, "For Legislative Staff, Policy Takes a Back Seat to Politics," *California Journal* (January 1987), 42–45.

19. Eric M. Uslander and Ronald E. Weber, "The 'Politics' of Redistribution: Towards a Model for the Policy-Making Process in the American States," *American Politics Quarterly* 3 (April 1975), 130–170.

20. Leonard Ritt, "State Legislative Reform: Does it Matter? *American Politics Quarterly* 1 (October 1973), 499–510, and Albert K. Karnig and Lee Sigelman, "State Legislative Reform and Public Policy: Another Look," *Western Political Quarterly* 28 (September 1975), 548–552.

21. Malcolm E. Jewell and Samuel C. Patterson, *The Legislative Process in the United States*, 3rd ed. (New York: Random House, 1977), 116.

22. *Baker* v. *Carr*, 369 U.S. 186 (1962).

23. Robert S. Lorch, *State and Local Politics: The Great Entanglement*, 2nd ed. (Englewood Cliffs, NJ: Prentice-Hall, 1986), 149–150.

24. Alan Rosenthal, *Legislative Life*, (New York: Harper & Row, 1981), 182.

25. Michael Engel, *State and Local Politics: Fundamentals and Perspectives* (New York: St. Martin's, 1985), 120–121.

26. Samuel C. Patterson, "Legislators and Legislatures in the American States," in Virginia Gray, Herbert Jacob, and Kenneth B. Vines, eds., *Politics in the American States* (Boston: Little, Brown, 1983), 165.

27. Alan Rosenthal, "If the Party's Over, Where's All that Noise Coming From?" *State Government* 57 (1984), 50–54.

28. Rob Gurwitt, "Cultures Clash as Old-Time Politics Confronts Button-Down Management," *Governing: The States and Localities* (April 1989), 47.

29. John Herbes, "17th-Century Counties Struggle to Cope with 20th-Century Problems," *Governing: The States and Localities* (May 1989), 42.

30. Lorch, 229.

31. Richard L. Engstrom and Michael D. McDonald, "The Electioin of Blacks to City Councils: Clarifying the Impact of Electoral Arrangements on the Seats/Population Relationship," *American Political Science Review* 75 (June 1981), 344–354. For an excellent source of research on the impact of district versus at-large elections, see Peggy Heilig and Robert J. Mundt, *Your Voice at City Hall* (Albany: State University of New York Press, 1984).

32. John J. Harrigan, *Political Change in the Metropolis*, 4th ed. (Glenview, IL: Scott, Foresman, 1989), 95–96.

33. Richard D. Bingham, *State and Local Government in an Urban Society* (New York: Random House, 1986), 404.

Chapter 10

Chief Executives

Americans are notorious for their distrust of executive power. The American Revolution was largely a war against royal governors, who were appointed by Britain's King George III, and who enforced unpopular laws. Consequently, early state constitutions and local charters significantly curbed the power of state and local executives and left legislatures largely unrestrained.

Over the course of American history, executives have gradually strengthened their role in state and local politics at the expense of legislatures. In our modern urban society, government has become larger and more pervasive. The need for full-time professional executives to manage government operations has increased. Since legislatures and local boards are composed chiefly of part-time amateurs, we depend heavily on chief executives and bureaucrats to offer solutions to our problems.

This chapter focuses on chief executives at both the state and local levels. Special attention is given to governors, mayors, city managers, and school district superintendents. The chapter examines what these chief executives do, why they have become more powerful, how their role in our intergovernmental system has evolved, and how individuals can influence their decisions.

THE FUNCTIONS OF CHIEF EXECUTIVES

Symbolic

Chief executives are our most visible politicians. Even citizens who know or care little about politics can usually identify the governor, mayor, and superintendent of schools. These executives symbolize their respective units of government; they are celebrities who receive a great deal of media attention and scrutiny.

Being a symbol is important for a chief executive because it enhances his or her **informal powers**. Unlike **formal powers**, which come from legal and constitutional provisions, informal power refers to influence — the power to persuade.[1] Because chief executives receive so much public exposure, they have many opportunities to influence public opinion. Modern chief executives are cognizant of the potential for influence of their "office," and most seek to build and embellish their symbolic role. They spend a significant portion of their time acting out this role through public appearances. For example, one study estimated that governors spend almost 30 percent of their time meeting with the general public and conducting ceremonial functions.[2] Public officials, especially elected ones, are likely to support an executive who is backed by the force of strong public opinion.

Informal power can come from sources other than the chief executive's symbolic function. For example, a governor who commands a strong and dominant party will find his or her influence enhanced. A mayor or school superintendent with a forceful personality will generally have more success in persuading others to see his or her point of view. Serving as the most important symbol of one's government, however, clearly gives a chief executive a unique advantage.

Administrative

The first responsibility of a chief executive is to administer laws by managing organizations called bureaucracies that constitute the executive branch. Executives direct and coordinate the activities of executive branch agencies so that policy goals can be achieved in an efficient manner. They also formulate new programs and modify old ones. Finally, chief executives interact with legislators, interest groups, and others who are inevitably involved in the implementation of public policy.

Executives are often held responsible for the actions and performance of the bureaucracy, but the amount of control they exercise over state or local bureaucrats is tempered by several factors. The size of the bureaucracy may make it difficult for executives to manage it. Whereas the city manager of Salem, Oregon, oversees about 100 people, the governor of California is responsible for 6000 state employees.

Executives' administrative responsibilities involve more than the technical difficulties of managing large organizations. Their management responsibilities are meshed in bureaucratic politics. Often agencies have entrenched interests that come from administering programs over a long period of time. Alliances of agencies with interest groups and other interested constituencies as well as with legislators and board members may dilute the ability of the chief executive to direct these agencies.

Executive control of the bureaucracy may depend to a great degree on the extent of the executive's power of appointment. Unlike the President, however, state and local chief executives often deal with department heads who are independently elected and thus have independent power bases. The civil service movement — a major reform in state and local governments in the twentieth century — has tempered executives' control over the bureaucracy. Even when a chief executive has extensive appointment power, problems may arise. If executives make appointments strictly on the basis of a merit system, they risk alienating loyal party members. If they employ the concept of patronage as the guiding principle for appointments, weak or incompetent appointees may result.

Chief executives must share their administrative power with legislatures. As we learned in Chapter 9, legislatures and boards have final authority over state and local budgets. This means that bureaucrats will always be responsive to legislatures to some degree. This becomes significant when the chief executive and the legislature or board disagree on substantive policy or program questions and goals. Thus executives' ability to manage the bureaucracy may depend on their relationship with the legislature.

Legislative

In introductory political science classes one learns that legislatures are responsible for passing laws and that executives are responsible for executing those laws. Before long one recognizes that this neat distinction of responsibilities does not describe modern American government accurately.

State and local chief executives are often described as chief legislators because of their prominent role in producing legislation. Their visibility allows them to set the direction of public policy, and legislative bodies often respond to the chief executive's agenda. Most executives assume their office with some type of **program**, that is, a series of policy proposals they and their advisers have developed during the campaign. The most important of these proposals become the chief executive's real agenda; this agenda reflects the executive's broad philosophy and goals. For example, a governor may come to office prepared to slash state spending and exercise "fiscal responsibility" or a newly elected mayor may be prepared to push for more stringent environmental regulations in the face of what he or she perceives as excessive or reckless commercial development.

Executives generally possess several advantages in dealing with legislatures. The prestige and influence that come from their symbolic function have already been discussed. In addition, they generally have superior staff resources and are much more likely to be full-time professionals.

Chief executives also play a dominant role in legislating when they execute laws because the manner in which a law is implemented often determines the very nature of that law. Chief executives and the bureaucrats who work for them often have a great deal of discretion in interpreting and applying laws. For example, a state legislature may decide that certain professions need to be regulated, but the regulatory agencies determine specific rules for the licensing and monitoring of those professions. A local superintendent and principal may be charged with interpreting and implementing a local school board's policy of limited corporal punishment. The power of executives and bureaucrats to make rules that have the force of law is discussed in more depth in Chapter 11.

Fiscal

Because chief executives occupy the central positions in state and local administrations and have general responsibility for their management, they can take a broad view of fiscal resources and spending priorities. Consequently, executives generally are charged with proposing changes in taxation and preparing budgets. These changes and proposals are submitted to legislatures, councils, or boards for review and final approval.

Chief executives may also have a broad view of resource and spending patterns because they generally have broader constituencies. A governor represents the whole state; a mayor speaks for all the citizens of a city. Although executives may be swayed by narrow interests or parochial concerns, they are more likely to consider the effects of a policy on the whole community.

Budgets are an important means of administrative control for executives. Most chief executives review the budget requests of departments and agencies and make final budget recommendations to legislatures or boards. Without such control, executives are handicapped in a test of wills with their bureaucracies. Although chief executives' power and influence over the budget vary, it is important for administrative agencies to have the support of the executive. This support often makes it possible to continue and expand these agencies' programs. Even more important, agencies that find themselves out of favor with their executives may face the prospect of executive veto power.

GOVERNORS

In the last ten years the importance of the states and their elected leaders has grown not only in the states but also within the context of our federal system of government. As the federal government has reduced its responsibility for domestic programs and services, the gap has been filled in part by the states. This trend has pushed the governorship into the leading position in the states. Governors are taking the initiative in sorting out the responsibilities the states will continue to perform and in pursuing the traditional functions of the states, such as education and criminal justice.

Governors have not always exercised the power and leadership that they do today. Historically there has been a gradual trend toward centralization of gubernatorial power. This trend has evolved through several historical phrases.

Historical Development of the Role of Governor

Early Legislative Dominance   The governors of the original 13 colonies were King George III's appointees. As agents of the Crown, those royal governors were symbols of tyranny to American colonists. The early experi-

Governor elect Douglas Wilder of Virginia. (Courtesy of Bettmann.)

ence with these royal governors left its mark; Americans are still notoriously suspicious of executive authority.

Unpleasant memories of colonial governors prompted early architects of state constitutions to fashion the role of the governor as a "powerless ceremonial officer." Most governors were selected by their own state legislatures to serve one-year terms. Most had no veto power and virtually no appointment power.[3] In contrast, state legislatures or "assemblies" acquired courageous reputations by standing up to tyrannical governors during the colonial period. Thus early American history was a time of state legislative dominance.

The 1800s and Jacksonian Democracy   The nineteenth century saw conflicting patterns in executive authority. Widespread corruption and incompetence in state legislatures fostered disillusionment with legislative power, and many people began to realize that stronger governors were needed to check the power of legislatures; some standard changes were made to increase governors' powers. The governorship became an elective position with a term of two or four years. Governors' powers were broadened to include the veto.

The enhancement of executive power in the early nineteenth century was followed by restrictions on that power. The movement toward "popular democracy" which characterized the Jacksonian period brought about the **long ballot**. This means that most state executives were elected independently and removed from control by the governor. These **plural executives**, or unintegrated executives, became the norm in most states in the 1800s. Thus even as governors gained independence from legislatures, they were able to exercise little control over their own branches of government.

The Progressive Era   Toward the end of the nineteenth century widespread corruption in state and local governments brought demands for reform. Most of the corruption was blamed on abuses by political parties. As we learned in Chapter 8, the dominance of the patronage system, or "spoils system," meant that elected officials appointed people who were of questionable integrity or were plain incompetent to government jobs. Progressive reformers pushed through a series of reforms that were supposed to "depoliticize" government. New policies aimed at limiting the power and abuses of political parties were put into effect in a number of states. Civil service systems were created to replace patronage with **merit systems**, and government commissions and boards were established that operated outside the control of elected officials.

Civil service systems and independent commissions were supposed to isolate executive bodies from partisan political influence. This meant that these bodies were isolated from the person who was supposed to be responsible for them: the elected chief executive. Typically governors had no power to appoint members to these boards and commissions or to remove them. Being governor was like being the manager of a large business, but without the power to hire and fire key personnel. Meanwhile, as urbanization and industrialization continued at a rapid pace throughout the first half of the twentieth century, the demand for government services generated larger state bureaucracies.

The Age of the Executive The first radical shift of power for governors occurred in 1918, when Governor Al Smith of New York commissioned a study on the reorganization of state government. The reforms proposed by Smith and subsequently adopted included a four-year term for the governor; gubernatorial appointment of all statewide officials except the lieutenant governor, attorney general, and comptroller; and the preparation of an executive budget by the governor for submission to the legislature.[4]

The real increases in executive power came in the 1950s and 1960s, when a number of states revised their constitutions. Governors often led the movement for state constitutional revision and in the process made sure their own interests received a hearing. Gubernatorial power was also enhanced by the "reapportionment revolution" of the early 1960s. Rural legislators had traditionally viewed strong executive power suspiciously. Redistricting corrected the overrepresentation of rural interests in state legislatures and gave urban constituencies more representation. Most important, the need for strong executive power became more apparent as state and local governments assumed greater responsibilities. Strong governors were a logical result of stronger, more active governments. Although gubernatorial power varies greatly among the states, it is clear that since the 1950s the executive branch has dominated governmental affairs in the statehouse.

The Modern Governor

Between the 1940s and the 1960s state governments were the object of a great deal of criticism and scorn. Characterized by corruption, malapportionment, and incompetence, state governments were referred to by such unflattering terms as the "weak sisters" and the "fallen arches" of the federal system. In 1961, *New York Times* columnist James Reston wrote that "state capitols are over their heads in problems and up to their knees in midgets."[5] Among the midgets Reston referred to were no doubt many state governors who possessed reputations as unprofessional good-time Charlies.[6]

But times have changed. Gradually the states have taken steps to reform their political institutions and processes. Governors have become creative and experienced professionals who use their formal and informal powers to transform their states. Modern governors have been compared to company chief executive officers (CEOs) who oversee sizable budgets, manage large organizations, and persuade their states to adopt new ideas and innovations. As Governor Bill Clinton of Arkansas (Box 10-1) says, "We're in a new and different period. It's a good time to be a governor."[7]

Institutionalization of the Governorship Governors are extraordinarily busy officials whose schedules are typically frenetic.[8] They gener-

Box 10-1 **Selling a Vision: Governor Bill Clinton and Education Reform in Arkansas**

Governor Bill Clinton of Arkansas is an excellent example of the new breed of modern governors occupying statehouses these days. A Rhodes scholar, Clinton was first elected governor in 1978 at the age of 32. Almost at once he mounted a statewide campaign to improve public schools. He wanted legislation to raise educational standards and teachers' pay. He proposed mandatory teacher competency tests, broader curricula, and tests that students had to pass to get out of the eighth grade. At the same time, he made what most people consider to be a foolish and risky assumption for a politician: He assumed that the people of Arkansas would accept a one-cent rise in the sales tax to pay for the improvements.

By most standards, Arkansas is one of the last places one would expect to find active and progressive government. The per capita income of its 2 million people ranks forty-seventh in the nation. More than a quarter of the adults can't read. The governor's salary — $35,000 — is the lowest in the nation, and the legislature averages only about 55 days a year in session. The oil and gas bust closed factories, and the farm depression reduced state revenues.

Governor Clinton insisted, however, that voters will accept tax increases "if you can show them where the money will go." Clinton and his wife launched a statewide campaign to do just that. They pulled out all the stops to build support for education reform. Governor Clinton sent Mrs. Clinton, his Yale law school classmate, to hold hearings in each of the state's 75 counties. They raised money from the business community for ads in the media. They gave out thousands of blue ribbons, asking people to wear them to broadcast their theme: "Our kids need a blue-ribbon education." And they drummed home the message that education means jobs.

The legislation faced powerful opposition, including the Arkansas Education Association, which dislikes tests for teachers. After the bill passed, the association persuaded the state house of representatives to repeal it, but the senate refused to go along, and the governor prevailed. As one of the new breed of governors, Clinton demonstrated how to talk about issues in ways that not only made sense to voters but moved them.

ally delegate some of their responsibilities to their staffs. The size of governors' staffs and the roles performed by staffers vary from state to state. In general, the governors of small, less populous states have smaller staffs than do those of large populous states. Thus governorships in smaller states tend to be more **personalized**, while governorships in larger states tend to be more **institutionalized**.

One leading student of the governorship suggests that it is in the mid-sized states, which appear to be in transition between personalized and institutionalized governorship, that the greatest burdens are placed on the governor. These states face problems similar to those of the larger states.

However, they have not yet established sufficient staff resources for the governor to discharge the responsibilities of the executive with greater ease.[9]

Gubernatorial staffers perform a number of important functions: speech writer, press secretary, budget officer, and policy adviser among others. Recent governors tend to be less likely to appoint campaign staffers to their personal staffs. This reflects a heightened awareness of the importance of staff members and their abilities,[10] since a person who knows how to direct a political campaign may not always be an expert on running the government. It also means that governors have a larger pool of knowledgeable staffers from which to select. The more recent capable executives and the more powerful gubernatorial office have attracted better individuals to serve as staffers in the governor's office.

Intergovernmental Responsibilities As the federal government struggles with the federal budget deficit, states are assuming more responsibility for government programs and services. This has not been an easy process for states that have to a certain degree weaned themselves from federal grant dollars. Federal grants to state and local governments grew from $7.9 billion in 1962 to $94.8 billion in 1981.[11] Until recently, federal grants constituted a rising portion of state and local budgets. In 1955 they made up 11.8 percent of the revenues for state and local budgets, and by 1982 that figure had increased to 25.4 percent.[12] Under the Reagan administration's "new federalism" policy, federal assistance to the states declined significantly.

The states have responded unevenly to cutbacks in federal funding.[13] However, a number of states led by progressive governors not only have moved to provide programs mandated by the federal government but have fashioned innovative solutions to problems that Washington has not addressed. Although states have long been recognized as policy experimenters or "laboratories of democracy," their assertiveness in policy leadership has grown in recent years. As two political scientists recently stated, "Policy innovation in the 1980's . . . is the beloved stepchild of the states, adopted from neglectful national parents."[14] There is no doubt that younger, more educated, more assertive governors whose formal powers have been strengthened are largely responsible for this surge of new activity.

Governors are adopting new strategies in their attempt to assume more control of intergovernmental affairs. Formerly federal agency directors dealt directly with state agency directors. In many states governors have moved to consolidate intergovernmental affairs under their supervision so that they can be more directly involved in communications with federal agencies.

Governors are also equipping themselves to be the chief lobbyists for their state governments by establishing Washington liaison offices to assist them in handling relations with the national government. In 1989, 36 states had such offices. The National Governors' Association, the most important governors' organization, has been strengthened significantly. It has changed from a part-time, largely ineffective annual conference to an association with substantial influence in the national political arena. These developments are helping governors play a much more active role in our intergovernmental system.

Recruitment, Tenure, and Compensation

In general, the formal qualifications to be a governor are not very restrictive. Most states stipulate age and citizenship requirements. More than four-fifths of the states have a minimum age requirement of 30 years, and 36 states require the governor to be a U.S. citizen. Forty-three states require state residency, with residence before an election ranging from one month to ten years. Twenty states add that the governor must be a "qualified voter," while a few prohibit persons convicted of bribery, perjury, or "infamous crimes" from serving as the governor. Some states have unusual or antiquated requirements. Montana prohibits persons of "unsound mind" from being governor, while Kentucky bans its governors from dueling.[15]

It is the unwritten requirements for governor that restrict most average citizens from the job. Governors are characteristically white male Protestants who are married and have children. They are generally well educated, with a career in law or business, substantial experience in public office, and the support of the state's party officials. Although most governors are middle-aged, they have been getting younger in recent years. The average age for all governors from 1951 to 1981 at the time of their first election was 47.4 years, compared with 51 years in the decade 1940–1950.[16] There is some evidence that younger governors are better governors. One study compared 117 "outstanding" governors from 1950 to 1975 with colleagues who were judged to have performed less well. There performances were correlated with factors such as prior political and governmental experience, legal training, education, age, formal powers of the office, and various characteristics of the individual states. Among these factors, the strongest predictor of performance was the governor's age upon taking office.[17] Although the authors admit that their findings are tentative, this study provides evidence that age is not a barrier to effective leadership.

The ability to lead effectively is also influenced by a governor's tenure, or the length and frequency of gubernatorial terms. A governor serving only a two-year term or one who cannot be reelected is immediately weaker than is one who does not operate under these restrictions. The length of the gubernatorial terms varies significantly. Governors in only three states — New Hampshire, Rhode Island, and Vermont — still have two-year terms. Three states — Kentucky, New Mexico, and Virginia — restrict the governor to a single four-year term, while 25 states restrict the governor to no more than two four-year terms. Twenty-two states place no restrictions on how many terms an individual can serve as governor.[18]

Although more is not necessarily better with respect to the length of time in office for a governor, short or restricted terms do hamper a governor's ability to complete an agenda. A new governor typically spends the first year in office getting adjusted to the demands of being the chief executive. Governors elected for a two-year term must immediately begin thinking about reelection, while those who cannot serve successive terms may quickly find themselves lame ducks. The governors regarded as most successful are those who can set long-range goals and see them through to completion.

It is possible for most legislatures to remove governors before the end of a term through the process of **impeachment**. The usual method is for the lower house to impeach, that is, bring formal charges against the accused, and the senate to hold a formal trial. If the accused is convicted in the senate, he or she is removed from office. Eighteen governors have been impeached, and eight have been convicted. The last governor to be convicted and removed from office was Evan Mecham of Arizona in 1988. Because of controversial remarks, many of which were considered racial slurs, a recall petition was started even before Mecham was elected. The petition was successful, and a recall election was scheduled for May 1988. However, after a grand jury indicted him in January 1988 on six criminal charges related to campaign finance violations, Mecham was impeached and convicted by the state legislature. After his removal from office, the Arizona Supreme Court canceled the recall election.

The good news for governors is that they are much better paid than they used to be. The median salary for governors in 1955 was $15,000, compared with $52,400 in 1981. Salaries range from $130,000 for the governor of New York to $35,000 for the governor of Arkansas. Although these are not exorbitant figures, they are high enough to attract competent and professional candidates.

The Governor as Manager

As chief executives of their states, governors have formal responsibility for a host of bureaucracies that control enormous amounts of money, employ thousands of people, undertake a variety of government programs, and have a direct impact on the lives of large numbers of people. Like private business managers, governors want these bureaucracies to perform well and efficiently at the lowest possible cost. Unlike private managers, however, governors operate with a host of **constraints** that may limit their ability to manage their own branch (Box 10-2).

The most obvious constraint on a governor's ability to manage is the separation and sharing of power's with the legislature and courts. Unlike a private-sector CEO, a governor generally has to get legislative approval to change the primary tasks or structure of executive agencies and departments. Since the legislature has final authority over administrative agency budgets, agencies often respond to the mandates of the legislature, which may or may not conflict with those of the governor.

Often governors try to direct or change agencies that are allied with organized interest groups. These organized interests form the agency's "con-

---

Box 10-2 **Different Views of the Governor as Manager**

Governor Michael Dukakis:

> I've got a colleague here at the Kennedy school who says you're really like an orchestra leader. You can't do it by yourself, and one of your most important jobs is to select the folks in the orchestra. And, you can't have all violins and all trombones. You have to have a variety of people. Whom you pick, how you pick them, and what kind of leadership and support, inspiration, and motivation you can provide as a chief executive has a great deal to do with whether or not you are successful.

Governor Calvin Rampton:

> [A] governor can shield himself from [getting burned by management]. I had subordinates who did my dirty jobs, like everybody else. If I felt a decision was necessary, but I knew it was not going to be well received, I had the decision announced by the department head. I don't think there is anything wrong with that. Being in the management role does not mean that you are going to be out there with your chest out taking the bullets all the time. You're more like the admiral of the flagship, sitting back in the bowels of the ship, letting someone else fire the shots—but you are making the decisions.

Source: Robert Dalton, "Governors Views on Management," in Thad L. Beyle and Lynn R. Munchmore, eds., *Being Governor: The View from the Office.* (Durham, NC: Duke University Press, 1983), 95.

---

stituency" and generally oppose any effort by a chief executive to change the organization or responsibilities of "their" agency. Consequently, governors may find that the changes they feel are essential to improving the performance or reducing the costs of an agency are resisted by key legislators who are responding to the pleas and complaints of client groups that would be adversely affected by the proposed changes.[19]

Despite these constraints, today's governors enjoy greater executive control. More staff resources, expanded appointment authority, and greater control of the budget process are narrowing the gap between a governor's responsibilities for management and the actual capacity of a governor to meet those responsibilities. Although executive management of the state bureaucracy encompasses a number of activities, the following four powers are among the most important: appointment, organization, budget, and crisis resolution.

Appointment Power   The power most fundamental to a governor as manager is the power of appointment. As Michael Dukakis, the governor of Massachusetts, stated, a governor's success "depends heavily on the quality and caliber of people he appoints."

However, gubernatorial appointment is limited by a number of factors. In nearly every state there are other statewide elected officials who share executive power and who are quite independent of the governor. These elected executives make up the plural executive and generally include the lieutenant governor, the secretary of state, the attorney general, and the state treasurer. In addition, some top administrative officials are appointed by boards or commissions rather than by the governor. Table 10.1 shows that of 1992 administrative positions, less than half (46.8 percent) are appointed by governors while 38.2 percent are appointed by boards, agency heads, or the legislature and 15 percent are separately elected. There is considerable variation among the states in the percentage of upper-level officials the governor may appoint, ranging from a low of 20.5 percent in South Carolina to a high of 86.8 percent in New York.

Table 10.1 HOW STATE ADMINISTRATIVE OFFICIALS ARE SELECTED

State	Total officials	Separately elected	Appointed, but not by the governor	Appointed by the governor (%)
Alabama	37	8	15	14 (38.9)
Alaska	45	2	29	14 (31.8)
Arizona	39	6	17	16 (42.1)
Arkansas	38	6	17	15 (40.5)
California	40	7	4	29 (74.4)
Colorado	37	5	15	17 (47.2)
Connecticut	43	5	17	21 (50.0)
Delaware	42	6	16	20 (48.8)
Florida	41	9	18	14 (35.0)
Georgia	35	8	18	9 (26.5)
Hawaii	19	2	3	14 (77.8)
Idaho	40	7	15	18 (46.2)
Illinois	31	6	3	22 (73.3)
Indiana	37	7	8	22 (61.1)
Iowa	40	7	6	27 (69.2)
Kansas	43	6	20	17 (40.5)
Kentucky	42	8	18	16 (39.0)
Louisiana	41	10	6	25 (62.5)
Maine	41	1	25	15 (37.5)
Maryland	42	5	18	19 (46.3)
Massachusetts	46	6	16	24 (53.3)
Michigan	41	4	23	14 (35.0)
Minnesota	41	5	10	26 (65.0)
Mississippi	35	11	10	14 (41.2)
Missouri	40	5	24	11 (28.2)
Montana	43	6	19	18 (42.9)
Nebraska	43	8	13	22 (52.4)
Nevada	44	6	22	16 (37.2)

continued

Table 10.1 HOW STATE ADMINISTRATIVE OFFICIALS ARE SELECTED (continued)

State	Total officials	Separately elected	Appointed, but not by the governor	Appointed by the governor (%)
New Hampshire	39	1	14	24 (63.2)
New Jersey	40	1	17	22 (56.4)
New Mexico	37	6	12	19 (52.8)
New York	39	3	3	33 (86.8)
North Carolina	44	10	13	21 (48.8)
North Dakota	40	12	15	13 (33.3)
Ohio	43	5	16	22 (52.4)
Oklahoma	39	8	17	14 (36.8)
Oregon	42	6	24	12 (29.3)
Pennsylvania	44	5	11	28 (65.1)
Rhode Island	42	5	17	20 (48.8)
South Carolina	40	9	23	8 (20.5)
South Dakota	44	7	16	21 (48.8)
Tennessee	43	2	21	20 (47.6)
Texas	39	6	24	9 (23.7)
Utah	39	6	15	18 (47.4)
Vermont	41	6	13	22 (55.0)
Virginia	37	3	4	30 (83.3)
Washington	44	9	18	17 (39.5)
West Virginia	40	6	15	19 (48.7)
Wisconsin	32	6	12	14 (45.2)
Wyoming	38	5	16	17 (45.9)
Totals	1992	299	761	932
50-state percentage		15%	38.2%	46.8%

Source: Thad L. Beyle and Robert Dalton, "Appointment Power: Does It Belong to the Governor?" in Thad L. Beyle and Lynn R. Munchmore, eds., *Being Governor: The View from the Office.* (Durham, NC: Duke University Press, 1983), 109–110. Reprinted by permission.

In addition to top administrative positions, governors have the power to appoint members of many of the regulatory and advisory boards and commissions that make up the state bureaucracy, but here the governor's power may also be limited: Most appointees serve fixed terms and cannot be removed, that is, fired, by the governor except for cause. Removal for cause means that the governor must prove that the appointee was not carrying out his or her duties. In a few states, removal may even require approval by the legislature.

In some states many subcabinet officials in the state bureaucracy may be selected through a civil service, or merit, system. This means that people who show they have the qualifications for a government position are hired, promoted, and fired by an independent civil service commission. Although civil service reform encourages the hiring of qualified people, it detracts from the governor's power to manage the bureaucracy. It is difficult for governors to control the bureaucracy if they have no power to hire and fire bureaucrats.

One recent study showed that governors have mixed feelings about civil service systems. On the one hand, governors feel that civil service regulations provide continuity in state government and free them to think about key appointments and major issues. On the other hand, they are opposed to extending civil service reform to top administrative officials because it makes those officials less responsive to the governor's policy goals.[20]

Organization Power   The power to create and abolish agencies and to reassign duties and functions among agencies and departments allows governors to emphasize their own programs and priorities. Governors restructure executive departments through **executive orders**. In the last 20 years governors have issued executive orders aimed at reorganizing the upper levels of the bureaucracy and generally streamlining the executive branch.

In most states, the legislature still has primary authority over reorganization of the bureaucracy. However, 16 states now grant the governor some type of reorganization authority. In most of these 16 states the governor is allowed to propose reorganization plans for the executive branch that take effect unless they are disapproved by the legislature.[21]

Reorganization of the bureaucracy may be sorely needed, but governors quickly realize the disadvantages of comprehensive efforts in this area. Reorganization is likely to disrupt the routines of the bureaucracies, cause a loss of morale among administrative officials, and cause the departure of key personnel. It also opens the door for power struggles, or turf battles, among agencies. These and other frustrations cause even the most energetic and progressive governors to hesitate before taking on the bureaucracy.

Budget Power   Almost all governors are given sole responsibility for preparing the first draft of the budget and submitting it to the legislature. This means that the state budget director is responsible to the governor directly or through the head of an intervening agency who is appointed by the governor. Only three states — Mississippi, South Carolina, and Texas — require their governors to share this budgetary power with other officials.

There are two reasons why the preparation, presentation, and execution of the budget by the governor are important. First, by overseeing the initial draft of the budget, the governor is assured that this draft reflects his or her overall philosophy on taxing and spending. Thus the governor sets the agenda for legislative debate and compromise. This gives the governor an advantage despite the fact that the legislature exercises final statutory authority over the budget. Second, initial control of the budgetary process gives the governor some control over the bureaucracy. Administrators who cooperate with the governor may discover that their slice of the budget pie is somewhat greater than that of uncooperative or hostile administrators.

The governor's budget generally carries a good deal of weight with the legislature because the governor, unlike the legislature, is in a position to weigh the needs of the entire state. In addition, governors are generally equipped with more staff resources. Legislators who feel compelled to dispute the governor's recommendations will find themselves at a disadvantage in terms of data and expertise. The governor's budget office is more likely to be equipped with professional staff members who are able to research the needs of the state and evaluate the performance of administrative agencies.

Despite these staff resources, the governor's influence over the budget varies considerably from state to state. In states with strong parties and strong governors, the governor is expected to take the lead in getting the party platform enacted. In those states, the budget is the source of funds for the platform on which the governor and his or her party campaigned for office. Thus the governor plays a much more dominant role than governors do in states where parties are weak and the governor is elected in a campaign with little policy content. In states with strong parties, the governor's budget message is the first step in showing whether promises made in the campaign will be kept.[22]

Crisis Resolution Power   Governors are often called on to respond to sudden demands placed on them by natural or synthetic crises. The former may include floods, hurricanes, ice storms, and earthquakes; the latter may include responses to strikes or riots. Whenever an emergency response is required, the governor is viewed as the person in charge. Often a governor's response to emergencies is made through a concurrent "military" role; the governor is the commander in chief of the state militia, or the National Guard, as it has come to be known in the states. The governor may call out the National Guard to protect property and preserve order if the situation seems to demand it. Many governors have found that emergencies preoccupy their administrations and take up a great deal of their time.[23]

The Governor as Chief Legislator

As the key representative of all the people in the state, the governor is expected to lay out a legislative program or agenda early in his or her administration. Often this program emerges during the campaign for office; it is usually formalized in the governor's initial address to the legislature and in subsequent "state of the state" speeches. Education reform, job development, tax reform, drug abuse prevention, and expanded health care are examples of problems that a governor may want to pursue aggressively.

Strategies of Influence   A successful governor knows that to influence the legislature effectively, it is necessary to use all available resources. These resources include the formal powers of the governor, such as budgetary power and the veto, but also include many informal techniques of persuasion. Persuasive power comes naturally from being governor; the office itself suggests respect and leadership.

The governor is most likely to take advantage of the public's feeling that he or she should set the state's governmental agenda. Indeed, a smart governor takes steps to educate the public and involve key public opinion leaders in the policy-making process. A case in point is Governor Richard Riley of South Carolina, a state where the governor's formal power over the legislature is very weak. Riley, determined to enact sweeping educational reforms in his state, established two blue-ribbon task forces on educational improvement that were made up of legislators, educators, and top business leaders. In preparing for the legislative session, Riley mobilized all his informal powers, especially public relations, media access, and personal popularity. He held public forums across the state to stir up the citizens for education reform. His efforts resulted in the Education Improvement Act of 1984, a sweeping reform of the state's educational system.[24]

Governor Riley provides an example of a governor's use of the "bully pulpit," that is, the visibility that comes with the office. Governors are regarded with a certain awe by the general public; when they speak, people listen. Their informal powers have been strengthened by the advent of the electronic media, especially television. Governors repeatedly appear on television and periodically hold press conferences to express their positions. Legislators seldom have the same opportunities to bask in statewide recognition.

Governors also try to persuade the legislature by lobbying. Though most are not as obvious as the governor of Ohio, who formally registered himself as a lobbyist before the legislature, a governor will always spend at least a portion of his or her time influencing legislation. Governors are assisted in their communications with the legislature by a legislative liaison officer and staff, although the staffers may not be formally called legislative liaisons. Examples of lobbying activities that governors and their staffs may engage in are talking to individual members of the legislature, discussing the legislative calendar with the legislative leadership, recruiting witnesses to testify before legislative committees, encouraging agencies or interest groups to lobby, and on occasion even preparing floor speeches for supportive legislators. In addition, Thad Beyle found in his study of 37 states that 75 percent of the governors' offices have an open door policy toward legislators; that is, legislators are allowed to see the governor whenever they want.[25]

The Veto The power to veto bills passed by the legislature was the one resource traditionally held by most eighteenth-century governors. Today that power is stronger and more flexible than ever (Table 10.2). All the states but North Carolina give governors the power to veto; 47 states give governors **line item veto** power.[26] This allows the governor to veto a single item within an appropriations bill rather than vetoing the entire bill. Ten states have adopted a hybrid form of item veto in which the governor can reduce the dollar amount of a specific budget item without eliminating that item altogether. Fifteen states now provide for **executive amendment**, in which a governor may veto a bill but then send it back to the legislature with

Table 10.2 STATES RANKED BY GOVERNOR'S VETO POWER

Very strong	Strong	Medium	Weak
Alaska	Alabama	Florida	Indiana
Arizona	Arkansas	Massachusetts	Maine
California	Kentucky	Montana	New Hampshire
Colorado	Tennessee	New Mexico	North Carolina
Connecticut	West Virginia	Oregon	Rhode Island
Delaware		South Carolina	Vermont
Georgia		Texas	
Hawaii		Virginia	
Illinois		Washington	
Idaho		Wisconsin	
Iowa			
Kansas			
Louisiana			
Maryland			
Michigan			
Minnesota			
Mississippi			
Missouri			
Nebraska			
New Jersey			
New York			
North Dakota			
Ohio			
Oklahoma			
Pennsylvania			
South Dakota			
Utah			
Wyoming			

Source: Council of State Governments, *The Book of the States, 1986–87* (Lexington, KY: Council of State Governments, 1987), 37–38.

recommended changes. If the legislature agrees to the governor's suggestions, the governor will sign the bill into law.

In 15 states the governor can **pocket veto** a bill when the legislature is not in session by withholding his or her signature for a specified period of time. However, in three of these states the legislature may reconvene to override the veto. If it does not, the bill dies.

It is possible for the legislature to override a governor's veto, but in all the states this requires more than a simple majority. Consequently, legislative override of a veto is rare: The proportion of overrides in all states is always less than 10 percent. In some states legislative override of the governor's veto almost never occurs. For example, during John Carlin's two terms as governor of Kansas, he signed 3085 bills and vetoed 129. Every one of his vetos was sustained.

The governor's power to veto is a formidable weapon, and often the threat of a veto is enough to kill or alter a bill to the governor's liking. Governors do not exercise the veto authority frivolously. When surveyed, a large majority agreed with the statement "Bills should be signed unless the governor has very strong objections." Governors generally exercise the "courtesy of notification" once they decide to veto a bill. This means that they usually notify the affected legislators and agency heads.[27]

Leading Stronger Legislatures   In the past few years there has been a modernization of state legislatures. Chapter 9 described how legislatures are becoming more professional: Sessions are longer, pay is higher, and staff support is increasing. More time and resources are allowing legislators to concentrate on overseeing the performance of the executive branch. In addition, reapportionment of legislative districts has resulted in greater representation of urban constituencies. These changes have made legislatures more equal partners with the executive in the formulation of state policy.

In a recent study the National Governors' Association (NGA) looked at changes in the institutional powers of governors from 1965 to 1985. The NGA uses six indexes to measure the formal powers of governors: the governor's tenure potential, appointment powers, and budget-making power; the legislature's budget-changing ability; and the governor's veto power and political strength in the legislature. The first three indexes measure the governor's power within the executive branch, while the second three concern the governor's power relative to the legislature. All the state governors were assigned point values based on the six indexes which indicated the strength of their formal powers. Table 10.3 shows these rankings. The most notable finding was that while governors' executive powers have been strengthened in the last 20 years, their powers over the legislature have decreased.[28]

The resurgence of state legislatures is not always advantageous for governors. Legislators are demanding a greater voice in state government and increasing the time they spend overseeing and evaluating the activities of the executive branch. However, while modernization of the legislature is sure to make a governor's relationship with the legislature more difficult, it is not a completely unwelcome change. Most governors find that informed, competent legislators are more in tune with their view of the state's problems. This is reinforced by the fact that legislatures are more representative of urban constituencies than they used to be. Often urban areas provide the margin of victory that governors need in a statewide election. Thus governors and legislators are more likely to agree that the needs of these urban areas should be addressed. Governor Rubin Askew of Florida expressed the view of many governors when he listed the rise of state legislatures as one of the three primary causes of a strengthened governorship.[29]

Table 10.3 A COMPARISON OF THE FORMAL POWERS OF GOVERNOR*

Very strong	Strong	Moderate	Weak	Very weak
Maryland (27)	Connecticut (24)	Alabama (22)	Maine (19)	Texas (16)
Massachusetts (27)	Louisiana (24)	Alaska (22)	Montana (19)	North Carolina (16)
New York (26)	Nebraska (24)	California (22)	New Hampshire (19)	South Carolina (14)
West Virginia (26)	Utah (24)	Georgia (22)	New Mexico (19)	
	Arkansas (23)	Illinois (22)	Virginia (19)	
	Colorado (23)	Iowa (22)	Nevada (18)	
	Florida (23)	Ohio (22)	Washington (18)	
	Hawaii (23)	Pennsylvania (22)	Mississippi (17)	
	Michigan (23)	Arizona (21)	Oregon (17)	
	Minnesota (23)	Delaware (21)	Rhode Island (17)	
	New Jersey (23)	Idaho (21)	Vermont (17)	
	North Dakota (23)	Indiana (21)		
	South Dakota (23)	Kansas (21)		
		Oklahoma (21)		
		Tennessee (21)		
		Wyoming (21)		
		Kentucky (20)		
		Missouri (20)		
		Wisconsin (20)		

*Score in points.

Source: Office of State Services, "The Institutionalized Powers of the Governorship: 1965–1985," *State Services Management Notes.* (Washington, DC: National Governors' Association, 1987), 14–17.

The Governor as Party Leader

A governor's success as party leader is vital to his or her success as governor. As a candidate, the future governor must put together a coalition to win the party's nomination; as governor, he or she must put together a legislative coalition to win approval of his or her policies. The governor's chances for success are enhanced if the governor's party members form a majority in the legislature, as long as this majority is not too large. If it is too large, different groups in the legislative party will form "factions" and probably will disagree with each other.

The best of all worlds for a governor is to represent a unified majority party in a state with a competitive two-party system. Because members of the governor's party must compete against members of the other party, it is in their best interests to support the governor and help the governor be successful. Because the governor is the leader of their party, this helps ensure their success as well. It is worth noting that the governor's role as leader of the party can put him or her at a disadvantage in a state with a divided government, that is, a state where the members of the governor's party are in a legislative minority.

The influence of the governor over the legislative party is also impacted by the governor's skills at leading the party. All governors have certain resources with which to influence party members, but their skill at using them marks the difference between a successful governor and an unsuccessful one. Successful governors use **patronage** — the power to make appointments and distribute favors — to their advantage. For example, a governor may appoint the friend of a legislator to a government position or a judgeship or award a contract to a firm in which that legislator is interested. Governors often campaign for their supporters in the legislature. Gubernatorial appearances at a rally or luncheon may make it easier for a legislator to raise money for a campaign. All this helps the governor establish allies in an attempt to sway the legislature.

LOCAL CHIEF EXECUTIVES

Chances are, your most direct and frequent encounters with political leaders will be with local executives. Local governments provide citizens with some of their most important and immediate public needs: education, health care, roads, sanitation services, police and fire protection, and recreational facilities. Local chief executives — mayors, city and county managers, and school district superintendents — have final responsibility to see that these services are delivered effectively. These local leaders, like all chief executives, are often in the limelight. A mayor attends the grand openings of industrial plants that will bring jobs and economic development to the city; a school superintendent speaks at sports banquets to honor the school districts' athletes. Like chief executives in general, they use this public exposure to enhance their persuasive power. However, like all chief executives, they bear the brunt of voter dissatisfaction if local problems develop.

Counties: Headless Horsemen

The county is a pervasive form of local government: Counties exist in all the states but Connecticut and Rhode Island. A county, unlike a city, is not created by local inhabitants to serve their unique local needs. Counties serve as an administrative arm of state governments. Originally counties stuck to their role as local agents of the state and largely administered state services such as tax assessment and collection, law enforcement, and road maintenance. However, in Chapter 5 we learned that counties are assuming more responsibility for local self-government, especially in densely populated and urbanized states.

The most obvious generalization about county chief executives is that there are none. Seventy-five percent of the nation's counties still have a **commission form** of government, with an elected county board and a number of independently elected officials. These elected officials often consist of a judge, sheriff, treasurer, clerk, auditor, coroner, and tax assessor. In general, none of these elected officials has centralized authority over the others. In a few states, the county judge presides over the county board but has few real executive powers such as the power of appointment and the power to veto board actions. In many states the judge is no longer an official of the county but is designated by the state to be part of the state judiciary.

As counties have taken over a larger range of activities and services, there has been a movement to restructure county government. The changes implemented by some county governments have centralized executive authority and/or made it more professional. The two forms of county government that incorporate these changes are the **council-administrator form** and the **council-elected executive form**.

The council-administrator form of government is the fastest growing type in American counties. It is a product of the municipal reform movement that resulted in the council-manager form of city government discussed in Chapter 9. An elected council creates policy and appoints a professional administrator to carry it out. The county manager is a trained public administrator who takes over the day-to-day management of the county, hires and fires county employees, and prepares budgets. The county manager is completely answerable to the county board and can be fired at the board's discretion.

The council-administrator form results in the professionalization of county government. It allows a highly trained specialist to provide professional leadership and frees county commissioners from day-to-day management. It is also the most likely change to be adopted at the county level because it does not require substantial changes in the structure of the county government: The jobs and power of county commissioners are not threatened, and voters are not asked to approve radical changes. Many of the criticisms leveled at the council-manager form of city government also apply to the council-administrator form. Some fear that a professional administrator is not as closely in tune with the needs of the community. Critics also worry that the county manager may exercise too much influence over elected commissioners because he or she has more knowledge and information about the day-to-day affairs of the county.

The council-elected executive form provides for an elected commission and an elected county executive or "county board president." The latter differs from the traditional county judge or county board chair chosen by peers at the first board meeting. The elected county board executive or president is the formal head of the county and frequently has appointment and veto powers that resemble those of a governor. This executive prepares the budget and the policy recommendations that are submitted to the board. A few counties combine both the council-administrator form and the council-elected executive form so that an elected county board president or the county board will appoint a professional manager.

Mayors

Whatever the political realities of municipal government, both the public and the media assume that the mayor is *the* chief executive. Mayors perform the most visible duties of city government: appearing at meetings, dinners,

Mayor Tom Bradley of Los Angeles. (*Source:* California Journal.)

and ribbon-cutting ceremonies; presiding over council meetings; handling emergencies; and meeting with state and federal leaders. Citizens with complaints about potholes in the streets or crime in the neighborhood are most likely to go to the mayor.

Chances are, a person who wants to be mayor is not expecting to get rich or have a full-time professional career. Unlike most other state and local chief executives, mayors are generally part-time officials. Most devote about 20 hours a week to the job and earn an average salary below $10,000. The larger the city, the more likely that the mayor's job will be full-time, although this is not always the case. During his four terms, San Antonio's mayor, Henry Cisneros, earned about $10,000 a year and supplemented his income by teaching at local universities. In recent years the job of big-city mayor has become more of a stepping-stone to higher office than it used to be. For example, former mayors Pete Wilson of San Diego and Richard Lugar of Indianapolis went on to serve in the U.S. Senate.

Selection of Mayors In most cities the mayor is elected directly by the people. Except in the Northeast, elections for mayor are usually nonpartisan. In about 10 percent of the nation's cities the council or commission selects one of its members to be mayor. This method is used chiefly in smaller cities. Such council-elected mayors are almost always politically weak. They do not have the force that comes from being directly elected by the people, and they usually represent only one district of the city.

Strong and Weak Mayors   In Chapter 9 we learned that the mayors can be either strong or weak depending on the form of city government. Under the *commission* and *council-manager forms* of city government, mayors are usually weak. They remain members of the council or commission, and their formal powers are usually limited to presiding over the council and serving as symbolic leaders of their cities. They have no authority to veto council actions and do not appoint the heads of city departments. The *mayor-council form* of city government can be classified as a *weak mayor* or *strong mayor* system. In weak mayor systems the mayor's appointment power is limited; some or all mayoral appointments may have to be approved by the council. The council, not the mayor, is likely to have control over the budget. In contrast, strong mayors often have many of the executive powers of a governor: significant appointment power, budget power, reorganization power, and veto power. The formal strength of a mayor is closely related to the size of a city; the strongest mayors are generally found in the largest cities, which are also the cities most likely to have strong mayor form of government.

It is important to remember, however, that all mayors have some informal influence that comes with the office. A mayor with a forceful personality and a flair for media attention can have a great deal of influence with the council and other city officials (Box 10-3). The potential use of *informal* resources is available to all chief executives.

The Roles of the Mayor   There are significant differences in the way mayors perform their job. These differences are likely to be based on two factors. The first is the extent of the mayor's legal and political resources. Does the mayor have sufficient revenue to launch new innovative programs? Is he or she a full-time mayor? Are there sufficient staff resources for the mayor to engage in policy planning, political work, and relations with the state and federal government?[30] The second factor is the mayor's subjective view of his or her role as mayor. On the one hand, a newly elected mayor may feel that his or her mission is to change the basic goals and policies of the city and thus may want to develop new programs or reorganize city government. On the other hand, a mayor may feel that his or her role is to deal individually with existing city problems without initiating new directions or goals. For a better understanding of these differences, we can divide the mayor's role into four types of leadership: the ceremonial mayor, the caretaker mayor, the program entrepreneur, and the crusader mayor.[31]

The *ceremonial mayor* is not likely to have a great deal of legal or political power or the desire to establish broad new goals and reshape city policy. This type of mayor has a modest staff and handles most problems individually. He or she generally relies on old friends and colleagues for support rather than trying aggressively to build new coalitions. The prototype of the ceremonial mayor is a personable, gregarious person who enjoys personal contacts with constituents and welcomes the opportunity to perform ceremonial tasks.

Box 10-3 **Personality and Mayoral Success: Biracial Politics in Mississippi**

Robert Walker is a former Legal Services lobbyist and NAACP field director. He is now the black mayor of Vicksburg, Mississippi, a city of more than 25,000 where a majority of the people who vote are white. Walker first won the mayor's job in a special election in the spring of 1989, outpolling his white opponent by a mere 263 votes. A year later, in June 1989, Walker was reelected to a full four-year term with more than 60 percent of the vote.

   Although blacks constitute a slight majority in Vicksburg, they cast no more than 45 percent of the vote. To get elected, Walker had to convince about a quarter of the white electorate that the city was ready for a black mayor. Walker appealed to these white votes by downplaying his advocacy role in the NAACP and repeatedly denying that he would require that a majority of the employees in city hall be black. After his election he kept his promise: "The first meeting I had, I told the department heads I didn't come to knock anybody out. Nobody who did his job had to fear for his job." The mayor continued to cultivate the confidence of white voters by taking a calm, cautious approach to city government.

   As expected, Walker's caution generated frustration and criticism from the city's black community. Where were the jobs for blacks? Where were the contracts for minority businesses? Still, Walker has agitated for change in a less publicized way. He wrote to Democratic Governor Ray Mabus to press Vicksburg's plans for inclusion in a state pilot housing program and said he wanted 25 percent of the construction contracts under that program to be set aside for black contractors.

   One of Walker's most pressing concerns will no doubt continue to be winning the confidence of the white community, and dealing successfully with the biracial politics of Vicksburg will require competence and hard work. But it will also require a special kind of personality that Robert Walker seems to possess.

Source: Alan Ehrenhalt, "For the Black Mayor of Vicksburg, Political Success Means Staying Calm," *Governing the States and Localities* (April 1989), 36–40.

The *caretaker mayor* is similar to the ceremonial mayor in many ways. This type of mayor does not establish an agenda with long-term goals but concentrates on maintaining traditional services or enhancing services that will produce political payoffs. Much of the mayor's time is spent attending to people with demands or complaints. However, a caretaker mayor has a bigger staff than that of the ceremonial mayor and is likely to delegate more authority to others.

The mayor may decide to act as a *program innovator*, that is, someone who establishes major goals and pushes for new or expanded programs to meet those goals. Only a portion of the mayor's time is spent reacting to complaints; the rest is used to carry out long-range objectives. The policy innovator makes waves. Changing the priorities of city government is going to upset entrenched interests.[32] Therefore, the program innovator will spend a great deal of time building alliances with major interest groups: the business community, federal agencies, the city council, organized labor, and universities, among others. This type of mayor is likely to have a large professional staff and will delegate authority to staff as well as to established bureaucracies.

The *crusader-mayor* is similar to the program innovator but lacks the legal and political resources that the innovator possesses. This type of mayor is very active and ambitious and has long-range goals for the city but relies on the force of personality and persuasive powers. He or she lacks the power to control city bureaucracies and motivates the public by means of a dramatic or crusading style of leadership.

These types are ideals, and a mayor cannot always be neatly classified as one of the four. However, they are useful to illustrate how the structure of the institution combines with the individual mayor's personality to create a style of leadership.

Mayors and the Intergovernmental System   Mayors determined to set and achieve long-range goals quickly realize that their success lies in large part in the hands of other governments. The most important of these governments is the state, which has legal authority over local governments. Many of the decisions that affect a mayor's ability to deal with city problems are made in the state capital. For example, a mayor who wants to establish or maintain important city programs relies on state aid for a large percentage of the revenues to fund those programs. The new interest in urban problems that has characterized state governments since the redistributing revolution of the 1960s has been both a blessing and a problem for mayors. On the one hand, states are more financially supportive of the efforts of cities to deal with urban problems. On the other hand, the trend has been for states to centralize decision making and reduce the autonomy of local officials.

In the early 1960s local governments began to rely heavily on federal aid to finance welfare, criminal justice, and health care programs. During the Reagan administration this aid was significantly reduced, and more cuts in the immediate future appear likely. The Gramm-Rudman-Hollings Act passed by Congress in 1987 imposes automatic cuts in the federal budget. One mayor called these cuts "urban terrorism" because of the reduction in aid to big cities they would bring.[33] Although this charge may be a bit extreme, the reductions will probably mean fewer street repairs, worsened bus service, the end of free tests for AIDS, and cuts in day care, job-training, education, and treatment programs for alcohol and drug abuse.

Despite mayors' dependence on the state and federal governments, the biggest constraint on their power is probably other local governments that are beyond a mayor's control. In most cities, huge policy areas are assigned to completely independent special district governments which are not even part of the city government. These "functional fiefdoms" are often run by a board of appointed officials who are independent of the mayor and city council and quickly develop their own set of vested interests. As noted in Chapter 5, the proliferation of these special districts fragments the policy-making process and makes it difficult to assign political accountability to any one official or government body. Thus the need for more unified leadership probably constitutes the single best argument for strengthening the power of the mayor.

Mayors and Economic Development For the past few years cities have been developing strategies for economic development that make them attractive to private industry. These efforts were pushed by the cuts in federal aid that took place during the Reagan administration. The Reagan and Bush administrations have instructed the cities "to wean themselves from dependence on federal aid and to prepare themselves for free-market competition."[34] Thus cities are behaving like entrepreneurs, striving for success in the national market.

Mayors play a critical role in the entrepreneurial strategies of the cities, and many mayors have been elected on economic development platforms. Mayors push for programs that will attract industry either directly or indirectly. For example, the mayor may persuade the city council to offer a firm tax incentives or below-market loans to upgrade the transportation or educational system to attract industry to the city. Bit-city mayors all over the country have led efforts to revitalize or "redevelop" downtown areas. Such revitalization entices businesses to locate in the city rather than a suburb; it also lures tourists to the city. All these strategies are designed to enhance the community's business climate.

Whereas members of the business community may advise the mayor on many issues, they are particularly involved in the politics of economic development. Mayors have created public-private partnerships, or *quasi-public organizations*, to promote economic growth. These organizations, typically made up of the mayor, city officials, and prominent members of the business community, often plan and work together to achieve a particular project or simply plan development strategies in general. For example, Denver's mayor, Federico Pena, worked very closely with the Denver Partnership, a downtown development corporation, to collaborate on a downtown master plan. The purpose of the plan was to direct and promote development in and around the central business district. A 27-member panel consisting of city officials, representatives of business interests, and community leaders served as the steering committee for the project. However, the Denver Partnership provided three-quarters of the initial funding and two-thirds of the staff for the project.[35]

The influence of the business community on economic development has generally been helpful to mayors. With the reduction of federal aid, many people believe that development policy provides the only lasting solution to the problem of financing local improvements. A mayor's efforts to attract or revitalize industry usually have wide support. However, this situation is not conflict-free. Neighborhood groups sometimes react suspiciously to economic development projects that threaten to disrupt their neighborhoods; they also may resent the time and resources devoted to economic development policies at the expense of neighborhood services. One of the most important challenges for mayors in the 1990s will be to create a consensus for development policies that benefit landowners and developers and at the same time generate a fiscal surplus that can be shared with the rest of the city (Box 10-4).

City Managers

The city manager holds a unique position in local government. Managers provide leadership but do not generally possess independent political power. They depend on elected officials for continued employment but are not political appointees. The manager is a trained professional public administrator who both assists and leads the council. Although managers establish contacts with leaders in the community, the manager is generally unable to build a power base to use against the council in battles of will. The manager's job is to inform elected officials, recommend actions those officials should take, and implement the policies they establish.

Although an increasing number of women are entering the field, the typical city manager is a white male in his thirties or forties who has a college degree. The average tenure is about five years. In earlier years, when managers were seen strictly as technicians, they tended to have an engineering background. Today, however, a city manager is likely to have a degree in the social sciences, specifically a bachelor's or Master's degree in public administration.

The Modern Role of the City Manager   The change in the credentials of city managers reflects the change in the nature of the job. Although managers administer city policies and manage city employees, they are taking a more active role in *making* policy. In council-manager cities, most policy originates with the manager, who presents a range of alternatives to the council and recommends a course of action. Managers are usually very powerful because they possess a near monopoly of technical information; almost all contacts with the municipal bureaucracy take place through the manager. Many managers prepare the city budget with little or no input from council members, and the council members often vote yes or no, that is, "up or down," on the manager's budget proposal. Managers even exercise control over the issues the council discusses; they meet with the presiding officer of the city council to prepare the agenda for council meetings.

Relationship with the Council   In Chapter 9 we discussed the advantages and disadvantages of the different forms of municipal government. A mayor-council system with a strong mayor is often the most appropriate

Box 10-4 **Need Neighborhood Services? Try Hiring the Neighbors**

Tom Fink, the mayor of Anchorage, Alaska, has found one answer to the problem of maintaining municipal services in the face of declining revenues. He has enlisted neighborhoods to provide neighborhood services. This neighborhood-based system for service delivery dates back to 1974, when the city contracted with a local group of users to maintain and operate the recently built midtown ice-skating arena. A new arena serving the city's northern area is now managed by a nonprofit community corporation.

Fink points to numerous success stories. The Anchorage Softball Association provides daily infield maintenance at two neighborhood softball complexes. The city continues to maintain the outfield areas on a less frequent basis. In return for the field and stadium maintenance provided by local summer league baseball teams, the city pays for the lights at the stadium—a pretty good deal when the days lengthen to 18 hours.

Community leaders in the predominantly low-income neighborhood of Mountain View have organized volunteers to spot and report zoning violations, remove abandoned vehicles and trash piles, and refurbish and maintain neighborhood recreational centers and parks. Municipal assistance has come in the form of design expertise and donated plants, cooperation and training from municipal zoning officials, and free dump passes for people willing to haul their own trash to the municipal landfill.

In all these cases both the city and the organization benefit. The neighborhood gets services it wants and needs, and the cost to the city is far less than that of hiring full-time workers to do the job. For example, the city is paying $60,000 over a four-year period for the maintenance of ski trails. If the city had to do the work itself, the cost, including employee benefits, would be more like $280,000.

Fink points out that there are potential pitfalls. Union difficulties may arise because of the displacement of municipal employees. Anchorage officials have always been careful not to replace employed workers with the less costly alternative. The idea has worked best when services that could not be staffed by the city under existing budget constraints are extended into new neighborhoods.

Another pitfall is a possible lack of consistent leadership within the neighborhood groups that take on the obligation to provide services. Fear that the group will not perform explains why the government hesitates to enter into such an agreement in the first place. The experience of Anchorage flies in the face of that belief largely because certain individuals have made these partnerships work. As Fink says, "Our successes have depended largely on the tireless effort of several dynamic individuals. Long-term continuation of the effort, should those individuals depart, could be problematic." As we point out consistently in this text, individuals, *do* make a difference in government.

Source: Tom Fink, "Need Neighborhood services? Try Hiring the Neighbors," *Governing: The States and Localities* (October 1989), 86.

form of government for a large city because the mayor is best equipped to hold many powerful interests together. However, a strong mayor-council system institutionalizes conflict in a traditional separation-of-powers arrangement. Neither the council nor the mayor can impose solutions on the other, and so resolution of conflict is often difficult.

A more harmonious relationship exists between the city manager and the council. No formal separation of powers exists, and its absence creates an atmosphere where a cooperative relationship between council and executive is possible. Other factors encourage harmony. Because the council appoints the manager, the two share similar goals for the community. Managers who can be fired at will by the council almost always work to advance the council's goals.

A survey of city officials in both council-manager and mayor-council cites showed that council-manager cities had significantly smoother relationships between the executive and the council. Table 10.4 indicates that *all* council members responding in the council-manager cities reported that the council and manager had a good working relationship, but only 56.5 percent of the council members in strong mayor-council cities shared this opinion. A very large majority (76.9 percent) of council members in council-manager cities reported that the manager generally provided the council with sufficient alternatives for making policy decisions, while only 29 percent of council members in mayor-council cities reported satisfaction with

Table 10.4   COUNCIL-EXECUTIVE RELATIONS

Description	Form of government*			
	Council-manager		Strong mayor-council	
	Council members agree (%)	Department heads agree (%)	Council members agree (%)	Department heads agree (%)
The council and manager (or mayor) have a good working relationship	100.0	75.7	56.5	52.1
The manager or mayor provides the council with sufficient alternatives for policy decisions	76.9	90.9	29.1	56.2
The council effectively draws on the expertise of the professional staff	76.9	76.1	54.2	47.9
Intervention by a council member is necessary to get an adequate response to a citizen's complaint	34.6	7.5	66.7	14.6

*The forms of government included six council-manager and five strong mayor-council cities.

Source: International City Management Association, *The Municipal Yearbook,* vol. 55 (Washington, DC: International City Management Association, 1988), 25. Reprinted by permission.

the range of alternatives. Council members in council-manager cities showed more confidence in executive expertise and the executive's ability to handle citizens' complaints.

These data should not give one the idea that conflict between manager and council does not exist. The fact that a city manager holds the job for only an average of about five years tells us that all is not paradise. Managers may resent council involvement in what they feel is their traditional role. Just as managers are becoming more involved in policy-making, politicians are becoming more involved and assertive in service delivery and the implementation of policy. Political problems may arise for a manager. Managers may become alienated from some members of the council if they come to be identified with one faction in a badly divided council. Managers are bureaucrats, and they are sometimes criticized for stereotypical bureaucratic behavior such as waste, inefficiency, and rigidity. A manager's unwillingness to be flexible may anger council members who are elected and who may be willing to bend policies for the good of their political futures.

School Superintendents

The job of school superintendents is often a paradox: they are among the most respected and yet most controversial of public administrators. Deference comes from the fact that the superintendent has a large degree of professional expertise on education. Since Americans place a great value on education, they are likely to respect educational "experts." However, education is a sensitive and value-laden process. Educational policy-making involves teachers who want to be paid sufficiently for their professional efforts and want to be part of the policy-making process. It involves parents who want their children to learn to read and write and compute but also want them to learn specific values. It involves taxpayers who want the whole process to be done at a reasonable cost.

What Superintendents Do A superintendent is hired by what is usually an elected school board to be a professional manager of the school district. The superintendent's responsibilities fall into four broad categories: personnel, financial management, administration, and curriculum and instruction. Hiring and firing a high school principal, recruiting a basketball coach, promoting a teacher to an administrative position, and hiring and firing the school system's budget director are all part of a superintendent's *personnel* responsibilities. As part of the *financial* responsibilities, superintendents, along with their staff, propose the district's budget and submit it to the board for approval; they also authorize expenditures for allocated funds. Superintendents *administer* the day-to-day operations of the school district, which can be anything from authorizing a school drug search to deciding on school bus routes. Finally, superintendents are primarily responsible for recommending and implementing changes in the schools' *curriculum*: organizing grade levels, deciding which courses to cut, and choosing which extracurricular activities to offer. Superintendents, depending on the school district, have varying amounts of responsibility for each of these areas.

A superintendent, like a city manager, is a professional administrator who is not expected to engage in partisan politics. In the minds of most Americans, a superintendent is a politically neutral figure, and he or she makes an effort to project an image of a person whose only interest is setting the best course for public education. In reality the superintendent probably has a set of goals for the school district, and the success of those goals depends on political support from the board and the community. Thus, like all chief executives, superintendents use their informal powers, which come from visibility and association with the public. Although superintendents do not rub elbows in the grimy world of partisan politics, they make frequent public appearances, give speeches to civic groups, issue press releases, and belong to several community organizations. As the authors of an important study note, a superintendent "appeals to the public on a subtle level by projecting himself as the foremost authority in the community over a policy area where knowledge rather than political influence should prevail."[36]

Relations Between Superintendents and Boards The typical local school board is composed of laypersons serving on a part-time basis. This and the fact that school districts have become larger and more complex to operate mean that boards are deferring more and more to the expertise and recommendations of the superintendent. This is especially true in large, urban, heterogeneous school districts which are run by large bureaucracies.

The tendency of superintendents to dominant boards does not mean that the relationship between the two is always harmonious. Indeed, the trend in the last few years has been toward increasing conflict. Several factors account for these disagreements. The superintendent may develop the attitude that he or she is the expert and view the school district as a personal possession, resenting any attempt by the board to infringe on his or her authority. Conflict may arise from the way the superintendent and the board view their roles. One study showed that in many areas, both felt they should have more authority.[37] For example, both parties felt they should have more authority over personnel matters. Thus this area of a superintendent's responsibility is ripe for a collision with the board. Newly elected board members may not understand the extent of their authority and feel that their role includes managing the day-to-day responsibilities of the district. Finally, certain issues in education policy that are especially controversial have generated conflict between boards and superintendents. The most prominent example is school desegregation.

Certain policies and procedures instituted by a school board or superintendent can help prevent or relieve conflict. To clarify the role of the board and the superintendent, it is a good idea for a district to have a district policy manual which defines the specific responsibilities of each party. A clear definition of roles and responsibilities will help resolve conflicts. Another helpful tactic is to discuss a problem as soon as it is identified. Not doing so means that the problem may fester and become bigger. One method for identifying problems is regular performance reviews for superintendents; these reviews make it possible for the board to raise its concerns before they become major issues. Boards also need to review their own performance periodically to see if they are fulfilling their roles properly. The superintendent should be involved in this review process.[38]

Conclusion

Chief executives at all levels—federal, state, and local—have common functions. All serve as symbols of their respective governments and in doing so command a certain amount of informal persuasive power. All chief executives administer public policy and direct and coordinate the actions of public bureaucracies. Most are responsible for initiating major policy goals and preparing and presenting budgets to legislative bodies.

Although Americans have harbored a general suspicion of executive authority, the strength of state executive power has been enhanced significantly since the 1950s and 1960s. This enhanced authority is evident in large, populous states which tend to have large gubernatorial staffs, that is, institutionalized governorships. However, recent evaluations of gubernatorial power have revealed that while the formal powers of governors over executive branches have increased, the powers of governors vis-à-vis legislatures have decreased.

Today's governors tend to be younger and more aggressive about pursuing innovative policy goals. The decline in federal aid to the states has forced the states to assume more initiative and responsibility for public programs. Although the states have responded unevenly, many progressive governors have demonstrated impressive leadership skills.

Among local chief executives, there is a great deal of variation in terms of the strength and centralization of authority. Although counties have traditionally decentralized executive authority in county commissions and other elected county offices, some large urban counties are using a manager or elected executive to manage county government. Mayoral authority varies from the weak mayor, found primarily in council-manager and commission forms of city government, to the strong mayor, found in mayor-council cities. There are significant differences in the way mayors perform their jobs. These differences are usually attributable to the amount of legal and political resources mayors possess and their subjective view of what their role should be. Mayors, like governors, find themselves constrained by other governments, not the least of which are the special district governments, or "functional fiefdoms," that exist beyond the control of general-purpose governments.

The city manager is a professional manager who both assists and leads the elected city council. In addition to their administrative duties, managers have assumed more responsibility for initiating and making policy. Because managers, unlike strong mayors, do not operate under a system of separation of powers, they generally enjoy more harmonious relationships with councils.

Whereas most special district managers operate in the shadowy confines of invisible governments, school superintendents are highly visible and often controversial. The superintendent enjoys a reputation as a respected professional. At the same time, the administration of the most sensitive public policies makes a superintendent vulnerable to criticism from both school boards and the general public. Although tension between superintendents and elected school boards is increasing, certain policies and procedures are useful in preventing or relieving conflict.

Study Objectives

1. Describe functions that are unique to chief administrators.
2. Identify factors in the 1950s and 1960s that were important in enhancing the power of governors.
3. In recent years there have been many changes in the office of governor. Discuss the concept of the modern governor.
4. Define what is meant by gubernatorial appointment power. Explain why there are often constraints on this power.
5. Explain why it is important for governors to have responsibility for preparing and submitting the first draft of the state budget.
6. Pretend that you are the governor of your state. Discuss the strategies that you would employ to influence the state legislature to adopt your legislative program.
7. Describe the four different roles of the mayor and try to provide an example of each.
8. Discuss the duties and responsibilities of city managers. Identify the basis for harmony between city managers and city councils. Identify potential causes of conflict between these managers and councils.
9. Describe the four broad responsibilities of school superintendents. Identify reasons for conflict between superintendents and school boards and suggest how such conflict can be prevented.

Glossary

commission form of county government Consists of an elected board and a number of elected officials such as county judge, county sheriff, and county clerk.
constraints Restrictions on the power of a governor that limit the control the governor exercises over legislative bodies and bureaucracies.

council-administrator form of county government Consists of an elected council that appoints a professional administrator to carry out council policy.

council-elected executive form of county government Consists of an elected commission and an elected county executive or county board president.

executive amendment Allows the governor to veto a bill and send it back to the legislature with recommended changes. If the legislature agrees to the governor's suggestions, the governor will sign the bill into law.

executive order A rule or regulation issued by the governor that has the effect of law. Executive orders are used to create or modify the organization or procedures of administrative agencies.

formal powers Governors' powers which come from legal and constitutional provisions.

impeachment Bringing formal charges against an executive official or judge. An official who is impeached and convicted is removed from office.

informal powers A chief executive's power to influence or persuade by virtue of holding a highly visible office.

institutionalized governorship Staff and bureaucracies established to assist the governor. It is usually found in larger states.

line item veto Allows the governor to veto a single item within an appropriations bill rather than vetoing the entire bill.

long ballot Most executives within state government are elected independently and are removed from control by the governor.

merit system Sometimes referred to as "civil service." People are hired for government jobs on the basis of their qualifications.

patronage Sometimes referred to as the spoils system. Parties have the power to dispense government jobs to the supporters of party politicians and policies.

personalized governorship The lack of staff or bureaucracies to assist the governor. It is usually found in smaller states.

program A series of policy proposals that governors or mayors and their advisers develop during a campaign.

plural executive Sometimes referred to as an unintegrated executive. Most high-level executive officials are independently elected by the voters in a state.

pocket veto A special veto power exercised by the governor at the end of a legislative session. Bills not signed by the governor die after a specified time.

Endnotes

1. The concept of persuasive power was most clearly described in Richard E. Neustadt's definitive study of the presidency, *Presidential Power* (New York: Wiley, 1960, 1980).
2. Coleman B. Ransone, Jr., *Governing the American States* (Westport, CT: Greenwood, 1978), 96 Copyright 1978 by the National Governors' Association.
3. Regina K. Brough, "The Powers of the Gubernatorial CEO: Variations Among the States," *Journal of State Government* 59 (July-August 1986), 59.
4. Regina K. Brough, "Strategies for Leaders Who Do Not Have a Lot of Power," *Journal of State Government* 60 (July-August 1987), 157.
5. Cited in David Wessel, "Can-Do Capitals: States Enlarge Roles as Congress Is Unable to Solve Problems," *Wall Street Journal* (June 28, 1988), 1.

6. Larry Sabato, *Goodbye to Goodtime Charlie: The American Governorship Transformed* (Washington, DC: Congressional Quarterly Press, 1983), 19.
7. Wessel, 1.
8. See, for example, "A Day in the Life of a Governor," in Center for Policy Research, *Governing the American States—A Handbook for New Governors* (Washington, DC: National Governors' Association, 1978), 10–20.
9. Thad H. Beyle, "Governors' Views on Being Governor," in Thad L. Beyle and Lynn R. Munchmore, eds., *Being Governor: The View from the Office* (Durham, NC: Duke University Press, 1983), 30. Also published in *State Government*, 52 (Summer 1979).
10. Ibid., 30.
11. Advisory Commission on Intergovernmental Relations, "The Question of State Government Capability," (Washington, DC: 1985), 6.
12. Ibid., 7.
13. Richard P. Nathan and Fred C. Doolittle, *The Consequences of Cuts: The Effects of the Reagan Domestic Program on State and Local Government* (Princeton, NJ: Princeton University Urban and Regional Research Center, 1983).
14. Ann O'M. Bowman and Richard C. Kearney, *The Resurgence of the States* (Englewood Cliffs, NJ: Prentice-Hall, 1986), 27.
15. Sabato, 19–20.
16. Ibid., 31.
17. Lee Sigelman and Roland Smith, "Personal, Office and State Characteristics as Predictors of Gubernatorial Performance," *Journal of Politics* 43 (February 1981), 169–180.
18. Thad L. Beyle, "The Governors, 1986–87," in Council of State Governments, *The Book of the States*, (Lexington, KY: CSG, 1988), 30.
19. James K. Conant, "Gubernatorial Strategy and Style: Keys to Improving Executive Branch Mangement," *Journal of State Government* 59 (July-August 1986), 82.
20. Thad L. Beyle and Robert Dalton, "Appointment Power: Does It Belong to the Governor?" in Beyle and Munchmore, eds., 113.
21. Although the U.S. Supreme Court has ruled that the legislative veto violates the separation of powers provision of the U.S. Constitution, the ruling does not apply to states.
22. Sarah McCally Morehouse, *State Politics, Parties, and Policy* (New York: Holt, Rinehart & Winston, 1981), 250–251.
23. See Milton Shapp's comments in Center for Policy Research, *Reflections on Being Governor* (Washington, DC: National Governors' Association, 1981), 34.
24. Richard C. Kearney, "How a 'Weak' Governor Can be Strong: Dick Riley and Education Reform in South Carolina," *Journal of State Government* 60 (July-August 1987), 150–156.
25. Thad L. Beyle, "The Governor as Chief Legislator," in Beyle and Munchmore, eds., 134–137.
26. Beyle, *Book of the States, 1988–89*, 30.
27. Beyle, "The Governor as Chief Legislator," 140.
28. Office of State Services, "The Institutionalized Powers of the Governorship: 1965–1985," in *State Management Notes*, (Washington, DC: National Governors' Association, 1987) 14–17.
29. Sabato, 80.

30. Jeffrey Pressman, "The Preconditions for Mayoral Leadership," *American Political Science Review* 66 (June 1972), 512–513, 522.

31. For an extensive discussion of these categories, see Pressman, "The Preconditions for Mayoral Leadership," John P. Kotter and Paul R. Lawrence, *Mayors in Action: Five Approaches to Urban Government* (New York: Wiley, 1974), chap. 7, and John J. Harrigan, *Political Change in the Metropolis*, 4th ed. (Glenview, IL: Scott, Foresman, 1989), 202–205.

32. Robert L. Lineberry and Edmund P. Fowler, "Reformism and Public Policies in American Cities," *American Political Science Review* 61 (September 1967), 701–716.

33. Thomas G. Donlan, "The Oxen that Roared: Politicians Speak Out about the Effects of Gramm-Rudman Budget Cuts," *Barrons*, (February 10, 1986), 27.

34. Dennis R. Judd and Randy L. Ready, "Entrepreneurial Cities and the New Politics of Economic Development," in George E. Peterson and Carol W. Lewis, eds., *Reagan and the Cities* (Washington, DC: Urban Institute, 1986), 210.

35. Ibid., 226.

36. L. Harmon Zeigler and M. Kent Jennings, with G. Wayne Peak, *Governing American Schools: Political Interaction in Local School Districts* (North Scituate, MA: Duxbury, 1974), 152.

37. Donald T. Alvey and Kenneth E. Underwood, "School Boards and Superintendents: How They Perceive Each Other," *Education Digest* 51 (February 1986), 46–49.

38. J. G. Hayden, "Superintendent-School Board Conflict: Working It Out," *Education Digest* 52 (April 1987), 11–13.

Chapter
11

The Many Limbs of the Executive Branch

Laws initiated and approved by chief executives and passed by legislatures are put into effect by employees of the executive branch. These employees work in agencies, bureaus, departments, divisions, and offices that are collectively referred to as bureaucracies. Bureaucrats are the public officials most likely to come into contact with the average citizen. A real estate salesperson who wants to be licensed, an out-of-work carpenter who claims unemployment compensation, and a high school senior seeking admission to a state university all deal with public bureaucracies and bureaucrats.

Since the Great Depression and Franklin Roosevelt's New Deal of the 1930s, the size and scope of federal, state, and local governments have increased dramatically. The growth in government programs has been accompanied by an expanding bureaucracy to do the work. Most of the atten-

(Courtesy of Conklin/Monkmeyer.)

tion to and criticism of this trend have focused on the "bloated" federal bureaucracy, but in recent years the growth of state and local bureaucracies has exceeded that at the federal level. In 1953, 63 percent of all public employees worked for state and local governments; in 1986, the figure was 83 percent.[1]

The expanding size of administration is another source of the irritation and suspicion that Americans have always felt for bureaucracy. Ronald Reagan's remark in his inaugural speech of 1981 that "government is not the solution to the problem, government is the problem" echoes the sentiments of many citizens. However, the size of the bureaucracy is a direct result of the services that citizens demand. We expect state and local governments to provide free public education, investigate cases of child abuse, maintain recreational parks, solve crimes and put people in jail, and regulate utility companies. It is the employees of the executive branches of our state and local governments who do all these things.

Criticism of bureaucrats derives not so much from what they do but from the conflicting standards of performance that we expect them to meet. The public expects bureaucrats to be both *effective* and *responsive*. These two goals are not the same; they may even contradict each other. **Effectiveness** is the degree to which an administrator's decisions are more likely than are alternative choices to bring about the desired outcomes, that is, to make policies work.[2] We expect the employees of public agencies to make their decisions on the basis of technical expertise, not on the basis of pressure from politicians (Box 11-1). We demand that the managers of public bureaucracies run their agencies smoothly and effectively, that is, "run them like a business."

Box 11-1 **The Problems of the Texas State Board of Insurance**

In January 1989, the Texas State Board of Insurance found itself the target of two of the toughest politicians in Texas: Attorney General Jim Mattox, an all but announced candidate for governor, and State Senator John Montford, a former Marine officer and prosecutor. Charges of waste, cronyism, and patronage were echoed by Mattox's remark that the agency was carrying on an "incestuous relationship with the industry it regulates." Montford, chair of the powerful Senate State Affairs Committee, initiated hearings to investigate the agency and called for the resignation of its three commissioners.

The two politicians and other critics of the insurance board believe that the board has been "captured" by the interest it is supposed to regulate. In other words, the insurance board is controlled by the insurance industry in Texas. Instead of regulating the insurance industry to protect the interest of the public, the insurance board takes a proindustry position. At the very least, the board may overlook abuses by individual insurance companies or fail to enforce state regulations that these companies violate.

Although **capture** of state regulatory agencies does not always occur, several factors inevitably encourage it. The most important factor is the need for insurance regulators to be "experts." Selling insurance these days is a complicated business. Thus many of those charged with regulating the insurance industry come from the industry itself. Who else is going to be as familiar with the business as insurance executives are? Who else is going to be as *effective* at insurance regulation?

When these executives finish their stint as appointed insurance commissioners, they probably will return to their insurance companies. Going from an industry to a regulatory board and back to the industry is known as the **revolving door syndrome**. This syndrome helps account for the allegations of capture of regulatory agencies by the industries they regulate.

The process of capture illustrates the problem of conflicting standards for bureaucracy. On the one hand, we want those who regulate the private sector to be effective, that is, knowledgeable about what they are doing. On the other hand, we want these executives and the bureaucrats who work for them to respond to the interest of the public in general. Sometimes, as the problems of the Texas State Board of Insurance reveal, it is hard to live up to both standards.

Responsiveness is the extent to which decisions by bureaucrats reflect the preferences of the community or the officeholders authorized to speak for the public.[3] When bureaucrats implement public policies, we insist that they be sensitive to the needs and demands of the public and accountable to the elected politicians who represent the public. There are times when the most effective decisions are not the most responsive. For example, the parole and probation of criminal offenders may be more effective than incarceration in the rehabilitation of these offenders. Chances are, however, the

Box 11-2 Awards for Creative Nonresponsiveness

James Boren is a former bureaucrat who is concerned about bureaucratic nonresponsiveness and red tape. In 1972, after years of tangling with unbending bureaucrats, he quit the Foreign Service and founded the International Association of Professional Bureaucrats.

The association awards the ''Order of the Bird'' to agencies and companies that exhibit truly ''creative nonresponsiveness.'' Each trophy is a Boren original featuring a featherless, potbellied bird customized for the award winner. American Airlines won a plane-shaped bird wearing smoked glasses for trying to make a pilot fly after two eye operations and the revocation of his license by the Federal Aviation Administration. A Budweiser distributor in New York got a bird for frustrating participants in a recycling program by demanding that 31,920 cans be examined to see if each one actually came from New York. (They found $4.62 worth of out-of-state cans.)

Boren has proposed that paper-pushing bureaucrats could end war. Proclaiming the motto ''Peace through better documentation,'' he urges an exchange of military personnel between the United States and the Soviet Union, saying that the resulting increase in paperwork will leave ''no time for Star Wars.''

Source: *The Giraffe Gazette* 5(2) (Spring, 1989), 3.

public prefers, if not demands, incarceration. The failure of state and local government employees to meet either of these goals inevitably evokes the wrath of the public and its elected representatives.

In this chapter we will examine the functions bureaucracies perform, the ways in which state and local executive branches are organized to do business, the role of state and local bureaucracies in our federal system, and the ways in which individual citizens can participate in bureaucratic decision making. Finally, we will discuss ideas and reforms that are designed to make state and local bureaucracies more effective and/or responsive (Box 11-2).

FUNCTIONS OF BUREAUCRACY

In theory, the job of the executive branch is to implement and enforce policies made by legislatures and chief executives. However, in practice, the activities of executive agencies go far beyond this technical division of responsibilities. Bureaucrats *do* execute policy, but they are also involved in making policy and reviewing its impact. For this reason we will examine three major functions of bureaucracy: administration, rule making, and adjudication.

Administration

"Administer" is another word for "execute," "enforce," or "apply." The oldest job of executive branches is to administer laws and policies established by policymakers. Once policymakers decide on a policy or course of action, they must direct an executive agency to put that policy into effect. The agency makes specific decisions that are needed to put the policy in place and assumes the day-to-day tasks of carrying it out. For example, a county commission may decide to allocate county funds for a county park and recreation center; the county parks and recreation department is responsible for collecting user fees from persons who use the county facility and for overseeing its maintenance. A state that is required to implement federally mandated controls on the use of pesticides may assign regulation to a state agency that spells out for chemical firms, farmers, and aerial spraying firms just which pesticides can be used and the limits on that use. Thus policymaking without administration means no policy at all.

Rule Making

In addition to *executing* policy, modern bureaucracies are playing an increasingly larger role in *making* policy. Industrialization, urbanization, and the technological complexity of our society mean that elected officials require the help of experts to make policy decisions. Legislatures, especially the part-time variety that are found in many state and local governments, are simply not able to address many technical problems with specific solutions. To execute these specific solutions, legislatures delegate authority to executive agencies to draft rules or guidelines. These rules lay out the specific actions to be taken to achieve the goal of the policy. For example, most state legislators agree on the need to regulate medical services. Without regulation, the public may be harmed by unqualified or unscrupulous doctors, some making exaggerated claims for "cures" and treatments and some simply playing roles for which they have no training. However, most state legislators know very little about the highly technical field of medicine. Hence, regulation of physicians is the responsibility of the state medical board.

The delegation of authority to executive agencies is referred to as **bureaucratic discretion**. Some people say that the delegation of broad rule-making authority to administrative agencies is one of the most important characteristics of contemporary American government.[4] Bureaucratic discretionary authority *is* a cause for concern. Because agency rules or regulations have almost the same impact as laws, the authority to make these rules gives the bureaucracy **quasi-legislative power**. Critics worry that the bureaucracy has become a fourth branch of government and that bureaucratic discretion violates the principle of separation of powers. They are worried that the powerful executive officials who make these rules are not responsive either to elected representatives or to the public. Still, delegation of authority to the bureaucracy is a necessity of modern government. The large number of problems that face elected officials and the technical nature of the solutions to these problems force bureaucratic experts to assume responsibility. Furthermore, legislators depend on experts from the bureaucracy for advice in revising old laws and making new ones.

Revising Rules: Adjudication

Just as legislatures have willingly yielded legislative power to administrative agencies, the courts have given these agencies judicial power. Agencies decide more cases and controversies than do courts of law. A disagreement that results from an agency rule is generally decided by the rule-making agency itself. A court may eventually hear a case involving a disputed agency rule, but only *after* the agency reviews and rules on the case. For example, a welfare client deprived of benefits or a public housing tenant faced with eviction may demand a hearing by the appropriate agency. These hearings resemble court trials; an aggrieved party is usually represented by counsel and may bring in sympathetic witnesses to testify in his or her behalf. If the protesting party is still not satisfied after the hearing, he or she may appeal to the courts.

The power of administrative agencies to judge cases involving agency rules is referred to as **quasi-judicial power**. Agencies are given this power because the number of rules subject to dispute and the technical nature of those rules make it necessary for bureaucrats to assume a central role in their interpretation.

The significance of administrative agencies becomes obvious when one considers that they combine all three traditional institutional functions: legislative, executive, and judicial. Agencies make rules that have the force of law, execute those rules, and judge the validity of those rules.

THE NATURE OF BUREAUCRATIC ORGANIZATION

To effectively administer laws passed by legislatures and rules established by agencies, state and local executive branches must possess many of the characteristics of classic bureaucracies.[5] To varying degrees, these characteristics include division of labor, expertise, hierarchical organization, and standardized procedures.

1. *Division of labor.* The responsibilities of bureaucrats are subdivided in various ways so that agencies are like people on an assembly line, each having a specific function to perform.

2. *Expertise.* The division of labor in bureaucracies allows employees to become experts in specific areas. Bureaucrats concentrate their attention on specific problems and deal day in and day out with the same tasks. Employees of public bureaucracies are likely to have job security, and most expect to spend their working careers in their agency or department. Thus long years of experience add to their expertise.

3. *Arrangement of the various units of the bureaucracy in a hierarchy, that is, a pyramidal form of organization.* Authority flows down from a single top administrator—a governor or mayor—and responsibility flows up the pyramid.[6] Almost everyone in every bureaucracy has a boss and, unless one is at the bottom of the hierarchy, some subordinates.

4. *Standardized procedures.* State and local bureaucracies, like all bureaucracies, operate in accordance with fixed rules and regulations, that is, "by the book." Communications are generally formalized through memos, and permanent records are kept of bureaucratic actions. All these formal rules help bureaucracies function effectively.

According to people who study organizations, these characteristics help assure that public services are delivered effectively. However, as we've noted, an organization that is effective may not be politically responsive to the public in general. Hence, state and local bureaucracies deviate from these classic characteristics. The managers of executive branches are not usually experts and career bureaucrats but elected or appointed officials. State and local bureaucratic structures may not follow the pyramidal form of organization in which final authority and responsibility are placed in the hands of a governor or mayor. In short, state and local executive branches deviate from the classic characteristics of bureaucratic structure in order to enhance accountability to the public and to the elected officials who represent the public.

ORGANIZATION OF STATE EXECUTIVE BRANCHES

Students of American national government know that the federal executive branch is organized in a cabinet-style structure that gives the President the authority to appoint and remove the heads, or secretaries, of cabinet-level departments. Although 36 states have so-called cabinet systems, very few give the governor authority to appoint or remove important cabinet-level officials.[7] As Table 11.1 shows, the lieutenant governor, secretary of state, attorney general, and treasurer are generally constitutionally created positions that are elected by the public. In states with Jacksonian constitutions the voters elect department heads in other policy areas, such as agriculture, commerce, and education. As noted earlier, the election of these **plural executives** denies the governor control over the executive branch, fragments decision making, and ultimately makes it difficult for the electorate to assign responsibility.

Table 11.1　METHODS OF SELECTION OF STATE EXECUTIVE OFFICIALS

State	Lieutenant governor	Secretary of state	Attorney general	Treasurer
Alabama	E	E	E	E
Alaska	E	*	GB	GB
Arizona	*	E	E	E
Arkansas	E	E	E	E
California	E	E	E	E
Colorado	E	E	E	E
Connecticut	E	E	E	E
Delaware	E	GS	E	E
Florida	E	E	E	E
Georgia	E	E	E	A
Hawaii	E	*	GS	A
Idaho	E	E	E	E
Illinois	E	E	E	E
Indiana	E	E	E	E
Iowa	E	E	E	E
Kansas	E	E	E	E
Kentucky	E	E	E	E
Louisiana	E	E	E	E
Maine	*	L	L	L
Maryland	E	GS	E	L
Massachusetts	E	E	E	E
Michigan	E	E	E	GS
Minnesota	E	E	E	E
Mississippi	E	E	E	E
Missouri	E	E	E	E
Montana	E	E	E	A
Nebraska	E	E	E	E
Nevada	E	E	E	E
New Hampshire	*	L	G	L
New Jersey	*	GS	GS	GS
New Mexico	E	E	E	E
New York	E	GS	E	GS
North Carolina	E	E	E	E
North Dakota	E	E	E	E
Ohio	E	E	E	E
Oklahoma	E	GS	E	E
Oregon	*	E	E	E
Pennsylvania	E	GS	E	E
Rhode Island	E	E	E	E
South Carolina	E	E	E	E
South Dakota	E	E	E	E
Tennessee	*	L	SC	L
Texas	E	GS	E	E
Utah	E	*	E	E

continued

Table 11.1   METHODS OF SELECTION OF STATE EXECUTIVE OFFICIALS (continued)

State	Lieutenant governor	Secretary of state	Attorney general	Treasurer
Vermont	E	E	E	E
Virginia	E	GB	E	GB
Washington	E	E	E	E
West Virginia	*	E	E	E
Wisconsin	E	E	E	E
Wyoming	*	E	GS	E

*No specific chief administrative official or agency in charge of function.

E = elected by public; G = appointed by governor; GS = appointed by governor and approved by senate; GB = Appointed by governor and approved by both houses of legislature; A = Appointed by administrative official or board; L = Elected by legislature; SC = Elected by state supreme court.

Source: Council of State Governments, *The Book of the States, 1986–87* (Lexington, KY: Council of State Governments, 1987), 53.

The Lieutenant Governor

One of the most confusing roles in state executive branches is that of the lieutenant governor, who in many states has both executive and legislative functions. The lieutenant governor usually presides over the state senate, casting a tie-breaking vote when necessary. In some states this official assumes more important legislative functions, and the power to appoint committee chairs, schedule debate, and assign bills to committees can make a lieutenant governor a powerful force in state politics.

In most states the lieutenant governor's primary executive responsibility is to succeed the governor if the governor dies, retires, is impeached, or becomes incapacitated. This position in the line of success makes this office the main stepping-stone to the governorship, and many view it as a kind of training ground for governors. Indeed, the list of lieutenant governors who moved up to higher office reads like a *Who's Who of American Government:* Governor Mario Cuomo of New York, former Senator Thomas Eagleton of Missouri, Governor Charles Robb of Virginia, Paul Laxalt, adviser to President Reagan and former senator from Nevada, and Senator Paul Simon of Illinois.[8] However, the office bears the brunt of criticism and jokes because its occupant often does little but wait around to become governor. A recent lieutenant governor of Nevada expressed his frustration with the job when he said that he spent most of his time "checking the obituaries to see if I should be in Carson City."[9]

However, the office of lieutenant governor is becoming more significant. One of the most important trends is that of electing the governor and lieutenant governor as a team. Rather than have the voters select the lieutenant governor as a separate and independent executive, 22 states have the candidates for governor and lieutenant governor from each party run as a team. This encourages compatibility between the two and avoids the embarrassment and friction of having a governor and lieutenant governor from different parties. A lieutenant governor who is a member of a partisan team is much more likely to support the governor and can be an invaluable source of influence over the legislature.

Another noteworthy trend is the increase in the executive or administrative role of lieutenant governors. Thirty states now authorize the governor to delegate executive duties to the lieutenant governor, and governors in other states have done this without explicit authority. Although governors who run as part of a team are more likely to assign their lieutenant governors executive responsibilities, almost all governors do so to some extent.[10] Some states even make the lieutenant governor the head of one or more executive departments. In Indiana, for example, the lieutenant governor is director of the department of commerce and commissioner of agriculture. In Georgia, the lieutenant governor sits on the state's economic development council, finance and investment commission, and building authority.[11]

Despite the trend toward expansion of the executive role, the legislative role of the lieutenant governor is not in decline in most states. In the 20 states where the lieutenant governor runs independently of the governor, he or she presides over the state senate in all but 1 (Louisiana). In the 22 states where the two officials run as a team, the lieutenant governor presides over the senate in 13.[12] The legislative role of the lieutenant governor is a controversial one. Critics believe this role detracts from his or her executive responsibilities, undermines support for the governor's authority, and is inconsistent with the doctrine of separation of powers. Supporters of a powerful legislative role for the lieutenant governor claim that it allows him or her to serve as a liaison between the executive and legislative branches, keeping lines of communication open.

Department Heads and Top Administrators

The governor and lieutenant governor are assisted in the administration of state government by the executives who supervise the state bureaucracy. These officials may be the head of executive departments such as commerce, health, or agriculture and are often referred to as commissioners. Top administrators may also supervise state boards, agencies, or regulatory commissions. These department heads and top administrators occupy a crucial position in state government because they serve as intermediaries ("middlemen") between the governor and the civil servants or career bureaucrats.

Selection of Administrators   Although constitutionally created positions such as attorney general, secretary of state, and state treasurer are selected by voters, most department heads, agency directors, and state board members are appointed by the governor with the consent of the state senate. Some of these officials may be selected by a state board or commission. The governor's power of appointment of state board or commission members may not give the governor the control over these organizations that this power implies because the appointments are made on a staggered long-term basis; the terms are usually six years. The governor does not have a majority of his or her own appointees for the first two years of the term, and carry-over appointees from the previous administration continue to exercise control over board policy.

Because a majority of top-level administrative offices are patronage positions, that is, are appointed by the governor, they encourage bureaucratic responsiveness to the governor's policies and programs. However, what is supposed to work in theory is not always achieved in reality. Executives have difficulty controlling departments and agencies for several reasons. The sheer size of the agency may make it hard for the director to keep up with what is going on. Even more important is the fact that the department head or director is a "temporary" employee, while middle managers and lower-level bureaucrats are permanent civil service employees who have more knowledge and experience and may be reluctant to follow directions from someone they see as a stranger and an amateur.

Profile of the Modern State Administrator   What kind of person occupies top-level administrative positions in state government? Are these administrators representative of the public in general? How have the characteristics of state administrators changed over the years? Given the fact that much of our experience with state government involves contacts with the agencies and departments these administrators supervise, these are important questions. A continuing study conducted by the American State Administrators Project (ASAP) helps answer these questions. The study surveyed state agency heads every five years from 1964 through 1984, and the results reveal important data concerning the representativeness and professionalism of these executives.[13]

The democratic ideal suggests that public organizations should maintain work forces that are representative of the people they serve. We can see from Table 11.2 that the heads of state agencies do not reflect the characteristics of the public at large. The survey for 1984 shows that the majority of these administrators are white males with graduate degrees. However, we can also see that over the past 20 years women and minorities have made some progress. For the first time since the surveys began, more than 10 percent of the respondents in 1984 were women, and the percentage of black respondents doubled.

The study also indicates that state administrators are becoming younger and more educated. In 1978, the median age of agency heads dipped below 50 years for the first time, and the trend toward younger administrators continued in 1984. Over one-fourth of the respondents in 1984 were "baby boomers." The graduate degree seems to be a growing prerequisite for administrators. The self-educated executive who learns by "hard knocks" solely "on the job" is becoming a thing of the past.[14]

Table 11.2 PERSONAL AND BACKGROUND CHARACTERISTICS OF STATE ADMINISTRATORS

	1964 (%)	1968 (%)	1974 (%)	1978 (%)	1984 (%)
Age					
Under 40	13	14	17	22	25
40–49	28	29	31	33	33
50–59	35	38	33	31	28
60 and over	24	19	19	14	14
Mean	52	50	50	48	47
Median	53	51	50	49	47
Sex					
Male	98	95	96	93	89
Female	2	5	4	7	11
Ethnic background					
White	98	97	96	92	90
Black	1	1	2	2	5
American Indian				1	0.7
Asian	1	2	2	4	3
Hispanic	0	0	0	1	2
Education					
High School or less	15	7	4	3	2
Some college	19	18	13	11	6
Bachelor's degree	25	15	18	15	15
Some graduate study	25	16	17	14	14
Graduate degree	40	45	47	56	63

Source: American State Administrators Project. Cited in Peter J. Haas and Deil S. Wright, "The Changing Profile of State Administrators," *Journal of State Government* 60 (November-December 1987), 270–278. Reprinted with permission, copyright by the Council of State Governments.

The Civil Service

Most employees in state executive branches are not political appointees but are part of a civil service or merit system. This means that these employees are hired because they take a test that proves they are qualified to perform a particular job; employment is based on merit rather than political connections or patronage.

Federal Influence Civil service reform was initiated by the federal government with the passage of the Pendleton Act in 1883. Reformers were disgusted by what they perceived as abuses of patronage, or the spoils system, in which incompetent people were given government jobs primarily because of their connections with politicians and political parties. The act itself, however, was stimulated by the assassination of President James A. Garfield in 1881 by a disappointed office seeker. Passage of the Pendleton Act stimulated the growth of state civil service systems. New York promptly established a civil service commission that year, and Massachusetts followed suit in 1884.

In 1939 the federal government provided the most important impetus for states to adopt merit systems. The federal Social Security Act passed in that year requires governments receiving federal aid money to use a merit system to staff agencies that implement programs with that money. Between 1940 and 1973, 33 states adopted comprehensive merit systems for all state agencies. Today, about three-fourths of the states have comprehensive civil service systems and the rest have limited coverage involving one or more agencies.[15]

The federal government further influenced state and local personnel practices by passing the Hatch Act in 1939. This act prevents federal employees from participating in partisan political activity, that is, running for political office, managing political campaigns, circulating petitions, and other similar activities. Following the federal lead, legislatures in all the states adopted "little Hatch Acts" of their own to limit the political activity of state employees. Although all the states prohibit this activity, some are more restrictive than others.

How Merit Systems Work   You will recall that a merit system implies that people are hired and paid according to the work they do rather than the political pull they have. Thus the first step in installing a merit system is *job classification*. Jobs are grouped into different categories according to the type of work performed and are arranged hierarchically. Jobs that require the most training, expertise, and responsibility are at the top of the hierarchy, while those which require the least are at the bottom. The classification of jobs is also necessary in order to construct exams that test the competency of the people competing for those jobs. Applicants are elevated on the basis of their exam scores, academic credentials, and job experience. Other criteria, such as military service and affirmative action, also may be considered. In most states supervisors follow the so-called rule of three, meaning that they hire one of the top three applicants.

After a period of time—usually five years—an individual in a civil service position is given **tenure**. This means that the individual can be fired only for reasons that are specified in state law. Tenure makes it very difficult for a supervisor to fire an employee. To dismiss a civil service employee, cause for dismissal must be presented to a civil service commission. Examples of cause for dismissal include repeated failure to follow an administrator's directive and misuse of official power. The rationale behind tenure is that it protects nonpolitical employees—civil service employees—from interference by and pressure from politicians.

Civil service commissions generally run state merit systems. These are nonpartisan independent boards whose members are usually appointed by chief executives and approved by legislative bodies. The commission's responsibilities include describing and classifying jobs, designing tests, and laying out rules for promotion, retirement, dismissals, and other personnel matters.

The Pros and Cons of Merit Systems The value of a professional bureaucracy that is familiar with the day-to-day operations of government is obvious. These employees provide the continuity and expertise that are often missing in states where governors and legislatures are transient and part time. Taxpayers like to know that public employees are qualified and competent to perform the functions they are hired to perform.

However, the disadvantages of the merit system have also become obvious. Employees in a civil service system may not respond willingly to elected or appointed managers. Protected by tenure, they feel little incentive to promote a manager's goals; they can simply "wait the manager out." Thus civil service employees are insulated from political pressure but are also insulated from political or "democratic" control. The ability of the officials we elect to political office to govern effectively is restricted by a permanent and politically independent bureaucracy.

The permanence and expertise of professional bureaucrats also give them power over elected and appointed officials. Bureaucrats are experts on procedures and programs within their areas of specialization. Legislators and top-level administrators depend on bureaucratic experts for information. All this means that bureaucrats—the government officials least accountable to the public in general—are playing an increasingly important role in policy-making.

The Pros and Cons of Patronage Systems A patronage, or spoils, system means that elected chief executives give government positions (as well as contracts and other special favors) to those who have supported their election effort. In most cases, these supporters are members of the chief executive's party. In general, the disadvantages of a merit system are the same as the advantages of a patronage system. Government employees are very responsive to elected officials because their jobs and careers depend on the goodwill and success of the official who appoints them. Chief executives are able to surround themselves with loyal subordinates who support their views and help them redeem their campaign pledges.

As we learned in Chapter 8, strong parties—those with the authority to provide inducements or rewards for party workers—are likely to be more responsive to the public in general. If the party in power does not deliver on its promises, it is possible for the voters to "throw the rascals out." Thus patronage systems promote responsiveness.

The primary disadvantage of patronage systems is the lack of continuity and expertise. Dispensing jobs to loyal supporters does *not* guarantee that these supporters are qualified to perform the increasingly complicated functions of modern government. It also does not give them the experience to learn these functions, since even popular chief executives step down from office after a few years. Thus patronage systems may sacrifice effectiveness for responsiveness.

Reorganization of State Executive Branches

Throughout the twentieth century governors have engaged in executive branch **reorganization**, that is, reshaping the way in which departments, agencies, boards, and commissions are organized. There is no doubt that reorganization was long overdue. States had hundreds of state agencies standing alone, often without any central direction and coordination. This fragmentation of power and responsibility made it hard for governors to achieve their policy goals. Critics charged that agencies possessed overlapping functions and often duplicated services. Thus reorganization was meant to address both political and administrative concerns. Governors would have more control over the state bureaucracy, and the bureaucracy would be run more effectively and efficiently.

Most of the major efforts by states to reorganize their executive branches resulted from similar activities at the federal level. At the national level, reorganization followed three major studies: the Taft Commission of 1910–1913, the Brownlow Committee initiated by President Roosevelt in 1937, and the Hoover Commission of 1947–1949.[16] The most recent wave of state executive reorganization, prompted by the Hoover Commission and by reapportionment, was the most extensive. Between 1965 and 1977, 21 states launched major reorganization efforts and virtually all the rest undertook some reorganization.[17]

Goals of Reorganization   Although states did not always adopt them, the following goals were set up as the standards of reorganization:

1. Concentrate more authority and responsibility in the hands of the governor. The governor should have more appointment and removal power.
2. Consolidate boards, agencies, and commissions into a few departments with broad functional responsibilities. The heads of these departments should be appointed by the governor, not elected.
3. Abolish boards and commissions used for administrative work and replace them with single executives.
4. Coordinate staff services—budgeting, accounting, purchasing, personnel—into a single department. In the language of bureaucracy, the personnel, finance, legal, and other units of a bureaucratic organization constitute its *staff* services.
5. Ensure that there is an independent audit of the executive branch, preferably by a legislatively appointed auditor.
6. Provide for a governor's cabinet, whose members he or she appoints, to advise the governor on policy matters and help eliminate duplication and overlap of functions.[18]

Although the response in the states has been uneven, substantial progress has been achieved in goals 1, 2, 4, and 5. There is no doubt that the power of governors has been strengthened. Between 1964 and 1981, all but eight states reduced the number of top executive officials who are elected. North Carolina reduced its elected executives from 110 to 10; Nevada, from 42 to 6. In most of these cases, election was replaced by gubernatorial appointment. As Chapter 10 pointed out, many governors were also given the power to reorganize their executive branches through executive orders.

Consolidation of agencies has taken place particularly in the areas of environmental protection, transportation, and human services. By 1978, 42 states had grouped staffed services under departments of finance or adminis- tration, although few states group all staff functions in these departments. By 1979, two-thirds of the states had an independent auditor designated by the legislature.[19]

Progress has been much less extensive for goals 3 and 6. Multimember boards and commissions are still used widely in state government, although some have been consolidated. A number of states did provide for a cabinet system—36 by 1979. However, the creation of a cabinet system took sec- ond billing to the decision to appoint rather than elect department heads. A governor who does not have the power to appoint cabinet secretaries is not likely to view the cabinet as a useful advisory body. Thus goal 1—the concentration of authority in the hands of the governor—was a much more significant goal than was the creation of cabinet systems per se.[20]

Resistance to Change   Implementation of these reorganization goals seems like such a logical and rational thing to do that one may wonder why the goals have not been adopted universally. The reason is that reorganiza- tion is a highly *political* process. There is often strong support for maintain- ing separately elected officials so that people can have more direct influence or because that is the traditional way of doing things. Recall that Americans have always been suspicious of centralized executive power. Certainly agency heads will resist consolidation into a larger department that threatens their authority. Special-interest groups often have a close working relation- ship with a specific agency (perhaps have even captured the agency) and do not want to see it subsumed into a larger, less accessible department. These and other obstacles mean that proponents of reorganization face a difficult task.

An Example of State Bureaucratic Organization: The Texas Public Education System

One of the most important areas of policy administered by state and local bureaucracies is education policy. All 50 states have local school districts and authorize local school boards to govern them. Although these local boards administer important day-to-day policy, their authority is limited severely by state legislation.

The bureaucratic arrangements in most states reflect the control that the state exercises over local school districts. In almost every state government, the primary policy-making body is the state board or commission of educa- tion. The board is assisted by the chief executive official, usually called the commissioner or superintendent of public education. These chief executive officials are selected in a variety of different ways: In 29 states they are appointed by the state board or commission, in 16 states they are elected by the people of the state, and in 5 states they are appointed by the governor. The implementation of state education policy is the responsibility of the state department of education, which usually is a very large bureaucracy.

The Texas Public Education Bureaucracy Because the organization of the public education bureaucracy in Texas is typical of that in many states, it is useful in illustrating the administration of this complex state and local policy. Figure 11.1 illustrates how Texas organizes the bureaucracy to implement public education. The legislature and the state board of education have broad decision-making power for public education in Texas. The state board of education, whose members are elected for four-year overlapping terms from 15 districts, establishes general rules and guidelines, approves organizational plans, submits budget recommendations to the legislature and governor, and contracts for the purchase of textbooks. The legislature approves the budget for the state's share of the cost of public education.

Much of the decision making concerning education is left to the Texas Education Agency (TEA) and the local school boards. The TEA, whose administrators are appointed by the state board, handles such general policy matters as curriculum, teacher certification, and school accreditation. The chief administrator of the TEA is the commissioner of education, who is appointed to a four-year term by the state board. The commissioner, an experienced educator assisted by a professional staff, acts as a kind of state superintendent, making recommendations to the lay state board.

The day-to-day operation of public schools is the responsibility of locally elected school boards. These boards approve local school budgets, set tax

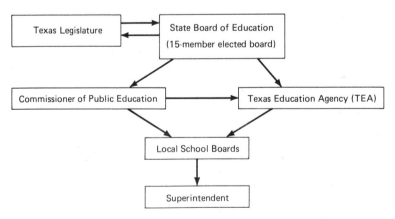

Figure 11.1 Organization of the public education bureaucracy in Texas.

rates, arrange financial audits, make personnel decisions, establish local salary schedules, and approve construction contracts. Because local school boards are composed of part-time laypersons, one of their most important decisions is to hire a professional, that is, a superintendent, whose job is to manage the daily operation of the district.

Where Do You Fit In? Pondering the organization and functions of this large state and local bureaucracy may intimidate the average citizen, but individuals determined to influence education policy are given a variety of opportunities to do so in our example. The members of the major policy-making bodies — the legislature, the state board of education, and the local school boards — are elected. All make policy in open accessible forums. In addition, many of the day-to-day decisions that affect citizens most directly are made at the local level. Local boards and officials are generally sensitive to the values and concerns of their immediate communities. Although citizens do not elect a superintendent, the fact that the superintendent is a local official makes him or her one of the most accessible bureaucrats.

BUREAUCRATS IN THE INTERGOVERNMENTAL SYSTEM

State agency heads and administrators are intermediaries in the intergovernmental system. Every year billions of dollars are channeled through state agencies by the federal government to achieve national goals. A number of costly programs are administered jointly by the federal and state governments, including medical care for the poor (Medicaid), traditional welfare programs such as Aid to Families with Dependent Children (AFDC), highways, sewage treatment, education, and public and low-cost housing programs. Thus state administrators play a crucial role in the successful implementation of these federal grant-in-aid programs.

In 1978, approximately 70 percent of state agency heads reported that their agencies received federal aid. Although this figure dropped to 59 percent in 1984, it is still significant. At present about 15 percent of state agencies receive *more than half* their funding from the federal government.[21]

Effects of Federal Dollars

An important consequence of federal revenues to states has been the increase in the number of state agencies. This increase has come about because of the requirement of many federal grants to have a "single state agency" administer federal funds. States have often been required to create new agencies to meet this condition. The proliferation of these new agencies has made it even harder for a governor to control the bureaucracy and has been a factor in gubernatorial calls for reorganization.

Federal aid also may loosen the ties that state administrators feel toward other state officials, the legislature, and the governor. An agency head charged with implementing important federal programs may rely on the federal government for a substantial degree of funding and is also likely to have a close working relationship with federal bureaucrats. For example, a state welfare administrator may be closer to officials in the Department of Health and Human Services in Washington, DC, than to state officials. The same is true of bureaucrats in other functional areas, such as transportation, waste management, law enforcement, education, and housing.

The tightly knit relationships between federal and state bureaucrats are sometimes referred to critically as **functional fiefdoms** by elected officials. These officials feel that bureaucrats within these functional areas become unmanageable and unresponsive; elected officials lose control over policy as bureaucrats collaborate among themselves. It is true that these functional fiefdoms are strengthened by the large number of complex federal regulations that apply to the programs that state governments administer. Program officials find it necessary to keep in contact with each other to decipher and interpret regulatory requirements.

Relations of State and Local Administrators

A major political development of the twentieth century has been the growing state dominance over local governments. Changing revenue and spending patterns tell some of the story. The local share of state and local revenues declined from 83 percent in 1902 to well under half that figure today. In spite of this, the local share of state and local *spending* is 61 percent. In other words, local governments spend more money than do state governments even though they raise less.[22] States are spending more to subsidize local governments. As you might expect, state-local relationships are coming more and more to resemble parent-child relationships: As states spend more money on local government programs and services, they exercise more control over local programs.

Another interesting indication of the growing centralization of power in state-local relationships is the development of state departments of community affairs. Although these organizations were nonexistent before 1960, all the states had some form of community affairs agency by 1980.

State departments of community affairs provide examples of how state administrators serve as intermediaries in the intergovernmental system. A large portion of the federal aid meant for local governments is channeled through state governments. For example, community development grants are distributed to states by the federal Department of Housing and Urban Development (HUD). These grants can be used for a whole range of activities, including land acquisition, street improvement, sewage treatment systems, parks and playgrounds, and the elimination of slums. States decide which activities will be funded. State community development departments or agencies then distribute these monies to local governments, which use them for local development projects.

Surveys of state administrators show that their attitude toward playing the role of intermediaries may be changing. Until recently the heads of state agencies were nearly unanimous in believing that federal aid to local governments should be channeled through the states. Recently, however, administrators have become less convinced that this channeling is necessary. The reason for the changing attitude may be that the national regulations and requirements attached to federal grants make administering them more and more expensive for the states.[23]

REFORMING THE BUREAUCRACY: CURRENT ISSUES

As state and local bureaucracies continue to grow, politicians and academics recommend changes that they believe will make these bureaucracies more effective and responsive. Some of the changes have been more successful than others; many have been controversial. The following discussion examines how these reforms are supposed to work in theory, how they have developed in reality, and their impact on the way state and local governments operate. Among the most prominent issues and changes are budget reform, the development of state and local employee unions, the contracting out of public services to private firms, more openness and participation in state and local governments, and new legislative strategies for controlling the bureaucracy.

Budgeting and Budget Reform

"Budgeting" means planning how to spend money, and as you might guess, it is the heart of governing. Deciding who gets what through a budget is our leaders' way of deciding what government does and what its most important functions are.

The Budget Process In all but three states the governor has responsibility for planning the state budget and submitting it to the legislature. Thus the budget is the governor's most potent weapon in controlling the state administration. A governor's budget plan reflects proposed expenditures in a **fiscal year**. A fiscal year is a financial year, not a normal calendar year. For example, many states have fiscal years that begin July 1 and end June 30. The traditional reason for using fiscal years was that legislatures generally met in the spring. By summer the decisions about state agency budgets were finalized so that those agencies could begin spending money.

Once the governor's budget is submitted (if not before), the intensely political process of approving the budget swings into gear. State agencies, organized interest groups, and other interested parties lobby the legislature intensely to make sure their share of the budget pie is retained or increased. Legislators who are supposed to think about the interest of the state or city in general are bombarded with information and arguments from narrow, well-organized special interests.

Although some zealous legislators with a cause work for extreme changes in the budget, most prefer not to deviate from the status quo in a radical fashion. To do so is to invite the wrath of the bureaucrats and special interests that find themselves threatened by big changes in the budget. For this reason, the budgeting process has traditionally been incremental. **Incremental budgeting** is a relatively comfortable process for most of the actors involved. The proposed budget is based on figures in the previous year's budget plus a little more. Agencies may request money for a few new programs and overestimate the amount needed for old ones. Governors and legislators review agency requests and make some cuts. Agencies get what they need, governors and legislators get credit for holding down spending, and everybody is satisfied through not thrilled by the whole process.

Once money is *appropriated* by the legislature, the final step in the budget process is to make sure the money is spent in the way the legislature intended. The process of looking at agency expenditures to see if they are legal and accurate is called **auditing**. In most states auditing is performed by an official selected by the legislature. In about a dozen states the auditor is popularly elected. Both election and appointment by the legislature are methods that help ensure that auditors are independent of the executive branch agencies they are charged with checking.

Budget Reforms   As comfortable as incremental budgeting is for politicians, interest groups, and agencies, it is not without vehement critics. These critics say that old programs are seldom reviewed, long-range planning is difficult, and in general not enough scrutiny is placed on the budgeting process. Agencies, they argue, should be asked to justify their programs, not just their increments, from the bottom up. Budgeting should be used to prioritize state and local programs and services so that those which are not needed can be thrown out completely.

In the early 1970s budget reforms were adopted by many states and local governments in an attempt to avoid or minimize incrementalism. These reforms are often referred to by their initials; two of the most important are **planning-programming-budgeting systems (PPBS)** and **zero-based budgeting (ZBB)**. PPBS was first implemented by the U.S. Department of Defense in the early 1960s and proved so impressive that several states adopted it. In general, this system emphasized the overall goals of agencies rather than year-to-year spending items. Expenditures were lumped together in comprehensive program packages such as health and welfare or crime. Rather than justifying line items in the budget, agencies justified their requests in terms of their program objectives. Agencies were also supposed to analyze and present alternative methods for achieving their objectives.[24] Because PPBS was extremely complicated and time-consuming and because it failed to consider the political forces that prevail in the budget process, it was largely unsuccessful.

In the late 1970s, President Jimmy Carter proposed that the federal government adopt the ZBB plan he had introduced as governor of Georgia.

In theory ZBB assumes that agencies justify why they should get any money at all, that is, why they should get more than zero dollars, rather than why they should get increments above the previous year's appropriation. Each department budget is broken down into a series of related activities called decision packages. Managers at each level review each proposed activity and are supposed to cut back or eliminate those which are not necessary. In some cases departments rank their programs in order of priority. ZBB, like its predecessor PPBS, is supposed to encourage a thorough analysis of programs as well as a planning process.

However, ZBB has never been implemented in its pure form. Several states have adopted hybrid forms that can realistically be put into place in the highly politicized budget process. Ironically, ZBB in its present form reverts to the incremental process it was supposed to replace. In most states each agency prepares three alternative levels of funding for each activity in its decision package. The three alternative levels are (1) the current level of funding, (2) a level 90 percent of the current level, and (3) the level requested by the agency. Rather than starting at a zero level of funding, the agency actually starts at 90 percent.

The disparity between the theory and practice of ZBB illustrates the basic flaw in most budget reform schemes. Reformers assume that budgeting is taking place in a political vacuum where there is plenty of time for a thorough analysis of state programs from top to bottom. This ignores the fact that politicians who make budget decisions are operating in a whirlwind of intense political interests, with little time and a scarcity of information and staff resources.

Some scholars find that ZBB and similar reforms have resulted in longer-range views and a more thorough evaluation of programs.[25] However, bureaucrats object to the increased time and paperwork these reforms require and are not always convinced that the results justify the extra effort. Nevertheless, ZBB and similar reforms are indications that the public management profession is constantly experimenting with ways to organize government activities more efficiently and spend tax dollars more effectively. By experimenting with new techniques of budget management, technology, and delivery, many city managers, school superintendents, state agency directors, and other public employees usually categorized as bureaucrats attempt to help the public get the most services for the least money.

State and Local Employee Unions

In recent years public employee unions have increased in size and political influence. Today about 40 percent of state and local employees belong to unions, although union membership is most prevalent among local employees, particularly clerks, teachers, police officers, fire fighters, and nurses. Two of the largest unions are the AFL-CIO affiliated American Federation of State, County, and Municipal Employees (AFSCME) and the Service Employees International Union (SEIU). Teachers make up nearly one-fifth of all state and local employees, and many are represented by the National Education Association (NEA).

State and local employee unions have grown for a number of reasons. Public employees have followed the lead of other groups, such as minorities and women, who have organized to protect their rights and promote their interests. The most important reason for the growth of unions is probably economic. For years public employees felt that their pay was inferior to that of similar workers in the private sector, and for a while this perception was accurate. Between 1975 and 1982 pay gains in the public sector lagged behind those in the private sector by about 8 percent. However, since 1981, whether from the influence of unions or for other reasons, pay increased by about the same percentage in the two sectors.[26] Although many states have kept up with the average pay increases since 1981, some have lagged significantly behind.

Comparing Public and Private Unions   Like their private counterparts, public unions organize state and local employees and represent workers in **collective bargaining** with management to improve pay and working conditions. Whereas private unions try to get job security for their workers, this is not as great a concern for public unions, whose workers may be protected through the civil service system.

Public unions are supposed to be denied one of the most potent weapons of unionization: the *right to strike.* Strikes by federal employees and almost all state and local employees are illegal. The rationale behind this prohibition is that public workers generally provide essential services; denial of these services causes serious disruptions in the community. Anyone denied the services of policy officers, fire fighters, garbage disposal workers, or school-teachers would probably agree with this rationale. Nonetheless, laws against striking are difficult to enforce, and illegal strikes often take place. Workers who strike must ultimately be prosecuted and punished by elected officials, and very few politically sensitive public officials are willing to imprison or fine striking teachers or fire fighters.

Public unions face other obstacles in their attempts to bargain with management, including the problem of "elusive authority" and the ability of governments to resist union pressure. It is difficult for the representatives of public unions to work out complex or sensitive agreements with management because management often consists of the legislature or another elected board. In a state or local agency the immediate manager — the agency head — is merely an agent of the legislature or board and has no real authority to bargain with the union. Another problem for these unions is the ability of governments to resist pressure. Unlike private businesses, governments have continuing sources of revenues through taxes and are not pressed to produce profits. Therefore, they can choose to ignore or postpone workers' demands or wait out strikes. The fact that revenues are raised through taxes adds to the government's resistance. Very few elected officials are enthusiastic about granting salary increases to state and local employees if it entails calling for tax increases.

However, public unions possess certain advantages over private unions. Just as elected officials may not have the incentive to punish illegal strikers, they do not always have the incentive of private managers to resist worker demands. Elected mayors who are in office for one or two terms may not have the desire or perseverance to stand up to powerful city unions. They are likely to feel pressure from disgruntled citizens denied police protection or garbage collection because of city strikes, or they may make long-term concessions such as greater pension benefits in lieu of immediate wage increases.

Another advantage for public unions is access to information. Open records laws mean that public employee unions have access to information about budgets that is not always readily available to private unions. This information may give them an advantage in the bargaining process.

Perhaps the most important advantage for public employee unions is their political clout. Although these unions have always engaged in lobbying and political action, many have increased this activity in recent years and have become powerful political forces. A good example is New York's Civil Service Employees Association (CSEA). The CSEA represents 250,000 government workers across the state, has its own lobbyist, and is playing an increasingly large role in the state's elections. It is widely credited with helping elect Mario Cuomo governor through hundreds of phone banks across the state and a massive union-run get-out-the-vote drive. It also successfully lobbied the state legislature for a bill which adds to the supplemental pensions collected by state and local employees.[27]

Unions Challenge Merit State and local employee unions are the object of criticism from several sources. Conservatives argue that public unions are unacceptable because they compromise the sovereignty of democratic government. Why should those who work for democratically elected leaders have an important role in making decisions?

Unions are also the object of criticism from "good government" liberals who claim that they interfere with the concept of merit. These critics argue that the across-the-board salary increases that unions press for negate the whole idea of giving increases only to those who deserve them. They use the same argument to criticize the unions' practice of demanding that seniority rather than merit form the basis of promotion and leadership. Finally, they are concerned that unions bring government employees back into the world of partisan politics. Recall that the primary goal of a merit system is to remove those who implement government policy—bureaucrats—from the realm of policy-making.

Union supporters reply that the competition among workers in a merit system lowers worker morale, that seniority is related to merit, and that politics already influences personnel decisions in many so-called merit sys-

---

Box 11-3 **Public Unions Push for Comparable Worth**

Is the job performed by an office secretary as valuable as that performed by a highway repair worker? Is the job of a nurse as valuable as that of a garbage truck worker? Those who support the concept of comparable worth charge that salaries for many jobs are lower not because they require less skill, training, or experience but solely because they are traditionally performed by women.

The concept of **comparable worth** implies that different jobs can be compared objectively to determine their relative value to the employer and that jobs that are of the same value should be paid equally. Thus comparable worth goes beyond the policy of equal pay for equal work. It demands equal pay for jobs of equal value.

In recent years state and local employee unions have taken up the cause of comparable worth by pressuring state and local governments to conduct evaluations of different jobs to determine if salaries should be boosted in job classes that are traditionally female. Unions have made some progress at the bargaining table. In 1986, AFSCME and the city of Chicago reached a $1.2 million agreement to raise salaries in about 60 job classes. Several states and municipalities—including Minnesota, Wisconsin, Iowa, New Jersey, and the city of Los Angeles—have comparable pay plans in place as a result of legislation or collective bargaining. Progress has been made in court as well. The most well-known comparable worth case, involving state workers in Washington and the AFSCME, ended in 1985 with an out-of-court settlement worth an estimated $482 million. Pay raises for 34,000 employees in female-dominated jobs are being phased in over a period of six years.

Although the implementation of comparable worth has been limited primarily to the public sector, it faces vigorous opposition from business groups which fear that the concept and its accompanying costs will filter into the private sector. Opposition also comes from citizens who resent the threat of higher taxes to pay for higher government wages. All these opponents argue that it is impossible to make objective comparisons among jobs that are not the same.

The issue of comparable worth is a controversial one, a political hot potato that is likely to be debated in state and local governments for quite some time.

---

tems. They also contend that merit is difficult to measure (Box 11-3). What some call merit may simply be favoritism on the part of those who recommend and make promotion decisions. Finally, they argue that without an organization representing them, public employees will not be treated fairly by their employers.

Contracting out Public Services: Privatization

One of the most significant developments in state and local governments in recent years has been the trend toward **privatization**—providing public-sector services through private-sector contracts.

Contracting with private firms has been practiced by state and local governments for quite some time. States contract with private companies to build highways, and the federal government gives contracts to private corporations to build weapons systems. However, in recent years the prevalence and scope of private contracting have increased. A survey conducted by the International City Management Association in 1982 found that 41 percent of commercial solid-waste collection (garbage collection) and 34 percent of residential collection were being undertaken privately. Examples of other services carried out under private contract were street repair work (26 percent), utility billing (12 percent), vehicle towing and storage (78 percent), emergency medical service (13 percent), public hospital management (25 percent), building and grounds maintenance (19 percent), and data processing (22 percent).[28] Some local governments even contract out for police and fire protection, and several states are exploring the possibility of privately run prison systems.

The popularity of privatization reflects the prevailing political climate. Reduced federal aid and the reluctance of citizens to pay higher local and state taxes mean that governments are willing to try new strategies to save money. In addition, Ronald Reagan's and George Bush's well-known preference for private rather than public action only added fuel to privatization's fire. Almost all the arguments in support of contracting out are couched in terms of classic conservative economic principles. Supporters claim that contracting with private companies shrinks the size of government and reduces the cost of providing public services. Privatization reduces the "natural monopoly" that government enjoys in providing services. Efficiency is enhanced because several private firms, or "suppliers," compete among each other and with the government to provide the service at the lowest possible cost.

The results of some studies provide impressive support for privatization. One study of private versus public garbage collection found that private service cost about 30 percent less and was just as effective.[29] Another study looked at seven different services that were contracted out in the five-county Los Angeles area: street cleaning, janitorial services, residential garbage collection, payroll, traffic-signal maintenance, turf maintenance, and street-maintenance. For all these services except payroll, public-sector expenses were higher, ranging from 37 percent more for tree trimming to 96 percent more for street maintenance.[30]

Some people are concerned about the trend toward contracting out. The most serious problem, they say, is the potential loss of control that may occur as government gives more responsibility to the private sector. Will a private garbage collection firm be as responsive to citizens who complain about inadequate service as a municipal agency is? Does a state really want to surrender authority over its prison system to a private company? In this view, too much privatization leads to a loss of government responsibility and, consequently, a loss of citizen control.

There are other concerns. Public unions resist privatization because of the threat it poses to their workers, and they have cause to be worried. The loss of jobs by government workers who are displaced by private contractors is sometimes unavoidable. A related question is the effect that privatization has on minorities and affirmative action. Government employment has been an especially valuable means of progress for minorities, and there is no guarantee that this progress will continue when jobs are shifted from the public sector to the private sector.

Some critics even question the efficiency argument of those who support an expanded role for the private sector. Competition is not always present; a few large firms may dominate. The most obvious example is the enormous waste and inefficiency that we have witnessed on the part of defense contractors. Moreover, critics maintain that for every story lauding the efficiency of private enterprise, there is an example of inefficiency, waste, and corruption. One example is the New York Human Resources Administration, which canceled several contracts for custodial and printing services because of large cost overruns. What happens, the critics ask, when private firms fail to live up to their contracts? Governments may be left with serious disruptions of service because of poor performance by private firms or because those firms face bankruptcy after bidding too low in order to win contracts.

State and local governments should approach privatization with caution. There are situations where contracting out can reduce costs and increase efficiency. It can also bring fresh ideas and approaches into established programs. The possibility of contracting out may even stimulate public employees to perform better. However, governments should be aware of its limitations and potential problems.

Openness in Government

Bureaucracies by nature are undemocratic. Bureaucrats are supposed to follow rules, that is, go by the book, without paying attention to the individual preferences of their clients. Most employees in a government agency are not elected, and some are not always concerned about being responsive to prevailing political attitudes. They prefer to make decisions on the basis of their technical expertise, out of the interfering and uninformed view of the general public. When mismanagement or abuse of discretionary authority does occur in a public agency, there is a tendency for bureaucrats to close ranks and protect themselves against the prying eyes of the press and public. Although bureaucrats are supposed to be responsive to elected leaders, we have already seen that many civil service and career bureaucrats are insulated from real control by elected officials.

In the last few years there has been persistent pressure by organized citizens' groups such as Common Cause to open up government decision making and make it more accessible to the general public. Reforms began at the federal level and have gradually spread to the states. These changes have made both state legislatures and executive agencies more accessible to the average citizen and have made it easier to detect mismanagement and abuse in public agencies. Among the most important reforms are open meetings (sunshine laws), open records laws, increased protection for whistle-blowers, and citizen participation requirements.

Sunshine laws require that public bodies — legislative committees, city councils, state and local agencies, and other similar bodies — open all meetings to the public except in special circumstances specified by law. Examples of these circumstances might be sensitive personnel questions and a discussion of the legal strategies involved in a lawsuit. In such circumstances the board or agency may meet privately in "executive session." Although all states have adopted open meetings laws, some are more rigorous than others. Most states require advance notice of meetings, and many require that detailed minutes of meetings be made available to the public.

Sunshine laws allow the public to participate in the decision-making process of legislative committee members and public bureaucrats. Open meetings requirements open the often critical decisions made by executive agencies for comment and scrutiny. For example, a state public utility commission that decides to request a multimillion-dollar rate increase must face the rate-paying public in its deliberations.

There is a growing sense, however, that having meetings open to the public is not such a good idea. Often those who attend public meeting are members of special-interest groups. It is much harder for legislators or bureaucrats to resist pressure from these groups when they are present and breathing down their necks. Other factors have lessened the enthusiasm for open meetings. Meeting in private saves time; it also allows public figures the chance to ask "dumb" questions and not be embarrassed. Most impor-

Citizens attend an open public hearing. (*Source:* San Marcos Daily Record.)

tant, many people claim that it is easier to compromise and devise solutions to difficult and politically sensitive problems without the watchful and critical eye of the press or special-interest groups. Despite these problems, sunshine laws are alive and well in state and local governments.

Perhaps even more important in giving the public access to state and local agencies are **open records laws**, which allow access to most of the records and information held by public agencies. The big push for access to information came after the Watergate scandal in the early 1970s. By 1983 all but two states—Delaware and Mississippi—had adopted open records laws.

States generally exempt certain records from public scrutiny. For example, access to the grades of a person attending a state college is generally denied to protect individual privacy. Although states vary in the extent to which they encourage and enforce freedom of information, in recent years most states have strengthened their open records laws.

Occasionally corruption or mismanagement in a public agency is revealed by an employee of the agency itself. These individuals become frustrated with what they perceive as abuses by the agency and buck the tendency of bureaucrats to close ranks in the face of potential criticism. Individual bureaucrats who open up to public view the abuses or mismanagement of their agencies are called **whistle-blowers**. These courageous individuals refuse to go along with or perpetuate policies they feel are damaging to the public and lay aside ambition for promotion and good relations with colleagues to challenge the status quo. Indeed, in the past whistle-blowers were almost always denied promotions within their agencies or were even fired.

In 1978, the federal Civil Service Reform Act strengthened protections for whistle-blowers, and some states followed suit. However, whistle-blowers are far from invulnerable. Even if they receive legal vindication, they almost always continue to be ostracized by their colleagues (Box 11-4). It would be a mistake to imagine that we can rely on these individuals to expose the abuses of bureaucracy; most people find it difficult to display the dirty laundry of the agency employing them.

In recent years state and local governments have instituted *citizen participation procedures* to encourage individuals to get involved in public decision making. These procedures have been established through local ordinances, state laws, and requirements or "strings" in federal grant-in-aid programs to state and local governments. They have opened up opportunities for citizens to become immediately involved in the policy-making process. State and local agencies are being advised by citizen advisory committees; some state governments and almost all local governments are holding public hearings on proposed budgets and nonfiscal matters such as zoning changes. Some cities and counties, especially those over 100,000 in population, are using citizen surveys to provide representative samples of citizen views. Forty-eight states have administrative procedures acts which govern

---

Box 11-4 **A Whistle-Blower Speaks Up**

Irwin Levin is an example of a determined individual who bucked the system. Levin, of New York City, New York, was a senior supervisor in the Brooklyn field office of Special Services for Children. Levin complained persistently to his superiors about the negligence, incompetence, and gross errors of judgment of overloaded or inexperienced welfare workers assigned to cases of suspected child abuse. He discovered that 11 children had died who could have been saved if the city had made meaningful changes in the system. When no one responded, Levin went to the press with confidential files. For his actions he was fined, suspended without pay for four months, demoted, and transferred.

After several years Levin was finally vindicated, but the problem of ineffective social services remains.

Source: "The Giraffe Honor Roll," *The Giraffe Gazette* 3(4) (Summer 1987), 1,2.

---

rule making by administrative agencies and allow for citizen input into the rule-making process.

The impetus for these requirements came in the early 1970s, when the federal government began incorporating citizen participation requirements into federal aid programs. To receive federal aid, state and local governments were forced to adopt various participatory procedures. For example, one of the federal government's most popular grant-in-aid programs — the community development block grant (CDBG) — allows communities to choose from a wide variety of programs and policies designed to rebuild and preserve urban areas. Communities that apply for these funds (and almost all do) must assure the Department of Housing and Urban Development (HUD) that they will (1) provide citizens with information on the amount of funds available and the range of activities that may be undertaken, (2) hold at least two public hearings to obtain citizens' views, and (3) allow citizens to participate in the development of the application.

Some observers note the disadvantages that accompany the proliferation of citizen participation procedures. These procedures are time-consuming and costly. Even more important, the citizens who are drawn to the process are not truly representative of the general public, but tend to represent special-interest groups. Some public officials feel that the procedures are merely "pro forma," that is, exist to fulfill a desire for more citizen involvement but don't really work. Despite these criticisms, democracies are *supposed* to be characterized by a full and free interchange of information between the people and their elected representatives and appointed administrators. Expanding citizen participation procedures allows us to come closer to this ideal.

Advocates of formal citizen participation requirements argue that these requirements help involve a broad cross section of citizens on a regular basis. Without these requirements, public officials would almost surely make decisions based on input from only the most vocal or most affluent citizens and might get a very distorted view of community needs. Citizen participation requirements do *not* assure that groups normally left out of the decision-making process will be heard, but they do give these groups more of an opportunity to participate.

Citizen participation requirements not only increase opportunities for broader citizen involvement, they also may increase the *efficiency* of the policy-making process and the *effectiveness* of policy. Citizens who actively participate in the process of decision making allow public officials to get information *before* the decision is made so that delays caused by unexpected citizen opposition are minimized. Public officials may build support for a policy so that citizens cooperate more fully with officials when it is time to implement that policy. In addition, informed and active citizens can help state and local officials monitor the effectiveness of government programs and can sometimes suggest midcourse corrections.

Legislative Control of the Bureaucracy

State and local legislatures are supposed to oversee their respective bureaucracies to make sure that policy is implemented the way the legislature intended. This legislative **oversight** has grown in importance as legislatures delegate more authority to executive agencies. As noted earlier in this chapter, state legislatures often appoint auditors to monitor spending by administrative agencies. In recent years state legislatures have devised other legal tools to help them control expanding bureaucracies. Here we discuss two of the most important tools: sunset laws and the legislative veto.

Sunset Legislation   Pioneered by Colorado in 1976, **sunset laws** specify that agencies be "sunsetted," that is, terminated, unless the legislature passes a law to re-create them. A typical sunset process works like this. The legislature reviews the state insurance board, the agency charged with regulating the state's insurance industry. After an extensive review, the legislature passes a bill re-creating the state insurance board, perhaps with some changes. If for some reason the legislature fails to enact a law re-creating the board, the board will cease to exist. After an established period—usually 10 or 12 years—the state insurance board comes up for sunset review again. The innovative part of this process is that for the first time the agency is responsible for proving the need for its existence.

Thirty-five states and some municipalities have adopted sunset laws. The typical sunset process has the legislature examine a specific number of agencies—usually 20 to 30—during a legislative session. Some states have "comprehensive" sunset laws, meaning that all or almost all state agencies are reviewed. Some states restrict sunset review to regulatory agencies.

The hope behind sunset reform is that unnecessary or wasteful agencies will be allowed to die. Because it holds out the promise of shrinking government, sunset has been advocated by conservatives. Indeed, one study found that sunset laws tend to be adopted in states that have a "negative orientation to government," that is, institutionally weak legislatures, governors with limited formal powers, conservative Democratic parties, and low levels of expenditures.[31] However, most studies have found that sunset rarely results in the abolition of agencies. Rather, it tends to result in moderate changes in the operating procedures of agencies and, in some cases, improved performance.[32]

Legislative Veto   As state legislatures delegate more authority to the bureaucracy to make rules and interpret statutes, steps have been taken by some legislatures to promote a greater review of these rules. Twenty-nine states have established the **legislative veto**, which means that the legislature —often a legislative committee— has the authority to veto rules that are not reasonable or do not meet the original intent of the legislature. The legislative veto was also exercised by the U.S. Congress until 1983, when the Supreme Court declared it unconstitutional. The Supreme Court ruling cast some doubt on the future of the often controversial use of the legislative veto in the states.

Not surprisingly, the legislative veto tends to be used in states with full-time legislatures that have the time and staff resources for careful review of actions by state agencies. Proponents of the legislative veto argue that it provides a check on bureaucratic excesses and enables the legislature to ensure that agency regulations are consistent with legislative statutes. Critics charge that it violates the principle of separation of powers and serves as a tool for powerful special interests that want to block controversial programs.[33]

Conclusion

The first and oldest job of the executive branch is to implement and enforce policies made by legislatures and chief executives. The hands-on job of implementing policy is performed by bureaucrats who work in executive agencies, bureaus, commissions, and boards. The size and scope of these state and local bureaucracies are expanding in response to the growing demands on government in recent years.

In addition to implementing laws and policies, executive agencies are given discretionary authority by legislatures to design rules and regulations. These rules act as guidelines laying out the specific details necessary to put policies into effect. Agencies also adjudicate disputes involving their own rules; that is, they decide initially if their rules are reasonable. Appeals to a court are possible but generally are permitted only after one has exhausted the administrative review process.

Bureaucracy is often the object of criticism. The criticism arises not so much because bureaucrats are stupid or lazy but because they are judged by the different and often conflicting standards of effectiveness and responsiveness. Although bureaucrats may function with competence and effectiveness, they may not always be sensitive and responsive to the demands of the public or to the elected officials who represent the public.

To achieve responsiveness and accountability to elected officials, reformers feel that governors should be given the power to appoint top executives. These executives, acting as intermediaries between the governor and career bureaucrats, will work to achieve the policy goals of the governor. Gubernatorial appointment, however, provides no guarantee that governors will control state bureaucracies. Staggered terms for appointees and a permanent civil service may discourage the bureaucracy's responsiveness to the policies and programs of the governor.

The establishment of civil service systems in the states was influenced by the institution of a merit system at the federal level. Today about three-fourths of the states have comprehensive merit systems, and the rest have limited coverage. Because merit systems help ensure that public workers are employed on the basis of their qualifications and expertise, these systems encourage a more professional bureaucracy. However, government bureaucrats protected by tenure are not likely to be as responsive to democratically elected representatives.

Recent surveys indicate that state administrators are becoming younger, more educated, and a bit more representative of women and minorities, although women and minorities still hold only a small percentage of top state administrative jobs. State administrators have also assumed an increasingly important role in the intergovernmental system. These administrators execute important federal programs and receive a significant portion of their funding from federal agencies. States have also gradually tightened control over local governments through state control of federal pass-through funds and increased state funding of local programs.

In recent years there have been a number of reforms and other developments designed to make state and local bureaucracies more effective and responsive. Budget reforms such as planning-programming-budgeting systems and zero-based budgeting are designed to replace incremental budgeting with a comprehensive "bottom-up" review of programs. These reforms have in general had disappointing results because they fail to take into account both the time constraints and the political realities of the budget process.

Public employees have been organizing and joining unions in increasing numbers in response to what they perceive as pay inferior to that received for similar employment in the private sector. Although public unions lack the legal right to strike in most states, they do possess advantages. Among the most important advantages is their increasing political clout. However, unions face challenges from those who see them as a threat to the concept of merit. Their clout is also being undermined by the increasing tendency of state and local governments to contract out services to private firms.

Pressure from Common Cause and other "good government" groups has resulted in more openness in government. Public bodies, including state and local agencies, are subject to open meetings and open records laws that give the press and the average citizen access to information. Some people are concerned, however, that too much openness may constrain the decision-making process or allow undue influence by special interests.

Legislatures have strengthened their oversight function and have instituted innovations such as sunset legislation. Sunset laws force legislatures to review administrative agencies on a periodic basis. Legislative review is necessary because agencies automatically go out of existence unless they are re-created by legislative statute. State legislatures also employ the legislative veto to review agency rules and guidelines, although the future of the legislative veto has been put into question by the U.S. Supreme Court's ruling that it is unconstitutional at the federal level.

Study Objectives

1. Explain why bureaucracy is often the object of criticism. Describe how the concept of capture of regulatory agencies discussed in Box 11-1 illustrates the problems of modern bureaucracy.
2. Identify the three functions of executive branch agencies and boards.
3. Describe the changes that are making lieutenant governors influential executive actors.
4. Define the term "civil service." Identify and discuss both the advantages and disadvantages of a civil service system.
5. Discuss the extent to which states have met the standards or goals of reorganization of their executive branches.
6. Describe the effect federal aid has had on state executive branches and administrators.
7. Explain why most budgeting processes are incremental. Discuss why most budget reforms that are intended to provide comprehensive long-range views of government programs are not likely to be successful.
8. Proponents of merit systems argue that unions challenge the concept of merit. Explain why they make this charge. Describe the responses union supporters offer to their critics.
9. Define the term "privatization." Describe the arguments of those who support privatization and the concerns of those who view it skeptically.

10. Explain why sunset laws are supposed to help shrink government and discuss whether this in fact occurs.

Glossary

auditing The process of examining a state or local government agency's expenditures to see if they are legal and accurate.

bureaucratic discretion The delegation of authority to administrative agencies by legislatures. Agencies use this authority to establish legally binding rules or regulations.

capture A regulatory agency comes to be controlled by the industry or interest that it is supposed to regulate.

collective bargaining Negotiation about the terms and conditions of employment between an employer and a union representing the employees.

comparable worth A demand made by women's groups in recent years. Different jobs can be compared objectively to determine their relative value to the employer; jobs that are of the same value should be paid equally.

effectiveness A standard applied to bureaucracy. The degree to which an administrator's decisions are more likely than are alternative choices to bring about the desired outcomes.

fiscal year Designates the cycle of a budget year, *not* a normal year.

functional fiefdoms The exclusive relationships that develop among federal, state, and local bureaucrats who administer specific functional areas such as transportation, law enforcement, or welfare. Elected officials sometimes feel that bureaucrats within these fiefdoms are not responsive to them and to the public they represent.

incremental budgeting The process of proposing budgets based on figures in the previous year's budget plus a little more.

legislative veto The legislature—often a legislative committee—has the authority to strike down agency rules that do not meet the original intent of the legislature.

merit system The system of hiring government employees on the basis of their qualifications; employment is based on merit rather than political connections or patronage.

open records laws Allow citizens to gain access to most of the records and information held by public agencies.

oversight The process conducted to make sure that administrative agencies implement policies the way the legislature intended.

planning-programming-budgeting systems (PPBS) Budget reforms that emphasize the overall goals of agencies rather than year-to-year spending items.

plural executive Chief executive officials and department heads are elected, making them independent of control by the chief executive.

privatization The process of providing public-sector services through private-sector contracts.

quasi-judicial powers The power of administrative agencies to judge cases involving agency rules or regulations.

quasi-legislative powers The authority of the bureaucracy to make rules or regulations that have the force of law or legislation.

reorganization Reshaping, usually through executive order, the way in which departments, agencies, boards, and commissions are organized.

responsiveness A standard applied to bureaucracy. The extent to which decisions by bureaucrats reflect the preferences of the community or the officeholders authorized to speak for the public.

revolving door syndrome The process by which bureaucrats pass from industry to a regulatory board and back to industry. This syndrome is one of the reasons why agencies are captured by the industries they regulate.

sunset laws A form of oversight. Specify that agencies be "sunsetted," that is, terminated, unless the legislature passes a law to re-create them.

sunshine laws Require that all public bodies open all meetings to the public except in special circumstances specified by law.

tenure The right to hold a position or office free from arbitrary dismissal. Public employees in the civil service and teachers achieve tenure after serving a probationary period.

whistle-blower An individual who exposes to public view the abuses or mismanagement of his or her agency.

zero-based budgeting A budget reform that forces agencies to justify why they should get more than zero dollars rather than an incremental increase. In reality, agencies generally start with 90 percent of their budgets rather than a zero amount.

Endnotes

1. *Special Analyses: Budget of the United States: Fiscal Year 1988* (Washington, DC: Office of Management and Budget, 1987), I-1–I-11.
2. Francis E. Rourke, *Bureaucracy, Politics, and Public Policy*, 3rd ed. (Boston: Little, Brown, 1984), 6.
3. Ibid., 4.
4. Gary C. Bryner, *Bureaucratic Discretion: Law and Policy in Federal Regulatory Agencies* (New York: Pergamon, 1987), 1.
5. The "classic" characteristics of bureaucracy are often taken from Max Weber. See H. H. Gerth and C. Wright Mills, trans., *From Max Weber: Essays on Sociology* (New York: Oxford University Press, 1946), 196–239.
6. Richard C. Elling, "State Bureaucracies," in Virginia Gray, Herbert Jacob, and Kenneth N. Vines, eds., *Politics in the American States: A Comparative Analysis*, 4th ed. (Boston: Little, Brown, 1983), 250.
7. Advisory Commission on Intergovernmental Relations, *The Question of State Government Capability* (Washington, DC: ACIR, 1985), 149.
8. Arthur English and John J. Carroll, "The Lieutenant Governor: New Directions for a Neglected Office?" Paper delivered at the 1988 meeting of the Southern Political Science Association, November 3, 1988, p. 2.
9. Lieutenant Governor Myron E. Leavitt of Nevada, *U.S. News and World Report* (November 5, 1979), 53–54. Cited by Larry Sabato, *Goodbye to Good-Time Charlie: The American Governorship Transformed*, 2nd ed. (Washington, DC: Congressional Quarterly Press, 1983), 74.
10. Thad L. Beyle and Nelson C. Dometrius, "Governors and Lieutenant Governors," in Thad L. Beyle and Lynn R. Munchmore, eds., *Being Governor: The View from the Office* (Durham NC: Duke University Press, 1983), 148.

11. English and Carroll, 10.

12. Ibid., 8.

13. Peter J. Haas and Deil S. Wright, "The Changing Profile of State Administrators," *Journal of State Government* 60 (November-December 1987), 270–278.

14. Ibid., 271–272.

15. *The Question of State Government Capability*, 164–165.

16. Ibid., 144.

17. Thomas H. Clapper and Thad L. Beyle, "Organizing State Government to Be Managed," in Thad L. Beyle, ed., *State Government: CQ's Guide to Current Issues and Activities, 1987–88* (Washington, DC: Congressional Quarterly, 1987), 125. This article also appeared in the *Comparative State Politics Newsletter* (August 1986), 13.

18. A. E. Buck, *The Reorganization of State Governments in the United States* (New York: Columbia University Press, 1938), 14.

19. *The Question of State Government Capability*, 147–149.

20. Ibid., 148–149.

21. Haas and Wright, 276.

22. David C. Nice, *Federalism: The Politics of Intergovernmental Relations* (New York: St. Martin's, 1987), 146–147.

23. Haas and Wright, 276.

24. James Ramsey and Merlin H. Hackbart, *Innovations in State Budgeting: Process, Impact* (Lexington, KY: Center for Public Affairs, 1980), 6.

25. Kenneth Howard, *Changing State Budgeting* (Lexington, KY: Council of State Governments, 1973), 167.

26. Bureau of Labor Statistics and Richard E. Schumann, "State and Local Government Pay Increases Outpace Five-Year Rise in Private Industry," *Monthly Labor Review* 110 (February 1987), 18–20.

27. Matt Talmer, "New York's Civil Service Employees Association: A New Political Look," *Empire State Report Magazine* (September 1984), 7–8.

28. Results of the survey cited by Donna Dudek, "Going Private . . . Paying Less?" in Thad L. Beyle, ed., *State Government: CQ's Guide to Current Issues and Activities, 1988–89* (Washington, DC: Congressional Quarterly, 1988), 156.

29. E. S. Savas, *Privatizing the Public Sector: How to Shrink Government* (Chatham, NJ: Chatham House, 1982), 93.

30. Barbara J. Stevens, ed., *Delivering Municipal Services Efficiently: A Comparison of Municipal and Private Service Delivery—Summary* (Washington, DC: U.S. Department of Housing and Urban Development, June 1984).

31. David C. Nice, "Sunset Laws and Legislative Vetoes in the States," *State Government* 58 (Spring 1985), 27–32.

32. Cynthia Slaughter (now Opheim), "Sunset and Occupational Regulation: A Case Study," *Public Administration Review* 46 (May-June 1986), 241–245.

33. Nice, 27.

Chapter
12

The Search for Justice: Law and the Judiciary

The central goal of government in a liberal democracy is to provide justice. To the extent that they operate as intended, all political institutions contribute toward the production of justice. Some institutions, however, are specifically oriented toward creating and dispensing justice, while others attempt to promote justice as a by-product of their operation. In this chapter and Chapter 13 we will examine some of the institutions which undertake to create and dispense justice in the process of administering the law.

If everyone in our society agreed about what is just (and what is unjust), the administration of justice and the enforcement of law would be a much easier task. The good news is that there is a considerable amount of agreement, without which we could not survive as a nation-state. The sobering news is that our society will never agree on everything. In part this simply

(Courtesy of Forsyth, Monkmeyer.)

reflects the human condition, but it also reminds us that we are one of the most diverse societies on the face of the earth, certainly the most heterogeneous liberal democracy to last 200 years on this planet.

The following pages will attempt to demonstrate how we survive as a diverse people by examining (1) the different kind of law used to promote order and justice, (2) the structure of the state and local court systems, (3) the role of lawyers and bar associations, and (4) the methods for selecting and removing judges.

THE NATURE OF LAW

The word **law** has at least two very important and related meanings. A particular law is a rule, statute, or ordinance issued by a unit of government.[1] The law against rape and the laws against burglary and robbery are examples of statutes. These laws are collected in **codes**.

"Law" is also used in a general sense to refer to the entire body of principles, rules, and statutes created by the various legislative bodies and government agencies. When we use the term as if "the law" were some awesome, majestic force, it is not only this body of law but also the notion that even powerful individuals have to obey the rules to which we refer. We have a government of laws. Law is created by legislative bodies and judges. It is then interpreted by judges and enforced by prosecutors and police officers, all working within the particular political culture of a state or nation. Using this definition, "law" is a constantly changing entity which reflects the values and ideas of a society. The goal of the legal process — the creation, interpretation, and enforcement of the law — is justice.

Law and Justice

Law and justice are not synonymous. Justice involves acting in accordance with values and ideals; law involves acting in accordance with rules and procedures. **Justice** may be thought of as fair treatment, but justice is not an inevitable consequence of law. One mark of a civilized people is its resolve to make justice an outcome of the legal system.

Law involves a process for making rules and pursuing justice. Since justice is best pursued calmly and systematically, a major feature of every legal system is the maintenance of order. Sometimes law represents a compromise between competing interests, but at other times law supports some interests at the expense of others.[2] Therefore, law originates from both consensus and conflict, depending on the issue and the times. In a liberal democracy, we can use political resources to influence lawmaking, law enforcement, and the interpretation of law.

In some societies, the **rule of men** operates. One person (in some countries, a few people) decides what the law is and how it should be applied. In this system, the winner in a dispute is determined by the characteristics of those involved: who is strongest, most clever, most politically powerful, or most willing to use drastic means to win.

Our legal system is based on the **rule of law**. This means that legal questions refer at some point to a written document and are resolved in a formal process. Citizens may disagree about what is meant by that written document, but their disagreements are resolved in a formal process which occurs in a court of law, and all sides agree more or less to abide by the decision. The rule of law is a major ingredient in the pursuit of justice in modern society.

Law in a Federal System

The federal Constitution is the supreme law of the land, and although the states have constitutions, they cannot make laws in violation of the federal Constitution. If they do, the laws are challenged and struck down as unconstitutional.

Two doctrines mesh state and federal law. Both derive from the federal Constitution. The first — the **full faith and credit clause** of the Constitution —applies to civil matters. It requires that each state recognize contracts made in other states. Thus a will made in Oregon will be valid in Florida, and a contract signed in Arizona must be honored in New York. The second —

the **doctrine of incorporation** — applies the federal Bill of Rights to the states by using the due process clause of the Fourteenth Amendment. Thus, no person may be deprived of the rights guaranteed in the Bill of Rights without due process of law.

One example of the doctrine of incorporation is the application of most of the rights contained in the first ten amendments of the federal constitution — the Bill of Rights — to state as well as federal courts. Those rights, called **civil liberties**, are promises that the state will not arbitrarily and capriciously abridge the freedom of individuals. In return, the state demands that citizens obey its laws. Civil liberties promise that individuals cannot be imprisoned by an unjust government like that of the British in the colonies prior to the Revolutionary War.

Among the civil liberties are those deemed very important by the citizens of the United States: (1) the right to assemble, (2) the right of free speech, (3) the right to be free from cruel and unusual punishment, (4) the right to be free from unreasonable search and seizure, (5) the right to be free from self-incrimination, and (6) the right not to be deprived of life or liberty without due process of law.

At times, judges have decided that a *practice* at the state level is in violation of the federal Constitution even though it has been common in state courts for a long time. For instance, the rule that illegally gathered evidence could not be used in a criminal trial, known as the exclusionary rule, was the law only in federal courts. However, in a 1960 ruling, *Mapp* v. *Ohio*,[3] the Supreme Court decreed that the practice by states of admitting illegally obtained evidence in criminal trials was a violation of the due process clause of the Fourteenth Amendment. In light of this ruling, the exclusionary rule was incorporated into the laws of all states.

THE FORMS OF LAW

The American legal system contains four major categories of law: (1) common law, (2) equity law, (3) statute law, and (4) administrative law. All these categories have evolved in light of the federal Constitution and have developed in response to the particular demands of a modern democracy. In addition, civil and criminal law are two major types of law woven throughout these categories.

Common Law

Law evolving out of the efforts of judges to settle cases and disputes by using the customs of the common people is called **common law**. The American system of common law is based on the system of law which originates in medieval England.

Common law today is still judge-made law, and its application is sometimes the subject of much discussion and disagreement. Common law is

---

Box 12-1 **Common Law in Action**

An example of the application of common law can be found in *Rodriguez* v. *Bethlehem Steel Company*. Mrs. Rodriguez sued Bethlehem Steel because her husband had been injured in an accident which was allegedly caused by the negligence of the steel company. As a result of the accident, he was unable to do the sorts of things husbands normally do, including having sexual relations with his wife. Mrs. Rodriguez said she could no longer be a wife to her husband but instead had become his nurse. She wanted to sue for loss of consortium but was unable to do so. Common law held that a woman has no personal rights except through her husband. As a result, Mrs. Rodriguez could not sue for loss of consortium, or the loss of her husband's love and services as a husband. However, the California Supreme Court ruled that women are no longer the chattel of their husbands. Instead, it ruled that women are independent individuals who have all the rights of men, including the right to sexual relations with their spouses and the right to sue for the loss of that right. Common law, "inspired by natural reason and an innate sense of justice, and adopted by common consent for the regulation and government of the affairs of men," gave Mrs. Rodriquez the right to sue for redress of her situation.

Source: 12 Cal 3d 282, 525 P.2d 669 (1974). See Stanley Mosk, "The Common Law and the Judicial Making Process," *Harvard Journal of Law and Public Policy* 11(1)(Winter 1988), 35–41.

---

created when judges apply a general principle, often found in the precedents supplied by other cases, to situations not fully covered by statute law. **Stare decisis**[4] is the judicial practice of applying a previously used legal principle to a set of facts to settle a legal dispute (Box 12-1). Each case becomes a precedent for those which follow and is applied by judges in similar situations unless a good reason not to do so can be found.

Common law is flexible and practical and permits older law to be applied to modern situations. Because it is flexible, law evolves and changes. Because judges constantly interpret the law in light of previous ruling and modern practice, it is difficult to know with certainty what the law *is* at any given time. All the lawyers know is what the law has been until this time and this judge's ruling.

Equity Law

Equity law arises from the attempt to prevent wrong which cannot be remedied by damages.[5] It is also judge-made law. A request for equity is a request for fairness; it is often a request that some action be prevented on the grounds that permitting the action would make it impossible to achieve equity at a later date. Equity law had its beginnings in the English equity courts of the fourteenth century. Equity courts provided a place where a commoner could plead with the monarch for fairness on the basis that common law could not provide it. A number of states have separate equity courts, but whether separate courts are maintained or their functions are subsumed in other courts, the American system of jurisprudence recognizes the obligation to provide equity.

For instance, suppose a developer has purchased a tract of land on which several 2000-year-old gingko trees stand. A conservation-minded citizen may request that a judge stop the developer from destroying the trees by blocking development of the land until the issue can be decided in court at a later date. In this case, the citizen will argue that if the developer were permitted to continue the tree destruction and if a court were to decide at a later date that the development should not occur, no one would be able to bring the trees back. In pursuit of equity, the judge may issue an **injunction**, or a judicial ruling that prohibits an action, in this case the destruction of the trees by the developer. Or the judge may issue a **writ of mandamus** requiring another official—a sheriff, for example—to intervene. A writ of mandamus is a judicial ruling that commands an action to be done, in this case the preservation of the trees. This is an example of equity law: providing equity through preventive rulings by a judge. (If the developer destroys the trees despite the judicial ruling, the judge can find the developer in **contempt of court** and summarily fine or jail the developer.)

Statute Law or Civil Law

Although it is interpreted and applied by judges, **statutory law** is written and enacted by a legislature. When they conflict, statutory law overrides common law, although many statutes are based on common law. Thus the two traditions complement more than compete with each other.

All criminal law is statutory law. In criminal cases, the accused is prosecuted by the government since all crimes are against the public order even though private property or individuals may be harmed as well. If a behavior is not expressly forbidden in written law, it is not a crime no matter how wrong the people in the culture may think it is. The disadvantage of a pure system of civil or statutory law is the difficulty of writing laws which cover all situations. In the American system of justice, statutory law is combined with common law to bring about justice.

Administrative Law

One form of law that often is overlooked is law made by administrative bodies. State legislatures and local governing boards often create administrative agencies to enforce their legislative intentions. Examples of such agencies are housing agencies, civil service boards, and state revenue agencies. **Administrative law** deals with rate making, operating rules, the rights of individuals and firms regulated by administrative agencies, and the power of certain courts to review or overturn decisions made by administrative agencies.

These government agencies make rules and regulations to govern the work they do and the population with which they deal, as described in Chapter 11. These rules are like laws, and quasi-judicial hearings take place in administrative tribunals every day. Because of the widespread use of administrative agencies to regulate important aspects of economic and social life, more people are affected by administrative law than are affected by statute law.[6] For instance, suppose a police officer in a police department operating under civil service rules and regulations is fired by the police chief. The officer may have the right to appeal the firing to a civil service board. The board listens to the appeal in a hearing and makes a legal ruling about whether the agency followed its own rules in firing the officer. Once rendered, this ruling can be appealed to a higher court, and statutory, common, or equity law may be applied. This entire process takes place under civil service law created by a state legislature and the rules and regulations made by the local civil service board in light of the law.

Civil Law and Criminal Law

An important distinction which organizes our thinking about law is the dichotomy between civil law and criminal law. **Criminal law** is made up of codes which prohibit and occasionally require certain behaviors. Criminal laws contain sanctions or punishments to be applied if the law is violated. The sanctions may consist of fines, confinement, or execution.

Criminal law is statute law; there are no longer common law crimes. Criminal law is prosecuted by local, state, and federal governments; the government or state is the complainant, and the accused person becomes the defendant. The majority of criminal law cases are handled by state courts.

Criminal law can be divided into two categories: Felonies and misdemeanors. The exact qualities of a felony vary from state to state, but in general felonies are crimes punishable by death or more than a year in prison. Examples of felonies are murder, rape, robbery, and arson. Misdemeanors are all other crimes and are considered to be less serious than are felonies. The penalties usually range from fines to jail terms of less than a year. Examples of misdemeanors are traffic violations, petty theft, and disorderly conduct.[7]

Civil law includes every legal action other than criminal proceedings. Examples of civil law are contract law, which applies to the nature of agreements between individuals or corporations; domestic or family law, which applies to husband, wife, and child relationships; and tort law, which covers civil wrongs, not based on contracts, allegedly done by one or more citizens against another. An example of an action brought under domestic law would be divorce, the request for dissolution of a marriage; an example of an action brought under tort law would be libel,[8] the accusation that an individual has been maliciously defamed in print by another person.

Although civil law and criminal law are mutually exclusive, a specific behavior can be penalized under both systems. For example, rape is a criminal offense, and a rapist may be convicted in a criminal court. A woman who has been raped can also bring a civil suit against the rapist in order to recover damages. Motor vehicle theft is also a criminal offense, but the person whose car has been stolen can file a civil suit against the thief to recover damages.

The Law and the Search for Justice

Law is both a product of and a guide for continuing the search for justice. The American system of law is a combination of common law, statutory law, equity law, and administrative law. One reason for this mixed system is the inability of common law, with its emphasis on economic laissez-faire and the right of landowners, to provide a basis for modern industrial society.[9] English common law reflected the complex mutual obligations of the feudal society in which it developed. Land and property rights were something more than mere economic resources; they described an individual's station in life. Those who had property were superior in terms of status, prestige, and power; those without property were clearly inferior. The emphasis on economic opportunity and social equality in the United States made changes in common law necessary if Americans were to live up to the ideal of equality for all. Nevertheless, common law remains an important part of the American legal system.

The method by which justice is sought in the American court system is called the **adversarial system** of justice or the adversarial process. Ideally it assumes that in a contest between two well-prepared adversaries, the plaintiff and the defendant, the truth will emerge. Each case is a dispute to be settled in a court of law by following a set of rules, with each side having certain rights and obligations. Each side is expected to present its best case; the hope is that as a result of this proceeding, the truth will emerge and justice will be achieved.

THE JUDICIARY: COURTS AND CASES

Despite complaints about judicial activism, the American judiciary is a passive institution. Courts and judges do not initiate legal action or legislation. Rather, they must wait for citizens or agents of the state to bring business to them.

The business of judges and courts can be classified in terms of two dichotomies: (1) civil and criminal cases and (2) original and appellate jurisdictions. Some courts deal with all four categories, and some specialize. Each category has a vocabulary and procedures that distinguish it from the others, but all four employ the adversarial ideal in the search for justice.

Civil Cases

Civil cases begin when an attorney files a complaint on behalf of a **plaintiff** against a respondent. The plaintiff is the complaining party and may also be known as the petitioner or appellant. The **respondent** is also known as the appellee or defendant. To initiate a civil case, the attorney for the plaintiff must accomplish three things: (1) choose the appropriate court, (2) have the complainant sign a **summons**, or a complaint against the respondent that gives notice requiring the respondent to appear in court to answer the charges, and (3) explain the charges to the court and request a remedy.

It is sometimes necessary early in the proceedings to issue a **subpoena** to compel the presence of the respondent. If the respondent fails to appear, the court may hold that person in contempt of court and levy additional penalties. A **subpoena duces tecum** requires the respondent to bring something, usually records or other possessions, to the court. Both forms of subpoena must always be served in person.

When the defendant appears in court, he or she must enter a plea. The defendant may admit the truth of the complaint or deny the complaint and begin the process of defense. Unless the defendant is able to repudiate the jurisdiction of the court or disallow the legality of the complaint or unless the staff or plaintiff withdraws the charge, the case will proceed.

Discovery, the next step in civil cases, takes place outside the courtroom. Discovery is the formal and informal exchange of information between the sides in a lawsuit. When the discovery occurs in a formal setting, it is called a **deposition**, and the questions and answers are officially and accurately recorded in sworn testimony. Written questions, called **interrogatories**, may also be submitted with a request for written answers during discovery.

The pretrial stage follows discovery. Because going to trial is a time-consuming and financially draining operation for all the participants, including the court, procedures have developed to reduce its likelihood. Many judges require pretrial hearings or conferences between the two parties in hopes that their differences can be settled before trial. Arbitration between the two parties may also be used. Many courts require arbitration in some situations for at least two reasons. First, it helps to reduce the civil caseload; second, there may be other paths to justice than one which results in a winner and a loser.[10] If no decision can be reached through pretrial hearings or arbitration, the case goes to trial.

During the trial, both sides present their cases in the best light. In civil cases, a **preponderance of evidence**—the superior weight or quality of evidence—is the principle by which verdicts are decided.[11] Common law required a petty trial jury of 12 persons, and a verdict required a unanimous decision. Today some civil cases are decided by a judge, and verdicts do not have to be unanimous, although they must be more than a simple majority. In the interest of efficiency, juries now can include as few as six people.

The verdict or finding in civil cases involves decisions about the points raised by the plaintiff and, if appropriate, an assessment of damages and court costs. A plaintiff may win the case but receive little or no damages and even have to pay all or part of the court costs in addition to attorney's fees.

Criminal Cases

Criminal cases are brought to the court's attention when the state attempts to charge an individual with a crime. Charges may be brought in two ways:

(1) by **indictment** or true bill,[12] a charge drawn up by a prosecutor and brought by a **grand jury**, a group of approximately 12 to 23 individuals chosen by the prosecutor, and (2) by a **bill of information**, an accusation made under oath by a prosecuting attorney before a court.[13] All states use grand juries, and most states permit the use of a bill of information to bring charges in some criminal cases.

The next step is the same in both civil and criminal cases: The defendant must indicate a plea. In a criminal case, the plea is entered at the **arraignment**, where the defendant hears the charges against him or her and enters a plea of guilty or not guilty. Bail may also be set, and the defendant can be freed by paying a certain amount of money to guarantee his or her appearance at the trial.

If the plea entered is not guilty, the process of defense begins. The defendant may try to deny the court's jurisdiction or the legality of the complaint in order to get the state to drop the charge.

The pretrial stage comes next. In criminal cases, a common feature of the pretrial stage is **plea bargaining**. This is a process in which the prosecutor and the defendant, through the defense attorney, negotiate the punishment to be assigned in return for a guilty plea.

Plea bargaining operates under two different models: (1) the *consensus* model and (2) the *concessions* model.[14] In the consensus model, the most commonly used process, prosecutors, defense attorneys, and judges can be thought of as a courtroom work group sharing agreements about the "worth" of certain kinds of cases.[15] Certain cases and charges have a standard worth, "a going rate." Cases involving serious crimes committed by defendants with prior records are worth more than others and typically result in a plea of guilty, with a more severe penalty.

The concessions model occurs when the worth of a case is unclear because the case is not routine. The defendant may have information with which to bargain for concessions from the prosecution. The sides "haggle" with one another, with each side getting and giving concessions in the process of arriving at the plea. The defendant's attorney communicates the outcome of the bargaining process to the defendant, and they decide whether to plead guilty or go to trial. If the defendant is unwilling to plead guilty, the case is taken to trial.

Plea bargaining is advantageous to prosecutors, defense attorneys, and defendants since it eliminates the cost and uncertainty of a trial.[16] It is frequently encouraged by judges as well, though often in covert ways. Former judge Abraham Blumberg reports that some judges help cooperating defense attorneys by arranging a "slow plea of guilty," which is a brief "mock" trial presided over by the judge for the benefit of an attorney whose clients insist on demonstrating their innocence in a trial.[17] Cooperating attorneys may also receive favorable sentences for their clients in return for guilty pleas and the circumvention of a trial.

In criminal cases, the most common disposition of a felony arrest which is not rejected or dismissed is a guilty plea, not a trial. Data gathered from a number of urban courts show that in 1979, 45 percent of all felony arrests ended in guilty pleas while only 5 percent ended in trials; half of all felony arrests ended in dismissal or rejection of the indictment. Guilty pleas outnumbered trials by a margin of ten to one.[18] Many authors argue that too often the criminal courts are in fact dispositional rather than adversarial.[19]

Dispositional justice refers to the tendency, common in criminal justice bureaucracies, to emphasize the efficient processing of cases through plea bargaining. Hence, there is a predisposition in favor of making a deal rather than seeking the truth.[20] The consequence of dispositional justice is to reduce the likelihood that a defendant will receive the protection of the law promised in the Bill of Rights—the defendant's civil liberties. Although dispositional justice is more efficient and cost-effective than is the cumbersome adversarial process, it ensures that defendants will not have a jury trial, be permitted to examine witnesses against them, or be permitted to examine the process by which the evidence against them was discovered. As a result, it fails to protect the defendant against the power of the state to punish arbitrarily.

If a case does go to trial, two assumptions guide the process in the criminal court: (1) The defendant is assumed to be innocent until proved guilty, and (2) guilt must be proved beyond a reasonable doubt. The burden of proof is on the state to demonstrate that the defendant is guilty. In addition, the criteria for guilt are more rigorous than they are in civil cases.

An adversarial system of justice is a very inefficient system for resolving civil or criminal disputes. It is often more cost-effective and less time-consuming for each side to negotiate a settlement, with each party giving up something to get something else, than it is to fight to the bitter end in a court of law. As a result, plea bargaining in criminal cases and pretrial negotiation in civil cases are common. The trials that occur constitute only a fraction of all cases in which trials could take place. Whether you want to promote this kind of negotiated justice is something to consider. It is one of several issues affecting the search for justice that will confront you as a future decision maker.

THE JUDICIARY: COURTS AND JURISDICTIONS

Because the United States has a dual system of governments—federal and state—it also has a dual court system. Not only does the federal government make and enforce law, all 50 state governments do so as well. State court systems are created by state constitutions, as was discussed in Chapter 4. Except in the appellate process, where the leap from state to federal courts is made, state courts are separate from the federal system.

The vast majority of cases are filed in state courts. Eighty million cases were filed in state courts in 1983. By comparison, slightly fewer than 278,000 cases (241,842 civil cases and 35,872 criminal cases) were filed in

Table 12.1   STATE COURT CASE FILINGS FOR 1983 AND 1987

	1983	1987
Civil	12,839,400	16,027,139
Criminal	10,511,116	11,271,768
Juvenile	1,142,271	1,338,737
Total	24,492,787	28,637,644
Traffic	57,287,920	65,634,297
Total, including traffic	81,780,707	94,271,941

Sources: For 1983, Carla Gaskins, Eugene Flango, and Jeanne Ito, *Case Filings in State Courts, 1983,* Bureau of Justice Statistics (Washington, DC: GPO, 1984), 2; for 1987, *State Court Caseload Statistics: Annual Report 1987* (Williamsburg, VA: National Center for State Courts, 1989), 18, 20.

federal courts in the same year.[21] (See Table 12.1 for the number of court filings in state courts in 1983 and 1987.)

State court systems vary in terms of the names given to the different courts and in terms of structure. Nevertheless, there is a general pattern of hierarchical structure shared by state court systems (Figure 12.1). At the top of each system is a court of last appeal, variously known by one of several names, including supreme court and court of last appeals. The second level of courts is the appellate courts; beneath them are the trial courts and specialized trial courts.

Although some discernible court structure exists in all states, most state court systems are not well integrated. In 29 states, trial courts at the same level have overlapping jurisdiction, and the levels and courts do not communicate readily with one another.[22] To develop more efficient systems of justice, five states — Illinois, Idaho, Iowa, Minnesota, and South Dakota — and the District of Columbia have created two- or three-tier court systems that permit ease of access and clearly defined jurisdictions. Their trial courts have been consolidated into a single trial court with jurisdiction over all cases and proceedings. The courts at each level have distinct boundaries and separate budgets, with centralized rule-making authority. Although unification of court systems will not solve all the problems faced by the courts, it can reduce the confusion which exists in many state court systems[23] (Figures 12.2 and 12.3).

Courts of Last Appeal

State courts of last appeal are at the top of the hierarchy. All states have at least one court of last appeal, and two states have two courts, one to handle civil cases and the other to handle criminal cases. Called supreme courts in 43 states and by various names (supreme judicial court, court of appeals, court of criminal appeals) in the others, these are the last courts at the state levels to which appeals can be made.

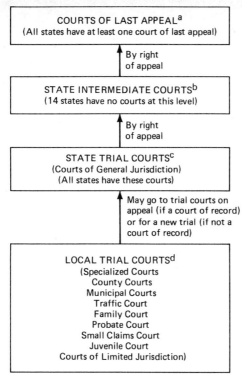

COURTS OF LAST APPEAL[a]
(All states have at least one court of last appeal)

↑ By right
of appeal

STATE INTERMEDIATE COURTS[b]
(14 states have no courts at this level)

↑ By right
of appeal

STATE TRIAL COURTS[c]
(Courts of General Jurisdiction)
(All states have these courts)

↑ May go to trial courts on
appeal (if a court of record)
or for a new trial (if not a
court of record)

LOCAL TRIAL COURTS[d]
(Specialized Courts
County Courts
Municipal Courts
Traffic Court
Family Court
Probate Court
Small Claims Court
Juvenile Court
Courts of Limited Jurisdiction)

[a] Also known as Supreme Court, Supreme Court of Appeals,
Supreme Judicial Courts, Court of Appeals, and Court of Criminal Appeals.

[b] Also known as Court of Appeals, Intermediate Court of Appeals, and
Court of Criminal Appeals.

[c] Also known as Superior Court, Chancery Courts, Circuit Court, District
Court and Court of Common Pleas.

[d] These courts have limited jurisdiction, though they may have original
jurisdiction and may be courts of record.

Figure 12.1 The general structure of state court systems.

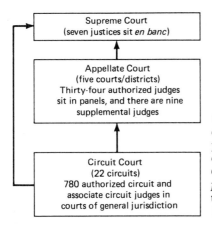

Supreme Court
(seven justices sit *en banc*)

Appellate Court
(five courts/districts)
Thirty-four authorized judges
sit in panels, and there are nine
supplemental judges

Circuit Court
(22 circuits)
780 authorized circuit and
associate circuit judges in
courts of general jurisdiction

Figure 12.2 The Illinois state court system has been unified to provide a more efficient system of justice. (*Source: State Court Caseload Statistics: Annual Report 1987* [Williamsburg, VA: National Center for State Courts, 1989], 147.)

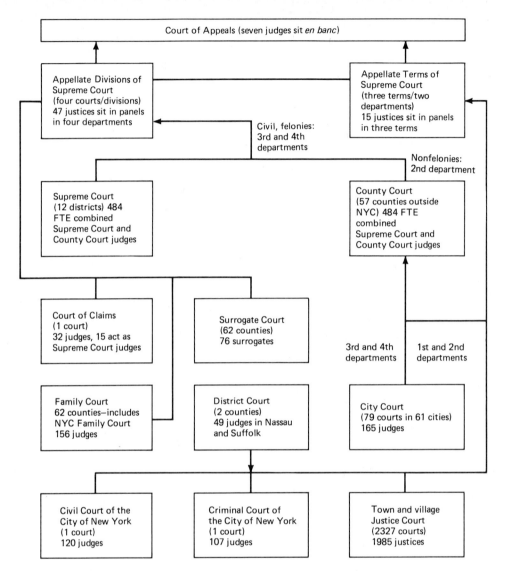

Figure 12.3 The New York state court system has overlapping jurisdictions, making communication between the many courts less efficient. (*Source: State Court Caseload Statistics: Annual Report 1987* [Williamsburg, VA: National Center for State Courts, 1989], 166.)

Courts of last appeal do not accept all cases referred to them from the intermediate appellate level.[24] They accept cases only on the basis of questions of law; that is, they decide whether the law was interpreted or applied fairly. They decide whether the defendant received justice in terms of the law. Courts of last appeal may set common law, examine statutory interpretation, or interpret the state constitution. The United States Supreme Court, which hears only a fraction of the cases appealed to it, demands that state remedies be exhausted before it will hear a case. Thus, the few cases selected to be head by the Supreme Court have been heard previously in state courts of last appeal.

Intermediate Courts of Appeal

State intermediate courts of appeal hear cases which are appealed from the lower courts. Appellate courts do not have original jurisdiction; they can hear only cases which have been appealed to them from a lower court. Although appeals to the state court of final appeal can be made from state intermediate appellate courts, most cases are not appealed beyond the intermediate appellate courts because of the cost of such appeals and the low acceptance rate by the final court.

Intermediate appellate courts have different names in different states, including courts of appeal (26 states), appellate courts (2 states), and various names in other states. Fourteen states have no intermediate appellate courts, and four states have two major courts at this level.[25] Some states have an intricate system of appellate courts with numerous judges; note the elaborate appeals process for New York State shown in Figure 12.3.

State Trial Courts

State trial courts, the next level of courts, have *general jurisdiction*, which means they can hear any type of case which comes up in their area, civil or criminal. They are courts of *original jurisdiction* because cases start or originate there, and they can also hear cases appealed to them from lower courts and administrative tribunals. When appeals come from local trial courts and most administrative tribunals, the cases are heard **de novo**, as completely new cases. State trial courts carry the responsibility for much of the work done in state courts and therefore have broad authority.

Within each state there are several territorial jurisdictions called districts or circuits. The state trial court within the district has jurisdiction in the territory. Among the common names for these courts are circuit court (18 states), superior court (13 states), and district court (16 states). These courts hear both civil and criminal cases.

Local Trial Courts

Local trial courts are courts of *limited jurisdiction*, which means they can hear only specific kinds of cases (juvenile court, traffic court, probate court) or cases which occur within a particular area (county court, municipal court). County courts are established by state governments and deal with violations of state and local ordinances and laws. Municipal courts are established by cities to deal with violations of local ordinances and state laws. These courts deal almost exclusively with criminal violations; most of their

Box 12-2 **The Small Claims Court**

If you believe that you have been cheated but the amount of the loss is not enough to justify hiring a lawyer, you have another option. You can take your grievance to small claims court, where you will be able to represent yourself for only the small cost of filing fees. To find the small claims court, look in the telephone book. If you see no listing under the municipal or county headings, call the justice of the peace or a county court clerk for the location of the small claims court. In some areas, small claims cases are handled by a justice of the peace.

When you find the small claims court, there will be forms to complete and a small filing fee to pay. There is usually someone there to help you complete the forms and give you advice about the court process. The following guide may help you decide whether to file in small claims court.

To file in small claims court:

1. Your claim must be based on a sound legal concept.

2. You must have evidence to support your claim.

3. Your claim must be within the dollar limitation of the jurisdiction of the court.

4. You must file your claim within a specified period of time.

5. You must file your claim with the court that has jurisdiction over your case.

6. Many courts require and common sense dictates that you contact the other party and attempt to resolve the dispute before going to court.

7. In injuries to property or person, you must be able to prove that intentional or negligent behavior was the cause of the injury.

Source: Gayle L. Niles and Douglas H. Snider, *Woman's Counsel: A Legal Guide for Women* (Denver: Arden, 1984), 32–34.

time is taken up by misdemeanor traffic violations. Many towns do not want to bear the cost of municipal courts and thus do not establish them.

Both county and municipal courts may be courts of original jurisdiction. They are also generally the first *courts of record*. Courts of record have three characteristics: (1) Transcripts of the precedings are available, (2) decisions are appealable, and (3) judges preside over the proceedings.

These courts solve local problems. Courts such as traffic court, juvenile court, and family court serve a specific community and may alleviate local social problems. Among the most successful of such courts are the small claims courts, where citizens can settle minor disputes involving relatively small sums of money. Individuals plead their cases to the judge without the services of a lawyer. These courts are streamlined and permit the quick dispensation of justice (Box 12-2).

Justice of the Peace Courts

The justice of the peace court is the lowest court at the state level and is presided over by a justice of the peace (JP). Individuals who become JPs are not required to be lawyers or to have any particular training before being elected (usually) or appointed (less often) to the post. Some states do require training when the justice of the peace takes office. The duties of a justice of the peace vary but customarily involve civil cases of less than $300, misdemeanors, and other services for a fee. These services may include conducting marriage ceremonies, certifying deaths, and notarizing documents.

Cost of State and Local Court Systems

The burden of funding the court system in the United States is carried by state and local governments. These governments funded 91 percent of all court payrolls and over 80 percent of all prosecution and legal service payrolls in the United States in 1985. Salaries for public defender offices are funded almost exclusively by state and local governments.[26]

In comparison to corrections and police protection, judicial systems are among the least costly agencies in the justice system. Table 12.2 shows the costs of a court system to state and local governments. Note that courts account for less than 18 percent of all justice system costs at the local level;

Table 12.2 COURT SYSTEM EMPLOYMENT AND PAYROLLS: OCTOBER 1985

	Total employment	October payroll($)
Total state justice system	443,383	878,889,000
Total state court system only	175,725	217,149,000
Total local justice system	885,560	1,698,005,000
Total local court system only	91,011	296,714,000
Judicial (courts only)		
State	61,082	151,678,000
Total local	115,967	171,344,000
County	88,291	134,529,000
Municipal	27,676	36,815,000
Prosecution and legal services		
State	23,926	53,164,000
Total local	54,025	111,763,000
County	35,657	72,154,000
Municipal	18,386	39,609,000
Public defense		
State	6,003	12,307,000
Total local	5,733	13,607,000
County	5,476	12,956,000
Municipal	257	651,000

Source: Timothy J. Flanagan and Katherine M. Jamieson, *Sourcebook of Criminal Justice Statistics, 1987,* U.S. Department of Justice, Bureau of Justice Statistics, (Washington, DC: GPO, 1988), 151.

the court system accounts for one-quarter of the cost for the entire justice system at the state level.

THE JUDICIARY: LAWYERS AND JUDGES

Most judges are lawyers, and if you are interested in becoming a judge, you should plan on going to law school and becoming a lawyer first. The following discussion about lawyers may help you decide if law is a career you'd like to pursue, but be sure to read Box 12-3 to learn about law school before you decide.

Lawyers: Gatekeepers of the Legal System

The classic image of the attorney in the courtroom—tireless, moral, partisan, and above all concerned with justice—is the stuff of many books and movies. However, real lawyers are average people with typical life problems which, as is true of all persons in the legal system, may encourage them to find solutions which fall short of the romantic ideal portrayed by Perry Mason. This is not meant to demean lawyers or to impugn their motives. They are, in fact, pivotal to the search for justice in the United States.

The number of persons practicing law increases every year. In June 1988, the Department of Labor reported that more than 759,000 lawyers and judges were working in the United States, up from 716,000 in June 1987.[27] Of those lawyers, 600,000 were males and 159,000 were females.[28] However, as the number of lawyers increases, the distribution of legal services and the public's perception of the legal profession continue to be areas of concern for the nation's legal system (Table 12.3).

Lawyers "Man" the Litigious Society Lawyers are the "principal gatekeepers" for noncriminal cases since would-be litigants must seek their

Table 12.3 PUBLIC RATINGS OF THE HONESTY AND ETHICAL STANDARDS OF LAWYERS AND POLICE OFFICERS: 1988.
Question: How would you rate the honesty and ethical standards of the people in these different fields?

	Very high (%)	High (%)	Average (%)	Low (%)	Very low (%)	No opinion (%)
Druggists	14	52	29	2	1	2
College teachers	10	44	35	5	1	5
Police officers	10	37	39	8	3	3
Lawyers	3	15	45	23	10	4
Realtors	3	10	47	27	7	6

Source: Katherine M. Jamieson and Timothy J. Flanagan, *Sourcebook of Criminal Justice Statistics, 1988*, Bureau of Justice Statistics, (Washington, DC: GPO, 1989), 192.

Box 12-3 So You Want to Be a Lawyer

If you want to be a lawyer, you must overcome a series of obstacles. The first is earning a bachelor's degree with a very good grade point average. You do not have to major in any particular area, although classes which emphasize critical thinking skills, logic, and writing will help once you get into law school.

Getting into law school is the second obstacle. Law schools use grade point averages and scores on the Law School Admission Test (LSAT) as important criteria for admission. They also may consider other criteria, such as improvement in grade point average, college activities, ethnic background, a personal interview or written essay (often requested on admission forms), and letters of recommendation. Very prestigious law schools may consider the college where the bachelor's degree is earned and the difficulty of the undergraduate curriculum.

You should take the LSAT seriously because law schools do. Some students take courses to prepare for the exam. You must decide if your pocketbook will permit such a course; you must also decide if your skills require it. Write to the Law School Admissions Council/Law School Admissions Services, Box 2000, Newtown, PA 18940-0989, or call (215) 968–1001 for more information about law school admissions.

Deciding which law schools to apply to is important. You should consider where you want to practice law and then decide whether you want to attend a law school with a national reputation or a local law school which may or may not be prestigious. Consider whether you need to attend school at night or part time and check to see which law schools permit you to do so. Consider whether you can get an additional degree while earning the law degree. Be sure to apply to several law schools in case you are not admitted to the school of your choice.

Once in law school, your life will change dramatically. You will learn the case law approach, a method of examining related cases that focus on an area of law and then applying the information in those cases to the case you are studying. Law school professors expect you to find and think about the material on your own. They do not tell you what you should know, but they will call on you in class and expect you to have the answers. Law school is anxiety-provoking until you learn the case method, how to study, and how to be prepared for class.

If you want to be a lawyer in order to make a great deal of money, law school is where you should make your mark. Starting salaries for lawyers are high for the students in the upper 10 percent of a class (an average of over $40,000 in most large cities), but mediocre students can expect ''to devote considerable time and energy to securing a first job they consider acceptable.''

Once finished with law school, you will have to pass a state bar exam to become a lawyer. You may work in a law firm as a clerk or research assistant before taking the exam, but ''passing a bar'' admits you to the practice of law. In 1987, more than 40,000 persons became eligible to practice law, adding to the more than 700,000 already practicing. It should be obvious that the competition between lawyers is significant.

Source: *The Official Guide to U.S. Law Schools 1990–1991*, (Newtown, PA: Law Services Publications, 1990), 2, 10.

services; their control over civil litigation may be thought of as a monopoly.[29] Although many lawyers work for governments (state, local, and federal) and private industry, the significant majority are in private practice. Lawyers make their living by representing clients in actual and potential lawsuits. As a result, more than *16 million* civil suits were filed in state and local courts in 1987.[30] The frequency with which lawsuits are filed and the number of readily available attorneys to do the filing produce the belief that disputes should be settled in court. As a result, the courts are glutted with lawsuits to which time, money, and effort must be allocated. The question which must be asked is whether justice can result from this overloaded legal system.

Nevertheless, the dissemination of legal services to those who need them in civil matters is uneven. Surprisingly, middle-income individuals may be represented less adequately on a regular basis than are people of any other economic level. The business community is likely to be best served by private law firms and the poor in large cities are likely to be well served by various government agencies.[31] Many middle-class individuals must rely on word-of-mouth information from friends and acquaintances when choosing a lawyer; they may have to rely on the same attorneys who wrote their wills instead of using a specialist. Other middle-income individuals may be unable to afford an attorney's fees and so may be unable to obtain legal assistance.

A number of authors have been interested in the degree to which private attorneys represent the interests of their clients as opposed to their own interests, particularly in the criminal courts. In such analyses, a distinction is made between courthouse regulars and out-of-town attorneys. Defense attorneys who regularly appear before the same judges and must negotiate with the same prosecutors are likely to be more concerned with their relationships with the courtroom work group than with their clients' welfare.[32] Members of the work group share a similar problem: All must manage their burdensome caseloads and attempt to keep the justice system working. This provides the impetus for dispositional justice — the efficient processing of cases through the criminal justice system — by emphasizing plea bargaining. There is some evidence that this situation also occurs in the practice of civil law when the attorney's client or case cannot generate a large fee.[33]

Attorneys who come in from other communities as "hired guns" have little to lose in their relationships with local justice officials and are more likely to fight for the interests of their clients; by contrast, outsiders may be unaware of the rules and expectations in the local court, putting them at a disadvantage in negotiations and rulings.[34] This is true whether the case is in civil or criminal court. In this case, attorneys are obligated to do what they can to secure a positive verdict for their clients. (See Box 12-5 for an example of the lengths to which attorneys will go to gain an advantage in a major case.)

Lawyers are the only individuals permitted to practice law or conduct out-of-court legal business (Box 12-4).[35] In more than half the states, lawyers are required to be dues-paying members of the state bar in order to practice

Box 12-4 The Paralegal: Another Career in the Judiciary

It is not necessary to become a lawyer or a judge to work in law. The Labor Department estimates that the fastest growing occupation for the next ten years will be the paralegal profession. Not only does the employment outlook look optimistic for paralegals, but the average national salary is between $22,000 and $25,000, with a Dallas law firm paying some paralegals nearly $100,000 (though this is very unusual).*

A *paralegal* is a legal assistant, someone who is trained to help lawyers research cases and prepare briefs. Paralegals may even prepare preliminary versions of legal documents and interview witnesses. They are often central to the activity of a law firm or administrative agency, and the work is important as well as exciting.

There are three routes to becoming a paralegal: (1) two-year associate of arts programs, (2) four-year baccalaureate programs, and (3) professional certification. Associate degree programs typically involve a two-year training program and can be begun after one graduates from high school. They are housed in community colleges, universities, and ''proprietary'' schools (profit-making businesses offering training, similar in nature to beauty schools and truck driver schools).

Some colleges and universities have established four-year degree programs which offer in-depth training as well as a liberal arts education. Most certificate programs require at least a year of college work, and some require a bachelor's degree. Completion of all the work required for graduation may take up to two years. Certification programs are also offered at colleges, universities, and proprietary schools.

Recommending one kind of program over another would be a mistake because different practices and views exist in different parts of the country. To decide which program is best for you, talk to paralegals working where you want to work. Ask where they went to school and which kinds of programs they recommend. Ask about job opportunities in the area. If the Department of Labor is correct, there should be many opportunities!

*Paul Marcotte, ''$100,000 a Year for Paralegals?'' *The Paralegal* 4(2) (1988), 1. See also Alice Fins, *Opportunities in Paralegal Careers* (Lincolnwood, IL: VGM Career Horizons, 1985).

law in that state.[36] This system is known as the **integrated bar**, a name used to avoid the negative connotations of a union shop. The integrated bar is, despite the name, a closed shop, which means that people must join the union, in this case the bar, if they want to work. A voluntary bar exists in fewer than half the states; it does not require membership in order to practice law, but attorneys still must pass a bar exam to practice law in those states.

State legislatures establish bar associations but typically place them under the control of the state judiciary. The first unified or integrated state bar was established in North Dakota in 1921, and the idea became popular in state legislatures during the Depression, when voluntary bar associations were unable to sustain sufficient membership.[37] The integrated bar makes powerful political groups of state bar associations, since the dues collected may be used to fund any number of activities, including lobbying for proposed legislation, legal aid programs, and improvements in the justice system. Bar associations are also typically responsible for testing would-be lawyers, accrediting law schools, and disciplining attorneys. They may also respond to the economic and social problems of particular states in order to ameliorate those problems.[38]

The power of integrated bar associations to propose or lobby for legislation is one reason they are under attack by numerous groups, including state legislatures that are beginning to demand that bar associations become voluntary. Indeed, many people support the idea of voluntary bar associations in states with mandatory associations, arguing that the required dues can be used to support programs that many dues-paying attorneys do not support.[39]

As we shall see in the text section, bar associations are especially powerful in states with the Missouri Plan method of judicial appointment. Critics of the Missouri Plan say that it trades the influence of political parties for the influence of bar associations. Integrated bar associations with unified views of appropriate judicial appointment are thus made even more powerful. Such power makes the complete demise of the integrated bar unlikely but does ensure a continued attack on it.

Judges: The Individuals in Charge

The classic image of the judge — impartial, unemotional, rational, and above all fair — is the stuff of many books and movies, but judges are individuals, with their own life experiences and world views. Are judges more similar to one another than they are to the average American, and if so, why is that the case? The following sections are intended to help answer this question and provide some insight into the judge's contribution to the search for justice.

Although judges have traditionally enjoyed high status, in recent years they have also been publicly criticized, leading to demands for judicial accountability. In large part these criticisms have been aimed at federal judges and their rulings on civil rights and civil liberties, but local courts are not without their critics. (For example, note in Table 12.4 that many people believe their local courts are too lenient with offenders.) Demands for judicial accountability tend to focus on how judges are selected.

Who Becomes a Judge?   Judges traditionally have been male attorneys from upper-middle-class or upper-class families who have been active in politics and have demonstrated party loyalty. State courts are still heavily dominated by white males, although there are signs that this is likely to change with the increase in the number of women and minorities graduating from law school.[40] However, in 1985 women accounted for less than 8 percent of all judges at each level of state judiciaries.[41] Judges also tend to be middle-class or upper-middle class individuals, since most of them have had

Table 12.4 1987 ATTITUDES TOWARD THE SEVERITY OF LOCAL COURTS BY DEMOGRAPHIC CHARACTERISTICS*

	Too harsh (%)	Not harsh enough (%)	About right (%)	Don't know (%)
National	3	79	12	6
Females	3	80	11	6
Male	4	78	14	6
Whites	2	81	12	5
Black and other	7	70	14	9
College	3	77	14	6
High school	3	84	9	4
Grade school	5	71	18	7
Republican	2	86	10	2
Democrat	4	78	13	6
Independent	4	76	12	8
18–20 years	0	76	17	7
21–29 years	4	78	9	8
30–49 years	4	78	13	5
Over 50 years	2	82	2	4
Professional	2	80	13	5
Clerical	2	81	12	5
Manual	5	78	11	5
Farmer	2	82	12	2

*In answer to the question, "In general, do you think the courts in this area deal too harshly or not harshly enough with criminals?"

Source: Timothy J. Flanagan and Katherine M. Jamieson, *Sourcebook of Criminal Justice Statistics, 1987*, Bureau of Justice Statistics (Washington, DC: GPO, 1988), 142–143.

the education and finances to complete law school. As Henry Glick points out,

> Most judges also are "local boys who made good." Recruitment politics generally requires a close tie to state and local politics, resulting in judges who have always been close to home. There are some exceptions, especially in the fast growing states, but lawyers who leave home probably have a difficult time establishing sufficient ties to a new community to make them acceptable as local judges. Winning elections or an executive appointment usually requires careful nurturing of a political career. This means developing contacts, establishing a record of service to a political party, holding lesser posts in the community, and being well known to fellow lawyers and other prominent groups. Consequently, state judges normally have been born and raised in the same state as the court on which they serve, and have held one or more nonjudicial political jobs such as state legislator and prosecuting attorney or have been a local judge. They are also likely to be a member of the political party that dominates politics in their area. In short, they are typically political insiders and long-standing local residents.[42]

How Are Judges Selected? The selection of judges is a major issue confronting those concerned with justice. There are two basic approaches to judicial selection: *election* and *appointment*. Federal judges acquire their positions exclusively through appointment, but states use both election and appointment. Those who advocate election of judges argue that this process makes judges accountable to citizens. Those who advocate appointment argue that the judiciary should be independent of popular opinion and loyal only to the law. Both appointment and election involve a certain amount of risk. The appointment method permits the person who does the appointing to choose unfit political associates to be judges. However, elections do not assure that judges will remain independent of popular opinion or political contributors and thus raises questions about the impartiality of the judiciary (Box 12-5).

The six methods for selecting judges are (1) partisan elections, (2) non-partisan elections, (3) appointment by the governor, (4) merit selection at some level of the judicial system, (5) legislative elections, and (6) selection by sitting judges.[43] These methods have been combined in an attempt to produce merit selection plans with the strengths of both appointment and election. Under the **California Plan**,[44] the governor nominates one person for each judgeship. If that person is confirmed by the commission on judicial appointments, he or she becomes a judge who must stand for election at the next general election. This election is a referendum on the judicial record compiled while in office; the judge does not have an opponent. If elected, the judge sits on the bench for a 12-year term and can be reelected as often as the electorate returns a majority of positive votes.

The **Missouri Plan**, an amendment to that state's constitution in 1940,[45] also combines election and appointment. It has been more popular than the California Plan. Nonpartisan nominating boards nominate three qualified candidates for each vacant judgeship, and the governor appoints the judge from those nominations. After a period of not less than a year, the judge stands for election in an unopposed, nonpartisan ratification by the electorate. If ratified, the judge secures the position for a period of years that depends on the level of the judgeship. Fourteen other states have developed variations on the Missouri Plan, including permitting judges to run opposed on partisan or nonpartisan ballots at some point after initial ratification in the case of some judgeships.[46]

Judges in courts of last appeal are chosen by a variety of methods, including partisan election (10 states), nonpartisan election (13 states), and some version of the Missouri Plan (14 states)[47] (Table 12.5). They serve terms of six years to life. In 15 states, the term is six years; in 12, it is eight years; and in 12, it is ten years.

The chief justice in courts of last appeal is chosen in different ways. In 17 states, the chief justice is chosen by the other justices; in 12 states, the chief justice is appointed by the governor with the consent of the legislature. In seven states the chief justice is elected, and in seven the chief justice is the judge with the greatest seniority of service.

Box 12-5 **The Election of Judges and Campaign Contributions**

The following excerpt is taken from a book describing the competition between Texaco and Pennzoil for Getty Oil and the subsequent legal battle, much of which took place in the Houston, Texas, courts. Joe Jamail represented Pennzoil, in whose favor the suit was ultimately resolved, much to the surprise of many people who had examined the merits of the case. The campaign contribution from Jamail is mentioned frequently as a clue to many of the rulings in the case.

The majority of states elect their local judges, but every Texas judge from the county bench to the state Supreme Court must withstand the onslaught of partisan elections. The reason is rooted in the state's Reconstruction Constitution of 1869, in which the carpet baggers gave the governor the power to appoint some ten thousand political officials around the state. When Texas finally bade farewell to the Yankees, the locals saw to it that virtually every important political job in the state—including every judge from the county level up—was controlled by the voters.

In modern times, conducting a judicial re-election campaign posed little problem in the numerous rural burgs of Texas, where little was required of incumbents beyond some handshaking at the livestock show or county fair. But in a town like Houston, the fourth largest city in America, voters in a single election day might face choices for three Supreme Court races, fifteen appeals-court races, thirty-seven state district court races and seventeen county court races. The only hope of assuring re-election was name recognition, and in a county with so many candidates and so many voters that could be obtained only through money, most coming from lawyers and law firms. Big money.

State District Judge Anthony J. P. Farris, a curmudgeonly former U.S. attorney with a long white mustache and rather mournful eyes, was facing no opposition in the 1984 Republican Primary but expected to have a Democratic opponent in the fall. And his campaign chairman was fretful over the dearth of campaign funds raised to date. Even Joe Jamail, a big-time judicial donor who sat on the steering committee of the judge's campaign, had donated a paltry $100.

On March 5, 1984, Judge Farris was assigned jurisdiction over all pretrial legal matters in *Pennzoil* v. *Texaco*. Two days later, he received a campaign check for $10,000, four times greater than the largest amount he had previously received. It came from Joe Jamail.

Source: Thomas Petzinger, Jr., *Oil and Honor: The Texaco-Pennzoil Wars*, (New York: Putnam, 1987), 282.

Intermediate appeals court judges are chosen in the same fashion as are justices in courts of last appeals in all but three states (Table 12.6). They serve terms of six years to life. In 16 states, the term is six years; in 8 states, it is eight years; and in 6 states, it is ten years. Trial court judges are selected in a number of ways, but the Missouri Plan (10 states), partisan election (12

Table 12.5   STATES AND THEIR METHODS OF SELECTING COURT OF LAST APPEAL JUDGES

Missouri Plan	Partisan election	Nonpartisan election
Alaska	Alabama	Georgia
Arizona	Arkansas	Idaho
Colorado	Illinois	Kentucky
Florida	Mississippi	Louisiana
Indiana	New Mexico	Michigan
Iowa	North Carolina	Minnesota
Kansas	Pennsylvania	Montana
Maryland	Tennessee	Nevada
Missouri	Texas	North Dakota
Nebraska	West Virginia	Ohio
Oklahoma		Oregon
South Dakota		Washington
Utah		Wisconsin
Wyoming		

Source: Council of State Governments, *The Book of States, 1986–87* (Lexington, KY: (CSG, 1987)).

states), and nonpartisan election (17 states) are the most common methods of selection.[48] Terms of office can be four years (9 states), six years (24 states), or eight years (7 states).

Does It Matter How Judges Are Selected?   Are there any differences between appointed and elected judges? Although a final answer is not available, a study of state supreme court justices in four states found that the adoption of a particular judicial role — liberal lawmaker versus conservative law interpreter — was based on personal values and appeared to be unrelated to methods of judicial selection.[49] It is likely that the type of selection makes little difference in determining who becomes a judge, since regardless of the method, selection is made from the same general group of people: middle-class lawyers with political contacts.[50]

Does either type of selection produce superior judges? Again, the answer is that the selection process probably makes little measurable difference, if any, in the average quality of judges. Studies show that sitting judges are rarely rejected by voters under the merit plans — the Missouri and California plans — and that judges voted into office are almost always returned to office.[51] Since the group from which these judges were originally selected contained similar types of persons, there is no reason to believe that on average these two processes lead to significantly different outcomes.

The major difference between partisan election (and governor appointment) and merit plan selection has to do with who has the most influence. Political parties are most influential in states where judges are elected or appointed by the governor with little meaningful challenge by others (the

Table 12.6   STATES AND THEIR METHODS OF SELECTING COURT OF INTERMEDIATE
APPEAL JUDGES

No court	Missouri Plan	Partisan election	Nonpartisan election
Delaware	Alaska	Alabama	Georgia
Maine	Arizona	Arkansas	Idaho
Mississippi	Colorado	Illinois	Kentucky
Montana	Florida	New Mexico	Louisiana
Nebraska	Indiana	New York	Michigan
Nevada	Iowa	North Carolina	Minnesota
New Hampshire	Kansas	Pennsylvania	Ohio
North Dakota	Maryland	Texas	Oregon
Rhode Island	Missouri		Washington
South Dakota	Oklahoma		Wisconsin
Utah	Tennessee		
Vermont			
West Virginia			
Wyoming			

Source: Council of State Governments, *The Book of States, 1986–87* (Lexington, KY: CSG, 1987).

California Plan), but in states which emphasize some variation of the Missouri Plan with a nonpartisan nominating body selecting a pool of qualified candidates, the group most often represented in the nominating process has a great deal of power. That group is usually the state bar, and its influence is institutionalized in such plans. Where the Missouri Plan is used, bar politics have replaced party politics in the selection of judges.[52] Neither electing judges nor appointing them under the Missouri Plan has been shown to produce demonstrably more competent or less biased judges.

How Important Is the Influence of Judges' Party Affiliation?   An analysis of the judicial behavior of all elected appellate judges confirms that there are "basic decision-making differences between Democratic and Republican judges in courts selected under partisan nomination and election procedures."[53] Although party affiliation does not explain all appellate judicial behavior, it explains more than does any other variable, including age, gender, class, and ethnicity.[54]

The implication of these findings is that voters can influence court systems in states that permit the election of judges at some point in the process *if* they know the judges' party affiliation and the meaning of that affiliation in the state in which they live. This is important because appellate judges, whether at the intermediate level or the final level, make decisions which are policy-oriented. Their decisions have implications for policies concerning the rights of the poor and the wealthy, women and men, adults and children, and taxpayers and welfare recipients as well as criminals and victims. If research continues to show the relevance of party affiliation to judicial decision making, individuals who want judges to be accountable to the electorate rather than independent of it should lobby on behalf of reforms which permit voters to use parties in selecting judges.

How Are Judges Removed from Office?   Like judicial selection, the removal of judges is an issue of judicial accountability. Some states may have more than one method for removing judges. The most common methods are impeachment, removal by the court of last appeal, and the use of a special court selected on a case-by-case basis.

Most states have more than one method for removing judges from office. Charges which can lead to removal include the claim that judges can no longer fulfill the obligations of the job because of illness or accident or that they have been convicted of a felony. Forty-three states permit the impeachment of judges, by far the most common method of judicial removal. Thirty-four states allow the court of last appeals to remove judges, and 17 states convene a court of the judiciary to remove judges after the receipt and investigation of charges by a state judicial commission. Twelve states permit the court of last appeals to remove judges for cause without an investigation by a state judicial commission.

Just as the trend is away from gubernatorial appointment of judges, it is also away from gubernatorial removal of judges. Two states permit governors to remove incapacitated judges, and one state permits the governor to remove judges for criminal convictions. In 13 states, the governor can remove judges with the concurrence of two-thirds of the legislature.

While an emphasis on accountability has led to the election of judges, the right to recall judges through election exists in only four states. One state permits the state legislature to remove judges by legislative resolution. Two other states permit the removal of district judges by a local tribunal.

THE JUDICIARY: COURT REFORM

Among the problems confronting state and local courts, three are particularly important because they interfere with the administration of justice: Judges are burdened by excessive caseloads, courts are at times burdened by inadequate or unpredictable funding, and communities are often burdened with less able judges. Although no single answer or model has been developed, state and local governments are developing some promising solutions.[55]

State Funding   In more than half the states, state governments have assumed the responsibility of financing all state and local courts. Opposition to state funding often occurs among local officials who fear the loss of revenues produced in municipal courts through filing fees and various fines. Some people believe that state funding will not solve the resource problems in state and local courts and that sources of funds at both the state and local levels are necessary in many instances.

Judicial Accountability   Judicial independence is a means to an end —justice— and so is the effort to make judges accountable by using performance evaluations. The bars in several states have canvassed their members in formal evaluations of judges. This method relies on practicing attorneys. An approach used in Nebraska and in the U.S. Ninth Circuit surveys individuals involved in court cases: Plaintiffs and defendants are asked about the performance of the judges in their cases.[56] This approach is being tested in a number of locales and can be expected to be an increasingly common feature of court systems in the future. If nothing else, it offers the eventual evaluators — the electorate — a useful data base on which to make decisions.

Judicial Caseloads and Judicial Salaries   A major concern of individuals who care about the search for justice are the questions of whether judges have more work than they can effectively handle and whether judges are being adequately paid. The typical judge has a caseload which makes trials unavailable to most citizens. These caseloads invite plea bargaining in criminal cases, encouraging defendants to forfeit their day in court. These caseloads also result in pressure to submit civil cases to binding arbitration, even at the appellate level, thereby reducing the likelihood of a trial.

The problem of the judicial work load is compounded by the salaries paid to judges. Although many citizens believe they would be happy with the typical judge's salary, the fact is that judges as practicing attorneys can on the average make a significantly higher salary than they can as judges. It may feel good to tell judges to go work as attorneys if money is their sole concern, but as citizens of the United States we must be concerned with motivating capable women and men to become judges. Unrealistic caseloads and low salaries may make becoming a judge less attractive, reducing the number of would-be judges and lowering the quality of judges.

One approach to making the job more attractive is the judicial sabbatical. As a response to the problems of caseload and salary, the sabbatical provides judges with a chance to rest as well as catch up on their reading on law and changes in the law. Another approach has been to reduce judicial caseloads by permitting judges to censure parties who use inappropriate delaying tactics. A third strategy has been the various innovations in scheduling cases which rigidly docket predictable cases and permit more leeway for cases with less predictability.

Conclusion

These proposals for court reform result from discussions concerning the kind of court system that Americans want. These are extraordinarily important discussions, the kind in which the citizens of a democracy should participate in order to maintain the rule of law and secure justice. The search for justice is a constant quest to secure the goal which sets civilized individuals apart from those without regard for human rights and civil liberties. It involves all governmental institutions, including law enforcement and corrections. It is to these two institutions that we turn in Chapter 13.

Study Objectives

1. Identify the differences between law and justice.
2. Identify the differences between the rule of law and the rule of men.
3. Identify the differences between common law, statutory law, equity law, and administrative law.
4. Identify the differences between civil law and criminal law.
5. Delineate the steps in the civil court process.
6. Delineate the steps in the criminal court process.
7. Explain the reasons for the decline of the adversarial court system and the rise of the dispositional system.
8. Identify and discuss the levels of state court systems.
9. Identify the six ways in which judges are chosen.
10. Delineate the differences between judges chosen under the Missouri Plan and those who are elected.
11. Describe the importance of political parties in the election of judges.
12. Identify the various kinds of jurisdictions which apply to courts
13. Identify the cases which are handled in state and local courts.
14. Identify the following terms:

due process	summons
subpoena	subpoena duces tecum
bill of information	grand jury
discovery	deposition
interrogatory	integrated bar

Glossary

adversarial system A system of justice, also called the adversarial process. Assumes that justice and the truth will emerge as a result of a contest, governed by constitutional guarantees of due process, between two well-prepared adversaries: the plaintiff and defendant.

administrative law Law made by administrative agencies, including law concerned with rate making, operating rules, the rights of individuals or firms regulated by administrative agencies, and the power of certain courts to review or overturn decisions made by administrative agencies.

arraignment Occurs when the defendant hears the charges against him or her and enters a plea of guilty or not guilty.

bill of information An accusation against an individual made under oath by a prosecuting attorney before a court, which may begin the criminal process against that person.

California Plan A method of selecting judges in which the governor nominates one person for each judgeship. If that person is confirmed by the commission on judicial appointments, he or she must stand for election at the next general election. If elected, the candidate sits on the bench for a 12-year term.

civil law Has two common uses; may refer to statutory law or to all law which is not criminal law.

civil liberties The legal rights guaranteed to all citizens by the Bill of Rights, including but not limited to the right to free speech, the right to trial by a jury of one's peers, and the right to be free from unreasonable search and seizure.

codes Collections of laws or a complete set of interrelated laws.

common law Judge-made law.

contempt of court Applied to an act which lessens the dignity of the court, interferes with the work of the court, or constitutes willful disobedience of a judge or a court order. It may result in punishment by fine, incarceration, or both.

criminal law Statute law, made up of codes which prohibit and occasionally require certain behaviors. Violations can result in fines, confinement, or execution.

De novo Means "completely new." A de novo trial is a new trial, ordered by a judge or an appeals court, which begins again as a completely new case.

deposition The taking of sworn testimony outside of court during the discovery portion of a lawsuit.

dispositional justice The tendency, common in criminal justice bureaucracies, to emphasize efficient processing of cases through plea bargaining.

discovery A formal and informal exchange of information between two sides in a lawsuit.

doctrine of incorporation Applies the federal Bill of Rights to the states by using the due process clause of the Fourteenth Amendment.

en banc The practice of having all the justices of a court sitting and hearing the same case. Most state courts of last appeal sit en banc. Sometime the term is spelled "in banc" or "in bank."

equity law Law made by judges in an attempt to prevent a wrong.

full faith and credit clause A clause in the Constitution which requires that each state recognize contracts made in other states.

grand jury A group of approximately 12 to 23 individuals, chosen by the prosecutor, whose task it is to review criminal charges and bring formal indictments.

indictment A formal accusation of a crime made against a person by a grand jury. The grand jury usually acts at the request of a prosecutor.

injunction A judicial ruling that prohibits an action.

integrated bar A state bar system which requires lawyers to be dues-paying members of the bar in order to practice law in that state.

interrogatories Written questions submitted with a request for written answers during discovery.

justice Often defined as fair treatment.

law Has two meanings. A rule, statute, or ordinance issued by a unit of government. Also used in a general sense to refer to the entire body of principles, rules, and statutes which has been created by the various legislative bodies and government agencies.

Mapp* v. *Ohio A landmark decision by the U.S. Supreme Court ruling that the practice by states of admitting illegally obtained evidence in criminal trials is a violation of the due process clause of the Fourteenth Amendment to the Constitution.

Missouri Plan A method of selecting judges. Nonpartisan nominating boards nominate three qualified candidates for each vacant judgeship, and the governor makes appointments from among these nominees. After a period of time the judge stands for election.

National Center for State Courts Located at 300 Newport Avenue, Williamsburg, VA, 23187-8798. Gathers and freely disseminates data and other information about state trial courts.

paralegal A legal assistant, working in a law firm or administrative agency, who is trained to help lawyers research cases, prepare briefs, prepare preliminary versions of legal documents, and interview witnesses.

plaintiff Also known as the petitioner or appellant. The complaining party in a civil case.

plea bargaining A process in which the prosecutor and the defendant, through the defense attorney, negotiate the punishment to be assigned in return for a guilty plea.

preponderance of evidence The superior weight or quality of evidence. The principle by which verdicts are decided in civil cases.

respondent The apellee or defendant; the party against whom a complaint has been filed in a civil case.

rule of law A system of governing in which decisions are based on a set rules which are written and are known to many.

rule of men A system of governing in which decisions are based on the whims of individuals rather than a set of rules.

stare decisis Latin for "let the decision stand." The judicial practice of applying a previously used legal principle to a set of facts to settle a legal dispute.

statutory law Law which is enacted by a legislature.

subpoena A court's order to a person that he or she appear to testify.

subpoena duces tecum A court order that a person appear and bring certain documents when he or she testifies.

summons A writ delivered by an authorized person to inform the recipient that a lawsuit has been filed against the recipient.

writ of mandamus A judicial ruling that commands that an action be done.

Endnotes

1. Jack C. Plano and Milton Greenberg, *The American Political Dictionary* (New York: Holt, Rinehart & Winston, 1989), 240.
2. Richard Quinney, *The Social Reality of Crime* (Boston: Little, Brown, 1970), 35.
3. 81 S. Ct. 1684 (1961).
4. *Stare decisis* is Latin for "let the decision stand."

5. Plano and Greenberg, 232.

6. Ibid., 217.

7. Ibid., 243.

8. Libel can also be prosecuted as a criminal offense, though this is rare.

9. Henry J. Abraham, *The Judicial Process: An Introductory Analysis of the Courts of the United States, England, and France* (New York: Oxford University Press, 1986), 17.

10. See Marcia J. Lim, "The State of the Judiciary," in Council of State Governments, *The Book of the States, 1986–87* (Lexington, KY: Council of State Governments, 1987), 149.

11. Danile Oran, *Law Dictionary for Nonlawyers* (St. Paul, MN: West, 1985), 234.

12. The prosecutor carries the charge to the grand jury. If the grand jury does not believe that the charge is unwarranted, it can issue a no true bill, and thus no one is indicted.

13. Plano and Greenberg, 235.

14. James B. Eisenstein, Roy B. Flemming, and Peter F. Nardulli, *The Contours of Justice: Communities and Their Courts* (Boston: Little, Brown, 1989), 120–121.

15. Herbert Jacob, *Urban Justice: Courts, Lawyers, and the Judicial Process* (Boston, Little, Brown, 1978), 174–181.

16. For a discussion of plea bargaining as a method of achieving justice, see Arthur Rosett and Donald R. Cressey, *Justice by Consent: Plea Bargains in the American Courthouse* (New York: Lippincott, 1976).

17. Abraham S. Blumberg, *Criminal Justice: Issues and Ironies* (New York: New Viewpoints, 1979), 236, 257–262.

18. Barbara Boland and Brian Forst, *The Prevalence of Guilty Pleas*, U.S. Departement of Justice, Bureau of Justice Statistics (Washington, DC: GPO, 1984), 1.

19. For a discussion of this issue, see Blumberg, *Criminal Justice*, Herbert Jacob, *Urban Justice: Law and Order in American Cities* (Englewood Cliffs, NJ: Prentice-Hall, 1973), and Jerome Skolnick, *Justice Without Trial* (New York: Wiley, 1975).

20. For a discussion of the myth of the adversarial system, see Blumberg, *Criminal Justice*, and J. Q. Wilson, *Thinking About Crime* (New York: Vintage, 1977), 201–204.

21. Daniel McGillis, *The Federal Civil Justice System*, U.S. Department of Justice, Bureau of Justice Statistics (Washington, DC: GPO, 1987), 4.

22. *State Court Caseload Statistics: Annual Report 1987* (Williamsburg, VA: National Center for State Courts, 1989), 17.

23. G. Alan Tarr, "Court Unification and Court Performance: A Preliminary Assessment," *Judicature* 64(8) (March 1981), 356–368.

24. The distinction made here is between appeals based on questions of fact and those based on questions of law. Questions of fact refer to the facts of the case: Was the murderer driving a red or a green car? Did the burglar steal a piano or a bassoon? These kinds of disputes are not settled in courts of last appeal. Rather, such courts examine the fairness of the trial, the appropriateness of the judge's rulings, or the admissibility of the evidence.

25. Computed from *The Book of the States, 1986–87*, 156–171.

26. Timothy J. Flanagan and Katherine M. Jamieson, *Sourcebook of Criminal Justice Statistics, 1987*, U.S. Department of Justice, Bureau of Justice Statistics (Washington, DC: GPO, 1988), 15.

27. *Employment and Earnings*, Bureau of Labor Statistics (Washington DC: GPO, June 1988), 30.

28. Ibid., 30.

29. Jacob, 35.

30. *State Court Caseload Statistics, Annual Report, 1987*, 18.

31. Jacob, *Urban Justice*, 44, and James S. Eisenstein and Herbert Jacob, *Felony Justice: An Organizational Analysis of Criminal Courts* (Boston: Little, Brown, 1977), 285.

32. See Blumberg, *Criminal Justice*, 227–246, and Eisenstein and Jacob, *Felony Justice*, 50.

33. Douglas Rosenthal, *Lawyer and Client: Who's in Charge?* (New York: Russell Sage, 1976.)

34. See, for instance, Alan Dershowitz, *Reversal of Fortune* (New York: Random House, 1985), and F. Lee Bailey, *The Defense Never Rests* (New York: Stein & Day, 1971).

35. William C. Louthan, *The Politics of Justice* (Port Washington, NY: Kennikat, 1979), 82.

36. See Dayton D. McKean, *The Integrated Bar* (Boston: Houghton Miffin, 1963), for a discussion of the history and ethics of integrated state bars.

37. Myrna Oliver, "Bar Wars," *California Lawyer* 8 (January-February 1988), 30–33.

38. For a discussion of one such response by the Minnesota bar, see J. Kenneth Myers, "The Role of the Bar in Troubled Times—A Minnesota Perspective," *Alabama Law Review* 38(3) 1987, 637–657.

39. Mark Thompson, "Is a Voluntary Statewide Bar in the Works?" *California Lawyer* (8, January-February 1988), 34–35.

40. Henry R. Glick, *Courts, Politics, and Justice* (New York: McGraw-Hill, 1983), 87.

41. Karen L. Tokarz, "Women Judges and Merit Selection Under the Missouri Plan," *Washington University Law Quarterly* 6(3) 1986, 915.

42. Glick, 87–88.

43. Abraham, 23. Selection by sitting judges is used only to choose chief justices of the supreme courts in 18 states.

44. Adopted in 1934 by a voter initiative and referendum.

45. Abraham, 38.

46. Computed from *The Book of the States, 1986–87*, 156–171.

47. Computed from *The Book of the States, 1986–87*, 156–171, and Flanagan and Jamieson, 110.

48. Computed from *The Book of the States, 1986–87*, 156–171.

49. John T. Wold, "Political Orientations, Social Backgrounds, and Role Perceptions of State Supreme Court Judges," *Western Political Quarterly* 27 (1974), 239–248.

50. Glick, 88–89, and Philip L. Dubois, *From Ballot to Bench* (Austin: University of Texas Press, 1980), 246.

51. Abraham, *The Judicial Process*, 40–41, Adlai E. Stevenson, "'Reform and Judicial Selection," *American Bar Association Journal* (November 1978), 1683–1685, and Henry Robert Glick and Kenneth N. Vines, *State Court Systems* (Englewood Cliffs, NJ: Prentice-Hall, 1973), 46–50.

52. Jacob, 72.

53. Dubois, 248.

54. Ibid.

55. See Lim, 146–154.

Chapter
13

The Search for Justice: Crime, Police, and Corrections

CRIMINAL JUSTICE

A government that tolerates crime cannot long maintain its legitimacy, yet a society must provide some measure of justice for its residents, even those accused of crimes. The question that must be answered is, What is meant by justice in the criminal justice system?

Various definitions exist. During a criminal trial the prosecutor asks the jury to convict the accused to deter others from committing crimes. At the end of the trial, the victim or the victim's loved ones may argue that the convicted person should be punished as harshly as the victim was abused in retribution for the suffering that was inflicted. The convicted person's fam-

(Courtesy of Kim Bradley, San Marcos Daily Record.)

ily may argue in favor of rehabilitation because the accused is "sick" and should be in a facility which can help him or her return to a normal life.

These conflicting claims about the appropriate consequences of a criminal trial reflect only a small portion of the disagreement about the nature of justice in America. The question whether we should seek deterrence, retribution, rehabilitation, or some combination of these elements, is one for which there is no simple answer. Nevertheless, we must ask difficult questions and examine some difficult — and surprising — facts in order to make the choices that we will face in the future.

CRIME, VICTIMIZATION, AND IMPRISONMENT

National polls frequently show that crime is an issue of great concern to Americans, yet crime, like poverty, is a permanent feature of society. The issue is not whether or when we will eliminate crime but how much of it we can tolerate and how much personal wealth and freedom we will sacrifice to it. This section will examine the nature and extent of criminal behavior in the United States; subsequent sections will scrutinize efforts by individuals working together to reduce the debilitating effects of crime.

Although crime is a national problem, reducing crime is the responsibility of state and local governments. Funding the "war" on crime is also the responsibility of state and local governments, with little help coming from the federal government.[1] Controlling crime and providing justice within limited budgets constitute a challenge for governments and for the individuals who assist in this undertaking.

What Is Crime?

Crime is the violation of statutory, criminal law; all criminal laws provide for some form of punishment. Criminal statutes clearly delineate the nature of each crime, permitting police officers, attorneys, and judges to make distinctions between similar acts. Murder is more than the killing of one human being by another. To be defined as murder, the killing must be willful, and it cannot be justified by the situation. It cannot be a matter of self-defense or the defensible killing of a citizen by a police officer in the line of duty. Similarly, burglary is not simply stealing; in fact, a burglary may not involve theft at all! To be defined as burglary, the act must include unlawful entry of a structure with the intention to commit a felony (Box 13-1).

How Are Crimes Counted?

There are two methods of counting crimes in the United States: (1) police reports tabulated by the Federal Bureau of Investigation (FBI) and (2) victimization reports compiled by the Bureau of Justice Statistics (BJS).

The FBI has gathered crime statistics from police departments in the United States since 1930 and now publishes crime report summaries every three months. Each year the FBI publishes the *Uniform Crime Reports*, an annual summary of the crime statistics received from police departments.

The FBI reports two different forms of crime data: crimes reported and arrests made. *Crimes reported* refers to crimes originally reported by citizens or the police. *Arrests* refers to the number of arrests, not the number of persons arrested. If a person reports that he or she was both robbed and beaten, that report counts as two crimes, one crime of robbery and one crime of assault; if three individuals are arrested for robbing and beating that person, those arrests count as three arrests for robbery or three arrests for assault (or some combination of three robberies and assaults) depending on the local police department's method of counting and reporting crime. It is important to recognize, however, that most crimes are not reported to the police; as a result, another method of measuring the amount of crime — victimization studies — has been developed.

Victimization studies consist of research about victims and serve as a

Box 13-1 *Uniform Crime Report* Definitions

The Federal Bureau of Investigation amasses data from more than 95 percent of the police departments in the United States every year and publishes the data in a document entitled *Crime in the U.S.* This publication is usually referred to as the *Uniform Crime Reports* and contains information about crimes reported to the police, persons arrested, and law enforcement personnel. The definitions are used to define the *Crime Index*, those crimes considered by the FBI to be the most serious in the United States. Among these crimes are the following:

Murder and nonnegligent manslaughter . . . is the willful (nonnegligent) killing of one human being by another. The classification of this offense, as for all other Crime Index offenses, is based solely on police investigation, as opposed to the determination of a court, medical examiner, coroner, jury, or other judicial body. Not included in the count for this offense classification are deaths caused by negligence, suicide, or accident; justifiable homicides; and attempts to murder or assaults to murder, which are scored as aggravated assaults. . . .

Forcible rape . . . is the carnal knowledge of a female forcibly and against her will. Assaults or attempts to commit rape by force or threat of force are also included; however, statutory rape (without force) and other sex offenses are excluded. . . .

Robbery is the taking or attempting to take anything of value from the care, custody, or control of a person or persons by force or threat of force or violence and/or putting the victim in fear. . . .

Aggravated assault is an unlawful attack by one person upon another for the purpose of inflicting severe or aggravated bodily injury. This type of assault is usually accompanied by the use of a weapon or by means likely to produce death or great bodily harm. . . . Attempts are included since it is not necessary that an injury result when a gun, knife, or other weapon is used which could and probably would result in serious personal injury if the crime were successfully completed. . . .

Burglary [is] the unlawful entry of a structure to commit a felony of theft. The use of force to gain entry is not required to classify an offense as burglary. Burglary . . . is categorized into three subclassifications: forcible entry, unlawful entry where no force is used, and attempted forcible entry. . . .

Larceny-theft is the unlawful taking, carrying, leading, or riding away of property from the possession or constructive possession of another. It includes crimes such as shoplifting, pocket-picking, purse snatching, thefts from motor vehicles, thefts of motor vehicle parts and accessories, bicycle thefts, etc. in which no use of force, violence, or fraud occurs. In the Uniform Crime Reporting Program, this crime does not include embezzlement, ''con'' games, forgery, and worthless checks. . . .

Motor vehicle theft is defined as the theft or attempted theft of a motor vehicle. This definition excludes the taking of a motor vehicle for temporary use by those people having lawful access. . . .

continued

Box 13-1 *(continued)*

> *Arson* is defined . . . as any willful or malicious burning or attempting to burn, with or without intent to defraud, a dwelling, house, public building, motor vehicle or aircraft, personal property of another, etc. Only fires determined through investigation to have been willfully or maliciously set are classified as arsons. Fires of suspicious or unknown origins are excluded.
>
> **Source:** *Uniform Crime Reports for the United States, 1987*, Federal Bureau of Investigation, U.S. Department of Justice (Washington, DC: GPO, 1988), 7, 13, 16, 21, 24, 28, 33, 36.

second method of counting crimes. The BJS began gathering victimization statistics in 1972 and now publishes an annual report summarizing the data. The data are collected in a national survey of a sample of households.[2] Those who report that a member of the household has been a crime victim are asked if a report has been made to the police. Thus, the BJS not only provides information about household victimization but also provides information about crime reporting by citizens to the police.

The BJS reports criminal incidents and victimizations. A **criminal incident** is a "specific criminal act involving one or more victims."[3] A **victimization** is a specific criminal incident that affects one person. An incident may involve a number of crimes, but the incident is counted only once and is categorized in terms of the most serious crime. In the example of the person who was both robbed and assaulted, the BJS would report that criminal incident as one robbery and one victimization. Thus, more crime occurs than is reported in the BJS annual report (and in *The Uniform Crime Report*).

How Much Crime Occurs in the United States?

All the statistics you will read in this chapter are estimates about the amount of crime that are based on police reports or interviews with victims. No one really knows how much crime occurs in the United States. The number of crimes counted depends on the method of counting. The FBI reports less crime than does the BJS. For instance, the FBI, using data that came to the attention of police departments, reported 1,489,170 violent crimes in 1986, but the BJS, based on victim reports, estimated that 5,515,450 violent crimes occurred.[4] Table 13.1 summarizes the statistics for 1986 reported by both agencies.

The disparities in the data gathered by the FBI and the BJS suggest that a great deal of crime is not reported to police agencies. Most unreported crime is property crime; however, violent crimes often are not reported if they are considered personal or private. Property crime often is not reported when the attempt was unsuccessful or the property was recovered.[5] Fear of reprisal

Table 13.1 CRIMES OF VIOLENCE AND PROPERTY OFFENSES REPORTED BY THE FBI AND THE BJS: 1986

	FBI	BJS
All crimes	13,211,900	34,118,310[a]
Rape[b]	91,460	129,940
Robbery[c]	552,775	1,009,160
Aggravated assault[c]	834,322	1,542,870
Burglary[c]	3,241,410	5,556,600
Motor vehicle theft	1,224,137	1,355,860
Larceny	7,257,153[d]	8,455,220[e]

[a]Refers to the number of victimizations, not the number of crimes.

[b]Includes attempts and completed acts; does not include statutory rape.

[c]Includes attempted and completed acts.

[d]Includes all larcenies reported to police.

[e]Includes only household larcenies.

Sources: Uniform Crime Reports for the United States, 1987, Federal Bureau of Investigation, U.S. Department of Justice (Washington, DC: GPO, 1988), 41, and Kelly H. Shim and Marshall DeBerry, *Criminal Victimization in the United States, 1986,* Bureau of Justice Statistics, U.S. Department of Justice (Washington, DC: GPO, 1988), 14.

is also a reason commonly given for not reporting crimes to the police (Box 13-2).

The FBI and the BJS also provide data concerning the rate of crime and victimization. A **rate** is a measure of the incidence of an event for a base population; the homicide rate is the number of homicides for every 100,000 persons. Rates are useful measures because they permit comparisons of different geographic areas and comparisons of the same area over time, regardless of the size of the population.

The variation in crime and victimization rates between areas of the country can be seen in Table 13.2. Although many Americans think that Eastern states are the most violent, the South contributes disproportionately to the reported rates of homicide and rape. Southern states contain less than 35 percent of the country's population, yet they contribute almost 42 percent of the reported homicides and 36 percent of the reported forcible rapes.[6]

It is useful to compare reported crime rates in the United States with the rates in other countries. Table 13.3 shows the number of reported crimes in the United States and Japan. Note that Japan, with approximately half the population of the United States, reports less than 10 percent of the number of homicides, less than 1 percent of the robberies, and less than 2 percent of the rapes reported in the United States. Note also that the data on U.S. crime in the table come from the FBI's *Uniform Crime Reports*, which have been shown to underestimate the amount of crime in the United States. Crime, it appears, is a much more common phenomenon in the United States than it is in Japan.

Box 13-2 **The Calculation of Crime and Victimization Rates**

Crime rates calculated by the Federal Bureau of Investigation are usually based on a population of 100,000 and are calculated by dividing the number of crimes reported by the population and multiplying by 100,000. If a country of 243,400,000 individuals reported 3,236,184 burglaries in one year, the computation of the *burglary rate* would look like this:

3,236,184/243,400,000 =
0.01329575 × 100,000 =
1329.6 burglaries per 100,000 inhabitants, or a burglary rate of 1329.6

That was, in fact, the burglary rate in the United States for 1987, according to the FBI.

Victimization rates are calculated in much the same way, although they are usually calculated on a population base of 1000, producing a victimization rate per 1000 inhabitants. According to the Bureau of Justice Statistics, the rate of robbery in 1987 was 5.2 robberies per 1000 persons and the rate of rape was 0.7 per 1000 persons. According to the FBI's *Uniform Crime Reports*, the national robbery rate was 213 robberies per 100,000 persons, or 2.13 per 1000 persons, and the national rape rate was 37.4 rapes per 100,000, or 0.374 per 1000 persons. In both cases the rates reported by the FBI are approximately half those reported by the BJS.

Source: *Uniform Crime Reports for the United States, 1987*, Federal Bureau of Investigation, U.S. Department of Justice (Washington, DC: GPO, 1988), 13, 16, 24, and Kelly M. Shim and Marshall M. DeBerry, *Criminal Victimization 1987 in the United States*, Bureau of Justice Statistics, U.S. Department of Justice (Washington, DC: GPO, 1988), 3.

Table 13.2   INDEX OF CRIME BY REGION, OFFENSE, AND POPULATION DISTRIBUTION: 1987[a]

Region	Population (%)	Crime index (%)	Violent crime (%)[b]	Property crime (%)[c]	Homicide
Northeast	20.7	18.0	21.5	17.6	17.2
Midwest	24.5	21.6	20.2	21.8	19.8
Southern	34.5	36.6	34.3	36.9	41.9
West	20.4	23.8	23.9	23.7	21.1
	100.0	100.0	100.0	100.0	100.0

[a]Columns do not add up to 100% because of rounding.

[b]Includes murder, forcible rape, robbery, and aggravated assault.

[c]Includes burglary, larceny-theft, and motor vehicle theft.

Source: Uniform Crime Reports for the United States, 1987, Federal Bureau of Investigation, U.S. Department of Justice (Washington, DC: GPO, 1988).

Table 13.3   CRIME IN THE UNITED STATES (POPULATION 243,000,000) AND JAPAN (POPULATION 121,672,000): 1986

	Japan		United States	
	Number reported	Arrest rate (%)	Number reported	Arrest rate (%)
Homicide	1,676	96.7	20,613	70
Robbery	1,949	78.5	542,775	27
Assault*	21,171	93.8	834,322	59
Rape	1,750	88.1	91,459	53

*Called infliction of bodily injury in Japan

Source: Uniform Crime Reports for the United States, 1987, Federal Bureau of Investigation, U.S. Department of Justice (Washington, DC: GPO, 1988), 41, and Homu Sogo Kenkyuko, *Hanzai Hakusho (White Paper on Crime)* (Tokyo, Japan: Finance Ministry, 1987), 6.

Another way of thinking about the amount of crime is to examine the change in crime rates over time. The *Uniform Crime Reports* indicates that there are over 5000 index crimes for every 100,000 persons in the United States, but that rate varied during the last ten years from a high of 5950 in 1980 to a low of 5031 in 1984. From 1978 to 1987, the rate increased 8.1 percent, from 5140 to 5550, but the increase from 1986 to 1987 was only 1.4 percent.[7]

The BJS reports a victimization rate of 96.1 for personal crimes (rape, robbery, assault, larceny) and a household victimization rate of 171.4 for burglary, larceny, and motor vehicle theft.[8] This represents a decline from a high of 130.5 in 1978. The household victimization rate has also declined from a high of 223.4 in 1978; it has been below 200 since 1983.[9]

Although the national crime rates have increased since 1973 according to the FBI, the victimization rates have declined steadily according to the BJS. These differences result from the methods used to acquire information. The FBI relies on citizens' reports to the police, while the BJS employs random polling of individuals in their homes. The crime increase reported by the FBI is therefore probably a result of an increase in citizen reporting of crimes rather than an increase in the actual crime rate.

Who are the Victims?

Crime is intraracial; the victim and offender are usually persons of the same race. This point is frequently misrepresented in television dramas and the print media. To examine Table 13.4 and to report only that blacks kill twice as many whites as whites kill blacks is to miss the point that the vast majority of murders is intraracial.

In crimes of violence with single offenders, whites are victims of white offenders in 80 percent of all cases and blacks are victims of black offenders

Table 13.4 MURDER IS INTRARACIAL

| Victim | Murderer | | |
	White (%)	Black (%)	Total (%)
White	45.5	5.4	50.9
Black	2.1	47.0	49.1
Total	47.6	52.4	100.0

Source: Andrew Hacker, ed., *U/S: A Statistical Portrait of the American People* (New York: Viking, 1983), 217.

in 84 percent of all cases. Whites are assaulted by whites in 84 percent of all assaults, and blacks are assaulted by blacks 83 percent of the time.[10]

Who becomes a victim varies according to the crime. Males are more likely than females to be victims of violent crimes and are also more likely to be the offenders (Box 13-3). Individuals between the ages of 12 and 20 have the highest rates of violent victimization, and blacks are more likely than whites to be victims of violent crimes. White females have the lowest rate of criminal victimization, and males who have never married have the highest rate of violent crime victimization.[11]

For crimes of theft, whites are more likely than blacks to be victims. Males once again have higher victimization rates than do females, and unmarried males have the highest victimization rates of all. Individuals between the ages of 12 and 20 are the most likely to be victims of theft. City dwellers are more likely than are suburbanites to be victims of theft, and rural residents are the least likely to be theft victims.[12]

Drugs and Crime

The relationship between drug use and crime is complex. Criminal offenders report much higher drug use than do persons in the general population, but 60 percent of these offenders report that use of drugs began *after* the first arrest.[13] One in three property offenders and one in four violent offenders report drug use prior to criminal acts, and about half the violent offenders report alcohol use prior to their crimes.[14]

Drug use is unlikely to be the cause of a criminal career, but it may serve as the precipitating event in criminal acts by increasing aggressiveness or decreasing inhibitions.[15] Drug use may also motivate offenders to commit property crimes to buy drugs.[16] The evidence suggests that attempts to reduce crime solely by reducing drug use are not likely to be successful since crime usually precedes drug use. The injustice of crime is seldom subject to simple solutions.

Who Goes to Prison?

Men who are poor and uneducated, have never married, and are under 30 years of age make up the greater part of all state prison populations. More

Box 13-3 **Who Are the Offenders?**

Information about persons arrested comes from the Federal Bureau of Investigation's *Uniform Crime Reports*. In general, males are arrested more often than females are, and the crimes for which males are arrested are more serious. In addition, while juveniles are frequently depicted as increasingly violent and criminal, the number of juvenile arrests is declining. The following snapshot of arrest data reported for 1987 is instructive.

Eighty-two percent of the persons arrested were males.

The number of females arrested increased 32.8 percent from 1978 to 1987 and 4.3 percent from 1986 to 1987.

Driving under the influence is the crime for which males are most often arrested, accounting for 14 percent of all male arrests.

The number of male arrests* increased 23.3 percent from 1978 to 1987 and 1.8 percent from 1986 to 1987.

The *number* (not rate) of arrests of persons under age 18 declined 7.9 percent from 1978 to 1987!

The number of arrests of persons age 18 or older increased 34.5 percent from 1978 to 1987.

Whites accounted for 68.7 percent of all arrests in 1987; blacks accounted for 29.5 percent of all arrests in the same period.

*Note that this is not the number of males arrested, since one male can account for a number of arrests; it is the number of *male arrests*, that is, arrests of males.

Source: *Uniform Crime Reports for the United States, 1987*, Federal Bureau of Investigation, U.S. Department of Justice (Washington, DC: GPO, 1988).

than half of all men sentenced to prison have been found guilty of serious crimes: murder, nonnegligent manslaughter, rape, robbery, aggravated assault, or burglary. At the end of 1987, there were 25,812 women in state prisons, or less than 5 percent of all state inmates.[17]

Blacks are overrepresented in prison populations. It may be useful to think about this issue in another way. Penologists use the terms the **prevalence of imprisonment** (the probability of being imprisoned on any given day) and the **lifetime prevalence of imprisonment** (the probability of being imprisoned during one's lifetime).[18] A national survey of inmate populations indicates that on an average day in 1982, *1 in every 49 adult black males* in the United States was in prison, compared with 1 in every 376 white males.

From 1978 to 1981, males were 26 times more likely to be imprisoned than were females. White females are the least likely segment of the population to be imprisoned; only 1 in 10,000 white females was incarcerated on an average day in 1982.[19]

A predicted rate of the lifetime prevalence of imprisonment can be calculated from 1979 imprisonment levels. During his entire life, a male is about 14 times more likely to go to a state prison than is a female. A black female is eight times more likely to serve a state prison sentence than is a white female. Blacks, regardless of sex, are six to seven times more likely to serve a state prison sentence at some time during their lives than are whites.[20]

We know a great deal about the people who go to prison: the crimes for which they have been convicted, the number of times they have been incarcerated, the length of time between incarcerations, the drugs they use, and other facts too numerous to list. What we do not know is how to keep them from returning to prison.

What Is the Rate of Return to State Prisons?   Penologists calculate a recidivism rate based on what Glaser called clear recidivism, a return to prison. Among males in state prisons in 1978, an estimated 61.3 percent had been incarcerated as a juvenile, adult, or both.[21] Assuming that the group of prisoners entering prison in 1979 is typical of previously released cohorts, it is estimated that about half those admitted to prison in 1979 will return to prison within the 20-year period following their release, but 14 percent of the total cohort will return within the first year. The risk of recidivism is greatest during the first few years after release.[22]

All things considered, the younger the person released from prison, the greater the likelihood of recidivism within the first year. Among inmates aged 18 to 24, an estimated 22 percent will return to prison during the first year after release and half will return within seven years after release.[23]

State and Local Programs for Crime Reduction

A number of programs to reduce or prevent crime have been implemented at the state and local levels. Many of the most innovative have been developed at the neighborhood level.[24] Although no program can eliminate crime, several approaches have reduced the amount of crime in certain areas, making citizens feel more secure in their homes and more positive about their communities.

Crime Stoppers   This is a national program that is implemented by the citizens and police in a community. It is intended to encourage citizen participation in crime deterrence by offering monetary rewards to individuals who provide information about crime and by involving individuals in raising money for the rewards.

The Crime Stoppers program operates through local newspapers and television stations. "Crimes of the Week" are featured, and a telephone number is provided; callers who provide information leading to the arrest and conviction of those guilty of a crime are promised large sums of money; they are also promised anonymity. Callers who provide information about other crimes also receive money in amounts that usually are determined by a local citizens' advisory board. This board works closely with police detectives to raise money, publicize the program, choose Crimes of the Week, and deliver rewards.

Although the impact of Crime Stoppers on crime rates may not be measurable, studies indicate that the program is a cost-effective way of solving felony cases which are unlikely to be solved by traditional methods.[25] Police investigators report that this program has been effective in providing evidence to "crack" difficult cases. Nationally, the program is said to have helped solve more than 92,000 felony crimes, convict more than 20,000 criminals, and recover $562 million in stolen property and narcotics.[26] Individuals who want to contribute to crime-fighting efforts in their community should consider a Crime Stoppers program.

Neighborhood Watch Programs These programs are often called Crime Watch, Block Watch, or Community Alert as well as Neighborhood Watch. They also involve individuals in crime prevention efforts in their neighborhoods and communities. Working with an agency, usually the local police department, residents form block groups and elect a block captain who is responsible for coordinating the efforts and schedules of the participants as well as integrating the group with neighboring block groups. Participants organize crime prevention programs, publish awareness newsletters, and designate safe houses for children to run to when danger threatens. The goal of such groups is to increase citizen awareness of the conditions under which crime is most likely to occur and thus reduce the likelihood of crime.

A variety of techniques have been developed in these programs to facilitate citizen awareness about crime, including telephone chains, newsletters, and meetings. Neighborhood Watch signs are placed in the neighborhood, and intensified surveillance is encouraged.[27] Local police departments are usually willing to participate in "operation identification" programs, which involve engraving citizens' property with identifying symbols, and "operation lockup" programs, which distribute security locks to citizens.[28]

The most common problem faced by block groups is maintaining citizen enthusiasm for the project, but studies of a program in Philadelphia indicate once more the importance of individuals who are willing to provide proper leadership. Innovative block watch captains, supported by local police officers, can keep programs alive and make a significant contribution to their communities.[29]

LAW ENFORCEMENT: THE CHALLENGE OF POLICING A FREE SOCIETY

Few persons in the United States are more aware of the principles of limited government described in Chapter 4 than are police officers, who must deal with the constraints of limited government on a daily basis. Police officers take an oath to maintain the peace and uphold the law, but they must do so in the context of a legal system designed to prevent the abuse of power. The rules which govern police officers (as well as attorneys, judges, correctional officers, and other officers of the court) restrict their ability to intercede in the lives of individuals. Whether these legal constraints also unnecessarily limit the ability of police officers to protect individuals from crime is an ongoing debate in our society.

An example of the restrictions on police officers is in order. Suppose two police officers patrolling an interstate highway see an old van painted with peace symbols and sporting several bumper stickers which advocate drug use and free love. A bearded man familiar to the police as a drug dealer is driving the van. In the van with him are three other men with long hair and beards. As a result of their experience, the police officers suspect that the van contains illegal drugs and other illegal items such as burglary tools or stolen goods. However, even if the police know that each of the men has a history of drug or burglary convictions, they may not legally stop the van to search it unless they have more than a suspicion. They must have **probable cause**— the right to infringe on the liberty of others because of a belief about their activities resulting from trustworthy information which could be interpreted by a reasonable person to mean that a crime is taking place (or has taken place) and that the person in question is (or was) a participant in that crime.[30]

There are conditions under which the police officers could stop the van. If they knew that a crime had been committed by persons fitting the general description of the men in the van, if one of the men was seen by the officers throwing a marijuana cigarette out the window, or if the van was clocked going faster than the speed limit, the police officers could stop the van. Under any of these conditions, as well as others, the officers would have a right to invade the privacy of the men by detaining them, and in some circumstances the officers could search the men and the van, seize any illegal substances or stolen goods, and arrest the occupants. These conditions constitute probable cause for believing a crime has been committed.

You may want to know why the police officers cannot simply stop the van if they believe the men have committed or might commit a crime. The reason is that individuals in the United States are protected from arbitrary and capricious interference in their lives by the government and its agents. Most people in the United States believe that it is better to have as much personal freedom or liberty as possible; if police officers were able to intercede easily in the lives of individuals, the personal freedom of individuals would be reduced.

Providing the police with more authority does not necessarily mean that police officers could by themselves reduce crime. In fact, police officers are simply part of a larger criminal justice system which has some impact on criminal activity. It is also important to understand that criminal justice systems are themselves part of the larger society and reflect the political culture of that society.

All other things being equal, according to scholars of comparative government and criminologists, the more efficient the criminal justice system, the lower the official crime rates in that country. However, it is also the case that efficient, coercive criminal justice systems tend to exist in societies whose people value order more than they value freedom.[31] We value individual freedom in this country. It is not likely that Americans would tolerate the idea of having their homes randomly searched and their property capriciously seized in order to reduce crime without mounting significant protest and demanding an end to the "police state."

The Number of Law Enforcement Personnel

Fighting crime is primarily a state and local activity. There are approximately 15,000 state and local law enforcement agencies in the United States; more than 12,000 of them are general-purpose local police forces, reflecting the emphasis placed by Americans on local control of the police.[32] The duties of these agencies include law enforcement, maintenance of order, and service to the community.

The number of law enforcement personnel has remained fairly stable since 1972. In 1987, there were 555,364 sworn officers and 202,144 civilians employed in law enforcement by state and local governments.[33] In recent years larger cities have had a higher ratio of law enforcement personnel to the total population than have suburbs and small towns. Cities of 250,000 or more had, on the average, 3.5 law enforcement employees per 1000 residents, the highest per capita average for all city population groups. The lowest per capita ratio was 2.1 law enforcement employees per 1000 residents for cities with populations below 50,000.[34]

Kinds of Law Enforcement Personnel

Law enforcement personnel can be divided into many categories. One basic distinction is that between sworn officers and civilians. **Sworn officers** are individuals who have undergone sufficient training to meet state requirements for fulfilling all the duties of the police role. These duties include detaining individuals, making arrests, and using deadly force. Civilians constitute all the other employees who work for any law enforcement agency. They include secretaries, many radio dispatchers and lab technicians, and crime investigators and other office workers. Civilians make up a quarter of all law enforcement personnel.[35]

It is also possible to classify law enforcement personnel by jurisdiction. Municipal law enforcement personnel usually work in city police departments, but they may be assigned to the city sheriff or the prosecuting attorney's office. The duties and activities of municipal law enforcement officers — urban police officers — will be covered in depth later in this chapter.

County law enforcement employees work in sheriff's departments, although a few large cities also have sheriffs who may be independent of or consolidated with the local municipal government.[36] In 1980, there were county sheriff's offices in all but 12 of the 3040 counties in the United States and state sheriff's offices in all states except Alaska. Sheriffs, who are elected in all states except Rhode Island and Hawaii (where they are appointed), typically perform the following duties: (1) maintaining a jail, (2) providing police protection, (3) maintaining court security, and (4) serving process papers.[37]

Nine of ten sheriffs are responsible for maintaining a jail. Although training is not required to be a sheriff, there are requirements in all states for becoming a sworn officer. Where sheriffs are sworn officers, they are often required to investigate crime, particularly in rural areas which are not patrolled by a police department. Sheriff's departments also provide security in courthouses and courtrooms. In addition, sheriffs may be required to serve papers informing individuals that they have been called as jurors or witnesses or that they have legal judgments against them and to serve summonses.

State police personnel are employees of agencies named the state police, the state highway patrol, or the state department of public safety. All the states except Hawaii have such an agency.[38] Within these agencies, officers are responsible for investigating violations of state statutes either in association with local police personnel or independently. Some state police agencies have specialized departments for investigating the sale and transportation of illegal drugs, white-collar crime, and organized crime, depending on the particular problems faced by the state, often as a result of its location. For instance, border states — Texas, Florida, California — have had specialized state police drug enforcement departments for decades, while Northeastern states — New York, New Jersey, Pennsylvania — have maintained state police organized crime departments for decades. In many states, the state police agency has almost complete responsibility for the investigation of white-collar crime, including consumer fraud and embezzlement.

Who Becomes a Police Officer?

The men and women who choose law enforcement as a career are average Americans with no unusual personality traits. In recent years an emphasis on professionalization has led to more sophisticated selection procedures, so that police officers are carefully selected from those who apply to be officers. Many states require psychological evaluations of would-be police officers to find individuals who can handle the pressures of police work; professional police departments demand an extensive background investigation of applicants for the same reason. To select the best officers, police administrators, often working with civilians who serve on police commissions or civil service commissions, interview potential police officers, asking about their ideas concerning police work, anticipated behavior in special situations, and views on deadly force and police discretion.

In 1987, 92 percent of all sworn officers were men and only 8 percent were women; however, 64 percent of all civilian law enforcement employees were women.[39] A 1983 survey of the 50 largest cities in the United States found that 14.5 percent of all sworn officers were black and 5 percent were Hispanic.[40]

What Do Police Officers Do?

More has been written about the activities of the urban police officer than about any other individual in law enforcement (except perhaps the private detective). Despite the portrayal on television and in the popular press, a police officer does not make a felony arrest or fire a weapon on an average tour of duty. On a typical day in a typical city, the average police officer spends the greatest amount of time on service activities and smallest amount on law enforcement activities.[41] Patrol officers spend much of their time driving around the city, answering calls from citizens and initiating calls on their own (Table 13.5).

The three basic categories of police officer activity are called the **components of the police role** by James Q. Wilson. The three components are as follows:

(1) law enforcement, which involves all those activities whose obligations end with an arrest or citation and in which law is used as a tool to punish
(2) order maintenance, which involves all those activities designed to restore order or avoid disorder and which may end in arrest, but only if order cannot be secured in any other way
(3) service, which involves all those activities designed to please the public by providing aid or service to members of the community[42]

Serious situations — those involving the law enforcement component — are likely to begin when a citizen "calls the cops." Formal intervention — detaining or arresting a suspect or issuing a citation — is most likely to occur when the police define an individual's activity as serious, dangerous to the individual or to others. (Table 13.5 describes the amount of time devoted to their various duties and the results of intervention by patrol officers in three cities.)

Table 13.5   POLICE ACTIVITY IN THREE CITIES BY TYPE AND FREQUENCY

Event type	Relative frequency (%)	Police-initiated (%)	Formalized (%)[a]	City
Serious[b]	11.3	3.9	72.8	Elyria
Serious[b]	6.5	10.4	—[c]	Columbia
Serious[b]	30.2	18.2	56.4	Newark
Less serious[d]	38.1	6.4	25.4	Elyria
Less serious[d]	38.5	17.6	—[c]	Columbia
Less serious[d]	35.3	25.3	24.4	Newark
Traffic events[e]	34.0	25.4	69.1	Elyria
Traffic events[e]	34.3	75.2	—[c]	Columbia
Traffic events[e]	9.8	32.4	62.7	Newark
Service events[e]	16.7	11.6	15.0	Elyria
Service events[e]	20.7	30.0	—[c]	Columbia
Service events[e]	23.2	56.7	19.4	Newark

[a]A record is made of the event, usually in the form of a citation, or an arrest.

[b]Usually involves the law enforcement component of the police role.

[c]Information unavailable.

[d]Usually involves the order maintenance component of the police role.

[e]Usually involves the service component of the police role.

Source: Jeffrey S. Slovak, Styles of Urban Policing: Organization, Environment, and Police Styles in Selected American Cities (New York: New York University Press, 1986), 64–100.

Why Do Police Officers Do What They Do?

Explaining why anyone does anything is a tricky business, but police behavior has been the subject of a great deal of research. Four aspects of police officers' lives have been found to be important in explaining police behavior: (1) training, (2) socialization into the role of police officers, (3) the policy established by the police department, (4) the stress of the daily demands of the occupation.

Training   All individuals who become police officers receive training, usually at a county or municipal training center. The training requirements in most states stress human relations and crisis intervention skills, weapons training, knowledge of law, and communications. Patrol techniques and criminal investigation skills, however, take up the majority of the training time. The use of firearms and self-protection are also crucial aspects, as is mastering the law and its intricacies. The goal of such training is to produce an officer who is courageous and suspicious, can exercise authority, and can cope with the constant threat of danger as well as the occasional possibility of corruption.

Police officers provide a number of services in every community. (Courtesy of Kim Bradley, San Marcos Daily Record.)

Socialization   Socialization—the process of learning the norms, values, and roles of the organization—overrides the influence of social class to produce a cadre of fellow officers. The process of socialization into the police role turns an average individual into a person who can cope with sights and activities few Americans know much about.[43] Police officers see violence and tragedy, hear curses directed at them, and feel hostility and rejection. At the same time, they intercede in troubled situations to help individuals and must do so with authority and dispassion.

The ability to handle all aspects of this difficult job must be learned. Much of the learning takes place after formal training in the socialization process, in which police officers come to learn what is expected of them by the individuals with whom they come into frequent contact: other police officers, good citizens, potential criminals, and momentarily misguided individuals.

Departmental Policy   Departmental policy is necessary because police officers must use **discretion**, the right to choose between two or more task-

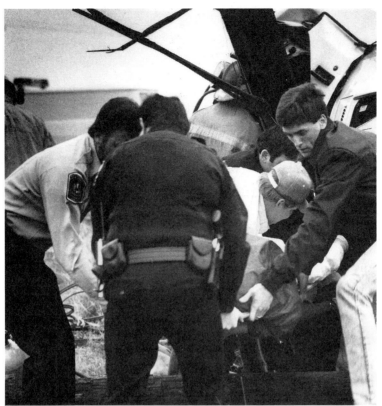

(Courtesy of Kim Bradley, San Marcos Daily Record.)

related alternatives regarding their work. Because police officers cannot deal with all the law violators they see — they simply do not have the time or resources — they must decide when individuals and situations merit official interest.

Remember the anecdote about the two police officers who see a van carrying several men suspected of having committed a crime? In this case, the officers have no legal right to stop the van, but if the van were traveling 10 miles over the speed limit, the situation would require the police officers to use discretion. Should they stop the van, or should they direct their attention toward other areas which might be more important? Police officers must regularly use discretion under circumstances much more complex and ambiguous than those described in this example.

James Q. Wilson has argued that controlling the discretionary decisions of patrol officers is one of the most important goals of police administrators.[44] To do this, administrators create departmental policy to guide the discretionary decisions of police officers. A particular kind of policy produces a particular style of policing. Since controlling discretion is so important, police behavior can be understood by studying departmental policy and the resulting **styles of policing**. There are three styles which tend to develop in particular kinds of communities.

A *legalistic* style of policing tends to develop in communities with a professional city manager–city council form of government in which the city manager acts to protect the police department from politicians and their demands for favorable treatment. Officers need not fear the wrath of the police chief when politicians or their friends are cited or arrested, because the city manager is there to defend the chief and the department. A mayor's child and a day laborer are likely to be similarly charged for similar behaviors.

Policy in a legalistic-style department emphasizes the law enforcement component of the police role; the goal is to enforce the law uniformly and efficiently. Policy is written, and it emphasizes aggressive application of the law. The law is used as a tool to punish individuals. Impartial, aggressive policing is most likely to occur in this style. As a result, this style produces the highest rate of traffic citations, official delinquents, and felony arrests among the three styles.

A *watchman* style of policing tends to develop in predominantly working-class communities which have spoils system forms of government. The winners of elections are able to appoint their supporters to important positions within the city government. In such communities, politicians have a great deal to say about who is the chief of police. Police officers are most likely to behave in a manner which will please the police administrators and therefore the politicians. A mayor's child may be permitted to carouse on the city square, while a day laborer may be arrested and charged with public intoxication for the same behavior.

Policy, which is for the most part unwritten, emphasizes the order maintenance component of the police role; the goal is to maintain order and avoid antagonizing powerful individuals while doing so. Policy demands that each officer consider the identity of an individual when making discretionary decisions. The law is used as a tool to maintain order in the community, and the specific charges at the time of arrest may be less important than the goal of detaining the individual. As a result, impartial, aggressive law enforcement is much less likely in this style of policing.

A *service* style of policing tends to develop in homogeneous middle-class communities where there is widespread agreement about the police role. Policy emphasizes service to the citizens of the community; officers are trained to be courteous and helpful. Police officers do not overlook crimes committed by community residents; if the crimes are considered serious (e.g., burglary, rape, homicide), they are handled in a legalistic style. If they are considered trivial (e.g., marijuana use, panty raids, curfew violations), they are likely to be handled in a watchman style. In this style, a mayor's child who is intoxicated in public may be handled more leniently than a day laborer engaged in the same behavior, but both will be treated punitively for drunken driving or burglary.

Stress Stress governs the role of the police officer in the society. It is the police officer who provides the most visible reminder of the potential for crime and violence, the seamy side of life in the United States.[45] Police work is stressful for several other reasons: (1) the conflict between civil liberties and order, (2) rejection by citizens, and (3) the threat of violence and the use of force.

Perhaps the most problematic aspect of police work is the necessity of protecting civil liberties while enforcing statutory law. This conflict between fighting crime and protecting civil liberties produces significant role strain among police officers. To cope with the stress, police officers adapt in a number of ways, including becoming overly aggressive, cynical, and unemotional.[46] They also may develop an "us-versus-them" attitude toward outside individuals and as a result withdraw into the police subculture.[47] To the extent that police officers withdraw, they become isolated from the average individual and may lose contact with good citizens.

Isolation increases the stress felt by police officers. Since police officers remind many people of things they would rather forget, citizens are less likely to befriend them,[48] adding to the feelings of isolation and rejection experienced by officers. This feeling is particularly troubling when police officers think about the risks they take for citizens who seem not to appreciate the work they do. The feelings of isolation and resentment, coupled with the demand that police officers enforce the law under due process guidelines, make police work very stressful.

Indicators of stress and role strain are higher than average rates of divorce and substance abuse among police officers. In 1986, a survey of major departments found that administrators viewed the potential for drug abuse among officers to be so significant that policies and procedures for dealing with the problem had been initiated.[49] Although it is difficult to generate statistics about suicide among police officers, it is generally believed that law enforcement officers are more likely to take their lives than are members of many other professions.[50]

The use of force makes the police officer's job very stressful. Police officers have an almost unrestricted right to use force, but Americans devalue the use of force, preferring education and intellect as methods of solving problems. However, since individuals occasionally use violence, the capacity for a legal response to the illegitimate use of force must exist. Nonetheless, since the use of force cannot be admired lest force become too popular (and therefore frequent), even those who have the legal right to use it suffer a loss of status and prestige because of their willingness to take on such an obligation. The phrase "It's a dirty job, but someone has to do it" surely applies to police work.[51]

Police officers and their families bear many of the costs of police work, but the public also suffers if police officers experience job-related problems. Police work is rarely done in public view, and secrecy sets the stage for the abuse of power. The private, stress-related problems of a police officer have the potential to become the public, legal problems of an individual.

Civil Liberties and Police Work

Discretion is an important and inevitable part of police work, but departmental policy can provide only general guidelines for the exercise of discretion. As a result, discretion has significant implications for civil liberties and the rule of law.[52]

Police officers may exercise discretion by ignoring or intervening in a situation. If intervention is chosen, police officers may do so informally (giving the individual a warning or a lecture) or formally (making an arrest or issuing a citation). If the decision is made to intervene formally, officers must be aware of the individual's legal rights. If those rights are violated, the subsequent arrest or citation may be declared invalid and the officer may be subject to disciplinary or legal procedures.

On the other hand, much of what police officers do is done in private, without meaningful public scrutiny; thus, police officers may be able to get away with illegal actions against individuals. Civil liberties (for instance, the right to be free from unreasonable search and seizure) are secure only to the extent that police departments require officers to ensure them and courts see to it that individuals receive them. The problems involved in policing a democratic society while maintaining sufficient order to protect regular commerce are significant, and their solutions are not without cost.

Future of Law Enforcement in the United States

A number of proposals have been generated to change police work. Some proposals are intended to make police work more efficient; others, to make it more just. A few are intended to reduce the stress experienced by police officers.

More Personnel?   One proposal for reducing the stress experienced by police officers is to increase the number of officers. More personnel should mean less work and therefore less stress. It should also mean more deterrence and therefore less crime.

There is some evidence that a dramatic increase in the number of police officers patrolling an area can reduce the amount of reported crime, but the hypothesis that more officers equals less crime is far from demonstrated. Early flawed studies seemed to show a relationship between increased patrols and crime reduction (and led to some dramatic increases in police department size), but subsequent studies have invalidated this relationship (the Kansas City Preventive Patrol Study) or suggested that the cost of such crime reduction is higher than individuals are willing to pay (the Rand Institute's New York City Subway Study).[53]

Whether more personnel would reduce the stress caused by overwork is not known. Although some police departments are understaffed by national standards, it is not clear that adding police officers reduces the amount of work for each officer. Adding officers many ultimately produce additional work, since citizens are more likely to call the cops if the police are able to come when called.

Take the Handcuffs off Police Officers?   One of the problems faced by police officers is the role strain caused by the conflict between fighting crime and protecting civil liberties. Some individuals have suggested that this conflict could be reduced or eliminated by reducing or eliminating due process. One rather frequent proposal is to reduce the rights of individuals by reducing the scope of the **exclusionary rule**, permitting more police intervention and thus reducing crime. (As noted in Chapter 12, the exclusionary rule is the legal guideline which says that illegally gathered evidence usually may not be used in a criminal trial.)

The attorney generals in the Reagan administration, William French Smith and Edwin Meese, asserted that the exclusionary rule, along with the Miranda warning, reduces the ability of police officers to enforce the law and therefore should be abolished.[54] Although the weakening or abolition of the exclusionary rule would clearly make the job of police officers easier in that they would be able to intervene more readily in the lives of individuals, it is not nearly as clear that such intervention would reduce the crime rate. A number of studies indicate that the exclusionary rule has very little impact on crime in either direction.[55] However, it is obvious that the elimination of the exclusionary rule would make the apprehension of criminals much easier, thereby making police officers' task of fighting crime more efficient and presumably more satisfying.

A recent limitation of the exclusionary rule is the *good faith exception*, which holds that evidence gained when officers unknowingly and in good faith serve an invalid warrant is admissible in court. The good faith exception now applies only to warrants containing errors created by a magistrate. If the exclusionary rule continues to be modified by the good faith exception, that evidence gathered by police officers who violate the civil liberties of individuals without actually intending to will be admissible in a court of law. Weakening or eliminating the exclusionary rule might reduce the role strain experienced by police officers, thus reducing the stress of the occupation, but it would also dramatically reduce the freedom and liberty of Americans.

Develop New Methods of Deploying Police Officers?   Some people have suggested this as a way of reducing job stress. The new approaches underscore community involvement as a method of reducing stress and crime at the same time.[56] One suggestion has been that police departments implement some version of the **team policing** approach to crime reduction. This approach is similar to strategies, used in Japan, of giving police officers "semipermanent" responsibility for a neighborhood or a part of a city.[57] Officers are expected to become familiar with the residents, thus increasing citizen confidence in the competence of police officers and increasing citizen willingness to provide information and support to the police.[58]

Team policing is a crime-fighting strategy. Since the police cannot adequately fight crime by themselves, they must secure community involvement if meaningful crime reduction is to occur. Advocates of this approach believe that successful crime fighting would significantly reduce the stress experienced by police officers.

An alternative to this is the **community service** approach, which is designed to mobilize neighborhood support by encouraging citizen participation in neighborhood management. Proponents of this approach believe that police officers should emphasize social work skills in dealing with individuals. Officers should consider many of their duties as responses to requests for help in dispute settling rather than demands that arrests be made. Integration and feelings of security with the community on the part of officers should result, enabling community members to demand higher standards of behavior from one another. James Q. Wilson, who does not advocate the community service approach, nevertheless argues that properly trained police officers "can help evoke a sense of community and a capacity for regulation where none is now found."[59]

The community service approach is not a crime-fighting approach but a method of helping the members of a community police themselves. Self-regulation should lead to crime reduction, proponents argue; perhaps more important for police officers, it could reduce citizen antagonism toward them, thus reducing their feelings of isolation and rejection.

It is important to recognize that although changes in police work may alleviate some of the stress and frustration found among police officers, such changes are not likely to reduce the overall crime rate significantly. Communities which experiment with new forms of police work may experience higher levels of order, but it is likely that the true criminals in those communities will simply move to more accommodating neighborhoods. The crime rate is a national social problem, not merely a local police problem.

What Can the Individual Do?

Individuals can contribute to local police departments in a number of ways. They can become active in civil service commissions, sit on civilian review boards, join police reserve units, participate in crime prevention organizations, and support state and local politicians who have similar ideas about law enforcement priorities.

Civil Service Boards Are Staffed by Individuals in the Community   Many municipal police departments are protected by civil service regulations. Cronyism is reduced in these departments because hiring and promotion are done through testing and interviews.

Departments governed by civil service regulations often have citizens on their personnel boards who interview aspiring officers. Employment and promotion are important decisions which can influence the course of police work in a city. Individuals interested in becoming involved in the police department should contact the personnel department of their local government.

Individuals Can Be on Civilian Review Boards in Some Police Departments These boards are composed of groups of citizens who review important police actions. Civilian review boards may examine the use of deadly force or undercover operations. Individuals who want to participate in civilian review boards should become involved in local politics and become known in the community for having an interest in these issues.

Police Reserve Programs Are Available to Individuals Some individuals want to do police work but do not want to make a career of it. They may be candidates for a local police reserve program. In most cases, reserve officers must meet the same employment standards as police officers meet. Civilian reserve officers are trained in the basics of police work and are teamed with police officers. Reserves are expected to donate their time doing routine police work, which occasionally becomes as exciting and dangerous as police work can be. If this sounds appealing to you, contact your local police department to see if a police reserve unit exists. If one does not exist, talk to the chief of police about starting one.

One of the most helpful things individuals can do is participate in crime prevention activities. These activities include but are not limited to those mentioned earlier: neighborhood watch programs, Crime Stoppers, and raising money for drug education and prevention efforts. Police officers cannot fight crime without citizen support; significant reductions in the crime rate will not occur unless individuals participate in crime prevention. If crime prevention sounds like something with which you would like to become involved, find out about the programs in your area. If no programs exist, start one.

Finally, individuals who care deeply about police issues, civil liberties, and crime reduction can become involved in the state and local political process. These issues are crucial to the maintenance of democratic societies. Become involved to make your views known. Support candidates who share your views. These activities are the lifeblood of a democratic society.

CORRECTIONS: THE CHALLENGE OF HUMANE AND EFFECTIVE PUNISHMENT

Like other debates involving the criminal justice system, the corrections debate centers on whether deterrence, retribution, or rehabilitation should be the goal of corrections. The treatment of incarcerated individuals is as important in a free society as is their treatment prior to conviction, since almost all persons who enter prison are released back into society, carrying with them the lessons learned in prison. Nevertheless, the first mandate for corrections departments is to control those who have been apprehended and sentenced.

The first goal of all American prisons is **custody** — containing prisoners within the prison. The second goal is **control** — retaining authority over prisoners' actions within the prison. Corrections officers are trained to respond to threatening situations first to maintain custody and then to maintain control. Policy does not permit administrators to accede to prisoner's demands even to gain the release of corrections officers who have been taken hostage. Custody and control are the most important rules in corrections.

The Types of Correctional Facilities

There are two forms of facilities designed to incarcerate adults for some period of time: jails and prisons. **Jails** are detention facilities designed to hold several kinds of persons for short periods of time, including those (1) awaiting arraignment or trial, (2) awaiting sentencing, (3) sentenced and awaiting transport to prison, (4) convicted of probation or parole violations, or (5) given a sentence of less than a year and a day.

In 1986, approximately 47 percent of jailed inmates had been convicted of a crime for which they were jailed; the other 53 percent were awaiting disposition of their cases and had not been convicted during the period of their incarceration.[60] Men, since they are the most often arrested, are the most common residents of jails; women accounted for only 8 percent of the jail population in 1986.[61]

Two thirds of all jails in the United States are small and were built to hold fewer than 50 inmates; these small jails house fewer than 15 percent of all jailed inmates. More than half of all jailed inmates are in jails which hold over 250 inmates.

Jail populations have a high volume of inmate turnover. In the year ending June 30, 1983, the 3338 local jails reported more than 16 million admissions and releases, for a national average of 44,000 "jail transactions" a day.[62]

Prisons are facilities designed to hold adults sentenced to a year or more. State prisons are typically thought of as having three levels of security: minimum, medium, and maximum. Maximum-security prisons, which are designed to house the most serious felons, pursue the goal of custody with seeming disregard of the consequences for inmates:

> The sixty maximum security prisons in the United States are surrounded by high walls or double fences, accompanied by manned towers. Electronic sensing devices and lights impose unremitting surveillance. The prisons have heavily barred and inside cell blocks with two to six tiers of cells, back-to-back. . . . To achieve full custodial control, as well as inmate surveillance, there are frequent searches of cells and inmates for weapons and other contraband. . . . Doors which might permit privacy are replaced by grilles of tool-resistant steel. Toilets are open and unscreened. . . . Body searches frequently precede and follow visits [by persons outside the prison]. . . . Fifty-six maximum security prisons,

built between 1830 and 1900 and since remodeled and expanded, are still in use — the backbone of the American prison system.[63]

Medium-security institutions commonly have fences rather than walls and have a variety of types of living quarters. Often inmates live in barracks or dormitories, and their privacy is less frequently invaded by corrections officers. Minimum-security prisons also may have barracks or dormitories, but supervision is less than is found in medium-security prisons. Inmates may work in fields or farms attached to the prison.

Imprisonment in the United States

The history of imprisonment is somewhat short. Until relatively recently, having a roof over one's head and three meals a day could hardly be considered punishment. Before the eighteenth century, mutilation and execution were the most common forms of punishment. In an ironic way, the American Revolutionary War ultimately led to the birth of prisons for two reasons: (1) the developing emphasis on republicanism and (2) the loss of the colonies as a "dumping ground for convicts."

The loss of the colonies made new forms of punishment necessary. At the same time, the philosophy of emphasizing the right of free people to choose their government (and therefore to reject an inhumane government) guided political philosophers to ward a **doctrine of utilitarian punishment**, in which punishment should be sufficiently severe to dissuade future criminal acts but no more severe lest the persons punished become unfit for living among good individuals.[64] Deterrence became the goal of the correctional system, and imprisonment was thought to be a more effective deterrent than execution, since the imprisoned individual would be around to serve as an example of the cost of crime.

The earliest prisons in the United States were penitentiaries in Pennsylvania requiring solitude and "penitence" (hence the name). The assumption that men (since almost all prisoners *were* men) given time to reflect on their misdeeds would reform themselves soon gave way to a harsher view of human potential. Prisons in the United States came to be modeled on the Auburn plan, which originally emphasized solitary confinement but soon gave way to a philosophy of corporal punishment, strict discipline, and arduous labor.[65]

Rehabilitation became the stated goal of many correctional systems after World War II. The **rehabilitative ideal** — the notion that inmates given the opportunity to change and be rehabilitated could do so — became popular. Various strategies, from individual and group therapy and behavior modification to job training and educational programs, were implemented.

Robert Martinson officially certified the failure of the rehabilitative ideal in 1974 with his survey of studies concerning rehabilitation.[66] His conclusion, widely reported and very influential, was that rehabilitation attempts in prisons, halfway houses, and reformatories are for the most part unsuccessful. Little evidence existed to support the idea that any past or current programs were demonstrably effective in rehabilitating convicted felons. The Martinson report proved to be the death knell of the rehabilitative ideal.

Incarceration in the United States Today

An emphasis on retribution and deterrence marks the current correctional system. Few corrections administrators today espouse rehabilitation as a goal or possibility. Educational and job training programs exist, but their primary contribution is to maintain order within the prison. **Warehousing** — confinement which makes no attempt to change inmates — is the dominant feature of prisons today.

Today's prisons have been shaped by two major societal changes: (1) the rights movements of the 1960s and (2) the expansion of due process by the Supreme Court during the same period.

The rights movements increased political awareness among all Americans. Blacks and Hispanics became conscious of the value of organized protest. That awareness went into the prison with black and Hispanic prisoners who organized political gangs. White prisoners have done the same, and most state prisoners now join gangs instead of remaining isolated.

The expansion of due process by the Supreme Court during the 1960s produced an awareness of prisoners' issues. Corrections officers have seen their right to discipline inmates sharply curtailed as federal courts have become involved in the day-to-day operations of the prison; one result of this loss of authority has been an increase in role strain among correctional officers.

How Many People Are in Prison?

By the end of 1987 there were over 500,000 persons in state prisons, for an incarceration rate of 212 sentenced prisoners per 100,000 residents.[67] This rate reflects a steady increase in the population of state prisons during the last 62 years, but the most dramatic increases have come during the last decade. From 1980 to 1986, state prison populations in the Northeast increased almost 11 percent and state prison populations in the West increased 14 percent. From 1980 to 1987, Alaska's prison population grew *209.5 percent*, and the states of California, New Hampshire, Hawaii, New Jersey, Arizona, and Nevada experienced increases of more than 140 percent.[68]

Why has there been such a dramatic increase in prison populations during the last decade? The answer is complicated, but much of it has to do with new sentencing and correctional philosophies. Despite a relatively steady rate of reported crime (and a declining victimization rate) during the late 1970s and the 1980s, there has been a demand for more and longer sentences. As a result, less emphasis has been placed on community-based programs and more emphasis has been placed on imprisonment, contributing to the increase in prison populations.

Prison overcrowding is a significant problem in a number of states. Most states are operating above capacity. At the end of 1987, state prisons were estimated to be operating at 105 percent of their highest capacity. In 1987, 16 states reported holding 12,220 prisoners in local jails because of prison overcrowding.[69] Leaders in several states are rethinking the emphasis on imprisonment and looking once again at funding community programs to reduce the costs of dealing with crime and pursuing justice.

The Corrections Officer

Much has been written about police officers, but corrections officers have received much less attention. However, there is little doubt that the job of the corrections officer is just as stressful as that of the police officer. Perhaps the lack of glamour in prison work contributes to the dearth of popular literature about and media attention to the prison guard. Whereas young men and women from all parts of the world may want to become police officers when they grow up, few dream of becoming a prison guard.

Who Becomes a Correctional Officer? Individuals working in adult and juvenile correctional facilities are predominantly male. As of June 30, 1986, more than 176,000 people had been hired by state governments to work in these facilities, and more than 106,000 of them were white males. In addition, there were 35,486 white females, 23,997 black males, and 10,699 black females working in state correctional facilities.[70] The typical requirements for becoming a corrections officer in a state facility are a high school degree or its equivalent and being at least 18 years old. Drug use, a criminal record, and an undesirable employment record are reasons for denying a person work as a corrections officer.

Correctional Work Is as Stressful as Police Work The stress experienced by corrections officers and, as a direct result, their families is related to a failure to include corrections officers in decision making about their work. Their stress is similar to that experienced by a secretary who has little or no control over the decisions made by the boss but who must nevertheless implement those decisions. Such situations produce high stress levels because the people implementing the policy have little influence over the policy.

Other sources of stress for prison guards are role ambiguity and role strain. Corrections officers are expected to maintain order—custody and control—within the prison or jail. Authority for carrying out their obligations is necessary, yet officers report that their authority has been reduced by court decisions. As a result, corrections officers must rely on personal aspects of their relationships with inmates to maintain order. At times they must overlook infractions; at other times they must punish inmates. Making such choices is stressful.[72] Because of these ambiguous task-related de-

---

Box 13-4 **AIDS in Prison**

Acquired immune deficiency syndrome (AIDS) promises to be a problem of the 1990s. AIDS poses a major problem for prisoners, corrections officers, and administrators. State inmate populations include a higher incidence of persons in the high-risk groups — intravenous drug users and males with homosexual contacts. As of October 1987, there were 1964 reported cases of AIDS in correctional institutions throughout the country.[71]

Housing and caring for inmates diagnosed with AIDS are critical issues. Screening inmates for AIDS without violating their rights is another important issue. Liability issues must be considered as well. If administrators are found liable for failing to protect inmates from AIDS infection, taxpayers will have to pay for judgments against those administrators.

Deciding what to do with inmates who are released from prison with AIDS is another problem. There are no legal justifications for retaining persons in prison past their release dates; moreover, AIDS is not grounds for incarceration. It may be in the long-term interests of citizens to be concerned about the adequacy of rehabilitation programs if unreformed inmates are released to prey on communities again.

---

mands, corrections officers report uncertainty about what is expected of them and discomfort with the conflicting demands of the job (Box 13-4).

Probation

Probation — the practice of deferring prison sentences by permitting convicted offenders to serve their sentences in the community under the supervision of the court — is an alternative to prison. Probation permits the rehabilitation of offenders who pose no threat to the community.

In 1986, the number of adults on probation increased by 6.4 percent, the eighth year in a row that such an increase occurred.[73] Ironically, the "get tough with felons" policy which has dominated corrections since the mid 1970s, producing larger prison populations, has also resulted in larger probation populations. Prisons cannot accommodate all persons convicted of felonies, and the probation population is increasing at a rate greater than that for the prison population.

Perhaps more surprising than the size of the probation population is its composition. A new concept has entered corrections literature: felony probation. Between one-third and one-half of all persons on probation have been convicted of felonies.[74] Perhaps most surprising to those who believe that harsh punishment is the key to correctional deterrence is Samuel Walker's conclusion about probation: It is "the one correctional treatment program that seems to work" by achieving its stated goals and serving "broader social needs."[75] It does not succeed with every offender, but it succeeds often

---

Box 13-5 **The Probation Officer: Social Worker with the Power to Imprison**

Probation officers have important roles in the criminal justice system. Supervising both juveniles and adults, a probation officer must make decisions about how cases will be processed (formally, informally, or by transfer to another court), sentence recommendations and the disposition of cases, and the form of supervision required in each case. In most cases, the probation officer must also provide supervision and make certain that the counseling or treatment which has been ordered is provided.

Probation officers experience significant role strain. They are expected to counsel offenders and help them with occupational and personal problems. In this way, they are treatment-oriented. At other times they must recommend revocation of probation and send probationers to jail or prison. This orientation toward social control is in conflict with the treatment orientation, producing role strain and conflict. However, probation officers participate in the most successful rehabilitation program in the criminal justice system.

Probation officers often have large caseloads and work long hours. Beginning salaries range from $12,768 in West Virginia to $31,644 in California, with an average of around $17,000. Most states require a bachelor's degree and related experience to become a probation officer.

Source: Timothy J. Flanagan and Katherine M. Jamieson, *Sourcebook of Criminal Justice Statistics, 1987* (Washington, DC: GPO, 1988), 81.

---

enough that Walker recommends maintaining the present system with only minor modifications.

Probation's success may not be a result of probation itself but rather of the fact that the persons who receive probation are good risks. It is also probable that avoiding prison and its corrupting effects will actually decrease the likelihood of a person's becoming a career criminal. It is not so much the effectiveness of probation but one's good fortune in avoiding the state prison which produces rehabilitation. Whatever the reason for its success, probation is one of the most effective correctional practices.[76] (See Box 13-5 for a discussion of the probation officer's job.)

Proposals

Public concern about taxes, prisons, crime, and criminals has produced a number of proposals for relief from all these "ills." Former Chief Justice Warren Burger helped popularize the idea of **prison industries** by advocating "factories within walls" as a necessary aspect of prison reform. Like most ideas, this one is not new. In early prisons, inmate labor was commonly sold to private employers. Not surprisingly, objections came from those private employers who did not benefit from the cheap labor. For the most part, prison industries disappeared during the Great Depression.

In January 1985 there were more than 25 private-sector prison industries.[77] A number of prison industry models exist, all of which have had some degree of success. The advantages for prisoners include the ability to earn a reasonable salary while in prison and, in some situations, to acquire a skill which can be helpful in getting a job after leaving prison. The advantages for employers involve low cost or free factory space and a flexible but readily available work force. State and local governments can anticipate increased revenues and more orderly inmates in the prisons.[78]

However, a number of problems continue to exist for prison employers. Prison industries suffer from decreased efficiency when prisoners do not want to work. Moreover, motivating an uneducated, unskilled work force presents problems for industries, especially those requiring extensive training. There are still unresolved legal issues concerning appropriate wages, hours, and liability. As prison industries become more common, some of these problems are likely to be solved.

Private-sector involvement in corrections has taken a second form. **Private prisons** are prisons built, managed, and sometimes owned by private firms or individuals. They represent an alternative to funding prison construction with tax dollars. Between 1980 and January 1, 1986, 13 private prisons and jails opened in six states.[79] The relative ease with which private industry can finance and build a facility compared with the bureaucratic demands of state and local governments increases the likelihood of private prisons in the future. Proponents argue that the private sector can manage prisons more efficiently and, consequently, less expensively than governments can; opponents note the legal problems associated with liability for the failure of private prisons. Current experience is insufficient to make adequate judgments about the future of private prisons, but there is some evidence that state and local governments can receive "more and better prison services for less money."[80]

The Debate Revisited: Deterrence, Rehabilitation, or Retribution?

This section began with a discussion of the debate concerning the ideal goal of prisons. Should prisons be organized to deter, rehabilitate, or provide retribution?

We do not know what, if anything, about the prison experience contributes to rehabilitation; penologists have for the most part abandoned the rehabilitative model and its definition of inmates as persons who can be changed for the better. More important, we do know that prisons punish by depriving prisoners of freedom, dignity, privacy, safety, and heterosexual contact. The fact that humans can become accustomed to these deprivations (and therefore not be deterred by them) should come as no surprise; one has only to examine the streets of Calcutta or the villages of Ethiopia to know that humans can become accustomed to the direst circumstances.

Whether prisons provide retribution or should provide sufficient retribution to satisfy those calling for it is ultimately a question of values. The instrumental question is whether the individuals who fund state and local governments can afford institutions which require inmates to retain their capacity for violence and become less civilized in order to survive. Although the thought of inflicting suffering on inmates may gratify individuals at a visceral level, the fact remains that almost all inmates ultimately leave prison to walk the streets in America again. If we consider the issue in these terms, the question becomes not "How much pain can we inflict on them to pay them back for what they have done to us?" but "What can we do while they are in prison to make them less likely to pay us back when they leave prison?"

Individuals who care deeply about issues related to imprisonment, civil liberties, and crime reduction must become involved in the state and local political process. These issues are among the most critical in a civilized society, and it is important that citizens be informed about them. It is also important that state legislators be knowledgeable. Individuals must insist that humane treatment of inmates be a part of the legislative program.

The Costs of Justice: Pay Now or Later?

Fighting crime is a major industry in the United States. The fight against crime and for justice is conducted primarily by state and local governments. The question is whether we are spending too much or too little and whether the money could be better spent in other kinds of programs.

State and local governments pay almost all the costs of law enforcement in the United States. Expenditures for police protection vary from state to state but are always high. Megastates such as California ($2.7 billion per year) and New York ($2.4 billion per year) spend more for police protection than do smaller, less prosperous states such as Mississippi ($112 million per year) and West Virginia ($80 million per year).[81]

In 1987, the budgets of all sheriff's departments, state agencies, and local police departments totaled more than $28 billion.[82] Local police departments accounted for more than $18 billion of this total, and sheriff's departments accounted for almost $7 billion. These budgets are funded by taxpayers who must decide whether these are effective methods of allocating revenues.

Expenditures for police protection have remained steady for the last few years. Until recently, expenditures for police employment in 88 large cities had increased 5.5 times (figures adjusted for inflation) between 1938 and 1982, from $80 million to $3 billion.[83] Police budgets as a percentage of total city budgets increased from 8 percent in 1940 to 14 percent in 1980.[84] The largest increase — 103 percent — came during the 1960s, in a time when the trend toward police professionalization was at its peak; since 1977, real expenditures have dropped slightly.[85]

State and local governments also bear most of the cost of imprisonment

Table 13.6   CORRECTIONS EXPENDITURES BY LEVEL OF GOVERNMENT FOR FISCAL YEAR 1985

Level of government	Expenditures ($)
Total state	8,080,703,000
Total local	4,246,865,000
Total county	3,197,603,000
Total municipal	1,049,262,000

Source: Sue Lindgren, Justice Expenditure and Employment, 1985, Bureau of Justice Statistics (Washington, DC: GPO, 1987), 3.

(Table 13.6). Over 60 percent of all corrections employees work for state governments, and another 35 percent work for local governments.[56] During the period 1971–1985, state government expenditures to operate correctional institutions increased by 511 percent while expenditures to build new facilities rose by 653 percent.[87]

County and municipal governments are also responsible for funding correctional operations. County expenditures for building and operating prison facilities, including jails and juvenile detention facilities, increased from 70 percent of all corrections expenditures in 1977 to almost 80 percent in 1985. Municipal expenditures in the same period increased even more, from 76 percent to 92 percent. At the same time, probation and parole programs experienced reduced funding as a result of the increased emphasis on warehousing.[88]

The cost of justice includes more than the tax dollars spent on apprehending and imprisoning criminals. There are costs for the persons who work in law enforcement and corrections and for those who are imprisoned. Finally, there is the cost to the society when inmates who might have been punished in other ways are released from prison.

The most significant question is whether it is possible to alleviate the human and monetary costs of reducing crime by funding programs which increase the likelihood that individuals in our society will have adequate nutrition, education, and health care. Since inmates in state prisons are not well educated, have often been psychologically deprived, and frequently have serious health problems, it may be possible to reduce the frequency of crime by attacking these problems. Programs which lessen these problems early in the lives of individuals may reduce those individuals' inclination to commit crimes later in life. Although no policy can eliminate crime, policies which reduce human suffering and offer an opportunity to pursue the American dream can surely reduce crime. Otherwise we will continue the present strategy of fighting crime, which is ultimately a strategy of paying too much, too late.

WHAT WE CAN DO AS CITIZENS IN THE COMMUNITY

Law enforcement and corrections cannot be expected to solve the crime problem by themselves. Citizen involvement in the process is crucial for two reasons: (1) Such involvement increases citizens' appreciation of the problems associated with law enforcement and (2) increases citizens' commitment to law-abiding behavior.

Why do citizens become more law-abiding when they are involved in the law enforcement process? Suppose all citizens in the United States who consider themselves to be law-abiding refused to purchase any item they *thought* might be stolen, *no matter how good a deal they seemed to be offered.* How long do you suppose burglars would continue to steal such items? How long do you suppose fences would be willing to buy stolen merchandise from thieves? What do you suppose would be the impact on the crime rate? It should be clear from this example that crime cannot flourish unless "good citizens" permit it to. If good citizens were involved daily in a community crime prevention effort, do you imagine that they would be as eager to buy stolen merchandise which had been obtained in violation of their very efforts? Some would, of course, since the desire for material possessions is an important part of our culture, but many, if not most, would not. Their commitments to the laws against theft would be strengthened by their efforts, and they would be less willing to encourage theft by purchasing stolen merchandise.

The alternative form of community crime prevention is, of course, vigilantism. Vigilante justice arises in the United States when citizens lose faith in the criminal justice system. When citizens pursue criminals without regard for the law, they become lawless and similar to those they pursue.

There may be no way to eliminate crime, but if the damaging effects of crime are lessened, it will be because individuals organize their communities in new and better ways to attack these problems. As members of a community, we have an obligation to contribute to the community; as property-owning members of that community, we have a monetary motivation for making it the best community possible. Whatever the motivation, communities do not persist or become better without the involvement of their members.

Conclusion

One of the purposes of order in a society is to provide a suitable context for the pursuit of "the good life," however that be defined. It is difficult to maintain order in a society as complex and heterogeneous as ours, in part because there are so many views of the good life. Maintaining order in such a society places a significant burden on those who are assigned the task. Police officers and corrections officers are constrained by law and cannot do whatever is most efficient or effective to restore or maintain order; rather, they are required to do what is legal under the state and federal constitutions. Because our society defines justice in terms of individual liberty, police officers may not do whatever is efficient to maintain and restore order on the streets. Because our society defines justice in terms of freedom from cruel and inhumane punishment, corrections officers may not do whatever is efficient to maintain and restore order in the prison.

There are significant costs of a criminal justice system like ours. There are monetary costs to the taxpayers, who must fund the police departments, prisons, and auxiliary agencies. There are emotional costs to the employees of police departments and prisons. There are emotional and physical costs to the "clients" of police and corrections officers. At times there are physical, emotional, and monetary costs to individuals when the clients of police and correctional officers are returned to the streets.

Alternative forms of police organizations have been suggested as possible ways of making police departments more effective without reducing the liberties of individuals. Some national figures have even suggested reducing civil liberties to provide more order. Penologists tout alternatives to prison as a way of reducing the debilitating effects of prisons, and others argue for private-sector involvement within the prisons to reduce the costs to taxpayers.

Providing both freedom and order may be the goal most difficult to obtain in a democracy. If that is the case, individual understanding of and involvement in the solutions is critical. For an elaboration of yet another problem, we go to Chapter 14.

Study Objectives

1. Identify the constraints on efficient crime fighting by police officers and the limits to efficient maintenance of order by corrections officers.
2. Identify the costs of police and corrections to our society.
3. Identify the number and kinds of police personnel.
4. Identify the proposals for reducing the costs of police work.
5. Identify the components of the police role.
6. Identify the styles of policing and explain why and where they develop.
7. Identify the reasons why police officers act as they do.
8. Identify the rehabilitative ideal and explain what led to its abandonment.
9. Identify the costs of constructing and maintaining correctional facilities.
10. Identify the three concepts of justice and their implications for the criminal justice system.

11. List the goals of correctional institutions.
12. List and discuss the characteristics of prisoners in the United States.
13. Discuss probation as a crime-fighting strategy.
14. Identify the proposals for reducing the problems in police and correctional work.
15. Identify the following terms:

probable cause	discretion
exclusionary rule	recidivism
prevalence of imprisonment	

Glossary

community service An approach to crime reduction designed to mobilize neighborhood support by encouraging citizen participation in neighborhood management and crime fighting.

components of the police role The concepts created by James Q. Wilson to describe the activities of police officers. The three components are law enforcement, order maintenance, and service.

Control Retaining authority over prisoners' actions within the prison. It is the second goal of American prisons.

crime The violation of statutory criminal law.

criminal incident A concept developed by the Bureau of Justice Statistics to measure victimization. It is defined as a specific criminal act involving one or more victims.

custody Containing prisoners within the prison. It is the first goal of American prisons.

discretion An inevitable aspect of the work of police officers and other law enforcement officials. It requires them to choose between two or more task-related alternatives in the course of their work.

doctrine of utilitarian punishment The idea that punishment should be sufficiently severe to dissuade future criminal acts but no more severe lest the persons punished become unfit for living among good individuals.

exclusionary rule The legal guideline which states that illegally gathered evidence usually may not be used in a criminal trial. The recent good faith exception to the rule holds that evidence gained when officers unknowingly and in good faith serve a warrant prepared invalidly by a magistrate is admissible in court.

jails Detention facilities designed to hold several kinds of persons for short periods.

lifetime prevalence of imprisonment The probability of being imprisoned during one's lifetime.

prevalence of imprisonment The probability of being imprisoned on any given day.

prison industries "Factories within walls" in which prison inmates can work to earn money and keep busy.

prisons Detention facilities designed to hold adults sentenced to a year or more.

private prisons Prisons built, managed, and sometimes owned by private firms or individuals. They represent an alternative to funding prison construction with tax dollars.

probable cause The right to infringe on the liberty of others because of a belief about their activities resulting from trustworthy information which could be interpreted by a reasonable person to mean that a crime is taking place (or has taken place) and that the person in question is (or was) a participant in that crime.

probation The practice of deferring prison sentences by permitting convicted offenders to serve their sentences in the community under the supervision of the court. It is an alternative to prison.

rate A measure of the incidence of an event for a base population.

recidivism rate The rate at which inmates return to prison.

rehabilitative ideal The belief that inmates who are given the opportunity to change and be rehabilitated will do so.

styles of policing Tendencies on the part of police officers to behave in a certain way. These tendencies, identified by James Q. Wilson, result from departmental policy. There are three styles of policing: legalistic, watchman, and service.

sworn officers Individuals who have undergone sufficient training to meet state requirements for fulfilling all the duties of the police role.

team policing An approach to crime reduction similar to strategies used in Japan. A group or team of police officers are given "semipermanent" responsibility for a neighborhood or a part of a city.

Uniform Crime Reports An annual summary of the crime statistics received from police departments in the United States. Published by the Federal Bureau of Investigation.

victimization A specific criminal incident that affects one person. An incident may involve a number of crimes, but it is counted only once and is categorized by the most serious crime.

victimization studies Consist of data about victims gathered in a national survey of a sample of households by the Bureau of Justice Statistics.

warehousing The current practice of confining inmates. No attempt is made to rehabilitate or change the inmates; instead, the goal is simple custody.

Endnotes

1. Katherine M. Jamieson and Timothy Flanagan, *Sourcebook of Criminal Justice Statistics, 1988*, Bureau of Justice Statistics (Washington, DC: GPO, 1988), 2–23.
2. Kelly H. Shim and Marshall DeBerry, *Criminal Victimization in the United States, 1986*, Bureau of Justice Statistics (Washington, DC: GPO, 1988), 111–112.
3. Ibid., 1.
4. *Uniform Crime Reports for the United States, 1987*, Federal Bureau of Investigation (Washington, DC: GPO, 1988), 41, and Shim and DeBerry, 14.
5. Shim and DeBerry, 10.
6. *Uniform Crime Reports for the United States, 1987*, 41.
7. Ibid., 4.
8. Shim and DeBerry, 3.
9. Ibid.
10. Ibid., 46.
11. Shim and DeBerry, 3.

12. Ibid., 3–5.
13. *Report to the Nation on Crime and Justice*, 2nd ed., Bureau of Justice Statistics (Washington, DC: GPO, 1988) 50, and Christopher Innes, *Drug Use and Crime* (Washington, DC: GPO, 1988), 1.
14. *Report to the Nation on Crime and Justice*, 51.
15. Nevertheless, 81 percent of state inmates reported that they were not daily users of a major drug during the month prior to arrest, and 65 percent reported that they had never been regular users of a major drug. For further information, see Innes, 1.
16. In fact, Charles Silberman reports that methadone maintenance programs might have actually increased criminal activity among some heroine addicts since "[b]y freeing young addicts of the need to spend most of their time 'chasing the bag,' methadone apparently gave them more time and energy to commit predatory crimes." For more information on this subject, see Charles E. Silberman, *Criminal Violence, Criminal Justice* (New York: Vintage, 1980), 244.
17. Patrick A. Langan, John V. Fundis, Lawrence A. Greenfeld, and Victoria W. Schneider, *Historical Statistics on Prisoners in State and Federal Institutions Yearend 1925–1986*, Bureau of Justice Statistics (Washington, DC: GPO, 1987), 3.
18. Patrick A. Langan, with the assistance of Lawrence Greenfeld, *The Prevalence of Imprisonment*, Department of Justice, Bureau of Justice Statistics (Washington, DC: GPO, 1985), 2.
19. Ibid., 3.
20. Lawrence A. Greenfeld, *Examining Recidivism*, Department of Justice, Bureau of Justice Statistics (Washington, DC: GPO, February 1985), 5.
21. Langan and Greenfeld, 1.
22. Ibid., 3–4.
23. Greenfeld, 3.
24. For a bibliography of community crime prevention programs, see *Topical Bibliography: Community Crime Prevention Programs* (Washington, DC: National Institute of Justice, no date).
25. Dennis Rosenbaum, Arthur L. Lurigio, and Paul J. Lavrakas, *Crime Stoppers: A National Evaluation of Program Operations and Effects* (Washington, DC: GPO, 1987), v.
26. Ibid.
27. James Garofals and Maureen McLeod, *Improving the Use and Effectiveness of Neighborhood Watch Programs*, Department of Justice, National Institute of Justice (Washington, DC: GPO, 1988).
28. If you are interested in learning more about crime prevention, write to the National Crime Prevention Council, Suite 540, 733 15th Street, NW, Washington, DC, 20005.
29. Peter Finn, *Block Watches Help Crime Victims in Philadelphia*, in *Research in Action*, National Institute of Justice (Washington, DC: GPO, 1986).
30. *Carroll v. United States*, 267 U.S. 132, 45 SCt. 280, 69 L.Ed 543 (125), cert. den. 282 U.S. 873, 51 S.Ct 78, 75 L.Ed 771.
31. Herbert Packer, *The Limits of Criminal Sanction* (Stanford, CA: Stanford University Press, 1968), 150.
32. Brian Reaves, *Profile of State and Local Law Enforcement Agencies, 1987*, Bureau of Justice Statistics (Washington, DC: GPO, 1989), 1.
33. Ibid.

34. *Uniform Crime Reports for the United States, 1987,* 227.

35. Ibid., 229.

36. *Justice Agencies in the United States: Summary Report, 1980,* Bureau of Justice Statistics (Washington, DC: GPO, 1980), 5.

37. Reaves, 6.

38. *Justice Agencies in the United States: Summary Report, 1980,* 6.

39. *Uniform Crime Reports for the United States, 1987,* 233.

40. Timothy J. Flanagan and Edmund F. McGarrell, *The Sourcebook of Criminal Justice Statistics—1985,* Bureau of Justice Statistics (Washington, DC: GPO, 1986), 58. There is dramatic variation in the percentage of sworn officers who are black. In Washington, DC, half of all officers are black while 70 percent of the population is black. In Honolulu, blacks make up less than 1 percent of all sworn officers and less than 2 percent of the population. The same variation exists for Hispanic officers. In El Paso, where 63 percent of the population is Hispanic, 57 percent of the officers are Hispanic. However, at least four cities have no Hispanic officers. In only one city (Toledo) is the percentage of blacks on the police force as high as the percentage of blacks in the community. In only two cities is the percentage of Hispanic police officers as high as the percentage of Hispanics in the community.

41. James Q. Wilson, *Varieties of Police Behavior* (Cambridge, MA: Harvard University Press, 1968), 5, and Jeffrey S. Slovak, *Styles of Urban Policing: Organization, Environment, and Police Styles in Selected American Cities* (New York: New York University Press, 1986), 64–100.

42. Wilson, 4–34.

43. Bernard Locke and Alexander B. Smith, "Police Who Go to College," in Abraham S. Blumberg and Arthur Niederhoffer, eds., *The Ambivalent Force* (Hinsdale, IL: Dryden, 1976), 164–168.

44. Wilson, 64–65.

45. John Clark, "Isolation of the Police: A Comparison of the British and American Situations," *Journal of Criminal Law, Criminology, and Police Science,* 56(3) (September 1965), 308.

46. Arthur Niederhoffer, *Behind the Shield: The Police in Urban Society* (Garden City, NY: Doubleday, 1969).

47. Jerome Skolnick, *Justice Without Trial* (New York: Wiley, 1975).

48. Ibid.

49. Barbara Manili, Edward F. Connors III, Darrel W. Stephend, and John R. Stedman, *Police Drug Testing,* National Institute of Justice (Washington, DC: GPO, 1987).

50. See especially Michael Heiman, "The Police Suicide," *Journal of Police Science and Administration* 3 (September 1975), 267–273. For a challenge to these assertions, see Arthur and Elaine Niederhoffer, *The Police Family* (Lexington, MA: Lexington Books, 1978), and Gail Goolkasian, Ronald W. Geddes, and William DeJong, *Coping with Police Stress,* National Institute of Justice (Washington, DC: GPO, 1985), 7–10.

51. Egon Bittner, *The Functions of the Police in Modern Society* (Cambridge, MA: Oelgeschlager, Gunn & Hain, 1980), 37.

52. Skolnick, *Justice Without Trail,* and Paul Chevigny, *Police Power* (New York: Pantheon, 1972).

53. For an extensive discussion of these issues, see James Q. Wilson, *Thinking About Crime* (New York: Vintage, 1983), 61–68.

54. Edwin Meese III, "Preparing the Police Agenda for the 1990's," *Law Enforcement News*, XIII(253) (August 18, 1987), 8, 11.
55. Samuel Walker, *Sense and Nonsense About Crime* (Monterey, CA: Brooks/Cole 1985), 91–98.
56. Jerome H. Skolnick and David Bayley, *The New Blue Line: Police Innovation in Six American Cities* (New York: Free Press, 1986).
57. David H. Bayley, *Forces of Order: Police Behavior in Japan and the United States* (Berkeley: University of California Press, 1976), and L. Craig Parker, Jr., *The Japanese Police System Today: An American Perspective* (New York: Kodansha International, 1984).
58. See especially Skolnick and Bayley, *The New Blue Line*, and Wilson, *Thinking About Crime*, 71–74.
59. Wilson, *Thinking About Crime*, 13.
60. Susan Kline, *Jail Inmates 1986*, Bureau of Justice Statistics (Washington, DC: GPO, April 1988), 1.
61. Ibid.
62. *Report to the Nation on Crime and Justice*, Bureau of Justice Statistics (Washington, DC: GPO, March 1988), 106.
63. Leonard Orlando, *Prisons: Houses of Darkness* (New York: Free Press, 1975), 52–53.
64. Edward L. Ayers, *Vengeance and Justice: Crime and Punishment in the 19th-Century American South* (New York: Oxford University Press, 1984), 37–40.
65. Clemens Bartollas, *Correctional Treatment: Theory and Practice* (Englewood Cliffs, NJ: Prentice-Hall, 1985), 5–6.
66. Robert Martinson, "What Works? — Questions and Answers About Prison Reform," *The Public Interest* (Spring 1974), 22–54.
67. Lawrence Greenfeld, *Prisoners in 1987*, Bureau of Justice Statistics (Washington D.C.: GPO, April, 1988), 1–2.
68. Ibid., 2.
69. Ibid., 4.
70. *1987 Juvenile and Adult Directory of Departments, Institutions, Agencies, and Patrolling Authorities* (College Park, MD: American Correctional Association, 1987).
71. Theodore M. Hammett, *Aids in Correctional Facilities*, Bureau of Justice Statistics (Washington, DC: GPO, May 1988), xvii.
72. James G. Fox, *Organizational and Racial Conflict in Maximum-Security Prisons* (Lexington, MA: Lexington Books, 1982), 19–33.
73. Thomas Hester, *Probation and Parole 1986* (Washington, DC: GPO, December 1987), 1.
74. Joan Petersilia, *Probation and Felony Offenders*, National Institute of Justice (Washington, DC: GPO, March 1985), 1, and Walker, 175.
75. Walker, 176.
76. Ibid.
77. George E. Sexton, Franklin C. Farrow, and Barbara J. Auerbach, *The Private Sector and Prison Industries*, National Institute of Justice (Washington, DC: GPO, 1985), 6.
78. Barbara A. Auerbach, George E. Sexton, Franklin C. Farrow, and Robert H. Lawson, *Work in American Prison: The Private Sector Gets Involved*, National Institute of Justice (Washington, DC: GPO, 1988).
79. *Report to the Nation on Crime and Justice*, 119.

80. Charles H. Logan and Bill W. McGriff, *Comparing Costs of Public and Private Prisons: A Case Study*, National Institute of Justice (Washington, DC: GPO, 1989), 8.

81. Katherine M. Jamieson and Timothy J. Flanagan, eds., *Sourcebook of Criminal Justice Statistics, 1986*, Bureau of Justice Statistics (Washington, DC: GPO, 1988), 4.

82. Reaves, 2.

83. Craig Uchida and Robert Goldberg, *Police Employment and Expenditure Trends*, 2. Bureau of Justice Statistics (Washington, DC: GPO, 1986).

84. Ibid., 1.

85. Ibid.

86. Sue Lindgren, *Justice Expenditure and Employment, 1985*, Bureau of Justice Statistics (Washington, DC: GPO, March 1987), 3.

87. Ibid., 4.

88. Ibid., 5.

The Search for Justice: Poverty and Welfare

POVERTY

Wealth and poverty are relative terms. What is thought of as poverty in Mississippi, the poorest state in the United States, may be considered a more than adequate life-style in Bhopal, India. However, while most poor people in the United States live better lives than do the poor in India and Mexico, they do suffer in comparison to middle-income and upper-income families. Moreover, their suffering is not merely a matter of psychological distress but a very real deprivation of adequate health care, housing, and nutrition as well as an increased likelihood of being a crime victim. The subject of this chapter is America's poor and attempts by state and local governments to improve their lives.

(Courtesy of Kim Bradley, San Marcos Record.)

Social scientists raise a number of questions about the poor: What causes poverty? What can be done about it? Are the poor equally distributed throughout the country? Is aid to the poor equal in different parts of the country? What is the impact of poverty programs on the poor? Does the impact of these programs justify their cost? These are among the questions to be answered in this chapter.

Although few social scientists believe that poverty can be eliminated, many feel that its more unfortunate effects can be ameliorated. Many people, including some social scientists, believe that poverty can be reduced through government programs. Others think that federal, state, and local governments have no obligation to provide aid to the poor. This chapter provides an analysis of the nature and causes of poverty and an examination of some of the programs sponsored by state and local governments to deal with poverty.

What Is Poverty?

The relativity of wealth and impoverishment has given rise to two ways of defining poverty. The first way, an **absolute definition of poverty**, defines poverty in terms of an objective standard, usually a governmental measure of subsistence. We will refer to an absolute measure of poverty — the poverty line — throughout this chapter. A second method of defining poverty is to use a **relative definition of poverty**. This method involves making a subjective judgment about the meaning of poverty in comparison to the standards of the society. John Kenneth Galbraith has suggested that even if individuals have enough income to survive, they may be considered poverty-stricken if their resulting life-style is considered by the community to be unacceptable or degrading.[1]

The way poverty is defined is a political issue. The Social Security Administration set the first **poverty line** in 1964 by estimating the lowest cost of feeding a family of four. Based on the Department of Agriculture's analysis of the consumption needs of families and a 1955 study showing that families of three or more spent roughly one-third of their income on food, the poverty line for families was set at approximately three times the cost of feeding a family. Smaller families and persons living alone have slightly higher costs, a fact that is taken into consideration when the poverty line is calculated. Although modest adjustments have been made to take inflation into account, the poverty line remains similar to its original formulation (Table 14.1). Thus we can think of the poverty line as three times the cost of feeding the members of a household and thereby create an absolute definition of poverty.

This official definition of poverty is criticized by many people. Some argue that the poverty line is too low and therefore overlooks many individuals who live in inadequate circumstances, fails to take into account the increasing disparity between the poor and the nonpoor, and underestimates the amount of poverty in the United States.[2] Others argue that the poverty line is too high and therefore includes many people who do not need or deserve aid because it ignores government transfer payments (noncash welfare payments such as food stamps and Medicaid), encourages underreporting of income, and overestimates the amount of poverty in the United States.[3] Many scholars have concluded that on balance the official poverty line neither exaggerates nor minimizes the amount of poverty in this country.[4]

An illustration of the political debate concerning the method of calculating the poverty line is given in Figure 14.1. The measure used prior to December 1988 (and used in this chapter unless otherwise noted) did not include the value of government aid such as food stamps, Medicaid, and Aid to Families with Dependent Children (AFDC).[5] When those programs are

Table 14.1 THE POVERTY LINE FOR A FAMILY OF FOUR AND MEDIAN FAMILY INCOME: SELECTED YEARS*

Year	Average income for a family of four ($)	Median family income ($)
1960	3,022	19,100
1965	3,223	21,968
1970	3,968	24,662
1975	5,500	24,039
1980	8,414	23,565
1981	9,827	22,995
1982	9,862	22,913
1983	10,178	23,131
1984	10,609	23,661
1985	10,989	24,072
1986	11,203	24,897

*For years prior to 1981, the average threshold for a nonfarm family of four is shown.

Source: U.S. Bureau of the Census, *Statistical Abstract, 1988,* (Washington, DC: GPO, 1989), 422, and Mark S. Littman and Eleanor F. Baugher, *Poverty in the United States*, U.S. Department of Commerce, Bureau of the Census (Washington, DC: GPO, 1988), 154.

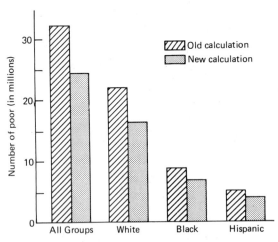

Figure 14.1 Changes in the method of calculating the poverty line have changed the number of officially poor people in the United States. (*Source:* Joanna Neuman, "Way poverty's assessed changed," *USA Today* [December 29, 1988], 4A.)

included, the number of persons considered poor drops from more than 32 million to less than 25 million. Advocates for a welfare system argue that the inclusion of such benefits in the measure of poverty masks the suffering of the poor; those opposed to the current welfare system suggest that the benefits constitute income and should be calculated since they contribute to the standard of living of poor people.

In 1986, the official poverty line for an average family of four was $11,203.[6] However, as we shall see, many persons and families whose incomes were below this line did not receive welfare payments, and many persons whose incomes were above the line did receive government payments. The reason for this paradox is that only 7 of the 59 major welfare programs use the poverty line as a "means test," that is, a criterion of eligibility; another 20 use some variation of the poverty line as a criterion.[7]

How Many Are Poor?

The United States began to calculate a poverty rate in 1959, when almost 40 million people (22 percent of the population) were poor. In 1983, there were over 35 million poor people, a 20-year high for the United States.[8] The **poverty rate**—the percentage of the population below the poverty line— was 15 percent, the highest rate since 1965. By 1987 the number of poor persons had dropped to less than 33 million, but even at that, *one of every seven* persons in the United States is poor.[9] (Figure 14.2 shows the changes in the poverty rate since 1959.)

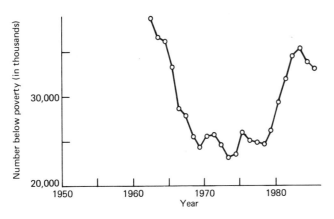

Figure 14.2 The poverty rate has changed over the last three decades. (*Source:* William O'Hare, *Poverty in America: Trends and New Patterns.* [Washington, DC: Population Reference Bureau, 1987], 7, 8, 43–44.)

The Causes of Poverty Among the Deserving Poor: Unemployment, Family Disorganization, Low Wages, and the Culture of Poverty

Well, it may come as no suprise that in a country as wealthy as the United States there are poor people. Many Americans, however, are not aware of the fact that there are more poor white people than poor black and Hispanic people combined (Figure 14.3). In Box 14-1 we take a closer look at who the poor are. This is necessary to help us decide how best to reduce poverty, and how to determine who among the poor "deserve" help and what the nature of that help will be. Poverty is sometimes seen as the just deserts of a life of sloth, but while the causes of poverty may occasionally include laziness, they are not exhausted by it. Being poor or becoming poor may be the result of many factors, including unemployment, family disorganization, and chronically low wages. In these cases, where poverty results from social and economic factors rather than individual failure, we may speak of a class of persons who deserve assistance from the government.

• *Unemployment* is the most common cause of poverty. Half of those who enter poverty do so because someone in their family has lost a job or has had his or her wages cut.[11] When the government fights inflation by encouraging unemployment, as the Reagan administration did, poverty is sure to follow. The recession of the early 1980s put almost 11 percent of the population out of work, producing the highest unemployment rate since the Great Depression.

Corporations and businesses do not always consider the welfare of their employees in making business decisions or make provisions for retraining or relocating the employees. Entire industries, such as the auto and steel industries in the 1970s, may reduce their work forces, causing widespread unemployment in many states. A local industry may relocate to another state or even a foreign country where wages are lower. A small business may become insolvent and reduce its work force or even close its doors. An individual may become ill and be unable to work. Unemployment can happen to anyone, and during the 1980s between 7 million and 11 million people were out of work.

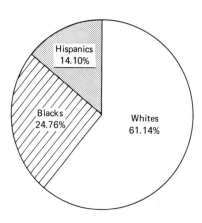

Figure 14.3 The majority of poor people in the United States are white. (*Source:* Mark S. Litman and Eleanor F. Baugher, *Poverty in the United States.* U.S. Department of Commerce, Bureau of the Census [Washington, DC: GPO, 1988], 5–12.)

Box 14-1 **Who Are the Poor?**

It is possible to think of the poor in dichotomous categories: the deserving and the undeserving poor, the working and the nonworking poor, the occasionally poor and the chronically poor, the elderly and the young, men and women, blacks and whites. These categories may convey the shape of poverty, but they cannot convey its consequences for the poor.

The majority of poor people in the United States are white and female and live outside of central cities. In 1986,

- More than 22 million whites were poor
- One of every eight white persons was poor
- 9 million black people were poor
- One of every three black persons was poor
- Half of all female-headed black households were poor
- 5 million Hispanics were poor (one of every four)[10]
- One-third of all families whose head of household was under age 25 had incomes below the poverty line

In 1987,

- More than 18 million females were poor
- 14 million males were poor
- 10 million people who worked were poor
- 21 percent of those under age 18 were poor
- 12 percent of those over 65 were poor

Regionally,

- 38 percent of the poor live in the South
- 19 percent live in the Northeast
- 36 percent live in central cities
- 38 percent live in rural areas
- 25 percent live in suburbs

Source: *The Forgotten Half: Pathways to Success for American Youth and Young Families* (Washington, DC: William T. Grant Foundation Commission on Work, Family, and Citizenship, 1988), 21, and William O'Hare, *Poverty in America: Trends and New Patterns*, (Washington, DC: Population Reference Bureau, 1989), 15, 43.

Family disorganization also produces poverty. Women and children are the most common victims of family disorganization and the most common victims of poverty. Women are likely to enter poverty when they become the head of a household; 38 percent of such households have incomes below the poverty line. Whether the new status is the result of divorce, widowhood, or an out-of-wedlock baby, it is likely to produce poverty.

The fact that more than half of all poor persons are female is known to those who study poverty. This overrepresentation of females in the poverty figures has been called the **ferminization of poverty**, but female-headed households have been poor in the United States since poverty figures began to be kept in 1959, when almost half of all female-headed households had income below the poverty level. In 1986, 12 percent of all families were below the poverty line, but 38 percent of all female-headed households and 50 percent of all black female-headed households were below the poverty line.[12]

Being born into a poor family is a third path into poverty. Twenty percent of all children in the United States live in poverty. Some social scientists believe that there is a **culture of poverty**, meaning that the poor are a distinct group with their own rules, ideas, and beliefs. The culture of poverty implies that the poor learn to be poor or fail to learn how to escape poverty and indeed transmit poverty as a way of life to their children. These theorists believe that poor children are likely to become poor adults who have their own poor children, thus continuing the culture and cycle of poverty.

The **underclass** is a term used to describe a particular group caught in the culture of poverty.[13] Coined by Gunnar Myrdal and popularized by Ken Auletta, the term describes "a third world rural and urban 'underclass' cut off from society, its members lacking 'the education and the skills and other personality traits they need in order to become effectively in demand in the modern economy.'"[14] Members of the underclass have been unable to take advantage of the increases in opportunity which resulted from affirmative action and are thus trapped in poverty. They have little hope of becoming conventional middle-class Americans.

Individuals enter poverty for reasons besides unemployment, family disorganization, and membership in the culture of poverty. Perhaps most shocking is the fact that some people enter poverty, or fail to leave it, even though they work full time.

Low wages are another cause of poverty. The **working poor** are rarely mentioned in the media, perhaps because the popular image of the poor is that they do not work or, worse, will not work. That image is in many cases false. Among the 20 million poor adults in 1986, fully half reported that they had worked during the year and more than a third reported that they had worked 50 weeks or more during the year.[15] Among those who worked fewer than 50 weeks (including those who did not work), a third reported they were keeping house and one in five reported they were looking for work.[16]

Even poverty-stricken women who have small children work. In 1986, more than 15 percent of all white women and almost 40 percent of all black women with children under age 6 were below the poverty line.[17] Among poor women with children under 6, 8 percent of white women and more than 17 percent of black women worked full time.[18]

If it seems difficult to believe that someone who worked full time could nevertheless be poor, imagine the situation of a mother of two children who works at a fast-food restaurant for 40 hours a week in 1986. Minimum wage is $3.35 an hour. If she is fortunate enough never to be sick, never to lose working time because of the illness of her children, and never to suffer the effects of violent crime, and if she can work 40 hours a week, 52 weeks a year, she can earn $134 a week, or $6968 a year. That places her and her children below the poverty line for a family of three (one adult and two children), which in 1986 was $8829.[19] Regardless of where she stands in relation to the poverty line, imagine what a mother faces when she must house, feed, and clothe two children on less than $9000 a year. Trying to save for college or even for Christmas with that income requires tenacity.

Many individuals in this society live on the brink of poverty. As long as they can work, they may be able to stay above the poverty line, but they may enter poverty if they become ill, are injured in an accident, acquire a new family member, or are victims of violent crime. Others have no choice about poverty: They are children who have had the bad luck to be born into poverty. For the deserving poor, entering poverty is a result of bad luck.

Failure to Work: The Undeserving Poor?

Do those who fail to work deserve poverty? Are there poor persons who somehow deserve their lot in life because of their lack of effort? Why don't the nonworking poor work? These are common questions about the poor.

Some nonworking poor individuals are elderly. In 1986, there were over 38 million Americans 60 years of age or older, among whom over 4.5 million had incomes below the poverty line. Many people 60 and over do work, and more than 420,000 of the poor over 60 did work, but more than 4 million did not. Of those who did not work, one-quarter reported that they were ill or disabled, half reported that they were retired, and the remainder said they were unable to find work or were keeping house.[20]

Many of the nonworking poor are not permitted to work. Children make up a significant proportion of the officially poor. One-fifth of all persons under age 18 live in poverty![21] Although few people suggest that nonworking children and the nonworking elderly should be denied welfare benefits, there is much less agreement about what can be expected of women with children. However, with the cost of child care increasing, it is not clear what women with several small children gain by working at low-paying jobs.

Those who are physically able to work must justify their failure to work. Charles Murray has suggested that many of the poor do not work because work and independence are less attractive than are welfare and dependency. In addition, he suggests that the behaviors that help the poor cross the poverty line have lost their former status.[22] In other words, he suggests that being dependent and on welfare does not have the social stigma it once had and that some poor people are not as willing to attempt an escape from welfare as they once were. This is particularly true, Murray argues, for unmarried fathers and fathers to be who avoid marriage and contribute to the out-of-wedlock birthrate, thus increasing the number of poor women and children. Welfare makes poverty sufficiently tolerable that the poor do not do all they can to avoid it.

William Julius Wilson suggests in rebuttal to Murray that many of the poor do not work primarily because they cannot find jobs for which they have suitable skills.[23] Inadequately educated and with few job skills, the poor have traditionally worked as semiskilled or unskilled laborers in central-city industrial centers.[24] In the last 20 years, however, advances in transportation and communication have permitted manufacturers, retailers, and construction industries to move from the central city, taking with them the blue-collar jobs commonly filled by the poor. To take the place of these employers have come information-processing and financial organizations, bringing with them opportunities for professional, or white-collar, employees. Thus the **urban industrial transition** and the resulting decline in employment opportunities have made finding work increasingly difficult for the urban poor.

A similar process has been at work in rural areas. The industries common to rural areas — agriculture, timber, mining, oil and gas production — have declined in the last decade, and unemployment rates have risen.[25] In addition, incomes have fallen in rural areas, and fringe benefits, especially pension plans, are less common than they are in urban areas. Poverty is increasing in rural areas, and the gap between urban and rural poverty rates is decreasing.

Thus we are left to ask whether some of the poor fail to work because they don't want to work or because they cannot find work. There is probably some truth to both positions. For some people, welfare no longer carries the stigma it once did, and they remain unmotivated to work. Many would work, however, if jobs were available or if they had the skills for the jobs that are available. A local government attempting to deal with the problem of poverty must consider both arguments if it is to develop comprehensive and effective policies for job creation, job training, and new education initiatives to deal with those who, for whatever reason, choose not to work.

Consequences of Poverty

Being poor has a number of detrimental consequences for the poor and the country in which they live. It means more than simply having a low income and results in more than simply a low standard of living. Being poor means being less likely to become educated, having a home, enjoy good health, or be safe from crime. These are the facts of life for poor people.

Education is one of the first areas in which the poor are at a disadvantage. To be successful in school, to learn to read, write, and analyze, children must have sufficient nourishment, rest, health, and parental involvement to be able to demonstrate their native ability. Poverty, hunger, and distracted parents reduce the possibility of success in school.

Poverty is related to education in another way. The "hidden curriculum" in American schools emphasizes learning the attitudes and values necessary for success in the United States. Students learn the value of disciplined labor, punctuality, and competition and winning. Just as important to educational success is the belief that what is said in the classroom has value and the faith that what one does in the classroom will have a payoff. However, children who are discouraged by the consequences of poverty may see little relevance of these values to their own lives; when they are not learned, these values make escape from poverty more difficult.

If a major goal of the American educational system is to prepare our youth for positions in the work force, the urban poor face another disadvantage. Inner-city schools, with their underfinanced classrooms and underpaid teachers, help "guarantee the future economic subordinacy of minority students."[26] Rural poverty is no less deprivating, and poor rural youth are no better prepared for skilled jobs in the labor force than are their brothers and sisters in the city. If anything, levels of education are lower in rural areas.[27] In both cases the school systems fail to produce students who have the language and self-presentation skills necessary to secure entry-level jobs in the skilled work force. For students who have little faith in the American dream, the public school system offers only another chance to fail.

Homelessness is often a consequence of poverty. Although our stereotype of the homeless is of hoboes and bag ladies, an increasing number of homeless people consist of families with children who once owned or were making payments on a home or rented a decent apartment until eviction. Having lost their homes, they live in their cars, on the street, or in shelters. Some cities rent hotel rooms for the homeless (Box 14-2).

Why do individuals and families lose their homes and become unable to find new ones? They become homeless for the same reasons they become poor: unemployment, low wages, family disorganization, and simple bad luck. The lack of low-cost housing in the United States is a major cause of the continuation of homelessness. Many families cannot make a down payment on a home because their wages are too low. They cannot rent suitable housing because of the size of their families, the cost of rental property, or both. The late Michael Harrington suggested that the term "homeless" should be changed to "uprooted" because physical shelter is only one aspect of the phenomenon. The most damaging aspect of being uprooted is the precarious nature of one's day-to-day living. As he puts it:

> A 'home' is not simply a roof over one's head. It is the center of a web of human relationships. When the web is shredded as a result of social and economic trends, a person is homeless even if he or she has an anonymous room somewhere.[28]

It is clear that homelessness is a threat to the well-being of a wide variety of people, an increasing number of them single women or women and their children.[29] Perhaps the following testimony from a hearing of the House Subcommittee on Housing and Urban Development in 1984 best demonstrates the personal nature of the problem:

Box 14-2 **Homeless, with Children, in America**

The following is an excerpt from *Rachel and Her Children: Homeless Families in America* by Jonathan Kozol. The author explored what happens to families with children when they have no home. Sometimes they live on the streets. Some cities find temporary housing for them in hotels and motels. This is a description of the consequences of such housing for a mother and her children who live in a room for which the city pays $63 a night to the Hotel Carter. The rooms are dirty, with broken windows and holes in the floor. Tourists rent newly renovated rooms on the floors above the first three floors, where the poor live. The rooms on the upper floors are painted and clean, with televisions and air conditioners. They rent for $35 a night.

As you will see, poor children who live in the Hotel Carter are not permitted to catch their school buses in front of the hotel because the management does not want the tourists to see them.

A mother of three children in the Hotel Carter tells me this: She was a teacher's aide, had worked for three years with retarded children, and was living doubled up with relatives when the death of one and the marriage of another forced her to the streets. She's been living in the Carter for two years.

"My rent allowance is $270. Places that I see start at $350. Even if you could pay it, landlords do not want you if you are homeless. 'Where do you live?' I say the Carter. That's the end of it. It's hard to do it. You psyche yourself. They want to check you out. You feel ashamed."

"It's the same with public school. The teacher asks, 'Where do you live?' You say the Carter. Right away they put you in a slot. Jennifer is in the fourth grade. . . . Do they put homeless kids in categories? 'Course they do!'" . . .

Food is short: "By the eighteenth of the month I'm running out. I have to borrow. They have got to eat. When we're low we live on macaroni and french fries. I can make a lot from two potatoes. When you're running low you learn to stretch. I don't have the money to buy meat. Even if I did, there's no refrigerator. It won't keep."

"Christmas last year, we stayed in our room. Christmas this year, we'll be here again. It's a lonely time for everybody. You know what scares [the other poor women in the hotel] the most? It's when the rent is due. You go to your welfare office. You're afraid there's a mistake. It happens for no reason. . . ."

"They told my kids: 'You have to use the back. You're not allowed to use the front.' They herd them down that corridor to the rear door. It doesn't hurt so much that they would want *me* to be hidden. It does hurt that they would want my children to be hid."

Do children know they are viewed as undesirables? Using the same exit that is used by the hotel to throw away the trash is pretty vivid. They leave with the trash. Perhaps they carry some of its stench with them into school. "We aren't going to get away with this," said Daniel Moynihan. . . . The twenty-first century, he said, "is going to punish us. . . ."

Source: Jonathan Kozol, *Rachel and Her Children: Homeless Families in America*, (New York: Crown, 1988), 156–158.

Ms. Vanover: I have been on the streets for five months now. I started in a very small town in New Hampshire where I held a variety of low paying jobs, barely enough to live on. . . . At the time, I was three months pregnant, very hungry for many days. I thank God there was a soup kitchen in the town. After my baby was born, I moved back home for several months. That didn't work out because my mother couldn't afford to feed both me and my baby. I thought maybe going to the big city might give me a better chance to find work. [She and her husband left, leaving the child with her mother in New Hampshire.] My husband is a Vietnam veteran and is having an impossible time trying to get benefits or a job. We have traveled the East coast, through New York, New Jersey, Philadelphia, and Washington, looking for work, but still nothing. It is impossible to find a job without a steady place to sleep. It is a vicious cycle, no mailing address, no telephone, no clean clothes, no showers, no bus fare, no nothing. In a few other cities there were shelters. Most often there were none. I have stayed in places that would frighten most people. I was frightened.[30]

Poor health and shorter lives are characteristics of those who are poor, perhaps because poverty reduces one's access to medical care. A study of more than 600 women who had cancer surgery at a hospital in Harlem shows a five-year survival rate of only 30 percent. The national average for black women is 60 percent, and for white women it is 70 percent. Dr. Harold Freeman, who began offering free breast exams at Harlem Hospital a decade ago, reports that the women patients there see physicians much later than do their wealthier female counterparts. "Getting into the medical system for diagnosis and later treatment may to the poor person be more painful than a painless lump."[31] In general, blacks have higher rates of death from cancer, with black males having the highest rates of all Americans.[32] Readily available health care is especially critical for mothers and children. Perhaps nowhere are disparities between middle-income Americans and the poor more apparent than in the infant mortality rates for black versus white babies. Black babies are twice as likely to die in the first year, a phenomenon related to the fact that a greater percentage of young mothers with poor health habits and poor prenatal care go on to have low-birth-weight babies.[33]

Poverty also reduces the likelihood of getting an adequate diet. Good nutrition is necessary for a healthy immune system.[34] A diet high in fat and low in protein is associated with poverty, producing obesity and illness. Black Americans have a life expectancy 5½ years shorter than that of white Americans, primarily because a larger percentage of the black population lives in poverty.[35] Perhaps more ominous, the gap in life expectancy between blacks and whites has again begun to increase.[36] Poor Southern whites also have higher than average death rates as a result of poverty.[37] An examination of life expectancy tables reveals that the average American Indian, a group that is the "poorest of the poor," dies 20 years earlier than does the average non-Indian.[38]

Poverty causes stress, and stress can produce disease. Stress in itself is not pathogenic, but chronic stress which is not channeled into physical exercise or ameliorated by social involvement has a debilitating effect on health.[39] Stress which is handled through the use of alcohol, tobacco, and drugs produces a significantly increased risk of chronic and disabling diseases, such as cancer and heart disease; coupled with a high-fat diet, this approach to dealing with stress is deadly.

Criminal victimization is another consequence of poverty. The poor are the most likely victims of violent crime and are commonly victims of property crime as well. The death rate from homicide for white males in 1985 was 8 per 100,000, but for black males it was almost 50, having declined from 67 in 1980.[40] One in every 31 black males dies as a result of homicide, while 1 in 179 white males will be a homicide victim.[41]

Household burglary rates are highest for those with a household income below $7500.[42] Violent crime rates are highest for the poor as well. Robbery, rape, and assault victims are most common in the income levels below $7500.[43] Violent victimization rates are higher for the unemployed, the divorced, and the never married, all characteristics more common among the poor.

Poverty is so damaging for the poor and the country in which they live that federal, state, and local governments have implemented relief or welfare programs in one form or another for the last half of this century. Delineating the costs and contributions of these programs is the goal of the next section.

Poverty and the Fifty States

The poor are not distributed equally among the states. The South has the greatest proportion of poor persons in the United States. Mississippi has the greatest percentage of people below the poverty line of any state, and Wyoming has the smallest percentage. The number of poor (not the percentage of poor people in the population) varies between states: New York, California, and Texas have the highest number of poor persons; Alaska, Wyoming, and Vermont have the fewest poor persons. (Figure 14.4 shows the distribution of the poor in states which have been selected to show the states with the highest and lowest ratios of poor to nonpoor people and a set of representative states between the extremes.)

THE SYSTEM OF WELFARE

Probably no governmental expense elicits more disagreement than the system of welfare. The disagreement is fueled by misunderstanding and misinformation but has its roots in the fundamental debate over the responsibility of government for the well-being of citizens. This section focuses on the dimensions of the welfare system and its cost to state and local governments.

Should We Have a Welfare System?

In recent years this has been a frequently asked question. It has been raised in part because middle-income Americans have begun to question the desirability of paying taxes to support a welfare system. However, we believe there are very good reasons for having some form of a welfare system.

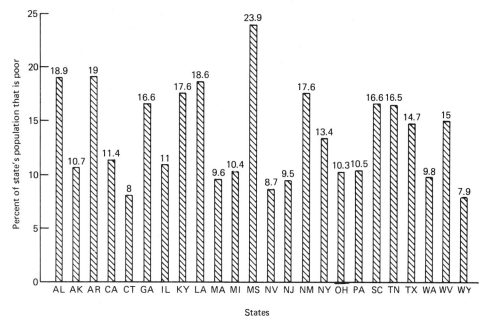

Figure 14.4 In 1979, the percentage of the population considered poor ranged from a high of 23.9 in Mississippi to a low of 7.9 in Wyoming. States selected to show range of poverty between states. The states with the highest (Mississippi) and lowest (Wyoming) percent of populations below poverty are shown, as well as a representative sample of states between the two extremes. (*Source: Statistical Abstract, 1989.*)

Maintaining the legitimacy of the political and economic systems is the first justification for a welfare system. If a government is to maintain the cooperation necessary for achieving national goals, it must be seen as being responsive to the needs of its citizens. In every society there are some individuals — the young, the disabled, the elderly — who cannot take care of themselves. Moreover, in our laissez-faire capitalist economy, low wages and the cost of private health insurance produce a tenuous way of life for many. For citizens who through no fault of their own cannot afford the necessities of life, the government must provide some form of aid to maintain the legitimacy of the polity and the economy.

Human resource investment is another justification for the system of welfare. Although there is a persistently poor underclass in the United States, it makes up less than 5 percent of the poor at any time.[44] Most poor persons fall into poverty and are able, with temporary relief, job training, or both, to once again become contributing, tax-paying members of their communities.

Humanitarian reasons are a third justification for a welfare system. Demonstrating compassion for the less fortunate is a hallmark of civilized societies. Whereas abandoning the disabled and the elderly may be acceptable in a subsistence-level society which cannot support unproductive individuals, a country as wealthy as the United States surely has an obligation to those who become poor despite their best efforts to do otherwise.

The arguments against welfare have to do primarily with its cost. Redistributive policies — policies which transfer earnings "from higher to lower income segments of the population" — have "negative consequences for local economies when the low income recipients are not needed by the local economy."[45] Although unskilled workers are at times needed to work in local industries, this is less often the case when manufacturing enterprises, as noted by William J. Wilson, change their character and location. Nevertheless, the arguments cited in support of aid to the poor have such a strong moral basis that governments are willing to honor them.

What Is Welfare?

In this chapter, **welfare** refers to means-tested social programs. **Means-tested** government programs are those based on some measure of income. The four major means-tested programs — **Aid to Families with Dependent Children (AFDC), Supplemental Security Income (SSI), Medicaid,** and **food stamps** — use a multiple of the poverty line to decide who is eligible for aid. For instance, the food stamps program provides stamps for families if their incomes are less than 130 percent of the poverty line. These are the typical welfare programs, designed to provide the poor with adequate food and shelter.

Most of the money spent by governments on social programs is not spent in means-tested welfare programs but in social insurance programs such as **Social Security, Medicare**, veterans' benefits, worker's compensation, student loans, and unemployment insurance. These social insurance programs, sometimes called **entitlements**, provide support for a wide range of people and are primarily directed toward middle- and upper-income Americans. These programs are designed to provide a safety net for middle- and upper-income American families should the breadwinner(s) become disabled or unemployed or die prematurely. These are also the programs intended to help America's elderly secure a dignified retirement. Such programs are not welfare programs.

The yearly government outlay for Social Security is larger than that for all means-tested programs put together.[46] Social Security benefits are not means-tested; they are provided regardless of income level. Only 20 percent of the funds distributed in the entitlement programs funded through Social Security go to the poor. Despite the fact that Social Security is not a welfare program, it nevertheless lifts one-quarter of the population — the families of the disabled, the elderly, and survivors — above the poverty line.[47]

Federal, State, and Local Governments: Partnership or Rivalry?

Until 1932, state and local governments assumed responsibility for public assistance. However, the Great Depression proved to be too much for most state and local budgets, and the federal government began to help state and local governments provide relief to families and individuals. At the end of the Depression, only the disabled, the blind, and orphans remained on the welfare rolls.

Assistance to state governments continued without meaningful changes during the 1950s, but the turbulence of the 1960s led to greatly expanded welfare rolls. Lyndon Johnson's Great Society programs declared a war on poverty, and Johnson attempted to fund it and the Vietnam war at the same time. The "war at home" lost support as the war abroad increased in intensity and cost. At the same time, the Johnson administration gave federal aid directly to local welfare programs in the South, bypassing the state governments which had blocked the poor from receiving aid. Not surprisingly, state officials became irate at losing the right to administer programs in their states, and the defection of Southerners from the Democratic party, which had begun as a result of civil rights initiatives in the Kennedy and Johnson administrations, continued in earnest.[48] Subsequent administrations have attempted to dismantle the Great Society programs, not without some success.

Recently, the Reagan administration attempted to reduce federal funding of welfare programs, hoping to force state and local governments to assume more of the cost. The most dramatic revamping of the welfare system since the Great Depression was legislated in 1988. The Family Support Act established the Jobs Opportunity and Basic Skills (JOBS) program, which requires each state to develop programs for poor families with children. The goal of JOBS is to decrease welfare dependency by providing remedial education and job training aimed at groups prone to welfare dependency, primarily members of the underclass. Each state has been required to submit a program to the Department of Health and Human Services by 1990. It is too soon to know whether this approach will work, although since it provides only a few hundred dollars per recipient per year, there is some doubt that it will accomplish its intent.[49]

In 1987, the federal government provided about 75 percent of the cost of welfare programs,[50] continuing the war on poverty as a federally supported struggle. Yet, as will be seen, the federal government cannot ensure that individuals in different states will receive similar levels of assistance. In fact, federalism makes that impossible; the poor experience deprivation in some states while having a much better standard of living in others.

Nor is the federal government inclined to do more than is necessary in funding state welfare programs. As noted, the Reagan administration attempted to make state and local governments assume more of the costs of welfare. Since this attempt came in the midst of taxpayer revolts in a number of states, it was not completely successful. At the same time, however, the federal government bestowed greater flexibility on the states in making major grant allocations. Nevertheless, the appropriate source and amount of funding for welfare programs continue to be a source of friction between governments as well as concern for those whose lives are constrained by the vagaries of intergovernmental politics.

State governments want the federal government to increase the amount of aid to the states while giving the states more leeway in administering the programs. There has been some support in Congress for this idea. Senator Daniel J. Evans, saying that "the current inequalities in AFDC are a national disgrace," argued for establishing minimum benefit and eligibility standards for AFDC and Medicaid while assuming full responsibility for funding those programs.[51] There is, as one might expect, much opposition to this "nationalization of welfare" suggestion; even many state and local officials argue, as did federal officials in the Reagan administration, that variations in the cost of living between states call for more flexibility at the local level.

The debate between governments concerning who should set welfare levels and who should administer programs is likely to continue. The next section examines those programs and discusses their costs for governments.

Federal, State, and Local Welfare Programs for the Poor

State and local governments receive funds from the federal government through three kinds of grants: categorical grants-in-aid, general revenue-sharing grants, and special revenue-sharing block grants. **Categorical grants-in-aid** are targeted at special categories of need. Such grants begin when the federal government enacts legislation offering funds to states which meet federal specifications. The states then pass legislation bringing them into compliance with the federal legislation. **Special revenue-sharing block grants** are federal funds offered to states to replace, at one time, numerous categorical grants-in-aid directed at a particular problem, such as job creation or community development. These block grants were used by the Reagan administration to reduce funding for welfare by consolidating previous categorical grants into block grants at a lower funding level.[52]

Currently, there are four major government welfare programs: AFDC, SSI, Medicaid, and food stamps. The costs of all four programs are shared by the federal and state governments, though the states pay less than half the costs of the programs. A brief summary of these programs follows.

Aid to Families with Dependent Children   This is a federal and state categorical grant-in aid program, with state governments paying approximately 45 percent of the cost. AFDC was established by the Social Security Act of 1935, and each state administers its own program. All families with children under 18 with one parent absent are eligible for AFDC cash benefits. In over half the states, two-parent families are also eligible when the father is out of work. The cost of AFDC to state and local governments is around $7 billion per year. Approximately 11 million persons receive benefits each year; only about one-fifth of the 20 million poor adults receive AFDC benefits.[53]

Supplemental Security Income   This program was established in 1972 to provide additional monthly cash payments to impoverished elderly, blind, and disabled persons. The federal government administers the program through Social Security Administration offices. State and local governments pay approximately 20 percent of the cost, which in 1986 was almost $12 billion. More than 11 million individuals — over 4 percent of the population — received SSI benefits.

Medicaid   This program was established in 1965 to help cover the medical costs of persons eligible for AFDC and SSI. Each state creates and administers its own program within broad federal guidelines. The states have a great deal of latitude in determining eligibility and kinds of benefits. Payments, which are made directly to those providing the services, generally hospitals and physicians, are also established by the state. State and local governments paid approximately $20 billion in 1986 to provide medical care to more than 21 million persons.

Food Stamps   This program, begun during the 1960s, distributes coupons redeemable for food to families and individuals with incomes under 130 percent of the poverty line. State welfare agencies administer the program under broad federal guidelines. The federal government provides almost all the funding for food stamps. In 1986, state governments funded 7 percent of the program, costing them about $900 million and providing benefits to approximately 20 million persons a month. State and local governments also provide assistance by administering various job training and creation programs. The Job Corps continues to train a small number of disadvantaged young people. A similar program, the Work Incentive Program, helps ADFC mothers find private-sector work. The Comprehensive Employment and Training Act (CETA) of 1973 was an attempt to provide job training programs and expand public-sector hiring of the poor. It was replaced in 1983 by the Jobs Partnership Training Act, which has the goal of uniting the government and the private sector in local efforts to provide jobs for displaced and disadvantaged workers.

States also receive funds through social services block grants, which can be used for in-home care of children and the elderly. In addition, states receive funds for the remedial or compensatory education of poor children under the Education and Consolidation Act of 1982 (Table 14.2).

How Much Does the Welfare System Cost?

The distinction between means-tested (welfare) programs for the poor and non-means-tested (entitlement) programs for all Americans is especially important in calculating the cost of the welfare system. The attack on the welfare system by President Ronald Reagan, who promised to reduce the federal government's expenditures for social programs, brought this distinction into sharp relief. Those who were eager for the reduction discovered that most of those expenditures went for entitlement programs, not welfare programs. Further, they found that significant cost reductions would have to come from entitlements. This section focuses on the costs of social welfare.

Table 14.2 FEDERAL AND STATE GOVERNMENT EXPENDITURES: 1986

Programs	Money spent in 1986 by governments ($ billions)	
	Federal	State
Social insurance[a]		
Social Security retirement	176.8	0
Social Security disability insurance	19.8	0
Unemployment insurance	15.4	0
Non-means-tested noncash benefits		
Medicare	62.7	0
Means-tested cash insurance[b]		
AFDC	9.5	8.2
SSI	10.3	2.5
Means-tested noncash benefits†		
Medicaid	25.0	19.7
Food stamps	12.5	0.9
Public and subsidized housing	12.5	0
Reduced-price school lunches	2.6	0
Social programs that do not provide direct benefits to individuals		
Employment and job training	1.7	0
Compensatory education aid	3.6	0.75
Social services block grants	2.6	0
Total	355	32.05

[a] For all citizens, through primarily helping middle-income citizens.

[b] For the poor.

Source: William O'Hare, *Poverty in America: Trends and New Patterns* (Washington, DC: Population Reference Bureau, 1989), and Mark S. Hoffman, ed., *The World Almanac and Book of Facts,* 1989, 543.

The cost of *public welfare programs* for state governments was more than $72 billion in 1986. This figure represents almost 20 percent of total general expenditures. The greatest expenditure by state governments is for education, though Massachusetts spent more for welfare than for education. In other states, public welfare is generally the second most costly category, but 13 states spent more for highways than for public welfare in 1986.[54]

Although all states provide for public welfare, there is significant variation in the amount spent. State expenditures for public welfare ranged from $11.5 billion in California down to $101 million in Wyoming. As a percentage of all expenditures, the outlay for welfare ranged from 29 percent in California down to 6.67 percent in Alaska.

Not only general state expenditures but AFDC payments vary by state as well. States are able to set the level of AFDC payments, producing a significant variation in the range of payments for a family of four. In 1987, the benefits for a family of four were highest in Alaska ($571) and California ($551); in the same time period, they were lowest in Alabama ($114) and

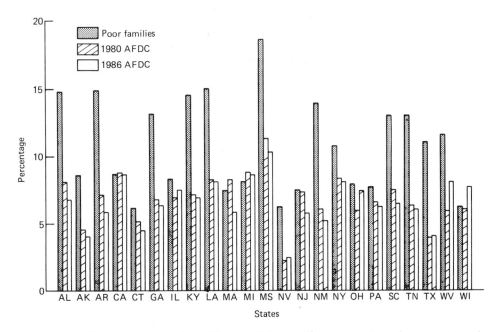

Figure 14.5 The percentage of families receiving welfare is not directly proportional to the percentage of poor persons in each state. (*Source: Statistical Abstracts, 1980, 1988.*)

Mississippi ($116). Figure 14.5 shows the variation in AFDC payments in states selected to show the states with the highest and lowest percentages of families above and below the poverty line and a representative set of states between the extremes.

AFDC payments to the average female-headed household with two children averaged less than $354 per month in 1987.[55] Such payments do not represent the entire cost of the assistance, however. Approximately 80 percent of AFDC families also receive food stamps, and over 90 percent receive Medicaid. About one-quarter of AFDC recipients also live in public housing, yet only approximately one-fifth of all impoverished adults receive AFDC benefits.

Several explanations have been offered for the grim circumstances of the poor: (1) They do not possess the political power of a PAC or interest group, (2) the political machines which once provided services in large cities have all but disappeared, and with them their services to the poor, (3) at-large elections have reduced the political power of the poor, and (4) nonpartisan elections have reduced the participation of the poor, and with a lack of participation comes a lack of political power.

These factors do not, however, explain why the poor in some states fare better than do those in other states. In all likelihood, the answer has to do with the traditional docility of the poor, particularly in Southern states, and the occasional activism of the poor, particularly in Northern and Western states. Pivens and Cloward[56] have demonstrated the relationship between welfare activism and increases in welfare budgets; thus one can expect that the more pliant the poor are, the less likely they are to receive increased benefits. The poor in the South, whose welfare payments traditionally have been lower and less sufficient, constitute a more passive population; hence politicians at the state and local level in the South do not have to respond as meaningfully to their needs as do politicians in the North and West, where the poor have threatened disorder.

Welfare myths fuel the debate about welfare. The myth that the poor won't work has been addressed in this chapter. However, there are other myths: that welfare recipients remain on relief forever, that lives of luxury are lived on welfare, that welfare recipients drive Cadillacs to pick up their food stamps, and that women have as many children as possible in order to get more welfare.

These myths are not supported by data. The majority of AFDC families receive aid for less than three years. As seen earlier, the average AFDC payment is less than $400 a month. On the average, the combined value of AFDC payments and food stamps equals 74 percent of the official poverty line. Only 7 percent of AFDC families own a car, and the average value of their cars is less than $2270. The average AFDC family has total assets of less than $900[57] and has only two children under the age of 18.[58] Surely these facts do not support the welfare myths.

Who Receives Welfare?

Welfare programs target two categories of people: the disabled, blind, or elderly poor and poor families with children. Many persons considered poor by government standards receive no government assistance of any kind; in 1985, only 59 percent of all persons considered poor received government assistance.[59] In 1984, 19 percent of households received means-tested benefits, but only 8 percent of households received some sort of means-tested cash assistance.[60] In 1983, less than 60 percent of officially poor households received benefits from one of the four major means-tested noncash assistance programs.[61]

Welfare recipients are typically young and female. Women make up 56 percent of the welfare population, since welfare rules favor women with children and the elderly. There are more elderly women than elderly men, and so women and children constitute the significant majority of welfare recipients. Although blacks and Hispanics have a much greater likelihood of going on welfare than do whites, the majority of people on welfare are white.[62] In 1986, 16 percent of all whites, some 31 million persons, received means-tested welfare. Fifty percent of all blacks (more than 14 million individuals) and 43 percent of all Hispanics (more than 6 million individuals) received means-tested welfare payments of some kind. One in three children received welfare, as did one in five elderly persons. Nationally, approximately one in five persons received some type of means-tested welfare (Figure 14.6).

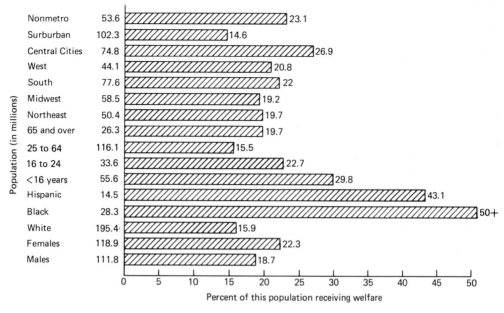

Figure 14.6 Welfare is received by individuals and families in all parts of the country, by all races and ethnicities, and by people of all ages and sexes. (*Source:* William P. O'Hare, *America's Welfare Population: Who Gets What?* [Washington, DC: Population Reference Bureau, 1987], 6.)

Does Welfare Make Any Difference?

Perhaps no debate has been joined more stridently than the debate over the value of welfare. Liberals argue that for many people welfare is a necessity without which life would be inhumane and survival doubtful (Box 14-3). Conservatives argue that welfare encourages sloth and perpetuates poverty. As in many such debates, there may be a kernel of truth in both sets of arguments.

Much of the debate about welfare has to do with its usefulness. Does giving welfare to the poor make their lives better or worse? Charles Murray, the leading critic of welfare, argues that welfare policies have actually made life worse. He believes that welfare discourages the effort and aspirations necessary for the poor to escape welfare; in fact, he suggests that the welfare system is a trap, built with good intentions but having the unintended consequence of encouraging dependency.

A counterargument advanced by John Schwarz is that a number of welfare programs, including CETA and Head Start, have had significant successes.[63] Michael Harrington, whose book *The Other America* revealed the extent of hunger and poverty in the early 1960s, has argued that if the welfare system is a failure, it is because it is underfunded. If the war in

Box 14-3 **A Day in the Life of a Welfare Worker**

In large metropolitan areas, welfare workers, schoolteachers, and police officers see the consequences of poverty daily. What follows is a firsthand account of hunger and poverty as described by an investigative reporter as she toured a Philadelphia slum with a welfare worker. Although it does not happen every day, this is the kind of experience with which a welfare worker frequently must deal.

Anna [Jones] and her nine children lived in a boarded-up section of North Philadelphia near Fifteenth Street and Susquehanna Avenue. Paint fell from the walls of tenement buildings, broken windows went unreplaced, and even the shattered glass seemed never to be picked up. . . . These were the streets the Jones kids played in and walked through when they went to school. But when I found them, the children had been going to school less and less. Inside the school's administration office there was a steadily growing fear that these children were in danger of starving to death. The school officials were still a little afraid to say anything definitive, afraid of making a mistake. But one nurse involved with the case admitted that the kids were getting worse. After that, the school counselor wrote a letter to the Department of Welfare explaining that a caseworker found the house unfit for human habitation and that on a recent visit to the house the children were found eating a box of laundry starch.

As we stood shivering in front of Mrs. Jones's house, the counselor explained that there were plenty of other cases like this in Philadelphia — some were worse. In the dark living room, Mrs. Jones sat huddled in a bathrobe, on the only piece of furniture in the house, a torn green couch, partially covered by a dirty sheet. A plastic trash bag covered one of the broken windows but the wind tore through the others, past the living room into the empty kitchen, and down the rubbish strewn, mouse-infested stairway to the cellar.

"Mrs. Jones, do you have any food in the house?" the counselor had asked.

"Yes, I have food."

We looked in the refrigerator. The only thing there was some kind of orange liquid that had spilled and hardened along the bottom shelf and a single can of solidified fat. The kitchen hadn't one item of food. A pot sat on the hot plate with an old tea bag floating in its cold water.

The children came downstairs dressed in the school outfits given to them by the Department of Welfare at the beginning of the year. These were still quite new, perhaps because the children had attended school so little. They came in silently and lined up, trembling without coats, behind the couch. Their hands were numb with cold, but they stood there, like little Spartans in their mother's army, determined to be loyal to her.

"Are you cold?" I asked.

"No," said a nine-year-old girl, speaking for the group.

"Are you hungry?"

"No."

"When did you eat last?"

"We're not hungry," she said deliberately.

"Does your mother have food?"

"Yes," she said. "She does."

continued

Box 14-3 *(continued)*

It was as if those kids had memorized a liturgy before their mother brought them down from the bedroom, where they slept on torn, filthy mattresses without sheets or blankets or pillows. Or perhaps hunger and cold had numbed them beyond feeling. The four-year-old didn't move. He simply stared off into space and the seventeen-month-old infant just sat there drinking water from a bottle. I was told she had never uttered a word.

Before I left I saw something in the eyes of one of the children. A desire to communicate something. He was Paul, a boy of eight, but his physical growth had already been retarded by about three years. I bent down. "Would you like to come back to school with us?" I asked. "It's warm at school and there are lunches."

He didn't say anything. He didn't have to. He just looked at me hard, for a long serious moment, then slowly he lifted his hand and gently, tentatively, touched my cold fingers with his. I smiled. His large brown eyes filled with tears. Then he nodded.

Source: Loretta Schwartz-Nobel, *Starving in the Shadow of Plenty*, (New York: G.P. Putnam's Sons, 1981), 41–43. Reproduced with the permission of G.P. Putnam's Sons Inc.

Head Start has enabled many poor children to have a better chance of succeeding in school. (Courtesy of Kim Bradley, San Marcos Record.)

Vietnam had not sapped the nation's will to fight the war on poverty, poverty could have been reduced significantly in the United States.[64]

There is some evidence that giving money to those who cannot work does reduce poverty. Prior to the mid-1970s, the poverty rate for elderly persons was higher than that for children. Now, however, with SSI, Medicare, and Social Security, the poverty rate among the elderly has declined until it is now lower than that of children.

The problem of poverty has always been with us, and it will not soon disappear. Although providing for any person's every need is probably counterproductive to that person's welfare, some kind of aid may be necessary to help the unwilling poor escape poverty and help their children make better lives for themselves. Many of us want to help those who do not deserve their poverty, but we want to withhold help from those who are poor because of indolence. The question then becomes one of who deserves welfare. Separating the worthy poor from the unworthy poor is important if the welfare system is to have legitimacy in the community.

A New Proposal: Workfare

This question raises the larger issue: How shall we help the worthy poor help themselves? Recent **workfare** programs have been hailed by both liberals and conservatives as a partial solution to the twin problems of poverty and welfare.[65] These programs, which have been successful when work is available, are designed to help the poor find work and then require that they continue to work. Specially trained personnel help the participants find suitable work, plan transportation, and arrange child care if necessary. Participation in a workfare program is mandatory; welfare benefits can be reduced or eliminated for those unwilling to participate in the program or put forth the effort necessary to find and keep a job.

Critics of workfare say that it is authoritarian and coercive. Its proponents say that current welfare programs are more repressive and create dependency and passivity. Workfare, the advocates suggest, can actually help the poor develop the skills and values vital to earning a better way of life. This debate has not been resolved, and workfare will continue to be proposed as an answer to some of the problems created by welfare systems in the United States.

Conclusion: What We Can Do in Our Communities

Community efforts begin with the ideas of individuals who are able to organize others in the pursuit of a goal. The individuals who accomplish such goals are no different from you and your friends; they simply have taken a step beyond thinking to doing. Several examples of individuals making a difference in their communities follow. Perhaps they will provide answers to the problems in your community.

The problems associated with teenage pregnancy and motherhood have prompted a number of communities, including Norfolk, Virginia, and Rochester, New York, as well as several in Appalachia and Louisiana, to establish "resource mother" projects.[66] Neighborhood women who have successfully reared their own children are enlisted as counselors for local pregnant teenagers. Their task is to reduce the likelihood of future pregnancies and provide positive maternal role models. There is some evidence that the program is successful. Lawton Chiles, retired Florida senator, says, "Our studies indicate that if a girl has a baby by age 13, she'll have three by age 18. Well, where resource mothers have been used, the repeat rate has been cut in half."[67]

The problems of hunger and homelessness prompted Nancy Bissell and Gordon Packard to organize the Saint Martin's Soup Kitchen in Tucson, Arizona, which fed 240 people a day until the city closed the facility because of neighbors' complaints. Undaunted, Ms. Bissell and Mr. Packard established the Primavera Foundation, which hired 15 homeless men to renovate a dilapidated motel. The motel, which became a home for mentally and physically handicapped people, was followed by a 70-bed temporary shelter. Volunteers provide counseling, meals, and job leads.[68]

Millard Fuller was a millionaire by the time he was 30, so he chose another goal: He decided to eliminate substandard housing in the United States. He founded Habitat for Humanity, an organization with the goal of providing affordable housing to the poor. Joining with Clarence Jordan, he organized the Fund for Humanity, a pool of capital to buy housing materials and offer mortgages to those too poor to qualify for bank loans. Volunteers offered their labor, and Fuller recruited national figures, including former President Jimmy Carter, to participate in the project. Today Habitat for Humanity is a national organization which has built more than 4000 homes since 1976.

An average Habitat home of 1000 square feet sells for less than $30,000. The average homeowner has a monthly mortgage payment of around $150, usually less than the rent for substandard housing in the area. Homeowners participate in a sweat equity program: Not only do they help build their own homes, they also agree to help build other homes. Fuller insists that Habitat volunteers are not caseworkers; they are coworkers with homeowners in the Habitat for Humanity program.[69]

The children in South Providence, Rhode Island, had no park to play in, so Mark Toney organized the children of the area to lobby for a new park. Toney's political organization, Direct Action for Rights and Equality (DARE), helped convince city leaders that a park was necessary. DARE has also registered voters, improved school facilities, and instituted a fuel assistance program for poor families. The strength of DARE comes from an involved, dues-paying membership made up of blacks, Asians, Hispanics, and whites. Toney, who graduated from Brown University, uses classic community organization strategies to encourage local officials to become concerned about DARE's issues.[70]

The farming crisis of the 1980s had led to the foreclosure of over

300,000 farms. Helen Waller of Circle, Montana, was appalled by the crisis and decided to do something about the hardships facing farmers. She organized 47 farm groups in 35 states to create the Save the Family Farm Coalition, an organization which was responsible for legislation changing the credit provisions of 1987 farm legislation. Now lobbying for the Family Farm Act to be passed in 1990, Waller says you can fight city hall and can change things in Washington, DC. She knows because she had done it.[71]

You can make the kind of contributions to your community that Nancy Bissell, Gordon Packard, Millard Fuller, Mark Toney, and Helen Waller have made, or you may have another idea. What is important is taking the first step by putting your ideas into action and organizing your community to solve its own problems of poverty.

Study Objectives

1. Identify two kinds of definitions of poverty that social scientists use.
2. Explain how the poverty line was created.
3. List the major reasons for becoming poor.
4. Describe the culture of poverty.
5. List how many people are poor in the United States.
6. Explain how Charles Murray and William Julius Wilson disagree about the causes of poverty.
7. Delineate the characteristics of the underclass.
8. Identify the kinds of people who are poor in the United States.
9. List the consequences of poverty.
10. Explain why people become and remain homeless.
11. Describe how the poor are distributed across the states.
12. Explain how welfare payments vary between the states.
13. Describe the difference between welfare and entitlements.
14. Describe how much the system of welfare costs the federal government.
15. Identify how much the system of welfare costs state and local governments.
16. Describe the consequences of the welfare system.
17. Describe workfare as a solution to welfare dependency.

Glossary

absolute definition of poverty Defines poverty in terms of an objective standard, usually a governmental measure of subsistence such as the poverty line.

Aid to Families with Dependent Children A federal and state welfare program, established by the Social Security Act of 1935, administered by each state for all poor families with children under 18 with one parent absent. In over half the states, two-parent families are also eligible when the father is out of work.

categorical grants-in-aid Federal strategies for funding state and local governments, with the funds targeting special categories of needy persons.

culture of poverty The belief that the poor are a distinct group with their own rules, ideas, and beliefs. This implies that the poor learn to be poor or fail to learn how to escape poverty and transmit poverty as a way of life to their children.

entitlements Social insurance programs, such as Social Security, Medicare, veterans' benefits, worker's compensation, student loans, and unemployment insurance, which provide a safety net for middle-income people.

feminization of poverty Refers to the fact that females are overrepresented in poverty figures. This has been known since poverty figures began being kept in 1959, when almost half of all female-headed households had incomes below the poverty level.

food stamps A program, begun during the 1960s, which distributes coupons redeemable for food to families and individuals with incomes under 130 percent of the poverty line. It is administered by state welfare agencies, but the federal government provides almost all the funding.

means-tested Refers to government welfare programs based on some measure of income. The four major means-tested programs are Aid to Families with Dependent Children, Supplemental Security Income, Medicaid, and food stamps.

Medicaid A means-tested welfare program established in 1965 to help cover the medical costs of persons eligible for AFDC and SSI.

Medicare An entitlement program which was established by the Social Security Amendment of 1965 to provide health insurance programs for those drawing social security or old age benefits.

poverty line A measure of poverty established by the Social Security Administration in 1964. The lowest cost of feeding a family of four is multiplied by three to determine the proportion of income spent on food by the average middle-income family.

poverty rate The proportion or percentage of the population below the poverty line.

relative definitions of poverty Make a subjective judgment about the meaning of poverty in comparison to the standards of the society. John Kenneth Galbraith has suggested that even if individuals have enough income to survive, they may be considered poverty-stricken if their life-style is considered by the community to be unacceptable or degrading.

Social Security Refers to all those programs established under the Social Security Act of 1935. Among the entitlement programs currently referred to as social security programs are old age insurance, survivors insurance, unemployment insurance, temporary disability insurance, Medicare, and supplemental security income. Welfare programs which are implemented under the Social Security Act include Aid to Families with Dependent Children, Supplemental Security Income, and Medicaid.

special revenue-sharing block grants Federal funds offered to states to replace, at one time, numerous categorical grants-in-aid directed at a particular problem, such as job creation or community development.

Supplemental Security Income A means-tested welfare program established in 1972 to provide additional monthly cash payments to impoverished elderly, blind, and disabled persons.

underclass A term coined by Gunnar Myrdal. Refers to a third world rural and urban class cut off from society, lacking the education, skills, and personality traits needed to take advantage of the increases in opportunity which resulted from affirmative action, and thus trapped in poverty.

urban industrial transition The move from the central city by manufacturers, retailers, and construction industries, taking with them the blue-collar jobs commonly filled by the poor. In their place have come information-processing and financial organizations, with concomitant opportunities for professional or white-collar employees and a loss of opportunity for the urban poor.

welfare Means-tested social programs.

working poor The one-third to one-half of all adults whose incomes place them below the poverty line but who do in fact work, often 50 weeks or more during the year.

workfare Programs that require welfare recipients to work in order to get benefits while acquiring job skills or a high school diploma.

Endnotes

1. John Kenneth Galbraith, *The Affluent Society* (New York: New American Library, 1958), 251.
2. One strong argument against the poverty line is that middle-class people tend to spend about one-fourth of their income on food. Therefore, many reason, the basic cost of food should be multiplied by four to determine the official poverty line. As it is, the poor are doomed to substandard incomes.
3. For an interesting discussion of both perspectives, see Bonnie Szumski, ed., *Social Justice: Opposing Viewpoints*, (St. Paul, MN: Greenhaven, 1984), 57–97.
4. William Julius Wilson, *The Truly Disadvantaged: The Inner City, the Underclass, and Public Policy*, (Chicago: University of Chicago Press, 1987), 171.
5. Joanna Neuman, "Way Poverty's Asssssed Changed," *USA Today* (December 29, 1988), 4A.
6. Mark S. Littman and Eleanor F. Baugher, *Poverty in the United States*, U.S. Department of Commerce, Bureau of the Census (Washington, DC: GPO, 1988), 154.
7. William O'Hare, *America's Welfare Population: Who Gets What?* (Washington, DC: Population Reference Bureau, 1987), 3.
8. William O'Hare, *Poverty in America: Trends and New Patterns* (Washington, DC: Population Reference Bureau, 1989), 43.
9. Littman and Baugher, 5.
10. Mark S. Hoffman, ed., *World Almanac and Books of Facts, 1989* (New York: St. Martin's, 1989), 542.
11. O'Hare, *Poverty in America*, 15.
12. Littman and Baugher, 5.
13. A variety of definitions, few of them concise, have been used for the term "underclass." Some authors, such as Ken Auletta, include the mentally ill and some criminals. For a more scholarly definition, see Sara McLanahan and Irwin Garfinkle, "Single Mothers, the Underclass, and Social Policy," *Annals of the American Academy of Political and Social Science* 501 (January 1989), 92–104.
14. Ken Auletta, *The Underclass* (New York: Random House, 1982), 27.

15. Littman and Baugher, 2.
16. O'Hare, *Poverty in America*, 23.
17. Littman and Baugher, 61.
18. Ibid.
19. Ibid., 154.
20. Ibid., 55.
21. Ibid., 27.
22. Charles Murray, *Losing Ground: American Social Policy 1950–1980* (New York: Basic Books, 1984), 178–179.
23. Wilson, *The Truly Disadvantaged.*
24. John D. Kasarda, "Urban Industrial Transition and the Underclass," *Annals of the American Academy of Political and Social Science* 501 (January 1989), 26–47.
25. William O'Hare, *The Rise of Poverty in Rural America*, (Washington, DC: Population Reference Bureau, 1988), 5.
26. Wilson, 103.
27. O'Hare, *The Rise of Poverty in Rural America*, 9.
28. Michael Harrington, *The New American Poverty*, (New York: Penguin, 1985), 101.
29. Patricia A. Sullivan and Shirley Damrosch, "Homeless Women and Childen," in Richard D. Bingham, Roy E. Green, and Sammis B. White, eds., *The Homeless in Contemporary Society*, (Beverly Hills, CA: Sage, 1987), 82–98.
30. Quoted in Rene I. Jahiel, "The Situation of Homelessness," in *The Homeless in Contemporary Society*, 97–118.
31. "He Explores Link to Poverty," *USA Today*, (March 29, 1989), 2A.
32. Rita Rubin, "Black Health," *Dallas Morning News* (February 6, 1989), 6D–7D.
33. Ibid.
34. Jane E. Brody, "Intriguing Studies Link Nutrition to Immunity," *New York Times*, (March 2, 1989), 21, 24, 25.
35. Rubin, 6D–7D.
36. Philip J. Hilts, "Racial Life Expectancy Gap Widens," New York Times News Service, *Austin-American Statesman*, (October 9, 1989), A4.
37. Paul Clancy, "Doctor's Cancer Crusade," *USA Today*, (March 29, 1989), 2A.
38. Harrington, 221.
39. Richard Totman, *Social Causes of Illness* (New York: Pantheon, 1979).
40. U.S. Bureau of the Census, *Statistical Abstract, 1988* (Washington, DC: GPO, 1989), 81.
41. Marianne W. Zawitz, ed., *Report to the Nation on Crime and Justice*, Bureau of Justice Statistics (Washington, DC: GPO, 1988), 28.
42. Ibid., 27.
43. Ibid.
44. O'Hare, *America's Welfare Population*, 21.
45. Paul E. Peterson, *City Limits* (Chicago: University of Chicago Press, 1981), 43.
46. O'Hare, *America's Welfare Population*, 3.
47. Congressional Budget Office, *Poverty Status of Familes* (Washington, DC: GPO, June 1987).
48. Frances Fox Pivens and Richard A. Cloward, *Regulating the Poor* (New York: Pantheon, 1971).
49. O'Hare, *Poverty in America*, 44.
50. O'Hare, *America's Welfare Population*, 10.

51. *Summary of Welfare Reform Hearings—1986*, (Washington, DC: ACIR, 1987), 11.
52. Steve Burghardt and Michael Fabricant, *Working Under the Safety Net: Policy and Practice for the New American Poor*, (Beverly Hills, CA: Sage, 1987), 158.
53. O'Hare, *Poverty in America*, 44.
54. Council of State Governments, *The Book of States, 1988–89*, (Lexington, KY: CSG, 1989), 245.
55. O'Hare, *America's Welfare Population*, 8.
56. Pivens and Cloward, *Regulating the Poor*.
57. O'Hare, *America's Welfare Population*, 7.
58. Ibid., 5.
59. Ibid.
60. Ibid., 4.
61. Ibid., 31.
62. Ibid., 6.
63. John E. Schwarz, *America's Hidden Success: A Reassessment of Twenty Years of Public Policy*, (New York, Norton, 1983).
64. Harrington, *The New American Poverty*.
65. Lawrence M. Mead, "The Logic of Workfare: The Underclass and Work Policy," *Annals of the American Academy of Political and Social Science* 501 (January 1989), 156–169.
66. William Raspberry, "A Good Start in Life," *Austin American-Statesman* (October 17, 1989), A8.
67. Ibid.
68. *Giraffe Gazette* V(1)(1989), 15.
69. Don Winbush, "A Bootstrap Approach to Low-Cost Housing," *Time* (January 16, 1989), 12–13.
70. William O. Beeman, "Door Knocker Extraordinaire," *Mother Jones*, (January 1989), 29.
71. Pat Dawson, "High Noon in the Heartland," *Mother Jones*, (January 1989), 32–33.

Chapter 15

Paying for It: The Revenue-Expenditure System

In this chapter we conclude our exploration of the interaction between the individual and the governments by discussing the cost of using government to solve problems — the price we pay for it. The price has at least two parts.

One part of the price is called the government **budget**. A budget is a plan for getting and spending money. The getting, or income, side of the budget is called *revenue*. In some states the legislative committee that deals with revenue bills is called the ways and means committee. Expenditures are usually dealt with by appropriations committees, which spend money by allocating or appropriating it to the departments or agencies which actually spend it. If there is less revenue than there is expenditure, the budget is unbalanced. State and local governments cannot print extra money the way the federal government can, and so they must revise the budget to reduce expenditures, find more revenue, borrow the money, or find a way to get another unit of government to pay for the proposed programs. An ongoing intergovernmental problem in virtually every state is the tendency for too many state legislatures to make local governments bear most of the costs of new programs.

The second part of the price to be paid is the human and social consequences of *not* acting to solve problems or not acting fast enough — in other words, doing a "half-fast" job of alleviating human suffering. Two familiar observations summarize this part of the price of failing to deal with serious social, environmental, and human problems: "There is no such thing as a free lunch" and "You can pay me now, or you can pay me later."

The first observation reaffirms the fact that virtually everything has a price, and the second reminds us that there is a time frame involved. The cost often goes up while we delay paying it.

THE BUDGET: A PLAN FOR PAYING FOR IT

The budget constitutes one of the most important sets of decisions that political actors try to influence. Decisions about budgets often involve life-and-death matters. Usually these issues are abstract and distant. When the likelihood of highway death is increased by decisions to cut funds for enforcing the speed limit or for inspecting trucks and keeping unsafe ones off the highway, the consequences can be treated as statistics rather than living, dying, or maimed individuals. Sometimes, however, these life-and-death decisions involve real people whom the decision makers have come to know (Box 15-1).

In November 1987, Coby Howard died of leukemia for want of a $100,000 bone marrow transplant operation that his family could not afford. He was 7 years old. To blame the government of Oregon or even the director of the Oregon Adult and Family Services Department for the deaths of particular individuals is both unfair and unrealistic, because these tragedies are happening in every state. Political leaders have to make tough decisions, and they do not make them lightly. Freddye Webb-Petett is the administrator who had to decide on the funding recommendation that affected a whole category of human lives, including Coby Howard's. She keeps a picture of Coby on her desk to remind her on a daily basis of something which she already knows: Government decisions about money have consequences for real people.[1]

Nine Influences on Governmental Budgets

Among the many influences on the budget of a unit of government, there are at least nine which you have encountered in earlier chapters of this book.

Box 15-1 **Budgets Involve Life-and-Death Decisions**

Donna Arneson, a 36-year-old single mother with no health insurance and no savings, was one of several victims of a 1988 decision by the state of Oregon not to provide funds for organ transplants. Although the chances of a successful operation were only about 50 percent, a liver transplant was Mrs. Arneson's only hope to live more than a few weeks beyond the end of the legislative session.

As new surgical techniques, drugs, sophisticated organ donor systems, and after-care methods have raised the hopes of many people doomed to die, the demand for transplant operations has increased dramatically in this decade. The number of heart transplants increased more than 20-fold from 1981 to 1987. Transplant operations cost between $150,000 and $250,000 and thus are beyond the means of most Americans.

The expense of the operation and the high mortality rate (about 50 percent) make for tough decisions for state officials charged with stretching scarce medical and social service funds as far as possible. Among the recipients of the 19 medical transplants — bone marrow, heart, liver, and pancreas — that Oregon covered between 1985 and 1988, only 9 have survived. During the past two years the state legislature has adopted a series of changes that will provide increased access to basic medical care for about 24,000 low-income people a year. The total cost of these reforms will be over $18 million.

These medical expenditures may provide early diagnosis and preventive care that will avoid the risk, expense, and high mortality rates of transplant operations. In the meantime, people who need these operations and cannot afford them wait to die.

Source: Michael Specter, "Oregon Legislators Face Up to the Hard Job of 'Playing God,'" *Washington Post National Weekly Edition*, (February 15, 1988), 33.

The Legislature   This is the body that passes the several laws that are collectively referred to as the budget. At a minimum, the legislature passes at least one appropriations bill, which at the state level is sent to the executive branch for approval. If the existing revenue laws will yield enough to pay for the appropriations, then new tax bills may not be needed. However, between 1984 and 1988 every state passed some form of revenue legislation. In 1988 alone, all but 14 states revised their tax laws.[2]

Legislatures also evaluate the expenditure of funds. This includes watchdog and sunset review functions, in which legislators determine whether agencies should be assigned more appropriate tasks, whether they are using their funds properly, and whether one or more agencies should be abolished, significantly reorganized, or made part of another agency or department.

The Executive Branch   This branch of the government plays four roles in the budgetary process at the state level and at least three at the local level. First, the chief executive at the state level and in many local governments prepares the budget submitted to the legislature and is expected to lobby for its approval. Second, once the legislature passes tax and appropriations (spending) bills, the chief executive in all states but one (North Carolina) has the power to veto them. In some states the governor has a **line item veto**. This pertains only to appropriations and means that the governor can strike out specific items without having to veto the whole bill. Except in municipalities with a strong mayor system, most local government constitutions do not give the executive branch a veto.

The third role of the executive branch is spending the money appropriated to it. This involves the several agencies in the executive branch which perform a variety of services and enforce regulations. A special set of activities constitute a fourth role: collecting taxes and accounting for the expenditure of funds through preaudit and postaudit procedures.

Preaudits occur when an official called an auditor or comptroller certifies that there is enough money in an agency's budget for a particular kind of expenditure. For example, among the separate categories in a typical agency's budget one finds supplies, personnel, contracts, and equipment. The money in these categories is not always interchangeable (fungible), and thus it is necessary for someone to certify that the money is going to be spent appropriately.

Periodically, after money has been spent, another auditor, sometimes from a different agency, examines the agency's records to make sure that the money was actually spent appropriately — that the bills have been paid and that the correct individuals or organizations received the money.

The Judicial Branch   This branch gets involved in the budget when it hears challenges to the legality of the ways in which various agencies spend money or collect it as taxes or fees, hears challenges to the constitutionality of tax or appropriations laws, and prosecutes and tries the cases of individuals accused of breaking tax laws or spending government money inappropriately. Both the judicial and the legislative branches also spend money. They need staff and equipment to perform their functions, just as the executive branch does.

The Political Culture   The budget is affected through the myths and beliefs generally accepted in a region or state about what is appropriate for government to spend money on and what the most appropriate sources of revenue are. Political culture is one reason why there are so many different patterns of taxing and spending among states which are rich as well as among those which are poor.[3]

The amount of money spent on a given program is not determined simply by the wealth of the economy in the area where a unit of government is located. Table 15.1 provides a comparison of the states in terms of differ-

Table 15.1   PER CAPITA WELFARE EXPENDITURES AND STATE-LOCAL WEALTH

State*	Per capita welfare expenditures	Rank	Index of state-local wealth	Rank
Alabama	167.19	49	74.3	48
Alaska	585.80	2	176.9	1
Arizona	192.88	43	98.7	19
Arkansas	232.73	34	73.3	49
California	478.19	5	117.8	9
Colorado	242.70	30	116.8	10
Connecticut	379.60	11	135.2	4
Delaware	201.47	41	121.4	6
Florida	183.73	45	105.1	14
Georgia	255.80	28	94.0	26
Hawaii	290.80	23	113.3	11
Idaho	182.42	47	76.9	45
Illinois	328.21	18	95.9	23
Indiana	260.38	26	86.9	38
Iowa	291.39	22	83.7	40
Kansas	217.81	38	95.7	24
Kentucky	296.54	19	76.4	47
Louisiana	247.46	29	90.1	34
Maine	452.27	7	94.5	25
Maryland	330.51	17	107.6	12
Massachusetts	571.86	3	123.5	5
Michigan	466.47	6	96.2	22
Minnesota	389.87	9	102.4	16
Mississippi	235.98	31	65.3	50
Missouri	219.21	37	92.7	29
Montana	292.71	21	88.0	37
Nebraska	260.38	27	91.2	32
Nevada	146.34	50	146.8	3
New Hampshire	233.06	33	119.4	8
New Jersey	365.44	14	120.5	7
New Mexico	233.17	32	91.3	31
New York	682.99	1	106.8	13
North Carolina	206.80	40	88.3	36
North Dakota	351.37	16	93.9	27
Ohio	375.26	12	90.8	33
Oklahoma	289.08	24	98.1	20
Oregon	227.30	35	93.3	28
Pennsylvania	385.71	10	89.7	35
Rhode Island	504.44	4	91.9	30
South Carolina	183.57	46	78.6	43
South Dakota	215.19	39	77.8	44
Tennessee	292.91	20	83.5	41
Texas	173.63	48	103.5	15
Utah	219.38	36	80.4	42

continued

Table 15.1   PER CAPITA WELFARE EXPENDITURES AND STATE-LOCAL WEALTH (continued)

State*	Per capita welfare expenditures	Rank	Index of state-local wealth	Rank
Vermont	367.37	13	99.4	18
Virginia	195.30	42	100.7	17
Washington	353.95	15	97.8	21
West Virginia	260.98	25	76.4	46
Wisconsin	409.11	8	85.8	39
Wyoming	191.20	44	150.7	2
U.S. Average	$291		100	

*The top ten states in per capita welfare expenditures are printed in bold. The ten wealthiest states are underscored.

Source: Advisory Commission on Intergovernmental Relations, 1986 *State Fiscal Capacity and Effort*, (Washington, DC: ACIR 1988), 12; and U.S. Department of Commerce, Bureau of the Census, *State Government Finances in 1988* (Washington, DC: U.S. Government Printing Office, 1989), 51.

ences in welfare expenditures and wealth (i.e., the ability to afford high welfare payments).[4] Only Alaska, California, and Massachusetts lead in *both* wealth and welfare expenditure. Nearly all the high-welfare-effort states — many of which are not wealthy — are states with a moralistic political culture. Although the average AFDC payment in wealthy states is higher than the average payment in poor states, the variation within each category (poor states and rich states) suggests that politics and political culture have more than a little to do with this difference.

An interesting pairing is Florida and New York. Both states rank high in wealth (fifteenth and fourteenth) and the percentage of the population which is in poverty (about 13 percent in 1979). However, Florida ranks forty-fifth in per capita welfare expenditures, while New York ranks first.[5]

Note that the second and third wealthiest states, Wyoming and Nevada, provide limited assistance to families on welfare. Neither state has a moralistic political culture, and in both at least 5 percent of the population is in poverty.

Institutions   The relative strength of institutions has a great effect on the size and shape of a budget. Interest groups and parties attempt to influence how money is appropriated and how revenues are acquired. We observed earlier that the business community is overrepresented in both weak and strong interest group systems. Although companies can play a positive role, as they do in Battle Creek (Chapter 5), they can also use their influence in the political economy to prevent positive action on issues such as workplace safety, economic regulation, and the way funds are raised. Borrowing from rather than taxing the rich is greatly favored as a revenue method by banks and investment law firms.

When interest groups predominate in a state without countervailing political institutions such as strong parties and strong institutions of government, the budgetary result is often less money spent on programs to benefit the have-nots and less effort made to protect the environment.[6]

Decision Makers   The personality and perceptions of every decision maker involved in the process of designing, passing, and executing the budget affect the role these people play in shaping the content of the budget and the way it is administered. To those seeking to influence the budget of a particular unit of government, these factors are very important.

Prior Decisions   Budget decisions of the past have an impact on the ones a society has to make in the present and in the future. "You can pay me now or pay me later," says the auto mechanic who is trying to get you to buy an oil change and a new oil filter now instead of an engine overhaul later. The mechanic has a point, since an engine overhaul costs about 50 times as much as the clean oil filter which prevents it. In the context of governmental budgets, we sometimes pay for *not* doing things — by not paying now, we pay much more later.

Decisions of Other Governments   Decisions made by one government may affect the budgets of other governments. When a school district builds a new school, the city or county has to deal with the budgetary consequences of increased traffic on nearby roads. In an intergovernmental system, each government affects one or more other governments. When the state legislature assigns functions to local governments without providing the resources to pay for them, the legislature is in essence passing on tax increases or service cutbacks.

When the federal government borrows huge amounts of money, it affects the ability of other governments to borrow. When the federal government cuts back on social programs, it requires state and local government budget makers to confront decisions about taking up the slack or dealing with the human and political consequences of reductions in programs such as education, health, housing, transportation, and environmental protection.

Political Activities by Individuals   The political activities of individuals and groups influence budgetary decisions. Money is seldom appropriated by legislatures unless it is clear that some individuals want it to happen so much so that they will invest political resources (time, energy, and talent) to advocate that appropriation.

Redistribution: What Gets Paid for and Who Pays

Decisions about taxing and spending have a redistributive effect. **Redistribution** refers to government actions which alter the existing pattern of opportunities to live a better life. The term is most often used to identify actions which assist the have-nots.

Thus, after the effects of inheritance, biology, good luck, bad luck, and the uneven distribution of economic opportunities have had an impact on the resources available to individuals, the government may attempt to influence the life chances of individuals by using its powers to tax, spend, and regulate. It may increase opportunities for education, jobs or job training, and good health and decent housing by taxing and by spending.

Redistribution occurs because almost any set of rules is likely to distribute costs and benefits unevenly. For example, the rules of basketball tend to benefit tall people with exceptional leaping ability; the rules of ice hockey don't.[7] A decision by the federal government to fight inflation by maintaining a 5 percent unemployment rate does not affect stockbrokers and carpenters equally, nor does it affect states and communities in the same way.

Redistribution is most often thought of in terms of spending in the form of cash or cash equivalent payments (AFDC, unemployment compensation, food stamps) or in the form of services (free public education, subsidized medical care). Redistribution can also occur in the form of regulations which cost the government money to enforce or cost businesses money to comply with, usually both. The minimum-wage law for example, is a government regulation that redistributes money from employers to employees.

Many benefits are available to the have-nots only if the government pays for them. The haves, by contrast, are in an economic position to pay for most of these benefits privately. They can enjoy clean water, health care, swimming pools, an education for their children, and even private police protection whether the government pays for them or not.

Not all government policies are redistributive in the way we have defined the term. When some individuals bear a heavier tax burden than do others, the inequalities in society may be reinforced rather than modified. Furthermore, some government spending policies also reinforce inequalities. Public funds are occasionally spent on programs that are more likely to benefit the haves than the have-nots (Box 15-2).

The fourth item in Box 15-2 suggests that the way in which a government raises and spends money (and how much) has an impact on whether a budget is redistributive. Thus, budget decisions not only involve life and death, they also involve social justice and influence the structure of opportunity for the next generation.

Budget Choices: The Art of the Possible

In making decisions about taxing and spending, chief executives and legislators at the local and state levels face a number of difficult choices even if they decide to spend no more than they did the previous year. These choices can be summarized under four courses of action. First, they can spend the same amount this year as last year on every program. In effect, this means cutting each program the same amount, because every year inflation reduces

Box 15-2 Reinforcing Inequality: Selected Examples

1. Providing funds for an elaborate highway system linking suburban shopping centers, upper-class residential neighborhoods, and downtown offices benefits the haves. An alternative could be to pay for public transportation for the many poor people who don't have cars or vans or to build people movers (like the ones in airports) in the central cities to make it easier to get around the city.

2. A state that spends a lot of money on a low-tuition higher educational system on the one hand and on a bare minimum elementary and secondary educational system on the other hand is reinforcing inequality. Since upper-class and middle-class children are better prepared at home for even the worst primary and secondary school system (by parents who read to them, buy them coloring books, make them watch "Sesame Street," and correct their grammar), they are much more likely to survive under-funded primary and secondary schools. Thus they will be able to take advantage of the state's opportunities for higher education, while the children of parents with limited education and teaching skills will be less likely to do so.

   Redistribution could be advanced by a well-financed state-supported system of pre-primary, primary, secondary, and remedial education. This might increase the opportunities for more of the children of the have-nots to overcome the disadvantages of poverty and nonsupportive home environments while they learn job skills or make it to college.

3. Spending money on research, information, and technical assistance to businesses and investors instead of on retraining, unemployment benefits, or worker's compensation to those injured or made ill on the job can reinforce inequality.

4. Borrowing instead of raising taxes to pay for government buildings and facilities often reinforces inequality. Millions of dollars in public money are paid to lawyers and brokers who design bond packages so that public credit can be used to pay more public money in interest to the wealthy individuals who buy the bonds. In buying bonds, the wealthy lend money at interest to the public instead of paying taxes to finance whatever the bond issue was designed to pay for in the first place. Not only does paying for facilities with bonds triple the cost of a facility, the interest earned by the bondholders is usually exempt from taxation.

the number of things a fixed amount of money can buy. Thus to buy the same services that were bought the year before, the budget for each program would have to be increased.

The second choice is to take inflation into account and attempt to keep some programs at the same service level rather than the same dollar level. This means that budget makers have to decide where to cut if they do not wish to find new sources of revenue. This choice involves concentrating the cuts in a few programs in order to offer the same level of services in others. Third, budget makers can improve some services by cutting others. Fourth, if new problems arise — and they often do — whole new programs must be funded out of cuts in other programs.

The choices are not often as simple as spend or don't spend. Avoiding waste, promoting efficiency, and attempting to walk the fine line between responsibility to the next generation and attending to the realities of the present one are difficult tasks. That is why politics is sometimes referred to as *the art of the possible*. Creating and enacting budgets for state and local governments are the essence of the art of the possible.

The Fiscal Year

The **fiscal year** is a 12-month period used for bookkeeping purposes. "Fiscal" and "financial" both mean "having to do with money." A fiscal year is also known as a budget year. During the weeks of transition between fiscal years, accounting officials and those responsible for implementing budgets often communicate in jargon (Box 15-3).

At the end of a fiscal year, or budget year, the books are closed. Most agencies with unspent money on their ledgers cannot transfer it to the next year's budget. One way of looking at this unspent money is to say that these agencies saved the taxpayers' money; another way is to say that they failed to put to use all the resources given to them.

The federal fiscal year begins on October 1 and ends on September 30. Until 1974, it began on July 1 and ended on June 30. Forty-six states continue to use the latter dates for their fiscal years. Alabama and Michigan have adopted the new federal year, and Texas uses September 1. With few witticisms that weren't heard the year before, state officials in New York open the books on April 1. Although 21 states draw up two-year, or biennial, budgets, these budgets still consist of two separate fiscal years.[8]

Most local governments have a fiscal year that coincides with that of the state or with the calendar year. Within a state, most local governments usually all have the same fiscal year. Budgeting for many local governments, particularly large ones, is a process not all that different from the one we will describe for state governments in the following pages. The more local is the government, the more likely is the process to be less formal and take place over a shorter time span.

Agency Budget Requests

Throughout a given department, each subunit prepares a budget request (proposal) to be sent on to the next level. One of the major responsibilities of an official in charge of a major government unit — whether it is a large department within a state government, an agency within a department, or a university — is to negotiate with the subunits responsible to him or her in order to put together a budgetary request that makes the agency look good. A "good-looking" budget request is usually larger than the one for the year

---

Box 15-3 **Fiscal Year Frustrations**

''I'd like this supplies order charged to FY 91, if possible.''

''I'm sorry, the books for FY 91 closed yesterday; you'll have to wait until we start the '92 budget.''

''But I submitted the order weeks ago. It got hung up in Dean Whipsnade's office. That's why I'm delivering it personally now.''

''I wish I could help you, but the director of accounting was very firm in our staff meeting this morning about accepting any more orders for processing on the '91 budget. You might try to get Dean Whipsnade to call the director.''

''Thanks anyway, but the dean is out of town, and the acting dean won't do it. I should have followed up on this earlier.''

The foregoing conversation meant that the chair of a university department just missed the opportunity to buy a few hundred dollars worth of supplies for the next fiscal year with money from this fiscal year — money he or she may have been squirreling away for months with penny-pinching economies.

Now the unspent money gets returned to the state treasury or to the university's reserve fund if it is allowed to have one. The supplies, which have to be purchased anyway, will be purchased from the new fiscal year's budget. By saving money on supplies, the chair was planning on buying a new computer for the department. That computer might have saved even more money in stationery and secretarial time. That's why the chair is frustrated.

---

before (but not too much larger) and usually contains some (but not too many) new programs.

The larger the budgetary unit is, the more levels there are and the more opportunities for duplication and waste. Thus the larger the budgetary unit, the more formal the process of putting together the budget.

Agency officials receive proposals not only from the people they work with but also from interest groups and individuals who would like the agency to take on new responsibilities. Getting a proposal on an agency's budget request is no small accomplishment. Most agency officials are receptive to good ideas, especially those which result in an obvious justification for a bigger budget.

The Budget and You

The decision budget makers have to make about resources are not unlike those you make in deciding whether to become involved in the political system. Participation has a price, but so does nonparticipation. Thus, when you choose not to use some of your political resources to influence decisions, you make a decision for which you may pay later.

The observation that there is no such thing as a free lunch certainly applies to the politics of state and local governments. We cannot enjoy a life free of politics without paying for it by having others make decisions for us. Part of the price is that some of the decisions may be bad ones. The observation about paying later applies both to political participation and to spending money.

EXPENDITURES: WHERE DOES THE MONEY GO?

State and local governments spend over $700 billion a year. This amounts to approximately 17 percent of the gross national product (GNP).[9] The GNP is a figure which is used to represent the total annual output of all the final goods and services in the national economy expressed in terms of market value.[10]

Government Contributions to the GNP

State and local government expenditures are not simply amounts of money taken from the economy. They are contributions to it, and understated contributions at that. State and local government contributions to the GNP are measured by the budgets, which include the salaries paid as well as the goods produced. The GNP does not measure all the value added (or preserved) by government action. The salaries of schoolteachers, for example, can be measured as part of the GNP. However, the value added to the sum total of knowledge and skill possessed by each student is not measured and thus cannot be included in the GNP. The years of productive tax-paying life added to individuals who are talked out of suicide or guided out of drug addiction by social workers or school counselors do not get included either, any more than does the value of the property and lives saved by police, fire, and emergency medical services.

The Growth of Government Spending

When this century began, national, state, and local governments combined spent about 8 percent of the GNP. By 1975 this figure was about 30 percent, and it has stayed at about that level ever since. Although the federal government accounts for much of the increase, the state-local portion more than doubled, from 5 percent to more than 12.

The growth of state and local spending both in percentage terms and in total sums is largely a result of social, economic, and technological changes, including the industrial and automotive revolutions discussed in Chapter 1. It is much more expensive to operate a heterogeneous metropolitan society than it is to operate a homogeneous rural society. Not only are there more people to serve, the metropolitan setting demands more types of services. Whether we need more units of government to offer them is a point we discussed in Chapter 5.

Economic growth is often accompanied by inflation, a factor that creates serious problems for budget makers. Between 1967 and 1984 the purchasing power of the dollar declined from 100 cents to 37 cents.

It is partly due to the efforts of the public management profession, political leaders, and citizen groups to make government more efficient that the decline in the purchasing power of the dollar has not led to a 63 percent increase in the cost of state and local government or an equivalent decline in services. Although some of those economies were in the form of more effective use of dollars, some involved passing on the costs of inflation to public servants, who in some years received the same paychecks but fewer groceries.

Major State and Local Functions: What We Pay For

The Council of State Governments has identified over 50 functions that are performed by many if not most state governments.[11] A recent study of city government identified a list of 67 functions performed by some but not all city governments.[12]

The three biggest state expenditures account for nearly 60 percent of the total. They are aid to local governments, welfare, and education. Welfare and education are also the services for which most state aid is intended. The three biggest local government expenditure items are education, public utilities, and public safety, which together account for over half of total local government expenditures.

In examining total figures, it is important to recall that there is a considerable variety of service offerings at the local level within any state and a considerable difference in the amount of state assistance given to local governments. Furthermore, states grant resources and assign responsibilities to local governments in different ways. Table 15.2 provides one indication of the variety of combinations of state and local services by indicating state shares of total state and local expenditures. The state participation in state-local spending ranges from 40 percent in Nebraska to 77 percent in North Dakota. Among the megastates the range is not that different. Texas spends 47 percent of state and local funds, while California spends 61 percent. Thus, wealth and economic development are not the reasons for this variation. As we've observed before, a great deal depends on the political system and the willingness of individuals to work within it.

In addition to the diversity of ways in which state and local governments share responsibility for offering services, there is considerable diversity in the services each state-local system offers. Table 15.3 provides a basis for comparing the 50 states in terms of the amount of money spent by each state government in certain major human investment areas. In addition to diversity among the several states, there is considerable diversity within individual states because local politics as well as state politics matters.

Table 15.2 STATE GOVERNMENT SPENDING IN 1986 AS A PERCENTAGE OF TOTAL STATE AND LOCAL GOVERNMENT SPENDING

State	State spending ($ thousands)	Total state and local spending ($ thousands)	State spending as a percentage of total
Nebraska	2,204,924	5,462,989	40.4
Florida	13,739,762	29,394,554	46.7
Texas	20,781,744	43,807,796	47.4
Tennessee	6,080,204	12,707,922	47.8
Arizona	5,047,152	10,291,312	49.3
Colorado	4,952,058	9,984,770	49.6
Georgia	8,530,053	16,213,375	52.6
Kansas	3,521,814	6,612,361	53.3
Utah	3,070,914	5,947,084	55.9
New York	43,138,967	76,861,262	56.1
Illinois	17,822,767	31,293,419	57.0
Oregon	4,925,280	8,499,419	57.9
Minnesota	8,581,248	14,730,853	58.3
New Hampshire	1,348,160	2,304,855	58.5
Missouri	6,476,921	10,970,494	59.0
South Carolina	9,396,491	15,486,619	60.5
Michigan	17,562,829	28,963,185	60.6
California	57,370,220	93,900,571	61.1
Indiana	7,548,021	12,311,297	61.3
Washington	9,668,571	15,745,160	61.4
Pennsylvania	19,010,295	31,135,025	61.9
Iowa	4,852,394	7,825,102	62.0
South Dakota	1,074,034	1,733,351	62.0
Maryland	8,131,927	12,965,809	62.7
Nevada	1,916,667	3,049,643	62.8
Virginia	8,872,739	14,126,323	62.8
Wisconsin	9,124,918	14,466,957	63.1
Alabama	6,437,616	10,169,956	63.3
Montana	1,642,736	2,561,911	64.1
Ohio	19,010,295	29,469,576	64.5
Massachusetts	12,449,251	19,268,076	64.6
Louisiana	8,217,991	12,659,176	64.9
Wyoming	1,632,973	2,518,039	64.9
Connecticut	6,009,104	9,219,723	65.2
Oklahoma	5,629,075	8,630,815	65.2
South Carolina	5,640,568	8,593,507	65.6
Mississippi	3,853,688	5,817,823	65.9
New Jersey	16,043,098	24,124,325	66.5
Idaho	1,516,579	2,246,995	67.5
Arkansas	3,355,403	4,947,605	67.8
Vermont	1,094,716	1,561,579	70.1
Kentucky	5,791,162	8,147,150	71.1
Maine	2,156,438	3,008,413	71.7

continued

Table 15.2   STATE GOVERNMENT SPENDING IN 1986 AS A PERCENTAGE OF TOTAL STATE AND
LOCAL GOVERNMENT SPENDING (continued)

State	State spending ($ thousands)	Total state and local spending ($ thousands)	State spending as a percentage of total
Delaware	1,415,325	1,965,750	72.0
Rhode Island	2,167,041	2,915,912	74.3
Alaska	4,220,878	5,666,498	74.5
New Mexico	3,300,139	4,369,471	75.5
West Virginia	3,621,314	4,795,160	75.5
Hawaii	2,471,954	3,253,506	76.0
North Dakota	1,537,190	2,002,744	76.8
U.S. total	481,173,750	783,192,890	61.4

Source: Texas House of Representatives, *Final Report: Select Committee on Tax Equity*, (Austin, TX: 1989), table 47.

Table 15.3   PER CAPITA STATE SPENDING AND RANKS FOR SELECTED FUNCTIONS: 1988

State	Education	Rank	Welfare	Rank	Hospital	Rank	Highways	Rank	Police	Rank
Alabama	736.28	14	167.19	49	109.83	7	165.97	35	12.04	40
Alaska	1809.90	1	585.80	2	49.82	39	836.04	1	64.72	1
Arizona	630.39	25	192.88	43	20.44	50	301.16	3	26.39	8
Arkansas	602.17	34	232.73	34	57.32	35	181.11	27	10.73	42
California	841.29	7	478.19	5	62.00	33	97.04	50	23.07	10
Colorado	630.03	26	242.70	30	75.35	23	176.46	28	10.59	43
Connecticut	562.37	40	379.60	11	168.65	1	227.48	13	24.36	9
Delaware	906.17	5	201.47	41	71.04	27	260.09	8	41.47	2
Florida	532.38	42	183.73	45	34.80	46	153.55	38	17.56	25
Georgia	623.42	29	255.80	28	72.18	25	152.71	39	16.28	29
Hawaii	803.94	9	290.80	23	104.25	8	105.09	48	3.30	50
Idaho	617.29	30	182.42	47	28.70	49	219.12	16	16.37	28
Illinois	513.34	45	328.21	18	45.29	41	167.14	34	15.45	33
Indiana	658.90	20	260.38	26	65.20	29	162.57	36	13.40	36
Iowa	784.13	10	291.39	22	95.91	14	248.05	10	11.56	41
Kansas	599.61	35	217.81	38	93.08	17	198.01	21	8.17	48
Kentucky	695.27	15	296.54	19	57.00	36	216.09	17	20.09	15
Louisiana	610.17	32	247.46	29	127.05	4	146.01	43	22.57	12
Maine	627.71	27	452.27	7	43.11	42	170.83	31	18.63	19
Maryland	524.31	44	330.51	17	63.29	31	269.36	6	39.90	3
Massachusetts	559.97	41	571.86	3	119.97	5	114.28	47	23.10	11
Michigan	661.87	19	466.47	6	99.01	13	133.82	45	18.00	23
Minnesota	762.86	11	389.87	9	103.41	9	205.79	18	17.62	24
Mississippi	605.87	33	235.98	31	71.81	26	150.41	40	12.93	38
Missouri	572.44	39	219.21	37	73.33	24	148.72	41	15.77	31
Montana	592.00	37	292.71	21	41.56	43	276.21	5	19.38	17

continued

Table 15.3 PER CAPITA STATE SPENDING AND RANKS FOR SELECTED FUNCTIONS: 1988 (continued)

State	Education	Rank	Welfare	Rank	Hospital	Rank	Highways	Rank	Police	Rank
Nebraska	466.86	48	260.38	27	93.72	15	224.09	14	16.17	30
Nevada	653.52	22	146.34	50	34.30	48	199.27	20	15.69	32
New Hampshire	616.37	31	233.06	33	49.04	40	186.31	24	18.37	20
New Jersey	920.81	3	365.44	14	88.63	18	204.93	19	34.38	5
New Mexico	680.24	17	233.17	32	102.47	10	242.22	12	20.82	13
New York	307.21	50	682.99	1	160.35	2	102.10	49	19.54	16
North Carolina	748.13	13	206.80	40	77.41	22	169.00	33	17.06	26
North Dakota	819.34	8	351.37	16	87.65	19	282.01	4	10.24	44
Ohio	581.89	38	375.26	12	80.86	20	148.69	42	9.94	47
Oklahoma	639.59	24	289.08	24	78.24	21	190.68	22	12.57	39
Oregon	529.44	43	227.30	35	93.28	16	188.10	23	20.19	14
Pennsylvania	488.48	47	385.71	10	70.97	28	184.46	25	18.32	21
Rhode Island	626.82	28	504.44	4	119.97	6	159.51	37	18.74	18
South Carolina	428.40	49	183.57	46	101.70	11	145.17	44	18.14	22
South Dakota	688.64	16	215.19	39	36.85	45	222.77	15	15.13	34
Tennessee	492.31	46	292.91	20	64.64	30	174.70	29	9.98	46
Texas	599.03	36	173.63	48	58.82	34	169.99	32	10.18	45
Utah	851.63	6	219.38	36	100.97	12	172.63	30	14.27	35
Vermont	753.59	12	367.37	13	40.69	44	243.15	11	34.16	6
Virginia	658.15	21	195.30	42	129.75	3	257.87	9	36.50	4
Washington	917.17	4	353.95	15	62.19	32	182.38	26	16.84	27
West Virginia	678.69	18	260.98	25	34.80	47	260.74	7	13.12	37
Wisconsin	651.62	23	409.11	8	56.05	37	133.13	46	6.88	49
Wyoming	1013.61	2	191.20	44	55.63	38	472.17	2	29.15	7

Source: U.S. Department of Commerce, Bureau of the Census, *State Government Finances in 1988* (Washington, DC: U.S. Government Printing Office, 1989), 51.

While Table 15.3 provides some idea of the tremendous variation in the willingness of states to spend money on various services, Table 15.4 indicates the variety of services offered by several major cities. Clark and Ferguson developed a measure of municipal service offerings called the **functional performance index,**[13] which takes into account differences in the cost of services as well as the number of services offered. Thus, the index score takes into consideration the fact that some services are more expensive than others. Collecting solid waste, for example, is much more labor intensive and involves more equipment and land than does sweeping the streets. A low functional performance score may mean that a city offers few expensive services or some inexpensive ones, whereas a high score indicates a fairly comprehensive offering of all or nearly all 67 types of major services.

Table 15.4 is instructive not only because it indicates the wide range of service efforts put forth by various cities in general but also because it provides an example of the variation within a single state. In California,

Table 15.4 FUNCTIONAL PERFORMANCE SCORES FOR EIGHTEEN MAJOR CITIES

City, State	Functional performance score*
Baltimore, MD	567
Boston, MA	409
Chicago, IL	98
Cleveland, OH	64
Detroit, MI	158
Fort Worth, TX	31
Houston, TX	38
Indianapolis, IN	211
Jacksonville, FL	182
Los Angeles, CA	78
Memphis, TN	294
Milwaukee, WI	65
New York, NY	583
Philadelphia, PA	193
Phoenix, AZ	73
St. Louis, MO	142
San Francisco, CA	250
San Jose, CA	44

*Functional performance scores take into account the fact that some services are more expensive than others; thus, the *type* of as well as the *number* of services is reflected in each city's score.

Source: Terry Nichols Clark and Lorna Crowley Ferguson, *City Money: Political Processes, Fiscal Strains, and Retrenchment* (New York: Columbia University Press, 1983), 53. Reprinted by permission.

three cities — San Francisco, Los Angeles, and San Jose — have considerably different levels of service offerings.

The study in which the functional performance index was developed was conducted after New York City teetered on the brink of bankruptcy in 1975. There was a great deal of concern at the time that all the older Eastern cities might face similar problems as a result of increased service loads and declining tax bases. Clark and Ferguson examined demographic, financial, and political data on over 50 cities across the country to determine the causes of and solutions to **fiscal strain**, the inability to meet debt and expenditure obligations with existing revenues.[14]

Their major finding was that the process of urban decay is neither irreversible nor automatic. As Table 15.4 indicates, Baltimore and Boston are Northeastern cities with functional performance scores similar to that of New York. However, neither Baltimore nor Boston experienced the financial crises that New York did in the 1970s, even though they experienced some of the same problems in terms of job losses and demographic changes. According to Clark and Ferguson, the major reason for the financial stability of Baltimore and Boston was political leadership. Political leadership, even in cities with high service offerings, can deal successfully with fiscal strain.

Fiscal strain determinants are twofold, including both city fiscal policies and private sector resources. Informed analysts should consider each. Our twofold approach shows that population and job loss can bring fiscal strain, but only if local leaders do not adapt. To write off most older northeastern cities as "poor risks" is an enormous simplification, denigrating local leaders by assuming that they cannot adapt to private sector changes.[15]

The ability of leaders to lead depends in part on their personal abilities. Individuals matter, as we've noted a time or two. Leadership is also influenced by the nature of the political system in which they operate. Thus, political culture and political institutions are major factors in determining whether a particular state or local government will make a major or a minimal effort within the confines of available resources to offer social services and promote redistribution.

THE REVENUE SYSTEM

Our treatment of revenue will be somewhat more extensive than that of spending for at least three reasons: (1) the antitax bias of the American political culture, (2) the unfairness of the tax system in nearly every state, and (3) the need to deal with unfamiliar terms and concepts that are critical for an informed analysis of budget issues. In this section we will examine some of the major sources of revenue, with particular attention to eight tax sources identified by the Advisory Commission on Intergovernmental Relations (ACIR), ten criteria for evaluating state-local revenue systems identified by the National Conference of State Legislatures, and two useful analytical concepts developed by the ACIR for comparing and contrasting state and local revenue systems.

About half of state and local government revenue comes from the first item listed in Box 15-4: taxes. The percentage of revenue based on taxes rises to 63 percent when we include the 14 percent contributed by grants-in-aid which are paid for by federal taxes. Thus taxes are far and away the largest single source of state and local revenue. Even a portion of the category, "charges and miscellaneous," includes a variety of user fees and other transactions, some of which are virtually the same as taxes.[16]

Thus we will focus most of our attention on the major revenue source — taxes — and leave for your term papers an exploration of sources such as speed traps (fines and fees) and gambling (lotteries and pari-mutuel betting) as ways of raising revenue. As noted earlier, we focus on taxes not only because they are the major source of revenue but also because they are levied so unfairly in most states. Examining the fairness or unfairness of the sytem by which we pay for our governments seems worth including in a text dedicated to promoting informed and enlightened participation in the politics of the state and local government.

Box 15-4 **Revenue Sources for State and Local Governments**

1. Eight types of taxes: general sales, selected sales, licenses and fees, property, corporate income, personal income, severance, and estate and gift

2. Intergovernmental transfers, such as grants-in-aid and shared taxes

3. A wide variety of government enterprises, such as utilities and transit systems, toll roads and bridges, and state-owned liquor stores

4. The sale of monopoly rights or franchises to enterprises such as cable, taxi, and utility companies

5. The rent or sale of assets, such as land, buildings, and trees, coal, and other natural resources

6. Interest on money invested

7. Fines and penalties

8. Borrowing, usually but not always from wealthy individuals, insurance companies, and mutual investment funds

9. Fees or assessments for services such as park admission, survey work, and snow removal and improvements such as curbs and road construction

---

No New Taxes: The Promise of Free Lunches

One of the most potent political slogans in America is "no new taxes." This appeals to different categories of individuals for entirely different reasons. The net effect of the slogan is usually to preserve the biases built into the existing sytem of taxes and expenditures — the status quo.

For example, if our tax system relies largely on a percentage of what we spend, then those who can live comfortably without spending all they earn have an advantage: They have money left over each year to devote to untaxed activities such as speculating, saving, and investing. If we allow individuals and businesses to deduct from their taxable income (as business expenses) the money spent giving gifts (honoraria, fees, campaign contributions) directly or indirectly to public officials in order to gain access to them, we further bias the taxation system (and the political system) in the direction of those with money to pay for honoraria, fees, and helicopter rides.

To individuals who are disadvantaged by the biases of the status quo — the have-nots — the slogan "no new taxes" promises that their current tax burden will not be made even worse. Thus they are encouraged to believe that the tax rates affecting them won't increase if the "no new taxes" candidate is elected. In virtually every state, the poor and the middle class bear a heavier tax burden than do the rich.[17] Since there are so many poor people and since this unfairness is so widespread, the "no new taxes" message has a ready mass audience.

To those who are given advantages by the status quo, "no new taxes" means that there will be no changes in the current mix of taxes. No new *types* of taxes (there are about eight basic types) will be introduced, nor will the emphasis on particular types be changed. The message to them is that the distribution of burdens will not be reformed in the direction of fairness. Obviously, many of the rich are not too excited about such changes. To put it another way, they are highly motivated to contribute to the campaigns of "no new taxes" candidates.

Lest we be accused of fomenting class warfare here, we hasten to point out that in many states and communities the effort to make the taxation system more equitable has been led by wealthy individuals who know their taxes will go up if the biases in the taxation system are changed.

From the mid-1970s onward, the slogan "no new taxes" has been elevated to the level of a credibility test for political candidates from the White House to the county courthouse. One of the ironies of this slogan is that compared with the citizens of other industrialized nations, Americans are not heavily taxed. Table 15.5 represents the percentage of GNP paid in taxes to all levels of government during 1985 in 20 industrial nations.

The modern antitax movement began quietly in about 1974 in several medium-size cities across the country. It was particularly strong in cities with a high proportion of middle-class voters who, though liberal in the sense of supporting individualism, tolerance, and freedom of opportunity, were conservative in terms of using government funds to solve social problems. In 1978 the media focused on Proposition 13 in California, which was directed at property taxes, and the antitax movement gained national attention.[18] The fact that property taxes in general have ceased to be an accurate indicator of an individual's wealth was not the focus of the antitax movement; the supporters of the movement were not interested in reforming the system of taxation. In effect it was both an antigovernment and an antitax movement. Instead of making the system of paying for government more just, it sought to reduce both taxes and government.

According to Clark and Ferguson, "no new taxes" is part of the political culture learned by many Americans:

> Americans revolt against taxes when the tax bite is still lower than in many other countries. National factors reinforce fiscal conservatism for Americans: the absence of a feudal past, the correspondingly egalitarian ideology, individualist Protestantism, the frontier with vast areas of individual farming (reinforcing isolation), abundance of natural resources, isolation from other countries, and few wars.[19]

The Reagan and Bush administrations have certainly helped reinforce the antitax, antigovernment dimension of our culture. One of the promises

Table 15.5   TAX REVENUES AND GNP IN SELECTED NATIONS: 1985

Nation	Tax revenues as a percentage of 1985 GNP
United States	29.2
Australia	30.3
Austria	42.5
Belgium	46.9
Canada	33.1
Denmark	49.2
Finland	37.3
France	45.6
Greece	35.1
Italy	34.7
Japan	28.0
Netherlands	45.0
New Zealand	34.3
Norway	47.8
Portugal	31.1
Spain	28.8
Sweden	50.5
Switzerland	32.1
United Kingdom	38.1
West Germany	37.8

Source: U.S. Bureau of the Census, *Statistical Abstract of the United States, 1988* (Washington, DC: Government Printing Office, 1989).

of Reagan's 1980 campaign was to "get government off our backs." By continuing to spend at previous rates after cutting taxes, the Reagan administration at least indirectly promoted the notion that there really is such a thing as a free lunch. "Read my lips, 'No new taxes,'" a 1988 Bush campaign theme, has perpetuated this notion.

The price of policies based on the free-lunch myth is indicated in part by the fact that each year we now pay $100 billion more in interest on the national debt than we did in 1979.[20] In the absence of new revenue, the only way to pay for the tripling of the national debt has been to cut other programs. The effect of tax cuts for the rich and program cuts for the poor has been a massive eight-year shift toward the reinforcement of inequality.[21] Furthermore, since 87 percent of the national debt is owed to the wealthy American citizens and financial institutions that buy government bonds, the debt has reinforced inequality further. According to Heilbroner and Bernstein, two respected economists,

> It seems fair to say, therefore, that the government debt is a net expense for the lower three-quarters of the nation, and a net benefit for the upper one-quarter. Thus one very real but largely overlooked aspect of the interest burden lies in its impact on the distribution of income.[22]

The rest of the nation now provides interest income for the wealthiest one-quarter. At the same time social programs to aid the poorest quarter have been significantly reduced. State and local governments are now in the process of attempting to cope with the consequences of this shift toward inequality. Some governments, as we shall see, are trying harder than others.

Types of State and Local Taxes

According to the Advisory Commission on Intergovernmental Relations, virtually all tax sources used by state and local governments fall into one of eight categories: general sales, selective sales, licenses and fees, property, personal income, corporate income, estate and gift, and severance. Table 15.6 indicates the percentage of total tax revenue collected by state and local governments that each of these sources represents.

General Sales   This is a tax on the gross receipts of all retail sales. The tax is collected at the point of sale, and the business then pays the state on a monthly or quarterly basis. The state then allocates the local government share, if any.

Selected Sales   This tax is imposed on particular kinds of commodities. Among the items most frequently subjected to a selected sales tax are motor fuels, alcoholic beverages, tobacco products, insurance premiums, public utility bills, amusements, and pari-mutuel gambling.

Licenses and Fees   These taxes are levied at a flat rate in order to raise revenue and/or regulate. Among the most frequently taxed subjects are

Table 15.6   COMPONENTS OF THE REPRESENTATIVE REVENUE SYSTEM IN 1986

Tax source	Percentage of total
General sales taxes	19.6
Selective sales taxes	8.5
License taxes	2.8
Personal income taxes	16.1
Corporate income taxes	4.3
Property taxes	24.2
Estate and gift taxes	0.6
Severance taxes	1.4
Other taxes	3.4
Rents and royalties	1.6
Mineral leasing	0.1
User charges	17.4
Total	100.0

Source: Advisory Commission on Intergovernmental Relations, *State Fiscal Capacity and Effort: 1986*, (Washington, DC: ACIR, 1989), 4.

motor vehicles, motor vehicle operators, corporations, various occupations, firms engaged in the manufacture or distribution of alcoholic beverages, and hunting and fishing permits.

Property   There are three types of property: (1) real estate (land and improvements on it), (2) movable property (cars, paintings or home furnishings, equipment, and unsold commercial inventory), and (3) intangible property (stocks, bonds, securities, and other paper claims on wealth).

Many taxing authorities classify property according to its economic use. A frequently used scheme includes four categories of taxable property: residential, commercial, agricultural, and public utility. Each category may be taxed at different rates. Some categories, such as commercial, include real property and movable property such as heavy equipment.[23]

Personal Income   This is a tax on the net annual income of an individual after certain deductions are allowed. It is levied only on one's income. The principle of taxing according to income or ability to pay sometimes is employed in administering other taxes. Agricultural land in some states is taxed not on its market value (which may be quite high) but on the income derived from the crops or livestock raised on it (which may not be very much).

In 31 states property tax relief for people with low incomes is provided by means of **circuit breaker laws**, which limit the amount of property tax that can be collected on an individual's home or apartment. The circuit breaker is a percentage of the resident's income that can be collected in property tax regardless of the market value of the residence. After the specified percentage of income is reached, the property tax is turned off, just as circuit breakers cut off electricity when the load the wires must carry becomes too heavy.

In 25 of the states that use it, the circuit breaker applies to renters as well. It is assumed that a specific percentage of a tenant's annual renal payment represents the landlord's effort to pass on all or part of the property tax. In those states the elderly or disabled cannot be asked to pay more than a fixed percentage (from 15 to 25 percent) of their net income in property taxes whether they own or rent.[24]

Corporate Income   This is a tax on the net income or profits of a corporation or business firm. A corporation or firm with no profits pays no income tax. Most states levy this type of tax, and most firms prefer it to a corporate franchise or license tax which must be paid regardless of the profitability of the business in a given year.

Estate and Gift   These taxes are imposed on the transfer of property by gift or via a will. They are usually levied on large estates.

Severance   This tax is levied on the act of removing natural mineral products from the ground. The most common items taxed are coal, oil, and gas.

Determining the Mix

Numerous patterns emerge from the variety of ways in which several thousand state and local governments make use of the eight types of taxes. There are differences in the rates charged for each particular tax and in the exemptions or relief allowed. Some units of government do not use certain taxes at all. Six states do not tax corporate incomes, and ten do not tax net personal incomes.[25] Most states have vacated the property tax, leaving it as a revenue source for local governments. In many states certain taxes, such as sales or personal income, are optional for particular local governments.

There are two important taxation patterns. The first is the tendency for certain types of governments to use certain types of taxes. States rely largely on income and sales taxes, general-purpose local governments (municipalities, counties, and townships) rely largely on property and sales taxes, and school districts in all but a few states rely most exclusively on property taxes.[26]

The second important feature of any state-local tax system is the dominance of state government. Although the economy and the federal government have a significant influence on state and local revenues, the major source of decisions about the state-local tax mix is the state government, especially the state legislature. State governments have the power to levy taxes; limit, grant, or deny tax sources to local governments; and require local governments to perform functions that require revenue. Any discussion of reforming or evaluating the state-local revenue system in the 50 states tends to focus on the institutions empowered to change the entire system—the state legislatures and the governors.

Ten Characteristics of a Good State-Local Revenue System

According to the National Council of State Legislatures, a good state-local revenue system has ten characteristics. Although some of their criteria require more elaboration than do others, all are worth some attention.[27] In evaluating revenue systems, we naturally focus on taxes, the major source of state and local government revenue. Most of the following concepts can be applied to particular types of taxes as well as to entire revenue systems.

Coherence A high-quality state-local revenue system should consist of elements that function well together as a logical system. The state legislature, which is the major revenue policymaker, should design a reporting system to monitor the effects of state tax decisions on both the economy and local governments. Particular attention should be paid first to the *exemptions* that the state requires local governments to grant on property taxes. To be exempt is to be excused from an obligation. In many states the legislature declares that certain kinds of property or a portion of the value (the first $5000, for example) of property is exempt from taxation. If a state prevents local governments from using other tax sources, a property tax exemption can lead to serious reduction in the tax base of a local government. When a legislature requires (mandates) local governments to offer new or expanded services at the same time it cuts their revenue base, the legislature is putting these local governments in a double bind.

Reliability   A high-quality revenue system should produce revenue in a reliable manner. Reliability involves stability, certainty, and sufficiency.

Stability means that a tax system should not reinforce downturns in the economy and should help siphon excess income in inflationary times. Taxes on income and sales do this; taxes on property and various per unit taxes such as licenses do not.

Certainty means that there is a high probability that the tax yield will remain the same from year to year. Taxes on selected items that are not likely to be purchased in poor economic times fail to meet the certainty criterion. A sales tax system that is narrowly based also may fail to meet this criterion. In poor economic times discretionary income for luxury items, clothing, and home furnishings is reduced, but various services and necessities are still purchased. A broadly based sales tax thus promotes certainty.

Sufficiency means that a revenue system includes enough taxes to pay for the services and programs that the community feels are appropriate. A sufficient or adequate tax system should make use of taxes that grow at least as fast as the economy does.

Diversity   A high-quality revenue system should have substantial diversification of revenue sources over reasonably broad bases. A diverse revenue system should use a variety of taxes which require every sector of the economy to contribute. The ACIR recommends that a state-local tax system have the following mix of taxes: Sales and property taxes should constitute 20 to 30 percent of total revenue, personal income taxes should supply 20 to 35 percent, and the remainder should come from a combination of corporate taxes, user fees, and selective sales taxes.[28]

Equity   A high-quality revenue system should be fair. The minimum aspects of an equitable system are that (1) it shields genuine subsistence income from taxation, (2) it is proportionate or progressive, not regressive, and (3) horizontal equity should be observed; that is, all households with the same income should pay approximately the same tax.[29]

Subsistence means barely adequate to meet the most basic needs: shelter, food, and clothing. Medical care, recreation, education, and transportation, though essential to getting and keeping a job, are seldom provided by a subsistence income. It is impossible to shield a subsistence income from a sales tax, but there a methods for shielding the poor from the effects of other types of taxes. Circuit breakers can reduce the effects of a property tax on the poor. Using some kind of income tax and then exempting those below a certain income level would increase the dependence of a tax system on the ability to pay rather than the necessity to spend.

Vertical equity means that individuals in all income categories bear the same burden (not the same size tax bill). The **tax burdern** is the percentage of one's income paid in taxes. This is also known as the *effective rate* (ER).[30] Vertical equity is sometimes referred to as the ability to pay.

Table 15.7 shows the distribution of the ability to pay in the U.S. economy. The total population is divided into five categories of families according to income received in 1986. Each *quintile*, or 20 percent, of the population contains the same number of people. However, the quintiles do not receive the same amount of income.

The poorest 20 percent of the population received 4.6 percent of the total personal income earned in 1986. Thus, their ability to pay taxes for solving problems is rather limited. This quintile included an estimated 32.4 million persons below the poverty level. As you may recall from Chapter 13, the poverty level in 1986 was $5572 for an individual and $11,203 for a family of four.

By contrast, the top quintile, although constituting only 20 percent of the population, received 43.7 percent of the total personal income earned in the United States. The ability of this group to pay taxes is greater than that of the bottom three categories combined.

Thus, as Table 15.7 suggests, the percentage of the total income acquired by each of the income categories (or classes) leaves some people with a much greater ability to pay than others.

Beyond the notion of "soak the rich," which is always appealing to those of us who aren't, there are three justifications for employing vertical equity as a principle on which to base a tax system:

1. Those with high incomes have more to lose if a mutually agreed upon system of law and order, enforcement of contracts, and protection of property breaks down. Therefore, they should pay a larger amount — but not necessarily a higher percentage of their income — to maintain this system.

Table 15.7   DISTRIBUTION OF ABILITY TO PAY AMONG FIVE CATEGORIES OF U.S. HOUSEHOLDS

Category	Top income in category ($)	Percentage of total personal income in U.S. received by individuals in category*
Top 20%	Over 100,000,000	43.7
Second 20%	50,370	24.0
Third 20%	35,015	16.8
Fourth 20%	24,020	10.8
Fifth 20%	13,886	4.6

*Figures do not add up to 100 because of rounding.

Source: U.S. Bureau of the Census, *Current Population Reports, 1986*, (Washington, DC: U.S. Government Printing Office, 1987).

2. Those with high incomes have more to spend after paying for the basic necessities. Therefore, their *surplus* is being taxed, not their food, shelter, and clothing budgets, as in the case of a subsistence income.

3. Many of those with high incomes would willingly contribute a proportionate share of their income to pay for society but are reluctant to do this unless the rest of those with high incomes do so as well. Therefore, a taxation system requires everyone to do what some would do anyway.

Since efforts by human beings to reach a target such as tax equity do not always hit dead center, we use three additional terms in discussing vertical equity: proportionate, regressive, and progressive. A **proportionate tax** or tax system is one that hits the target of vertical equity. This type of tax system requires each individual to contribute to the cost of government in proportion to income received. In a proportionate tax system each individual bears the same tax burden, that is, has the same effective tax rate.

The other two systems depart from proportionality in opposite directions. A **regressive tax** system misses the target of proportionality by favoring the top income categories. The burden gets lighter as income increases. A **progressive system** misses the target in the direction of redistribution. The burden increases as income increases. The tax burden is lighter for the poor and heavier for the rich.

According to Donald Phares, who has done extensive research on tax equity among the states, all local tax systems are regressive, and only three states have progressive systems (California, Delaware, and Iowa). In only one state (Delaware) is the total state-local system even mildly progressive. Table 15.8 compares state-local tax systems using an index developed by Daniel B. Suits.[31] Using the most recent data available, Phares calculated the index scores for local, state, and state-local tax systems. According to this index, a score of −1 means that a tax system is totally regressive in that the have-nots pay the entire tax bill. An index score of +1 is completely progressive. Although recent tax law revisions in some states may alter the scores slightly, the basic pattern is unlikely to change unless significant tax reforms are instituted to move state-local tax systems in the direction of equity or perhaps even progressivity.[32]

The regressive nature of most state-local tax systems is largely associated with the types of taxes used in a state-local tax system (as well as the rates, which emphasize some taxes more than others). Regressive systems tend to depend on property and sales taxes. Progressive systems may use these taxes but depend to a much greater extent on corporate and personal income taxes.

Although it may be obvious that a tax on incomes will be proportionate or slightly progressive, the regressive impact of sales and property taxes is not quite so apparent. Property tax regressivity occurs because the value of one's residential property is often unrelated to one's income. For example, many elderly people on a modest retirement income who live in a house they bought 30 years ago are faced with an unpleasant consequence of urban

Table 15.8   EQUITY OF STATE TAX SYSTEMS*

State	Total state taxes	Total local taxes	Total state and local taxes
Alabama	−0.09	−0.15	−0.10
Alaska	−0.04	−0.08	−0.05
Arizona	−0.09	−0.12	−0.10
Arkansas	−0.08	−0.12	−0.09
California	0.04	−0.12	−0.04
Colorado	−0.04	−0.11	−0.07
Connecticut	−0.02	−0.13	−0.06
Delaware	0.06	−0.11	0.02
Florida	−0.13	−0.12	−0.11
Georgia	−0.05	−0.11	−0.07
Hawaii	0.00	−0.11	−0.03
Idaho	−0.03	−0.07	−0.04
Illinois	−0.04	−0.08	−0.06
Indiana	−0.04	−0.09	−0.06
Iowa	0.02	−0.08	−0.02
Kansas	−0.03	−0.07	−0.04
Kentucky	−0.03	−0.13	−0.05
Louisiana	−0.07	−0.07	−0.07
Maine	−0.04	−0.17	−0.07
Maryland	−0.04	−0.11	−0.06
Massachusetts	0.01	−0.16	−0.06
Michigan	0.01	−0.12	−0.06
Minnesota	0.04	−0.15	−0.02
Mississippi	−0.09	−0.14	−0.10
Missouri	−0.04	−0.14	−0.08
Montana	0.00	−0.07	−0.04
Nebraska	0.00	−0.07	−0.04
Nevada	−0.09	−0.11	−0.09
New Hampshire	−0.06	−0.18	−0.12
New Jersey	−0.03	−0.17	−0.10
New Mexico	−0.09	−0.15	−0.10
New York	0.07	−0.10	−0.02
North Carolina	−0.04	−0.11	−0.05
North Dakota	−0.02	−0.07	−0.04
Ohio	−0.01	−0.11	−0.05
Oklahoma	−0.03	−0.11	−0.06
Oregon	0.05	−0.10	−0.03
Pennsylvania	−0.01	−0.16	−0.06
Rhode Island	−0.01	−0.13	−0.06
South Carolina	−0.05	−0.12	−0.06
South Dakota	−0.08	−0.08	−0.08
Tennessee	−0.08	−0.10	−0.09
Texas	−0.13	−0.06	−0.09
Utah	−0.03	−0.14	−0.07
Vermont	0.00	−0.20	−0.07

continued

Table 15.8 EQUITY OF STATE TAX SYSTEMS* (continued)

State	Total state taxes	Total local taxes	Total state and local taxes
Virginia	−0.06	−0.12	−0.08
Washington	−0.06	−0.10	−0.07
West Virginia	−0.07	−0.10	−0.07
Wisconsin	0.02	−0.14	−0.03
Wyoming	−0.11	−0.04	−0.07
U.S. average	−0.04	−0.12	−0.07

*Index scores range from a completely progressive +1 to a completely regressive −1. Proportionality is 0.00.

Source: Donald Phares, "State and Local Tax Burdens Across the Fifty States," *Growth and Change* (April 1985), 39.

growth. When they bought that home, it was in a residential neighborhood on the edge of the city, but now it may occupy prime commercial land. Since land and property are taxed at their market value, these older citizens have property tax bills that do not reflect their income. For a significant portion of our population, the value of the property they own increases faster than their income does.

Many homeowners regard property taxes as being almost as obnoxious as the federal income tax. Roger J. Vaughn observes that the problem exists at least partially because only real estate is taxed. The value of stocks, bonds, paintings, jewelry, and expensive home furnishings are not taxed.

> Tax payers, angry about spiralling property taxes, have a hard time knowing who to blame—the assessor, the school board, the city council, or the county board. But much of the blame must be borne by the inequity of the tax itself. Real estate, the only real asset for low and moderate-income households, is but a small share of the assets of the relatively affluent. Yet property taxes are usually limited to real estate, making the tax relatively regressive.[33]

The property tax may lead to inequities in the business community as well. A business which owns a lot of expensive heavy equipment may have a higher tax burden than does one which makes the same profit without using equipment.

Sales tax regressivity occurs not only because it is administratively impossible to shield the poor from its effects but also because virtually the entire income of a poor family is subject to the sales tax. Poor families must spend all their income each year simply to feed, shelter, and clothe themselves. A wealthy family, even though it enjoys a higher standard of consumption (steaks instead of hot dogs, exclusive restaurants instead of fast food), will still have a goodly portion of its income available for investment, speculation, and savings, which usually are not subject to a sales tax.

Even in the 21 states where sales of food and prescription drugs are tax-exempt, the relief provided by this exemption reduces but does not remove regressivity. Next time you check your grocery bill, note the relatively modest portion of it actually devoted to food. In states with sales taxes, the rest of one's grocery bill — aspirin, shampoo, soap, dog food, paper towels, scouring powder, and so on—is subject to the tax. Furthermore, while grocery store food is not taxed, restaurant food is. In the interest of sanity, working mothers are likely to treat their families to occasional fast-food meals. Thus, a poor family's food budget is not exempt from taxation.

Horizontal equity means that people in the same income category are taxed at the same rate regardless of where they live. Not only is there economic inequality among states, there are also inequalities within states. Local governments differ considerably in terms of their ability to pay for services because they do not have equal tax bases. A school district which is able to raise revenue because it is located over a large pool of oil will not have to tax homes and businesses at a very high rate. A school district or city with little or no valuable commercial or industrial land will have to levy a higher tax rate on residential property.

The difference in tax bases of local governments is sometimes called **fiscal disparity**. Within the federal system, the national government and many state governments have made an attempt to take fiscal disparities into account in designing grant-in-aid programs. A major issue in many state legislatures is whether enough of an effort has been made by the state to deal with fiscal disparities which lead to inequalities in educational opportunity, health care, and other social services.

The consequences of fiscal disparities within any particular state can be reduced if the state government is willing to provide grants, share revenue, or pay for the cost of certain services. A study by the ACIR on the extent to which state expenditure patterns reduce interjurisdictional fiscal disparities indicated considerable variation among the states. State payments were classified as reducing fiscal differences if they directly or indirectly dealt with welfare and Medicaid or were based on local needs such as large school populations.

The states use a variety of methods for promoting horizontal equity. Some states have attempted to reduce disparities with revenue-sharing programs such as that used in North Dakota. In that state 5 percent of state income tax revenue is reserved for a program which distributes funds to local governments according to their level of poverty and the size of the population in the jurisdiction.[34] Massachusetts has assumed full fiscal responsibility for local court costs. The Minnesota Fiscal Disparities Act provides that all additions to the commercial real estate tax base be shared among the local governments in that metropolitan area. In Hawaii, there are no local school districts; education is funded completely by the state.

Efficiency   Within this criterion the National Association of Legislatures includes four related concepts. The first two are closely related: First, the tax system should be understandable to the taxpayer; second, it should be easy to comply with. There should not be a lot of complicated forms and a variety of different tax payment deadlines. One reason for the popularity of the sales tax is that it is relatively easy for a member of the general public to pay and does not require complicated calculations or forms. Income taxes, by contrast, often require a fair amount of emotional distress and intellectual effort. The complexity and effort are at least partially responsible for the fact that the federal income tax is consistently viewed as the least fair of the five major taxes collected in the intergovernmental system, even though, according to the ability-to-pay standard, it is one of the most fair. As Table 15.9 shows, the state income tax is viewed the most favorably. Thus, the public is not resistant to being taxed according to ability to pay. It's the difficulty of understanding and other dimensions of inefficiency that seem to bother people.

The third dimension of administrative efficiency includes the notion of low administrative costs. In a tax system that is administratively efficient, the tax can be collected without using most of the returns to pay for collecting it. This is another reason why property taxes are not popular. The property tax involves a series of labor-intensive steps every year for each piece of property in a taxing jurisdiction, as Box 15-5 indicates. Few tax systems would be as expensive to set up from scratch today as the property tax system.

Lotteries and pari-mutuel betting are often recommended as nontax revenue sources. Although the issues are too complex to deal with here, it is instructive to consider the amount of the "take" in a lottery system which is used up in prizes and administration (as well as advertising to promote the sale of lottery tickets, an activity whose appropriateness is worth some thought). After prizes and administrative costs, about 40 percent of lottery ticket sales are left for the state treasury.[35] Few other taxes would be used very long if 60 percent of the take was devoted to collection costs.

The fourth characteristic of an efficient tax sytem is that it does not unnecessarily interfere with private economic decisions such as home improvements, industry location, individual savings, and business investment. An economically efficient system should be competitive with tax systems in

Table 15.9　RESPONDENTS' ANSWER TO "WHICH DO YOU THINK IS THE WORST TAX—THAT IS, THE LEAST FAIR?"

Type of tax	1988 (%)	1983 (%)	1980 (%)
Federal income tax	26	35	36
Social Security tax	17	0	0
Local property tax	24	26	25
State sales tax	15	13	19
State income tax	9	11	10
Don't know	9	15	9*

*Figures may not sum to 100 because of rounding.

Source: ACIR, *Changing Attitudes on Government Taxes 1988*, (Washington, DC: U.S. Government Printing Office, 1988), 22.

Box 15-5 **Collecting the Property Tax**

1. Inspect to see if improvements have increased the market value.

2. Calculate the market value.

3. Notify the owner of the appraised value.

4. Convene an appeals board to hear appeals for changes in appraisal.

5. Render decisions on appeals and deal with the consequences, sometimes lawsuits.

6. Taxing authority holds a public hearing to discuss the tax rate. If the authority intends to raise the tax rate, notification must be published in newspapers and hearings must be scheduled.

7. Taxing authority deliberates and sets a tax rate. After the tax rate is set, there may be a referendum to reverse it (sometimes called a rollback election).

8. After a waiting period for rollback petitions has elapsed, hold the referendum (election) and await the results.

9. Alternatively, calculate the tax bill.

10. Distribute the tax bills.

11. Administer appeals.

12. Alternatively, verify documentation of applications for exemptions such as circuit breakers, homestead exemptions, and farm and ranch property exemptions.

13. Record and deposit the payments.

14. Collect delinquent payments.

other states or communities without relying heavily on tax incentives that favor certain businesses or industries over others or on industry-specific taxes that treat one type of business—telecommunications, utilities, banks—differently from others.

Accountability A high-quality revenue system should be explicit. There should be no hidden tax increases. There should be a notification and appeals process such as the one we have described. Many states now have "truth in taxation" laws that local taxing authorities must follow. However, few state legislatures deal adequately with the impact of their own decisions on local governments. Thus, state mandates requiring expensive administrative procedures or requiring that new services be offered at the local level are not always funded adequately by the legislature.

One way of improving accountability is to publish **fiscal notes** as part of all proposed state laws. A fiscal note is an estimate of the cost of the proposed law to the state or local government. The note alerts local governments and their state associations to attend hearings and propose alternatives or work for appropriations to reimburse expenditures. Otherwise, the local governments must raise local taxes to pay for the state-mandated actions or cut existing services.

Tax expenditure reports are another way to promote accountability.[36] A tax expenditure is the amount of revenue lost by granting an exemption to a tax. Every year interest groups for particular firms or industries seek specific exemptions from various taxes. Some of the loopholes created involve considerable costs to the government. In many cases the problem that the exemption is supposed to solve could be dealt with more efficiently and simply by a spending or loan program.[37]

Effectiveness A high-quality revenue system should be administered professionally and uniformly both throughout the state and within individual jurisdictions. Saving money by paying auditors, appraisers, and tax analysts poorly or by failing to provide adequate resources such as computers, software, and staff is a false economy. If the public becomes aware that some individuals are able to escape their fair share of the agreed upon tax burden, revenues may drop off and the system will become even more expensive to repair later.

One of the criticisms of the use of sales taxes with numerous exemptions is that the average convenience store clerk becomes the person who decides whether certain goods are taxable. The use of amateur tax collectors results in a variety of tax bills with little relationship to the law or to fairness or efficiency. A local NBC reporter was charged seven different amounts of sales tax on the same basket of goods in seven different pharmacies in New York, where the state exempts "drugs and medicines" from the sales tax. Confusion arose from anomalies such as the fact that sterilized cotton is exempt while nonsterilized cotton is not and that Prell shampoo is regarded as taxable by some pharmacies while Head and Shoulders is regarded as tax-exempt because it is intended to treat dandruff.[38]

Jurisdictional Parity A high-quality revenue system should result in enough equalization of the resources available to local governments that these governments can provide an adequate level of services. This is one of several areas where taxing and spending are related. State money is spent or given in local government grants so that local jurisdictions with inadequate tax bases do not have to overtax individuals and businesses and thus drive them away.

Despite fiscal disparities, horizontal equity should be maintained not only to make the tax system fair but also to provide a basic minimum level of services for all the citizens in the state. This is particularly important in the field of human resources and education. A region or community which cannot afford to prepare the next generation for leadership and citizenship is doomed to a cycle of dependency on the rest of the state.

Intergovernmental Responsibility A high-quality state-local revenue system should minimize intergovernmental tax competition and tax incentives for businesses. The evidence is overwhelming that taxes are not a particularly important factor in locating a business. The factors taken most seriously by businesses looking at an area are the quality of life, the availability of markets and raw materials, and labor costs.[39]

Table 15.10 compares the rankings of state-local systems in terms of their attractiveness to business with the rankings of states in terms of the actual locations of Japanese manufacturing plants. As the table indicates, the total number of plants in the ten states with the most attractive business tax climate is 138, whereas the total for the ten states with the worst business tax climate is 240. Clearly, considerations other than taxes are at work here.

Table 15.10 SELECTED TAX CLIMATE FACTORS

State	ACIR business tax ranking	Number of Japanese manufacturer locations
Alabama	5	12
Alaska	20	23
Arizona	11	4
Arkansas	13	6
California	50	167
Colorado	20	1
Connecticut	19	3
Delaware	16	0
Florida	12	5
Georgia	23	39
Hawaii	25	4
Idaho	29	0
Illinois	6	34
Indiana	13	17
Iowa	48	4
Kansas	25	2
Kentucky	9	10
Louisiana	40	0
Maine	39	1
Maryland	35	8
Massachusetts	32	9
Michigan	45	30
Minnesota	49	3
Mississippi	6	0
Missouri	1	5
Montana	43	1
Nebraska	20	6
Nevada	30	5
New Hampshire	10	3

continued

Table 15.10   SELECTED TAX CLIMATE FACTORS (continued)

State	ACIR business tax ranking	Number of Japanese manufacturer locations
New Jersey	4	40
New Mexico	32	0
New York	44	23
North Carolina	13	15
North Dakota	30	0
Ohio	17	18
Oklahoma	42	7
Oregon	37	8
Pennsylvania	34	20
Rhode Island	46	0
South Carolina	7	7
South Dakota*	3	0
Tennessee	2	19
Texas	23	23
Utah	25	1
Vermont	37	1
Virginia	7	9
Washington	36	34
West Virginia	47	2
Wisconsin	41	3
Wyoming	28	0

*South Dakota levies a 6 percent tax on the profits of banks and financial corporations.

Sources: Robert Kleine and John Shannon, *Characteristics of a High Quality State-Local Tax System* (Washington, DC: U.S. Advisory Commission on Intergovernmental Relations, September 1985), cited in Billy Hamilton and Tome Lineham, "Taxes and Economy: State and Local Taxes and Their Impact on Economic Development," *Rethinking Texas Taxes*, vol. 2, (Austin, TX: Texas House of Representatives, 1989) 207–215; and "Vital Statistics," *U.S. News and World Report*, (February 1, 1988), 73.

The persistence of the myth that tax subsidy equals plant location seems due in a large part to the existence of organizations which have a stake in it. As we observed in Chapter 7 on interest groups, many organizations depend on dues paid by businesses for their income. One of the best ways to demonstrate the value of an organization to its business clients is to promote low taxes. Thus a good deal of the pressure for special treatment for businesses in the tax system — in order to promote a "good business climate" for business location — comes from the numerous business interest groups already in the state or community. According to the National Conference on State Legislatures,

> Tax concessions are not cost-effective. State and local government revenues forgone through tax expenditures are greater than benefits derived by recipient firms. It is unlikely that any form of tax concession can be cost-effective.[40]

Many state and local tax breaks end up as subsidies for the federal government. The more profitable for the business in terms of not paying local or state taxes, the more corporate income tax the federal government collects. Furthermore, the fact that federal tax law allows firms to claim state and local tax payments as deductible business expenses means that differences in taxes between states or between local governments become even more irrelevant in regard to business location. The leveling effect of this deduction is sometimes called the **federal offset**.[41]

According to Rasmussen and colleagues, one of the most cost-effective ways to attract new business is to provide **loan guarantees** rather than tax breaks. A loan guarantee means that the government doesn't lend any money — a bank does — but agrees to pay back the loan if the business fails. Even if 22 percent of the money lent is not repaid, the ratio between the cost of the state guarantee payments to the lending institutions and the benefits received by the businesses is more favorable than is any tax incentive.[42]

Pragmatism   A high-quality revenue system should not be used as an instrument of social policy to encourage particular activities, such as business investment and personal saving. Taxes are inefficient in rewarding or encouraging behavior; they are almost by definition negative in effect.[43] Thus, a pragmatic tax system is based on the realization that taxes may be used to discourage behavior such as smoking, drinking, polluting, and gambling.

Taxes also can be used to reimburse governments for the indirect costs that arise from certain kinds of behavior. For example, evidence is mounting that working in an office where smoking takes place is a serious threat to one's health. Thus, many feel it appropriate for smokers to contribute more than others do to cancer research and treatment centers for cancer victims. In sum, using tax exemptions to encourage behavior results in tax expenditures; using taxes to discourage behavior results in revenue.

Although all ten characteristics of a good revenue system are important to know about, it may be worth considering some priorities in terms of participation. Fairness or vertical equity seems particularly appropriate for a political system which values equality of opportunity. If you do not work for tax reform, it seems fairly certain that you will pay a price in your state unless you are or become one of those who benefit from a regressive system and wish to continue that benefit.

We now move from evaluating the components of tax systems to two criteria for determining the political link between state-local wealth and state-local willingness to use that wealth to solve problems.

Tax Capacity and Tax Effort: Comparing the Fifty States

These two concepts were developed about 20 years ago by the ACIR to help Congress design grant-in-aid formulas. Many states have adopted them in designing some of their own grant-in-aid programs for local governments.

Tax capacity is the amount of revenue that would be collected in a unit of government if every one of the eight tax sources were taxed at the average rate for that source. Tax capacity is a way of identifying the tax base of a unit of government. It is also a measure of fiscal disparity. The concept is so useful that many states are beginning to use tax capacity data in devising grant-in-aid formulas for local governments.

Tax capacity is reported in billions of dollars. To make comparison easier, the ACIR has created a tax capacity index for each state which takes population into account and is scaled so that 100 is the per capita tax capacity of the average state. Thus the index score for each state is a percentage of the average. As Table 15.11 indicates, Arkansas has a tax capacity that is 73.3 percent of the average, while Wyoming has a tax capacity that is 150.7 percent of the average. In designing a grant program which takes tax capacity into account, Arkansas might expect a little more help than Wyoming.

Table 15.11 THE REPRESENTATIVE TAX SYSTEM: 1986

	State-local tax capacity		State-local tax effort	
	Index	Rank	Index	Rank
Alabama	74.3	48	86.4	40
Alaska	176.9	1	168.4	1
Arizona	98.7	19	98.5	20
Arkansas	73.3	49	90.7	34
California	117.8	9	95.3	26
Colorado	116.8	10	83.4	44
Connecticut	135.2	4	94.1	29
Delaware	121.4	6	81.0	46
Florida	105.1	14	76.5	48
Georgia	94.0	26	88.6	37
Hawaii	113.3	11	105.0	11
Idaho	76.9	45	89.7	35
Illinois	95.9	23	106.0	10
Indiana	86.9	38	94.3	28
Iowa	83.7	40	112.9	6
Kansas	95.7	24	96.4	24
Kentucky	76.4	47	89.3	36
Louisiana	90.1	34	90.8	33
Maine	94.5	25	98.8	19
Maryland	107.6	12	98.9	18
Massachusetts	123.5	5	103.4	12
Michigan	96.2	22	118.2	4
Minnesota	102.4	16	107.8	8
Mississippi	65.3	50	96.7	23
Missouri	92.7	29	81.6	45
Montana	88.0	37	103.2	13

continued

Table 15.11   THE REPRESENTATIVE TAX SYSTEM: 1986 (continued)

	State-local tax capacity		State-local tax effort	
	Index	Rank	Index	Rank
Nebraska	91.2	32	96.2	25
Nevada	146.8	3	65.2	49
New Hampshire	119.4	8	61.6	50
New Jersey	120.5	7	102.7	15
New Mexico	91.3	31	87.8	39
New York	106.8	13	151.5	2
North Carolina	88.3	36	91.5	31
North Dakota	93.9	27	88.6	38
Ohio	90.8	33	103.0	14
Oklahoma	98.1	20	84.7	42
Oregon	93.3	28	98.3	21
Pennsylvania	89.7	34	101.4	17
Rhode Island	91.9	30	111.0	7
South Carolina	78.6	43	93.5	30
South Dakota	77.8	44	95.0	27
Tennessee	83.5	41	83.7	43
Texas	103.5	15	79.1	47
Utah	80.4	42	106.5	9
Vermont	99.4	18	91.4	32
Virginia	100.7	17	85.1	41
Washington	97.8	21	102.7	16
West Virginia	76.4	46	98.0	22
Wisconsin	85.8	39	133.5	3
Wyoming	150.7	2	116.5	5

Source: Advisory Commission on Intergovernmental Relations, *State Fiscal Capacity and Effort: 1986* (Washington, DC: Government Printing Office, 1986) 12.

Tax effort is an attempt to measure the willingness of state leaders and citizens to pay for government out of available resources. Some state-local systems, of course, don't have a big tax base. Others are comparatively wealthy, but the decision makers have chosen not to use government to solve problems or have chosen to pay for programs by borrowing. Either way, the next generation is faced with the bills. Tax effort is an attempt to take the tax base (tax capacity) of each state-local system into account in measuring willingness to pay.

A state which realizes its capacity (taxes all eight of its resource bases at the average state rate) will have a tax index score of 100 (or 100 percent of its capacity). A state which raises more than its capacity is taxing at an above-average rate for at least some of the eight tax sources. Both Alabama (74.3) and Arkansas (73.3) are states with comparatively poor tax capacities. However, the tax effort index scores indicate that Arkansas tries harder to pay its own way than does Alabama. The tax effort index is calculated by dividing the tax revenue (money actually collected in taxes) by the tax capacity.

If one is designing a grant program which takes effort into account, states such as Nevada and New Hampshire, with very low tax efforts (65.2 and 61.6, respectively), might not do very well. Taking both tax effort and tax capacity into account, they would not expect to receive as much help as would any of the three states mentioned above. Whereas both Nevada and New Hampshire have tax capacities over 100, Alabama and Arkansas have much lower tax capacities and much higher efforts. Wyoming has a higher tax capacity than Nevada or New Hampshire, but it also tries harder, as Table 15.11 indicates.

Conclusion: Regressivity and Redistribution

We began this book by presenting three simple notions: (1) that individuals matter — they can change society or they can help preserve the essential values and institutions in a society in the midst of change, or both, (2) that state and local governments are among the major institutions in society for helping human beings achieve a higher quality of life, and (3) that if these two notions are even partially true, individuals ought to pay careful attention to their state and local governments and participate in shaping the decisions they make.

This chapter has advanced the notion that we can do better in terms of making our revenue systems more efficient and more equitable. If seeking social justice, making the institutions of government more efficient and responsive, and preserving our environment are among your goals, then sooner or later someone will ask you how to pay for those goals. Will it mean new taxes? One possible answer is yes — for the undertaxed. By revising state-local tax systems in a slightly progressive direction, simply by making sure that the rich pay the same percentage as the poor, we can raise billions of state-local dollars without increasing the burden of the poor or the middle class by one penny.

With that frightening thought we wish you well in your efforts to improve the relationships between and among individuals and the governments.

Study Objectives

1. Identify the two parts of the price to be considered in deciding whether to use government to solve problems.
2. Identify the factors which influence the budget.
3. Identify the major steps in the budget-making process.

4. Identify the ten characteristics of a high-quality state-local revenue system developed by the National Conference on State Legislatures.
5. Identify the principles involved in defining and promoting equity in a system of taxation.
6. Identify the approximate percentage of total personal income that the first and fifth quintiles of the population obtain.
7. Identify the reasons for basing a tax system on the principle of vertical equity.
8. Identify the negative nature of taxation.
9. Compare and contrast expenditures on the spending side of the budget with expenditures on the revenue side.
10. Compare and contrast tax capacity and tax effort.

Glossary

budget A plan for getting and spending money.

certainty A high probability that the tax yield will remain the same from year to year.

circuit breaker laws Limit the amount of property taxes that can be collected on an individual's home or apartment. The circuit breaker is a percentage of the resident's income that can be collected in property taxes regardless of the market value of the residence.

federal offset A term which refers to the fact that the federal corporate income tax tends to reduce differences in state-local tax systems. Thus, offering tax breaks to businesses may simply produce profits on which the businesses pay federal taxes.

fiscal disparity The difference in the tax bases of local governments and thus in their ability to offer services to their residents.

fiscal notes An estimate of the cost of a proposed law to the state or local government.

fiscal strain The inability to meet debt and expenditure obligations with existing revenues.

fiscal year A 12-month period used for bookkeeping purposes. Also known as a budget year.

functional performance index A method of comparing the service offerings of major American cities by examining not the amount of money spent but the mix of services. The index score takes into consideration the fact that some services are more expensive to offer than are others.

horizontal equity People in the same income category are taxed at the same rate regardless of where they live or whether their income comes from capital gains or wages.

line item veto Pertains only to appropriations; the governor can strike out specific items without having to veto the whole bill.

loan guarantee A promise by a unit of government to repay a loan if the borrower doesn't. This means that banks will lend money to a business because they know that they aren't assuming any risk. It is a method of subsidizing and thus attracting a new business to a community. Given the possibility that a business may fail and leave the government holding the bag, loan guarantee programs must be carefully managed.

preaudits Occur when an official called an auditor or comptroller certifies that there is enough money in an agency's budget for a particular kind of expenditure.

progressive system One in which the tax burden increases as income increases. The tax burden is lighter for the poor and heavier for the rich.

proportionate tax Requires each individual to contribute to the cost of government in proportion to income received. In a proportionate tax system each individual bears the same tax burden, or has the same effective tax rate.

redistribution Refers to government actions which alter the existing pattern of opportunities to live a better life. Redistribution is most often used to identify actions which assist the have-nots.

regressive A tax whose rate decreases as the income of those taxed increases. Another way of stating this is that in a regressive tax system, the poor pay more.

stability A tax system should not reinforce downturns in the economy and it should help siphon excess income in inflationary times.

subsistence Barely adequate to meet the most basic needs: shelter, food, and clothing.

sufficiency A condition that exists when a revenue system includes enough taxes to pay for the services and programs that the community feels are appropriate.

tax burden The percentage of one's income paid in taxes. Also known as the effective rate (ER).

tax capacity The amount of revenue that would be collected in a unit of government if every one of the eight tax sources were taxed at the average rate for that source.

tax effort An attempt to measure the willingness of state leaders and citizens to pay for government out of available resources.

tax expenditure The amount of revenue lost by granting an exemption to a tax.

vertical equity Individuals in all income categories bear the same burden (not the same size tax bill).

Endnotes

1. Michael Specter, "Oregon Legislators Face Up to the Hard Job of 'Playing God,'" *Washington Post National Weekly Edition*, (February 15, 1988), 33.
2. Advisory Commission on Intergovernmental Relations, *Significant Features of Fiscal Federalism: 1989*, (Washington, DC: ACIR, 1989), 28–30.
3. For an alternative interpretation, see Thomas R. Dye, *Politics in States and Communities* (Englewood Cliffs, NJ: Prentice-Hall, 1988), 476.
4. Ibid.
5. U.S. Department of Commerce, Bureau of the Census, *State Government Finances in 1988* (Washington, DC: Government Printing Office, 1989), 51.
6. Sarah McCalley Morehouse, *State Politics, Parties and Policy* (New York: Holt, Rinehart & Winston, 1981), 303.
7. Woody Allen claims to have attended a boxing match at which a hockey game suddenly broke out.
8. Council of State Governments, *The Book of the States, 1988–89*, (Lexington, KY: Council of State Governments), 225.
9. *Significant Features of Fiscal Federalism: 1989*, vol. 1, 2 and 12.

10. Jack C. Plano and Milton Greenberg, *The American Political Dictionary* 8th ed (New York: Holt, Rinehart & Winston, 1989), 356.
11. *The Book of the States, 1988–89*, 54–62.
12. Terry Nichols Clark and Lorna Crowley Ferguson, *City Money: Political Processes, Fiscal Strains, and Retrenchment*, (New York: Columbia University Press, 1983), 317–318.
13. Ibid., 53.
14. For a more detailed definition, see Clark and Ferguson, *City Money*, 43–50.
15. Clark and Ferguson, 13.
16. U.S. Bureau of the Census, *Statistical Abstract of the United States, 1988*, (Washington, DC: Government Printing Office, 1989), 262.
17. Donald Phares, "The Role of Tax Burden Studies in State Tax Policy," in Steven D. Gold, *Reforming State Tax Systems.* (Denver, CO: National Conference of State Legislatures, 1986), 81.
18. Clark and Ferguson, 110.
19. Ibid., 182.
20. Robert Heilbroner and Peter Bernstein, *The Debt and the Deficit* (New York: Norton, 1989), 26.
21. Congressional Budget Office study cited in *Austin American Statesman* (February 17, 1990), 10.
22. Heilbroner and Bernstein, 50.
23. *Significant Features of Fiscal Federalism*, 103.
24. Steven D. Gold, ed., *The Unfinished Agenda for State Tax Reform*, (Denver: National Conference of State Legislatures, 1988), 171.
25. *Significant Features of Fiscal Federalism*, 34–35.
26. Gold, 48.
27. The discussion which follows is based largely on Steven D. Gold, "Principles of a High Quality State Revenue System," and Steven D. Gold and Corina L. Eckl, "Appendix Checklist of Characteristics of a Good State Revenue System," in Gold, 47–63.
28. Robert Kleine and John Shannon, *Characteristics of a High Quality State-Local Tax System* (Washington, DC: ACIR, 1985), 15.
29. "Principles of a High Quality State Tax Revenue System," 52.
30. Donald Phares, "State and Local Tax Burdens Across the Fifty States," *Growth and Change*, (April 1985),34–35.
31. Daniel B. Suits, "Measurement of Tax Progressivity," *American Economic Review*, 67(4) (September 1977), 747–752. Cited in "State and Local Tax Burdens Across the Fifty States," 42.
32. See, for example, Michael Barker, ed., *State Taxation Policy* (Durham, NC: Duke University Press Policy Studies, 1983); Donald Phares, *State-Local Tax Equity: An Empirical Analysis of the Fifty States* (Lexington, MA: Lexington Books, 1973); Donald Phares, *Who Pays State and Local Taxes?* (Cambridge, MA: Oelgeschlager, Gunn, and Hain, 1980), and Joseph Pechman and Benjamin Okner, *Who Bears the Tax Burden?* (Washington, DC: Brookings Institution, 1974).
33. Roger J. Vaughn, "State Taxation and Economic Development," in Barker, *State Taxation Policy*, 48.
34. Barker, 46.
35. Elder Witt, "States Place Their Bets on a Game of Diminishing Returns," in Thad L. Beyle, *State Government: CQ's Guide to Current Issues and Activities, 1988–89* (Washington, DC: Congressional Quarterly, 1988), 206.

36. Robert Cline, "Personal Income Tax," in *Reforming State Tax Systems*, 207.

37. David Rasmussen, Marc Bendick, and Larry Ledebur, "A Methodology for Selecting Economic Development Incentives," *Growth and Change* (January 1984), 18–25.

38. *Reforming State Tax Sysems*, 135.

39. Barker, 80.

40. Larry C. Ledebur and William W. Hamilton, "The Failure of Tax Concessions as Economic Developmpent Incentives," in *Reforming State Tax Systems*, 112.

41. Richard D. Pomp, "Simplicity and Complexity in the Complexity of a State Tax System," in *Reforming State Tax Systems*, 112.

42. Ledebur and Hamilton, 113.

43. Gold, *The Unfinished Agenda*, 55.

Index

Administrative law, 412–414
Adversarial system, 414, 417
Advisory Commission on Intergovernmental Relations (ACIR), 78, 80, 84, 87, 153, 157, 158, 215, 532, 544, 551
Agglomerations, 38
Agricultural interest groups, 218–221
Aid to Families with Dependent Children (AFDC), 387, 485, 498, 500, 502, 503, 520, 522
Amendment, 96, 110, 112, 114, 117, 119, 123, 296
American Assembly, 280
American Bar Association, 213
American Farm Bureau Federation, 218
American Federalism, 56, 58, 60–62, 66, 75
  Litmus test (of Federalism), 70
  Union of governments, 61, 89
  Union of people, 61–62, 89
American Federation of State, County, and Municipal Employees (AFSCME), 391
American Indian Movement, 218
American Medical Association, 213
American Political Science Association, 214
American Revolution, 136, 297, 333, 468
Anglo, 12
Annexation, 149, 155, 158
Anti-federalists, 55, 260
Appointmenteering, 185, 189–191, 219
Appointment power, 298
  of mayors, 322
Apportionment, 119, 298, 299
Appropriations bill, 315, 349, 517
Appropriations committee, 315, 515
Appropriations laws, 518
Aristotle, 2, 15, 24

Arraignment, 416
Askew, Reubin, 205, 351
Associated Milk Producers Incorporated, 218
At-large election, 276, 278, 279, 317, 319, 322, 324, 329
Authority, 31, 38
Automotive revolution, 37, 526

Baker v. Carr, 299
Battle Creek, Michigan, 155–156, 159, 520
Belief system, 32
Bicameralism, 69, 306, 315, 328
Biennial sessions, 298, 301
Bill of information, 416
Bill of Rights, 72, 74, 100, 110, 116, 119, 410, 417
Blanton, Ray, 10–11
B'nai B'rith, 218
Board of Property Tax Equalization, 106
British Parliament, 69
Brownlow Committee, 384
Brown v. Board of Education, 74
Bryan, William Jennings, 298
Budget, 515
Budget Bill, 315
Budget-Making, 291, 315, 351
Bureaucracy, 15, 328, 334–335, 344, 347, 371, 373–376, 379, 383, 387
Bureau of Census, 49, 133
Bush, George, 242, 359, 395, 535
Business interest groups, 212–213

California Plan, 431, 434
Campaigning, 29, 44, 164, 175, 177, 192, 204–205, 222, 225, 308, 316, 319–320, 327–329, 335, 341, 343, 348, 353, 382, 534–535

Carlin, John, 350
Carter, Jimmy, 6, 390, 509
Casework, 295
Census of Governments, 39
Charters, 60, 130, 131, 132, 141–142, 152, 296, 333
Checks and balances, 103, 292, 324
Chief administrative officer (CAO), 133
Chief Executive Review and Comment procedure, 79
Chief executives, 77, 79, 80, 106, 112
Chief Justice, 431
Circuit breaker laws, 537
Circuit Court, 421
Citizen participation procedures, 397–399
Citizens Conference on State Legislatures, 300
City councils, 132, 133, 141, 143, 156, 174, 187, 197, 218, 233, 272, 276, 318, 320, 358, 359, 360, 365, 397, 543
City managers, 133, 291, 321–324, 329, 334, 335, 360–363, 391, 461
City of Tacoma v. Taxpayers, 77
Civil case, 414, 415, 417, 423, 436
Civil law, 410, 413, 427
Civil liberties, 410, 417, 429, 437
Civil service, 133, 191, 192, 277, 338, 346, 380, 381–383, 392, 396, 398, 402, 412, 413, 456, 465
Civil Service Reform Act, 398
Clinton, Bill, 339
Closed primaries, 281, 282
Collective bargaining, 213, 392
Commissioner's court, 317
Commission system, 323, 324, 353, 356
Committee on Economic Development, 153, 154
Committee on Ways and Means, 314
Common Cause, 216, 217, 225, 228
Common law, 410, 411
Concurrent Powers, 72
Confederations, 56
Conference committee, 315
Connecticut Compromise (Great Compromise), 57
Consolidated Metropolitan Areas (CMAs), 38
Congressional townships, 136
Constitutional Commissions, 120–121
Constitutional Convention, 56, 57, 58
Constitutional conventions, 119–120, 121
Constitutional government, 98, 100, 112
Contempt of court, 412, 415
Continental Congress, 136, 161
Conventional political participation, 165
Corporate income tax, 537–538, 550
Council-administrator system, 132, 354
Council-manager system, 131, 132, 133,

321–322, 324, 354, 356, 360, 362, 365
Council of Governments (COGs), 78–80, 83
Council of State Governments (CSG), 80, 83, 215, 527
Counties, 37, 77, 79, 80, 84
County boards, 143, 149, 316–318, 324, 329, 353–354
County Commissioner's Court, 141, 187, 317
Court
  Justice of the Peace, 423
  juvenile, 421–422
Court of Last Appeals, 418, 435
Court reform, 435, 437
Courts of Record, 422
Criminal case, 412, 414, 415–417, 418, 421, 436
Criminal law, 410, 412, 413
Crisis Resolution Power, 348
Cultural pluralism, 48–49

Daley, Richard, 272, 274, 277
Davis v. Bandemer, 300
Dealignment theory, 266
Declaration of Independence, 40, 41, 297
Defensive incorporation, 144, 149–151
Delegate, 55, 58, 60, 120, 165, 247
Delegated powers, 70–71
Delegate role, 294
Demonstrations, 165, 185, 188–189
de novo, 421
Deposition, 415
Dillon's Rule, 139, 140–141, 149, 152
Direct primary, 277–279
Disclosure, 231–232
Discovery, 415
Dispositional justice, 417, 427
Doctrine of incorporation, 410
Dred Scott Decision, 139

Education reform, 348, 349
Electioneering, 185, 191, 206, 208, 219, 232
Electoral college, 69, 264, 265
Electoral party, 244, 247, 254, 259, 262, 279, 280, 282–283
Elitism, 228–229
Employee unions, 389, 391–393
Endorsing Conventions, 247, 281, 282
Enumerated powers (expressed powers), 70
Environmental Defense Fund, 216
Equal Rights Amendment, 44
Equity law, 410, 411–412, 413, 414
Estate and Gift tax, 537
Ethnic groups, 24, 27, 29, 47–48, 217, 272
Ethnic interest groups, 218

Ethnic organizations, 204, 217
Exclusionary zoning, 150
Executive amendment, 349
Executive Office of the President, 79
Executive orders, 65, 80, 120, 347, 385
ex post facto, 72
Expressed powers (enumerated powers), 70, 152

FAIIR criteria, 301, 304
Fair Labor Standards Act of 1938, 65, 66
Family Court, 422
Family Farm Act, 510
Farm Bureau Federation, 227
Farmers Union, 226
Federal Election Campaign Act, 206
Federalism, 55, 242
Federalist Papers, 47, 55, 211
Federalists, 55, 260
Federal offset, 550
Federal Regional Councils, 87
Fiscal disparity, 82, 544, 547, 550
Fiscal federalism, 81, 84, 87
Fiscal notes, 87, 546
Fiscal strain, 531
Fiscal year, 389, 524
Flash cards, 20
Formal powers, 322, 334, 339, 341, 342,
    348, 351, 356, 365, 401
Fourteenth Amendment, 74, 100, 299, 410
Fox, the, 166, 167, 171, 172, 189
Fox River, 166, 167, 172
Fragmented executive branch, 133
Franklin, Benjamin, 58
Frost Belt, 90
Full faith and credit clause, 409
Functional fiefdoms, 359, 365, 388
Functional performance index, 530, 531

*Garcia v. San Antonio Metropolitan Transit
    Authority*, 65
General Law, 131, 141, 152
General Motors, 212, 229
General purpose government, 134, 142, 316,
    317, 324, 365
General Revenue Sharing Program, 84
General sales tax, 536
Gerrymandering, 299
Giraffe Project, 15–16, 166
Government, defined, 25
Governor, 11, 64, 73, 74, 78, 79, 82, 103,
    106, 115–116, 119–120, 142, 175, 205,
    215, 230, 233, 240, 244, 246–247, 263,
    334, 337–353, 365, 376–379, 383–384,
    387, 389, 401–402, 431, 434, 435, 518,
    538

Graham, John, 16
Gramm-Rudman-Hollings law, 358
Grand jury, 416
Grant in aid, 5, 7, 75–76, 79–81, 85–88,
    90, 242, 305, 341, 387–389, 398, 399,
    499–501, 533, 544, 547, 550–551, 553
Grant programs, 5, 7
Grassroots lobbying, 185, 187–188, 205, 223
Great Compromise, (Connecticut
    Compromise), 306
Great Depression, 239, 264, 274, 316, 370,
    428, 473, 488, 498–499
Greenpeace, 166–167

Hamilton, Alexander, 47, 56, 62
Hatch Act, 382
Hightower, Jim, 220–221
Home Rule, 131, 139, 141–142, 152
Hoover Commission, 384
Horizontal equity, 539, 544, 547
Housing Act of 1954, 79

Ideology, 32, 40
Impeachment, 110, 292, 343, 435
Implied Powers, 71–72, 140
Incorporation, 139–140
Incremental budgeting, 390
Independent school districts, 134, 142
Index of competition, 252
Indictment, 416
Industrial revolution, 34, 35–36, 46, 130, 138
Informal power, 334, 339, 349, 364
Initiative, 109, 119, 298
Injunction, 412
Integrated bar, 428–429, 437
Interest groups, 15, 76, 110, 122, 144, 146,
    147, 185, 188, 199, 203, 211, 234, 238,
    239, 242, 244–246, 254, 259, 277, 278,
    280, 282–285, 290, 292, 294, 304, 307,
    309, 311, 315, 321, 328, 334–335, 343,
    349, 358, 385, 389–390, 397, 399, 520,
    525, 547, 549
intergovernmental, 215
misrepresentation by, 226–227, 234
and PACs, 208–209
and Political Parties, 209–210
potential, 223
real, 222
Intergovernmental Relations (IGR), 18, 75, 76
Intermediate courts of appeal, 421
International City Management Association
    (ICMA), 132, 215, 395
Interrogatories, 415
Iron Law of Oligarchy, 224
Issue public, 183
Item veto, 349

Jackson, Andrew, 105–106, 267, 297
Jacksonian constitutions, 376
Jacksonian Democracy, 105–107, 201, 338
Jay, John, 47, 56, 61
Judges, 409, 410, 411, 412, 414, 415, 425,
    427, 429–435
  appointments of, 292
Jurisdiction, 25, 33, 34, 37, 39, 149, 314,
    414, 415, 416, 417–422, 455
Justice of the Peace Courts, 423
Juvenile Court, 421, 422

Labor unions, 42, 213, 273
La Follette, Robert, 298
Lakewood plan, 152
Law School Admission Test (LSAT), 425
Lawmaking, 290, 311, 316
Lawyer, 408, 411, 425–428, 430, 434
League of Latin American Citizens (LULAC),
    218
League of Women Voters, 216
Legislative committees, 121
Legislative staff, 122, 219, 303, 327
Legislative veto, 400, 401, 403
Legitimacy, 31, 128, 144, 153
Liberalism, 100, 103, 104
Licenses and fees tax, 536
Lieutenant Governor, 106, 284, 307, 316,
    339, 345, 376, 378–379
Line item veto, 315, 518
Litigation, 185, 194, 427
Loan guarantees, 204, 550
Lobbying, 179, 185, 187, 191, 208, 219, 227,
    232, 243, 290, 341, 349, 389, 393, 429,
    435, 509, 518
Lobbyists, 290, 304, 309, 314, 328, 341
Local interest groups, 218
Locke, John, 40, 47, 289
Long ballot, 141, 201, 273, 338
Loyal opposition, 258, 259, 260

McCulloch v. Maryland, 114
Machine politics, 269–274
Madison, James, 47, 56, 211, 227, 289
Madisonian theory, 294
Majority leader, 244, 307–308
Majority rule, 104, 112
Majority whip, 307
Malapportionment, 296, 299, 339
Mandates, 84–85, 90
Mapp v. Ohio, 410
Marshall, John, 71, 72, 114, 115
Mayor, 64, 78, 79, 105, 132, 133, 157, 215,
    233, 269, 272, 316, 322, 334, 336, 353,
    354–359, 362, 365, 376, 393

caretaker, 357
ceremonial, 356
crusader, 358
program innovator, 357
strong, 322, 329, 518
weak, 321, 322
Mayor-council system, 133, 321, 322, 356,
    360–362
Mecham, Evan, 109, 343
Medicaid, 485, 498
Medlock, Ann, 16
Megalopolis, 38
Melting pot, 48–49, 272, 273
Merit system, 279, 338, 346, 381–383, 431,
    434
Metropolitan Organizations for People, 168
Metropolitan paradox, 24, 37, 39
Metropolitan Sprawl, 38–39
Metropolitan Statistical Areas (MSAs), 37–39
Minnesota Department of Natural Resources,
    7
Minnesota Fiscal Disparities Act, 544
Minority leaders, 244, 307, 308
Minority whip, 307
Missouri Plan, 429, 431–434
Mobilization, 167, 219, 223, 225
Moralistic political culture, 137, 520
Mothers Against Drunk Driving, 169
Municipalities, 39, 84, 108, 109, 130, 133,
    138–141, 142, 144, 149–151, 153, 158,
    318, 320, 323, 400
Mushiness index, 184

Nader, Ralph, 216
Nation, 24, 27, 33
Nation-state, 26, 27, 88, 407
National Association for the Advancement of
    Colored People (NAACP), 218
National Association of Counties, 78, 215
National Association of Manufacturers, 212
National Association of Towns and
    Townships, 215
National Chamber Alliance for Politics
    (NCAP), 209
National Conference of State Legislatures,
    78, 215, 303, 538, 544, 549
National Conservative Political Action
    Committee, 228
National Council of Churches, 217
National Education Association, 215, 392
National Farmers Union, 218
National Governors Association, 78, 215,
    341, 351
Nationalism, 27, 61
National League of Cities, 78, 215

National Municipal League, 96, 153
National Organization for Women, 216
National Short-ballot Association, 276
New Deal, 35, 370
New England township, 136
New York's Civil Service Employees
  Association (CSEA), 393
Nonpartisan elections, 241, 275–276, 277,
  320–321, 324, 329, 431, 434
Northwest Ordinance, 136
Northwest Territory, 137

OMB (Office of Management and Budget),
  79, 88
One-party systems, 258
Open primary, 251
Open records laws, 393, 397, 398, 403
Opportunity costs, 173–175, 177, 198
Original jurisdiction (courts of), 421–422
Oversight function (watchdog function), 80,
  290, 291–292, 305, 400, 403

PACs (Political Action Committees), 203,
  209–210, 225, 228, 232, 234, 238, 242,
  280, 282–285, 327–328
  and interest groups, 208–209
Paralegal (Lawyer's Assistant), 428
Parasitism, 150
Particularized contacting, 179, 185
Partisan elections, 278, 281, 431, 434
Partisan gerrymandering, 300
Partisan municipal elections, 281
Party caucus, 244, 284, 308, 311
Party cohesion, 244, 259, 260, 282
Party competition, 44, 258, 311
Party identification, 248–252
Party in office, 241–242, 244, 247, 259,
  280, 284
Party in the electorate, 248, 260
Patronage, 265–266, 268, 270, 277, 335,
  338, 353, 380–381, 383
Pendleton Act, 381
Personal income tax, 536–538, 541
Plaintiff, 414–415, 436
Planning-Programming-Budgeting Systems
  (PPBS), 390–391, 402
Platform (political party), 242, 247,
  283–284, 335, 348
Plea bargaining, 416–417, 427, 436
  concessions model, 416
  consensus model, 416
Plebiscitary Democracy, 105, 107–108, 110
Plural executives, 338, 345, 376
Plurality election, 262
Pocket veto, 350

Polis, 2, 25
Political consultants, 205, 242, 243, 251,
  280, 282–283, 285
Political culture, 39–46, 137, 165, 194, 199,
  243, 279, 284, 409, 454, 518, 520, 534
  individualistic, 43–44, 46
  moralistic, 43, 44, 46, 102
  traditionalistic, 41–42, 44, 46
Political economy, 2–3, 112, 191
Political efficacy, 197
Political machine, 43–44, 267–274, 319,
  320, 329
Political participation, 43, 203, 210, 238,
  268, 285, 526
  campaigners, 178
  communalists, 177–178
  complete activists, 178
  cumulative, 175
  hierarchy of activities, 174–175
  inactives, 175
  options, 170
  organizations, 177
  parochials, 176–177
  types of participants, 175–178
  voting specialists, 176
Political parties, 41, 43, 50, 185, 199, 203,
  209–211, 227, 229, 230, 232–234, 238,
  240, 246, 248, 251, 255, 259, 264, 268,
  270–271, 274, 276, 277–279, 280,
  283–284, 299, 300, 338, 381, 429–430,
  434
  definition, 240
  and interest groups, 209–211
Political resources, 29, 31, 112, 116, 140,
  155, 167, 169, 173–174, 177, 185, 187,
  189, 196, 218, 224, 229, 263, 268, 356,
  358, 365, 521, 526
Political socialization, 24, 39, 266, 267
Political system, 24, 25, 27, 28–29, 34, 40,
  41, 43, 44, 46, 50, 99, 105, 115, 128,
  144, 151, 165, 171–172, 176, 184, 201,
  203, 208, 210, 211, 212, 219, 222, 223,
  225, 228, 230, 231, 233, 234, 290
Politico role, 294
Politics, 2, 3, 16
  definition, 25
Powell's Paradox, 199, 211
Pre-audits, 518
Preponderance of evidence, 415
President of the Senate, 244, 308
President pro tempore of the Senate, 307
Pretrial, 415, 416, 417
Primary elections, 209, 246, 247, 248, 251,
  255, 256, 259, 261, 280, 282
Privatization, 394, 396

Progressive Era, 338
Progressive Movement, 298, 319
Progressive tax, 539, 541
Property tax, 534, 537–539, 541–543, 545
Proportional representation, 264
Proportionate tax, 539, 541
Public hearings, 107, 113, 120–121, 185, 187, 219, 309, 314, 327, 398–399
Public interest groups, 216
Public Interest Research Group (PIRG), 216
Public opinion, 30, 31, 164, 180–184, 185, 243, 334, 349
    direction, 183
    intensity, 183
    salience (public awareness of issue), 183
    stability, 184

Quasi-judicial hearings, 413
Quasi-judicial power, 375
Quasi-legislative power, 374
Quasi-public organizations, 359
Quayle, Dan, 243
Queens Citizens Committee Organization, 218

Racial gerrymandering, 300
Ragghianti, Marie, 9–11, 14, 15, 28
Rational-comprehensive model, 254
Reagan, Ronald, 305, 341, 358, 359, 371, 378, 395, 464, 488, 499, 500, 501
Reagan administration, 80, 85, 87
Reapportionment, 90, 298–300, 328, 339, 351, 384
Recall, 109, 115, 254, 298, 343
Redistribution, 521–522, 532, 541, 553
Referendum, 107, 109, 119, 155, 156, 192, 197, 254, 298, 431
Reform movement, 272, 274–278, 279, 321
Regional Justice Information System (REJIS), 158
Regressive tax, 116, 539, 541, 550
Representation, 58, 68, 110, 156, 222, 294–295, 300, 306, 319, 339, 351, 490
Representative government, 102, 107, 112, 255, 294
Representing by interest groups, 222
Republicanism, 102–103, 104, 294, 468
Respondent, 414–415
Responsible party model, 211, 253–254, 256, 258, 259
Right to strike, 392, 402
Riley, Richard, 349
Robinson v. Cahill, 96
Roosevelt, Franklin Delano, 6, 248, 370

Roosevelt, Theodore, 35, 298
Rule of law, 409, 437
Rule of men, 409

San Antonio Independent School District v. Rodriguez, 100
Save the Family Farm Coalition, 510
School boards, 132, 142, 187, 190, 201, 215, 276, 289, 324–325, 336, 363–364, 543
    school districts, 215, 316, 324, 334, 363, 364, 521, 538, 544
    superintendents, 353, 363
Selected sales tax, 536
Separation of powers, 58, 59, 103, 112, 132, 242, 252, 289, 316, 322, 366, 374, 379, 401
Service-Employees International Union, 391
Severance tax, 537
Short ballot, 276
Sierra Club, 216
Single member districts, 120, 264, 272, 279
Small Claims Court, 422
Smith, Al, 339
Social diversity, 82
Social Security (Medicare), 498
Socio-economic status (SES), 175, 193
Sovereignty, 63–65, 90, 393
Speaker of the House, 120, 244, 307, 308
Special districts, 39, 75, 130–133, 134, 142, 143–149, 150, 152–153, 157, 324, 358, 365
    managers, 366
Special majority, 117, 150
Stare decisis, 411
State constitutions
    differences with U.S. Constitution, 96, 116
    flaws, 113–114
    and local government, 96
State election codes, 245
State Supreme Courts, 184
Statutory law, 412, 414
Straight ticket, 281–282
Strive Toward Excellence in Performance (STEP), 7
Strong mayor form, 132, 133
Subpoena, 415
    duces tecum, 415
Subsistence income, 485, 539, 541
Sufficiency, 539
Summons, 415
Sun Belt, 90
Sunset laws, 400, 517
Sunset legislation, 292, 400–401, 403
Sunshine laws, 397–398

Superintendent of Schools, 132–133, 190, 324–325, 334, 336, 363, 365–366, 391
Superior Courts, 421
Supplemental Security Income (SSI), 498

Taft Commission, 384
Taney, Roger, 139
Tax burden, 147, 522, 534, 540–541, 543, 547
Tax capacity, 550–551
Tax effort, 44, 552
Tax expenditure, 2, 547
Texas Board of Education, 3
Texas Railroad Commission, 106
Three-fifths compromise, 57, 58
Tocqueville, Alexis de, 55, 211, 227
Townships, 33, 77, 78, 134, 136–137, 215, 245
Traffic Court, 421, 422
Truman, Harry, 6
Tweed, William Marcey, 271

Udall v. Federal Power Commission, 76
Unconventional political participation, 165
Unified executive branch, 133
Unincorporated Area, 148, 150, 152, 159
United States Chamber of Commerce, 209, 212

United States Conference of Mayors, 215
United States Congress, 5, 26, 64
  House of Representatives, 57, 67, 68–69, 78, 209, 215, 228, 244, 263, 292, 299, 300, 306, 314
  Senate, 57, 67, 68–69, 78, 209, 215, 228, 244, 263, 292, 306, 307, 314, 355
United States Constitution, 55, 59, 69–73, 95, 98, 100, 113, 114

Vertical equity, 540, 541, 550
Virginia House of Burgesses, 6, 68
voting, 110
  cues, 259
  participation rates, 173, 199
  registration, 191, 200

Whistleblower, 398
Wilson, Woodrow, 298
Writ, 194
  of Habeas Corpus, 72
  of injunction, 194
  of mandamus, 194, 412

Zero-based Budgeting (ZBB), 390–391, 402
Zoos, 4